Guide to the Ont
Health Information Protection Act

Guide to the Ontario Personal Health Information Protection Act

Halyna Perun
Michael Orr
Fannie Dimitriadis

Published in 2005 by

Irwin Law
347 Bay Street
Suite 501
Toronto, Ontario
M5H 2R7

www.irwinlaw.com

ISBN: 1-55221-100-2

Library and Archives Canada Cataloguing in Publication

Perun, Halyna
    Guide to the Ontario Personal Health Information Protection Act / Halyna Perun, Michael Orr, Fannie Dimitriadis.

Includes text of Personal Health Information Protection Act, 2004.
Includes bibliographical references and index.
ISBN 1-55221-100-2

    1. Ontario. Personal Health Information Protection Act, 2004. 2. Medical records—Ontario—Access control. 3. Medical Records—Law and legislation—Ontario. 4. Privacy, Right of—Ontario. I. Orr, Michael, 1962- II. Dimitriadis, Fannie III. Title.

KEO730.R42P47 2005   342.7108'58   C2005-904282-6
KF3827.R4P47 2005

The publisher acknowledges the financial support of the Government of Canada through the Book Publishing Industry Development Program (BPIDP) for its publishing activities.

Printed and bound in Canada.

1 2 3 4 5   09 08 07 06 05

Summary Table of Contents

Detailed Table of Contents

CHAPTER 3:
HOW *PHIPA* WORKS WITH OTHER LAW 111

CHAPTER 12:
RULES FOR RECIPIENTS OF PERSONAL HEALTH INFORMATION FROM HEALTH INFORMATION CUSTODIANS *487*

Foreword

Anecdotal evidence exists that flagrant abuses of patients' privacy and breaches of confidentiality are not things of the past. These abuses were first brought to light during the proceedings of a public inquiry, the Commission of Inquiry into the Confidentiality of Health Information, and described in its three-volume report in September 1980, a quarter of a century ago. It is true that some of them ended because of the glare of publicity associated with the inquiry, and that institutional and administrative practices were introduced to prevent or discourage others. Memories are short, however, and bad habits difficult to suppress permanently. The need to implement many of the inquiry report's 170 recommendations, though undeniable, did not result in comprehensive legislation in Ontario until the *Personal Health Information Protection Act* came into force on 1 November 2004.

A fundamental purpose of law is to attempt to reconcile conflicting interests that inevitably arise in society, and conflicts abound in the fields of privacy and confidentiality, the importance of which, in a free society and in health care, needs no elaboration here. The practical difficulty in effecting this reconciliation is probably the chief reason for the failure of the earlier attempts to enact legislation that was obviously highly desirable. At the several conferences and symposiums convened over the years to consider the announced imminence of remedial legislation, all speakers representing the many affected interests were unanimous in the view that privacy and confidentiality were essential values that must be protected but many, if not most, of them asserted a "right to know" that required an exception to be made in their cases. If all of these claimed exceptions were legislated, the result would be, not a protection-of-privacy Act, but an invasion-of-privacy Act, and thus the attempts to reconcile these claims with patients' interests were abandoned.

With the federal government's enactment of the *Personal Information Protection and Electronic Documents Act*, S.C. 2000, c. 5, which, though not entirely appropriate for the health field, would, in default of provincial legislation, nevertheless apply to significant parts of it, there developed a consensus in Ontario that the next attempt must not be permitted to fail. The *Personal Health Information Protection Act, 2004*, S.O. 2004, c. 3 is the result.

The evolution of the new protective legislation was not easy and was, therefore, necessarily slow. Time was required, and taken, to enable attitudes toward many of the principles recommended twenty-five years ago to change. Many examples could be given, but one in particular is illustrative. Recommendations 82–85 in the inquiry's report relate to the right, with appropriate safeguards, to access to one's own health information and the right to seek to have erroneous statements corrected. The inquiry report described the issue in this way:

> Certainly, no other issue has aroused such intense emotional reactions on the part of persons accustomed, by their own admission, to the paternalism of "protecting" patients from precise information.

After receipt of the report, the government of the day did not simply let it gather dust. Within months, it appointed a distinguished Canadian to a task force on

> the practical implications for the health care system and providers and consumers of care, of implementing the recommendations of the Commission of Inquiry into the Confidentiality of Health Information.

The issue that was discussed at the greatest length in the task force report, which was submitted in November 1981, was that dealt with in recommendations 82–85. The report cited the opposition of interested organizations and individual practitioners, and then set out the task force's own recommendation:

> It is recommended that before any decision is made to implement recommendations 82–85 of the Report that an *ad hoc* advisory task force of persons with expertise and experience be set up to examine all the implications of recommendations 82–85 and to advise the Minister whether these recommendations should be implemented as submitted or in modified form.

Gradually, the hostility to the concept waned and even before the Supreme Court of Canada's 1992 decision in *McInerney v. MacDonald*, acceptance could be discerned in many circles formerly opposed to the idea, which paved the way for the statutory endorsement it now has.

Critical as the right of privacy is, like every other right, it is not absolute and where it conflicts with other interests deemed more important it must yield to them, provided that the resulting impairment is as small as possible. Societal recognition must be given to such essential interests as health research, health-insurance administration, and public health. To minimize the importance of these interests to all of us, who are, after all, patients, would be a disservice. This legislation seeks to strike a balance by reconciling the opposing interests, to the extent that reconciliation is possible. Whether it is the right balance, time will tell. If experience shows that the balance is not right, that it unreasonably favours disclosure over privacy protection, the imbalance can, and one hopes, will be redressed. In the meantime, this legislation, although much overdue, is to be enthusiastically welcomed. We are fortunate to have as our guides through its complexity the very lawyers who have worked so long and hard to bring it into existence.

The Honourable Horace Krever
November 2004

Preface

This book is intended as a guide that will help those who are affected by the *Personal Health Information Protection Act, 2004* (*PHIPA*) to understand their obligations under the Act and how to comply in the easiest and most effective manner. This book also addresses the essential elements of the *Quality of Care Information Protection Act, 2004* (*QCIPA*) and the rights and obligations created by that Act. Explaining complex legislation in a manner that will be properly understood by all those affected, most of whom are not lawyers or privacy experts, has been a considerable challenge. Where the goals of accuracy and brevity pulled in opposite directions, we have given priority to accuracy. At the same time, as much as possible, we have tried to explain *PHIPA* in a manner that is as accessible and helpful as possible to everyone who needs to comply with this complex new legislation.

We generally make a point of explaining in detail any specialized terminology as it comes up in the Guide. As an additional resource, a glossary explaining terminology essential to understanding *PHIPA* is included in Appendix 1.

The chapters that follow explain *PHIPA* step-by-step in a sequence that generally follows the structure of *PHIPA* itself.

Chapter 1 introduces *PHIPA* by explaining the integral link between privacy and health care, and provides a short history of the development of health privacy legislation in Ontario.

Chapter 2 discusses who is covered by *PHIPA* and in respect of what they are covered. Since the Act applies primarily to "health information custodians" (or "custodians") as they collect, use, and disclose "personal health information," this chapter focuses on the definitions and nuances of these terms to set the foundation for understanding every aspect of *PHIPA*. This chapter also introduces the other parties with roles in *PHIPA*, including "agents" of custodians, and providers of goods and services to enable custodians to use electronic means in dealing with personal health information. The chapter then describes how *PHIPA* regulates the collection, use, and disclosure of health numbers, a special type of personal health information.

Chapter 3 discusses how *PHIPA* affects and is affected by provisions in other law, including other legislation applicable to the health sector and beyond, Ontario's public sector privacy legislation, and Canada's federal private sector privacy legislation.

Chapter 4 discusses the obligations of health information custodians under *PHIPA*, largely found in Part II of the Act. This chapter includes guidance to custodians on their obligations to maintain the accuracy and security of personal health information in their custody or control, as well as guidance on how to fulfil the Act's administrative requirements regarding accountability and information practices.

Chapter 5 details the requirements that a consent under *PHIPA* must meet. Consent is a key concept in *PHIPA*, because generally health information custodians are not permitted to collect, use, or disclose personal health information about a patient without the patient's consent unless *PHIPA* specifically provides otherwise in certain circumstances.

Chapter 6 deals with substitute decision-making, which is about who, apart from the patient, is entitled to make decisions or requests or to take steps on behalf of the patient. As this issue often arises when the patient is mentally incapable of making a decision on his or her own, the chapter also addresses capacity and procedures pertaining to determinations of incapacity.

Chapters 7 through 10 all deal with different aspects of the rules governing the collection, use, and disclosure of personal health information by health information custodians.

- Chapter 7 explains the general limiting principles, and other rules, that apply to all collections, uses, and disclosures of personal health information by custodians.
- Chapter 8 deals with collections, both direct and indirect, of personal health information by custodians.
- Chapter 9 deals with uses of personal health information by custodians.
- Chapter 10 deals with disclosures of personal health information by custodians.

Chapter 11 explains the rules relating to personal health information in the context of health research. These rules apply to health information custodians in their disclosures and uses of personal health information for research purposes and to researchers who receive personal health information from custodians for research. The chapter also deals with disclosures to prescribed health registries and certain specified bodies for health system planning and analysis, including prescribed health planning entities and health data institutes. (These terms are all briefly defined in the glossary in Appendix 1.)

Chapter 12 considers the restrictions that apply to non-health information custodians who receive personal health information from health information custodians, particularly the restrictions on their subsequent uses and disclosures of such information.

Chapter 13 discusses patients' right of access to their recorded personal health information.

Chapter 14 deals with patients' right to request correction to their recorded personal health information.

Chapter 15 details the various ways of enforcing the obligations of *PHIPA*, including a review by the Information and Privacy Commissioner, a court action for damages, or a prosecution for an offence under *PHIPA*.

Chapter 16 canvasses the scope of the regulation-making powers under *PHIPA* and the process for mandatory public consultation on draft regulations.

Chapter 17 discusses the *Quality of Care Information Protection Act, 2004*. Although not a part of *PHIPA*, *QCIPA* was part of the same bill as *PHIPA*, and relates, in a number of ways, to *PHIPA*. This chapter discusses how "quality of care information" is defined, how to establish a quality of care committee under *QCIPA*, and the restrictions on the use and disclosure of quality of care information. The chapter includes a brief discussion of analogous amendments to the *Regulated Health Professions Act, 1991* pertaining to quality assurance programs under that Act.

ACKNOWLEDGMENTS

The development of government legislation is a complicated undertaking involving a great many people. After Cabinet gives a "go ahead" for legislation to be developed, the Ministry sponsoring the legislation, working together with its legal counsel, provides instructions to the Office of Legislative Counsel (an office of the Ministry of the Attorney General), which is in charge of drafting all Ontario legislation.

We were the primary legal counsel advising the Ministry of Health and Long-Term Care on the development of *PHIPA* and *QCIPA*, and we have been involved in advising the Ministry on health privacy matters for several years.

However, we are not writing this book in our capacity as government legal counsel; we are writing solely in our personal capacities. Nothing in this book necessarily reflects the views or opinions of the Ontario Ministry of Health and Long-Term Care, the Ministry of the Attorney General, or the government of Ontario.

Twenty-three years elapsed between the time when the Honourable Horace Krever first recommended health privacy legislation and the introduction of the legislation that brought *PHIPA* into being. Over the years, a significant number of people in the Ontario government have been involved in the developments that ultimately led to the enactment of *PHIPA*. Elected representatives on the legislative committees reviewing the legislation, stakeholder groups, and individuals who, over time, provided hundreds of submissions on the detailed provisions of the legislation, also played a crucial role in helping to refine the legislation to a point where it could be passed with unanimous support in the Legislature. It has been our pleasure to work with a number of these individuals. While this is not the appropriate place to acknowledge the very important work of all these people, we feel compelled to mention two of them in particular.

As discussed above, the Office of Legislative Counsel is in charge of drafting all Ontario legislation. We would be remiss if we did not acknowledge the leading role of Michael Wood, Legislative Counsel, whose pen was the final determinant of the words of *PHIPA*. Starting in 1997, Michael was the lead Legislative Counsel working on health privacy legislation, and he exemplified the very high standards of professionalism and service upheld by the Office of Legislative Counsel.

We would also like to acknowledge the lead role of Carol Appathurai, Director of the Health Information, Privacy and Sciences Branch of the Ministry of Health and Long-Term Care. Carol was the Ministry's foremost official devoted full-time (and more) to the development of the final version of *PHIPA*. Her dedication — particularly the efforts she made to work with stakeholders in analyzing concerns with the bill and developing appropriate ways in which to address them — was instrumental in shaping a bill that would ultimately be passed with the unanimous support of the Legislature. Equally important was Carol's positive disposition, which made the long hours at the office much less noticeable. We are grateful for the opportunity to have worked with Carol and her team on this project.

With respect to the project of writing this Guide, we would like to acknowledge with thanks the support and various contributions of a number of individuals.

The Honourable Horace Krever has done us a great honour in writing the Foreword to this Guide. His role in spurring the development of *PHIPA* cannot be overstated. It is truly appropriate that his words accompany a work about legislation that hopefully represents a fitting culmination of one of the very important projects of his illustrious career in Ontario's public service.

We would also like to express our appreciation to Murray Segal, Ontario's Deputy Attorney General, for allowing us to take on this project outside our role as Crown counsel. It has not been easy to complete this time-consuming work together with the demands of our "day jobs," and in this connection we also gratefully acknowledge the support of Dianne Dougall, Director of the Legal Services Branch of the Ministry of Health and Long-Term Care.

We would like to extend our gratitude to all of our colleagues, both within and outside our Legal Services Branch, who gave their assistance with various aspects of the Guide, from reviewing chapters, discussing difficult issues, to connecting us with other helpful individuals. Special thanks go to Brian Beamish, Jacinthe Boudreau, Elizabeth Carlton, Saara Chetner, Mary Jane Dykeman, Patrick Hawkins, Lise Hendlisz, Priti Sachdeva, Liam Scott, Ruth Stoddart, Debbie Tarshis, and Joaquin Zuckerberg. They were a huge help to us in developing this Guide, though in the end, of course, we take full responsibility for the contents.

We would also like to thank our publisher, Jeffrey Miller, who was a true gentleman throughout this project, and our editors, Jo Roberts and Tali Golombek, whose patience and attention to detail and readability has made this book what it is.

There were certainly days when we regretted our employer's willingness to allow us to take on a monumental task like this outside of work hours, but on the whole it has been a tremendous experience. We hope that an explanation of this complex legislation, from some of us who worked most closely on its details, will be beneficial to all concerned.

1 Introduction

A. PRIVACY'S CONNECTION TO HEALTH CARE

The provision of health care is dependent on the availability of information. Without complete and accurate information about a patient, health care providers are challenged in determining appropriate treatment. Understanding this need, patients share information about themselves with health care providers and permit providers to acquire intimate details about themselves through the provision of health care itself. Often, this information is of such a private and sensitive nature that a patient may not even share it with family or friends. Disclosures of such information to the wrong people can cause a patient embarrassment, or even more tangible disadvantages.

Consequently, a patient generally does not make information available to a health care provider without developing expectations about the use of the information. A patient must trust a health care provider to use the information in the best interests of the patient. If patients cannot trust health care providers, and the organizations within which providers work, to keep their information confidential and secure, then patients will be faced with the choice between foregoing privacy and foregoing proper health care, neither of which is an acceptable alternative.

An important goal of health information privacy legislation is to create a framework in which this trust, so essential to the provision of health care, can be fostered in a consistent manner. This recognition of the relationship between privacy and health care is not new. At least since the days of the Hippocratic Oath,[1] people have recognized that health care, privacy, and confidentiality are integrally linked.

While information must be kept private and secure, it must also be available quickly for the purposes of health care. Enabling the effective and efficient sharing of personal health information for the provision of health care while, at the same time, ensuring that patients can trust that their information will be kept private is key to creating a workable framework for health information privacy.

It must also be remembered that the delivery of health care does not occur in a vacuum. Health care providers must be able to disclose information about the provision of health care for supporting functions, such as to claim and obtain payment for health care services, including payment by the Ontario Health Insurance Plan. A provider must also be able to disclose information to a professional governing body in the course of its investigation of professional misconduct, or where the disclosure is required to protect public health.

Finally, any health information privacy regime, particularly one developed in the context of a largely publicly funded health care system, needs to recognize and accommodate uses of personal health information for purposes that enable the effective planning and management of the health care system itself. Health care delivery relies on health education, research, planning, and administration, and each of these, in turn, relies on some degree of access to personal health information.

The lengthy public dialogue that occurred in Ontario during the years that led to the development of the *Personal Health Information Protection Act, 2004*[2] reflects the need to balance these various considerations and interests.

---

1   This premise that patient information must be kept confidential is reflected in the Hippocratic Oath, where the duty was first known to be articulated with respect to physicians. It is widely accepted today that this duty of confidentiality applies to a range of health care providers. See, for example, *Re Axelrod* (1994), 119 D.L.R. (4th) 37 (Ont. C.A.). The duty of confidentiality is part of a broader duty, often called a fiduciary duty, to act in the best interests of the patient: *McInerney v. MacDonald*, [1992] 2 S.C.R. 138.

2   S.O. 2004, c. 3, Sch. A [*PHIPA*].

B. THE DEVELOPMENT OF HEALTH INFORMATION PRIVACY LEGISLATION IN ONTARIO

1) *Krever Report*

For over two decades, since the publication of the seminal *Report of the Commission of Inquiry into the Confidentiality of Health Information*[3] in 1980, there have been demands for a comprehensive legislative framework in Ontario to articulate clear limits and rules for the use of patient information in the health care system. The Royal Commission of Inquiry into the Confidentiality of Health Records in Ontario, led by Mr. Justice Krever, as he then was, was established in 1977 as a result of allegations of improper police access to records of the Ontario Health Insurance Plan and patient records in health care facilities.

The work of the Commission included an extensive review of the law pertaining to health information in Ontario and an inquiry into the handling of such information in health care facilities and by health care providers. The *Krever Report* highlighted the inconsistent treatment of personal health information in Ontario. Having reviewed seventy-seven statutes and numerous regulations, Mr. Justice Krever concluded that most dealings with personal health information were not covered in any way by legislation.[4] Where they were, the legislation was often inadequate. Mr. Justice Krever found:

> When gathered together, the relevant sections may appear to comprise a formidable body of law. However, in this case, the whole is not greater than the sum of its parts. The whole is merely a collection of piecemeal provisions. No general code is established for the handling of health information. No comprehensive policy is reflected in the present legislation.[5]

The *Krever Report* was instrumental in identifying the discrepancies between existing legislation and common practices in health care facilities and among health care providers with respect to the collection, use, and disclosure of patient information. It was clear that legislation lagged behind the reality of how health information was handled in the health sector. That legislation should clearly identify and authorize legitimate uses of such information so as

---

3   Ontario, Royal Commission of Inquiry into the Confidentiality of Health Records in Ontario, *Report of the Commission of Inquiry into the Confidentiality of Health Information*, (Toronto: Queen's Printer, 1980) [*Krever Report*].

4   *Ibid.*, vol. 1 at 52.

5   *Ibid.*, vol. 1 at 51.

not to impede effective delivery of health care was one important theme of the *Krever Report's* 170 recommendations. The recommendations of the Report also urged identifying and effectively prohibiting unauthorized uses and disclosures of personal health information.

Mr. Justice Krever concluded that patients are generally prepared to relinquish some of their privacy to obtain the care they need. While patients do expect their health care providers to keep their information confidential, he noted that even the Hippocratic Oath recognizes that confidentiality may be abrogated with good cause.[6]

2) *Romanow Report*

Over twenty years after the release of the *Krever Report*, the Committee of the Canada Privy Council appointed the Honorable Roy Romanow, Q.C. as Commissioner to inquire into the future of Canada's public health care system and to recommend measures required to ensure a universally acceptable, publicly funded health system.[7] The Commissioner's findings were released on 28 November 2002 in the Commission on the Future of Health Care in Canada's final report to Canadians, Building on Values: The Future of Health Care in Canada.[8]

The *Romanow Report's* forty-seven recommendations addressed ten critical aspects of the health care system, including the role of information in the system.[9] The *Romanow Report*, although dealing with issues going beyond information and privacy issues, highlighted many themes similar to those in the *Krever Report*: the right of the patient to control access to his or her information; the concerns patients have about abuse or misuse of their information; the critical need for patients to have ready access to their own information; and the need for health information to improve the delivery of health care.[10] Similarly, both reports raised the concern that patients have about the use of infor-

---

6   *Ibid.*, vol. 1 at 8 and vol. 3 at 75.

7   P.C. 2001-569.

8   Canada, Commission on the Future of Health Care in Canada, *Building on Values: The Future of Health Care in Canada* (Ottawa: Commission on the Future of Health Care in Canada, 2002) [*Romanow Report*].

9   *Ibid.* at Chapter 3.

10 Recommendation 10 of the *Romanow Report* states: "Individuals should have ownership over their personal health information, ready access to their personal health records, clear protection of privacy of their health records, and better access to comprehensive and credible information about health, health care and the health system." The Report further recommended that "amendments should be made to the *Criminal Code of Canada* to protect Canadians' privacy and to explicitly prevent the abuse or misuse of personal health information, with violations in this area considered a criminal offense." See *ibid.* at 76.

mation technology in health care.[11] The *Romanow Report* concluded that "[p]rivacy rules have to strike the right balance between strict privacy protection procedures and the legitimate and important need for health care providers to access personal health information."[12] The *Romanow Report* called for consistent and clear privacy rules across the country.[13]

3) Impact of the *Charter of Rights and Freedoms*

Since becoming law, the *Canadian Charter of Rights and Freedoms*[14] has had a significant impact on health information privacy, as it has on many issues in the health sector. Although a right to privacy is not expressly set out in the *Charter*, it has been well-established through the jurisprudence of the Supreme Court of Canada that a right to privacy is recognized and protected by several provisions of the *Charter*.[15] Moreover, the Supreme Court has held, for example in *R. v. Mills*, that the right to privacy has the same status as other *Charter* rights, such as the right to make full answer and defence.[16] The Court there stated:

> The values protected by privacy rights will be most directly at stake where confidential information contained in a record concerns aspects of one's individ-

---

11   *Krever Report*, above note 3, vol. 2, Chapter 18. *Romanow Report*, above note 8, Chapter 3 at 80 noted that many Canadians worry that their personal health information, when shared in electronic health records systems, could be abused or misused.

12   *Romanow Report, ibid.* at 80.

13   *Ibid.*

14   Part I of the *Constitution Act, 1982*, being Schedule B to the *Canada Act, 1982* (U.K.), 1982, c. 11 [*Charter*].

15   Notably, s. 7, "Everyone has the right to life, liberty and security of the person and the right not to be deprived thereof except in accordance with the principles of fundamental justice"; s. 8, "Everyone has the right to be secure against unreasonable search or seizure"; and s. 15(1), "Every individual is equal before and under the law and has the right to the equal protection and equal benefit of the law without discrimination and, in particular, without discrimination based on race, national or ethnic origin, colour, religion, sex, age or mental or physical disability," and s. 15(2) "Subsection (1) does not preclude any law, program or activity that has as its object the amelioration of conditions of disadvantaged individuals or groups including those that are disadvantaged because of race, national or ethnic origin, colour, religion, sex, age or mental or physical disability." All of these provisions have been referred to as relevant to privacy rights. It should be noted that no cases to date explicitly review the right to privacy in relation to legislation governing personal health information. In fact, most cases that analyze the *Charter* with respect to an individual's right to privacy arise in the context of law enforcement and not health care. It is beyond the scope of this Guide to provide a comprehensive review of the *Charter* and its application to the right to privacy.

16   [1999] 3 S.C.R. 668 at para. 61 [*Mills*].

ual identity or where the maintenance of confidentiality is crucial to a therapeutic, or other trust-like, relationship.[17]

The Court concluded that the reasonable expectation of privacy protected by
section 8 of the *Charter*[18] "includes the ability to control the dissemination of
confidential information."[19]

Accordingly, the Supreme Court of Canada has recognized that individuals have a reasonable expectation of privacy in therapeutic records, such as
medical or counselling records.[20] Also, the Court has concluded that individuals have a reasonable legally protected expectation that samples taken for medical purposes will remain private and the information from them will not be
used for other purposes.[21] As the Supreme Court of Canada noted in *R. v.
Dyment*: "Grounded in man's physical and moral autonomy, privacy is essential for the well-being of the individual."[22]

It is also well-settled that the right to privacy, like other *Charter* rights, is
not absolute and must be balanced against legitimate societal interests.[23] Nevertheless, a legislative framework that balances protections for patients with
societal needs will be subject to careful scrutiny to ensure that any limits on
patient privacy are demonstrably justified.

4) Privacy Enhancements to Ontario Health Legislation following *Krever Report*

In the couple of decades after the release of the *Krever Report*, there were certainly enhancements to Ontario legislation to clarify the rules with respect to
personal health information. Regulations under the *Public Hospitals Act* were

---

17   *Ibid.* at para. 89.

18   *Charter*, above note 14, s. 8.

19   *Mills*, above note 16 at para. 80.

20   *Ibid.* at paras. 80–82. See also *R. v. O'Connor*, [1995] 4 S.C.R. 411 and *A.M. v. Ryan*,
      [1997] 1 S.C.R. 157.

21   *R. v. Dyment*, [1988] 2 S.C.R. 417 at 434 [*Dyment*]. See also *R. v. Dersch*, [1993] 3 S.C.R.
      768.

22   *Dyment, ibid.* at para. 17.

23   See *Dyment, ibid.* at para. 428 and *Mills*, above note 16 at paras. 54 and 86. Furthermore,
      according to s. 1 of the *Charter*, the rights and freedoms in the *Charter* are guaranteed
      "subject only to such reasonable limits prescribed by law as can be demonstrably jus-
      tified in a free and democratic society." If there is an infringement of the *Charter*,
      analysis then turns to s. 1 to determine if the infringement is "saved" by s. 1 as a justi-
      fied reasonable limit. The criteria for determining if an infringement is a justified rea-
      sonable limit have been set out in *R. v. Oakes*, [1986] 1 S.C.R. 103 at 135–39, and *Egan
      v. Canada*, [1995] 2 S.C.R. 513 at para. 182.

updated.[24] The *Mental Health Act* was amended to provide psychiatric patients with a right of access to and correction of their clinical records.[25] Regulations under the *Independent Health Facilities Act* were developed to include provisions governing the disclosure of patient records.[26] New laws, such as the *Health Cards and Numbers Control Act, 1991*,[27] the *Long-Term Care Act, 1994*,[28] the *Regulated Health Professions Act, 1991*,[29] and the *Social Work and Social Service Workers Act, 1998*[30] were all developed to include requirements concerning the handling of personal health information.

Of course, since 1988 and 1992 respectively, the *Freedom of Information and Protection of Privacy Act* and the *Municipal Freedom of Information and Protection of Privacy Act* provide legal frameworks for access to and privacy of personal information in the public sector, including provincial ministries, government agencies, and municipalities.[31]

These law reforms were all steps toward providing better privacy protections, but, because of their piecemeal approach, they continued the patchwork of rules and left significant areas without clear statutory rules. Accordingly, the *Krever Report's* summary, that "the only thing that may be said with certainty about the treatment of health records held by health-care institutions in Ontario is that there is no consistency in the province's legislation,"[32] continued to be the state of the law in Ontario until the coming into force of *PHIPA*. As noted by the Minister of Health and Long-Term Care in the Legislature during the second reading debate on Bill 31,[33] "Existing laws that deal with health

---

24   *Hospital Management*, R.R.O. 1990, Reg. 965, made under the *Public Hospitals Act*, R.S.O. 1990, c. P.40, revised as a result of *PHIPA* by O. Reg. 324/04.

25   R.S.O. 1990, c. M.7, s. 36, repealed by *PHIPA*, s. 90(12).

26   *General*, O. Reg. 57/92, made under the *Independent Health Facilities Act*, R.S.O 1990, c. I.3, and revised as a result of *PHIPA* by O. Reg. 364/04.

27   S.O. 1991, c. 1, repealed by *PHIPA*, s. 82. This Act regulated the collection and use of the health number.

28   S.O. 1994, c. 26. A number of provisions pertaining to personal records in the custody or control of service providers have been repealed by *PHIPA*, s. 89.

29   S.O. 1991, c. 18. The framework of this legislation enabled the creation of rules governing the conduct of regulated health professionals, including their handling of patient health records.

30   S.O. 1998, c. 3. The framework of this legislation enabled the creation of rules governing the conduct of social workers and social service workers, including their handling of client health records.

31   *Freedom of Information and Protection of Privacy Act*, R.S.O. 1990, c. F.31 [*FIPPA*]; *Municipal Freedom of Information and Protection of Privacy Act*, R.S.O. 1990, c. M.56 [*MFIPPA*].

32   *Krever Report*, above note 3, vol. 1 at 89.

33   Bill 31, *An Act to enact and amend various Acts with respect to the protection of health information*, 1st Sess., 38th Leg., Ontario, 2003, the short title of which was the *Health Information Protection Act, 2003* [Bill 31].

information apply in some health care settings and not in others. This legislation addresses those problems. This legislation begins to treat our health care system as a system."[34]

5) Past Ontario Initiatives for Health Information Legislation

Following the *Krever Report*, successive Ontario governments attempted to advance a uniform legal framework that would protect the confidentiality of health information, provide consistency in the way in which such information is used and disclosed, and set out rules to ensure proper safeguards are in place to keep that information secure.

a) 1996 Consultation Paper and 1997 Draft Legislation

In June 1996, when the Ontario Ministry of Health released its consultation paper, *A Legal Framework for Health Information,*[35] it seemed Ontario would become the first province in Canada to develop and implement comprehensive and specific rules for the handling of personal health information in the health system. The release of the paper was followed by regional round table meetings and resulted in over one hundred written submissions.

In November 1997, the Ministry of Health released the draft *Personal Health Information Protection Act, 1997* for public consultation.[36] Four thousand individuals and organizations received a plain language overview of the draft legislation for review and comment, while a further one thousand received both the draft legislation and overview. The Ministry also held regional consultation meetings across the province. It received over two hundred written submissions.[37] Clearly, there was a significant interest in this initiative in Ontario.

The 1997 Draft Legislation proposed a detailed legislative framework for the collection, use, and disclosure of personal health information, which included a right of access for individuals to their personal health records, a right to request a correction of such records, and avenues for complaints and redress. Its scope extended beyond traditional settings for the provision of health care to cover the activities of public and private insurers, children's aid societies, colleges of regulated health professions, programs providing social

---

34   Ontario, Legislative Assembly, *Official Report of Debates (Hansard)*, 1123 (30 March 2004) at 1850 (Hon. George Smitherman).

35   Ontario, *A Legal Framework for Health Information* (Toronto: Ministry of Health, 1996).

36   Ontario, *Personal Health Information Protection Act, 1997: Draft for Consultation* (Toronto: Queen's Printer for Ontario, 1997) [1997 Draft Legislation].

37   Ontario, Legislative Assembly, *Official Report of Debates (Hansard)*, 1137 (30 March 2004) at 2050 (Shelley Martel).

assistance and related benefits, and managers of electronic networks. With this wide scope, the draft generated extensive debate.

The 1996 Consultation Paper and the 1997 Draft Legislation provided a comprehensive precedent for the work undertaken in other jurisdictions, including Alberta, Manitoba, and Saskatchewan, which moved forward with their own dedicated health information privacy legislation.[38]

b)   Bill 159

Ontario's eventual first attempt to pass such legislation was unsuccessful. Bill 159, *An Act respecting personal health information and related matters,* was introduced in the Ontario Legislature on 7 December 2000.[39] The Bill, however, was so poorly received that it was ultimately left to die on the order paper after hearings that winter.[40]

In its treatment of consent, Bill 159 was simultaneously found both too strict and too lenient. The "informed consent" standard for the collection, use, and disclosure of personal health information, as adapted in Bill 159[41] from the "informed consent to treatment" model,[42] was criticized as setting an inappropriately high standard for information flows.[43] Ironically, the high standard set for consent naturally went together with the need to exempt many types of collections, uses, and disclosures of personal health information from the requirement for consent, so at the same time there was significant criticism that the Bill allowed too many disclosures of personal health information without consent,[44] including all disclosures between health care providers for health care

---

38   *Health Information Act,* R.S.A. 2000, c. H-5 (Alberta); *Personal Health Information Act,* C.C.S.M. 2002, c. P33.5 (Manitoba); *Health Information Protection Act, 1999,* S.S. 1999, c. H-0.021 (Saskatchewan).

39   Bill 159, *An Act respecting personal health information and related matters,* 1st Sess., 37th Leg., Ontario, 2000, the short title of which was the *Personal Health Information Privacy Act, 2000* [Bill 159].

40   The Legislature prorogued in March 2001.

41   Bill 159, above note 39, cl. 21(3).

42   *Health Care Consent Act, 1996,* S.O. 1996, c. 2, Sch. A, s. 11.

43   At the Committee hearings on Bill 159, Ms. Daphne Jarvis, partner with the law firm of Borden, Ladner, Gervais argued persuasively that the same standard for informed consent to treatment should not apply to consent for the sharing of personal health information: "The concept of informed consent, in our view, very badly translates into consent for the purpose of collection, use and disclosure of information. There is not that interface, and to expect there to be such an interface between an individual and the health provider or institution is simply unreasonable and impractical, and it will result, we fear, in chaos." [Ontario, Legislative Assembly, Standing Committee on General Government, *Official Report of Debates (Hansard),* G-1001 (27 February 2001) at 1450 (Daphne Jarvis)].

purposes.[45] Under Bill 159, patients could not reliably opt out of such disclosures short of withdrawing from the treatment to which the disclosure related.

The Ontario Medical Association objected strongly to what was called the "directed disclosure" provision in the Bill, which would have empowered the Ministry of Health and Long-Term Care to compel health care providers to disclose information from patient charts directly to the Minister for the purposes of planning and management of the health system. In his presentation to the Standing Committee on General Government, the President of the Ontario Medical Association at the time iterated:

> The OMA does not believe that Bill 159 has any possible claims to legitimacy as a privacy bill if it does not rectify the sweeping intrusion by the government into its citizens' personal lives. This legislation should be about the protection of data and not the collection of data.[46]

A number of presenters to the Standing Committee also criticized the Bill as containing too many regulation-making powers, where policy could be determined by Cabinet and not be transparent to the public.[47] The Information and Privacy Commissioner of Ontario, Dr. Ann Cavoukian, was also concerned about the lack of sufficient investigation and order-making powers for her office as the office responsible for enforcing the legislation.[48] For these and

---

44   The president of the Ontario Medical Association urged that Bill 159 be significantly revised: "In its current form, Bill 159 sets the stage to open patients' medical information to unprecedented access and to undermine the trust relationship that exists between physicians and their patients." [Ontario, Legislative Assembly, Standing Committee on General Government, *Official Report of Debates (Hansard)*, G-965 (27 February 2001) at 0930 (Dr. Albert Schumacher).]

45   According to the Information and Privacy Commissioner, under Bill 159, "individuals have relatively little control over the collection, use and disclosure of their personal health information. ... [U]nder Ontario's bill [159] individuals have no way in which to prevent their health information from being shared freely among health care providers." [Ontario, Legislative Assembly, Standing Committee on General Government, *Official Report of Debates (Hansard)*, G-826 (8 February 2001) at 1400 (Dr. Ann Cavoukian).]

46   Ontario, Legislative Assembly, Standing Committee on General Government, *Official Report of Debates (Hansard)*, G-965 (27 February 2001) at 0930 (Dr. Albert Schumacher).

47   See further <www.ontla.on.ca/hansard/house_debates/37_parl/session1/ L115.htm>: Mr. David Christopherson's (NDP MPP, Hamilton West) response to Elizabeth Witmer, then the Minister of Health, in the Legislature at the introduction of the Bill. Also, the Ontario Information and Privacy Commissioner, for example, focused on this issue stating: "In almost every part of the legislation, key issues are left to be addressed in the regulations, leaving far too much to be decided at a later date in a non-public forum." [Ontario, Legislative Assembly, Standing Committee on General Government, *Official Report of Debates (Hansard)*, G-827 (8 February 2001) at 1400 (Dr. Ann Cavoukian).]

other reasons, the Commissioner, although a champion of Ontario's health information privacy legislative initiative, urged that substantial changes be made to the Bill before final passage by the Legislature.[49] The then federal Privacy Commissioner was much less supportive of Bill 159, squarely attacking it as "an assault on health privacy rights, not a defence of them."[50]

c) Impetus of *PIPEDA*

Following the end of Bill 159 in 2001, the looming presence of the new federal private sector privacy legislation, the *Personal Information Protection and Electronic Documents Act*,[51] began to play an increasingly significant role in encouraging all provinces, including Ontario, to develop and enact privacy legislation of various scopes.

PIPEDA was passed in April 2000 by the federal government and came into force in stages.[52] Before January 2004, *PIPEDA* was limited in scope to organizations under federal jurisdiction, like banks and airlines. As of 1 January 2004,[53] however, *PIPEDA* would begin to apply to all organizations within the province that collect, use, or disclose personal information, including personal health information, in the course of commercial activities, unless the province had "substantially similar" legislation applicable to such organizations in place, and federal Cabinet had ordered an exemption.[54]

---

48   Ontario, Legislative Assembly, Standing Committee on General Government, *Official Report of Debates (Hansard)*, G-828 (8 February 2001) at 1410 (Dr. Ann Cavoukian).

49   Ontario, Legislative Assembly, Standing Committee on General Government, *Official Report of Debates (Hansard)*, G-825 (8 February 2001) at 1350 (Dr. Ann Cavoukian). The Commissioner stated: "Please, let's do whatever we have to do to bring in legislative protections to ensure the privacy and confidentiality of health information. Again, this speaks in favour of fixing this decidedly imperfect bill rather than scrapping it."

50   The federal Privacy Commissioner stated, at the hearings on Bill 159, in part:

> The legislation appears designed, in fact, to ensure that the government of Ontario and a virtually unlimited range of other organizations and individuals could have unrestricted access to the most private health information of every Ontarian. ... As for Bill 159, I don't believe a law that is so fundamentally flawed in virtually every provision can readily be fixed. The government would have to rework nearly every section, reverse nearly every policy thrust and rethink nearly every assumption, which would be a massive task with so complex a piece of legislation. My suggestion would be to scrap it and start afresh in a new spirit.

> [Ontario, Legislative Assembly, Standing Committee on General Government, *Official Report of Debates (Hansard)*, G-857 (8 February 2001) at 1150 (George Radwanski).]

51   S.C. 2000, c. 5 [*PIPEDA*], Part 1, Protection of Personal Information in the Private Sector.

52   *Ibid.*

53   *Ibid.*, s. 30, which specifies when *PIPEDA* comes into force for which sectors.

54   *Ibid.*, s. 26(2).

PIPEDA was the federal government's response to a European Parliament directive that prohibits personal data relating to citizens of member states from being transferred to a country outside the European Union, unless that country ensures an adequate level of protection for such data,[55] as decided by the European Commission. If a country does not have an adequate level of protection, members of the European Union must prevent the transfer of personal data to that country. The European Commission has determined that *PIPEDA* provides "an adequate level of protection."[56]

Stakeholders in the health sector were concerned about the impact that *PIPEDA* would have on their operations, should it apply to them. First, *PIPEDA* was enacted to address the needs of electronic commerce and was not designed for the complexities of the health system.[57] The rule in *PIPEDA* that

---

55   Directive 95/46/EC of the European Parliament and of the Council of 24 October 1995 on the protection of individuals with regard to the processing of personal data and on the free movement of such data [Directive]. Official Journal L 281, 23/11/1995 P.0031-0050, online: <http://europa.eu.int/comm/internal_market/privacy/law_en.htm>. The Directive came into force on 24 October 1998, and was intended to be implemented by national legislation by all member states on or before that date. Its purpose is to provide protection for data within the European Union, to protect the right to privacy respecting the processing of personal data, and to facilitate the free flow of personal data within the European Union among the member states in compliance with the Directive. Member states may only transfer data to a country outside the European Union if the country has an "adequate level of protection," under Article 25(6) of the Directive.

56   32002D0002. 2002/2/EC: Commission decision 20 December 2001 pursuant to Directive 95/46/EC of the European Parliament on the adequate protection of personal data provided by the Canadian *Personal Information Protection and Electronic Documents Act* (notified under document number C (2001) 4539). Official Journal L 002, 04/01/2002 P.0013-0016, online: <http://europa.eu.int/smartapi/cgi/sga_doc?smartapi!celexdoc!prod!CELEXnumdoc&lg=EN&numdoc=32002D0002&model=lex>.

57   This concern had been noted by the Ontario Ministry of Health, in its submission to the Senate Committee on Social Affairs, Science and Technology reviewing *PIPEDA* as Bill C-6, *An Act to support and promote electronic commerce by protecting personal information that is collected, used or disclosed in certain circumstances, by providing for the use of electronic means to communicate or record information or transactions and by amending the Canada Evidence Act, the Statutory Instruments Act and the Statute Revision Act*, 2d Sess., 36th Parl., 1999, (assented to 13 April 2000) [*Ontario Ministry of Health Submission to the Standing Committee on Social Affairs, Science and Technology Regarding Bill C-6* (Toronto, Ministry of Health, December 1999) at 2]. This is also highlighted in the Ministry's overview of *PHIPA*: Ontario, *Personal Health Information Protection Act, 2004: An Overview for Health Information Custodians* (Toronto: Ministry of Health and Long-Term Care, August 2004) at 34, online: <www.health.gov.on.ca>.

express consent should be obtained for all sensitive information, combined with the provision that personal health information was almost always to be considered sensitive, suggested that express consent was the required norm for collections, uses, and disclosures of personal health information for health care.[58] Stakeholders in the health sector considered this requirement to be unduly inflexible and onerous.[59] Second, the uncertain application of the legislation, based on the uncertainty of the term "commercial activities," was seen as a major problem, as was the fact that the legislation would not be able to provide a consistent framework of privacy standards across the health sector.[60]

The unevenness and uncertainty of application of *PIPEDA* to the health sector, combined with the rules in that Act that did not reflect the needs of the health system, were critical reasons for moving forward with a made-in-Ontario approach.

---

58   *PIPEDA*, above note 51, s. 7, Schedule 1, s. 4.3.4. Industry Canada has confirmed that *PIPEDA* does apply to personal information collected, used, and disclosed in the health sector in the course of commercial activities by, for example, private pharmacies, laboratories, and health care providers in private practices. See *PIPEDA Awareness Raising Tools (PARTs) Initiative for the Health Sector* published by Industry Canada, online: <http://e-com.ic.gc.ca>.

59   See the following excerpt from the joint letter from the presidents of the Ontario Hospitals Association and the Ontario Medical Association to the Federal Ministers of Industry and of Health online: <www.oma.org/phealth/OHA-OMALetter06-23-03.pdf>:

> We believe that consent can and must be operationalized in such a way so as to not unduly constrain the ability of health care professionals to provide care, and that in some limited circumstances exemptions to express consent are warranted to ensure the effective delivery of care. We do not believe that *PIPEDA*, drafted with the goal of protecting the privacy of information in respect of electronic commercial transactions and requiring express consent of the individual achieves this critical balance and hence, application of this legislation to the health care sector is both inappropriate and unworkable.

60   For example, the president of the Ontario Medical Association explained to the Standing Committee on General Government during the hearings on Bill 31 that "[t]here is tremendous confusion in the system as all the players struggle to understand which, if any, of their activities are captured by *PIPEDA*. For example, based on the most recent commentary coming from the federal government, it would seem that physicians would be in *PIPEDA* for their office work but out of *PIPEDA* for their hospital work .... We desperately need a uniform set of rules that will apply throughout the health care system and fit with the reality of practice." [Ontario, Legislative Assembly Standing Committee on General Government, *Official Report of Debates (Hansard)*, G-41 (26 January 2004) at 1510 (Dr. Larry Erlick).]

d) *Privacy of Personal Information Act, 2002*

In December 2002, the Ministry of Consumer and Business Services released draft information privacy legislation for consultation.[61] Known as the draft *Privacy of Personal Information Act, 2002* (*POPIA*) and developed in consultation with the Ministry of Health and Long-Term Care, the stated impetus of *POPIA* was to provide comprehensive privacy legislation that would be considered substantially similar with *PIPEDA*, and hence relieve Ontario organizations from complying with the federal legislation, which was otherwise going to begin to apply to the whole commercial sector on 1 January 2004.

POPIA was a comprehensive but cumbersome proposal, as it contained two completely separate sets of rules, one pertaining to personal health information in the hands of health information custodians and the other applying both to personal information of all kinds in the broader private sector and non-health personal information in the hands of health information custodians. *POPIA* was designed to regulate not just the health sector, but also the broader private sector, including almost all non-governmental organizations from businesses to not-for-profit organizations, and even political parties and religious organizations.

The lessons learned from Bill 159 were reflected to a large degree in the health information privacy provisions adapted into the framework of *POPIA*. However, despite ongoing public statements on behalf of the government that the legislation would be introduced in time to take effect before *PIPEDA's* 1 January 2004 effective date for the commercial sector, this draft legislation was not ultimately introduced as a bill.

C. BILL 31: *HEALTH INFORMATION PROTECTION ACT, 2004*

As the clock ticked closer to *PIPEDA's* 1 January 2004 date for taking effect in the broader commercial sector, the need to move forward quickly with privacy legislation grew. The need was particularly pronounced for health care providers, who would be most adversely affected by having to comply with *PIPEDA*.

---

61   Ontario, *A Consultation on the Draft Privacy of Personal Information Act, 2002* (Toronto: Ministry of Consumer and Business Services, 2002), online: <www.cbs.gov.on.ca/mcbs/english/pdf/56XSMB.pdf>.

1) Introduction of Bill 31

As a result, the introduction of *PHIPA* in the Legislature on 17 December 2003,[62] received the overwhelming approval of health care sector stakeholders.[63] *PHIPA* appears as Schedule A to the *Health Information Protection Act, 2004.*[64] The other schedule to that Act is the *Quality of Care Information Protection Act, 2004.*[65] Both Acts proceeded together through the legislative process as the two parts of Bill 31, and the substantive provisions of both Acts came into force on 1 November 2004.

PHIPA builds on the Canadian Standards Association Model Code for the Protection of Personal Information[66] and reflects the ten fair information principles of that Code. In this way, *PHIPA* is consistent with *PIPEDA*, to which the Code is appended as a schedule and, accordingly, has the force of law.[67]

Although *QCIPA* did not garner a lot of attention in the Legislature, it is nonetheless a critical complement to *PHIPA.*[68] For the first time in Ontario, "quality of care information," defined under *QCIPA* to include, essentially, the information generated by or for designated committees aimed at improving health care within a health care institution, is shielded from disclosure in proceedings and elsewhere. The provisions of *QCIPA* should enable such institutions to foster the kind of frank and open discussions among health care practitioners within the institution that are necessary to find ways to provide the best possible quality of care.[69]

---

62 *PHIPA* was set out in Schedule A to Bill 31, see above note 33.

63 See the presentations of, for example, the University Health Network, the Canadian Mental Health Association, Ontario Division, the Ontario Medical Association, and Ontario College of Social Workers and Social Service Workers to the Standing Committee on General Government during the first day of the Standing Committee on General Government hearings on Bill 31. [Ontario, Legislative Assembly, Standing Committee on General Government, *Official Report of Debates (Hansard),* (26 January 2004).]

64 S.O. 2004, c. 3, Sch. A.

65 S.O. 2004, c. 3, Sch. B [*QCIPA*].

66 CSA Privacy Code. "Principles set out in the National Standard of Canada Entitled Model Code for the Protection of Personal Information, CAN/CSA-Q830-96" set out in Schedule 1 of *PIPEDA,* above note 51. How the provisions of *PHIPA* compare with the ten privacy principles set out in the CSA Privacy Code is discussed in greater detail in Chapter 3.

67 *PIPEDA,* above note 51.

68 *QCIPA* incorporated provisions in somewhat modified form that had been part of Bill 159, above note 39, and the 1997 Draft Legislation, above note 36. It first appeared as a proposed stand-alone Act in *A Consultation on the Draft Privacy of Personal Information Act, 2002,* above note 61.

69 See Chapter 17 for a detailed discussion of that Act.

Bill 31 moved swiftly through the legislative process. The Legislative Assembly's Standing Committee on General Government conducted public hearings on the Bill in four cities, and heard from over fifty organizations and individuals. The Committee carried out clause-by-clause consideration of the Bill twice, both before and after second reading debate on the Bill. Each time, the Committee accepted about one hundred amendments to the Bill to address issues that were raised by stakeholders, for example enhancing the investigative powers of the Ontario Information and Privacy Commissioner as the oversight official for the Act.[70] By the time of debate at third reading, all three parties unanimously supported the Bill.[71] The spirit of co-operation that emanated from all sides of the Legislature in ushering in *PHIPA* and *QCIPA* reflects not only a widespread readiness and desire for such legislation, but also the significant comfort level of stakeholders with its provisions.

2) Significant Differences between *PHIPA* and Bill 159

The key problems identified in the context of Bill 159 were addressed in *PHIPA* in a manner that appears to have allayed most serious criticism.

Unlike Bill 159, *PHIPA* requires consent for most collections, uses, and disclosures between health information custodians for health care purposes, but the requirements for establishing such a consent have been tailored to ensure that health care providers can continue to operate in an efficient manner. Particularly, the adoption of the "knowledgeable" consent model in *PHIPA*, in place of the "informed consent" requirement, and the rule that health care providers may imply consent for the sharing of personal health information for the provision of health care, while at the same time allowing patients to "lock out" certain information from being shared with health care providers, appear to have struck the right balance between on the one hand

---

70 The Legislative Assembly's Standing Committee on General Government held hearings on Bill 31 on January 26, 27, & 28, in Toronto, and on February 3, 4, & 5 in Kingston, London, and Sault Ste. Marie respectively. Clause-by-clause consideration of Bill 31 by the Committee occurred on 9 February 2004. The Bill was reported as amended to the Legislature on 22 March 2004. Second Reading occurred on 8 April 2004, followed by further clause-by-clause consideration by the Standing Committee on 28 April 2004. Third Reading of Bill 31 took place on 17 May 2004, followed by Royal Assent on 20 May 2004. See the legislative history of Bill 31, online: <www.ontla.on.ca/library/bills/381/3138i.htm>.

71 Third reading of Bill 31 passed unanimously with seventy-two ayes and zero nays. Ontario, Legislative Assembly, *Official Report of Debates (Hansard)*, 2280 (17 May 2004) at 1412.

respecting individual privacy and, on the other, facilitating the provision of health care.[72]

Further, the directed disclosure provisions in Bill 159 that many health care stakeholders perceived as a significant intrusion by government into patient files were tempered by the creation of an arms-length health data institute, so that necessary analysis may be conducted for planning and management of the health system without the need for the provision of any identifiable personal health information to the government, except with the specific approval of the Information and Privacy Commissioner. The introduction of the health data institute into *PHIPA* appears to have provided an innovative solution to address both the concern for the confidentiality of that patient information and the need for the proper planning and administration of the health system.

Finally, the introduction of a mandatory public consultation process in the development of regulations under *PHIPA* and *QCIPA* has provided an assurance to health sector stakeholders that they will continue to be involved in the enhancement of the legislative framework, which is especially important given the significant range of matters under the legislation that are subject to regulations.

In large measure, *PHIPA* reflects numerous recommendations made by Mr. Justice Krever in his report and provides a framework for the implementation of many recommendations of the *Romanow Report*.

3) Goals of *PHIPA*

The purposes of *PHIPA*, set out explicitly in the legislation, are

- to establish rules for the collection, use, and disclosure of personal health information about individuals that protect the confidentiality of that infor-

---

72 In a presentation to the Ottawa Hospital, Ontario's Information and Privacy Commissioner noted this balance:

> One of the most important features of *PHIPA* is the implied consent model that applies to health care providers within the circle of care. Effective health information privacy legislation has to strike the right balance between allowing health care professionals to quickly pass on the information needed for patient care to another health professional, while restricting unauthorized disclosure. *PHIPA* does just that. While *PHIPA* builds in extensive privacy protection, it was designed not to interrupt the actual delivery of health care services.

> See, *Managing Personal Health Information under Ontario's New Health Information Protection Act*, a presentation by Dr. Ann Cavoukian to the Ottawa Hospital (7 December 2004), online: <www.ipc.on.ca>.

mation and the privacy of individuals with respect to that information, while facilitating the effective provision of health care;

- to provide individuals with a right of access to personal health information about themselves, subject to limited and specific exceptions;
- to provide individuals with a right to require the correction or amendment of personal health information about themselves, subject to limited and specific exceptions;
- to provide for independent review and resolution of complaints with respect to personal health information; and
- to provide effective remedies for contraventions of the Act.[73]

The dual focus of the first purpose statement is particularly notable. Privacy and confidentiality must be protected, but the protection must continue to allow and, indeed, facilitate the effective provision of health care to patients.

In part, *PHIPA* facilitates the effective provision of health care by providing consistent rules for the collection, use, and disclosure of personal health information across the health system so that information can be shared as necessary for maintaining the continuity of care, with assurance that the information will have the same protection wherever it moves.[74] *PHIPA* also supports the effective provision of health care by providing clear and practical rules about the ability to share information where appropriate to support health research, health planning, and quality improvement activities.[75]

The legislation is subject to a review by a committee of the Legislature, which must begin no later than 1 November 2007.[76] Within one year after beginning that review, the committee is required to make recommendations to the Legislature concerning amendments to the Act.[77] It is clear, therefore, that the dialogue as to whether the legislation achieves the right balance between privacy of and access to personal health information will continue.

---

73   *PHIPA*, s. 1.

74   As stated by the Minister of Health and Long-Term Care in the Legislature during the second reading debate on Bill 31. "The protections in Bill 31 give people confidence that no matter where they receive care, their personal health information is safe and secure. Public trust is at the heart of this bill" [Ontario, Legislative Assembly, *Official Report of Debates (Hansard)*, G-1121 (30 March 2004) at 1845 (Hon. George Smitherman).]

75   See, *Personal Health Information Protection Act: The Role of the IPC*, a presentation by Dr. Ann Cavoukian, Information and Privacy Commissioner to the Ministry of Health and Long-Term Care, (21 September 2004), slide 3, online: <www.ipc.on.ca>.

76   *PHIPA*, s. 75(a).

77   *Ibid.*, s. 75(b).

2 Application of the Legislation: Who and What Is Covered?

A. OVERVIEW OF SCOPE OF *PHIPA*

The *Personal Health Information Protection Act, 2004*[1] primarily governs the collection, use, and disclosure of personal health information by health information custodians.[2] Further, the Act provides patients[3] with a right to request

---

1   S.O. 2004, c. 3, Sch. A [*PHIPA*].
2   Both "personal health information" and "health information custodian" are defined in *PHIPA* and discussed in detail below.
3   "Patient" is used largely throughout this book as the most immediately understandable term to refer to the person who is the subject of personal health information. *PHIPA* uses the term "individual" to refer to the subject of personal health information. "Individual" is defined to mean "the individual, whether living or deceased, with respect to whom the information was or is being collected" (see *PHIPA*, s. 2). Of course, not all persons and entities in the health sector use the word "patient" in all contexts to describe recipients of health care services. Depending on the context, the subject of the personal health information may more appropriately be called a "client" or "resident," etc. or may be a patient, outpatient, former patient, or deceased patient. Nevertheless, for consistency and ease of reference, this Guide commonly uses the term "patient" to refer to all of these. Furthermore, when referring to a "patient" or "individual" providing a consent, making a request (e.g., for access or correction), providing an instruction, or taking some other step, the word "patient" or "individual" also can be read as including the patient's "substitute decision-maker" (see *PHIPA*, s. 25, and Chapter 6). The Guide does not generally repeat the phrase "patient or his or her substitute decision-maker, as the case may be," but in general, references to "patient" include references to the patient's substitute decision-maker.

access to and correction of their records of personal health information held by health information custodians. *PHIPA* also imposes administrative require-ments on custodians with respect to records of personal health information. In other words, recognizing that the collection, use, and disclosure of personal health information in the health sector requires special rules, *PHIPA* focuses on personal health information in the health sector specifically.

For the most part, persons who *PHIPA* identifies as health information custodians are those who would be expected to fall into that category as a result of their role in the health care sector. They are persons who gather, create, and hold personal health information as a fundamental aspect of their work. They are persons who are accustomed to dealing with sensitive health information, and most have long been subject to confidentiality requirements.[4]

Although it focuses on health information custodians, *PHIPA* also extends its reach to apply in a narrower manner to persons who are not custo-dians, but to whom a health information custodian disclosed personal health information. The Act refers to these persons as "recipients."[5] In addition, *PHIPA* recognizes that health information custodians will often act through agents, and creates rules governing the activities of such agents in handling personal health information. Further, the Act governs the activities of persons who provide services to health information custodians to enable the custodians to use electronic means to deal with personal health information. Finally, *PHIPA* governs the activities of all persons with respect to health numbers.

The scope of the Act could have been different. The Act could have been drafted so as to apply to the collection, use, and disclosure of personal health information by all entities, and not focus primarily on the activities of health information custodians. Alternatively, the Act could have been drafted to address the collection, use, and disclosure of all personal information, rather than only personal health information.[6] Canada's federal *Personal Information Protection and Electronic Documents Act* establishes rules for the collection, use, and disclo-

---

4   Confidentiality requirements for physicians date back to ancient times and the Hippo-cratic Oath. Legislation governing regulated health professionals and hospitals have included confidentiality requirements for some time. See, for example, *Professional Misconduct*, O. Reg. 856/93, ss. 1(1)[10] and 1(2), made under the *Medicine Act, 1991*, S.O. 1991, c. 30. Professional organizations have also included confidentiality require-ments in their codes of ethics. See Canadian Medical Association, Code of Ethics (Update 2004), which includes provisions concerning the privacy and confidentiality of a patient's personal health information, online at <www.cma.ca>.

5   The term "recipient" is used in the heading for *PHIPA*, s. 49(1).

6   As discussed in Chapter 1, in February 2002 Ontario's Ministry of Consumer and Business Services released *A Consultation on the Privacy of Personal Information Act, 2002*. The draft legislation, which was prepared in consultation with the Ministry of

sure of personal information in the course of commercial activities.[7] The scope of *PHIPA* is not qualified in such a way. A health information custodian's disclosure of personal health information is governed by *PHIPA*, however, regardless of whether the disclosure occurs in the context of a commercial activity.

This chapter discusses the application of *PHIPA* in four parts. First, the chapter discusses who is covered by the Act. This discussion centres largely on the definition of "health information custodian," which includes an explanation of related concepts such as "health care practitioner," "health care," and "custody or control," but also includes *PHIPA's* application to non-custodians, including agents of custodians, recipients of personal health information from custodians, and persons who provide services to custodians to enable them to use electronic means to handle personal health information. Second, the chapter discusses what is covered by *PHIPA*, which involves a detailed explanation of the term "personal health information." Third, the chapter explains the detailed rules contained in *PHIPA* relating to the collection, use, and disclosure of the health number, and the use of the health card. Finally, the chapter describes three key terms in the Act: collect, use, and disclose. This chapter thus discusses several key concepts and sets a foundation for understanding the Act.

B. WHO IS COVERED?

1) Health Information Custodians

a) Who Is a Health Information Custodian?

i) Definition

The concept of a "health information custodian" is central to the application of *PHIPA*. The term "health information custodian" is a defined term in the Act, and thus has a more precise meaning than simply someone who has custody of personal health information.[8] Only those persons captured by one of the cat-

---

Health and Long-Term Care, was drafted so as to apply to the health sector and to business and not-for-profit sectors outside the health sector, with separate rules for personal health information in the health sector. However, legislation of this scope was not introduced. See Ontario, *A Consultation on the Draft Privacy of Personal Information Act, 2002* (Toronto: Ministry of Consumer and Business Services, 2002), online: <www.cbs.gov.on.ca/mcbs/english/pdf/56XSMB>.

7   S.C. 2000, c. 5, s. 4(1)(a) [*PIPEDA*].

8   *PHIPA*, s. 3. Note, however, that no person is a custodian unless it has "custody or control of personal health information as a result of or in connection with" its role: *PHIPA*, s. 3(1).

egories of health information custodians in the definition of that term are considered custodians for the purposes of the legislation. Health information custodians include the following persons or organizations:[9]

- a health care practitioner, or a person who operates a group practice of health care practitioners;
- a service provider under the *Long-Term Care Act, 1994* who provides a community service to which that Act applies;.
- a community care access corporation;
- a person who operates a public hospital;
- a person who operates a private hospital;
- a person who operates a psychiatric facility;
- a person who operates an institution under the *Mental Hospitals Act*;
- a person who operates an independent health facility;
- a person who operates an approved charitable home for the aged;
- a person who operates a home or joint home under the *Homes for the Aged and Rest Homes Act*;
- a person who operates a nursing home;
- a person who operates a care home under the *Tenant Protection Act, 1997*;
- a placement co-ordinator under the *Charitable Institutions Act, Homes for the Aged and Rest Homes Act*, or *Nursing Homes Act*;
- a person who operates a pharmacy;
- a person who operates an ambulance service;
- a person who operates a home for special care;
- a person who operates a centre, program, or service for community health or mental health whose primary purpose is the provision of health care;
- an evaluator or an assessor under the *Health Care Consent Act, 1996* or the *Substitute Decisions Act, 1992*, respectively;
- a medical officer of health or a board of health;
- the Minister of Health and Long-Term Care, together with the Ministry of Health and Long-Term Care;
- Canadian Blood Services;
- a public health laboratory; and
- any other person that the regulations made under the Act identify as a health information custodian.

Because the meaning of the terminology used in the definition of "health information custodian," as summarized above, is not necessarily immediately apparent, a brief description of each category of health information custodian follows.

---

9   *PHIPA*, s. 3(1), General, O. Reg. 329/04, s. 3 [*PHIPA* Regulation].

ii) Categories of Health Information Custodians

a. A health care practitioner[10]

PHIPA defines the term "health care practitioner"[11] to include the following persons:

- registered drugless practitioners who provide health care;[13]
- regulated social workers and social service workers who provide health care;[14] and
- any other person whose primary function is to provide health care for payment.

The term "health care practitioner" is discussed in further detail below.[15]

b. A person who operates a group practice of health care practitioners[16]

Health care practitioners sometimes decide to work together as a group. Indeed, the government of Ontario has encouraged this practice through the introduction of frameworks such as "Family Health Teams."[17] A "group practice of health care practitioners" may take a variety of forms. In some cases, one practitioner will have other practitioners act on his or her behalf. In such instances, for the purpose of *PHIPA*, the practitioner may be the "person who operates the group practice," and the other practitioners may be his or her agents. In other instances, two or more health care practitioners may choose to establish a partnership,[18] to practise as a group. In recent years, practitioners have been able to take advantage of the opportunity to establish a professional corporation. Where a group practice is incorporated, the professional corporation is the "person who operates the group practice" and the practition-

---

10   *PHIPA*, s. 3(1)[1].

11   *Ibid.*, s. 2, definition of "health care practitioner."

12   Schedule 1 to the *Regulated Health Professions Act, 1991*, S.O. 1991, c. 18 [*RHPA*] lists the following regulated health professions: audiology and speech-language pathology; chiropody; chiropractic; dental hygiene; dental technology; dentistry; denturism; dietetics; massage therapy; medical laboratory technology; medical radiation technology; medicine; midwifery; nursing; occupational therapy; opticianry; optometry; pharmacy; physiotherapy; psychology; and respiratory therapy.

13   Drugless practitioners, including naturopaths, are registered under the *Drugless Practitioners Act*, R.S.O. 1990, c. D.18 [*DPA*].

14   Social workers and social service workers are regulated by the Ontario College of Social Workers and Social Service Workers pursuant to the *Social Work and Social Service Work Act, 1998*, S.O. 1998, c. 31 [*SWSSWA*].

15   See Section (B)(1)(b) below.

16   *PHIPA*, s. 3(1)[1].

17   Health care providers, such as physicians, nurse practitioners, and other health care professionals, may establish Family Health Teams to provide primary health care services.

18   *PHIPA*, s. 2 defines "person" to include a partnership, association, or other entity. The *Interpretation Act*, R.S.O. 1990, c. I.11, s. 29(1) provides that "person" also includes a corporation. It may also include an individual.

ers are agents of the corporation.[19] A health information custodian who is a person operating a group practice of health care practitioners may have agents who are not health care practitioners, as well.

c. A service provider under the *Long-Term Care Act, 1994*[20] who provides a community service to which that Act applies[21]

Many people are familiar with service providers, generally corporations, that provide services to the public in the community, pursuant to a contract with a community care access corporation.[22] Such services include "community services,"[23] which consist of community support services, including meal and transportation services and adult day programs; homemaking services, such as housekeeping and shopping; personal support services, such as personal hygiene activities; and professional services, including nursing, dietetic, and social work services.

d. A community care access corporation[24]

The Minister of Health and Long-Term Care designates community care access corporations [CCAC] as such pursuant to the *Community Care Access Corporations Act, 2001*.[25] There are approximately forty-two CCACs in Ontario. CCACs arrange for and authorize the provision of health care in patients' homes by service providers[26] under the *Long-Term Care Act, 1994*; authorize services for special needs children in schools; authorize the admission of patients into long-term care homes;[27] and provide information and referrals to the public about other community agencies and services.[28]

---

19 *Business Corporations Act*, R.S.O. 1990, c. B.1, s. 3.2(2) provides that only members of a profession can hold shares in a professional corporation and the officers and directors of the corporation must be shareholders.

20 See the *Long-Term Care Act, 1994*, S.O. 1994, c. 26, s. 2 [*LTCA*] definition of "service provider" for a more detailed meaning of that term.

21 *PHIPA*, s. 3(1)[2].

22 Such service providers may be agents of a community care access corporation, or health information custodians in their own right. Community care access corporations and the service providers with which they contract should ensure that the service provider's status under *PHIPA* is clear, perhaps by including provisions in their service agreements to describe their relationship.

23 *LTCA*, above note 20, ss. 2(3)–(7).

24 *PHIPA*, s. 3(1)[3].

25 S.O. 2001, c. 23, s. 2(1) [*CCACA*].

26 See Section (B)(1)(a)(ii)(c) above, for a discussion of "service providers."

27 See below for a discussion of the work of CCACs as placement co-ordinators under the *Nursing Homes Act*, R.S.O. 1990, c. N.7 [*NHA*]; *Charitable Institutions Act*, R.S.O. 1990, c. C.9 [*CIA*]; and *Homes for the Aged and Rest Homes Act*, R.S.O. 1990, c. H.13 [*HARHA*].

28 *CCACA*, above note 25, s. 5 sets out the objects of community care access corporations.

e. A person who operates a hospital within the meaning of the *Public Hospitals Act*[29]

Public hospitals are the health care facilities with which people are typically most familiar.[30] They are independent non-profit organizations usually incorporated pursuant to corporations legislation, such as the *Corporations Act*,[31] or by a private Act of the Legislature. Public hospitals are classified as general hospitals, convalescent hospitals, hospitals for chronic patients, active treatment teaching psychiatric hospitals, active treatment hospitals for alcoholism and drug addiction, and regional rehabilitation hospitals, and they are graded for further classification.[32] Public hospitals must comply with the *Public Hospitals Act* and regulations made under that Act. Many public hospitals are also designated as psychiatric facilities under the *Mental Health Act* and provide a variety of in-patient and out-patient mental health services, in addition to the medical, surgical, and other services provided at public hospitals.

f. A person who operates a private hospital[33]

Private hospitals are generally distinguishable from public hospitals, the complex health care organizations with which people are most familiar. The former are smaller health care facilities, often focused on a particular treatment.[34] Pri-

---

29 *PHIPA*, s. 3(1)[4][i]. In the case of a public hospital, a corporation overseen by the hospital's board is almost invariably the person who operates the hospital. *Public Hospitals Act*, R.S.O. 1990, c. P.40, s. 1 [*PHA*] provides that "board" means the board of directors, governors, trustees, commission, or other governing body or authority of a hospital.

30 *PHA*, *ibid.*, s. 1 provides that "hospital" means "any institution, building or other premises or place established for the treatment of persons afflicted with or suffering from sickness, disease or injury, or for the treatment of convalescent or chronically ill persons that is approved under this Act as a public hospital."

31 R.S.O. 1990, c. C.38.

32 *Classification of Hospitals*, O. Reg. 321/01, made under the *PHA*, above note 29, s. 1(1). The hospitals, their classifications and grades are set out in the list maintained by the Minister of Health and Long-Term Care pursuant to the *PHA*, s. 32.1(2) and available on the website of the Ministry of Health and Long-Term Care, online: <www.health.gov.on.ca>.

33 *PHIPA*, s. 3(1)[4][i]. *Private Hospitals Act*, above note 29, s. 3(1) prohibits a person from using a house as a private hospital unless the person has a licence issued under that Act before 29 October 1973, or a renewal of such a licence. The Minister of Health and Long-Term Care has not issued such licences since 1973. The "person who operates" a private hospital is the licensee, which may be a corporation. Under the *Private Hospitals Act*, s. 7(4), where the licensee is a corporation, the Minister may refuse to renew its licence if the Minister is not satisfied as to the character of each director and officer of the corporation and as to his or her fitness to direct, manage, or be associated with the operation of the private hospital.

34 *Private Hospitals Act*, *ibid.*, s. 1 provides that "private hospital" means a house in which four or more patients are or may be admitted for treatment, other than

vate hospitals form a small part of Ontario's health care system, with only eight private hospitals currently providing services in the province under the *Private Hospitals Act.*

g.   A person who operates a psychiatric facility[35]

The term "psychiatric facility" is defined in the *Mental Health Act* to mean a facility for the observation, care, and treatment of persons suffering from a mental disorder, and designated as such by the Minister.[36] There are over seventy psychiatric facilities in Ontario. Many public hospitals are also designated psychiatric facilities under the *Mental Health Act.* Although they may be exempt from providing any of these services,[37] facilities designated as psychiatric facilities must provide: in-patient services; out-patient services; day care services; emergency services; and consultative and educational services to local agencies.[38]

h.   A person who operates an institution under the *Mental Hospitals Act*[39]

Institutions under the *Mental Hospitals Act* are commonly referred to as provincial psychiatric hospitals.[40] These psychiatric hospitals are owned by the province of Ontario and managed by Ministry of Health and Long-Term Care

---

(a) an independent health facility within the meaning of the *Independent Health Facilities Act* or a hospital within the meaning of the *Public Hospitals Act,*
(b) repealed,
(c) a children's residence licensed under Part IX (Licensing) of the *Child and Family Services Act,* or
(d) a lodging house licensed under a municipal bylaw.

35   *PHIPA*, s. 3(1)[4][i]. Almost invariably, the person who operates the psychiatric facility will be a corporation, such as a hospital corporation. *Mental Health Act*, R.S.O. 1990, c. M.7, s. 1(1) [*MHA*] provides that "officer in charge" means "the officer who is responsible for the administration and management of a psychiatric facility." The officer in charge of a psychiatric facility would be an agent of the corporation who operates the psychiatric facility.

36   *MHA, ibid.*, s. 1(1). The *MHA*, s. 80.2 provides the Minister of Health and Long-Term Care with the power to designate facilities.

37   *MHA, ibid.*, s. 80.2(1).

38   *General*, R.R.O. 1990, Reg. 741, made under the *MHA, ibid.*, s. 4(1).

39   *PHIPA*, s. 3(1)[4][i]. *PHIPA*, s. 3(2) makes it clear that the officer in charge of the institution within the meaning of the *Mental Hospitals Act*, R.S.O. 1990, c. M.8 is the person who operates the institution. The *MHA*, s. 1 provides that "officer in charge" means the officer of the Ministry of Health and Long-Term Care who is appointed as the superintendent or hospital administrator of an institution.

40   *MHA, ibid.*,s. 1 provides that "institution" means an institution under this Act and includes every approved home connected therewith. Section 2 of that Act provides that that Act applies to such institutions as are designated from time to time by the regulations.

pursuant to the *Mental Hospitals Act*. At the time of writing, there are three such institutions in Ontario: Penetanguishene Mental Health Centre; North Bay Psychiatric Hospital; and Whitby Mental Health Centre. Together, these hospitals provide a range of mental health services on both an in-patient and out-patient basis. These services include children's and seniors' mental health programs, forensic programs for mentally disordered offenders, and in-patient rehabilitation services.[41] Psychiatric hospitals are also designated psychiatric facilities under the *Mental Health Act*, and they comply with that Act in providing certain mental health services.

i. A person who operates an independent health facility[42]

Independent health facilities are licensed out-of-hospital facilities that provide health care services.[43] Services may include diagnostic facilities, including radiology, ultrasound, magnetic resonance imaging, nuclear medicine, and sleep studies, or in-treatment or surgical facilities, such as plastic surgery, dermatology, and ophthalmology.

---

41 See the Ministry of Health and Long-Term Care website for additional information concerning such institutions, online: <www.health.gov.on.ca>.

42 *PHIPA*, s. 3(1)[4][i]. *Independent Health Facilities Act*, R.S.O. 1990, c. I.3, s. 3(1) [*IHFA*] prohibits a person from establishing or operating an independent health facility except under the authority of a licence issued by the Director of Independent Health Facilities, who is an employee of the Ministry of Health and Long-Term Care appointed by the Minister. For independent health facilities, the person who holds a licence to operate an independent health facility is the person who operates the facility. A person who holds a licence may be a corporation.

43 *IHFA*, *ibid.*, s. 1(1) provides: "independent health facility" means
  (a) a health facility in which one or more members of the public receive services for or in respect of which facility fees are charged or paid, or
  (b) a health facility or a class of health facilities designated by the Minister under section 4(2)(b),
  but does not include a health facility referred to in section 2.
    The *IHFA*, s. 2 provides that it does not apply to the following health facilities, persons, places, or services:
  1. An office or place in which one or more persons provide services in the course of the practice of a health profession,
    i.   for or in respect of which the only charges made for insured services are for amounts paid or payable by the Plan as defined in the *Health Insurance Act*, and
    ii. for or in respect of which no facility fee is requested from or paid by the Province or any person.
  2. A service or class of services that is exempt by the regulations.
  3. A health facility or class of health facilities that is exempt by the regulations.
  4. A person who is or a class of persons that is exempt by the regulations.

j.   A person who operates an approved charitable home for the aged[44]

Charitable homes for the aged are a type of long-term care home. Long-term care homes are facilities that provide care that is appropriate for people who, while not in need of hospital care, require twenty-four-hour nursing care and supervision within a secure setting. Long-term care homes offer a greater level of personal care and support than retirement homes or supportive housing. Charitable homes[45] are usually owned by non-profit corporations, such as those established by faith, community, ethnic, or cultural groups.

k.   A person who operates a home or joint home under the *Homes for the Aged and Rest Homes Act*[46]

Like a charitable home for the aged, homes and joint homes under the *Homes for the Aged and Rest Homes Act* are long-term care homes. Homes for the aged are typically owned and operated by municipalities.[47] Many municipalities are required to provide a home for the aged in their area, either on their own or in partnership with a neighbouring municipality.

l.   A person who operates a nursing home[48]

Nursing homes are the most common type of long-term care home.[49] Nursing homes provide health care to patients who, while not in need of twenty-four-

---

44   *PHIPA*, s. 3(1)[4][ii]. *CIA*, above note 27, s. 3 provides: "Where the Minister is satisfied that any corporation without share capital having objects of a charitable nature ... is, with financial assistance under this Act, financially capable of establishing, maintaining and operating a charitable institution and that its affairs are carried on under competent management in good faith for charitable purposes, the Minister may approve such corporation for the purposes of this Act." The person who operates the approved charitable home for the aged is the corporation who receives the Minister of Health and Long-Term Care's approval under the *CIA*, s. 3.

45   *CIA*, *ibid.*, s. 1 provides that "approved charitable home for the aged" means a building, the buildings, or the parts of a building or buildings approved under section 3 of the *Charitable Institutions Act* as a home for the aged.

46   *PHIPA*, s. 3(1)[4][ii].

47   *HARHA*, above note 27, s. 1 provides that "home" means a home for the aged established or maintained under this Act or a rest home established and maintained under this Act; "joint home" means a home of two or more municipalities or councils of bands, as the case may be.

48   *PHIPA*, s. 3(1)[4][ii]. *NHA*, above note 27, s. 1(1), provides that "licensee" means a person who is the holder of a licence under that Act. *NHA*, s. 4(1) prohibits any person from establishing, operating, or maintaining a nursing home except under the authority of a licence issued by the Director under that Act. The licensee is the person who operates the nursing home. Generally, the licensee is a private corporation.

49   *NHA*, *ibid.*, s. 1(1) provides that "nursing home" means any premises maintained and operated for persons requiring nursing care or in which such care is provided to two or more

hour hospital care, require twenty-four-hour availability of nursing care and high levels of personal care. Nursing homes may be operated by a range of for-profit or not-for-profit organizations.

m. A person who operates a care home[50]

Care homes are often described by their owners or operators as "rest" homes, "retirement" homes, "lodging" homes, or "seniors'" homes. The *Tenant Protection Act, 1997* defines a care home as a residential building or complex where people live so that they can receive care services, whether or not receiving the services is the primary purpose of the occupancy.[51] "Care services" are defined by that Act as health care services, rehabilitative or therapeutic services, or services that provide assistance with the activities of daily living.[52] By regulation, the following services are also included in the definition of "care services": nursing care; administration and supervision of medication prescribed by a medical doctor; assistance with feeding; bathing assistance; incontinence care; dressing assistance; assistance with personal hygiene; ambulatory assistance; and personal emergency response services.[53] The primary reason for living at

---

unrelated persons, but does not include any premises falling under the jurisdiction of
  (a) the *Charitable Institutions Act*,
  (b) the *Child and Family Services Act*,
  (c) the *Homes for the Aged and Rest Homes Act*,
  (d) the *Mental Hospitals Act*,
  (e) the *Private Hospitals Act*, or
  (f) the *Public Hospitals Act*.

50   *PHIPA*, s. 3(1)[4][ii]. A "landlord" within the meaning of the *Tenant Protection Act, 1997*, S.O. 1997, c. 24 [*TPA*] is the person who operates a care home. *TPA*, s. 1(1) provides that "landlord" includes the following:
  (a) the owner of a rental unit or any other person who permits occupancy of a rental unit, other than a tenant who occupies a rental unit in a residential complex and who permits another person to also occupy the unit or any part of the unit;
  (b) the heirs, assigns, personal representatives, and successors in title of a person referred to in clause (a); and
  (c) a person, other than a tenant occupying a rental unit in a residential complex, who is entitled to possession of the residential complex and who attempts to enforce any of the rights of a landlord under a tenancy agreement or this Act, including the right to collect rent. The term "rental unit" means any living accommodation used or intended for use as rented residential premises, and "rental unit" includes a unit in a care home.

51   *TPA, ibid.*, s. 1(1).

52   *Ibid.*, s. 1(1).

53   *General*, O. Reg. 194/98, s. 6(1). Further, the following services are included in the definition of "care services" if they are provided along with any service set out above: recreational or social activities; housekeeping; laundry services; and assistance with transportation: O. Reg. 194/98, s. 6(2).

the home need not be to receive care services. The levels of care services provided vary from home to home.[54]

n.   A placement co-ordinator[55] under the *Charitable Institutions Act,*[56] *Homes for the Aged and Rest Homes Act,*[57] or *Nursing Homes Act*[58]

Placement co-ordinators under these Acts determine a patient's eligibility for admission to such facilities and have the role of authorizing the admission of patients into such facilities. Placement co-ordination is a key component of the work of community care access corporations. All persons requesting admission to a long-term care facility must apply to the placement co-ordination services of the community care access corporation to have their eligibility determined.

o.   A person who operates a pharmacy[59]

Pharmacies are familiar health resources in communities. The *Drug and Pharmacies Regulation Act* provides that "pharmacy" means premises in or in part of which prescriptions are compounded and dispensed for the public or drugs are sold by retail.[60] At a local drugstore, the "pharmacy" is the part of the store where drugs are dispensed.

p.   A person who operates an ambulance service[61]

The delivery of ambulance services is governed by the *Ambulance Act.*[62] Upper-tier municipalities and designated delivery agents are responsible for the provision of land ambulance services. The Ministry of Health and Long-Term Care

---

54   See the website of the Ontario Rental Housing Tribunal for additional information about care homes and the *TPA*, online: <www.orht.gov.on.ca>.

55   *PHIPA*, s. 3(1)[4][ii].

56   Above note 27, s. 9.6(2).

57   *Ibid.*, s. 18(2).

58   *Ibid.*, s. 20.1(2).

59   *PHIPA*, s. 3(1)[4][iii]. The *Drug and Pharmacies Regulation Act*, R.S.O. 1990, c. H.4, s. 139(1) [*DPRA*] prohibits a person from establishing or operating a pharmacy unless a certificate of accreditation has been issued in respect thereof. However, *DPRA*, s. 142(1) provides that no corporation may own or operate a pharmacy unless the majority of the directors of the corporation are pharmacists. Further, no person other than a pharmacist or a corporation complying with the requirements of s. 142 may own or operate a pharmacy: *DPRA*, s. 144(1).

60   *DPRA, ibid.*, s. 117(1).

61   *PHIPA*, s. 3(1)[4][v]. *Ambulance Act*, R.S.O. 1990, c. A.19, s. 1(1) provides that "ambulance service" means, subject to subs. (2), a service that is held out to the public as available for the conveyance of persons by ambulance. Persons who operate ambulance services include municipalities, designated delivery agents, and the Ministry of Health and Long-Term Care.

62   See *Ambulance Act, ibid.*, s. 1 for definitions of terminology related to the delivery of ambulance services, including "upper tier municipality," "delivery agent," and "air ambulance services."

sets standards for the delivery of land ambulance services and monitors compliance with those standards.[63] The Ministry is also responsible for the delivery of air ambulance services.

q.   A person who operates a home for special care[64]

The *Homes for Special Care Act* defines a home for special care as a home for the care of persons requiring nursing, residential, or sheltered care.[65] Generally, homes for special care provide long-term and permanent supportive housing to persons who are or who have been consumers of mental health services. Accommodation is provided in conjunction with care, such as nursing care and assistance with the activities of daily living. The program encourages residents to integrate into the community by offering an alternative housing option to care in an institution.

r.   A person who operates a centre, program, or service for community health or mental health whose primary purpose is the provision of health care[66]

This category of health information custodians is broad and may capture many health care organizations, programs, and services that do not otherwise fall into any of the more specific categories of health information custodians discussed above. For example, this category would clearly include community health centres, which are not-for-profit corporations that provide primary health and health promotion programs in a community. There are fifty-four community health centres in Ontario, each established and governed by a community-elected volunteer board of directors.[67] However, the term "centre, program or service for community health or mental health" appears to go beyond

---

63   See, for example, *General*, O. Reg. 257/00, made under the *Ambulance* Act, above note 61, which addresses such matters as the certification of operators of ambulance services and the standard of patient care and of transportation that such operators meet, as set out in Ministry of Health and Long-Term Care publications.

64   *PHIPA*, s. 3(1)[4][vi]. *Homes for Special Care Act*, R.S.O. 1990, c. H.12, s. 5(1) [*HSCA*] provides that the Minister of Health and Long-Term Care may license homes for special care and may renew or cancel the licences on such terms and conditions as the regulations prescribe. *General*, R.R.O. 1990, Reg. 636, made under the *HSCA* s. 29(1) provides that the Minister may issue a licence to a home for special care if the home complies with that Regulation and the Minister finds the home suitable for the reception and care of residents. The person who operates a home for special care is the person who holds the licence.

65   *HSCA, ibid.*, s. 1.

66   *PHIPA*, s. 3(1)[4][vii].

67   Community health centres are not governed by legislation specific to such centres. See the Ministry of Health and Long-Term Care website for additional information concerning community health centres, online: <www.health.gov.on.ca>.

simply "community health centres" to include other centres, programs of services that are primarily involved in providing health care, including mental health care. Mental health centres, programs or services may include a range of health care, including many of the programs and services provided by many not-for-profit agencies, such as the Canadian Mental Health Association.

s.   An evaluator or an assessor[68]

An evaluator is a person who, under the *Health Care Consent Act, 1996*, may determine whether an individual is capable with respect to his or her admission to a care facility[69] and with respect to a personal assistance service provided in a care facility. Pursuant to the regulation made under that Act, an evaluator must be a nurse, occupational therapist, physician, psychologist, physiotherapist, audiologist, speech-language pathologist, social worker, or social service worker registered to practise in Ontario.[70]

Similarly, an assessor under the *Substitute Decisions Act, 1992* is a person qualified to determine an individual's capacity to make decisions about his or her finances or personal care.[71] The regulations made under the *Substitute Decisions Act, 1992* specify the classes of persons permitted to act as assessors.[72] To be qualified to conduct assessments, one must be a nurse, occupational therapist, physician, psychologist, social worker, or social service worker registered to practise in Ontario.[73] Physiotherapists, audiologists, speech-language pathologists, though authorized to act as evaluators, are not permitted to act as assessors. Assessors are also required to successfully complete a training program,[74] and fulfil any additional requirements set out in those regulations.[75]

---

68   *PHIPA*, s. 3(1)[5].

69   Under the *Health Care Consent Act, 1996*, S.O. 1996, c. 2, Schedule A, s. 2(1) [*HCCA*] provides that "care facility" includes a long-term care home under the *Nursing Homes Act*, the *Homes for the Aged and Rest Homes Act*, or the *Charitable Institutions Act*, above note 27.

70   *Evaluators*, O. Reg. 104/96, made under the *HCCA*, *ibid.*, s. 1.

71   The *Substitute Decisions Act, 1992*, S.O. 1992, c. 30, s. 1(1) [*SDA*] provides that "assessor" means a member of a class of persons who are designated by the regulations as being qualified to do assessments of capacity. The *SDA* governs, among other matters, what may happen when a person is not mentally capable of making certain decisions about his or her own property or personal care. Personal care includes health care, nutrition, shelter, clothing, hygiene, and safety.

72   *Capacity Assessment*, O. Reg. 238/00, made under the *SDA*, *ibid.*

73   *Ibid.*, s. 1(1.1).

74   *Ibid.*, s. 1(1)(b).

75   See Ontario, *A Guide to the Substitute Decisions Act* (Toronto: Ministry of the Attorney General, 2000), online: <www.attorneygeneral.jus.gov.on.ca/english/family/pgt/sdaact.asp>.

t.   A medical officer of health or a board of health[76]

Public health units, established for particular geographical areas, are governed by boards of health and administered by a medical officer of health who is appointed by the board of health.[77] There are approximately thirty-seven public health units in Ontario. The duties of a medical officer of health are set out in the *Health Protection and Promotion Act* and include causing the inspection of the health unit served by a medical officer of health for the purpose of eliminating the effects of health hazards in the health unit and reporting to the Ministry of Health and Long-Term Care in respect of reportable diseases and in respect of deaths from such diseases that occur in the health unit served by the medical officer of health.

The provision in *PHIPA's* definition of "health information custodian" suggests that either the medical officer of health or the board of health could be a health information custodian. The *PHIPA* Regulation clarifies that, where there is a medical officer of health, the medical officer of health is recognized as the health information custodian with respect to all the functions performed under the responsibility of the medical officer of health, and the board of health is not the custodian with respect to those functions.[78] Further, the medical officer of health is recognized as a single custodian with respect to all these functions, and there would not be another custodian recognized performing these functions.[79] To the extent that the board of health could be recognized as a custodian, it would only be with respect to separate matters that were not within the responsibility of the medical officer of health performing his or her duties.

u.   The Minister of Health and Long-Term Care, together with the Ministry of Health and Long-Term Care

The Ministry of Health and Long-Term Care is responsible for administering Ontario's health care system and providing services to people in Ontario through such programs as health insurance, drug benefits, assistive devices,

---

76   *PHIPA*, s. 3(1)[6]. *PHIPA* Regulation, above note 9, s. 3(2) provides that a medical officer of health, together with a board of health, are a single health information custodian.

77   *Health Protection and Promotion Act*, R.S.O. 1990, c. H.7, s. 62(1) [*HPPA*]. *HPPA*, s. 64 provides that a person is not eligible for appointment as a medical officer of health unless (a) the person is a physician; (b) the person possesses the qualifications and requirements prescribed by the regulations for the position; and (c) the Minister approves the proposed appointment.

78   *PHIPA* Regulation, above note 9, s. 3(2).

79   *Ibid.*

care for the mentally ill, long-term care, home care, community and public health, and health promotion.[80] It also regulates health facilities such as hospitals, nursing homes, and independent health facilities, and co-ordinates emergency care services.[81] The Minister of Health and Long-Term Care has charge over the Ministry and all its functions.[82] The Minister is one health information custodian together with the Ministry.[83]

v.   Canadian Blood Services

The regulation made under *PHIPA* prescribes Canadian Blood Services as a health information custodian.[84] Established in 1998, Canadian Blood Services is a not-for-profit, charitable corporation established pursuant to Part II of the *Canada Corporations Act*. Its mission is to manage the blood and blood products supply for Canadians. Canadian Blood Services' work includes the collection and screening of blood, the processing of blood into components and products for administration to patients, the management of the Unrelated Bone Marrow Donor Registry, and research into transfusion medicine.[85]

w.   A public health laboratory[86]

The Minister of Health and Long-Term Care has the power to establish public health laboratories.[87] Including the central laboratory in Toronto, there are twelve public health laboratories in Ontario. Public health laboratories carry out testing to support public health activities and programs relating to reportable, emerging, and other public-health-relevant diseases.[88]

---

80   *Ministry of Health and Long-Term Care Act*, R.S.O. 1990, c. M.26, s. 6.

81   See the Ministry's website for more information about the Ministry, online: <www.health.gov.on.ca>.

82   *Ministry of Health and Long-Term Care Act*, above note 80, s. 3(1).

83   Under *FIPPA*, below note 164, the Ministry, not the Minister, is the "institution" subject to *FIPPA*. The reference in *PHIPA*, s. 3(1)[7] to the custodian being "the Minister, together with the Ministry of the Minister if the context so requires" appears to allow the Ministry as a *FIPPA* institution to be treated as the same entity as the Minister, which in turn simplifies the application of *PHIPA*, s. 8 to the Ministry and Minister.

84   *PHIPA* Regulation, above note 9, s. 3(1). Canadian Blood Services is prescribed as a single health information custodian for all its functions. See Section B(1)(c) below for a discussion of one entity's operation of multiple facilities, programs, and services.

85   See Canadian Blood Services' website for more details, online: <www.cbs.on.ca>.

86   *PHIPA* Regulation, above note 9, s. 3(3).

87   *HPPA*, above note 77, s. 79(1) provides that the Minister of Health and Long-Term Care may establish and maintain public health laboratory centres at such places and with such buildings, appliances, and equipment as the Minister considers proper. Although established and maintained by the Minister, public health laboratories are separate health information custodians from the Minister together with the Ministry of Health and Long-Term Care: *PHIPA* Regulation, above note 9, s. 3(3)(a).

x. Any other person or class of persons prescribed by the regulations made under the Act as a health information custodian[89]

At the time of writing, Canadian Blood Services and public health laboratories are the two categories of health information custodians designated by regulation.[90]

iii) Looking behind the Terminology

Certain types of health care organizations may be health information custodians even though their inclusion in the above list is not immediately apparent. For example, consider the term "care home."[91] Although, perhaps, not obvious, this terminology includes many homes that are more commonly known as "retirement homes" or "rest homes." Consider, also, the example of a hospice. Although the list of health information custodians in *PHIPA* does not include the word "hospice," hospice work is provided in such varied ways that it can be captured by the definition of "health information custodian" in different ways. Some hospices are classified as public hospitals, while other hospice work is carried out as a "program of community health." Other aspects of the definition of "health information custodian" may capture other hospice work. It is important to look behind the words in the list of health information custodians to understand its scope.

iv) Health Information Custodian in Connection with Custodian's Work

A person in the list of health information custodians set out above is a custodian only where the person has custody or control of personal health information as a result of or in connection with performing the person's powers or duties or the work described in the list.[92] A person is not a health information custodian with respect to personal health information that the person holds in a personal capacity (e.g., information held through unrelated volunteer work) or in a different professional capacity (e.g., information held as a result of carrying out an investigation for a professional governing body).

v) "A Person Who Operates"

As mentioned above, the definition of the term "health information custodian" often refers to "a person who operates" a particular facility, program, or service.[93]

---

88   See the Ministry of Health and Long-Term Care's website for additional information about public health laboratories, online: <www.health.gov.on.ca>.

89   *PHIPA*, s. 3(1)[8].

90   *PHIPA* Regulation, above note 9, ss. 3(1) & (3).

91   *PHIPA*, s. 3(1)[4][ii].

92   *Ibid*, s. 3(1).

93   *PHIPA*, s. 3(1)[4]. Sections 85.2(1) & (3) of Schedule 2 to the *Regulated Health Professions Act, 1991*, above note 12, the Health Professions Procedural Code, include similar

PHIPA defines the word "person" to include "a partnership, association or other entity."[94] In many cases, the "person" that operates such a facility, program, or service is a corporation.[95] Legislation may require a person to hold a licence, or obtain the approval of the Minister of Health and Long-Term Care or other body, or enter into an agreement, in order to provide a service or operate a facility. In such instances, the person who operates the service or facility is the one who was approved, holds the licence, or entered into the agreement. The manager, director, chief executive officer, or chairperson generally is not the person who operates the facility or service for the purposes of *PHIPA*.[96]

vi) Not all Entities with Personal Health Information Are Health Information Custodians

A number of entities whose duties involve personal health information are not listed as health information custodians. This list of non-custodians includes professional governing bodies,[97] such as the College of Physicians and Surgeons of Ontario, insurance companies, children's aid societies, and hospital foundations.

vii) Exclusions from Who Is a Health Information Custodian

PHIPA excludes three categories of persons from the definition of health information custodian.[98]

First, certain "agents"[99] of health information custodians, including employees of custodians, are not custodians themselves. Agents acting for or on behalf of custodians, in doing so, take on a different role with respect to per-

---

language, as those provisions of the Code place obligations on "a person who operates a facility."

94   *PHIPA*, s. 2, definition of "person."

95   *Interpretation Act*, above note 18, s. 29(1) provides that a "person" also includes a corporation.

96   This is often apparent from a statutory, regulatory, or contractual context, under which a particular person is authorized, licensed, or contracted to operate the facility or service. Generally, this will be a corporate entity rather than a particular person who holds a certain position in that corporate entity. The appointment of a new chairperson or chief executive officer by a corporation operating a health facility does not make the facility a new custodian.

97   "Professional governing bodies" refers to the *RHPA* Colleges and also the Board of Regents under the *DPA*, above note 13, and the Ontario College of Social Workers and Social Service Workers under the *SWSSWA*, above note 14. "*RHPA* Colleges" refers to a College within the meaning of the *RHPA*, above note 12, which provides a framework for the regulation of twenty-three health professions in Ontario, including physicians, nurses, and dentists. Such a College is the governing body of the health profession to which it relates.

98   *PHIPA*, s. 3(3).

99   *Ibid.*, s. 2 defines the term "agent." See Section B(2) below for a discussion of agents.

sonal health information. A person who is the agent of a health information custodian and who is also a health care practitioner, a service provider under the *Long-Term Care Act, 1994* who provides a community service, or an evaluator or assessor is not a health information custodian when performing a power, duty, or work on behalf of the custodian.[100] For example, each of a nurse who is an agent of a hospital, a dental hygienist who is an agent of a dental surgeon, an audiologist who is an agent of a medical officer of health, and a psychologist who is an agent of a community mental health centre, would not be health information custodians when acting in that capacity.[101]

Nevertheless, in some cases, a health care practitioner may be employed by or in the service of another health information custodian, but remain a custodian in his or her own right. This scenario may arise where personal health information that a health care practitioner uses is in the custody and control of the practitioner, and the practitioner's disclosure of the information to the custodian is restricted.[102] Where this is the case, the custodian employer would not be able to permit the employee practitioner to use or disclose the information on the employer custodian's behalf, as the employer would not have the power to do so itself.[103] Rather, the health care practitioner would require authority to use and disclose information him- or herself as a health information custodian, and otherwise ensure his or her compliance with the Act.

Second, a person who would otherwise be a health information custodian, and who is authorized to act for or on behalf of another person who is not a health information custodian, is not a custodian if the authorized person's work does not include the provision of health care.[104] This is a common situation. Health professionals have a wide range of skills and knowledge of value

---

100 *PHIPA*, s. 3(3)[1]. See Section B(1)(a)(ii) above for a description of each of these categories of persons.

101 Of course, as agents, such persons will also be subject to all the restrictions of the Act, in addition to any requirements or restrictions imposed by the health information custodian of whom they are an agent: *PHIPA*, s. 17.

102 This may be the case of personal health information in the custody or control of an occupational health physician in a hospital, for example. See the *Occupational Health and Safety Act*, R.S.O. 1990, c. O.1, s. 63.

103 *PHIPA*, s. 17(1)(a) provides that health information custodian may only permit an agent to use or disclose personal health information on the custodian's behalf if the custodian is authorized to use or disclose the information. *PHIPA*, however, speaks to a custodian using and disclosing personal health information that is in the custodian's custody or control: *PHIPA*, s. 2, definitions of "use" and "disclose."

104 *PHIPA*, s. 3(3)[2]. For a discussion of these custodians and health care practitioners who act for or on behalf of a person who is not a health information custodian, see Section B(1)(b)(iii), below. See Section B(1)(b)(ii) below for a discussion of "health care."

to employers that extends beyond the provision of health care. Therefore, a physician who is employed by an insurance company to provide services that do not constitute health care, such as the review of claims documentation, is not a health information custodian when acting in that capacity. A pharmacist employed to promote a company's nutritional supplements to pharmacies also would not be a health information custodian when acting in that capacity. However, as discussed further below, where the authorized person provides health care in the course of his or her duties for the non-custodian, then he or she will be considered a health information custodian.

Finally, the Minister of Health and Long-Term Care is not a custodian when acting on behalf of ministries and other institutions that are not health information custodians.[105]

PHIPA also excludes three other categories of persons from the definition of "health information custodian."[106] First, an aboriginal healer who provides traditional healing services to aboriginal persons or members of aboriginal communities is excluded from the definition of custodian.[107] An aboriginal midwife who provides traditional midwifery services to aboriginal persons or members of an aboriginal community is also excluded.[108] Third, the Act excludes from the definition of custodian a person who treats another person solely by prayer or spiritual means in accordance with the tenets of the religion of the person giving the treatment.[109] These categories reflect an ongoing approach to the regulation of persons who provide such services. Their exclusion from the definition of "health information custodian" in *PHIPA* is consistent with the provisions of the *Regulated Health Professions Act, 1991*.[110]

---

105   *PHIPA*, s. 3(3)[3].

106   *Ibid.*, s. 3(4).

107   *Ibid.*, s. 3(4)[1].

108   *Ibid.*, s. 3(4)[2].

109   *Ibid.*, s. 3(4)[3]. In their submission on Bill 31, *An Act to enact and amend various Acts with respect to the protection of health information*, 1st Sess., 38th Leg., Ontario, 2003 [Bill 31], to the Standing Committee on General Government, representatives of the Anglican, Evangelical, Lutheran, and Roman Catholic Churches in Ontario stated: "We believe that the most reasonable way to solve the problem addressed in this brief is to include chaplaincy services in the definition of health care, and chaplains employed by or accredited by a health information custodian as health care practitioners. This will allow chaplains to obtain access to personal health information and oblige them to safeguard it." See Ontario, Legislative Assembly, Standing Committee on General Government, *Official Report of Debates (Hansard)*, G-002 (26 January 2004) at 1320 (Bishop George Elliott). Ultimately, the Committee did not accept this recommendation. However, see Chapter 5 for a discussion of s. 20(2) and other provisions concerning the use and disclosure of personal health information to representatives of religious organizations.

110   *RHPA*, above note 12, s. 35(1) provides that it does not apply to (a) aboriginal healers providing traditional healing services to aboriginal persons or members of an aboriginal

PHIPA also includes a regulation-making power to permit the exclusion of other persons or classes of persons from being considered health information custodians under *PHIPA*.[111]

b) Health Care Practitioners

i) Definition

For the most part, there should be little difficulty in identifying a health information custodian as such. One type of health information custodian that may, in some cases, be a challenge is "health care practitioner."[112] *PHIPA* defines the term "health care practitioner"[113] to include the following persons when they provide health care:

- regulated health professionals, such as physicians, nurses, speech language pathologists, and dental surgeons;[114]
- registered drugless practitioners;[115]
- social workers and social service workers;[116] and
- any other person[117] whose primary[118] function is to provide health care for payment.[119]

In addition to members of regulated health professions, members of unregulated health professions, such as acupuncturists, psychotherapists,

---

community or (b) aboriginal midwives providing traditional midwifery services to aboriginal persons or members of an aboriginal community. In addition, *RHPA*, s. 29(1)(c) excludes from the definition of "controlled act" (i.e., those activities that only certain health care professionals can provided), "treating a person by prayer or spiritual means in accordance with the tenets of the religion of the person giving the treatment."

111 *PHIPA*, s. 73(1)(c). As of the time of writing, no regulations have been made pursuant to this regulation-making power.

112 Another example of a custodian that may sometimes be a challenge to identify, for the same reasons discussed in this part, is a "centre, program, service for community health or mental health whose primary purpose is the provision of health care": *PHIPA*, s. 3(1)[4][vii].

113 *PHIPA*, s. 2, definition of "health care practitioner."

114 For a list of regulated health professions, see above note 12.

115 Drugless practitioners, including naturopaths, are registered under the *DPA*, above note 13.

116 Social workers and social service workers are regulated by the Ontario College of Social Workers and Social Service Workers pursuant to the *SWSSWA*, above note 14.

117 *PHIPA*, s. 2 defines "person" to include a partnership, association, or other entity. The *Interpretation Act*, above note 18, s. 29(1) provides that "person" also includes a corporation. It may also include an individual.

118 In some instances, health care may constitute one aspect of a person's functions. Consider, for example, the work of a firefighter or a lifeguard. Although perhaps, at times, providing health care as part of their work, firefighters, lifeguards, and many other persons do not have "health care" as their "primary function."

119 *PHIPA* does not define the word "payment." However, it may include payment in kind.

practitioners of traditional Chinese medicine, or traditional Chinese medicine herbalists are also captured by the term "health care practitioner" where the practitioner's primary function is the provision of health care for payment.[120] Further, persons whose primary function is to provide health care for payment are "health care practitioners," even if they are not part of a recognized "profession," such as, persons employed by supportive housing providers[121] to provide health care to residents.

The regulation made under *PHIPA* clarifies that a person who provides fitness or weight-management services is not a "health care practitioner."[122]

ii) What Is "Health Care"?

A person is only a health care practitioner when the person provides health care.[123] Therefore, to understand the scope of the term "health care practitioner" it is necessary to understand the meaning of the term "health care," another defined term in *PHIPA*.[124] Health care means any observation, examination, assessment, care, service, or procedure that is done for a health-related purpose and that is carried out or provided:

- to diagnose, treat, or maintain an individual's physical or mental condition;
- to prevent disease or injury or to promote health; or
- as part of palliative care.

The regulations made under the Act clarify that "a procedure that is done for a health-related purpose," and therefore health care, includes taking a donation of blood or blood products from an individual.[125] The Act specifically provides that "health care" also includes the compounding, dispensing, or selling of a drug, a device, or equipment or any other item to an individual, or for the use of an individual, pursuant to a prescription. It further includes community services that are identified in the *Long-Term Care Act, 1994* and provided by service providers.[126] Community services[127] under that Act include community

---

120 *PHIPA*, s. 2, paragraph (d) of definition of "health care practitioner."

121 *Social Housing Reform Act, 2000*, S.O. 2000, c. 27, s. 2 defines "supportive housing provider."

122 *PHIPA* Regulation, above note 9, s. 2(1).

123 This is evident for each of *PHIPA*, s. 2, clauses (a) to (d) of the definition of "health care practitioner."

124 *PHIPA*, s. 2, definition of "health care."

125 *PHIPA* Regulation, above note 9, s. 1(1).

126 See discussion of service providers, above, in Section B(1)(a)(ii).

127 Where a person provides such services outside the scope of the *LTCA*, above note 20, the service would not constitute "health care" unless it is also done for a "health-related purpose."

support services,[128] homemaking services,[129] personal support services,[130] and professional services.[131]

In most cases, whether a service falls within the definition of "health care" will be obvious. In other instances, however, it may not be clear whether an activity constitutes "health care" for the purposes of *PHIPA*. The Ministry of Health and Long-Term Care provides the following guidance in public explanatory material about *PHIPA*:

> The definition of "health care" refers to an examination, procedure, etc. "that is done for a health-related purpose." The inclusion of this language, "health-related purpose," limits the scope of the definition of "health care" so as to exclude many activities, etc. from "health care." If the sole way in which a person would be captured by the definition of "health information custodian" would be through the language "a person whose primary function is to provide health care for payment" in the definition of "health care practitioner," it is necessary to consider whether the services that [the person] provide[s] are performed for a "health-related purpose." Transportation services, for example, are generally not provided "for a health-related purpose." Similarly, assessments of potential parents performed to assist an adoption [agency] to decide whether to place a child with the potential parents are not provided "for a health-related purpose." Therefore, the services of the person in question and the services to be provided must be considered to determine whether he or she is a "health information custodian."[132]

The meaning of the term "health care" should be considered in the broader context of the Act. As discussed above, the scope of the Act focuses on a cate-

---

128 *LTCA, ibid.,* s. 3(4) identifies the following as community support services: meal services; transportation services; caregiver support services; adult day programs; home maintenance and repair services; friendly visiting services; security checks or reassurance services; social or recreational services; providing prescribed equipment, supplies, or other goods; and services prescribed as community support services.

129 *LTCA, ibid.,* s. 3(5) identifies the homemaking services, including housecleaning; doing laundry; ironing; mending; shopping; banking; paying bills; planning menus; preparing meals; caring for children; and services prescribed as homemaking services.

130 *LTCA, ibid.,* s. 3(6) includes personal hygiene activities and routine personal activities of living as personal support services.

131 *LTCA, ibid.,* s. 3(7) includes the following as professional services: nursing services; occupational therapy services; physiotherapy services; social work services; speech-language pathology services; and dietetics services.

132 Ontario, *Personal Health Information Protection Act, 2004: An Overview for Health Information Custodians* (Toronto: Ministry of Health and Long-Term Care, August 2004) at 34, online: <www.health.gov.on.ca>.

gory of persons called health information custodians, generally found in the health care sector. *PHIPA* does not regulate the collection, use, and disclosure of personal health information by all persons. An interpretation of the term "health care" should be consistent with this focus. "Health care" should not be interpreted so as to broaden the scope of the Act so that it no longer has the health care sector as its focus.

The interpretation of the term "health care" should also reflect the policy of section 20(2) of the Act. This provision permits health care practitioners and specified health information custodians who collect personal health information from a patient or another health information custodian to assume the individual's implied consent to the collection, use, and disclosure of that information for the purpose of providing health care or assisting in the provision of health care, unless the patient expressly instructs otherwise.[133] A very broad reading of the definition of health care, and thus the definition of health care practitioner, can run contrary to the policy behind this provision, which can be described as facilitating collections, uses, and disclosures in the health care system that individuals generally expect to occur without requiring express consent.[134] Would it be reasonable to assume, without the individual expressly indicating so, that a patient consents to a physician's disclosure of the individual's personal health information to a weight loss company, personal trainer, or life coach? Or would a patient expect to have a greater role in decisions concerning such persons' collection, use, and disclosure of personal health information? The response to this question may be useful in some instances in interpreting the term "health care," particularly as it applies in the definition of "health care practitioner."

iii) Health Care Practitioners Employed by Non-Health Information Custodians
Many health care practitioners are employed or retained by persons who are not health information custodians. The list of such health care practitioners is extensive and includes audiologists and speech language pathologists employed by boards of education, social workers employed by children's aid societies, massage therapists employed by hotels or recreational facilities,

---

133   See Chapter 5 for a discussion of this provision.

134   A similar conclusion can be reached with respect to *PHIPA*, s. 38(1)(a), which permits a health information custodian to disclose personal health information about a patient to the same categories of health information custodians as those listed in *PHIPA*, s. 20(2), including health care practitioners, "if the disclosure is reasonably necessary for the provision of health care and it is not reasonably possible to obtain the individual's consent in a timely manner," unless the patient has expressly instructed the custodian not to make the disclosure.

occupational health nurses or physicians employed by manufacturers, a person who is employed by a supportive housing provider to provide health care, and persons who provide health care in and nurses employed by government bodies to provide services in correctional facilities or youth justice facilities.

PHIPA does not exclude these employee health care practitioners from the definition of the term "health information custodian."[135] Therefore, where these practitioners provide health care as part of their duties, they are, as individuals, health information custodians separate from their employers.[136] An employer generally does not become a health information custodian by employing or retaining a health care practitioner. As custodians, these practitioners must act in accordance with *PHIPA* and fulfil the obligations of custodians under that Act. In addition, it is important to note that a practitioner's provision of personal health information to his or her non-custodian employer is a disclosure of personal health information under *PHIPA*, which can only be made in accordance with *PHIPA*'s rules relating to disclosures, which usually requires the express consent of the patient to whom the information relates, unless *PHIPA* authorizes a disclosure without consent in the circumstances.[137]

Where several health care practitioners are employed or retained by the same non-custodian to provide health care as part of their duties, they may work together to facilitate the fulfilment of their obligations as health information custodians under *PHIPA*. For example, the practitioners may jointly develop their information practices, including determining how to store records of personal health information, and their public written statements. They may all designate one person to act as their contact person.[138] Even where they act together in this way, however, each health care practitioner is a separate custodian under *PHIPA* and has all the duties of a custodian.[139] While co-operating in this manner makes the health care practitioners' compliance with

---

135 *PHIPA*, s. 3(3)[2] does not apply to exclude persons from being health information custodians who provide health care in the course of their duties.

136 Note that "personal health information" does not include identifying information contained in a record that relates primarily to an employee or other agent of a custodian if the record is maintained for a purpose other than the provision of health care to the employee or agent: *PHIPA*: s. 4(4). See Section C(1)(f), below.

137 See Chapter 10 for a discussion of disclosures of personal health information without consent.

138 See Chapter 4 for a discussion of these obligations.

139 These duties include: to appoint or act as "contact person" (*PHIPA*, s. 15); to develop and comply with "information practices" (*PHIPA*, s. 10); to ensure accuracy (*PHIPA*, s. 11) and security (ss. 12 & 13) of personal health information; and to make available a written public statement (*PHIPA*, s. 16(1)). See Chapter 4 for more detail.

PHIPA more convenient, it does not affect the substance of their obligations under *PHIPA*.

To further facilitate the fulfilment of their obligations under *PHIPA*, health care practitioners employed by persons who are not health information custodians should seek the assistance of their employers. It is in an employer's interest to ensure that its employees are able to comply with the law in an efficient manner, and in a manner that will harmonize as much as possible with the employer's operations. Such health care practitioners should also look to their professional governing bodies and other professional organizations for guidance on how to facilitate their compliance with the Act.

c) Multiple Facilities and Custodians

At times, one organization will operate more than one health facility,[140] such as multiple nursing homes. Generally, *PHIPA* deems such an organization to be a separate custodian with respect to the personal health information of which it has custody or control as a result of or in connection with operating each of the facilities that it operates.[141]

There are exceptions to this general rule. First, a person who operates a public hospital[142] and any of the facilities, programs, or services described in paragraph 4 of the definition of "health information custodian"[143] is deemed to be a single health information custodian for the operation of the public hospital, and the other facilities, programs, and services.[144] Consequently, a hospital with several sites is one health information custodian. Furthermore, a hospital that operates a psychiatric facility, laboratory, pharmacy, and a mental health program, for example, is one health information custodian together with all such services. Similarly, a community care access corporation that provides community services[145] and that also acts as a long-term care placement co-ordi-

---

140 The term "facility," according to *PHIPA*, s. 3(5), refers to the different types of facilities referred to in s. 3(1)[4].

141 *PHIPA*, s. 3(5).

142 See Section B(1)(a)(ii)(e) above for a discussion of the phrase "a person who operates a hospital within the meaning of the *Public Hospitals Act*" as it appears in *PHIPA*, s. 3(1)[4][i].

143 Some of the facilities, programs, and services that *PHIPA*, s. 3(1)[4] describes include: public hospitals; psychiatric facilities; nursing homes; pharmacies; laboratories; community health programs; and mental health programs.

144 *PHIPA*, s. 3(6)[1].

145 See Section B(1)(a)(ii)(c), above, for a discussion of the phrase "a service provider within the meaning of the *Long-Term Care Act, 1994* who provides a community service to which that Act applies," as it appears in *PHIPA*, s. 3(1)[2].

nator[146] is deemed to be a single health information custodian for both types of functions.[147] Likewise, Canadian Blood Services is prescribed as a single health information custodian for all its functions.[148] Each public health laboratory is also a single health information custodian in respect of all its functions.[149]

Where these exceptions do not apply, an organization that operates several facilities and is deemed to be a separate health information custodian for each facility may wish to be permitted to act as a single unified custodian in respect of two or more of the facilities. Furthermore, in certain circumstances, other separate health information custodians may also wish to be permitted to act together as a single custodian for their operations. The Act provides two ways in which custodians can be deemed to be, or permitted to act as, a single unified custodian.

First, health information custodians can be prescribed by a regulation made under *PHIPA* to be deemed to be a single health information custodian for the custodians' operation of multiple facilities.[150] A regulation establishing Canadian Blood Services as a single health information custodian for all its functions is one example of the use of this regulation-making power.[151]

Alternatively, a health information custodian, or two or more custodians, can make an application to the Minister of Health and Long-Term Care for an order permitting all or some of the applicants to act as a single health information custodian on behalf of those facilities, powers, duties, or work that the Minister specifies.[152] To make the order, the Minister must be of the opinion that the order is appropriate in the circumstances,[153] having regard to

- the public interest;
- the ability of the applicants to provide individuals with reasonable access to their records of personal health information;
- the ability of the applicants to comply with the requirements of the Act; and

---

146 See Section B(1)(a)(ii)(n) above for a discussion of placement co-ordinators described in s. 9.6(2) of the *CIA*, s. 18(2) of the *HARHA*, or s. 20.1(2) of the *NHA*, all above note 27.
147 *PHIPA*, s. 3(6)[2].
148 *PHIPA* Regulation, above note 9, s. 3(1). See Section B(1)(a)(ii)(v) above for a discussion of the functions of Canadian Blood Services.
149 *PHIPA* Regulation, *ibid.*, s. 3(3)(a). See Section B(1)(a)(ii)(w) above for a discussion of public health laboratories.
150 *PHIPA*, s. 3(6)[3]. See Chapter 16 for details about the process for making regulations.
151 *PHIPA* Regulation, above note 9, s. 3(1). See also *PHIPA* Regulation, ss. 3(2) & (3).
152 *PHIPA*, s. 3(7).
153 *Ibid.*, s. 3(8).

- whether permitting the applicants to act as a single custodian is necessary to enable them to effectively provide integrated health care.

The Minister can include terms in the order that the Minister considers appropriate.[154] In addition, the Minister can broaden the scope of an order so that any class of health information custodians that the Minister considers to be situated similarly to the applicants is permitted to act as a single health information custodian.[155] To extend an order in this way, the Minister must be of the opinion that such an order is appropriate, having regard to substantially the same factors as mentioned above.[156]

No hearing is associated with these types of orders of the Minister of Health and Long-Term Care.[157] The Ministry has developed instructions for applicants[158] seeking such orders. In addition to basic administrative information about the applicants, the instructions describe the information applicants should provide to assist the Minister in considering the appropriateness of the order, including the following:

- a description of the facilities, powers, duties, or work for which an order of the Minister is sought;
- an explanation of why the applicant(s) believe(s) that the order would be in the public interest;
- a description of how applicant(s) would be able to provide patients with reasonable access to their records of personal health information if permitted to act as a single health information custodian as proposed by the applicant(s);
- an explanation of how an order would enhance the ability of the applicant(s) to effectively provide integrated health care;
- an explanation of how an order would affect the applicant's ability to comply with the Act; and
- a description of any measures or safeguards that the applicant(s) propose(s) to take in order to ensure that the purposes of the Act, and the applicant's ability to comply with the Act, are not impeded by the requested order.

---

154 *PHIPA*, s. 3(8).

155 *Ibid.*, s. 3(9).

156 *Ibid.*

157 *Ibid.*, s. 3(10).

158 The Ministry of Health and Long-Term Care's "Instructions for Application for Minister's Order under s. 3(8) of the *Personal Health Information Protection Act, 2004*" are available on the Ministry's website, online: <www.health.gov.on.ca>.

The instructions for an application to the Minister also indicate that the Minister reserves the right to request further information to assess the appropriateness of the proposed order. Therefore, there may be instances in which the Ministry may contact applicants to discuss their applications in additional detail.

Before applying for such an order, health information custodians should consider whether the order is really necessary to enable the custodians to operate in an effective manner with respect to personal health information. Custodians should consider that many of the perceived advantages of being allowed to operate as a single unified custodian can be reached even in the absence of such an order; for example, by collaboration between the custodians affected in developing information practices and written public statements, and, possibly, in appointing a common contact person for all of them. Custodians should also analyze in detail the required information flows between the various health information custodians, keeping in mind that as long as they are operating as separate custodians, transfers of information between them, even if transmitted through a common contact person, are considered to be disclosures and must be made in accordance with *PHIPA's* rules for disclosures of personal health information.[159]

d) "As If It Were a Health Information Custodian"

In several instances, the regulations made under *PHIPA* indicate that a person may undertake an activity "as if [the person] were a health information custodian" for the purposes of a particular section of *PHIPA*.[160] These provisions permit persons who are not health information custodians to undertake an activity with respect to personal health information in the same manner that health information custodians may do so under the Act. For example, prescribed planning entities may disclose personal health information as if they are health information custodians for the purposes of section 44 of *PHIPA*.[161] Therefore, prescribed planning entities can disclose personal health information to researchers in accordance with the research rules in *PHIPA* applicable

---

159 *PHIPA*, s. 6(1). Where a custodian may operate as one unified single custodian with respect to multiple facilities, powers, duties, or work, then transfers of personal health information between the facilities, etc. will be considered "uses" of the information, and not "disclosures," and thus would be subject to different rules. See Chapters 9 and 10, which discuss uses and disclosures of personal health information.

160 For example, *PHIPA* Regulation, above note 9, ss. 13(4), 13(5), 14(4), 14(5), 18(3), and 18(4).

161 *PHIPA* Regulation, *ibid.*, 18(4).

to health information custodians.[162] However, the persons to whom such provisions refer are not thereby health information custodians. The Act merely permits them to undertake activities in the way in which health information custodians may do so.

e) "Custody or Control"

i) Relevance of Concepts

A person is only a "health information custodian" while having custody or control of personal health information as a result of or in connection with performing the person's powers or duties or the work described in the applicable part of the definition of "health information custodian."[163] What does it mean to have "custody or control" of personal health information? To understand this phrase, it is useful to consider its history.

ii) Custody or Control in FIPPA/MFIPPA

a. Background

The expression "custody or control" has a history in Ontario's public sector privacy and access to information legislation, the *Freedom of Information and Protection of Privacy Act* and the *Municipal Freedom of Information and Protection of Privacy Act*.[164] Whether records of personal information are considered to be in the custody or under the control of an institution subject to one of those two Acts has been the focus of several of the Information and Privacy Commissioner's orders, in addition to judicial consideration. Although considered in that different context,[165] it is useful to understand how the language "custody or control" has been interpreted for the purposes of that legislation.

In considering the issue of "custody or control" in the context of the public sector legislation, institutions must be found to have either "custody" or

---

162 For example, the disclosure may be made after a research ethics board's approval of the researcher's research plan. See Chapter 11 for a discussion of the rules applicable to health information custodians in disclosing personal health information to researchers.

163 *PHIPA*, s. 3(1).

164 R.S.O. 1990, c. F.31, s. 10(1) [*FIPPA*] and R.S.O. 1990, c. M.56, s. 4(1) [*MFIPPA*] respectively, provide individuals with a right of access to a record or a part of a record in the custody or under the control of an institution, subject to the exceptions identified in the Act. *FIPPA* became law in Ontario in 1988. *MFIPPA* followed shortly thereafter in 1991.

165 The differences are discussed below. The most obvious difference is that *PHIPA* refers to "custody or control" of personal health information, not just of records of personal health information.

"control" of the record in question in order to trigger obligations under those Acts. It is not necessary that institutions have both "custody" and "control." *PHIPA* is also clear that having either custody or control is enough to make a health information custodian subject to the Act.[166]

In addition, in the context of *FIPPA* and *MFIPPA*, the Office of the Information and Privacy Commissioner has found that the terms "custody" and "control" should be given broad and liberal interpretation in order to give effect to the purposes and principles of the legislation.[167]

Further, the Office of the Information and Privacy Commissioner, in the context of *FIPPA* and *MFIPPA*, has stated that it is not possible to establish a precise definition of the words "custody" or "control" as they are used in public sector privacy legislation, and then simply apply those definitions in each case. Rather, it is necessary to consider all aspects of the creation, maintenance, and use of particular records, and to decide whether the institution has "custody" or "control" in the circumstances of a particular fact situation.[168]

The consideration of several factors assists in determining whether an institution has "custody" or "control" of particular records. A 1989 order of the Office of the Information and Privacy Commissioner[169] listed the following factors as being particularly relevant:

1) Did an officer or employee of the institution create the record?
2) What use did the creator intend to make of the record?
3) Does the institution have possession of the record, either because it has been voluntarily provided by the creator or pursuant to a mandatory statutory or employment requirement?
4) If the institution does not have possession of the record, is it being held by an officer or employee of the institution for the purposes of his or her duties as an officer or employee?
5) Does the institution have a right to possess the record?
6) Does the content of the record relate to the institution's mandate and functions?
7) Does the institution have the authority to regulate the record's use?

---

166 *PHIPA*, s. 3(1).
167 Order P-120, Ministry of Government Services (22 November 1989), online: <www.ipc.on.ca> [P-120].
168 Order P-271, Algonquin College of Applied Arts and Technology (12 February 1992), online: <www.ipc.on.ca> [P-271].
169 P-120, above note 167. This early order from the Commissioner's Office has been relied on regularly in subsequent orders.

8) To what extent has the record been relied upon by the institution?
9) How closely is the record integrated with other records held by the institution?
10) Does the institution have the authority to dispose of the record?

The Office of the Information and Privacy Commissioner has also found that whether an institution has a statutory power or duty to carry out the activity that resulted in the creation of the record is also relevant to establishing "custody or control."[170]

The above factors are not an exhaustive list of all factors that should be considered by an institution in determining whether a record is "in the custody or under the control" of an institution, but they help provide some guidance.[171]

b. Custody

The fact that there may be limits on the institution's ability to govern the use of the records is relevant to the issue of whether the institution has control of the records, but it does not preclude an institution from having custody.[172]

One order provides:

> The Oxford Dictionary defines ... "Custody" ... as "guardianship; care."
>
> ...
>
> "Custody" is defined in *Black's* [*Law Dictionary*, 5th ed.] as "the keeping, guarding, care, watch, inspection, preservation or security of a thing, carrying with it the idea of the thing being within the immediate personal care and control of the person to whose custody it is subjected.[173]

When considering whether an institution has custody of a record, bare possession does not amount to custody for purposes of public sector privacy legislation. In order for there to be "custody" in the legal sense there must also be some right to deal with the records and some responsibility for their care and protection.[174] This suggests that an institution to which an unsolicited record is sent will not necessarily be considered to have custody of the record until it takes some step to accept that record into its care. However, it has been held

---

170 Order P-912, Ontario Criminal Code Review Board (21 April 1995), online: <www.ipc.on.ca> [P-912].
171 See above note 164.
172 Order P-239, Ministry of Government Services (5 September 1991), online: <www.ipc.on.ca> [P-239].
173 P-120, above note 167.
174 P-239, above note 172; P-271, above note 168.

that physical possession of a record is often strong evidence of custody, and only in unusual circumstances could it successfully be argued that an institution did not have custody of a record in its actual possession.[175]

The following examples of matters where institutions under *FIPPA* were found to have custody of records provide further guidance as to how the term "custody" may be applied in practice. In the context of *MFIPPA*, where a hospital sent a patient's medical record to the police, with the patient's consent, the record in the police files, was treated as being in the custody or control of the police, even though the police did not request the record from the hospital.[176] In the context of *FIPPA*, the Office of the Information and Privacy Commissioner has determined that notes made by an employee of an institution as a panellist in a job competition conducted on behalf of the institution were in the control of the institution, despite the fact that the panellist had taken the notes home, because the employee created the notes for the purpose of documenting employment-related concerns, which she subsequently introduced into the employment context.[177] Also in the context of *FIPPA*, the Commissioner's office has found that minutes of meetings of the Board of Directors of the Canadian Blood Agency were in the custody of the Ministry of Health when a representative of the Ministry received the minutes and retained them with other Ministry records.[178]

c. Control

An IPC order provides:

> The Oxford dictionary defines "control" as the "power to direct; command." …

> *Black's Law Dictionary* (5th Edition) defines "control" as meaning "power or authority to manage, direct, superintend, restrict, regulate, govern, administer or oversee."

The Court of Appeal of Ontario has held that the absence of evidence that an *FIPPA/MFIPPA* institution has actually exercised control over particular records will not necessarily advance the institution's argument that it, in fact,

---

175   P-120, above note 167.

176   Order M-128, Metropolitan Toronto Board of Commissioners of Police (6 May 1993), online: <www.ipc.on.ca>.

177   Order P-41, Ministry of Tourism and Recreation (2 March 1989); Order P-257, Ministry of Community and Social Services (29 November 1991); Order P-1105, Ministry of Agriculture, Food and Rural Affairs (24 January 1996); online: <www.ipc.on.ca>.

178   Order P-1291, Ministry of Health (14 November 1996), online: <www.ipc.on.ca>.

has no control.[179] The issue is whether the institution has the power to control the record, not whether it has actually exercised that power.

Other IPC orders[180] set out the following questions for consideration of the issue of control of records:

- Does the institution have a statutory power or duty to carry out the activity resulting in the creation of the records?
- Is the activity a "core," "central," or "basic" function of the institution?
- Are there any contracts between the institution and the third party giving the institution the right to possess or control the records?
- Who paid for the creation of the record?
- To what extent did the institution rely or intend to rely on the record?
- Who owns the record?

Again, some concrete examples of matters where institutions under *FIPPA* were found to have control of records help to show how the term "control" may be applied. In the context of *FIPPA*, the Office of the Information and Privacy Commissioner has determined that notes made by an employee of an institution as a panellist in a job competition conducted on behalf of the institution were in the control of the institution, despite the fact that the panellist had taken the notes home.[181] The Court of Appeal, in the context of *FIPPA*, found that the Ontario Criminal Code Review Board had control of backup audio tapes prepared by the court reporter, an independent contractor, at its disposition hearings. As the sole purpose of creating the backup tape was to fulfil the Board's statutory mandate to keep accurate records, the Board had the power to limit the use to which the backup tapes may be put, and the Board was required to have access to all the records prepared by the court reporter in the event that an issue arises about the accuracy of either the record or the transcript.[182]

iii) Custody or Control in PHIPA

Given the direction of the Office of the Information and Privacy Commissioner on the issue of custody or control of personal information in the public sector, it is reasonable to assume that the Commissioner will take a similar

---

179 *Ontario (Criminal Code Review Board) v. Ontario (Information and Privacy Commissioner)* (1999), 47 O.R. (3d) 201 (C.A.). The dictionary definitions of "control" were cited in Order P-120, above note 167.

180 MO-1237, York Catholic District School Board (29 September 1999); MO-1242, City of Kitchener (19 October 1999), online: <www.ipc.on.ca>.

181 See above note 177.

182 *Ontario (Criminal Code Review Board) v. Ontario (Information and Privacy Commissioner)*, above note 179.

approach in interpreting the words "custody or control" as those words are used in *PHIPA*.[183]

However, one difference in the *PHIPA* context is notable. Under *PHIPA* it is not just records of personal health information, but personal health information itself that is referred to as being in the custody or control of a health information custodian.[184] This difference suggests that, unlike the case in *FIPPA* and *MFIPPA*, it may be possible to have custody or control of personal health information that is not in recorded form.

2) Agents

a) Generally

PHIPA recognizes that health information custodians will often act through agents. Indeed, some custodians will only act through agents.[185] The Act supports this practice by providing rules to help ensure that custodians and agents are appropriately accountable for their actions in respect of personal health information and setting out their respective roles and responsibilities.

b) Definition of "Agent"

Although the courts have developed a meaning for the term "agent" at common law, the meaning of the term "agent" in *PHIPA* does not rely on common law jurisprudence for its interpretation. The Act defines the term "agent" broadly as a person[186] who acts for or on behalf of a custodian in respect of personal health information for the purposes of the custodian.[187] A person who acts for his or her own purposes in respect of personal health information is not an agent. A person is only an agent when acting with the authorization of the custodian.[188] An agent may or may not have the authority to bind the custodian.[189] An agent may or may not be an employee; an agent may or may not be remunerated.[190]

---

183 *PHIPA*, ss. 2 (definitions of "disclose" and "use"); 3 (definition of "health information custodian"); 4(4); 8; 10(1); 12; 13; 15(3); 16; 17(1); 22(4); 49(3); 51; 52; 53; 60; & 72(1).

184 *PHIPA*, ss. 2 (definitions of "disclose" and "use"); 3 (definition of "health information custodian"); 4(4); 8; 10(1); 12; 17(1); 22(4)[2]; & 49(3) all refer to custody or control of personal health information.

185 Health information custodians that are corporations, such as public hospitals and long-term care homes, will operate through agents alone.

186 An agent need not be an individual. *PHIPA*, s. 2 defines "person" to include a partnership, association, or other entity. The *Interpretation Act*, above note 18, s. 29(1) provides that "person" also includes a corporation.

187 *PHIPA*, s. 2, definition of "agent."

188 *Ibid.*

189 *Ibid.*

190 *Ibid.*

c) Who Are Agents?

Agents of a health information custodian may be found within or outside the health information custodian's organization. A custodian's agents may include a wide range of persons who have different roles with respect to the custodian's personal health information. Some agents handle small amounts of personal health information, while other agents deal with the complete records of personal health information in the custodian's custody or control.

A health information custodian's agents may include, for example, any of the following persons who carry out functions with personal health information on behalf of the custodian:

- any employee of the custodian who deals with personal health information;
- information technology service providers;[191]
- contact persons, as defined in *PHIPA*;[192]
- providers of records management services;
- providers of information destruction services;
- accountants;
- bookkeepers;
- providers of transcription services;
- providers of claims management services;
- chaplains and other spiritual care providers;
- volunteers who visit patients;[193]
- food delivery agents;
- students training to be health care practitioners;[194] and
- legal counsel.

Health care practitioners, including physicians, nurses, physiotherapists, medical laboratory technologists, and occupational therapists, are often agents of health information custodians, like hospitals, long-term care facilities, and laboratories. As discussed above, a person, such as a health care practitioner, who would otherwise be a health information custodian but who is an agent of a health

---

191 Such a provider may or may not be an agent of the custodian. See Section B(3) below.

192 See of Chapter 4, Section B for a discussion of the role of a contact person, an agent whose role is identified in *PHIPA*, s. 15.

193 Though a volunteer may not have access to extensive personal health information, in the context of a facility like a hospital, even limited identifying information like the patient's name, as such, is considered personal health information.

194 *PHIPA*, s. 37(1)(e) provides that a health information custodian may use personal health information for educating agents to provide health care. See Chapter 9 for a discussion of this provision.

information custodian is not him- or herself a custodian in respect of personal health information that he or she collects, uses, or discloses while performing his or her powers or duties for the custodian for whom he or she is an agent.[195]

d)   Limitations on Activities of Agents

A health information custodian may permit his or her agents to collect, use, disclose, retain, or dispose of personal health information on the custodian's behalf where the custodian is permitted or required to collect, use, disclose, retain, or dispose of the information.[196] Generally, if the custodian does not have authority to deal with the information, the agent will not have the authority either.[197] In addition, the collection, use, disclosure, retention, or disposition of the information by an agent on behalf of a custodian must be in the course of the agent's duties, and not contrary to the limits imposed by the custodian, the Act, or any other law.[198] For example, an agent may not keep copies of records of personal health information for the agent's own use outside the scope of the agent's duties to the custodian. Likewise, where a custodian informs an agent that the agent must not use personal health information for the purpose of marketing the custodian's services, the agent must not proceed to do so. An agent is required to follow the instructions of the custodian except to the extent they are inconsistent with *PHIPA* or another law.[199]

Health information custodians hold decision-making powers with respect to personal health information in their custody or control. In some instances, a custodian may delegate decision-making powers to agents. Such a delegation is inevitable in the case of corporate health information custodians. Where a health information custodian does not delegate such powers, an agent may nevertheless carry out the decisions of the custodian. For example, a custodian may decide when it is appropriate to destroy personal health information, while an agent may be responsible for destroying the information after that period of time. Health information custodians always retain accountability for the personal health information that their agents handle on their behalf. For

---

195   *PHIPA*, s. 3(3)[1]. See Section B(1) above.

196   *PHIPA*, s. 17(1)(a).

197   As such, if an employee of a custodian, such as a health care practitioner, is collecting and using information that the custodian does not have authority to collect and use, it would appear that the employee cannot be acting as the agent of the custodian in that respect, and may instead be acting as a health information custodian in his or her own right. See above note 102 for an example in the context of occupational health and safety.

198   *PHIPA*, s. 17(1)(b).

199   *Ibid.*

the purposes of *PHIPA*, a health information custodian remains responsible for the personal health information in the custody or control of the custodian, even where the custodian authorizes the agent to act on its behalf.[200]

While *PHIPA* includes rules applicable to a health information custodian in working with an agent,[201] the Act also includes rules that an agent must follow in acting in that capacity.[202] Both have legal duties under *PHIPA*. Except where the law provides otherwise, an agent of a health information custodian must not collect, use, disclose, retain, or dispose of personal health information on the custodian's behalf unless the custodian permits the agent to do so.[203]

e)   Use and Disclosure by Agent: Exceptions to Limitations

There are several exceptions to the obligation of an agent of a health information custodian not to use or disclose personal health information on behalf of the custodian without the custodian's permission. One exception to this prohibition is where the use or disclosure of the personal health information is permitted or required by law, such as where the agent is required to disclose the information to comply with a requirement in legislation or pursuant to a court order.[204] An agent may also disclose personal health information without the custodian's authorization where the disclosure is necessary for the purpose of eliminating or reducing a significant risk of serious bodily harm to a person or group of persons.[205] Further, an agent may disclose personal health information without the custodian's authorization to professional governing bodies for the purpose of the administration or enforcement of the *Drug and Pharmacies Regulation Act*, the *Social Work and Social Service Work Act, 1998*, the *Regulated Health Professions Act, 1991*, or an Act named in Schedule 1 to that Act.[206] In

---

200 *PHIPA*, s. 17(1). It is interesting to note that the heading for s. 17(1) changed from "Custodian responsible for agents" to "Agents and information" after the first reading of Bill 31, above note 109.

201 *PHIPA*, s. 17(1).

202 *Ibid.*, s. 17(2).

203 *Ibid.*

204 *Ibid.* For example, an agent may be required to disclose personal health information to a medical officer of health pursuant to the *Health Protection and Promotion Act*, above note 77. See Chapter 3, Section A(3)(b), for a discussion of the phrase "permitted or required by law."

205 *PHIPA* Regulation, above note 9, s. 7(2)(i).

206 *Ibid.*, s. 7(2)(ii). Schedule 1 of the *RHPA*, above note 12, lists twenty-one health-profession-specific Acts, including the *Medicine Act, 1991*, S.O. 1991, c. 30; the *Occupational Therapy Act, 1991*, S.O. 1991, c. 33; the *Nursing Act, 1991*, S.O. 1991, c. 32; the *Midwifery Act, 1991*, S.O. 1991, c. 31; the *Dental Hygiene Act, 1991*, S.O. 1991, c. 22; and the *Pharmacy Act, 1991*, S.O. 1991, c. 36.

addition, an agent may disclose personal health information without the custodian's authorization to the Public Guardian and Trustee or a children's aid society so that these bodies can carry out their statutory functions.[207] These permitted disclosures parallel disclosures that health information custodians are permitted to make under *PHIPA*.[208] This mirroring of powers permits agents, including physicians, nurses, social workers, and other regulated professionals, to fulfil their responsibilities as professionals in the health care sector, or under other applicable law.[209]

Another exception arises in the context of risk management activities. Many health information custodians are members of organizations that provide them with medico-legal and risk management advisory services. The majority of hospitals in Ontario receive advice from Healthcare Insurance Reciprocal of Canada (HIROC);[210] and physicians receive advice from the Canadian Medical Protective Association (CMPA).[211] *PHIPA* permits a health information custodian to use personal health information "for the purpose of risk management, error management or for the purpose of activities to improve or maintain the quality of care or to improve or maintain the quality of any related programs or services of the custodian."[212] A custodian may provide personal health information to HIROC or the CMPA, where the organization is an agent of the custodian, for this purpose. Normally where an agent receives personal health information from a custodian of which it is an agent, the agent is not permitted to use the information for other custodians. However, a special provision in the *PHIPA* Regulation allows HIROC or the CMPA, as the case may be, to use the information, together with other such information that the organization has received from other custodians for the purpose of systemic risk management analysis.[213] The CMPA, for example, uses person-

---

207 *PHIPA* Regulation, *ibid.*, s. 7(2)(iii).
208 *PHIPA*, ss. 40(1), 43(1)(b), (c), (d), & 43(1)(e). See Chapter 10 for a discussion of these provisions.
209 For example, s. 85.1(1) of Schedule 2 to the *RHPA*, above note 12, the Health Professions Procedural Code, requires a member of a College of a health profession to file a report if the member has reasonable grounds, obtained in the course of practising the profession, to believe that another member of the same or different College has sexually abused a patient.
210 HIROC provides professional and general liability coverage and risk management support.
211 Operated on a not-for-profit basis, the CMPA is a mutual defence organization for physicians in Canada.
212 *PHIPA*, s. 37(1)(d).
213 *PHIPA* Regulation, above note 9, s. 7(1).

al health information that a physician member provides to it for the purpose of providing error management services to the physician, but it also uses the information for the broader purpose of systemic risk management analysis, of benefit to all physician members. The CMPA may analyze information from multiple members, perhaps from a class of physicians who practise in a particular field, to help members improve the care and services they provide to patients.[214] HIROC undertakes similar work for its members. However, in using the personal health information from multiple custodians, the CMPA and HIROC must not disclose personal health information provided to them by one health information custodian to another custodian.[215]

f) Sub-agents

In acting for or on behalf of a health information custodian,[216] an agent may seek the assistance of others in fulfilling its obligations to the custodian, provided it has the permission, express or implied, of the custodian to do so. For example, where a custodian contracts with a records management company to manage the custodian's records of personal health information, it is understood that the employees of the records management company will be carrying out the actual work. In such a situation, the agent will be responsible to the custodian for ensuring that its employees, or others acting on its behalf, comply with all the requirements and restrictions imposed on the agent under *PHIPA*[217] and by the custodian. *PHIPA* does not state explicitly whether such an employee or other person acting for the agent will be considered to be the agent of the custodian contracted on behalf of the custodian by the custodian's direct agent, or merely a person responsible to the agent.

Further, in general, *PHIPA* does not include requirements governing these relationships.[218] However, it would be prudent for a health information custodian to include in an agreement with an agent provisions that set out appropriate permissions and restrictions on the agent's further delegation of responsibilities to its employees and others, and that require the agent to

---

214 See the website for the CMPA for more information about the CMPA's work, online: <www.cmpa-acpm.ca>.
215 *PHIPA* Regulation, above note 9, s. 7(1)(ii).
216 *PHIPA*, s. 17(2).
217 Such requirements and restrictions are set out in *PHIPA*, s. 17.
218 Only under the *PHIPA* Regulation, above note 9, ss. 6(1)[3] and 6(3)[6] is the issue of sub-agents explicitly addressed, requiring those providing certain services to health information custodians to impose requirements on third parties retained to assist in providing services to health information custodians. See Section B(3)(d)(iii) below for a discussion of the obligations of health information network providers.

impose restrictions and controls to ensure that the restrictions imposed on the agent will be properly observed and the ultimate responsibility of the custodian will be effectively facilitated.[219] Even where a custodian does not require such an agreement, an agent of a health information custodian should ensure that the agent's employees and others facilitate and do not hinder the agent's obligations to the custodian. To ensure a common understanding, it may be appropriate for the agent to clarify in writing its relationship with these parties and their obligations with respect to personal health information.

g) Provision of Information to an Agent Is Not a Disclosure

The provision of personal health information by a custodian to his or her agent is not a disclosure of the information by the custodian, nor is the acceptance of the information by the agent a collection under *PHIPA*.[220] Instead, the provision of personal health information between a health information custodian and an agent of a custodian is considered to be a use of the information by the custodian. Therefore, for example, the provision of personal health information by a dental surgeon to the dental surgeon's accountant is a use of that information, not a disclosure. Further, the provision of personal health information by one agent of a health information custodian to another is a use of the information. Thus, the provision of personal health information by an admitting clerk in a hospital to a nurse in the hospital is a use of the information by the hospital.

A health information custodian who is permitted by *PHIPA* to use personal health information for a given purpose can provide it to the custodian's agent, who may use it for that purpose on behalf of the custodian.[221] For example, a custodian who is permitted to use personal health information to obtain payment for the custodian's provision of health care in accordance with the Act[222] may provide the information to the custodian's agent to use it for that purpose.

---

219 Similar to the restrictions set out in *PHIPA* Regulation, *ibid.*, s. 6(1)[3], contractual provisions might include the following requirements:

> [The agent] shall not permit its employees or any person acting on its behalf to be able to have access to the information unless the employee or person acting on its behalf agrees to comply with the restrictions that apply to [the agent] under this agreement and under *PHIPA*, and to facilitate [the agent's] compliance with this agreement and *PHIPA*. [The agent] shall be responsible to the custodian for anything done or omitted to be done by such employees or persons with respect to any personal health information that is subject to this agreement.

220 *PHIPA*, s. 6(1).
221 *Ibid.*, s. 37(2).
222 *Ibid.*, s. 37(1)(i).

By including these transactions concerning personal health information in the definition of "use," the Act requires the custodian to have authority to use the information in this way. The Act does not require the custodian to find additional authority to provide the information to the agent for this purpose.

The CSA Privacy Code includes concepts that appear to be consistent with this principle in *PHIPA*. The Code includes the following principle:

> An organization is responsible for personal information in its possession or custody, including information that has been transferred to a third party for processing. The organization should use contractual or other means to provide a comparable level of protection while the information is being processed by a third party.[223]

The Code thus appears to distinguish between "transfers" of information and "disclosures" of information. A transfer of personal information to a third party for processing evidently does not constitute a disclosure of the personal information to that third party. In this way, the CSA Privacy Code and *PHIPA* treat third-party processors and agents in a similar manner.[224]

h)   Notifying Custodian of Incidents

An agent of a health information custodian must notify the custodian at the first reasonable opportunity if the personal health information handled by the agent on behalf of the custodian is stolen, lost, or accessed by unauthorized persons.[225] The custodian and agent should have a clear understanding con-

---

223   CSA Privacy Code, 4.1.3. "CSA Privacy Code" is the term commonly used to refer to the Code incorporated in Schedule 1 of *PIPEDA*, above note 7, which Schedule is officially entitled "Principles Set Out in the National Standard of Canada Entitled Model Code for the Protection of Personal Information, CAN/CSA-Q830-96."

224   However, *PIPEDA*, above note 7, does not specifically address internal transfers of information or transfers to agents as a use, which has led to some difficulties in the interpretation of the *PIPEDA* rules for agents of organizations subject to that Act.

225   *PHIPA*, s. 17(3). It is necessary to distinguish unauthorized access from "access by unauthorized persons." The phrase "access by unauthorized persons" arguably does not include access by a person who is authorized to gain access. For example, if, through the use of a password, a nurse has access to the personal health information of all patients on a hospital's electronic patient record system, but should only use the password to access records about patients to whom she provides care, she is "authorized" to gain access, but access to particular records may be "unauthorized," as in the case where the nurse enters the wrong patient number and briefly views another patient's record momentarily. In contrast, a member of the hospital's cleaning staff who intercepts the nurse's password and gains access to the system would be an "unauthorized person" as well.

cerning the manner in which the agent should bring this information to the attention of the custodian to ensure that it is done effectively and expeditiously.[226] The notice to the custodian in turn permits the custodian to fulfil its obligations under the Act to notify the patient to whom the information relates where such a breach occurs.[227]

i) An Agent's Failure to Comply

Like others, an agent who is alleged to contravene *PHIPA* is subject to being investigated by the Information and Privacy Commissioner, who may, if the allegation is substantiated, make a number of different types of orders with respect to the person.[228] An agent may contravene *PHIPA* by collecting, using, disclosing, retaining, or disposing of personal health information in contravention of section 17(2). Wilfully collecting, using, or disclosing personal health information in contravention of *PHIPA* is also an offence.[229] Even where the agent's action is not necessarily the subject of the investigation, for example, where it is the custodian's compliance with *PHIPA* that is in issue, the Commissioner may make an order against the agent where it is necessary in order to ensure that the custodian complies with the order made against the custodian.[230] Wilful failure to comply with a Commissioner's order is an offence under *PHIPA*.[231] *PHIPA* makes an agent of a corporation that commits an offence under the Act a party to that offence, where the agent authorized the offence, or had the authority to prevent the offence from being committed but knowingly refrained from doing so.[232] Clear communications between a health information custodian and its agents are essential to ensure both the custodian's compliance with the Act, and the agent's compliance with the custodian's instructions, and the Act.

---

226 See Chapter 4, Section G for a discussion concerning a custodian's managing agents.

227 A health information custodian has an obligation to provide such a notice pursuant to *PHIPA*, s. 12(2).

228 See Chapter 15 for a discussion of the Commissioner's powers.

229 *PHIPA*, s. 72(1)(a).

230 *Ibid.*, s. 61(1)(h).

231 *Ibid.*, s. 72(1)(i)

232 *Ibid.*, s. 72(3).

3) Providers of Goods and Services to Enable Use of Electronic Means

a) Information Technology in the Health Care Sector

The information upon which health care providers depend to provide care to patients may lie in various locations, from physician offices to laboratories to hospitals to community care access corporations, and so on, each provider having gathered one part of the picture of a patient's health. The provision of health care in Ontario today involves multiple health care providers in a variety of settings, sometimes great distances apart. Information technology can connect these health care providers across different patient care settings and provide them with timely access to information they need to provide care.

Information technology is playing an increasingly significant role in the health care system. According to Ontario's Minister of Health and Long-Term Care, "... gone are the days where e-health will be treated as a dispensable expenditure. Information technology is essential to ... health care in Ontario."[233] The First Ministers' ten-year plan to strengthen health care highlighted the importance of information technology in the health care system in the upcoming years:

> Electronic health records and telehealth are key to health system renewal. ...
> Recognizing the significant investment that has been made and achievements
> to date, First Ministers agree to accelerate the development and implementa-
> tion of the electronic health record, including e-prescribing.[234]

Although it has the potential to increase the quality of health care provided to patients, the use of information technology, such as that required in the creation of electronic health records, also poses many challenges, particularly from a privacy perspective.[235] Therefore, it is crucial that legislative rules be in place to provide the framework within which technology can be used in the health care sector to its full potential. Privacy safeguards form part of this framework to ensure that patients will be willing and able to reap the benefits of the technology without losing confidence in the security of their sensitive health information. Indeed, information technology has the potential to

---

233   The Honourable George Smitherman, Minister of Health and Long-Term Care, "Ontario's Health Transformation Plan: Purpose and Progress," Presentation at St. Lawrence Market, Toronto (9 September 2004), online: <www.health.gov.on.ca/ english/media/speeches/archives/sp_04/sp_090904.pdf>.

234   Office of the Prime Minister, News Release, "A 10-year Plan to Strengthen Health Care" (16 September 2004), online: <www.pm.gc.ca/eng/news.asp?category=1&id=260>.

enhance the privacy and security of personal health information through such tools as access controls, audits trails to track access to records, and other privacy-enhancing technologies.

b) Building on Existing Requirements Applicable to Custodians

Many health information custodians have been accustomed to taking special steps to ensure security and confidentiality of personal health information when using electronic means to collect, retain, use, and disclose the information. For example, physicians, in creating and maintaining records in an electronic computer system, have been required to ensure that the system has various characteristics, including a password or other reasonable protection against unauthorized access, and the ability to maintain an audit trail.[236] The College of Chiropractors of Ontario has imposed similar obligations on chiropractors.[237] Similarly, regulations made under the *Public Hospitals Act* have required hospitals to take privacy-protective measures with electronic records. Boards of hos-

---

235 Information and Privacy Commissioner/Ontario, *Privacy Review: Chatham-Kent IT Transition Pilot Project* (22 April 2002), online: <www.ipc.on.ca> [Chatham-Kent Review].

236 *General*, O. Reg. 114/94, s. 20, made under the *Medicine Act, 1991*, above note 206, provides:

> 20. The records required by regulation may be made and maintained in an electronic computer system only if it has the following characteristics:
>
> 1. The system provides a visual display of the recorded information.
> 2. The system provides a means of access to the record of each patient by the patient's name and, if the patient has an Ontario health number, by the health number.
> 3. The system is capable of printing the recorded information promptly.
> 4. The system is capable of visually displaying and printing the recorded information for each patient in chronological order.
> 5. The system maintains an audit trail that,
>   i.   records the date and time of each entry of information for each patient,
>   ii. indicates any changes in the recorded information,
>   iii. preserves the original content of the recorded information when changed or updated, and
>   iv. is capable of being printed separately from the recorded information for each patient.
> 6. The system includes a password or otherwise provides reasonable protection against unauthorized access.
> 7. The system automatically backs up files and allows the recovery of backed-up files or otherwise provides reasonable protection against loss of, damage to, and inaccessibility of, information.

237 College of Chiropractors of Ontario, Record Keeping Standard of Practice S-002 (amended 30 November 2002), online: <www.cco.on.ca/record_keeping.htm>.

pitals have been required to ensure that electronic means used to prepare or keep records are designed and operated so that the records are secure from loss, tampering, interference, or unauthorized use or access.[238] Custodians remain obligated to comply with such requirements, as applicable.

c) Requirements Applicable to Custodians When Using Electronic Means

Under *PHIPA*, a health information custodian must comply with any requirements set out in the regulations whenever using electronic means to collect, use, modify, disclose, retain, or dispose of personal health information.[239] At the time of writing, the *PHIPA* regulation does not contain any such standards specific to a custodian's use of electronic means. Custodians remain, however, obligated to comply with *PHIPA*'s general requirement for all custodians to "take steps that are reasonable in the circumstances to ensure that personal health information in the custodian's custody or control is protected against theft, loss and unauthorized use or disclosure and to ensure that the records containing the information are protected against unauthorized copying, modification or disposal."[240] The power to develop additional rules, as needed, for electronic information practices may be important in ensuring on an ongoing basis that up-to-date rules are in place to address developments in technology, including the challenges and opportunities they present.

d) Requirements Applicable to Persons Who Provide Goods and Services

i) Generally

Often, health information custodians will rely on others with the necessary expertise to provide them with the electronic means to reap the benefits of information technology in their operations. Persons who provide goods or services for the purpose of enabling a health information custodian to use elec-

---

238 *Hospital Management*, R.R.O. 1990, Reg. 965, s. 34, made under the *PHA*, above note 29 [Reg. 965] provides:

> 34. (1) Where in this Regulation or under by-laws of a hospital a notation, report, record, order, entry, signature or transcription is required to be entered, prepared, made, written, kept or copied, the entering, preparing, making, writing, keeping or copying may be done by such electronic or optical means or combination thereof as may be authorized by the board.
>
> (2) The board shall ensure that the electronic or optical means referred to in subsection (1) is so designed and operated that the notation, report, record, order, entry, signature or transcription is secure from loss, tampering, interference or unauthorized use or access.

239 *PHIPA*, s. 10(3).
240 *Ibid.*, s. 12(1).

tronic means to collect, use, modify, disclose, retain, or dispose of personal health information must comply with the requirements set out in the regulations.[241] The regulation made under *PHIPA* imposes requirements on persons who provide such services.[242] These persons may or may not be agents of the custodian.[243]

ii) Non-Agents Who Supply Services

One set of requirements applies only to a person who supplies services that permit a health information custodian to use electronic means to handle personal health information, where the supplier is not an agent of the custodian.[244] These requirements are similar to the responsibilities of agents under *PHIPA*.[245] The requirements reflect the limited interaction that such service suppliers, as non-agents, are expected to have with personal health information in providing services to health information custodians. Further, they reflect that such persons do not have a decision-making role with respect to personal health information. Rather, they provide services to health information custodians to carry out the custodians' decisions.

Where a supplier of such services to a health information custodian is not an agent of the custodian, the supplier must not use any personal health information to which it has access in the course of providing the services, except as necessary in the course of providing those services or as required by law.[246] For example, it may be necessary for a supplier of such services to handle the information in order to repair a problem with the services. Further, the supplier must not disclose any personal health information to which it has access in the course of providing the services for the health information custodian, except as required by law, such as through a court order or a search warrant.[247] The supplier is also prohibited from permitting its employees or others acting on its behalf to have access to the information, unless they agree to comply with the

---

241 *Ibid.*, s. 10(4).

242 *PHIPA* Regulation, above note 9, s. 6. No direct requirements are currently imposed on persons who supply goods only and not services, though *PHIPA* Regulation s. 6(4)(b) applies to the relationship between a health information custodian and such a supplier of goods.

243 *PHIPA* Regulation, *ibid.*, s. 6(1) applies only to persons who are not agents, while *PHIPA* Regulation, s. 6(3) applies to persons whether or not they are agents.

244 *Ibid.*, s. 6(1).

245 *PHIPA*, s. 17(2).

246 *PHIPA* Regulation, above note 9, s. 6(1)[1].

247 *Ibid.*, s. 6(1)[2]. See Chapter 3, section A(3)(b) for a discussion of the phrase "required by law."

restrictions that apply to the supplier.[248] Typically, a supplier should ensure that such an agreement is set out in writing.

iii)   Requirements Applicable to Health Information Network Providers

a.   Health information network provider defined

The regulation made under *PHIPA* imposes requirements on persons that are "health information network providers," also referred to as "providers." A health information network provider is a person who provides services to two or more health information custodians, where the services are provided primarily to custodians to enable the custodians to use electronic means to disclose personal health information to one another.[249] The set of requirements in the regulation applies to all such providers, whether or not the provider is an agent of any of the custodians.[250] In this definition of a "health information network provider," the word "primarily" is a key term. It narrows the application of this definition significantly to exclude those persons who provide such services to all categories of persons, and not primarily to health information custodians. For example, a corporation that primarily provides electronic communications services to the general public for its personal use, such as a general telecommunications company, would not be subject to these requirements, even if some health information custodians relied on the company's services in the course of providing health care.

Further, the definition makes it clear that the term "health information network provider" only includes persons who provide services to at least two health information custodians. A person who provides services to one hospital, for example, to permit agents of the hospital at one site to provide personal health information to agents located at another site would not be captured by the definition. However, a corporation that provides services to three hospital corporations in a community to permit them to use electronic means to disclose personal health information about their overlapping patient populations to one another is an example of a health information network provider.[251]

---

248   *PHIPA* Regulation, *ibid.*, s. 6(1)[3].

249   *Ibid.*, s. 6(2). Bill 159, *An Act respecting personal health information and related matters,* 1st Sess., 37th Leg., Ontario, 2000, cl. 17(1) included requirements for persons termed "information managers," which included a person who provides information management or information technology services to a health information custodian. *PHIPA* does not use the term "information manager."

250   *PHIPA* Regulation, *ibid.*, s. 6(2).

251   This would appear to be the case even if the corporation providing the services was one of the three hospitals itself, as it would be a health information network provider with respect to the other two hospitals.

b. Requirements

A provider must comply with the following requirements in providing services to health information custodians.

- The provider must notify every applicable[252] health information custodian at the first reasonable opportunity if the provider accessed, used, disclosed, or disposed of personal health information other than in accordance with the regulations made under *PHIPA*.[253] For example, where a provider disclosed personal health information in an instance other than where required by law, the provider must notify the applicable custodian of that fact. The provider must also provide such a notice in a case where an unauthorized person accessed the personal health information.[254]

- The provider must provide to each health information custodian to which it provides services, and make available to the public,[255] a plain language description of the services that the provider provides to the custodians.[256] The description should be written in such a way that it is appropriate for sharing with the individuals to whom the personal health information relates as a way to be open about the role of information technology in the custodians' operations.[257] It should also include a general description of the safeguards that the provider has put into place to protect against unauthorized use and disclosure of the personal health information and to protect the integrity, security, and confidentiality of the information.[258] The inclusion of the word "general" to qualify the nature of the descriptions is significant. The provider need not include detailed information about the safeguards that have been put into place. Indeed, the provider must withhold from the public information that would put the security of the personal health information at risk.

---

252 Generally, it would appear that an "applicable" health information custodian would be the custodian that was party to the communication of the personal health information in question.

253 *PHIPA* Regulation, above note 9, s. 6(3). Similar language appears in *PHIPA*, ss. 12(2) & 17(3).

254 The term "unauthorized person" refers to a person other than the provider and a person who is not authorized to have access to the personal health information. See also above note 225.

255 *PHIPA* Regulation, *ibid.*, s. 6(3)[3][i].

256 *Ibid.*, s. 6(3)[2].

257 It is interesting to note that the Information and Privacy Commissioner recommended, in the context of her privacy review of the Chatham-Kent IT Transition Pilot Project, that such information be made available to patients. See Chatham-Kent Review, above note 235.

258 *PHIPA* Regulation, above note 9, s. 6(3)[2][i].

- The provider must make available to the public any directives, guidelines and policies of the provider that apply to the services, but only to the extent that these do not reveal a trade secret or confidential scientific, technical, commercial, or labour relations information.[259] For example, the provider must make available the acceptable use policy applicable to the services. However, as with the provider's description of the safeguards, the provider may withhold from the public any policies where disclosure would put the security of the personal health information at risk.

- The provider has a qualified obligation to provide an audit trail. Specifically, the regulation requires that "to the extent reasonably practical and in a manner that is reasonably practical," the provider must keep and make available to each applicable health information custodian, on the request of the custodian, an electronic record of

  i. all accesses to all or part of the personal health information associated with the custodian being held in equipment controlled by the provider, which must identify the person who accessed the information and the date and time of the access;[260] and

  ii. all transfers of all or part of the information associated with the custodian by means of equipment controlled by the provider, which must identify the person who transferred the information and the person or address to whom it was sent, and the date and time it was sent.[261]

This requirement describes the need to include, if and as practical, an audit trail as part of the services provided to the custodian. However, this obligation only arises where the personal health information is held in[262] or transferred by means of[263] equipment controlled by the provider. Where the custodian itself, and not the provider, controls the equipment in which the person health information is held, the provider is not required to provide the audit trail.

---

259 *Ibid.*, s. 6(3)[3][ii]. The words "to the extent that these do not reveal ..." such confidential information suggest that, where a directive, guideline, and policy contains such confidential information, the confidential information must, if reasonably possible, be severed from the document and the document then made available to the public. Only where it is not reasonably possible to sever the confidential information would the provider be justified in withholding the entire document.

260 *PHIPA* Regulation, *ibid.*, s. 6(3)[4][i].

261 *Ibid.*, s. 6(3)[4][ii].

262 *Ibid.*, s. 6(3)[4][i].

263 *Ibid.*, s. 6(3)[4][ii].

- The provider must perform an assessment of the services provided to the health information custodians, with respect to

  i. threats, vulnerabilities, and risks to the security and integrity of the personal health information, also known as a threat and risk assessment;[264] and

  ii. how the services may affect the privacy of the individuals who are the subject of the information, also known as a privacy impact assessment.[265]

- The provider must provide to each applicable health information custodian to which it is providing services a written copy of the results of the assessment of the services provided to the custodians, as described above.[266]

- The provider must ensure that any third party it retains to assist in providing services to a health information custodian agrees to comply with the restrictions and conditions that are necessary to enable the provider to fulfil its obligations under the regulations. For example, the third party should agree to comply with the restrictions on access to and disclosure of the personal health information. As a matter of good practice, this agreement between the provider and the third party should be in writing.

- The provider is required to enter into a written agreement with each health information custodian concerning the services provided to the custodian that

  i. describes the services that the provider is required to provide to the custodian;[267]

  ii. describes the administrative, technical, and physical safeguards[268] relating to the confidentiality and security of the information;[269] and

  iii. requires the provider to comply with *PHIPA* and its regulations.[270]

The health information custodians and the provider will likely include these requirements in one or more agreements that deal with other issues, as

---

264 *Ibid.*, s. 6(3)[5][i].

265 *Ibid.*, s. 6(3)[5][ii]. See Chapter 4, Section D(2)(d) for a brief discussion of privacy impact assessments.

266 *Ibid.*, s. 6(3)[5].

267 *Ibid.*, s. 6(3)[7][i].

268 The definition of "information practices" in *PHIPA*, s. 2 refers to the "administrative technical and physical safeguards and practices" of custodians. See Chapter 4, Section D for a discussion of a custodian's obligations concerning its information practices in *PHIPA*, s. 10(1).

269 *PHIPA* Regulation, above note 9, s. 6(3)[7][ii].

270 *Ibid.*, s. 6(3)[7][iii].

well. The provider may have a separate agreement with each custodian. Alternatively, there may be one agreement with the provider and all the custodians as parties to the agreement.

The provider can generally fulfil most of the above requirements concerning the provision of documents prior to its delivery of services to the custodian, and should do so.[271] The provider should also ensure ongoing compliance with these requirements, for example, by conducting assessments of threats and risks to the security of the personal health information on a regular basis and keeping the contents of the description for the public current.

iv)   Not a Disclosure to Provider

As discussed above, a health information custodian's provision of personal health information to an agent of the custodian constitutes neither a disclosure of the information by the custodian nor a collection by the agent.[272] *PHIPA* treats a custodian's reliance on a person who provides goods or services for the purpose of enabling a health information custodian to use electronic means to collect, use, modify, disclose, retain, or dispose of personal health information in a similar way. Generally, under *PHIPA*, where a custodian makes personal health information available to a person who is not acting as the custodian's agent, the custodian has disclosed the information to the person. Always treating this transaction as a disclosure, however, could effectively prevent custodians from using non-agent providers of goods and services to enable the custodian to use electronic means in relation to personal health information.

In order to enable the appropriate reliance on such providers, the regulation provides that a health information custodian who uses goods or services supplied by such a person, other than a person who is an agent of the custodian, is not considered in so doing to make the information available or to release it to that person for the purposes of the definition of "disclose" in the Act, provided that

a)   the person complies with the requirements in the regulations in supplying the services;[273] and

---

271   The Information and Privacy Commissioner recommended, in the context of her privacy review of the Chatham-Kent IT Transition Pilot Project, that vulnerability tests and network reviews be conducted "sufficiently long before going 'live' to have time to remedy vulnerabilities that may be identified." See Chatham-Kent Review, above note 235.

272   *PHIPA*, s. 6(1).

273   *PHIPA* Regulation, above note 9, s. 6(4)(a).

b) in the case of a person supplying goods to the health information custodian, the custodian does not, in returning the goods to the person, enable the person to access the personal health information except in accordance with the regulations.[274]

Therefore, where three hospitals rely on a provider of network services to permit the hospitals to disclose information to one another, in doing so, the hospitals should not be regarded as disclosing information to the provider as well, as long as the requirements of the regulation are met, as discussed above. As a further example, a health information custodian that purchases a computer from a supplier, and then stores personal health information on the computer, may only return the computer to the supplier for repairs either if the personal health information is removed first or if the provider complies with the restrictions on a non-agent electronic service provider, as discussed above.[275]

4) Recipients

As discussed above, *PHIPA* focuses on health information custodians. However, the Act also extends its reach to persons who are not custodians, but to whom a health information custodian disclosed personal health information. The Act refers to these persons as "recipients."[276] The Act limits a recipient's authority to use and disclose personal health information that it receives from a health information custodian.[277] These limitations apply to a recipient's use and disclosure of the personal health information, even if the recipient received the information before 1 November 2004, the day on which the Act came into force.[278] Those limitations are discussed in detail in Chapter 12.

---

274 *Ibid.*, s. 6(4)(b). The phrase "in accordance with the regulations" refers to *PHIPA* Regulation, s. 6(1).

275 See Chapter 4, Section K for a discussion of the appropriate disposal of records of personal health information. The supplier in this example would not, however, appear to be a health information network provider, as that term is defined in *PHIPA* Regulation, *ibid.*, s. 6(2).

276 *PHIPA*, heading for s. 49(1).

277 These limitations are primarily found in *PHIPA*, s. 49. Institutions under *FIPPA* or *MFIPPA*, above note 164, and persons employed by or acting on behalf of such institutions, are generally not considered recipients for the purpose of these provisions: *PHIPA*, s. 49(5); *PHIPA* Regulation, above note 9, s. 23(1).

278 *PHIPA*, s. 7(1)(b)(ii).

C. WHAT IS COVERED?

1) What Is Personal Health Information?

a) Generally

Generally, *PHIPA* governs the collection, use, and disclosure of "personal health information" and a patient's access to and correction of records of "personal health information." The term "personal health information" is defined[279] fairly broadly and, subject to some limitations[280] and expansions,[281] includes identifying information[282] about an individual in either oral or recorded form, if the information fits into one or more of the categories set out below, such that the information

- relates to the physical or mental health of the individual, including information that consists of the health history of the individual's family;
- relates to the providing of health care to the individual, including the identification of a person as a provider of health care to the individual;
- is a plan of service within the meaning of the *Long-Term Care Act, 1994* for the individual;
- relates to payments or eligibility for health care in respect of the individual,
- relates to the donation by the individual of any body part or bodily substance of the individual or is derived from the testing or examination of any such body part or bodily substance;
- is the individual's health number; or
- identifies an individual's substitute decision-maker.

Each of these categories is discussed in greater detail below. However, in order to fully understand the meaning of the term "personal health information," it is first necessary to consider several overarching aspects of this definition.

b) "Oral or Recorded Form"

The definition of "personal health information" includes information in both oral and recorded form.[283] The distinction between information in oral form

---

279 *PHIPA*, s. 4.

280 *Ibid.*, s. 4(4).

281 *Ibid.*, s. 4(3); *PHIPA* Regulation, above note 9, s. 4.

282 *PHIPA*, s. 4(2), definition of "identifying information." See Section C(1)(d) below.

283 *Ibid.*, s. 4(1). Contrast this language with that found in Bill 159, above note 249, cl. 2(1), which provided that "personal health information" means information relating to an individual, whether or not the information is recorded." In this respect, the language in Bill 159 had the potential to include a greater range of information than the definition of "personal health information" in *PHIPA*.

and information in recorded form is an important one in the context of a patient's right of access to his or her record of personal health information, as the right of access only applies to records of personal health information.[284]

Any personal health information in recorded form is by definition contained in a record. *PHIPA* defines the term "record" broadly to mean a record of information in any form or in any medium, whether in written, printed, photographic, or electronic form or otherwise.[285] The expression "record of personal health information"[286] covers a range of records that extends beyond the "health record," "medical record," or "clinical record" commonly found in health care settings. In the health care sector, "records" are found in a variety of media, including x-ray films, computer diskettes, microfiche, videotape, audiotape, and echocardiogram tape. Photographs,[287] digital images, dental impressions, and printed sonogram images may also be records of personal health information.

Consider, however, the status of substances such as blood samples, hair, and tissue samples. Are such substances "records" of personal health information? The Act does not address this issue specifically.[288] Such substances contain information about the patient from whom the sample is taken. Persons with the appropriate skill and knowledge are able to extract this information through analysis of the substance. However, it appears that such substances do not constitute "personal health information" within the meaning of *PHIPA*, as the information is not in "oral or recorded form." Although the definition of "record" refers to a record of information being "in any form or medium," the examples included in the definition, that is, records in written, printed, photographic, or electronic form, all refer to records in media in which a person

---

284 *PHIPA*, s. 52(1).

285 *Ibid.*, s. 2, definition of "record." A record, however, does not include a computer program or other mechanism that can produce a record: *PHIPA*, s. 2, definition of "record." Therefore, a health information custodian that receives a request for access to a record of personal health information about a patient is not required to provide the patient with access to a microfiche reader or word processing program used to produce the record, in addition to the record itself.

286 This expression appears in, for example, *PHIPA*, ss. 14, 53, and 55.

287 For example, Reg. 965, above note 238, s. 20, provides that a hospital may photograph medical records and notes, charts, and other material relating to patient care for the purpose of retaining the contents thereof in lieu of the original documents where the photographing of the documents is carried out in accordance with procedures established by the board of the hospital after considering the recommendations of the medical advisory committee.

288 Materials prepared by the Ministry of Health and Long-Term Care and the Information and Privacy Commissioner do not state a position on this matter.

recorded the information, directly or indirectly.[289] The same cannot be said of information contained in a blood sample.

In addition to the meaning of the term "record," other aspects of *PHIPA* also lead to the conclusion that such substances were not intended to constitute records of personal health information for the purposes of *PHIPA*. For example, the Act includes provisions concerning a patient's right of access to a record of personal health information about him- or herself.[290] However, it does not appear that the Act was developed to facilitate a patient's access to substances like blood samples.[291] The provisions in *PHIPA* that give a patient a right of access to records of personal health information in the custody or

---

289 A regulation made under *PHIPA*, s. 73(1)(d) could eventually clarify explicitly whether such a substance may constitute a record of personal health information.

290 *PHIPA*, s. 54(1)(a), for example, refers to a patient's entitlement to a copy of a record on request, but does not specify how this provision would apply where the information was contained in such a substance. *PHIPA*, s. 1, which sets out the purposes of the Act, also gives no suggestion that the Act governs the collection, use, and disclosure of such substances. If such substances were meant to be considered "records" of personal health information, further provisions would have been needed dealing with special issues relating to such "records."

291 It is interesting to consider whether *PIPEDA*, above note 7, purports to regulate the collection, use, and disclosure of such substances. The legislative history of Bill C-54, *An Act to support and promote electronic commerce by protecting personal information that is collected, used or disclosed in certain circumstances, by providing for the use of electronic means to communicate or record information or transactions and by amending the Canada Evidence Act, the Statutory Instruments Act and the Statute Revision Act*, 1st Sess., 36th Parl., 1997–98, the predecessor to Bill C-6, *An Act to support and promote electronic commerce by protecting personal information that is collected, used or disclosed in certain circumstances, by providing for the use of electronic means to communicate or record information or transactions and by amending the Canada Evidence Act, the Statutory Instruments Act and the Statute Revision Act*, 2d Sess., 36th Parl., 1999, (assented to 13 April 2000), suggests that the definition of "personal information" was amended in a way that broadened its scope to include information that was not in any recorded form. Prior to the review of the Standing Committee on Industry, the definition of "personal information" in Bill C-54 read as follows: "personal information means information about an identifiable individual that is recorded in any form." The definition was amended to read:

> personal information means information about an identifiable individual but does not include the name, title or business address or telephone number of an employee of an organization. (cl. 2(1))

The deletion of the words "that is recorded in any form" could be interpreted as having the effect of including information that was not in any recorded form, such as DNA or blood samples. See Parliamentary Research Branch, Law and Government Division, "Legislative Summary of Bill C-54: Personal Information Protection and Electronic Documents Act," LS-337E by John Craig (Ottawa: Library of Parliament, 1999), online: <www.parl.gc.ca/common/Bills_ls.asp?Parl=36&Ses=1&ls=C54>.

control of health information custodians do not include any special considerations for access to such substances, which would surely have been required if such substances were to be treated as records of personal health information.

Where a sample from a patient is accompanied by labelling information, such as the patient's name, health number, and the purposes for which the sample was collected, such as for a particular test, the information on the label is clearly in recorded form and constitutes personal health information. Similarly, written results of tests conducted on the sample, such as tests to determine whether the patient from whom the sample was taken is infected by a particular virus or is prone to develop a particular condition would constitute a record of personal health information. However, the sample itself would not appear to be personal health information, even when labelled, since the sample itself is not in oral or recorded form.

c) "About an Individual"

In order for information to be captured by the term "personal health information," it must be "about an individual." *PHIPA* defines the term "individual" to mean in relation to personal health information, "the individual, whether living or deceased, with respect to whom the information was or is being collected or created."[292] Through the use of the word "individual" in the definition, the Act clarifies that the information must relate to a human being, rather than a corporation or other legal entity. Throughout most of this Guide we refer to an "individual" as so defined as a "patient," since though the appropriate term may vary from context to context, that appears to be the most concrete and intuitively understandable term to express this concept.

In order to be personal health information, information need not be about a human being who is living; the individual may be deceased. However, the Act does not apply to personal health information about an individual after the earlier of 120 years after the record containing the information was created and 50 years after the death of the individual.[293] Finally, personal health information is about the individual with respect to whom the information was or is being collected or created. Therefore, where a health care practitioner collects information concerning a patient's mother, for example as part of his or her collection of information about the family health history of the patient,[294] the

---

292 *PHIPA*, s. 2, definition of "individual."

293 *Ibid.*, s. 9(1).

294 Family health history is specifically mentioned in *PHIPA*, s. 4(1)(a). See Section C(1)(e)(ii) below for a discussion of the phrase "family health history" and the impact of this aspect of the definition of "personal health information."

information is about the patient. This is important when considering several aspects of the Act.

d) "Identifying Information"

To constitute "personal health information," the information must be "identifying information," a term that is defined to mean information that identifies an individual or that it is reasonably foreseeable in the circumstances could be utilized, either alone or with other information, to identify an individual.[295] Information may identify an individual in various ways, including by name, unique identifying number,[296] address, biometric information (e.g., iris features, facial measurements),[297] photographic images, or through a combination of information. The issue of whether particular information constitutes identifying information is not always black and white. "Data identifiability can be characterized as a continuum or sliding scale, in which the divisions between degrees of 'identifiability' and 'anonymity' are not always clear cut."[298]

But when is it "reasonably foreseeable in the circumstances" that the information could be used to identify an individual, either alone or with other information? *PHIPA* does not provide detailed guidance on the meaning of this phrase.[299] However, it is probable that it is reasonably foreseeable in the circumstances that information can be used to identify an individual when the recipient of the information is known to have access to other information that, when combined with the information that it received, would identify the individual to

---

295 *PHIPA*, s. 4(2).

296 As an example of a unique identifier, Reg. 965, above note 238, s. 12(1) provides that every administrator shall ensure that each patient who is admitted to a hospital is issued a register number. The register number is an example of an identifier.

297 *PHIPA* does not specifically refer to biometric information. The *Electronic Commerce Act, 2000,* S.O. 2000, c. 17 provides that "biometric information" means information derived from an individual's unique personal characteristics, other than a representation of his or her photograph or signature. The *Ontario Disability Support Program Act, 1997,* S.O. 1997, c. 25, Sch. B, includes a similar definition.

298 Canadian Institutes of Health Research, Privacy Advisory Committee, *Guidelines for Protecting Privacy and Confidentiality in the Design, Conduct and Evaluation of Health Research: Best Practices Consultation Draft* (Ottawa: April 2004) at 25, online: <www.cihr-irsc.gc.ca> [CIHR Best Practices].

299 The Standing Committee on General Government amended the definition of "identifying information" that was included in Bill 31, above note 109, at first reading, which provided that "identifying information" means information that identifies an individual or for which there is a reasonable basis to believe that it could be utilized, either alone or with other information, to identify an individual. See Ontario, Legislative Assembly, Standing Committee on General Government, *Official Report of Debates (Hansard),* G-208 (9 February 2004) at 1050.

whom the information relates.[300] Where a health information custodian disclosing information that is otherwise non-identifying is not aware, and has no reason to foresee, that the recipient will be able to link the disclosed information to other accessible information to identify a specific patient, the information being disclosed may not be regarded as "identifying information." As a result, it is necessary to consider the resources of the recipient of the information. Information disclosed to a recipient with access to extensive data holdings may be identifying information. The same information disclosed to a person with no known ability to access data may not be personal health information.

Various types of information relating to a patient may allow the patient to be identified with various degrees of probability. The collection of certain data elements may increase the likelihood of a patient being identified. These data elements include the following:

- geographic location (e.g., location of residence, location of health event, especially where the location is not heavily populated);
- names of health care facilities and providers;
- rare characteristics of the patient (e.g., unusual health condition); or
- highly visible characteristics of the patient (e.g., ethnicity in certain locales).[301]

In the context of *FIPPA*, the Office of the Information and Privacy Commissioner has supported a conclusion that the "identifiable" threshold may be met where the information to be disclosed would lead one to identify a group of fewer than five individuals to whom the information may relate.[302] The

---

300 The issue of when health information is "identifying" has been the subject of discussion in related contexts. The Canadian Institutes of Health Research [CIHR], for example, considered the issue in the context of its recommendations on the interpretation and application of *PIPEDA* in the health research context to the Privacy Commissioner of Canada. In its recommendations, CIHR suggested "information about an identifiable individual" include information that can be linked with other accessible information by a reasonably foreseeable method to identify an individual. See Canadian Institutes for Health Research, *Recommendations for the Interpretation and Application of the Personal Information Protection and Electronic Documents Act (S.C. 2000, c. 5) in the Health Research Context* (30 November 2001), online: <www.cihr-irsc.gc.ca/e/publications/pdf_24020.htm>.

301 CIHR Best Practices, above note 298 at 25.

302 See, for example, Order P-644, Ministry of Health (14 March 1994), online: <www.ipc.on.ca>. See also Privacy Complaint Report PC-030036-1, Ministry of Health and Long-Term Care (27 May 2004), online: <www.ipc.on.ca>, in which the investigator for the Commissioner found that an incorrectly faxed document containing a patient's first name, last initial, date of birth, and information related to the patient's health, constituted personal information for the purposes of *FIPPA*, above note 164.

Office of the Information and Privacy Commissioner has also had the opportunity to consider the impact of one data element, the postal code, on the identifiability of an individual. An adjudicator concluded, in one case, where the information at issue included postal codes, in the absence of other information from which individuals may be identified, the information as a whole was not identifiable information.[303]

As a result of this reference to "identifying information" in the definition of "personal health information," it is necessary to distinguish health information that is not "identifying information," from "personal health information." *PHIPA* does not apply to a custodian's collection, use, and disclosure of health information that is not "identifying information." Where the information no longer constitutes "identifying information," the custodian may then disclose that information, as the Act would not regulate the custodian's disclosure of such information.

A variety of terms are used in the health care sector to describe the form in which health information is presented. "Aggregate health information," "anonymized health information," and "summary health information" are a few examples of such terms. However, these terms do not make it clear whether information is "personal health information." Health information can be compiled in aggregate form and yet still be identifying information. Similarly, information may remain identifying information even if the name of the patient to whom the health information relates is disassociated from the health information. Only when health information is stripped of its identifying potential to the extent that it is no longer "identifying information" is it therefore no longer personal health information.

PHIPA permits a health information custodian to use personal health information without the consent of the patient to whom the information relates for the purpose of modifying the information in order to conceal the identity of the patient.[304] Personal health information can be modified or "de-identified" to the point that it is no longer personal health information. "De-identifying" information under *PHIPA* means to make the information so it is not "identifying information." More specifically, *PHIPA* defines the term "de-identify," in relation to personal health information of an individual, to mean

---

303 The issue of whether full postal codes may be identifying information may depend on such factors as the facts of the case, the locations in question, and the other types of information that are linked to the postal code. See Order PO-2131, Ontario Lottery and Gaming Corporation (20 March 2003), online: <www.ipc.on.ca>.

304 *PHIPA*, s. 37(1)(f).

the removal of any information that identifies the individual or that it is reasonably foreseeable in the circumstances could be utilized, either alone or with other information, to identify the individual.[305]

e) Association with Health

As well as being in oral or recorded form, about an individual, and "identifying information," personal health information must also be associated with a patient's health or health care in some way.[306] The nature of the association can vary and include any one of a number of different types of information, as discussed in more detail below.

i) *Personal Health Information That "Relates to the Physical or Mental Health of the Individual"*

Personal health information includes identifying information about a patient that "relates to the physical or mental health" of the patient.[307] The expression "physical or mental health" is not described in *PHIPA*, but is clearly expansive. It is reasonable to assume that this language will be interpreted broadly, so as to ensure that such information benefits from the protections included in the Act. It can include information ranging from symptoms that a patient is experiencing to a health care provider's comments about the patient's prognosis. Consider the following additional examples of information that relates to the health of a patient: a diagnosis of the condition of a patient; concerns that a patient has expressed about the condition of his or her health; results of diagnostic tests; results of predictive genetic tests; the fact that a patient is deceased;[308] and the degree of pain a patient experiences from a condition. Information that relates to the physical or mental health of the patient would include the patient's health history. Clearly, information that "relates to the physical or mental health" of the patient is an expansive concept, although not without limits.[309]

---

305 *PHIPA*, s. 47(1), in the context of a health data institute's disclosure of information to the Ministry of Health and Long-Term Care.

306 This is subject to the mixed record rule, discussed below at Section C(1)(g).

307 *PHIPA*, s. 4(1)(a).

308 The fact that an individual is deceased is information about the individual's physical health. *PHIPA* makes it clear that "individual" includes a deceased individual: *PHIPA*, s. 2, definition of "individual."

309 Contrast this aspect of the definition of "personal health information" to that contained in Bill 159, above note 249, cl. 2(1), which provided that personal health information means information about an individual that is identifying information and that relates to the physical or mental health or well-being of the individual. *PHIPA's* definition does not include a reference to "well-being."

ii)   "Health History of the Individual's Family"

PHIPA clarifies that personal health information includes identifying information about a patient that consists of the health history of the patient's family, and that this type of information is considered information that relates to the patient's physical or mental health.[310] This provision of the Act makes it clear that the Act does not impede the common and appropriate practice of physicians and other health care providers of collecting information from patients about the health status and history of the patient's parents and other family members. In doing so, the health care provider would not be regarded as collecting the personal health information about the family member, but of the custodian's patient, and thus would not require the consent of the family member to do so. A health information custodian may also collect the health history of a patient's family for purposes other than the provision of health care, where *PHIPA* permits.

A related issue arises over the status of genetic information. Genetic information can be described as information concerning the hereditary characteristics of an individual or concerning the pattern of inheritance of such characteristics within a related group of individuals.[311] It can also be defined more narrowly to include only results of testing a patient's genetic materials. Apparently commenting on genetic information as more narrowly defined, the Office of the Information and Privacy Commissioner stated that "[n]o information about an individual could be more personal."[312] It can be argued that genetic information is unique because it relates not only to the patient from whom the information was collected, but also to some extent to the patient's blood relatives.

PHIPA does not include special rules for genetic information.[313] Some genetic information relates to the physical or mental health of an individual. The definition of "personal health information" in the Act includes some categories of genetic information. For example, personal health information

---

310   *PHIPA*, s. 4(1)(a).

311   Council of Europe — Committee of Ministers. Recommendation No. R (97) 5 of the Committee of Ministers of Member States on the Protection of Medical Data. Adopted by the Committee of Ministers on 13 February 1997 at the 584th meeting of the Ministers' Deputies.

312   Information and Privacy Commissioner/Ontario, *Submission to the Ontario Law Reform Commission, Project on Genetic Testing* (September 1992), online: <www.ipc.on.ca> at 3, referring to an individual's "genetic code."

313   *A Consultation on the Privacy of Personal Information Act, 2002*, above note 6, which included special rules governing an individual's consent to the collection, use, and disclosure of genetic information.

includes predictive genetic test information that is derived from a test of an individual's gene products or chromosomes and that indicates a susceptibility to illness, disease, impairment, or other disorders, whether physical or mental, as this information clearly relates to the patient's physical or mental health.[314] Genetic information about a patient derived from a predictive genetic test of a bodily substance of the patient constitutes that patient's personal health information, and the patient may consent to its use and disclosure, despite the fact that it may also relate to the patient's blood relatives.

iii) "Relates to the Providing of Health Care to the Individual"

Clearly there is overlap among the various categories of the definition of "personal health information," such as information that "relates to the physical or mental health of the individual" and information that "relates to the providing of health care to the individual."[315] Whether information relates to the providing of health care to a patient is obviously dependent on the definition of "health care." The term "health care" is a defined term in *PHIPA*,[316] and, as discussed above, means any observation, examination, assessment, care, service, or procedure that is done for a health-related purpose and that

- is carried out or provided to diagnose, treat, or maintain an individual's physical or mental condition;
- is carried out or provided to prevent disease or injury or to promote health; or
- is carried out or provided as part of palliative care.

The Act makes it clear that health care includes the compounding, dispensing, or selling of a drug, a device, equipment, or any other item to a patient for a health-related purpose, or for the use of a patient, pursuant to a prescription. It also includes community services identified in the *Long-Term Care Act, 1994* and provided by service providers.

A variety of information can relate to the providing of health care to a patient, such as the fact that an individual was admitted to a hospital as a patient; information concerning an assessment of a patient for an assistive device, such as a wheelchair; the fact that a patient is undergoing physical therapy; and the fact that a pharmacist dispensed medication to a patient.

314　*PHIPA*, s. 4(1)(a). The Ministry of Consumer and Business Services, *A Consultation on the Privacy of Personal Information Act, 2002, ibid.*, s. 2 included such a definition of "genetic information."

315　*PHIPA*, s. 4(1)(b).

316　*Ibid.*, s. 2, definition of "health care." See Section B(1)(b)(ii) above for a detailed discussion of this term.

iv) Provider Information

In addition, it is clear that the simple identification of an identifiable patient's health care provider as such constitutes personal health information, as *PHIPA* explicitly states that information that "relates to the providing of health care to the individual" includes "the identification of a person as a provider of health care to the individual."[317] The rationale behind this inclusion is understandable. Indicating, for example, that Dr. X is a patient's oncologist, clearly implies sensitive personal health information about the patient.

At the same time, however, information that identifies a health care provider in a professional capacity without identifying the provider's patient does not constitute personal health information. Personal health information consists of "identifying information about an individual ... if the information ... relates to the providing of health care to the individual, including the identification of a person as a provider of health care to the individual."[318] Where an individual patient cannot reasonably be identified from the information, the information is not personal health information. Thus, for example, information about the prescribing records of a particular identified physician is not to be treated as personal health information where it does not directly or indirectly identify a patient.

This result accords with the efforts of the Information and Privacy Commissioner to ensure that evolving health sector privacy legislation distinguishes between "personal information" and "professional information." In her response to the Ministry of Health and Long-Term Care consultation on privacy rules for the health sector, the Commissioner stated:

> ... we believe the definition of personal health information should be drafted to ensure that information about the employment and business responsibilities, activities and transactions of individual health service providers is not included. This type of information may be used to objectively assess the quality of provider services and should be considered professional in nature rather than personal health information.[319]

---

317 *PHIPA*, s. 4(1)(b).

318 *Ibid.*

319 Information and Privacy Commissioner/Ontario, *Submission to the Ministry of Health and Long-Term Care in Response to Ontario's Proposed Personal Health Information Privacy Legislation for the Health Sector (Health Sector Privacy Rules)* (October 2000), online: <www.ipc.on.ca>. The Commissioner's comments concerning information about health care practitioners contained in an audit report of access to a patient's electronic patient record, as set out in the Commissioner's report on the University Health Network's response to breaches in patient privacy, are consistent with her response to the Ministry's consultation paper:

The federal *PIPEDA* excepts "professional information" from the meaning of "personal information," thus also making the distinction between "personal information" and "professional information." *PIPEDA* makes it clear that the term "personal information" does not include the name, title, business address, or telephone number of an employee of an organization.[320] At times, however, the line between professional information and personal information has been the subject of dispute.[321]

This aspect of the definition of personal health information is also important in the context of *PHIPA'a* fundraising rules, which govern the personal health information that a health information custodian can collect, use, and disclose for fundraising purposes with a patient's implied or express consent. *PHIPA* does not regulate a health information custodian's use and disclosure of information that is not personal health information, only information that is personal health information. While a person's name and address alone do not necessarily constitute personal health information and thus may not be subject to the Act's fundraising rules, such information does constitute per-

---

> ... the information about physicians and other ... staff on the audit report is professional information, relating to professional services performed, not personal information. For example, the name, job title and department of a particular ... physician or staff member in a publicly-funded hospital is information about that individual in his or her employment capacity, not their personal capacity, and should not be protected from disclosure.

Information and Privacy Commissioner/Ontario, *Privacy Assessment: University Health Network's Response to Recent Breaches of Patient Privacy* (30 July 2002), online: <www.ipc.on.ca>.

320 In *PIPEDA*, above note 7, s. 2(1), "personal information" is defined as information about an identifiable individual, but does not include the name, title, business address, or telephone number of an employee of an organization.

321 The Privacy Commissioner of Canada has had the opportunity to consider the distinction between "personal" information and "professional" information under *PIPEDA*. In two separate complaints to the Commissioner, an individual and a physician complained that a corporation was improperly disclosing personal information by gathering and selling data on the prescribing patterns of physicians without their consent. In 2001, the Commissioner issued his finding that provider information, both in the form of an individual prescription and in the form of patterns determined from multiple prescriptions, did not fall within the definition of personal information: *PIPEDA Act* Case Summary #14, "Selling of information on physicians' prescribing patterns," 21 September 2001, online: <www.privcom.gc.ca>. See also *PIPEDA* Case Summary #15, "Privacy Commissioner releases his finding on the prescribing patterns of doctors," 2 October 2001, online <www.privcom.gc.ca>. By clearly requiring a connection between information concerning a health care provider and an identifiable patient to constitute personal health information, the language in *PHIPA* should avoid this area of contention.

sonal health information when it is exhibited in a manner that makes it reasonable to assume that the person's relationship to the custodian was a health care provider/patient relationship. When a name and address are contained in a list that is labelled as, or will be known or reasonably assumed to be, a list of patients of a hospital, for example, then the information is considered to be personal health information and subject to *PHIPA*. Indeed, even a sheet of labels of names and addresses in a physician's recycling bin may constitute personal health information in some circumstances, such as where it is reasonable to assume from the context that the individuals named on the labels are the physician's patients.

v) "Plan of Service within the Meaning of the Long-Term Care Act, 1994"

Identifying information in the form of a patient's plan of service within the meaning of the *Long-Term Care Act, 1994* constitutes personal health information.[322] A plan of service is a document that an agency must develop when providing community services, as defined under that Act.[323] It includes such information as the patient's requirements for care and the level of services to be provided to the patient.[324]

vi) "Payments or Eligibility for Health Care"

The inclusion of identifying information that "relates to payments or eligibility for health care"[325] in the definition of "personal health information" reflects the potential sensitivity of such information. Information that relates to either payments or eligibility for health care may suggest the nature of the health care itself.[326] Further, payment information may reveal the condition of the patient that necessitated the care for which payment is provided or for which the

---

322 *PHIPA*, s. 4(1)(c).

323 *LTCA*, above note 20, s. 2(3) provides that "community services" are community support services, including meal and transportation services and adult day programs; homemaking services, such as housekeeping and shopping; personal support services, such as personal hygiene activities; and profession services, including nursing, dietetic, and social work services.

324 *LTCA*, *ibid.*, s. 2(1) defines the term "plan of service" to mean a plan of service developed or revised by an approved agency under s. 22. Section 22 of that Act provides that when a person applies to an approved agency for any of the community service that the agency provides or arranges, the agency must assess the person's requirements, determine the person's eligibility for services, and develop a plan of service that sets out the amount of each service to be provided to the person.

325 *PHIPA*, s. 4(1)(d).

326 For example, billing codes that dental surgeons use to receive payment from insurers communicate the oral health care that the dental surgeon provided to a patient.

patient seeks care. The expression "eligibility for health care" includes eligibility for coverage under the *Health Insurance Act*[327] or for any other insurance or payment arrangement with respect to health care.[328] For example, the fact that the Ontario Health Insurance Plan made a payment to a physician for his or her provision of a particular treatment to a patient constitutes personal health information about the patient.[329] Similarly, the fact that an insurance company has reimbursed a patient for payments made by the patient toward the cost of specific health care services constitutes personal health information about the patient. A determination by the Ministry of Health and Long-Term Care that a patient is eligible for payment in respect of the patient's purchase of a hearing aid, for example, is also personal health information about the patient.

vii) Donation of Body Parts or Bodily Substances and Testing Thereof
The definition of personal health information includes information that relates to the donation by an individual of any body part or bodily substance of the individual or that is derived from the testing or examination of any such body part or bodily substance.[330] In Ontario, the donation of tissue, both *inter vivos* and *post-mortem*, is governed by the *Trillium Gift of Life Network Act*.[331] The fact that a person consented to the removal of tissue from his or her body for the purpose of transplanting it in accordance with that Act constitutes personal health information of that person. Similarly, the fact that a person donated blood to Canadian Blood Services also constitutes personal health information about that person.[332] Any testing of such body parts or bodily substances (for example, information derived from testing done to ensure donor/recipient compatibility or testing of blood products to ensure the safety of the supply of

---

327 R.S.O. 1990, c. H.6 [*HIA*].

328 *PHIPA* Regulation, above note 9, s. 1(4).

329 This information, and that in the next two examples, combines information about health care provided to the individual together with information about the individual's eligibility for coverage in respect of that health care. Information that relates solely to the individual's eligibility for coverage without reference to any services received or sought by the individual is also personal health information.

330 *PHIPA*, s. 4(1)(e).

331 R.S.O. 1990, c. H.20. Section 1 provides that "tissue" means a part of a living or dead human body and includes an organ but, unless otherwise prescribed by the Lieutenant Governor in Council, does not include bone marrow, spermatozoa, an ovum, an embryo, a foetus, blood, or blood constituents.

332 Canadian Blood Services is a health information custodian: *PHIPA* Regulation, above note 9, s. 3(1).

333 See Section C(1)(b) above.

blood products) is also personal health information under *PHIPA*. As noted above, the tissue or bodily substance itself is not personal health information.[333]

viii) Health Number

Another category of information included in the definition of "personal health information" is the health number. *PHIPA* provides that a "health number" means the number, the version code, or both of them assigned to an insured person within the meaning of the *Health Insurance Act* by the General Manager within the meaning of that Act.[334] This specific reference to the health number is consistent with the special rules in *PHIPA* concerning the collection, use, and disclosure of health numbers as both recognize the unique characteristics and role of the health number in the health care sector. *PHIPA* includes rules specific to any person's collection, use, or disclosure of another person's health number, as discussed in Section D below. The categories of information included in the definition of "personal health information" do not include a reference to any other specific identifier.[335]

ix) Substitute Decision-maker

The identification of a person as the substitute decision-maker of a specific patient is also expressly included in the definition of personal health information.[336] Generally, *PHIPA* defines the term "substitute decision-maker," in relation to a patient, to mean a person who is authorized under the Act to consent on behalf of the patient to the collection, use, or disclosure of personal health information about the patient.[337] Similar to the identification of a person as the

---

334 *PHIPA*, s. 2, definition of "health number."

335 For example, a register number, which must be issued to patients admitted to hospitals, as required by Reg. 965, above note 238, s. 12(1), is not included specifically in the definition of "personal health information." Nor is a health insurance number from an insurer or from another jurisdiction listed specifically as personal health information, though as noted above it may be personal health information if it can be reasonably be expected in the circumstances to identify the patient.

336 *PHIPA*, s. 4(1)(g).

337 *Ibid.*, s. 2, definition of "substitute decision-maker," which refers to the definition in *PHIPA*, s. 5(1). Given the definition of "substitute decision-maker" in *PHIPA*, it is not clear that the reference to substitute decision-maker in *PHIPA*, s. 4(1)(g) includes substitute decision-makers in other contexts. However, in many instances, a patient's substitute decision-maker for the purposes of *PHIPA* will also be the patient's substitute decision-maker for the purposes of other legislation, such as the *Health Care Consent Act, 1996*, above note 69: *PHIPA*, ss. 5(2), (3), & (4). Further, the identification of an individual's substitute decision-maker may also constitute personal health information because it relates to the mental health of the patient or relates to the providing of health care to the patient.

provider of health care to a patient, identifying that a patient has a substitute decision-maker may imply sensitive information about the patient, due to the common connection between incapacity and the use of a substitute decision-maker.[338]

f)   Exceptions to Definition of "Personal Health Information"

i)   *Employee or Agent Information*

Personal health information does not include identifying information contained in a record of the health information custodian if that identifying information relates primarily to employees or other agents of the custodian, and the record is maintained primarily for a purpose other than the provision of health care to the employees or other agents.[339] For instance, records that a health information custodian holds about the disability accommodation needs of an employee would fall outside the definition of personal health information. Although relating to the health of the employee, such records are specifically excluded from the definition of personal health information for the purposes of *PHIPA*. Likewise, generally, records concerning a custodian's employee's Workplace Safety and Insurance Board claim or concerning an occupational illness from which a custodian's employee suffers are not considered records of personal health information when held by the custodian in its role as employer.[340] The rationale for this approach seems clear. It is appropriate to regulate health information custodians, as employers, in the same manner as other employers with respect to the privacy of their employees' personal health information. As the Act does not focus on the regulation of the collection, use, and

---

338   The definition goes beyond this rationale, however, since all substitute decision-makers would be included equally, including those that may act for a mentally capable patient, such as a substitute decision-maker authorized in accordance with *PHIPA*, s. 23(1)[1][ii].

339   *PHIPA*, s. 4(4).

340   Within the meaning of the *Occupational Health and Safety Act*, above note 102, s. 1(1). For example, Reg. 965, above note 238, s. 19(1) requires the administrator of a hospital to ensure that a system is established for the keeping of records of personal health information for each patient of the hospital. Where a hospital maintains a record primarily for a purpose other than the provision of health care to the hospital's employees or other agents, the hospital does not maintain the record in connection with such an obligation. Where the hospital also admits the employee as a patient, however, then the hospital would be required to maintain a record concerning the employee as required by the regulation and that record would be a record of personal health information.

disclosure of employee health information by employers generally,[341] health information custodians are not regulated differently in this regard by the Act.[342]

ii)   Old Personal Health Information

PHIPA does not apply to personal health information about a patient after the earlier of 120 years after the record containing the information was created and 50 years after the death of the patient.[343] Therefore, although the information still technically constitutes personal health information, it can be collected, used, and disclosed without reference to the rules in the Act. This exemption from the Act may be important in the context of research, as the information may be useful for research purposes. Despite the exemption of this information from the Act, health information custodians are not prevented from continuing to handle the information as though *PHIPA* applied to it or in compliance with other privacy-sensitive practices.[344] A health information custodian may choose to protect that information in the manner that the custodian finds appropriate.

g)   Mixed Records: Expanding the Definition of "Personal Health Information"

The inclusion of what *PHIPA* terms "mixed records" in the definition of "personal health information" expands the breadth of the definition significantly. Basically, the Act provides that identifying information that is not health-related information constitutes personal health information for the purposes of the Act where it is found in a record that contains health-related identifying information, thus capturing much more information in the definition of "personal health information" than would otherwise be included.[345]

---

341   See Chapter 12 for a discussion of *PHIPA*'s impact on employers and other recipients of personal health information from health information custodians.

342   A similar exception is found in *FIPPA*, s. 65(6) and *MFIPPA*, s. 52(4), above note 164. *PIPEDA* only applies to personal information about employees of an organization that collects, uses, or discloses the information in connection with the operation of a federal work, undertaking, or business — that is, any work, undertaking, or business that falls within the legislative authority of the Parliament of Canada. See Office of the Privacy Commissioner of Canada, Fact Sheet: Application of the *Personal Information Protection and Electronic Documents Act* to Employee Records (18 May 2004), online: <www.privcom.gc.ca>.

343   *PHIPA*, s. 9(1).

344   An exception would be if another conflicting legal requirement applied to the information.

345   *PHIPA*, s. 4(3), and *PHIPA* Regulation, above note 9, s. 4. The provision in the regulation appears to effectively clarify the intent and operation of the mixed record rule in the Act.

The rationale for this approach to "mixed records" appears to be to simplify the application of *PHIPA*, especially for custodians that may be subject to other privacy requirements, such as those under *FIPPA*, *MFIPPA*, or *PIPEDA*.[346] Under the mixed record rule, all identifying information in any given record containing any health-related identifying information is deemed to be personal health information. Thus *PHIPA* applies to the entire record. The mixed record rule, however, does not apply to information that is not contained in a record. *PHIPA* does not regulate a health information custodian's disclosure of unrecorded information that is not personal health information.[347]

Such mixed records will emerge in a variety of situations. Records of health care practitioners and facilities often contain a substantial amount of information about patients that may not be health-related in all cases, such as a patient's financial information, nationality, or religious affiliation.[348] Where this kind of information is kept in a record that contains health-related information about the patient, all this information will be treated as "personal health information."

PHIPA includes rules that regulate the use and disclosure of personal health information by persons who are not health information custodians where they receive the information from a health information custodian.[349] *PHIPA* refers to these persons as "recipients." The mixed record rule impacts recipients who are not health information custodians in a different, less direct manner from how the rule applies to custodians.[350]

---

346 See Chapter 3 for more detailed information on the relationship of *PHIPA* and those three Acts.

347 In this instance, the term "personal health information" refers to health-related identifying information (namely, information identified in *PHIPA*, s. 4(1)), without the operation of the mixed record rule, which applies only to recorded information. However, in many instances, the disclosure of identifying information by a health information custodian will be personal health information as a result of aspects of the definition of "personal health information," particularly *PHIPA*, s. 4(1)(b); for example, if the disclosure effectively identifies the custodian as a provider of health care to the patient.

348 Often, however, such information would be related to a patient's health. For example, information about a patient's religious affiliation may relate to the nature of health care provided to an individual.

349 See Chapter 12 for a discussion of the rules applicable to recipients.

350 The focus of the *PHIPA* rules applicable to recipients is personal health information, regardless of whether the information is recorded, as can be seen from the fact that *PHIPA*, ss. 49(1) & (2) refer to personal health information, as opposed to records of personal health information. All identifying information contained in a record disclosed by a custodian to a recipient is considered "personal health information" and is subject to the recipient rules, provided that there is some health-related identifying

D. HEALTH CARDS AND NUMBERS

1) Background

PHIPA applies in a special manner to a particular kind of personal health information: the "health number." The Act defines "health number" to mean the number, the version code,[351] or both of them assigned to an insured person within the meaning of the *Health Insurance Act* by the General Manager of the Ontario Health Insurance Plan, more commonly known as OHIP.[352] Health numbers appear on the face of health cards[353] and are used to facilitate payments by the Ontario government for provincially-funded health resources.[354] Health numbers, and other numbers assigned by governments to uniquely identify individuals, raise significant privacy concerns. The concerns lie in the

---

information in the record. However, if the recipient moves any of the personal health information from the record received from the custodian into its own records, the other identifying information contained in the recipient's own record, that is, information that was not received from a custodian, does not thereby become subject to *PHIPA*. Where a health information custodian discloses personal health information orally to a recipient, only the identifying information that is health-related is personal health information and thus subject to the recipient rules. If the recipient then records the information received orally from the health information custodian, only the health-related identifying information received from the custodian will be covered by the recipient rules and not any other personal health information in the record. Nevertheless, for the sake of simplicity, a recipient may choose to treat all information that it receives from a health information custodian as personal health information so as to follow a uniform set of rules when using and disclosing the information. See Chapter 12 for details concerning the broader context of this issue.

351 A version code is a combination of two letters of the alphabet. Version codes are assigned when a health card is replaced as a result of loss, theft, or re-issuance. The version code is used for managing and controlling the OHIP system by identifying which health card is valid at the time of the service.

352 *PHIPA*, s. 2, definition of "health number."

353 *Ibid.*, s. 34(1) defines "health card" to mean a card provided to an insured person within the meaning of the *Health Insurance Act* by the General Manager of the Health Insurance Plan. The *HIA*, above note 327, s. 1 provides that "insured person" means a person who is entitled to insured services under the Act and the regulations. Section 1 also provides that "insured services" means services that are determined under s. 11.2 to be insured services.

354 In *PHIPA*, s. 34(1), provides "provincially funded health resource" means a service, thing, subsidy, or other benefit funded, in whole or in part, directly or indirectly by the government of Ontario, if it is health-related or prescribed. This definition is substantially the same as the definition that was found in the *Health Cards and Numbers Control Act, 1991*, S.O. 1991, c. 1 [HCNCA], repealed by *PHIPA*, s. 82.

use of such numbers as multi-purpose identification numbers to facilitate the linking of disparate information about an individual to create a more complete picture of his or her activities. Legislated privacy protections are viewed as necessary to ensure that the health number does not become used as a broad personal identifier, a result that is often referred to as "function creep."[355]

2) Special Rules for Health Numbers

The *Health Cards and Numbers Control Act, 1991* was enacted to restrict the collection and use of health numbers to a narrow set of situations.[356] As interest in maintaining the confidentiality of health numbers and health cards continues, *PHIPA* repealed that Act and incorporated its provisions, with some significant revisions and additions.[357] For the purposes of *PHIPA*, the health number is a particular kind of personal health information[358] with its own special rules. Because the Act's provisions concerning health numbers apply to all persons, they have a wider application than any other provisions in the Act, which, for the most part, apply only to personal health information in the hands of health information custodians or received from a custodian. These provisions are also notable because it is possible to contravene them without any specific intent (including, for example, by collecting a document that contains incidental references to a person's health number) and such contraventions may constitute an offence subject to a significant fine.[359] The Act applies to the collection, use, and disclosure of health numbers as of 1 November 2004, the day the Act came into force; *PHIPA* applies to uses and disclosures of the number even where the person collected the number prior to that date.[360]

3) Health Numbers and Health Information Custodians

The collection, use, and disclosure of health numbers by health information custodians is not restricted in a manner that differs from the collection, use, and disclosure of personal health information generally. In other words, for

---

355 For a discussion of such privacy issues in the context of the development of a "smart card," see the letter to David Tsubouchi, Chair of Management Board of Cabinet, from Information and Privacy Commissioner Ann Cavoukian, summarizing the Commissioner's position on smart cards (5 April 2001), online:<www.ipc.on.ca>.

356 *HCNCA*, above note 354.

357 *PHIPA*, ss. 34 and 82.

358 *Ibid*, s. 4(1)(f).

359 See Section D(7) below.

360 *PHIPA*, s. 7(1)(c).

health information custodians, the health number is simply treated as a category of personal health information that the custodian may collect, use, or disclose as permitted by the rules governing personal health information generally. In this way, the Act arguably provides health information custodians with greater flexibility to collect and use health numbers than they had in the past, as the *Health Cards and Numbers Control Act, 1991* included tighter restrictions on these activities in relation to health numbers. The *Health Cards and Numbers Control Act, 1991* restricted the collection and use of health numbers by all persons to a small number of circumstances.[361]

However, it is also important for a health information custodian to keep the general limiting principles of the Act in mind when collecting, using, and disclosing health numbers. As discussed below, a health information custodian must not collect, use, or disclose personal health information if other information would service the purpose of the collection, use, or disclosure, as the case may be.[362] In addition, a health information custodian must not collect, use, or disclose more personal health information than is reasonably necessary to meet the purpose of the collection, use, or disclosure, as the case may be. Thus, it may not always be appropriate for a health information custodian to collect, use, or disclose a health number, despite the absence of a specific restriction on that activity.

With these principles in mind, a health information custodian should consider whether it is reasonably necessary to include a person's health number in the information that the custodian collects, uses, or discloses. Where the health number is not reasonably necessary to meet the purposes of a particular collection, use, or disclosure, the health information custodian must not collect, use, or disclose it. Of course, there will be instances in which a health information custodian will collect a health number incidentally as part of a larger collection of personal health information. Often, it will not be reasonably possible to separate the health number from the remainder of the information so as not to collect it. For example, a health information custodian may collect records of

---

361 The *HCNCA*, above note 354, permitted a person to collect or use another person's health number for purposes related to the provision of provincially-funded health resources to that other person. In addition, a person who provided a provincially-funded health resource to a person who had a health card or health number could collect or use the health number for purposes related to health administration or planning or health research or epidemiological studies. The *HCNCA* did not restrict the disclosure of health numbers.

362 *PHIPA*, s. 30(1). See Chapter 7 for a more detailed discussion of these principles.

personal health information that include health numbers for the purpose of a proceeding in which the custodian is a party, although the custodian may not actually require the health numbers for that purpose. In such instances, it seems likely that the custodian's collection of the health number would be considered "reasonably necessary" to meet the purpose of the collection.

4) Health Numbers and Persons Who Are Not Custodians

a) Collection and Use

i) *Generally*

The collection, use, and disclosure of health numbers by a person who is not a health information custodian and not acting as an agent of a custodian[363] are restricted to specified purposes and circumstances.[364] Persons who are not health information custodians may not rely on an individual's consent for authority to collect and use the individual's health number. They may only collect and use another person's health number in relation to certain purposes or circumstances, as explained in greater detail below.

ii) *"Provision of Provincially Funded Health Resources"*

First, a person who is not a health information custodian may collect and use a health number for purposes related to the provision of provincially-funded health resources to the person to whom the number relates.[365] A "provincially funded health resource" is a service, thing, subsidy, or other benefit funded, in whole or in part, directly or indirectly, by the government of Ontario, if it is health-related or prescribed in the regulations made under *PHIPA*.[366] Examples of a "provincially funded health resource" include any services covered by OHIP as insured services for insured persons under the *Health Insurance Act*,[367] equipment for eligible persons funded by the Ministry of Health and Long-Term Care's Assistive Devices Program, and prescription drug products for eligible persons under the Ontario Drug Benefit Program.

---

363 *PHIPA* Regulation, above note 9, s. 1(8) clarifies that "a person who is not a health information custodian," as that phrase appears in *PHIPA*, s. 34 does not include, (a) a custodian's agent who is using or disclosing the information on behalf of the custodian in accordance with the Act, or (b) the individual or the individual's substitute decision-maker in respect of the individual's health number.

364 *PHIPA*, ss. 34(2), (3).

365 *Ibid.*, s. 34(2)(a).

366 *Ibid.*, s. 34(1).

367 See above note 327.

Clearly, where a person who is not a health information custodian actually provides a provincially-funded health resource to an individual,[368] the person's collection and use of an individual's health number in relation to that activity would be for a purpose "related to the provision of provincially funded health resources." Even where the person is not directly involved in the provision of the provincially-funded health resources to the individual, however, the person may still have the authority to collect and use the individual's health number on this basis. The words "related to" broaden the scope of activities that this section of *PHIPA* includes.[369] Organizations often ask parents of children who participate in their camps or on their sporting teams to include health numbers on emergency contact information forms. School boards and day care centres also ask parents to provide this information. Such organizations may collect and use a child's health number for the purpose of providing the health number to a hospital or physician, for example, in case the child requires health care.[370]

Again, the general limiting principles are important to keep in mind in applying this provision. A person who is not a health information custodian but who collects personal health information, including the health number, from a health information custodian, that is, a "recipient," is generally subject to the general limiting principles of the Act, as noted above.[371] Therefore, the recipient must not use the health number if the number is not reasonably needed for the purpose for which it is to be used. Of course, where the law requires that the recipient use the health number, perhaps through a requirement to include it on a form specified by the Ministry of Health and Long-Term Care, the recipient may do so.

---

368 Because an activity involving "provision of a provincially funded health resource" would likely be caught by the definition of "health care," and the definition of "health information custodian" captures those persons whose primary function is to provide "health care" for payment, it is not clear when a person who is not a health information custodian will provide a provincially-funded health resource.

369 See *R. v. Nowegijick*, [1983] 1 S.C.R. 29 and *Slattery (Trustee of) v. Slattery*, [1993] 3 S.C.R. 430, where the court considered the meaning of the phrase "relating to" and other connecting phrases.

370 See also Information and Privacy Commissioner/Ontario, *Frequently Asked Questions: Health Cards and Health Numbers* (8 November 2004), online: <www.ipc.on.ca> [IPC FAQs], which contemplates a collection for this purpose.

371 *PHIPA*, s. 49(2). Section 49(2) does not apply to institutions within the meaning of *FIPPA* and *MFIPPA*: *PHIPA*, s. 49(5). See Chapter 12, Section E for a more detailed discussion of the application of the general limiting principles to recipients.

iii) Purpose for Which It Was Disclosed

Secondly, a person who is not a health information custodian may collect and use a health number for the purposes for which a health information custodian has disclosed the number to the person.[372] The scope of this provision is directly related to the scope of the power of a health information custodian to disclose an individual's health number. The ability of a person who is not a health information custodian to rely on this provision of *PHIPA* to collect and use health numbers depends on the interpretation of the purpose for which the health information custodian disclosed the health number to the person.[373]

iv) Health Administration, Planning, and Research

A person who is not a health information custodian also may collect and use a health number if the person is identified in the regulations and the person is collecting or using the health number for purposes related to health administration, health planning, health research, or epidemiological studies.[374] Such a person may collect health numbers for these purposes from any source, including the individual to whom the number relates. With the exception of the term "research," *PHIPA* does not include definitions of these terms, although they do appear in other provisions of the Act, as well.[375] This language is carried over from the *Health Cards and Numbers Control Act, 1991*.[376] Consequently, it may be appropriate to interpret these terms in accordance with their ordinary meanings. The following persons may collect and use health numbers for these purposes:[377]

- Workplace Safety and Insurance Board;[378]
- prescribed health registries described in section 37(1)(c) of the Act and listed in section 13(1) of the *PHIPA* Regulation;[379]

---

372 *PHIPA*, s. 34(2)(b).

373 See Chapter 12, Section C(2) for a discussion of the interpretation of language similar to the "purpose for which it was disclosed," as it appears in *PHIPA*, s. 49(1).

374 *PHIPA*, s. 34(2)(d).

375 *Ibid.*, s. 2, definition of "research." The term "planning," for example, appears in *PHIPA*, s. 45(1). Further, the phrase "health planning or health administration" appears in *PHIPA*, s. 50(1)(d)(ii).

376 *HCNCA*, above note 354, ss. 2(2)(b) and 2(3). No judicial consideration of the *HCNCA* is reported.

377 *PHIPA* Regulation, above note 9, s. 11.

378 *Ibid.*, s. 11(1).

379 *Ibid.*, s. 11(2). "Prescribed health registry" refers to a person prescribed pursuant to *PHIPA*, s. 39(1)(c) who compiles or maintains a registry of personal health information for the purposes of facilitating or improving the provision of health care or relating to the storage or donation of body parts or bodily substances. At the time of

- prescribed planning entities described in section 45(1) of the Act and listed in section 18(1) of the *PHIPA* Regulation;[380] and
- a researcher that conducts research in accordance with the Act.[381]

v)   Purposes of a Proceeding

PHIPA's restrictions on a non-custodian's collection and use of a health number do not apply to a person who collects and uses a health number for the purposes of a proceeding.[382] For example, as part of the information that a plaintiff in a civil action discloses during the discovery process, a defendant may collect

---

writing, prescribed health registries include Cardiac Care Network of Ontario in respect of its registry of cardiac services; INSCYTE (Information System for Cytology etc.) Corporation in respect of CytoBase; London Health Sciences Centre in respect of the Ontario Joint Replacement Registry; and the Canadian Stroke Network in respect of the Canadian Stroke Registry. See also Chapter 11 for a discussion of prescribed health registries.

380   *PHIPA* Regulation, *ibid.*, s. 11(3). A "prescribed planning entity" is an entity that is prescribed in the regulation, pursuant to *PHIPA*, s. 45, to which a health information custodian is permitted to disclose personal health information for the purpose of analysis or compiling statistical information with respect to the management, evaluation, or monitoring of the allocation of resources to, or planning for, all or part of the health system, including the delivery of services. Prescribed planning entities, at the time of writing, include Cancer Care Ontario; the Canadian Institute for Health Information; the Institute for Clinical Evaluative Sciences; and the Pediatric Oncology Group of Ontario. See also *PHIPA*, s. 34(5). See Section D(4)(a)(vi)(b) below.

381   *PHIPA* Regulation, *ibid.*, s. 11(4). The *PHIPA* Regulation provides that certain entities are able to use personal health information for the purpose of carrying out research as though they are health information custodians. See, for example, *PHIPA* Regulation, s. 13(4) concerning a prescribed health registry's use of personal health information for the purpose of carrying out research in accordance with the Act. See also *PHIPA* Regulation, s. 18(3) concerning a prescribed planning entity's use of personal health information for the purpose of carrying out research in accordance with the Act.

382   *PHIPA*, s. 34(5)(a). *PHIPA*, s. 2 defines the term "proceeding" to include a proceeding held in, before, or under the rules of a court; a tribunal; a commission; a justice of the peace; a coroner; a committee of a College within the meaning of the *RHPA*, above note 12; a committee of the Board of Regents continued under the *DPA*, above note 13; a committee of the Ontario College of Social Workers and Social Service Workers under the *SWSSWA*, above note 14; an arbitrator; or a mediator. However, where the person received the health number from a health information custodian, before using the health number for the purpose of a proceeding, the person must ensure that it is permitted to do so in accordance with *PHIPA*, s. 49, which restricts a person's use and disclosure of personal health information generally where the person received the personal health information from a health information custodian. See Chapter 12 for a detailed discussion of the restrictions on a recipient's use and disclosure of personal health information.

the plaintiff's health number. Likewise, a lawyer may collect a client's health number for the purpose of collecting information on the client's behalf in the course of preparing for a proceeding in which the client is a party. In some instances, the health number itself will not be needed, but the documents that the person collects may include the number.

vi) Collection and Use by Specific Categories of Persons

a. Regulators of health professions

A person who is not a health information custodian may collect and use a health number if the person is the governing body of health care practitioners who provide provincially-funded health resources and is collecting or using health numbers from any source for purposes related to its duties or powers.[383] Such bodies include professional governing bodies, including colleges established under the *Regulated Health Professions Act, 1991*,[384] such as the College of Physicians and Surgeons and the College of Nurses, and the College of Social Workers and Social Service Workers established under the *Social Work and Social Service Work Act, 1998*.[385] Such professional governing bodies may, therefore, collect a person's health number as part of the records of personal health information that it collects in the course of investigating the activities of a member.[386]

b. Prescribed planning entities

The restriction on the collection and use of health numbers does not apply to a prescribed planning entity identified in the regulations made under section 45(1) of *PHIPA*[387] where the entity collects and uses health numbers in the

---

383 *PHIPA*, s. 34(2)(c). *HCNCA*, above note 354, s. 2(4) included a similar provision. Further, *PHIPA*, s. 34(2)(c) may overlap with *PHIPA*, s. 34(2)(b) in some instances and may also provide professional governing bodies with authority to collect and use health numbers. Where a health information custodian discloses personal health information, including the health number, to a professional governing body pursuant to *PHIPA*, ss. 43(1)(b), (c), or (d), it is authorized to collect and use the health number for a purpose set out in those clauses pursuant to *PHIPA*, s. 34(2)(b). *PHIPA*, s. 34(2)(c) may be of most relevance to a professional governing body's authority to collect and use the health number from non-health information custodians.

384 Above note 12.

385 Above note 14.

386 Sch. 2 of the *RHPA*, above note 12, the Health Professions Procedural Code, ss. 75–79 address the powers of investigation of the Registrar of health profession colleges. See also Part VI of the *SWSSWA*, above note 14, for the powers of the Registrar of the Ontario College of Social Workers and Social Service Workers.

387 *PHIPA* Regulation, above note 9, s. 18(1).

course of carrying out its functions under section 45 of the Act.[388] Health numbers may be one element of the data that such an entity collects from health information custodians.

c.   Health data institute

The restriction on the collection and use of health numbers by persons who are not health information custodians does not apply to a health data institute[389] that collects and uses health numbers in the course of carrying out its functions under sections 47 and 48 of *PHIPA*.[390] When required to do so by the Minister, health information custodians must disclose personal health information, including health numbers, to a health data institute, and the health data institute may collect and use those health numbers as part of its analysis and linking of the personal health information.

d.   Archives

An archive that is permitted to accept transfers of records of personal health information under *PHIPA*[391] or under the regulation[392] is permitted to collect health numbers incidentally to receiving such transfers.[393] This authority to collect health numbers is important, since it will usually not be practical for an archive to comb through the records for the purpose of finding and removing any reference to health numbers before accepting such a transfer.[394] Furthermore, such archives may use health numbers for research purposes under the same rules that apply to health information custodians; namely, with the approval of a research ethics board.[395]

---

388   *PHIPA*, s. 34(5)(b).
389   Health data institutes are approved under *PHIPA*, s. 47(9). See Chapter 11, Section D for a discussion of health data institutes.
390   *PHIPA*, s. 34(5)(c).
391   *Ibid.*, s. 42(3)(b).
392   *PHIPA* Regulation, above note 9, ss. 14(2) & (3).
393   *Ibid.*, s. 14(4)(a). Such a collection is also permitted by *PHIPA*, s. 34(2)(b) in the case of transfers from custodians under *PHIPA*, s. 43(3)(b).
394   This authority is particularly relevant to personal health information transferred under *PHIPA* Regulation, *ibid.*, ss. 14(2) & (3). Where the information is transferred to an archive under *PHIPA*, s. 42(3)(b), though, since that section authorizes the custodian to disclose the health number along with any other personal health information, the collection by the archive of the personal health information including the health number would be authorized under *PHIPA*, s. 34(2)(b).
395   *PHIPA* Regulation, *ibid.*, ss. 14(4) & (5).

b) Disclosure

i) Generally

The disclosure of a health number by a person who is not a health information custodian is further restricted. A non-health information custodian is prohibited from disclosing another person's health number except as required by law or as set out in the regulations.

ii) As Required by Law

A person who is not a health information custodian may disclose another person's health number as required by law. For example, where records of personal health information that include health numbers are held by a person who is not a health information custodian but who is the subject of a search warrant or court ordered disclosure, the person would be required to disclose the health number pursuant to the warrant or court order. Similarly, the disclosure may be mandated by statute or regulation.[396] The statute may specifically mention the disclosure of the health number or may require the disclosure of any information at the request of an official granted authority under the statute to require the disclosure.

iii) Purpose Related to Provision of Provincially-funded Health Resources

The regulation provides that any person who is not a health information custodian may disclose a health number for a purpose related to the provision of provincially-funded health resources.[397] For example, as discussed above, organizations often ask parents of children who participate in their camps or on their sporting teams to include health numbers on emergency contact information forms. These organizations may disclose the health number of a child to a hospital, for example, where the child is taken there for treatment.[398] Likewise, a school board may disclose a student's health number to a medical officer of health as part of the student's immunization information. Each of these disclosures of the health number would be a disclosure of the health number for a purpose related to the provision of a provincially-funded health resource.

iv) Purpose of a Proceeding

PHIPA's restrictions on a non-custodian's disclosure of a health number do not apply to a person who discloses a health number for the purposes of a proceeding.[399] The person would need to ensure that the disclosure of the health

---

396 For a discussion of the phrase "required by law," see Chapter 3.

397 *PHIPA* Regulation, above note 9, s. 12(1).

398 See also IPC FAQs, note 370, above.

399 *PHIPA*, s. 34(5)(a).

number was consistent with other relevant restrictions in the Act including those applicable to a person who is not a health information custodian but receives personal health information from a health information custodian.[400]

v) Disclosures by Specific Categories of Persons

The regulations also describe some situations in which certain categories of persons can disclose the health number.

a. Researchers

Researchers who receive a health number from a health information custodian,[401] or who use a health number in accordance with the use provisions in *PHIPA*[402] may, in certain circumstances, disclose the health number to a prescribed health registry, to a prescribed planning entity, or to another researcher. A researcher's disclosure to one of these parties is permitted where the disclosure is either part of a research plan approved by a research ethics board in accordance with the requirements in the Act, or necessary for the purpose of verifying or validating the information or the research.[403] Because prescribed planning entities and prescribed health registries, as well as some researchers, hold comprehensive information, a disclosure of personal health information that includes health numbers by a researcher to such a party may be necessary for the purpose of verifying or validating information for research where the integrity of the researcher's information is questionable, and the disclosure would serve to ensure confidence in or enhance the information's integrity.

b. Prescribed health registries

A prescribed health registry may disclose a health number for the purposes of its functions in facilitating or improving the provision of health care or that relate to the storage or donation of body parts or bodily substances.[404]

c. Prescribed planning entities

The restriction on the disclosure of health numbers by persons who are not health information custodians does not apply to a prescribed planning entity

---

400 *PHIPA*, s. 49. This section restricts a person's use and disclosure of personal health information generally where the person received the personal health information from a health information custodian. See Chapter 12 for a detailed discussion of the restrictions on a recipient's use and disclosure of personal health information.

401 Pursuant to *PHIPA*, s. 44.

402 Pursuant to *PHIPA*, s. 37(1)(j).

403 *PHIPA* Regulation, above note 9, s. 12(2).

404 *Ibid.*, s. 12(3).

where the entity discloses health numbers in the course of carrying out its functions under section 45 of *PHIPA*.[405] Such an entity may disclose health numbers in the course of carrying out its functions, which include compiling statistical information about the management or planning of the health system.

d. Health data institute

The restriction on the disclosure of health numbers by persons who are not health information custodians also does not apply to a health data institute where the health data institute discloses health numbers in the course of carrying out its functions under section 47 and 48 of *PHIPA*.[406] Therefore, where the health data institute discloses personal health information to the Minister of Health and Long-Term Care pursuant to section 48(1) of the Act, which is only permitted to occur in exceptional circumstances where the disclosure is specifically approved by the Information and Privacy Commissioner, the health data institute may include, as part of the personal health information, health numbers, where health numbers were named in the Minister's proposal as identifiers to be disclosed.[407]

e. Workplace Safety and Insurance Board

The Workplace Safety and Insurance Board may disclose a person's health number in the course of exercising its powers under section 159 of the *Workplace Safety and Insurance Act, 1997*.[408] For example, under that Act, the Board may disclose a person's health number in order to arrange or make payments for the person's health care.[409]

f. Archives

PHIPA authorizes an archive that is permitted to accept transfers of records of personal health information under the Act[410] or under the regulation[411] to disclose health numbers for research purposes under the same rules that apply to

---

405 *PHIPA*, s. 34(5)(b).
406 *PHIPA*, s. 34(5)(c). Since *PHIPA*, s. 47 does not involve a health data institute's disclosure of personal health information to the Minister, as only de-identified information may be disclosed to the Minister under that section, the reference to s. 47 in this section is only relevant in considering a health data institute's collection and use of health numbers.
407 *PHIPA*, s. 48(4)(b).
408 *PHIPA* Regulation, above note 9, s. 12(4). The *Workplace Safety and Insurance Act, 1997*, S.O. 1997, c. 16, Sch. A, s. 159 sets out the powers of the Workplace Safety and Insurance Board.
409 *Workplace Safety and Insurance Act, 1997, ibid.*, s. 33(2).
410 *PHIPA*, s. 42(3)(b).
411 *PHIPA* Regulation, above note 9, ss. 14(2) & (3).

health information custodians; namely, with the approval of a research ethics board.

Furthermore, an archive that acquired records of personal health information under *PHIPA*, and that ceases to comply with the conditions set out in the regulations, must transfer those records, including any health number that may be contained in them, to a compliant archive that is willing to receive them.[412]

5) Recipients of Health Numbers

The restrictions on the collection, use, or disclosure of a health number by a person who is not a health information custodian apply regardless of whether the person receives the health number from a health information custodian, another person who is not a health information custodian, or directly from the individual whose number it is. *PHIPA's* restrictions on the ability of persons who are not health information custodians to use and disclose health numbers apply despite the general "recipient rules" relating to a recipient's use and disclosure of personal health information.[413] Therefore, a person who receives personal health information that includes the health number may not use or disclose the health number unless the Act's rules concerning health numbers permit the use or disclosure, even if the person could use or disclose the remainder of the information pursuant to *PHIPA's* recipient rules.

6) Requiring Production of Health Card

Because the majority of residents of Ontario have a health card, organizations often accept the health card as a form of identification. Only a person who provides a provincially-funded health resource to an individual can require that individual to produce his or her health card.[414] Given the broad definition of "health information custodian" and "health care," in practice, only a health information custodian or a person acting on behalf of a custodian would appear to have the authority to require the production of a health card.[415]

---

412   *Ibid.*, s. 14(2).

413   *PHIPA*, ss. 34(2) & (3). Both of these sections specify that they operate "despite s. 49(1), which contains the general exceptions to the recipient rules. See Chapter 12 for a more detailed discussion of the rules applicable to recipients.

414   *PHIPA*, s. 34(4). Other persons are prohibited from requiring the production of another person's health card.

415   The "provision of a provincially funded health resource" would likely be caught by the definition of "health care," and the definition of "health information custodian" captures those persons who provide "health care." However, only custodians that provide

Accepting a health card from a person who presents his or her health card voluntarily is different from requiring a person to produce his or her health card. A person who does not provide a provincially-funded health resource to an individual may accept a health card that an individual produces in cases where the Act authorizes the collection of the health number; for example, for a purpose related to the provision of provincially-funded health resources. Where the person does not provide a provincially-funded health resource but permits an individual to present his or her health card to fulfil a purpose for which the Act does not authorize the collection of health numbers, such as for identification purposes, the Information and Privacy Commissioner has indicated that the person may accept the health card to fulfil this purpose. However, in doing so, the person must not take note of, record, photocopy, collect, or use the health number on the face of the card.[416]

7) Offences

PHIPA treats contraventions of the provisions of the Act related to health numbers and health cards seriously. Under the Act, it is an offence to require the production of an individual's health card, except if it is required by a person who provides provincially-funded health resources to the individual who has the card.[417] Further, a non-health information custodian who collects, uses, or discloses another person's health number in contravention of the Act is guilty of an offence under the Act.[418] No wrongful intention is required to be found guilty of this offence. A person accused of such an offence may defend the charge on the basis that he or she took all reasonable care in the circumstances to avoid committing the offence. On conviction, persons guilty of such offences are liable to significant fines of up to $50,000 for individuals and $250,000 for corporations.[419]

---

health care that is considered a "provincially funded health resource" could rely on this provision.

416 IPC FAQs, above note 370.
417 *PHIPA*, s. 34(4). *HCNCA*, above note 354, s. 3 created the same offence.
418 *PHIPA*, s. 72(1)(f). No persons were prosecuted for an offence under *HCNCA*.
419 For a more detailed discussion of offences under *PHIPA*, see Chapter 15.

Table A: *Summary of Health Number Rules for Non-Health Information*
             Custodians

Collection and Use of Health Number	Disclosure of Health Number
Basic Rule: *PHIPA*, s. 34(2): A person who is not a health information custodian must not collect or use another person's health number.	**Basic Rule:** *PHIPA*, s. 34(3): A person who is not a health information custodian must not disclose another person's health number.
Exceptions to and Exclusions from Basic Rule	
• *PHIPA*, s. 34(2)(a): may collect or use for purposes related to provision of provincially-funded health resources to person to whom number assigned • *PHIPA*, s. 34(2)(b): may collect or use for purposes for which health information custodian disclosed number • *PHIPA*, s. 34(2)(c): governing body of health care practitioners who provide provincially-funded health resources may collect or use for purposes related to body's duties or powers • *PHIPA*, s. 34(2)(d); *PHIPA* Regulation, s. 11[1]: Workplace Safety and Insurance Board may collect or use for purposes related to health administration, health planning, health research, or epidemiological studies • *PHIPA*, s. 34(2)(d); *PHIPA* Regulation, s. 11[2]: prescribed health registry may collect or use for purposes related to health administration, health planning, health research, or epidemiological studies • *PHIPA*, s. 34(2)(d); *PHIPA* Regulation, s. 11[3]: prescribed planning entity may collect or use for purposes related to health administration, health planning, health research, or epidemiological studies • *PHIPA*, s. 34(2)(d); *PHIPA* Regulation, s. 11[4]: researcher who received the health number as part of information that a custodian disclosed to researcher for research in accordance with *PHIPA* or that researcher uses for research in accordance with *PHIPA* may collect or use for purposes related to health administration, health planning, health research, or epidemiological studies • *PHIPA*, s. 34(5)(a): may collect or use for the purpose of a proceeding	• *PHIPA*, s. 34(3): may disclose as required by law • *PHIPA* Regulation, s. 12(1): may disclose for a purpose related to provision of provincially-funded health resources • *PHIPA* Regulation, s. 12(2): researcher may disclose to prescribed health registry, if disclosure is part of research plan approved under *PHIPA*, s. 44, or if disclosure is necessary for purpose of verifying or validating the information • *PHIPA* Regulation, s. 12(2): researcher may disclose to prescribed planning entity, if disclosure is part of research plan approved under *PHIPA*, s. 44, or if disclosure is necessary for purpose of verifying or validating the information • *PHIPA* Regulation, s. 12(2): researcher may disclose to researcher, if disclosure is part of research plan approved under *PHIPA*, s. 44, or if disclosure is necessary for purpose of verifying or validating the information • *PHIPA* Regulation, s. 12(3): prescribed health registry may disclose for the purpose of its registry functions • *PHIPA* Regulation, s. 12(4): Workplace Safety and Insurance Board may disclose in course of exercising its powers under the *Workplace Safety and Insurance Act*, s. 159 • *PHIPA*, s. 34(5)(a): may disclose for the purpose of a proceeding • *PHIPA*, s. 34(5)(b): prescribed planning entity may disclose for purpose of carrying out its functions under *PHIPA*, s. 45 • *PHIPA*, s. 34(5)(c): health data institute may disclose in course of carrying out its functions under *PHIPA*, ss. 47 and 48 • *PHIPA* Regulation, s. 14(4)(c): Archives of Ontario or archives that fulfil requirements of *PHIPA* Regulation, s. 14(1) may disclose

Exceptions to and Exclusions from Basic Rule	
• *PHIPA*, s. 34(5)(b): prescribed planning entity may collect or use for purpose of carrying out its functions under *PHIPA*, s. 45 • *PHIPA*, s. 34(5)(c): health data institute may collect or use in course of carrying out its functions under *PHIPA*, ss. 47 and 48 • *PHIPA* Regulation, s. 14(4)(a): Archives of Ontario or archives that fulfil requirements of *PHIPA* Regulation, s. 14(1) may collect where collection is incidental to receipt of records • *PHIPA* Regulation, s. 14(4)(b): Archives of Ontario or archives that fulfil requirements of *PHIPA* Regulation, s. 14(1) may use for research carried out in accordance with *PHIPA* as though the archive is a health information custodian	to a researcher in accordance with *PHIPA* as though a health information custodian • *PHIPA* Regulation, s. 14(4)(c): Archives of Ontario or archives that fulfil requirements of *PHIPA* Regulation, s. 14(1) may disclose to prescribed planning entity in accordance with *PHIPA* as though a health information custodian • *PHIPA* Regulation, s. 14(4)(c): Archives of Ontario or archives that fulfil requirements of *PHIPA* Regulation, s. 14(1) may disclose to health data institute in accordance with *PHIPA* as though a health information custodian

E. "COLLECT," "USE," AND "DISCLOSE" DEFINED

1) Generally

PHIPA uses four words to describe a health information custodian's primary transactions concerning personal health information: collect, use, disclose, and access. With the exception of the word "access," the Act sets out a specific meaning for each term (see below). A health information custodian can collect, use, or disclose personal health information whether the information is in oral or recorded form, although a custodian is only required to provide a patient with access to personal health information that is in recorded form.[420]

Although the Act focuses on the activities of health information custodians, the definitions of the terms "collect," "use," and "disclose" apply to the actions of persons who are not health information custodians as well as to custodians. For example, the provisions in the Act concerning the collection, use, and disclosure of health numbers[421] apply to the actions of persons who are not health information custodians, as do the rules concerning persons who are not health information custodians but receive personal health information from a custodian.[422] In interpreting these rules, the definitions of "collect," "use," and "disclose" in the Act apply.

---

420 *PHIPA*, s. 52(1).
421 *Ibid.*, s. 34.
422 *Ibid.*, s. 49.

To set a proper foundation for understanding the application of *PHIPA*, it is useful to examine these words in detail to understand their meaning and appropriate usage.

2) "Collect"

The term "collect" is defined in *PHIPA* to mean, in relation to personal health information, "to gather, acquire, receive or obtain the information by any means from any source."[423] The word "collection" has a corresponding meaning.[424] A health information custodian's receipt of personal health information from an agent of the custodian is not a collection.[425]

Subject to the restrictions in the Act, a health information custodian may collect personal health information in various ways, whether directly from the patient to whom the information relates, or indirectly from a source other than the patient, which source may or may not be a health information custodian. A health information custodian may collect personal health information made available to it in oral form or recorded form. A custodian may be considered to be collecting personal health information in certain circumstances, even when the custodian is receiving the information in oral form and not recording it, such as where the custodian requested the information and/or subsequently relied on it.

Sometimes, a custodian collects personal health information as a result of seeking the information. For example, a midwife collects personal health information directly from a patient when the patient responds to the midwife's questions concerning her health history. A chiropractor collects personal health information directly when a patient submits a completed form to a chiropractor describing courses of treatment that he or she has undergone in the past to deal with his or her back pain.

In other instances, a custodian collects information without having sought the information. Through the inclusion of the terms "acquire" and "receive" in the definition of the term "collect," *PHIPA* suggests that a health information custodian may be passive in the act of collecting, at least provided that the custodian can be found to have taken custody or control of the information. A dietician, for instance, may collect personal health information from a family physician when the dietician receives information pertaining to a patient from

---

423   *PHIPA*, s. 2, definition of "collect."
424   *Ibid.*
425   *Ibid.*, s. 6(1). Further, where a health information custodian provides personal health information to the custodian's agent, the agent does not "collect" the information. The provision of the information is a "use of the information": *PHIPA*, s. 6(1).

the physician upon the physician's referral of the patient to the dietician. A hospital may collect personal health information about a patient from a paramedic as the paramedic describes the patient's condition to an emergency room physician while bringing the patient into the hospital.

The Act is silent on what to do with unsolicited information, although it does require that records of personal health information that a custodian has in its custody or under its control are retained and disposed of in a secure manner.[426] Where there are professional or institutional standards or guidelines pertaining to unsolicited information, a health information custodian should follow them. Otherwise, where a health information custodian receives a record of personal health information that he or she did not request and does not need, the custodian should return the record to the sender or destroy it in a secure manner.[427]

3) "Use"

The term "use" is defined in *PHIPA* to mean, in relation to personal health information in the custody or under the control of a health information custodian or a person, "to handle or deal with the information, but does not include to disclose the information."[428] The word "use" as a noun has a corresponding meaning.[429] As the definition suggests, "use" of personal health information covers a variety of common activities ranging from organizing it to recording it in another medium. "Use" also includes relying on the information to undertake another activity, such as providing health care, carrying out research, evaluating services, or contacting the patient to whom the information relates.[430] The Act also permits a health information custodian to use personal health information without the consent of the patient to whom the information relates for the purpose of disposing of the information or modifying the information in order to conceal the identity of the patient.[431]

In the past, persons in the health care system may have viewed any kind of transfer of information as a "disclosure" of the information. The Act, however, makes it clear that the provision of personal health information by a

---

426 *PHIPA*, s. 13(1).

427 *Ibid.*, s. 13(1).

428 *Ibid.*, s. 2, definition of "use."

429 *Ibid.*

430 *Ibid.*, ss. 37(1)(a), (j), (c), & (g) provide that a health information custodian can use personal health information for such purposes without consent.

431 *Ibid.*, s. 37(1)(f).

health information custodian to an agent of the custodian, or the provision of personal health information by one agent of a custodian to another, or from the agent to the custodian, and the associated receipt of the information constitute a "use" of the information by the custodian; it is neither a disclosure by the one transferring the information nor a collection by the one receiving it.[432] A custodian's release or making available of personal health information to a person who is not the custodian's agent continues to constitute a "disclosure." Therefore, in a facility setting, for example, where nurses, physicians, physiotherapists, clerical staff, and others who are agents of the custodian update the record of a patient, view the record to carry out their responsibilities, or discuss a patient's progress, as authorized by the custodian, their activities with respect to the personal health information constitute "uses" of the information. Similarly, where an information management professional is retained to manage the records within the facility and is handling the records of personal health information for this purpose, the health information custodian has not "disclosed" the information to the professional; rather, the custodian has authorized the information management professional to "use" the information on the custodian's behalf for the purposes of records management.

4) "Disclose"

The term "disclose" is defined to mean "to make the information available or to release it to another health information custodian or to another person," but it does not include to "use" the information.[433] The term "disclosure" has a corresponding meaning.[434] Further, as discussed above in the context of the meaning of the term "use," the term "disclose" does not include a health information custodian's provision of personal health information to an agent of the custodian to use on the custodian's behalf. The term does not, therefore, apply to transfers of information between a custodian and its agents.[435]

A health information custodian can go about disclosing personal health information in different ways. A health information custodian may disclose personal health information orally or by sending recorded information to another person. An optometrist, for example, discloses personal health information when mailing to the Registrar of Motor Vehicles a written report of the name and clinical condition of a person who suffers from an eye condition that

---

432   *PHIPA*, s. 6(1).
433   *Ibid.*, s. 2, definition of "disclose."
434   *Ibid.*
435   *Ibid.*, s. 6(1).

makes it dangerous for the person to operate a motor vehicle, as required under the *Highway Traffic Act*.[436] A pharmacist discloses personal health information when informing a physician over the telephone that a patient is taking medication that may interact with the medication that the physician prescribed to the patient. An orthodontist discloses personal health information when transmitting through electronic means information concerning a patient's treatment to the patient's insurer. A custodian may also be found to disclose personal health information by leaving a voicemail recording of personal health information on a person's answering machine or by posting personal health information on a website.[437]

Through the inclusion of the phrase "to make the information available" the definition of the term suggests that a health information custodian may be passive in the act of disclosing. For example, a health information custodian who leaves a record of personal health information in a reception area where a patient to whom the information does not relate could read it has disclosed the personal health information by "making it available" to that patient. A health information custodian may arguably disclose personal health information unintentionally as well. A health information custodian who inadvertently sends a report that contains personal health information to the wrong address, where the report is read, may be found to have disclosed the personal health information.[438] Indeed, a disclosure of personal health information may arguably arise as a result of theft of the information.[439]

---

436 *Highway Traffic Act*, R.S.O. 1990, c. H.8, s. 204(1).

437 See Privacy Complaint Report MC-010036-1 and MC-010032-1, York Region District School Board and York Catholic District School Board (15 May 2003), online: <www.ipc.on.ca>, which considers a situation in the context of *MFIPPA* involving personal information made available on a website and through an automated phone system.

438 If the envelope is not opened and thus the report is not read, the sending of the report to the wrong address arguably would not constitute a "disclosure," provided that the envelope itself did not include personal health information.

439 The Office of the Information and Privacy Commissioner has come to this conclusion in the context of *FIPPA*. See Privacy Complaint Report PC-030043-1, Ministry of Labour (23 February 2004) online: <www.ipc.on.ca>, which considers an incident involving the theft of employment standards files from an office of the Ministry of Labour. See also Privacy Complaint Report PC-020054-1, Ministry of the Attorney General (26 June 2003) online: <www.ipc.on.ca>, which considered a matter involving the theft of a laptop computer from an Assistant Crown Attorney's car. Although *FIPPA* does not define the word "disclose," the Commissioner, consistent with conclusions reached in the context of *FIPPA*, may conclude under *PHIPA* that a disclosure may arise as a consequence of theft of information in the custodian's custody or control.

In the definition of "disclose" in section 2 of *PHIPA*, the expression "to make the information available or to release it to another health information custodian or to another person" does not include a person's providing personal health information to someone who provided it to or disclosed it to the person, whether or not the personal health information has been manipulated or altered, if it does not contain any additional identifying information.[440] This provision makes it clear that a custodian's returning of personal health information to the person who provided it to the custodian in the first place is not to be treated as a disclosure, even if the custodian returns the information in a different form. Although perhaps not required, this clarification is useful to ensure that the term "disclose" is not interpreted to include this type of transaction.

5) "Access"

Unlike the terms "collect," "use," and "disclose," *PHIPA* does not define the term "access." The term "access" is generally used to describe a health information custodian's provision of a record of personal health information about a patient to the patient and the patient's receipt of that record.[441] The Act distinguishes a health information custodian's provision of personal health information to a person other than the patient to whom the information relates from the custodian's provision of the information to that patient. While the former constitutes a disclosure of personal health information, the latter constitutes the patient's access to his or her personal health information. Therefore, in describing this transaction between a health information custodian and a patient, it is more appropriate to use the term "access," as opposed to "disclose" and "collect."

---

440 *PHIPA* Regulation, above note 9, s. 1(3).

441 Provision of personal health information to the patient's substitute decision-maker would similarly be treated as providing access. See Chapter 6 for a discussion of a substitute decision-maker's authority to make a request for access to a patient's record of personal health information.

3 How *PHIPA* Works with Other Law

A. GENERALLY

To implement the rules set out in the *Personal Health Information Protection Act*,[1] it is important for custodians and others to understand how the provisions in *PHIPA* relate to provisions in other legislation. This chapter discusses the interaction between *PHIPA* and

- other legislation and law generally, especially health sector legislation;
- Ontario's public sector privacy legislation,[2] a matter of special interest for those health information custodians that are also subject to that legislation; and
- the federal private sector privacy legislation,[3] a matter of special interest for any non-governmental health information custodians engaged in commercial activities.

---

1   S.O. 2004, c. 3, Sch. A [*PHIPA*].
2   Ontario's public sector access to information and protection of privacy legislation is the *Freedom of Information and Protection of Privacy Act*, R.S.O. 1990, c. F.31 [*FIPPA*] and the *Municipal Freedom of Information and Protection of Privacy Act*, R.S.O. 1990, c. M.56 [*MFIPPA*].
3   *Personal Information Protection and Electronic Documents Act*, S.C. 2000, c. 5 [*PIPEDA*].

B. INTERACTION WITH OTHER LEGISLATION GENERALLY

1) Two Fundamental Policy Objectives

PHIPA's interaction with other legislation generally reflects a balance between two fundamental policy objectives: a consistent privacy framework across the health sector and the preservation of special rules applicable to certain activities in parts of the health sector.

a) Uniform Sector-wide Rules

PHIPA aims to provide uniform and consistent rules across the health sector, rather than a patchwork of different rules.[4] This objective is embodied in the rule set out in the Act that, in the event of a conflict between *PHIPA* and any other legislation, *PHIPA* prevails, subject to certain exceptions discussed below.[5] For this reason, *PHIPA* included a number of complementary amendments to health sector legislation to ensure consistency with *PHIPA's* approach.[6]

b) Existing Special Rules Preserved

Second, in addition to providing uniform rules that apply to the whole health sector, *PHIPA* aims to allow the continuing functioning of special rules particular to specific parts of the health sector. The most important example of this

---

4   Health Minister George Smitherman explained it: "Currently there are no consistent rules covering what information can be collected, and how that information can be used and disclosed. Existing laws that deal with health information apply in some health care settings and not in others. This legislation addresses those problems. This legislation begins to treat our health care system as a system, not just parts of it; all parts of it are covered." Ontario, Legislative Assembly, *Official Report of Debates (Hansard)*, (30 March 2004).

5   *PHIPA*, s. 7(2). See Section B(2) below.

6   For example, sector-specific provisions relating to disclosures of personal health information were generally removed from the *Mental Health Act*, R.S.O. 1990, c. M.7 [*MHA*] and *Long-Term Care Act, 1994*, S.O. 1994, c. 26 [*LTCA*], as were patients' access and correction rights under those statutes. Other provisions were added (*PHIPA*, s. 89 amending the *LTCA*; *PHIPA*, s. 90 amending *MHA*). Further, the three long-term care facility statutes, the *Nursing Homes Act*, R.S.O. 1990, c. N.6 [*NHA*], the *Charitable Institutions Act*, R.S.O. 1990, c. C.9 [*CIA*], and the *Homes for the Aged and Rest Homes Act*, R.S.O. 1990, c. H.13 [*HARHA*] were amended for consistency with *PHIPA*: *PHIPA*, ss. 77, 87, & 92. Regulations under health sector legislation were also modified for consistency with *PHIPA* and its regulation; for example, several provisions that authorized disclosures of a medical record without consent in certain circumstances were removed from *Hospital Management*, R.R.O. 1990, Reg. 965, made under the *Public Hospitals Act*, R.S.O. 1990, c. P.40 and from *General*, O. Reg. 57/92, made under the *Independent Health Facilities Act*, R.S.O. 1990, c. I.3.

are the provisions that collections, uses, or disclosures permitted under other laws without consent continue to be permitted under *PHIPA* without consent.[7]

Each of these two fundamental policy aspects of *PHIPA* will be discussed in turn.

2) *PHIPA* Prevails over Other Ontario Legislation

As a general rule, in the event of conflict between a provision of *PHIPA*, including its regulations, and a provision of any other Ontario legislation or regulations, the provision of *PHIPA* or its regulation prevails; that is, one must follow the *PHIPA* provision.[8]

This rule only applies, however, where it is not possible to comply with both provisions at the same time.[9] If it is possible to comply with both provisions, one must do so. For example, if a health information custodian is required under other legislation to retain records for a lesser period of time than that required by *PHIPA*[10] (without requiring the record to be destroyed after that time), one complies with both provisions by keeping the record for a longer period; that is, complying with the more stringent standard.

The *PHIPA* Regulation clarifies this rule. It provides that where *PHIPA* or its regulations permits a collection, use, or disclosure (or other action), and another act or regulation forbids the collection, use, or disclosure, this is considered a situation where "it is not possible to comply with both" provisions, and hence the *PHIPA* provisions take precedence, overriding the provision in the other act or regulation.[11] Therefore it appears that collections, uses, or dis-

---

7   Regarding collections of personal health information, see s. 36(1)(h), and note (g). Regarding uses, see s. 37(1)(k). Regarding disclosures, see s. 43(1)(h). See further Chapter 8, Section C(7) & (8); Chapter 9, Section C(12); and Chapter 10, Section P. It is noteworthy that all of these are subject to any requirements and restrictions that may be prescribed, allowing existing collections, uses, and disclosures to be narrowed or subject to additional requirements by means of regulations under *PHIPA*. See Chapter 16 on *PHIPA* Regulations. No such regulations have been put forward as of the date of writing.

8   *PHIPA*, s. 7(2). The rationale for this may be that given the broad scope of *PHIPA*, it was not possible to be confident that all statutory provisions that could possibly regulate the conduct of health information custodians for the collection, use, or disclosure of personal health information, and other matters covered by *PHIPA*, were being updated to repeal conflicting provisions, though it appears that an attempt was made to do this.

9   This is implicit in the terms of *PHIPA*, s. 7(2) and is also made explicit in s. 7(3).

10 Currently *PHIPA* does not have regulations setting a fixed retention period, but records that are subject to an access request are required to be retained until the request and any associated appeals or processes are exhausted: *PHIPA*, s. 13(2).

11 *General*, O. Reg. 329/04, s. 1(5) [*PHIPA Regulation*].

closures that are permitted under *PHIPA* can be carried out despite provisions in other acts that either forbid the collection, use, or disclosure or that restrict it; for example, by requiring consent or some form of approval.[12] This rule does not apply to a non-custodian who receives personal health information from a custodian; such a non-custodian may not disclose the information further where prohibited by law.[13]

There are a number of exceptions to this general rule that *PHIPA* prevails:

- Any provision of the *Quality of Care Information Protection Act, 2004*[14] prevails over *PHIPA*,[15] so "quality of care information," as defined in that Act, is not permitted to be disclosed under any of the provisions in *PHIPA* that permit or require disclosures of personal health information. Quality of care information may be disclosed only where permitted under *QCIPA*.[16]
- Where the other Act specifically provides otherwise, by stating expressly that one or more provisions in that Act prevail over *PHIPA*, then those provisions take precedence over conflicting provisions in *PHIPA*. For example,

  - *PHIPA*[17] amended the *Child and Family Services Act*[18] so that certain of its provisions, relating to a child's access to an assessment of whether the child is in need of protection,[19] relating to the duty to report a child in need of protection,[20] imposing restrictions on the disclosure of information obtained pursuant to a court order in a child protection matter,[21] and providing for the disclosure in certain circumstances of a record of a mental disorder by a service provider under that Act in connection with a legal proceeding,[22] all prevail over *PHIPA*.[23]

---

12   It should be noted though that such a collection, use, or disclosure is generally permitted but not required under *PHIPA*, as explicitly clarified in s. 6(3)(a) with respect to disclosures, apparently for greater certainty, and as such a custodian still has discretion to refuse to make the collection, use, or disclosure.

13   *PHIPA* Regulation, above note 11, s. 21(3). The rules relating to such recipients are discussed fully in Chapter 12.

14   S.O. 2004, c. 3, Sched. B [*QCIPA*].

15   *PHIPA*, s. 7(4); *QCIPA*, *ibid.*, s. 2.

16   See Chapter 17 for more information about quality of care information and the restrictions on its disclosure.

17   *PHIPA*, s. 78.

18   R.S.O. 1990, c. 11 [*CFSA*].

19   *Ibid.*, s. 54(5.1).

20   *Ibid.*, s. 72(9).

21   *Ibid.*, s. 74(5.1).

22   *Ibid.*, s. 183(6.1).

23   *Ibid.*, s. 74(5.1) states: "Subsection (5) prevails despite anything in the *Personal Health Information Protection Act, 2004*."

- The *Drug and Pharmacies Regulation Act*[24] was amended by *PHIPA*[25] so that the provision entitling a patient to be provided with a copy of any prescription that was presented to a pharmacist on behalf of the patient, except where otherwise directed by the prescriber, would apply despite anything in *PHIPA*.
- The *Health Care Consent Act, 1996*,[26] was amended by *PHIPA*[27] so that its provisions relating to the right of a substitute decision-maker for treatment decisions, or decisions relating to personal assistance services or placement in a care facility, to access an incapable patient's information as necessary for that purpose, would prevail over any *PHIPA* provisions to the contrary.[28]
- The restrictions on the disclosure of "quality assurance information," as defined in the Health Professions Procedural Code under the *Regulated Health Professions Act, 1991*,[29] as instituted through amendments in *QCIPA*,[30] prevail over *PHIPA*.[31]
- The *Health Protection and Promotion Act*[32] was amended by *PHIPA*,[33] so that the provision requiring a medical officer of health to report to a complainant regarding an occupational or environmental health hazard without including any personal health information about a person, other than the complainant, without that person's consent prevails over *PHIPA*.
- The *Long-Term Care Act, 1994*[34] was amended by *PHIPA*[35] so that the revised provisions of that Act relating to disclosures of personal health information in proceedings prevail over *PHIPA*.
- The *Mental Health Act* was amended by *PHIPA*[36] to provide that the rules in that Act pertaining to such matters as community treatment orders; the collection, use, or disclosure of personal health information in the

---

24 R.S.O. 1990, c. H.4, s. 157(1.1).

25 *PHIPA*, s. 80.

26 S.O. 1996, c. 2, Sch. A [*HCCA*].

27 *PHIPA*, s. 84.

28 *HCCA*, above note 26, ss. 22 and 43.

29 Health Professions Procedural Code [Code], Schedule 2 to the *Regulated Health Professions Act, 1991*, S.O. 1991, c. 18, s. 83.1(4) [*RHPA*].

30 *QCIPA*, above note 14, s. 11(2).

31 The reasons for this are similar to the reasons for *QCIPA* prevailing over *PHIPA*, as set out in the first example listed above. See Chapter 17 for more detail.

32 R.S.O. 1990, c. H.7, s. 11 [*HPPA*].

33 *PHIPA*, s. 86.

34 *LTCA*, above note 6, s. 35.1.

35 *PHIPA*, s. 89(13).

36 *Ibid.*, s. 90(5).

context of examining, assessing, observing, or detaining a patient; and the disclosure of information in proceedings, prevail over *PHIPA*.[37]
  – Confidentiality provisions in the *Occupational Health and Safety Act*[38] were amended[39] so that they prevail over *PHIPA*.

• Similarly, where the regulations under *PHIPA* specifically provide otherwise, by stating expressly that one or more provisions in another Act or regulation prevail over *PHIPA*, then those provisions take precedence.[40] Under the *PHIPA* Regulation the following confidentiality provisions prevail over *PHIPA*, meaning that one who is subject to these provisions may not disclose the information except as permitted under those provisions, despite any provision in *PHIPA* that would otherwise permit or require the disclosure.[41]

  – The confidentiality requirements in section 19(8) of the *Remedies for Organized Crime and Other Unlawful Activities Act, 2001*, which require a court order for certain types of disclosures to a "reviewing authority" prescribed under that Act.[42]
  – The restriction on the reporting by a regulated health professional to an *RHPA* College, without patient consent, of the name of a patient who may have been sexually abused, as set out in the Health Professions Procedural Code under the *Regulated Health Professions Act, 1991*.[43]
  – Confidentiality requirements on adoption information under the *Child and Family Services Act*.[44]

---

37 *PHIPA* amended the *MHA*, above note 6, to add a new s. 34.1, which provides that where there is a conflict between s. 35 and s. 35.1 of the *MHA* and a provision of *PHIPA*, s. 35 and s. 35.1 prevail over *PHIPA*.
38 R.S.O. 1990, c. O.1, s. 63 [*OHSA*]. This section contains several confidentiality requirements respecting information relating to the *OHSA*, including a requirement that "Except for the purposes of this Act and the regulations or as required by law … no person shall disclose any information obtained in any medical examination, test or x-ray of a worker made or taken under this Act except in a form calculated to prevent the information from being identified with a particular person or case."
39 *PHIPA*, s. 93.
40 *Ibid.*, s. 7(2).
41 *PHIPA* Regulation, above note 11, s. 5.
42 *Ibid.*, s. 5(3). This will generally only be of concern to one relying on a provision of the *Remedies for Organized Crime and Other Unlawful Activities Act, 2001*, S.O. 2001, c. 28, to authorize a disclosure. In such a case a more detailed review of the provisions of that Act will be required.
43 *PHIPA* Regulation, *ibid.*, s. 5(2), referring to s. 85.3(4) of the Code, above note 29. This restriction also applies to such reporting by a facility where a regulated health professional practises.
44 *PHIPA* Regulation, *ibid.*, s. 5(1), referring to *CFSA*, above note 18, ss. 165 and 168(3). The application of these confidentiality requirements is limited. The restrictions

- Confidentiality requirements on employers and employers' representatives for health information about workers relating to workplace safety insurance under the *Workplace Safety and Insurance Act, 1997*.[45]

- A further exception not explicitly referred to in *PHIPA* but that must be kept in mind is that any applicable federal legislation that conflicts with *PHIPA* will prevail over *PHIPA* for constitutional reasons. *PHIPA* is provincial legislation and the provincial Legislature does not have the power to make its legislation prevail over any applicable federal legislation.[46]

- Just as valid federal legislation prevails over *PHIPA*, so does the Canadian Constitution, which includes the *Canadian Charter of Rights and Freedoms*.[47] To the extent that a provision of an Act is found by a court to be inconsistent with the *Charter*, that provision would be "of no force or effect."[48] As discussed above in Chapter 1,[49] the *Charter* has been interpreted by the courts as recognizing and protecting a person's reasonable expectation of privacy in confidential information, particularly sensitive information like most personal health information. The *Charter* applies to government and government-controlled entities, whether or not they are acting under statutory authority,[50] and it also

---

under s. 165 apply only to adoption information held by the Minister of Community and Social Services (now the Ministry of Children and Youth Services), a children's aid society, a licensed "children's residence" as defined in s. 192 of the *CFSA*, or the registry maintained by the Registrar of Adoption Information. The restrictions under s. 168(3) apply only to a person who receives adoption information from the Registrar of Adoption Information.

45 *PHIPA* Regulation, above note 11, s. 5(4), referring to s. 181(3) of the *Workplace Safety and Insurance Act, 1997*, S.O. 1997, c. 16, Sch. A. This provision prohibits employers and employers' representatives from disclosing "health information received from a health care practitioner, hospital, health facility or any other person or organization about a worker who has made a claim for benefits unless specifically permitted by [that act]."

46 P. Hogg, *Constitutional Law of Canada* (Toronto: Carswell) (looseleaf), c. 16.

47 Part I of the *Constitution Act, 1982*, being Schedule B to the *Canada Act, 1982* (U.K.), 1982, c. 11 [*Charter*].

48 The Constitution, including the *Charter*, *ibid.*, "is the supreme law of Canada, and any law [including all federal and provincial statutes and regulations] that is inconsistent with the provisions of the Constitution is, to the extent of the inconsistency, of no force or effect." *Constitution Act, 1982*, s. 52(1). Any tribunal with the power to decide questions of law may apply this provision, though only a "court of competent jurisdiction" can make a formal declaration of invalidity that would create a binding precedent: See Hogg, above note 46, at 37-34 and 37-36 and cases cited in notes 147, 148, and 157 there. Under s. 33 of the *Charter*, however, federal parliament or a provincial legislature could expressly declare that an Act or a provision thereof shall operate "notwithstanding" a provision included in section 2 or sections 7 to 15 of the *Charter*, subject to the further restrictions set out in s. 33.

49 Chapter 1, Section B(3).

50 *Charter*, above note 47, s. 32(1), and see also Hogg, above note 46 at 34-16 to 34-18.

applies to action taken by anyone under statutory authority, for example under the authority of *PHIPA*, since the statutory authority is only effective to the extent that it is consistent with the *Charter*.[51] *PHIPA* should be interpreted and applied in a reasonable manner that is consistent with the *Charter*.[52]

A further way in which *PHIPA* extends uniformity to the rules regarding the collection, use, and disclosure of personal health information is in respect of the rules for consent. The rules for consent set out in *PHIPA* appear to be intended to apply not just within *PHIPA*, but also to any other Act that requires consent for the collection, use, or disclosure of personal health information by a health information custodian.[53]

3) Preservation of Special Sub-sector Rules

a) Provisions in *PHIPA* That Preserve Existing Legal Obligations

As stated above, a second theme of *PHIPA*'s interaction with other legislation is the preservation of many existing rules set out in other legislation covering specific parts of the health sector with respect to collections, uses, and disclosures of personal health information. The most notable examples are set out below.

- A health information custodian is allowed to collect personal health information about a patient indirectly, without the patient's consent, if other law[54]

---

51   *Constitution Act, 1982*, s. 52(1), and see Hogg, *ibid.* at 34-12.1 to 34-13.

52   The relevance of the *Charter* in various *PHIPA* contexts is discussed elsewhere in this Guide. See Chapter 1, Section B(3); Chapter 10, Sections M(1)(d) and P(3)(a). A full analysis of the *Charter* is beyond the scope of this Guide.

53   Section 18(1) states explicitly that the requirements that consent be the voluntary and knowledgeable consent of the individual relating to the information apply equally where any other Act requires the individual's consent to the collection, use, or disclosure of personal health information by a health information custodian. The reference to the consent needing to be the "consent of the individual" indicates that the substitute decision-maker rules of *PHIPA* are applicable. This is also indicated explicitly in s. 23(1). Furthermore, a custodian who is collecting, using, or disclosing personal health information based on a consent mentioned in another Act will generally be relying on the fact that the other Act's authorization brings the collection, use, or disclosure under *PHIPA*, since *PHIPA* also applies and authorizes the collection, use, or disclosure where "permitted or required by law," (as discussed further below). As such the collection, use, or disclosure appears to be under *PHIPA* itself, to which all the consent rules of *PHIPA* will apply.

54   Where *PHIPA* refers to a collection, use, or disclosure being authorized where permitted or required by law, as discussed here for collection and in the following two bullets on use and disclosure, the actual phrase used is where it is "permitted or required by law or by a treaty, agreement or arrangement made under an Act or an Act of Canada": ss. 36(1)(g) & (h), 37(1)(k), and 43(1)(h). The scope of this will be discussed below.

(including legislation and regulations), permits or requires the collection.[55] Furthermore, where another law permits or requires a person to disclose personal health information to a health information custodian, the health information custodian is thereby authorized by *PHIPA* to collect the information from that person with the consent of the patient.[56]

- Where other law permits or requires a health information custodian to use personal health information, that use is authorized under *PHIPA*.[57]
- Where other law permits or requires a health information custodian to disclose personal health information, that disclosure is authorized under *PHIPA*.[58] The Act clarifies that, where a provision in Any act or regulation prohibits disclosures, but the prohibition is subject to an exception, any disclosures falling within the scope of the exception are permitted.[59]
- Disclosures are also permitted in the course of a statutory "inspection, investigation or similar procedure," for the most part under other existing statutes, for the purpose of facilitating the investigation.[60]
- Agents of health information custodians are generally not permitted to collect, use, or disclose personal health information except as authorized by the custodian, but they are permitted to do so in the absence of the custodian's authorization if it is "permitted or required by law."[61]
- Similarly, a person who receives personal health information from a health information custodian (i.e., a "recipient"), generally cannot use or disclose the information for a purpose other than the purpose for which the infor-

---

55 *PHIPA*, s. 36(1)(h). See further Chapter 8, Section C(8).

56 *Ibid.*, s. 36(1)(g). The provisions with respect to collections authorized by other laws are discussed in greater depth in Chapter 8, Section C(7).

57 *Ibid.*, s. 37(1)(k). The provisions with respect to uses authorized by other laws are discussed in greater depth in Chapter 9, Section C(12).

58 *Ibid.*, s. 43(1)(h). The provisions with respect to disclosures authorized by other laws are discussed in greater depth in Chapter 10, Section P.

59 *Ibid.*, s. 43(2). For example, the exceptions set out in the *HPPA*, above note 32, s. 39(2), to the general non-disclosure requirement in s. 39(1) of that Act would be treated as permissions to disclosure, though literally they are only exceptions to a duty of confidentiality that otherwise does not indicate clearly a permission to disclose.

60 *PHIPA*, s. 43(1)(g). This section also permits disclosures in the course of an "inspection, investigation or similar procedure" under a warrant for the purpose of complying with the warrant. It should be noted that, to the extent the language of this provision allowing a disclosure "for the purpose of facilitating the investigation" may go beyond what is actually required by law, such disclosure will be discretionary. See Chapter 10, section D(3) for more detail.

61 *Ibid.*, s. 17(2).

mation was disclosed to the person in the first place (except where prohibited by law[62]), but may do so if it is permitted or required by law.[63]

- A health information custodian is not permitted to provide a patient with access to his or her record of personal health information to the extent that "another Act, an Act of Canada or a court order" prohibits the disclosure of the information to the patient in the circumstances.[64]

b) What Is Included as Permitted or Required "By Law"?

Most of the provisions referred to above include the phrase "permitted or required by law." *PHIPA* does not explicitly set out the scope of what is intended by the words "by law," however.[65] At a minimum this phrase likely includes other Ontario statutes and regulations. For reasons discussed below, the phrase "by law" also appears to include at least federal legislation and regulations, and probably court orders.

The Supreme Court of Canada has recognized that

> [t]he term "by law" might, in some circumstances, be construed as a broad incorporation of rules established by statute or by precedent in the common law. The expression "by law" might, in these circumstances, [which involved the interpretation of the phrase "unless some penalty ... is expressly provided by law" in section 116 of the *Criminal Code*] be read as a reference to the criminal law only; and finally might, if limited to statute law, refer to either federal statutes, provincial statutes, or both.[66]

While the result in that case, interpreting "by law" narrowly to mean only statute law, is not relevant because it depended on the word "expressly," which appears in the section of the *Criminal Code* that was the focus of that case, the excerpt from the judgment quoted above does assist in showing that, in some circumstances, the phrase "by law" may encompass both provincial and federal statutes, and also rules established by precedent in the common law.

It seems fairly clear that *PHIPA* intends that "by law" includes at least federal statutes and regulations in addition to provincial ones. This is evident

---

62   *PHIPA* Regulation, above note 11, s. 21(3).

63   *PHIPA*, s. 49(1). If the information was received before *PHIPA* came into force, however, the custodian may use or disclose the information for the purpose for which it was disclosed to the person, except where doing so is otherwise prohibited by law: *PHIPA* Regulation, *ibid.*, s. 20. For more detail see Chapter 12.

64   *PHIPA*, s. 52(1)(b).

65   There appears to be a power under s. 73(1)(e) to define this expression further by regulation, but no such regulation has been made at the time of writing.

66   *R. v. Clement*, [1981] 2 S.C.R. 468 at 476.

from a supplementary provision interpreting the power to disclose "where permitted or required by law," as follows:

> 43. (1) A health information custodian may disclose personal health information about an individual,
>
> ...
>
> (h) subject to the requirements and restrictions, if any, that are prescribed, if *permitted or required by law* or by a treaty, agreement or arrangement made under an Act or an Act of Canada.
>
> (2) For the purposes of clause (1) (h) and subject to the regulations made under this Act, *if an Act, an Act of Canada or a regulation made under any of those Acts specifically provides* that information is exempt, under stated circumstances, from a confidentiality or secrecy requirement, *that provision shall be deemed to permit the disclosure* of the information in the stated circumstances. [Emphasis added.]

This language fairly clearly implies that *PHIPA* intends that the term "law" includes not just Acts of Ontario, but also Acts of Canada (i.e., federal legislation) and regulations[67] made under either federal or provincial statutes.[68]

Whether the term "law" is broad enough to include laws in other jurisdictions, outside Ontario, therefore appears doubtful, though perhaps not beyond argument. Generally speaking, though, laws of jurisdictions outside Ontario do not *apply* to the operations of persons in Ontario, and it is clear that for a person to be "permitted or required by law" to do some act, the law in question would at least have to apply to the person in the circumstances.

It is also uncertain whether the term "law" is intended to include subordinate legislation, such as municipal bylaws and the bylaws of the *RHPA* Colleges, which can perhaps be characterized as delegated legislative power under

---

67 As for regulations, the Ontario *Interpretation Act*, R.S.O. 1990, c. I.11, s. 29(1) provides that, in every Act, unless the context requires otherwise, "Act" includes enactment. The term "enactment" is not defined. However, the Court of Appeal of Ontario, noting that the term "Act" as defined in the *Interpretation Act* includes "enactment," has found that "enactment" has been consistently interpreted to include an Act or regulation or any portion of an Act or regulation: *Women's Christian Association v. London & District Service Workers, Local 220* (1996), 90 O.A.C. 59 (C.A.) at para. 51.

68 In this context it would not be reasonable to interpret the more specific language set out in *PHIPA*, s. 43(2) as applying only to the "treaty, agreement or arrangement" part of (1)(h), since the language of (2) does not limit itself in that way, and the conclusion in (2) that "the provision shall be deemed to permit the disclosure" is broad.

the *Municipal Act, 2001*[69] or under the *Regulated Health Professions Act, 1991*,[70] respectively. On the one hand, one could argue that since this type of subordinate legislation is not specifically referred to in section 43(2), it is not intended to be included in the phrase "by law." On the other hand, one could argue that since regulations, which are a form of subordinate legislation, are implied by section 43(2) to be included as "law," other forms of subordinate legislation should equally be considered to be included.[71]

There is Canadian case law suggesting that the expression "by law" is broad enough to include a decision of a tribunal or person who is authorized to make an order or determination, such that the order or determination would be considered within the scope of the term "law" referred to in the phrase "permitted or required by law."[72] If so, then a custodian would be able to rely on a tribunal order as authority to disclose personal health information, for example.[73]

The phrasing of an exception to the access rights may also be helpful in understanding what is included in "law":

> 52. (1) Subject to this Part, an individual has a right of access to a record of personal health information about the individual that is in the custody or under the control of a health information custodian unless,
>
> (a) the record or the information in the record is subject to a legal privilege that restricts disclosure of the record or the information, as the case may be, to the individual;

---

69 S.O. 2001, c. 25, ss. 2 and 5.

70 Above note 29.

71 However, corporate bylaws and the like, which are not subordinate legislation (since although they are made under delegated legislative authority, are more in the nature of private contractual instruments) would likely not be considered "law."

72 *British Pacific Properties Ltd. v. British Columbia (Minister of Highways & Public Works)* (1980), 112 D.L.R. (3d) 1 (S.C.C.); and *Teledyne Industries Inc. v. Lido Industrial Products Ltd.* (1982), 68 C.P.R. (2d) 204 (F.C.T.D.) (decision under federal *Interest Act*, R.S.C. 1985, c.I-15 provision providing that where no interest rate is fixed under an agreement or "by law" the interest rate should be deemed to be 5 percent).

73 If the tribunal decision is simply making an order to fulfil a statutory requirement under Ontario or federal law, then the statutory requirement would be enough alone to authorize the disclosure under *PHIPA*. But in some cases a tribunal may have the power to make an order that goes beyond what is actually required in any case by the statute; that is the type of situation discussed in this paragraph.

The fact that such an order or determination was not referred to in s. 43(2) does not seem to prevent such an order or determination from being considered within the scope of what is "law," since s. 43(2) is interpreting a kind of *rule*, not a kind of order or determination, and hence one would not expect s. 43(2) to refer to an order or determination made under a law even if it was included in what is considered "law."

(b)   *another Act, an Act of Canada or a court order* prohibits disclosure to the individual of the record or the information in the record in the circumstances. [Emphasis added.]

It may be argued that the phrase "another Act, an Act of Canada or a court order" is intended to state the idea referred to by the term "law" in other contexts in a more precise way in the context of the access provisions.[74] If so, the phrase "by law" may be understood to include a court order, and perhaps by extension, a ruling of any other body making an order or determination under a statute. It would make sense that, where a statute requires compliance with an order or determination made by a person authorized by the statute to make it, the order or determination would then be considered akin to a requirement of the statute.

Where *PHIPA* refers to a collection, use, or disclosure being authorized where permitted or required by law, the actual phrase used is where it is "permitted or required by law or *by a treaty, agreement or arrangement made under an Act or an Act of Canada.*"[75] This phrase appears to be adapted from the language of the *FIPPA*, which provides that "[a]n institution shall not disclose personal information in its custody or under its control except, ... for the purpose of complying with an Act of the Legislature or an Act of Parliament, or a treaty, agreement, or arrangement thereunder."[76] An example of an agreement made under a statute is a service agreement made under the *Nursing Home Act*[77] between the operator of a nursing home and the Ministry of Health and Long-Term Care, which regulates and provides funding to long-term care facilities such as nursing homes. It would appear that if such an agreement permits or requires a type of collection, use, or disclosure, it would be authorized under these provisions in *PHIPA*.

c)   *PHIPA* Not to Be "Construed to Interfere" with Certain Matters

In a similar vein, the Act sets out a number of matters with which "nothing in this Act shall be construed to interfere."[78] In other words, the matter described appears to be intended to function independently of *PHIPA* without *PHIPA*

---

74   This argument is reinforced by the words in *PHIPA*, s. 9(2)(f), which provides that "Nothing in this Act shall be construed to interfere with ... (f) *any provision of any Act of Ontario or Canada or any court order*, if the provision or order, as the case may be, prohibits a person from making information public or from publishing information [emphasis added].

75   *PHIPA*, ss. 36(1)(g) & (h), 37(1)(k), and 43(1)(h) [emphasis added].

76   *FIPPA*, above note 2, s. 42(e); *MFIPPA*, above note 2, s. 32(e).

77   *NHA*, above note 6, s. 4(2).

78   *PHIPA*, s. 9(2).

imposing any direct restrictions or permissions on the matter in question. The Acts refers to the following matters in this way:

- *"anything in connection with a subrogated claim or a potential subrogated claim"*:[79] A subrogated claim is one in which one party has a right to make a claim in the name of the other; for example, where an insurer that has paid a loss under an insurance policy is entitled to advance a claim, in place of the insured against a third party who caused the loss to the insured.[80] The right to make a subrogated claim may arise under contract, express or implied,[81] or may also be provided by statute; for example, the right of the General Manager of the Ontario Health Insurance Plan (OHIP) under the *Health Insurance Act* to claim against anyone who has wrongly or negligently injured a person for the cost of OHIP insured services provided to the person as a result.[82]
- *"any legal privilege, including solicitor-client privilege"*:[83] A legal privilege is a judicially recognized exception to the general rule that all relevant information should be able to be required to be produced in a legal proceeding.[84] There are several types of legal privilege.[85] This provision in *PHIPA* would appear to

---

79   *PHIPA*, s. 9(2)(a).
80   B.A. Garner, ed., *Black's Law Dictionary*, 8th ed. (St. Paul, Minn.: Thomson West, 2004) at 1467.
81   *Ibid.* at 1468.
82   *Health Insurance Act*, R.S.O. 1990, c. H.6, ss. 30 & 31. A similar statutory right of subrogation can be found in the *LTCA*, above note 6, s. 59.
83   *PHIPA*, s. 9(2)(b).
84   D.A. Dukelow, ed., *Dictionary of Canadian Law*, 3d ed. (Toronto: Thomson Carswell, 2004) at 994.
85   Legal assistance will often be required in dealing with the complexities that can be involved with issues of legal privilege. The following information provides only a cursory overview. Under solicitor/client privilege, a person who receives legal advice from a lawyer is entitled to refuse to disclose the information about the advice or communications that took place in obtaining the advice. Another type of privilege is litigation privilege, under which a person who prepares a document in anticipation of litigation may refuse to disclose it. Related to this is settlement privilege, which allows a party to refuse to disclose communications, (which may contain the words "without prejudice") made in an attempt to settle a legal dispute or proceeding. A type of "case-by-case" privilege has also been recognized by the courts that allows information to be deemed privileged by a court in certain circumstances to protect various types of confidential communications. This form of "common law privilege," also referred to as the "Wigmore test," was adopted by the Supreme Court of Canada in *Slavutych v. Baker*, [1976] 1 S.C.R. 254. The four required criteria for such privilege to apply are essentially that (1) the communications in question originated with an expectation of confidentiality; (2) the confidentiality was essential to the task at hand; (3) the task requiring the confidential communication was an essential task from the point of view of the public interest; and (4) the damage in disclosing such information would be greater than the damage in maintaining the infor-

mean, for instance, that any discretionary or required disclosures under *PHIPA* may not be made if the information is subject to an existing legal privilege, unless of course the privilege is waived.[86] The Act specifically provides that a patient does not have a right of access to privileged information.[87]

- *"the law of evidence or information otherwise available by law to a party or a witness in a proceeding"*:[88] This appears to clarify that the issue of what disclosures can or must be made under *PHIPA*, whether with or without consent, is entirely separate from the law of what may be admissible in evidence in a proceeding. The second part of the clause, "information otherwise available by law to a party or a witness in a proceeding," may be understood to mean that *PHIPA* does not act as a restriction on disclosures for the purpose of proceedings that are authorized by some other law, particularly laws governing proceedings.[89] *PHIPA* contains provisions that permit disclosures of personal health information for a proceeding and in connection with "a contemplated proceeding" in a number of types of instances, which may also apply.[90]

- *"the power of a court or a tribunal to compel a witness to testify or to compel the production of a document"*:[91] This appears to mean that a witness before a tribunal or court, who the tribunal or court has the power apart from *PHIPA* to compel to testify or produce a record of personal health information, cannot excuse him- or herself by relying on any restrictions set out in *PHIPA*.[92]

---

mation as privileged. The problem with this type of privilege is that it must be validated by a court in the circumstances of the case at hand. The privilege is presumed not to apply until the four-criteria analysis referred to above is conducted and shows that the privilege is required in the circumstances: *R. v. Gruenke*, [1991] 3 S.C.R. 263.

86 This restriction may be relevant, for example with respect to the kinds of disclosures that may be permitted in and for proceedings. See Chapter 10, Section M for more discussion.

87 *PHIPA*, s. 52(1)(a).

88 *Ibid.*, s. 9(2)(c). This provision is similar to *FIPPA*, above note 2, s. 64(1), and *MFIPPA*, above note 2, s. 51(1).

89 Understood in this way, the latter part of this clause may simply be a context-specific statement of the general principle in s. 43(1)(h) that disclosures under other laws continue to be permitted under *PHIPA*. It may be noted that s. 9(2)(c) and s. 9(2) in general are not subject to any prescribed requirements and restrictions that may apply to 43(1)(h).

90 *PHIPA*, s. 41. See Chapter 10, Section M for a discussion of the provision for disclosure in proceedings.

91 *PHIPA*, s. 9(2)(d). This is similar to *FIPPA*, above note 2, s. 64(2), and *MFIPPA*, above note 2, s. 51(2).

92 Given the provisions in *PHIPA* that allow collections, uses, and disclosures of personal health information where permitted or required by law, this provision may be superfluous; however s. 9(2)(d) makes it clear that such required disclosures in proceedings cannot be narrowed by way of regulations in *PHIPA* the way other required collections, uses, and disclosures may be. The permitted disclosures to these bodies under s. 43 of *PHIPA* appear to overlap with this general provision at least to some extent.

- *"the regulatory activities of a College under the* Regulated Heath Professions Act, 1991, *the College under the* Social Work and Social Service Work Act, 1998 *or the Board under the* Drugless Practitioners Act":[93] These bodies are not actually health information custodians under the Act so they generally would not be directly affected by *PHIPA*;[94] therefore the meaning of the provision appears to be that anyone who is subject to the regulatory activities of one of these bodies cannot, on the basis of *PHIPA*, refuse to comply with any lawful requirements that are part of those regulatory activities.[95]

- *"any provision of any Act of Ontario or Canada or any court order, if the provision or order, as the case may be, prohibits a person from making information public or from publishing information":*[96] This may mean that, to the extent that any provision of *PHIPA* permits information to be made public or to be published, which might sometimes be possible, for instance with the provision allowing disclosures as necessary to avoid serious bodily harm,[97] such an action will nevertheless not be permitted if another law prohibits the information from being published or made public.

C. INTERACTION WITH ONTARIO PUBLIC SECTOR PRIVACY LEGISLATION

Understanding the relationship and interaction between *PHIPA* and Ontario's public sector privacy legislation, the *Freedom of Information and Protection of Privacy Act* (*FIPPA*) and the *Municipal Freedom of Information and Protection of Privacy Act* (*MFIPPA*) is important not just for the organizations directly affected (i.e., those organizations that are subject to both regimes) but also for persons who interact with these organizations or provide services to them.

---

93   *PHIPA*, s. 9(2)(e).
94   Like other non-health information custodians, such bodies are, however, subject to the recipient rules under s. 49 and the rules about the collection, use, and disclosure of the health number under s. 34.
95   Disclosures to these bodies by health information custodians "for the administration and enforcement" of any of those Acts that is applicable, is permitted under ss. 43(1)(b), (c), & (d).
96   *PHIPA*, s. 9(2)(f).
97   *Ibid.*, s. 40(1).

1) Overlaps between *FIPPA* or *MFIPPA* and *PHIPA*

a) Impact on Custodians

A relatively small, but significant, group of health information custodians listed in *PHIPA* are also "institutions" as defined in and subject to *FIPPA* or *MFIPPA*.[98]

The most significant of these is the Ministry of Health and Long-Term Care, which as well as being a health information custodian[99] is also an institution under *FIPPA*.[100] The provincial psychiatric hospitals operated by the Ministry are listed in *PHIPA* as health information custodians in their own right, separate from the Ministry custodian,[101] but they are part of the Ministry "institution" from the point of view of *FIPPA*.[102]

Ontario ministries other than the Ministry of Health and Long-Term Care, all of which are institutions under *FIPPA*,[103] may include health information custodians, particularly under that part of the definition of "health information custodian" that includes "a person who operates … a centre, program or service for community health or mental health whose primary purpose is the provision of health care."[104]

Several health information custodians are either institutions under *MFIPPA* or part of such an institution, including the following:

- municipal homes for aged under the *Homes for the Aged and Rest Homes Act;*[105]

---

98 An "institution" under *FIPPA* means every ministry of the Ontario government and every other agency, board, commission, corporation, or other body designated as such in *General*, R.R.O. 1990, Reg. 460, made under *FIPPA*. Under *MFIPPA*, an institution includes a municipality, school board, municipal service board, transit commission, public library board, board of health, police services board, conservation authority, district social services administration board, local services board, planning board, local roads board, and any agency, board, commission, corporation, or other body designated as an institution in *Institutions*, O. Reg. 372/91, made under *MFIPPA*.

99 *PHIPA*, s. 3(1)(7).

100 *FIPPA*, above note 2, s. 2(1), clause (a) of definition of "institution."

101 *PHIPA*, s. 3(1)[4][i] includes as a custodian a person who operates "an institution within the meaning of the *Mental Hospitals Act.*" Given the qualification in the introductory language to 3(1)[4], which says that the health information custodian is the person who operates the facility, etc., it would appear that the health information custodian is actually the Ministry in respect of the particular mental hospital in question, as distinct from the Ministry in respect of any of its other general activities.

102 These provincial psychiatric hospitals are operated by the Health Ministry but are not listed as separate "institutions" in *General*, R.R.O. 1990, Reg. 460, made under *FIPPA*.

103 *FIPPA*, s. 2(1), clause (a) of definition of "institution."

104 *PHIPA*, s. 3(1)[4][vii]. In such a case, the custodian would be the ministry in respect of that centre, program, or service.

105 Such a home is a health information custodians in its own right under s. 3(1)[4][ii] of *PHIPA*, and considered part of the municipality, the municipality being the "institu-

- a municipally operated ambulance service;[106] and
- a medical officer of health.[107]

For ease of reference, these health information custodians that are subject to both *PHIPA* and *FIPPA* or *MFIPPA*, because they are an "institution" under *FIPPA* or *MFIPPA* or part of such an institution, are referred to in the discussion that follows as "*FIPPA/MFIPPA* custodians."

b)   Which Rules Apply to *FIPPA/MFIPPA* Custodians?

i)   General Rule

As a general rule, *FIPPA/MFIPPA* custodians are covered by *PHIPA* rather than *FIPPA* or *MFIPPA* for any personal health information in their custody or control.[108] Remember, however, that the definition of personal health information includes *all* identifying information[109] within a record containing any health-related identifying information.[110] As such, any records containing health-related identifying information in the custody or control of the

---

tion" under *MFIPPA*, above note 2, s. 2(1), clause (a) of definition of "institution." The custodian is the "person who operates" the home, which is the municipality, in respect of that home.

106 Similarly, an ambulance service operated by a municipality is a health information custodian in its own right under s. 3(1)[4][v] of *PHIPA*, and considered part of the municipality, the municipality being the "institution" under *MFIPPA*. The custodian is the "person who operates" the ambulance service, which in such a case is the municipality in respect of that ambulance service.

107 Under the *HPPA*, above note 32, a medical officer of health is defined as "a medical officer of health of a board of health." A board of health is an "institution" under *MFIPPA*, s. 2(1), clause (b) of definition of "institution." Under *PHIPA*, s. 3(1)[6], "a medical officer of health of a board of health within the meaning of the *Health Protection and Promotion Act*" is a health information custodian. Under the *PHIPA* Regulation, above note 11, s. 3(2),

> Despite paragraph 6 of subsection 3(1) of the Act, the medical officer of health of a board of health within the meaning of the *Health Protection and Promotion Act* is prescribed as a single health information custodian with respect to the performance of his or her duties under that or any other Act.

A medical officer of health is a health information custodian under *PHIPA* and would apparently be considered as part of the *MFIPPA* institution which is the municipality.

108 *PHIPA*, s. 8(1).

109 *Ibid.*, s. 4(2).

110 As described in s. 4(1)(a) through (g). This is what is referred to as the "mixed record rule," set out in s. 4(3) of *PHIPA* and clarified by s. 4 of the *PHIPA* Regulation, above note 11. The mixed record rule helps simplify things for *FIPPA/MFIPPA* institutions, so they need only comply with one Act for any given record. Chapter 2, section C(1)(g) explains the mixed record rule.

FIPPA/MFIPPA custodian will be covered by *PHIPA*. Often this may include virtually all the records held by the organization, except for records that contain no personal health information, such as employee and supplier records[111] and some financial records.[112]

Records in the custody or control of a *FIPPA/MFIPPA* custodian that do not contain any personal health information will continue to be covered by *FIPPA* or *MFIPPA*, as the case may be.[113]

ii)   Exceptions to the General Rule

There are a number of exceptions to the general rule that *PHIPA*, rather than *FIPPA/MFIPPA*, governs personal health information in the custody or control of such organizations.[114] The provisions of *FIPPA* or *MFIPPA*, as the case may be, set out in Table A, below, continue to apply to *FIPPA/MFIPPA* custodians.

Table A: Provisions from FIPPA *or* MFIPPA *Applicable to Health Information Custodians That Are Institutions or Part of Institutions under Those Acts*

PHIPA Section	FIPPA Section	MFIPPA Section	Nature of Provision
8(2)	11	5	Mandatory disclosure in the public interest, subject to notice requirement where the "head" of the institution believes the "record reveals a grave environmental, health or safety hazard to the public."
	12	N/A	Mandatory non-disclosure of cabinet-related material.
	15	9	Mandatory non-disclosure of information where the disclosure may prejudice intergovernmental relations, or reveal confidential information received from another government or international organization of states.
	16	N/A	Mandatory non-disclosure of information where the disclosure may prejudice the defence of Canada or an ally or that may interfere with the detection, prevention, or suppression of espionage, sabotage, or terrorism.

---

111   *PHIPA*, s. 4(4) deems that employee and agent records are not "personal health information" even if they contain health-related identifying information.

112   Many financial records do not contain any heath-related identifying information about a patient. Financial records containing any personal health information (for example, patient trust accounts in long-term care facilities) would be covered by *PHIPA*.

113   *FIPPA/MFIPPA* are only excluded by *PHIPA*, s. 8(1) with respect to personal health information.

114   In some cases the *FIPPA/MFIPPA* provisions are allowed to apply directly, for example, as set out in s. 8(2) of *PHIPA*, while in other cases *FIPPA* or *MFIPPA* provisions are adopted into *PHIPA* by reference, for example, as in s. 52(1)(f) of *PHIPA's* access provisions. The discussion here deals with both kinds of provisions.

PHIPA Section	FIPPA Section	MFIPPA Section	Nature of Provision
8(2)	17	10	Mandatory non-disclosure of third-party confidential information relating to scientific, technical, commercial, financial, tax, or labour relations information (subject to certain conditions).
	33	N/A	Mandatory routine disclosures of manuals, directives, and guidelines of the institution respecting allocation of public rights, privileges, benefits, or obligations, or decisions that affect the public.
	35(2)	N/A	That the material under the above provision (s. 33 of *FIPPA*) shall be made available in a reading room in each institution.
	36	N/A	Administrative provision requiring the institution to provide certain administrative information to the Chair-person of Management Board (i.e., the Minister in charge of the government's internal operations) to enable the Chairperson to prepare certain materials required under other sections of *FIPPA*.
	44	34	Administrative provision requiring that all personal information held by the institution that is organized according to the identity of individuals be included in a "personal information bank," which is included in an annual public list of such banks.
8(3)	32(b)	25(1)(b)[115]	Administrative provision indicating that records of personal health information held by an institution that is a health information custodian must be included in the list of types of records prepared by or in the custody or control of the institution, published annually by the Chairperson of Management Board.
8(4)	10	4	The "general access" provisions in *FIPPA/MFIPPA* continue to apply to information that is not health-related identifying information. Thus, even though a record

---

115 Section 25 of *MFIPPA* as a whole is listed in s. 8(2) of *PHIPA* as a provision with which institutions that are custodians must still comply. Though the corresponding whole section from *FIPPA* is not listed in s. 8(2) of *PHIPA*, the effect and intention appears to be the same; that is, *PHIPA*-related records and duties would be included in the material required to be made publicly available under s. 25, as in effect provided by s. 8(3) of *PHIPA*. As a related administrative matter, s. 24 of *MFIPPA*, also listed in s. 8(2) of *PHIPA*, imposes administrative duties on the "Minister," who in this context is the Chair of Management Board of Cabinet, and is not a health information custodian. It seems that s. 24 is only applicable to custodians in that their duties as custodians of records of personal health information are within the scope of the Chair of Management Board's obligation to compile and publish information about the institution.

PHIPA Section	FIPPA Section	MFIPPA Section	Nature of Provision
			may be subject to *PHIPA*, anyone may still request access under *FIPPA/MFIPPA* to the information in the record that is *not* health-related identifying information.
8(5)	not specified	not specified	This transition provision indicates that *FIPPA/MFIPPA* continue to apply to any collection, use, or disclosure of personal health information, or request for access for personal health information, that was made before 1 November 2004.
43(1)(f)	42(c), (g), or (n)	32(c), (g), or (l)	In addition to the types of disclosures allowed for health information custodians under *PHIPA*, this provision allows health information custodians that are subject to *FIPPA/MFIPPA* to continue to be permitted to disclose personal health information, under certain provisions in those Acts, specifically: • for the purpose for which the custodian obtained or compiled the information, or "for a consistent purpose" [*FIPPA*, s. 42(c); *MFIPPA*, s. 32(c)]; • to an institution or law enforcement agency in Canada to aid in a law enforcement investigation [*FIPPA*, s. 42(g); *MFIPPA*, s. 32(g)]; and • to the government of Canada in order to facilitate the auditing of shared cost programs [*FIPPA*, s. 42(n); *MFIPPA*, s. 32(l)]. (In the case of the custodian that is subject to *MFIPPA*, a disclosure for this purpose can also be made to the government of Ontario under this provision of *MFIPPA*.)

52(1)(f)	49(a), (c), or (e)	38(a) or (c)	In addition to the other grounds on which a health information custodian is allowed to refuse to grant a patient access to his or her record of personal health information under *PHIPA*, custodians that are subject to *FIPPA/MFIPPA* may continue to refuse disclosures based on
			• the grounds set out in *FIPPA*, s. 49(a) or *MFIPPA*, s. 38(a), which include where the information is:
			  • cabinet information [*FIPPA*, s. 12];
			  • draft municipal bylaws, or information from deliberations in closed meeting [*MFIPPA*, s. 6];
			  • advice to government [*FIPPA*, s. 13; *MFIPPA*, s. 7];
			  • such that its disclosure would be prejudicial to law enforcement [*FIPPA*, s. 14 & 14.1; *MFIPPA*, s. 8];
			  • such that its disclosure would be prejudicial to intergovernmental relations [*FIPPA*, s. 15; *MFIPPA*, s. 9][116]

---

116 *MFIPPA*, s. 9 somewhat resembles *FIPPA*, ss. 15 & 16 as adapted to a more localized context. See the actual provisions for detail.

PHIPA Section Reference	FIPPA Section Reference	MFIPPA Section Reference	Nature of Provision
			• such that its disclosure would be prejudicial to the defence of Canada or an ally [*FIPPA*, s. 16; *MFIPPA*, s. 9];[117] • third-party information containing a trade secret or confidential scientific, technical, commercial, financial, taxation, or labour relations information [*FIPPA*, s. 17; *MFIPPA*, s. 10]; • information relating to the financial and economic interests of the institution or the government, etc. [*FIPPA*, s. 18; *MFIPPA*, s. 11]; • subject to solicitor/client privilege, or was prepared by counsel to the institution or government [*FIPPA*, s. 19; *MFIPPA*, s. 12]; • such that disclosing it would seriously threaten the safety or health of an individual [*FIPPA*, s. 20; *MFIPPA*, s. 13]; or • published or soon to be published [*FIPPA*, s. 22; *MFIPPA*, s. 15]. • the grounds set out in *FIPPA*, s. 49(c) or *MFIPPA* s. 38(c), which allow a refusal of access to evaluative or opinion material provided in confidence (e.g., a confidential reference letter) for job competitions or awarding government contracts or benefits where the disclosure would reveal the confidential source; and • the grounds set out in *FIPPA*, s. 49(e); namely, that the information is a "correctional record" where the disclosure would likely reveal information supplied in confidence (only applies to *FIPPA* custodian).
8(2),[118] 81, and 91	34	26	This provision requires the institution to report on matters relevant to its duties under *PHIPA*; for example, number of access requests received and dealt with under *PHIPA*.

In addition to the provisions noted in Table A above, under which certain sections or parts of *FIPPA* and *MFIPPA* continue to apply to personal health information in the hands of a *FIPPA/MFIPPA* custodian, there are a few other sections in *PHIPA* that set out special provisions for *FIPPA/MFIPPA* custodians. These special provisions are listed and described below.

---

117 *Ibid.*
118 Section 8(2) refers to s. 26 of *MFIPPA* but not s. 34 of *FIPPA*, but the intention that custodians that are *FIPPA* institutions should make an annual report that includes separate mention of their *PHIPA* duties is clearly evident from the amendment to s. 34(2) of *FIPPA* contained in s. 81 of *PHIPA*.

First, a *FIPPA/MFIPPA* custodian is provided with certain additional powers to collect personal health information from a source other than the patient.[119] These powers are similar in some respects to powers provided under *FIPPA* and *MFIPPA*. Specifically this type of custodian has the power to collect personal health information indirectly without consent where the purpose of the collection relates to

- investigating a breach of a law of Ontario or Canada or of an agreement,[120]
- the conduct of a proceeding or a possible proceeding,[121] or
- the statutory function of the custodian.[122]

Second, where research is to be conducted involving the use or disclosure by a *FIPPA/MFIPPA* custodian of both personal health information and other identifying information that is not personal health information, *PHIPA* allows a simplified approach. In such case the *PHIPA* rules relating to research apply to *all* the information, and the research rules under *FIPPA* or *MFIPPA* do not apply to *any* of the information, even to the information that is not personal health information.[123]

Furthermore, where a research agreement under either *FIPPA* or *MFIPPA* was in place prior to 1 November 2004, disclosures by the relevant *FIPPA/MFIPPA* custodian within the scope of the agreement may continue to be made after 1 November 2004, until the agreement expires.[124]

2) *PHIPA* Provisions Relevant to *FIPPA/MFIPPA* Institutions That Are *Not* Health Information Custodians

In addition to the special provisions of *PHIPA* relevant to *FIPPA/MFIPPA* custodians set out above, *PHIPA* also contains a small number of provisions that apply to *FIPPA/MFIPPA* institutions that are *not* custodians. These provisions are described below.

---

119 *PHIPA*, s. 36(1)(c).

120 *Ibid.*, s. 36(1)(c)(i). This indirect collection power is similar to that provided in *FIPPA*, s. 39(1)(g) and *MFIPPA*, s. 29(1)(g) relating to law enforcement.

121 *PHIPA*, s. 36(1)(c)(ii). This indirect collection power is similar to that provided in *FIPPA*, s. 39(1)(f) and *MFIPPA*, s. 29(1)(f).

122 *PHIPA*, s. 36(1)(c)(iii). This power is similar to that provided in *FIPPA*, s. 38(2) or *MFIPPA*, s. 28(2) based on the language "necessary to the proper administration of a lawfully authorized activity." What "statutory function" means in this context is dealt with in Chapter 8.

123 *PHIPA*, s. 37(4) regarding uses for research and s. 44(7) regarding disclosures for research. See also Chapter 11, Section B(2)(e).

a)   Recipient Rules

The rules in *PHIPA* governing subsequent uses and disclosures of information received by a non-health information custodian from a custodian do not apply to *FIPPA/MFIPPA* institutions.[125] The regulation clarifies that the recipient rules also do not apply to a person employed by or acting on behalf of such an institution.[126] Even the part of the recipient rules that can apply to custodians in respect of employee- or agent-related personal health information does not apply to *FIPPA/MFIPPA* institutions.[127]

However, *FIPPA/MFIPPA* institutions that are not health information custodians are specifically provided with the authority to collect personal health information from a health information custodian, but only where the custodian has authority to disclose it to the institution under *PHIPA*.[128] This provision appears to be intended to preserve a power that before *PHIPA's* coming into force would have been covered by *FIPPA* or *MFIPPA*. The power allowed an institution under one of those acts to collect personal information, including personal health information, from another such institution that was permitted by *FIPPA* or *MFIPPA* to disclose the information to the collecting institution.[129]

b)   Access

A *FIPPA* or *MFIPPA* institution that is not a health information custodian will continue to process access requests under *FIPPA* or *MFIPPA*, as the case may be, for personal health information in the custody or control of a health information custodian who is employed by or in the service of an institution under *FIPPA/MFIPPA*, where the record is in the custody or control of the custodian as part of the custodian's duties with the institution.[130] This will arise where a health care practitioner is employed by or in the service of such an institution, and the practitioner provides health care in that role, since the practitioner, in such circumstances, is considered to be a distinct health information

---

124   *PHIPA*, s. 44(8). For more detail see Chapter 11, Section B(9)(b).

125   *PHIPA*, s. 49(5). Exceptions can be made by regulation, but no such regulations have been made at the time of writing. See Chapter 12 for information about the restrictions imposed on recipients and the relevant exceptions.

126   *PHIPA* Regulation, above note 11, s. 23(1).

127   *Ibid.*, s. 23(2).

128   *Ibid.*, s. 19.

129   *FIPPA*, s. 39(1)(b); *MFIPPA*, s. 29(1)(b). With the advent of *PHIPA*, a disclosure of personal health information from a *FIPPA/MFIPPA* custodian would no longer be authorized by *FIPPA* or *MFIPPA*, but rather by *PHIPA*.

130   *PHIPA*, s. 51(3).

custodian under *PHIPA*.[131] An example of this relationship would be a speech language pathologist (a type of health care custodian) who is employed by a school board (an institution under *MFIPPA*). *PHIPA* specially provides that in such a case the custodian is not required to provide patients with access to their records of personal health information in cases where the patient is entitled to request access through the institution.[132]

D. INTERACTION OF *PHIPA* WITH FEDERAL PRIVACY LEGISLATION (*PIPEDA*)

1) Basic Principles of the Application of *PIPEDA*

As explained in Chapter 1, the *Personal Information Protection and Electronic Documents Act*[133] is the federal government's private sector privacy legislation.[134] *PIPEDA* has applied since 1 January 2001 to personal information[135] held by an organization that is a "federal work, undertaking or business," such as a bank or airline, about its employees.[136] "Organization" is broadly defined to include any "person" and thus could include even a sole practitioner.[137] *PIPEDA* does not apply to federal[138] or provincial[139] governmental institutions, among others.[140] Of importance to Ontario's health sector, *PIPEDA* has applied since 1 Jan-

---

131 Such a person is not within the scope of the exclusion in *PHIPA*, s. 3(3)[2], since the person's duties include providing health care.

132 *PHIPA*, s. 51(3). This is discussed in more detail in Chapter 13, Section B(3).

133 S.C. 2000, c. 5 [*PIPEDA*].

134 In this context, only the portions of that Act relating to privacy are relevant, and not the parts relating to electronic documents, so when we refer to *PIPEDA* here, it is the privacy provisions that are being referred to. These provisions are set out in Part I and Sch. 1 of *PIPEDA*.

135 Until 1 January 2002, however, *PIPEDA* did not apply to "personal health information" as defined in s. 2 of that Act. See s. 30(1.1) and (2.1).

136 *PIPEDA*, above note 133, s. 4(1)(b).

137 *Ibid.*, s. 2: " 'organization' includes an association, a partnership, a person and a trade union."

138 *Ibid.*, s. 4(2)(a).

139 The exclusion of the provincial government from the application of *PIPEDA* is based on the principle, set out in the federal *Interpretation Act*, R.S. 1985, c. I-21, s. 17 that the Crown is not bound by legislation unless the legislation provides otherwise.

140 *PIPEDA* also does not apply to individuals collecting, using, or disclosing personal information for personal or domestic purposes or to organizations collecting, using, or disclosing personal information for journalistic, artistic, or literary purposes: above note 133, s. 4(2).

uary 2004 to personal information that an "organization collects, uses or discloses in the course of commercial activities."[141] "Commercial activities" is defined in *PIPEDA* as "any particular transaction, act or conduct or any regular course of conduct that is of a commercial character, including the selling, bartering or leasing of donor, membership, or other fundraising lists."[142]

2)   The Application of *PIPEDA* to Ontario's Health Sector

First the application of *PIPEDA* to Ontario's health sector absent *PHIPA* is considered. In Section 4 below the interplay of *PHIPA* and *PIPEDA* is considered.

The federal Department of Industry (Industry Canada) has indicated publicly that *PIPEDA* would likely apply to the activities of health care providers in private practice (e.g., physicians and dentists), private pharmacies and medical laboratories, and private for-profit long-term care facilities and home care services.[143] According to Industry Canada, the source of the payment (e.g., whether a physician is being paid by the government, public or private insurance, or directly by the patient) would not affect whether the activity is "commercial."[144] Industry Canada has indicated that the core activities of public hospitals and municipal homes for the aged are not considered "commercial activities."[145] According to Industry Canada, the application of *PIPEDA* to the core activities of private non-profit long-term care facilities and home care agencies is unclear.[146] It should be noted that, although these are the published statements of Industry Canada, they are not legally binding, and a court or the Federal Privacy Commissioner could take a different view.[147]

---

141   *PIPEDA, ibid.*, s. 4(1)(a).

142   *Ibid.*, s. 2(1).

143   Industry Canada, *PIPEDA Awareness Raising Tools (PARTs) Initiative for the Health Sector, Questions and Answers,* questions 16 and 26. Industry Canada indicates on its website that this document was prepared in consultation with the federal Privacy Commissioner and "major healthcare associations," online: <http://e-com.ic.gc.ca/epic/internet/inecic-ceac.nsf/en/h_gvoo207e.html>. This document has been referred to approvingly by the Privacy Commissioner of Canada, Jennifer Stoddart, in a speech entitled "Privacy Laws & Health Information: Making It Work" (27 October 27 2004) in Regina, Saskatchewan [Speech], online: <www.privcom.gc.ca/speech/2004/sp-d_041027_e.asp>, and the document is linked from the Privacy Commissioner's website.

144   *Ibid.*, question 6.

145   *Ibid.*, questions 7, 23, 24, and 26.

146   *Ibid.*, question 26.

147   As mentioned in note 143, however, the current federal Privacy Commissioner appears to support these interpretations of *PIPEDA* from Industry Canada.

It is significant that the application of *PIPEDA* to an organization depends not on whether the organization is a commercial organization, but rather whether any activity or activities that it carries out is "of a commercial character." Furthermore, the reference to "the selling, bartering or leasing of donor membership or other fundraising lists" as commercial activities to which *PIPEDA* applies suggests that it is intended that some of the activities of not-for-profit organizations will be subject to *PIPEDA* after all. As a result, even for organizations, like hospitals, whose core activities are likely not commercial activities covered by *PIPEDA*, certain activities that the organization may engage in (e.g., television rentals, or trading fundraising lists) may nevertheless be covered by *PIPEDA* as "commercial activities."[148]

3) Uncertainties in *PIPEDA*

As alluded to in Chapter 1, the way *PIPEDA* applies to the health sector is widely viewed as problematic.[149]

- First, the uncertainty over what is considered a "commercial activity" covered by *PIPEDA* is a problem, as organizations need to know whether they are covered or not and often cannot answer this question with an acceptable degree of certainty.
- Second, the fact that *PIPEDA* applies to only the "commercial" parts of the health sector means that *PIPEDA* is not capable of providing consistent and comprehensive rules across the health sector, since the health sector includes a broad mix of commercial and non-commercial actors, including governmental organizations.

---

148 *Ibid.*, questions 6–7 and 24.

149 Chapter 1, Section B(5)(c). The Ontario Information and Privacy Commissioner, in a document entitled "Frequently Asked Questions: *Health Information Protection Act,*" <www.ipc.on.ca/docs/hfaq-e.pdf>, states:

> The application of *PIPEDA* to personal health information has raised a number of concerns. The requirements under *PIPEDA* were designed to regulate direct marketing, electronic commerce and other analogous activities and do not specifically address the unique circumstances encountered within the health care system.

At public hearings before the federal Standing Committee on Industry, 18 March 1999 presentations were made on the particular problems raised by *PIPEDA* for the health sector, by the Ontario Ministry of Health and Long-Term Care, the Canadian Medical Association, the Canadian Institute for Health Information, the Canadian Pharmacists Association, and the Canadian Dentists Association.

Furthermore, see the joint letter from the Ontario Hospitals Association and Ontario Medical Association to Industry Canada, dated 23 May 2003, online: <www.oma.org/phealth/OHA-OMALetter06-23-03.pdf>.

It should be noted that for constitutional reasons federal legislation may not be capable of having a broader application than *PIPEDA*. To the extent that the federal government based *PIPEDA* on the federal government's power under the *Constitution Act, 1867* to regulate "trade and commerce," it may not be possible to extend the reach of the legislation in the provincial sphere beyond "commercial activities."[150] Even going this far has been controversial and is the subject of a constitutional challenge before the Quebec Court of Appeal, which is expected eventually to lead to a ruling by the Supreme Court of Canada on the constitutionality of *PIPEDA*.[151] A leading text on Canadian privacy law concludes that *PIPEDA* is likely to be found unconstitutional in its application to "commercial activities."[152] Of course, if *PIPEDA* is found unconstitutional in its application to organizations, other than those traditionally subject to federal jurisdiction like banks and airlines, it would not apply to most, if any, organizations in Ontario's health sector.

A further difficulty with *PIPEDA* for the health sector, is the lack of clarity about the obligations that the legislation imposes on such fundamental matters as when it is necessary to obtain express consent, rather than implied consent, for a collection, use, or disclosure of personal health information. *PIPEDA* provides that "[a]n organization should generally seek express consent when the information is likely to be considered sensitive,"[153] and specifies that "medical records" are "almost always considered to be sensitive."[154] This suggests that health care organizations subject to *PIPEDA* cannot rely on implied consent for the collection, use, or disclosure of personal health infor-

---

150 *Constitution Act, 1867* (U.K.), 30 & 31 Vict., c. 3, s. 91(2). Industry Canada has stated publicly that *PIPEDA* is based on the exercise of this power: Health Information Custodians in the Province of Ontario Exemption Order (Industry Canada), C. Gaz. 2005, vol. 139, no. 6 [*Health Information Custodians*].

151 This constitutional challenge was commenced by the government of Quebec, by way of an Order in Council dated 17 December 2003, on the question whether *PIPEDA* was outside the constitutional legislative powers of the federal parliament.

152 C. McNairn & A. Scott, *Privacy Law in Canada* (Toronto: Butterworths, 2001) express doubt about the constitutionality of *PIPEDA* as it relates to provincial sector organizations. After a detailed discussion they conclude at 101: "All of these considerations lead inevitably to the conclusion that [*PIPEDA*], to the extent that its application is enlarged at the second stage of implementation [to all organizations engaged in commercial activities], is unlikely to withstand a constitutional challenge. Neither the trade and commerce power nor the peace, order, and good government power under the *Constitution Act, 1867* would appear to provide the necessary support to sustain the Act in that application."

153 CSA Privacy Code, Schedule 1 to *PIPEDA*, 4.3.6.

154 *Ibid.*, 4.3.4.

mation. Industry Canada, however, has indicated that implied consent is sufficient "for the primary use of personal information in the direct care and treatment of an individual patient, as defined in a circle of care," provided that the patient has been made aware of his or her privacy rights.[155] This may provide some comfort for health care providers who wish to continue to rely on implied consent, but it is uncertain whether such an approach will be ultimately confirmed by the courts as the correct interpretation of *PIPEDA*, as the language of *PIPEDA* does not explicitly support such an approach. As such, health care providers who wish to operate with certainty that their consent practices conform with *PIPEDA* may feel compelled to obtain express consent before collecting, using, or disclosing personal health information, unless a specific exception to the consent requirement applies.[156]

As discussed in Chapter 1, *PHIPA* was drafted in large part to ameliorate such uncertainties of *PIPEDA* in its application to Ontario's health sector.

4) Interaction between *PIPEDA* and *PHIPA*

For health information custodians covered by *PIPEDA*, how will *PHIPA* and *PIPEDA* interact to affect their obligations?

a) General Principle Governing Interaction of Federal and Provincial Legislation

There is a principle in Canadian constitutional law that, where there are conflicts between federal and provincial legislation, such that it is not possible to comply with both simultaneously, the terms of the federal legislation are "paramount;" that is, one must comply with the federal legislation.[157] As such, generally speaking where *PHIPA* conflicts with the provisions of any applicable federal legislation, such that it is not possible to comply with the terms of both, the federal legislation must be followed and *PHIPA* will be considered inoperative to the extent of the conflict.

b) *PIPEDA* and the "Substantially Similar" Rule

However, *PIPEDA* in effect incorporates an exception to this principle of paramountcy that allows a provincial privacy law, such as *PHIPA*, to prevail and

---

155 Industry Canada, *PIPEDA Awareness Raising Tools (PARTs) Initiative for the Health Sector, Questions and Answers,* question 40. This document can be found online: <http://e-com.ic.gc.ca/epic/internet/inecic-ceac.nsf/en/h_gv00207e.html>. As noted above, the federal Privacy Commissioner has expressed support for this document.

156 The relevant exceptions are set out in s. 7 of *PIPEDA*.

157 Hogg, above note 46.

displace the provisions of *PIPEDA* where the provincial legislation is "substantially similar" to *PIPEDA* and a federal exemption order is made. The application of *PIPEDA* to Ontario's health sector will likely be largely displaced by *PHIPA*, due to the operation of section 26(2) of *PIPEDA*, which states:

> 26(2) The Governor in Council may, by order, ...
>
> (b) if satisfied that legislation of a province that is *substantially similar to this Part* [i.e., the privacy provisions of *PIPEDA*] applies to an organization, a class of organizations, an activity or a class of activities, exempt the organization, activity or class from the application of this Part in respect of the collection, use or disclosure of personal information that occurs within that province. [Emphasis added.]

This exemption arises only where ordered by the "Governor in Council," which effectively means the federal cabinet. The exemption cannot be ordered unless the Governor in Council is satisfied that the provincial legislation is substantially similar to *PIPEDA*. However, even if the Governor in Council is satisfied that the provincial legislation is substantially similar, the Governor in Council is not *required* to order an exemption.

c) Criteria and Procedure for Attaining "Substantially Similar" Status

Industry Canada has published a notice in the *Canada Gazette* "to advise the public of the process that Industry Canada will follow for determining whether provincial/territorial privacy legislation that applies to the private sector will be deemed 'substantially similar' to [*PIPEDA*]."[158]

According to this notice, the highlights of the process are as follows:

- The process can be initiated either by a request from the relevant province or on the initiative of the Minister of Industry.
- The Governor in Council makes its order on the recommendation of the Minister of Industry.
- No exemption applies without such an order.
- The notice states that "Industry Canada will publish a notice in the *Canada Gazette* announcing the request for consideration pursuant to paragraph 26(2)(b) and inviting comments from the public. Such comments will be

---

158 Process for the Determination of "Substantially Similar" Provincial Legislation by the Governor in Council (Department of Industry), C. Gaz. 2002, vol. 136, no. 31, online: <http://canadagazette.gc.ca/partI/2002/20020803/html/notice-e.html#i10>.

considered in the preparation of the Minister's recommendation to the Governor in Council."[159]

- The Minister of Industry will also seek the views of the Federal Privacy Commissioner before making the recommendation.

The notice also sets out that in order to be considered "substantially similar," provincial legislation will be expected to:

- incorporate the ten principles set out in Schedule 1 to *PIPEDA* (the CSA Privacy Code), with a special emphasis on the principles of consent, access, and correction rights;
- provide for an independent and effective oversight and redress mechanism with powers to investigate; and
- restrict the collection, use, and disclosure of personal information to purposes that are appropriate or legitimate.

The notice stresses, however, that the manner in which provincial legislation embodies these elements is open to considerable flexibility. The notice states:

> By making use of the term "substantially similar" in the *PIPEDA*, the legislation affords provinces/territories the flexibility to adapt and tailor their own private sector legislation to the specific needs and conditions of their jurisdiction while meeting the intent of the Act. The former Minister of Industry told the Standing Senate Committee on Social Affairs, Science and Technology on December 2, 1999, "We are really looking for similar principles…. We are looking for independent oversight and we are looking for redress for individuals. We are not trying to prescribe in detail what provinces need to do" and later, "We are setting the general standard, and the provinces can legislate around it."

d) Factors in Considering PHIPA's "Substantially Similar" to PIPEDA

Particularly in light of Industry Canada's published statements that *PIPEDA* allows the use of implied consent in the "circle of care" for the provision of health care,[160] *PHIPA* has little difficulty meeting the standard described in the Industry Canada notice with respect to *PHIPA's* regulation of personal health information in the hands of health information custodians. Indeed, on 5 February 2005, as this Guide was being prepared for publication, Industry Cana-

---

159 Such a notice was published with respect to *PHIPA* on 5 February 2005. See note 166 below and accompanying text.

160 As discussed above in Section D(3) of this chapter.

da issued a notice indicating that *"PHIPA is substantially similar to PIPEDA"* and recognizing that *PHIPA* is based on the CSA Privacy Code.[161]

The federal Privacy Commissioner has indicated that, in her opinion, *PHIPA* is substantially similar to *PIPEDA*.[162] The Ontario Information and Privacy Commissioner, as well as the government of Ontario, requested the federal government to recognize the substantial similarity of *PHIPA* to *PIPEDA* to pass an order exempting health information custodians from *PIPEDA*.[163]

The following table highlights very generally how the elements of *PHIPA* align with the requirements of substantial similarity set out in the Industry Canada notice.

Table B: PHIPA's *Substantial Similarity to* PIPEDA

Essential Elements of "Substantial Similarity"	How *PHIPA* Provides This Element
Accountability Principle	• s. 17: custodian responsible for personal health information in its custody/control • s. 15: appoint contact person • s. 10: implement information practices • s. 16: provide written public statement
Principle of Identifying Purposes	• s. 18(6): notice of purposes • s. 16: written public statement
Consent Principle	• Part III: consent provisions • Part IV: collection, use, and disclosure (including s. 29 — requirement for consent, unless specific exception applies)
Principle of Limiting Collection	• s. 29: collection with consent must be necessary for a lawful purpose • s. 30: collections of personal health information limited to what is reasonably necessary • s. 18(1): no consent through deception or coercion
Principle of Limiting Use, Disclosure, and Retention	• s. 30: use and disclosure limited to what is reasonably necessary • s. 29: use and disclosure with consent must be necessary for a lawful purpose
Accuracy Principle	• s. 11: accuracy obligations • s. 55: correction rights

---

161   *Health Information Custodians*, above note 150. The contents of this notice are discussed in more detail below.

162   Jennifer Stoddart, Privacy Commissioner of Canada, Speech, above note 143. Ms. Stoddart stated:

> Our opinion is that the Ontario legislation is substantially similar to the federal law. We are confident that the Ontario Act will be deemed substantially so in due course. Currently, *PIPEDA* still applies in Ontario for personal health information used in the course of commercial activity. [Emphasis added.]

163   *Health Information Custodians*, above note 150.

Essential Elements of "Substantial Similarity"	How *PHIPA* Provides This Element
Safeguards Principle	• s. 12: security requirements • s. 10: information practices required
Openness Principle	• s. 16: requirement for written public statement
Individual Access Principle	• Part V: access and correction rights
Principle of Challenging Compliance	• s. 15: contact person responsible for internal complaints process • s. 16: written public statement to include details on internal and external complaint processes
Provide for an independent and effective oversight and redress mechanism with powers to investigate	• Part VI: Information and Privacy Commissioner has full powers to investigate and make binding remedial orders
Restrict the collection, use, and disclosure of personal information to purposes that are appropriate or legitimate	• s. 29: collection, use, or disclosure with consent must be necessary for a lawful purpose • s. 30: collection, use, or disclosure of personal health information limited to what is reasonably necessary

e)   Expected Scope of the Exemption Order

Industry Canada's "substantial similarity" process notice,[164] referred to above, includes the following discussion of exemptions with respect to "sector specific legislation":

> ... the Order can exempt organizations or activities governed by sector specific provincial/territorial legislation that is deemed substantially similar, e.g., provincial/territorial health information legislation which applies to organizations, such as pharmacies, that are engaged in commercial activities in the health sector.

The power to make such a selective exemption order, which may not cover all the collections, uses, and disclosures within a province that are subject to *PIPEDA*, is clear from the language of *PIPEDA*,[165] that

> [t]he Governor in Council may, by order, ... if satisfied that legislation of a province that is substantially similar to this Part [i.e., the privacy provisions of *PIPEDA*] applies to *an organization, a class of organizations, an activity or a class of activities, exempt the organization, activity or class from the application of this*

---

164 See above note 158.

165 *PIPEDA*, above note 133, s. 26(2).

Part in respect of the collection, use or disclosure of personal information that occurs within that province. [Emphasis added.]

On 5 February 2005, Industry Canada published a notice in the *Canada Gazette* of a proposed order to exempt from *PIPEDA* all health information custodians who are subject to *PHIPA*.[166] The proposed terms of the exemption were as follows:

> Any health information custodian to which the *Personal Health Information Protection Act, 2004*, S.O. 2004, c. 3, Schedule A, applies is exempt from the application of Part 1 of the *Personal Information Protection and Electronic Documents Act* in respect of the collection, use and disclosure of personal information that occurs within the Province of Ontario.

It would appear that this exemption order, if made, would exempt health information custodians and those acting on their behalf[167] from compliance with *PIPEDA* for collections, uses, and disclosures of personal information within Ontario.[168] Such an exemption order would not, however, appear to cover non-custodian recipients of personal health information from custodians who are subject to the recipient rules in *PHIPA*.[169]

As the notice provided a period of fifteen days for interested parties to make submissions on the proposed order, an exemption order, on the same or modified terms, may be made at any time.

f)   Until an Exemption Order Is Made: The Requirement for Dual Compliance

Until such an order is made, both *PHIPA* and *PIPEDA* apply to non-governmental[170] Ontario organizations that are health information custodians and

---

166   *Health Information Custodians*, above note 150, available online: <http://canadagazette.gc.ca/partI/2005/20050205/html/regle4-e.html>.

167   Whether or not they are mentioned explicitly in the exemption order, agents of custodians must, for practical reasons, be understood as being covered by the exemption of custodians.

168   The proposed exemption order refers to "personal information" rather than "personal health information," but the operation of the mixed record rule renders this distinction less important than may otherwise be expected. See Chapter 2, Section C(1)(g) for information on the mixed record rule. Note that although employee and agent information is excluded from *PHIPA's* definition of personal health information under s. 4(4), *PIPEDA* does not apply to employee information in any case, except in respect of federal works, undertakings, or businesses, as indicated in s. 4(1)(b) of *PIPEDA*. Custodians would only rarely be considered federal works, undertakings, or businesses. So, again, the practical significance of the distinction between personal information and personal health information in this context is reduced.

169   The recipient rules are discussed in Chapter 12.

170   More precisely, "non-governmental" here refers to organizations that are not part of the Crown, nor Crown agents.

that collect, use, or disclose personal health information in the course of commercial activities.[171] Though the two regimes are similar in many respects, one cannot assume that compliance with one scheme will mean compliance with the other. For example,

- An organization subject to both Acts appears to have an obligation to inform its patients of the existence of the right to complain to both the provincial Information and Privacy Commissioner and the federal Privacy Commissioner.[172]
- In a situation where *PIPEDA* requires express consent for a particular collection, use, or disclosure while *PHIPA* accepts implied consent, the custodian would be obligated to comply with the higher standard and to obtain express consent.
- The list of collections, uses, and disclosures permitted without consent under *PIPEDA* and *PHIPA* are somewhat different, and an organization that is subject to both Acts would have to ensure that the collection, use, or disclosure was permitted under both Acts before going ahead without consent. As a practical matter, since *PHIPA* permits collections, uses, and disclosures that are permitted or required by law, if the collection, use, or disclosure is permitted by *PIPEDA*, then it will therefore be permitted by *PHIPA*.[173] However, *PIPEDA* does not contain such a provision that would automatically allow any collection, use, or disclosure that is permitted by *PHIPA*, so it will be necessary to check to make sure that *PIPEDA* authorizes the collection, use, or disclosure, as the case may be.[174]

---

171 They may also both apply to persons other than health information custodians who are subject to *PHIPA*, as further detailed in Chapter 2, but the discussion here focuses on custodians, who are subject to comprehensive regulation under *PHIPA* with respect to their handling of personal health information.

172 Under *PHIPA* this obligation arises under s. 16(1)(d). Under *PIPEDA* the obligation appears to be limited to those who actually make an inquiry or complaint to the organization: 4.10.3 of the CSA Privacy Code.

173 *PHIPA*, s. 36(1)(g) & (h), 37(1)(b) & (k), and 43(1)(h).

174 *PIPEDA*, above note 133, s. 7 sets out the exceptions to the requirement that all collections, uses, and disclosures require "knowledge or consent." The provisions allowing disclosures without knowledge or consent are as follows:

> (3) For the purpose of clause 4.3 of Schedule 1, and despite the note that accompanies that clause, an organization may disclose personal information without the knowledge or consent of the individual only if the disclosure is
>
> (*a*) made to, in the Province of Quebec, an advocate or notary or, in any other province, a barrister or solicitor who is representing the organization;
>
> (*b*) for the purpose of collecting a debt owed by the individual to the organization;
>
> (*c*) required to comply with a subpoena or warrant issued or an order made by a court, person or body with jurisdiction to compel the production of information, or to comply with rules of court relating to the production of records;

Only in cases where there is a conflict between the two Acts and it is not possible to comply with both does the doctrine of the paramountcy of federal legislation oblige one to comply with *PIPEDA* and excuse one from complying with *PHIPA* to the extent of the inconsistency.[175] Given the provisions of both pieces of legislation, however, there is not a large scope for conflict, so generally the

---

(*c*.1) made to a government institution or part of a government institution that has made a request for the information, identified its lawful authority to obtain the information and indicated that

    (i) it suspects that the information relates to national security, the defence of Canada or the conduct of international affairs,

    (ii) the disclosure is requested for the purpose of enforcing any law of Canada, a province or a foreign jurisdiction, carrying out an investigation relating to the enforcement of any such law or gathering intelligence for the purpose of enforcing any such law, or

    (iii) the disclosure is requested for the purpose of administering any law of Canada or a province;

(*d*) made on the initiative of the organization to an investigative body, a government institution or a part of a government institution and the organization

    (i) has reasonable grounds to believe that the information relates to a breach of an agreement or a contravention of the laws of Canada, a province or a foreign jurisdiction that has been, is being or is about to be committed, or

    (ii) suspects that the information relates to national security, the defence of Canada or the conduct of international affairs;

(*e*) made to a person who needs the information because of an emergency that threatens the life, health or security of an individual and, if the individual whom the information is about is alive, the organization informs that individual in writing without delay of the disclosure;

(*f*) for statistical, or scholarly study or research, purposes that cannot be achieved without disclosing the information, it is impracticable to obtain consent and the organization informs the Commissioner of the disclosure before the information is disclosed;

(*g*) made to an institution whose functions include the conservation of records of historic or archival importance, and the disclosure is made for the purpose of such conservation;

(*h*) made after the earlier of

    (i) one hundred years after the record containing the information was created, and

    (ii) twenty years after the death of the individual whom the information is about;

(*h*.1) of information that is publicly available and is specified by the regulations;

(*h*.2) made by an investigative body and the disclosure is reasonable for purposes related to investigating a breach of an agreement or a contravention of the laws of Canada or a province; or

(*i*) required by law.

175   Hogg, above note 46.

requirement will be for dual compliance for those organizations covered by both Acts, until such time that an exemption order may be made.

g)   *PIPEDA's* Continuing Application

If the Governor in Council makes an order in respect of *PHIPA* consistent with the order set out in the notice of 5 February 2005, custodians will still have to comply with *PIPEDA* for their handling of collections, uses, and disclosures of personal information that do not occur entirely within the province, but that take place in the course of a commercial activity, since there is no mechanism in *PIPEDA* to prevent its application to cross-border transmissions in the course of a commercial activity.[176]

Any organizations subject to *PIPEDA* that are not included in the exemption order, or that are conducting activities that are not covered by the exemption order, will have to continue to comply with *PIPEDA*, together with any provisions of *PHIPA* that may apply to them, such as the provisions regulating the collection, use, and disclosure of the health number, which apply to all persons.[177]

---

176   The exemption order under *PIPEDA* is not capable of exempting such matters from the application of *PIPEDA*, so *PIPEDA* will continue to apply despite any exemption order. The proposed draft exemption order discussed above actually refers only to collections, uses, and disclosures that occur within Ontario.

177   *PHIPA*, s. 34.

Obligations of Health Information Custodians

A. GENERALLY

In addition to the substantive rules that the *Personal Health Information Protection Act*[1] imposes for the collection, use, and disclosure of personal health information and for providing patients with a right to access and correct their records of personal health information, the Act also imposes on health information custodians certain obligations consistent with fundamental principles of informational privacy and the confidentiality of personal health information. These basic requirements, largely set out in Part II of *PHIPA*, require a health information custodian to be accountable and open about the custodian's information practices to ensure patients are aware of the custodian's collection, use, and disclosure of patient information, and about avenues of recourse open for addressing any problems. Custodians must also ensure the accuracy and security of personal health information in their custody or control. These obligations embody several of the ten principles set out in the CSA Privacy Code, specifically accountability, accuracy, safeguards, and openness. The fulfilment of these requirements creates a transparency and assurance of reliability that serves to foster public trust in health care providers and in the health system overall.

---

1   S.O. 2004, c. 3, Sch. A [*PHIPA*].

B. ACCOUNTABILITY

1) Designating a Contact Person

Under *PHIPA*, all health information custodians are required either to designate a contact person, or to take on the role of contact person themselves.
While a health information custodian who is a natural person (such as a physician in private practice, as opposed to a corporation or partnership)[2] has the
option of either designating a contact person or performing the functions of a
contact person him- or herself, a custodian that is not a natural person (such
as a hospital or long-term care facility) must designate a contact person.[3]

In some instances, separate health information custodians may address
the requirement in the Act concerning the function of the contact person more
efficiently by appointing a common person to act as the contact person for
them all. This strategy may be attractive for health care practitioners who provide health care in the course of their employment duties for a non-health
information custodian (e.g., nurses and speech language pathologists employed
by a school board, or social workers and social service workers employed by a
children's aid society). They may all appoint a common person within the
employer's organization, perhaps a person with established responsibilities for
privacy or records management, to help them all comply with *PHIPA* in an
efficient and co-ordinated manner that will also be harmonious with the information practices of the employer's organization as a whole.[4]

The designation of one person as having the responsibilities of the contact
person does not mean that other agents of the health information custodian do
not participate in the fulfilment of the custodian's responsibilities under the
Act. The contact person can delegate duties to others with the custodian's permission. A health information custodian may give several agents specific
assignments with respect to the custodian's information practices. The contact
person, however, retains overall responsibility for the activities assigned by
PHIPA to contact persons, as described below in this chapter.

---

2   *PHIPA*, s. 2, definition of "person."

3   *Ibid.*, ss. 15(1), (2), and (4).

4   The contact person, however, must take care to ensure that he or she does not act as a
    conduit for personal health information through which the custodians may flow per-
    sonal health information to each other or to the employer where *PHIPA* does not
    authorize such a disclosure.

2) Role of a Contact Person

Under *PHIPA*, the contact person is deemed an agent[5] of the custodian and is authorized to perform five categories of activities on behalf of the custodian.[6] The contact person

a) facilitates the custodian's compliance with the Act;

b) ensures that all agents of the custodian are appropriately informed of their duties under the Act;

c) responds to inquiries from the public about the custodian's information practices;

d) responds to requests of a patient for access to or correction of a record of personal health information about the patient that is in the custody or under the control of the custodian; and

e) receives complaints from the public about the custodian's alleged contravention of the Act or the regulations.

The nature of the position of a "contact person" will depend largely on the size and complexity of the health information custodian. In larger facilities, such as hospitals, an agent dedicated to work arising from the custodian's obligations under the Act, such as a Chief Privacy Officer, may be a practical necessity. In other instances, the responsibilities of the contact person may be added to the duties of an employee or other agent, such as a health care practitioner, health information manager, or administrative assistant. An agent who acts as a contact person need not dedicate all his or her time to activities related to the health information custodian's obligations under the Act. Health information custodians with smaller operations, such as health care practitioners and community health centres, are more likely to take this latter approach. A sole practitioner may perform the duties of the contact person him- or herself.

C. DETERMINING WHAT IS REASONABLE

Where *PHIPA* does not delineate specific processes or actions for health information custodians, it typically requires custodians to act "reasonably." For example, health information custodians must take steps that are "reasonable in the circumstances" to protect personal health information. Custodians may

---

5   See Chapter 2, Section B(2) for a discussion of "agents."
6   *PHIPA*, s. 15(3).

keep records of personal health information in an individual's home in any "reasonable manner." Further, custodians must take "reasonable steps" to ensure the accuracy of personal health information.[7] The alternative, which would be to provide specific concrete standards for each type of activity being regulated across the health sector, would be a challenge and could easily result in the imposition of a standard appropriate for one context on another context, where a different standard would be more appropriate. Health information custodians under *PHIPA* include a broad range of different types of operations ranging from individual employees[8] or sole practitioners to organizations with thousands of employees. What is appropriate in one context can be very different from what is appropriate in another.

Of course, the advantage of adopting a "reasonableness" standard is its flexibility to adjust to any situation or circumstance that arrives. The challenge with such a flexible standard, though, is determining concretely what it requires in any given circumstance. What is meant by language in the Act such as "reasonable steps," "reasonable in the circumstances," and "reasonable manner"?

Black's Law Dictionary defines "reasonable" as "[f]air, proper, or moderate under the circumstances."[9] The concept of "reasonableness" is well-grounded in the law of negligence in common law jurisdictions, like Ontario. In determining whether a person has acted in accordance with the standard of care expected of him or her in the execution of his or her duty, the court considers the actions of the "reasonable person." Consider the portrait of the "reasonable man" in the Ontario Court of Appeal's judgment in *Arland and Arland v. Taylor*:

> I shall not attempt to formulate a comprehensive definition of "a reasonable man" of whom we so frequently speak in negligence cases. I simply say he is a mythical creature of the law whose conduct is the standard by which the Courts measure the conduct of all other persons and find it to be proper or improper in particular circumstances as they may exist from time to time. He is not an extraordinary or unusual creature; he is not superhuman; he is not required to display the highest skill of which anyone is capable; he is not a genius who can perform uncommon feats, nor is he possessed of unusual powers of foresight. He is a person of normal intelligence who makes pru-

---

7   *PHIPA*, ss. 11(1), 12(1), & 14(1).

8   An individual health care practitioner employed by a non-health information custodian is a custodian in his or her own right. See Chapter 2, Section B(1) for a discussion of "health information custodians."

9   B.A. Garner, ed., *Black's Law Dictionary*, 8th ed. (St. Paul, Minn.: Thomson West, 2004), *s.v.* "reasonable."

dence a guide to his conduct. He does nothing that a prudent man would not do and does not omit to do anything a prudent man would do. He acts in accord with general and approved practice. His conduct is guided by considerations which ordinarily regulate the conduct of human affairs. His conduct is the standard "adopted in the community by persons of ordinary intelligence and prudence."[10]

How does a health information custodian act as this "reasonable person" in handling personal health information? In some circumstances, it will be difficult to be certain about how a "reasonable" health information custodian should proceed in dealing with personal health information. The Information and Privacy Commissioner has stated that "'reasonable efforts' can be defined as what a privacy-conscious and prudent healthcare institution would do in similar circumstances."[11] "Prudent," however, does not require a health information custodian to act with such caution or apprehension so as to halt its entire operations. A "reasonable" custodian appropriately balances his or her responsibilities under the Act with his or her other duties, such as the provision of health care.[12] According to the Assistant Commissioner, to take reasonable steps does not demand a standard so high as to necessitate that every possible step be pursued.[13] A reasonable custodian makes decisions in light of the particular circumstances in which the custodian operates. Where *PHIPA* leaves flexibility in terms of how to approach an issue, a "reasonable" custodian considers accepted or general practices in determining the appropriate course of action. "Activities and practices on the margins of general practice will generally be more contentious."[14] Evidence of appropriate and accepted practices may be found in guidance from regulatory bodies, volunteer associa-

---

10 *Arland and Arland v. Taylor*, [1955] O.R. 131 (C.A.).

11 Information and Privacy Commissioner/Ontario, *Privacy Assessment: University Health Network's Response to Recent Breaches of Patient Privacy* (30 July 2002), online: <www.ipc.on.ca>. The Commissioner made this statement in commenting on whether the hospital that was the subject of the privacy assessment was making reasonable efforts to ensure that the privacy breaches related to electronic patient records did not re-occur.

12 Indeed, a purpose of *PHIPA* is to establish rules for the collection, use, and disclosure of personal health information that protect the confidentiality of that information while facilitating the provision of health care. See *PHIPA*, s. 1(a).

13 Investigation Report I94-012M (27 September 1994), online: <www.ipc.on.ca>.

14 This statement was made in the different, but related, context of workplace privacy. Mary O'Donoghue, "Reasonableness in the Context of Workplace Privacy" (Paper presented to *Workplace Privacy*, an Infonex conference, Toronto, 25 June 2001), online: <www.ipc.on.ca>.

tions, and legal advisors. Health information custodians should have up-to-date knowledge of the prevailing accepted practices.

The Information and Privacy Commissioner has not had the opportunity to communicate many of her views on the actions of health information custodians through reports and orders. Until then, to help clarify what actions are "reasonable" in particular circumstances, it is useful to consider the position of the Information and Privacy Commissioner in the context of public sector privacy legislation, the *Freedom of Information and Protection of Privacy Act*,[15] and the *Municipal Freedom of Information and Protection of Privacy Act*.[16] Although certainly not determinative of the Commissioner's approach under *PHIPA*, reports and orders under public sector privacy legislation provide important insight into the Commissioner's perspective. These are available on the Commissioner's website.[17] It is also helpful to look to the findings of privacy commissioners in other jurisdictions, such as Alberta, where there is more experience with health information privacy legislation, and Canada.[18]

D. INFORMATION PRACTICES

1) Requirement for Information Practices

A health information custodian is required to have in place and comply with "information practices" that fulfil the requirements of *PHIPA* and the regulations.[19] The Act defines the term "information practices" to mean "the policy of a health information custodian for actions in relation to personal health information, including,

a)   when, how, and the purposes for which the custodian routinely collects, uses, modifies, discloses, retains, or disposes of personal health information, and

---

15   R.S.O. 1990, c. F.31 [*FIPPA*].

16   R.S.O. 1990, c. M.56 [*MFIPPA*].

17   Online: <www.ipc.on.ca>.

18   Alberta, Manitoba, and Saskatchewan each have had health information privacy legislation in place for a few years. *Health Information Act*, R.S.A. 2000, c. H-5 (Alberta); *Personal Health Information Act*, C.C.S.M., c. P33.5 (Manitoba); *Health Information Protection Act, 1999*, S.S. 1999, H-0.021 (Saskatchewan). As well, since 1 January 2004, the *Personal Information Protection and Electronic Documents Act*, S.C. 2000, c. 5 [*PIPEDA*] has applied to organizations within Ontario that collect, use, or disclose personal information, including personal health information, in the course of commercial activities.

19   *PHIPA*, ss. 10(1) & (2). Currently, neither *PHIPA* nor the *PHIPA* Regulation, *General*, O. Reg. 329/04, detail requirements for a health information custodian's information practices.

b) the administrative, technical, and physical safeguards and practices that the custodian maintains with respect to the information."[20]

2) Putting Information Practices in Place

a) Building on Existing Practices

Many health information custodians have devoted considerable time and effort in the past to developing sound information practices. The Information and Privacy Commissioner has acknowledged that the fact that health information custodians are required to establish and implement information practices that comply with *PHIPA* does not necessarily mean that custodians are expected to completely set aside their existing policies and practices. The Commissioner has noted that the Act builds on existing policies and guidelines for health care professionals.[21] Many health information custodians, such as regulated health professionals, have a long history of practices that respect the privacy and confidentiality of personal health information and are able to draw upon such experience. Similarly, many health information custodians have taken steps to comply with federal privacy legislation, the *Personal Information Protection and Electronic Documents Act*,[22] which, like *PHIPA*, is based on the CSA Privacy Code, which also requires the implementation of such privacy conscious information practices.[23] Health information custodians can adapt the information practices that they have in place to ensure their compliance with *PHIPA*. To the extent that custodians do not already have such policies in place, or where the policies have gaps, they will need to review and adapt their existing practices with respect to information and describe revised practices in a policy in a manner that will comply with *PHIPA*.

b) Developing Information Practices

In developing its information practices, a health information custodian should consider the following questions:

---

20 *PHIPA*, s. 2. The reference to the "policy" of the health information custodian in the definition of the term "information practices" may be unclear to custodians, as a "practice" is typically differentiated from "policy," but custodians should keep this definition in mind.

21 Information and Privacy Commissioner/Ontario, *Frequently Asked Questions: Health Information Protection Act* (13 August 2004), online: <www.ipc.on.ca>.

22 *PIPEDA*, above note 18.

23 This term is commonly used to refer to the Code incorporated in Schedule I of *PIPEDA, ibid.*, which Schedule is officially entitled "Principles Set out in the National Standard of Canada, Entitled Model Code for the Protection of Personal Information, CAN/CSA-Q830-96" [CSA Privacy Code].

- From whom and for what purposes does the custodian collect personal health information?
- For what purposes does the custodian use personal health information?
- To whom and for what purposes does the custodian disclose personal health information?
- In what circumstances does the custodian seek consent for collections, uses, or disclosures of personal health information, and what form of consent does the custodian seek?
- How does personal health information flow within the custodian's practice or organization?
- Who within the custodian's practice or organization handles personal health information?
- How and where does the custodian store personal health information?
- How long does the custodian retain records of personal health information?
- How does the custodian dispose of personal health information when it is no longer required?
- Who in the organization is responsible for modifying personal health information when necessary, and under what circumstances and in what manner is information modified?
- What safeguards does the custodian currently have in place to protect personal health information?

Considering responses to such questions may assist a health information custodian to understand how the custodian creates, collects, uses, discloses, retains, and disposes of personal health information from the time the custodian first interacts with a patient. This information may also help the custodian to identify risks to the privacy and security of the personal health information in the custodian's custody or control and how the custodian currently addresses those risks. Identifying high-risk aspects of the custodian's information practices and gaps in the management of those risks will highlight any areas that require the custodian's further attention.

c) Documenting Information Practices

Although not a requirement of *PHIPA*, a health information custodian should document the custodian's information practices in writing in the way in which the custodian documents other policies. Documenting information practices in this way better enables the custodian's review of its information practices, whether as part of a scheduled audit or as privacy incidents arise. For example, should a privacy breach occur, the custodian should be able to explain whether the breach happened because an information practice did not exist or was deficient, or whether it was a result of a failure to disseminate or follow the information practice.[24]

Documenting information practices is not necessarily sufficient in itself, however. It is not enough for a health information custodian simply to have "information practices." The custodian must develop information practices that comply with the requirements set out in *PHIPA* and its regulations.[25] One of the key obligations that information practices must support is the general obligation of all custodians to "take steps that are reasonable in the circumstances to ensure that personal health information in the custodian's custody or control is protected against theft, loss and unauthorized use or disclosure and to ensure that the records containing the information are protected against unauthorized copying, modification, or disposal."[26] These steps include implementing security measures, as discussed below in this chapter.[27] Also, information practices must support collections, uses, and disclosures of personal health information, whether with or without consent, that are consistent with the requirements set out in Parts III and IV of the Act, which deal with consent, and collections, uses, and disclosures of personal health information.[28]

Furthermore, when developing information practices it is necessary to bear in mind the fact that, if a health information custodian uses or discloses

---

24   See, for example, Privacy Complaint Report PC-030013-1, Ministry of Health and Long-Term Care (25 August 2003), online: <www.ipc.on.ca>, which describes the safeguards that the Ministry of Health and Long-Term Care had put into place to prevent the theft of Ontario Health Insurance Plan health cards. When a clerk left her counter to speak to her manager at an irate client's request, the client stole several voided health cards from the top of her computer. The mediator of the Office of Information and Privacy Commissioner/Ontario found that the Ministry had reasonable measures in place to prevent unauthorized access to obsolete health cards. These measures included a policy on the disposal of obsolete health cards, which included a requirement that staff make cards non-reusable after receiving them and removing them from the database by cutting them into two or more pieces and placing the pieces into a "shred-it bin." The mediator noted that additional "shred-it bins" may be useful in some offices and that the policy should be clarified to ensure that staff understood that cards should be made non-reusable immediately upon receipt.

25   *PHIPA*, s. 10(1).

26   *Ibid.*, s. 12(1).

27   See Section F(4) below for a discussion of technical safeguards.

28   See Chapter 8, Chapter 9, and Chapter 10 for a discussion of a health information custodian's collection, use, and disclosure of personal health information; and Chapter 5 for a discussion of requirements with respect to a patient's consent to a health information custodian's collection, use, or disclosure of personal health information about the patient.

a patient's personal health information without the patient's consent in a manner that is outside the scope of the custodian's description of its information practices, as set out in the custodian's written statement, the custodian is generally required to provide notice of that fact to the patient.[29] To limit the number of instances in which this obligation will arise, the custodian should develop comprehensive information practices and ensure that the written statement reflects these practices.[30]

d) Evolution of Information Practices

In most cases, a health information custodian's information practices will not remain static. Health information custodians should review their documented information practices regularly to ensure that they remain appropriate for their operations. As the custodian's operations evolve, perhaps as a result of the introduction to new information technology, it is important to update the custodian's information practices to reflect the changes. A health information custodian should take steps to ensure that the contents of documented information practices are kept current to reflect actual practice. Scheduling and documenting a date for the review, and those who will be involved in the process, may help ensure that the review is undertaken.

Although not a general requirement in *PHIPA*,[31] a health information custodian may wish to undertake a privacy impact assessment, commonly known as a "PIA," to assess the impact of the introduction of a new information technology system to a program or a new program itself. According to the Information and Privacy Commissioner, "a failure to consider privacy in an information technology project, from the design stage to post implementation evaluation, can have widespread and damaging repercussions."[32]

---

29 *PHIPA*, s. 16(2). See Section E below for a discussion of the written statement and the notice requirements arising from a health information custodian's use or disclosure of personal health information in a manner that is outside the scope of the custodian's description of its information practices, as described in the custodian's written public statement.

30 *PHIPA*, s. 16(1) sets out the requirement for a written public statement. See Section E below for a discussion of the Act's requirement for a written public statement.

31 Although the Act does not include a requirement for a privacy impact assessment, the *PHIPA* Regulation, above note 19, s. 6(3)[5][ii], includes a requirement for an assessment of how the services of a health information network provider may affect the privacy of the individuals. See Chapter 2, Section B(3) for a discussion of the requirements that the Act imposes on "health information network providers."

32 Ann Cavoukian, Ph.D., Information and Privacy Commissioner/Ontario, "Putting the 'E' into Privacy: Privacy Tips for Technology Leaders" (Presentation to Centre for Leadership Technology Seminar, Toronto, 17 August 2000), online: <www.ipc.on.ca>.

A privacy impact assessment has three components:

- a description of the information or data flows associated with the proposed program or system;
- privacy analysis of the data flow, including a consideration of the proposed program's or system's compliance with applicable privacy legislation; and
- an analysis of privacy issues raised by the proposed program or system, including a risk assessment and a discussion of options available for mitigating the risks, if any.[33]

The privacy impact assessment is a helpful tool that health information custodians may use to ensure the consideration of all implications of a new information technology system or program on health information privacy.[34]

E. WRITTEN PUBLIC STATEMENT

1) Content of Statement

The "public face" of the health information custodian's information practices is the mandatory written statement that contains a general description of the custodian's information practices.[35] The statement must also describe how to contact the custodian or its contact person, where the custodian has designated a contact person.[36] In addition, the statement must include a description of how a patient may obtain access to or request correction of a record of personal health information about the patient that is in the custody or control of the custodian.[37] Finally, the statement must describe how to make a complaint to the custodian and to the Information and Privacy Commissioner.[38]

---

33   *Ibid.*
34   A detailed discussion of privacy impact assessments is beyond the scope of this Guide. For more information, see Freedom of Information and Privacy Office, Management Board Secretariat, *Privacy Impact Assessment Guidelines* (Ontario: June 2001), online: <www.gov.on.ca/MBS/english/fip/pia/>. See also, Canada, Treasury Board of Canada Secretariat, *Privacy Impact Assessment Guidelines: A Framework to Manage Privacy Risks* (Ottawa: Minister of Public Works and Government Services Canada, 2002), online: <www.tbs-sct.gc.ca/pubs_pol/ciopubs/pia-pefr/paipg-pefrld_e.asp>.
35   *PHIPA*, s. 16(1)(a).
36   *Ibid.*, s. 16(1)(b).
37   *Ibid.*, s. 16(1)(c).
38   *Ibid.*, s. 16(1)(d).

2) Making the Statement Available to the Public

PHIPA does not include detailed requirements for the provision of the state-ment to the public. Though the provisions in the Act do not explicitly require it, a health information custodian should consider notifying patients in some way of the availability of the written public statement. The Act requires that a custodian make the written public statement available to the public in a man-ner that is practical in the circumstances.[39] Specifically how this is to be done is not set out in the Act. A custodian should take the custodian's patient popu-lation into account in determining the most effective way in which to make the written statement available. A health information custodian may retain copies of the written statement at the location(s) from which the custodian operates, or keep copies at hand when providing services to a patient. A health informa-tion custodian may wish to provide the statement to the public as a brochure or pamphlet, wall poster, or via the custodian's website. Alternatively, a health information custodian may choose a combination of these methods, and "layer" the information for the public, beginning with a simple document and offering a greater level of detail in each layer.

Consider, for example, the "layered" approach reflected in the recommen-dations arising from the Information and Privacy Commissioner's privacy review of the Chatham-Kent IT Transition Pilot Project.[40] In response to the

---

39 *PHIPA*, s. 16(1). Various provisions in *PHIPA* refer to a custodian providing a patient with notice of an issue concerning personal health information. Consider the differ-ent language used in *PHIPA* regarding the provision of such notices. In addition to *PHIPA*, ss. 16(1) and 18(6), see also *PHIPA*, s. 20(4) (regarding a custodian that is a facility offering a patient the opportunity to withhold or withdraw consent to the pro-vision of information to a representative of a religious or other organization); *PHIPA*, s. 38(3) (regarding a facility offering a patient the option, at the first reasonable oppor-tunity after admission, to object to the disclosure of the fact that he or she is a patient in a facility, his or her location, and information about his or her general health sta-tus); and *PHIPA* Regulation, s. 10(2) (regarding, at the time of providing service to a patient, posting or making available to the patient, in a manner likely to come to his or her attention, a brief statement concerning the custodian's use and disclosure of information for fundraising purposes).

40 Information and Privacy Commissioner/Ontario, *Privacy Review: Chatham-Kent IT Transition Pilot Project* (22 April 2002), online: <www.ipc.on.ca> [Chatham-Kent Review]. The Commissioner conducted a privacy review of the Chatham-Kent IT Tran-sition Pilot Project after a newspaper reported allegations of insufficient safeguards for personal health information. E-Physician Project was a project of the Ministry of Health and Long-Term Care, Ontario Family Health Network, and the Ontario Medical Association that supported the use of information technology as part of the reform of the provision of primary health care in Ontario, and the Chatham-Kent IT Transition Pilot Project was one aspect of the E-Physician Project.

question of whether patients were being fully informed of what was happening with their personal health information, the Commissioner found that patients received only general information about what was happening. The Commissioner recommended that the parties involved in the project prepare a written sign or brochure that notifies patients of their physician's participation in the pilot project. The Commissioner recommended that signs should be posted in a prominent location in each physician's office and direct the patients to a website for more information. The Commissioner also recommended that the parties involved in the project prepare a plain language patient information fact sheet on the project. The fact sheet could be posted on a website, and hard copies could also be made available in the physicians' offices. These recommendations suggest that the Commissioner would support the provision of information to the public in a variety of ways and at various levels of detail.

3) Written Public Statement Distinguished from Notice of Purposes

It is important to distinguish the written public statement required by section 16(1) of *PHIPA* from the "notices of purposes" described in section 18(6) that may be made available to patients as a way of ensuring that a patient knows the purposes of the collection, use, or disclosure of personal health information about the patient.[41] All health information custodians must make a written statement that provides specific information available to the public. In contrast, health information custodians are not required to develop a "notice of purposes." A notice of purposes is only one way in which health information custodians can ensure that a patient upon whose consent they rely, is knowledgeable of the purposes of the custodian's collection, use, and disclosure of the patient's personal health information.[42] Health information custodians may choose to combine the written public statement with a notice of purposes, as their contents may overlap, and then rely on the one document to serve both purposes.

---

41 See Section B(2) of Chapter 5 for a discussion of a custodian's use of a notice to meet the Act's requirement that a patient's consent to the collection, use, or disclosure of personal health information about the patient be "knowledgeable."

42 Instead, a custodian may provide an oral explanation, or, in particular circumstances, it may be clear that the patient already knows the purposes. Furthermore, a custodian relying on an assumed implied consent to collect, use, or disclose information for the provision of health care, pursuant to *PHIPA*, s. 20(2), is entitled to assume that valid implied consent is provided, without the requirement for any "notice of purposes," unless aware that the patient has stated otherwise.

4) Operating Inconsistently with Written Statement

As noted above, additional obligations face any health information custodian that uses or discloses personal health information without the patient's consent outside the scope of the custodian's stated information practices, as set out in the custodian's written public statement. In such instances, a custodian must inform the patient of the uses and disclosures at the first reasonable opportunity, unless the patient does not have a right of access under *PHIPA* to a record of the information.[43] The custodian must also make a note of the uses and disclosures and keep the note as part of the records of personal health information about the patient.[44] This requirement makes the drafting of the written public statement, and the information practices on which the written statement is based, a particularly important task. A custodian should take a comprehensive approach in drafting its information practices and describing these practices for the purposes of the written statement, including both routine and unusual uses and disclosures, to minimize the frequency of these mandatory notices.

5) Updating Written Statement

In most cases, a health information custodian's information practices will not remain static. A new and legitimate use or disclosure of personal health information may be identified. Likewise, contact information for the custodian's contact person may change.[45] A health information custodian should take steps to ensure that the contents of the written statement are kept current. To ensure that an update is undertaken, the custodian may schedule and document a date for a review of the written statement, and assign responsibility for this task.

---

43   *PHIPA*, s. 16(2). Where a health information custodian uses or discloses personal health information about a patient that is not recorded in a manner that is outside the scope of the custodian's information practices, s. 16(2)(a), as drafted, would not require the custodian to provide such notice to the patient it, had the information been recorded, the patient would not have had access to the record. *PHIPA*, s. 52 describes exceptions to an individual's right of access to a record of personal health information about the individual in the custody or control of a health information custodian. See Chapter 13.

44   *PHIPA*, ss. 16(2)(b) & (c). This notation will enable the individual's access to the information, unless the individual does not have a right of access to the record under *PHIPA*.

45   A custodian may prefer to refer to the contact person's title only and omit references to the contact person's name, for example, where changes in the identity of the contact person are likely.

F. PRACTICES TO PROTECT PERSONAL HEALTH INFORMATION

1) What Is Security?

The protection of the privacy of information depends, in part, on the existence of security measures to protect that information. Information security can be described as the controls exercised to securely collect and hold information.[46] Information security consists of

- confidentiality: keeping information from other persons;
- integrity: ensuring that the information is not changed in the absence of authorization; and
- accuracy and availability: ensuring that the information is accurate and accessible as required.[47]

2) Requirements for Security

PHIPA requires health information custodians to take steps to avoid privacy and security breaches by imposing basic security requirements. A health information custodian must ensure that the records of personal health information it has in its custody or control are retained, transferred, and disposed of in a secure manner and in accordance with any requirements identified in the regulations made under the Act.[48] A health information custodian is required to take steps that are reasonable in the circumstances to ensure that personal health information in the custodian's custody or control is protected against theft, loss, and unauthorized use or disclosure.[49] These obligations apply regardless of whether the custodian's records of personal health information are paper-based or electronic.

What constitutes "a secure manner"? What circumstances should a health information custodian take into consideration in determining what steps are "reasonable" in a particular context? As discussed above, a reasonable health information custodian balances its obligations under the Act with the custodi-

---

46   Information and Privacy Commissioner/Ontario and Deloitte & Touche, *The Security-Privacy Paradox: Issues, Misconceptions, and Strategies* (August 2003), online: <www.ipc.on.ca> at 2.

47   *Ibid.* at 2.

48   *PHIPA*, s. 13(1).

49   *Ibid.*, s. 12(1). The term "unauthorized" means not authorized by the Act or its regulations.

an's other obligations, such as the provision of health care. A reasonable health information custodian acts in light of the circumstances in which the custodian operates.[50] According to the CSA Privacy Code, the nature of appropriate safeguards varies according to "the sensitivity of the information that has been collected, the amount, distribution, and format of the information, and the method of storage."[51] *PHIPA*, though, provides little specific direction in this regard. The benefit of *PHIPA*'s approach is that health information custodians have significant flexibility to determine how to best comply with the Act's security principles. The Act's requirements are technology-neutral and contain no specific technology recommendations.[52] They are also flexible enough to be adapted to what is appropriate for all health information custodians, whatever the size or complexity of their operations.

3) Guidance on Security Practices

In complying with *PHIPA*'s requirements concerning the security of personal health information, health information custodians should consider incorporating the guidance that their regulatory bodies, associations, and medico-legal advisors provide.

Many regulatory bodies, such as professional governing bodies, provide their members with detailed direction concerning the information practices that they must have in place. Professional governing bodies provide such direction in various forms, including through policies and standards of practice.[53] In

---

50   See Section C above. For example, in relation to the "reasonable steps" that a custodian must take to retain records of personal health information in a secure manner, the Office of the Information and Privacy Commissioner has indicated that "what is reasonable varies depending on the sensitivity of the information and the risks to which it is exposed," noting the size of an organization as one factor to consider. According to the Office of the Information and Privacy Commissioner, custodians must "scale security measures to fit their own circumstances." See Information and Privacy Commissioner/Ontario, Fact Sheet: Safeguarding Personal Health Information (January 2004), online: <www.ipc.on.ca>.

51   CSA Privacy Code, above note 23, Principle 4.7.2.

52   *PHIPA* does not include any regulations imposing specific security requirements. However, *PHIPA* does include regulation-making powers that would permit the development of such regulations. See, for example, *PHIPA*, s. 73(1)(h).

53   The College of Physicians and Surgeons of Ontario, for example, has informed its members through its bi-monthly communication, *Members' Dialogue*, that using e-mail or fax to transmit personal health information is not a secure method of transmission. Therefore, the College, together with the Information and Privacy Commissioner, has recommended that physicians use measures, such as encryption for e-mail, to transmit information more securely. The College has also advised its members that, when con-

many instances, compliance with such direction is mandatory. However, even where custodians retain discretion concerning whether to follow the direction of the professional governing body, they should be cautious in taking an approach that is inconsistent with the direction of the governing body.

Provincial and national professional associations also provide their members with guidance on information practices. For example, to assist hospitals with their compliance with *PHIPA*, the Ontario Hospital Association co-operated with others to develop the *Hospital Privacy Toolkit: Guide to the Ontario Personal Health Information Protection Act*.[54] The Ontario Medical Association developed a similar tool for physicians.[55] Even prior to the introduction of the Act, voluntary associations, such as the Ontario Association of Medical Laboratories, have provided their membership with guidance on such aspects of their information practices as the retention of records of personal health information.[56] Similarly, the Canadian Health Information Management Association has developed numerous publications dealing with a variety of issues, including record security and the electronic transmission of health information.[57] Guidance from such associations can be particularly useful for their members, as it often reflects a consideration of the membership's specific needs.

Many health information custodians are members of organizations that provide them with medico-legal and risk management advice. Most hospitals in Ontario receive advice from the Healthcare Insurance Reciprocal of Canada;

---

tacting patients, physicians may leave messages either with third parties or on an answering machine, although messages should not include detailed personal health information, such as diagnostic test results. See "Privacy Legislation," Members' Dialogue (November/December 2004), online: <www.cpso.on.ca>. See also College of Physicians & Surgeons of Ontario, Medical Records, Policy #11-00 (May/June 2001), online: <www.cpso.on.ca/Policies/medicalrec.htm>. See also College of Physicians & Surgeons of Ontario, "A Guide to Current Medical Record-Keeping Practices: A Focus on Record-keeping in the Office-based Setting" (February 2000), online: <www.cpso.on.ca/Publications/ med_record-keeping2.pdf>.

54 Ontario Hospital Association, *Hospital Privacy Toolkit: Guide to the Ontario Personal Health Information Protection Act* (Toronto: Ontario Hospital Association, September 2004).

55 *Physician Privacy Toolkit: Guide to the Ontario Personal Health Information Protection Act* (Toronto: Ontario Hospital Association, September 2004). The Ontario Association for Non-Profit Homes and Services for Seniors also updated a resource initially developed for *PIPEDA* to provide guidance on *PHIPA*, online: <www.oanhss.org>.

56 Ontario Association of Medical Laboratories, "Guidelines for the Period of Retention of Laboratory Records and Materials," Guidelines for Clinical Laboratory Practice, CLP 020 (Toronto, Ont.: January 2000), online: <www.oaml.com/PDF/CLP020.pdf>.

57 Canadian Health Information Management Association, *Electronic Transmission of Health Information Record Security.* See also Canadian Health Information Management Association, *Security of Computerized Health Information*, online: <www.chima-cchra.ca>.

physicians from the Canadian Medical Protective Association; and nurses from the Canadian Nurses Protective Society. As part of this advice, these organizations often provide members with guidance on information practices.[58]

Health information custodians may find the reports and orders of the Information and Privacy Commissioner useful in developing their information practices. Custodians may also refer to the Commissioner's guidelines and directions in the context of provincial public sector privacy legislation, *FIPPA* and *MFIPPA*. For example, the Commissioner has developed guidelines for institutions governed by provincial public sector privacy legislation concerning the preservation of privacy and confidentiality when staff work outside of the office.[59] Although not developed in the context of *PHIPA*, these tools may assist health information custodians in developing appropriate safeguards for personal health information, until such time as further guidance specific to *PHIPA* is available.[60]

With such guidance, health information custodians should recognize that they are not alone in establishing practices to protect the personal health information in their custody or control. Custodians across the health care sector grapple with the same issues. Custodians should work collaboratively with other custodians, and the relevant regulatory bodies and associations, to understand their approaches to informational privacy and draw on their expertise, work, and experiences.

4) Types of Safeguards

a) Three Categories of Safeguards

A health information custodian should incorporate three types of safeguards: (i) physical; (ii) administrative; and (iii) technical, corresponding to the three

---

58 See, for example, Canadian Medical Protective Association, "Protecting Personal Health Information: An Overview for Physicians" On the Record No. 1 (September 2002).

59 Information and Privacy Commissioner/Ontario, "Privacy and Confidentiality When Working Outside the Office" *Practices* No. 20, online: <www.ipc.on.ca>.

60 At the time of writing, the Office of the Information and Privacy Commissioner had developed the following documents: *A Guide to the Personal Health Information Protection Act*; *Frequently Asked Questions: Health Information Protection Act*; *Frequently Asked Questions: Regulations under the Health Information Protection Act*; and *Frequently Asked Questions: Health Cards and Health Numbers*. In addition, the Office had also begun to develop "fact sheets" specific to certain issues, including a fact sheet about safeguarding personal health information. In time, the Office of the Information and Privacy Commissioner will likely develop additional documents to assist health information custodians specifically with their compliance with *PHIPA*.

types of safeguards referred to in the definition of "information practices."[61] Physical safeguards include the physical measures, policies, and procedures that a health information custodian follows to protect personal health information in the custodian's custody or control, in addition to related premises and equipment, from natural and environmental hazards and unauthorized access. Administrative safeguards, on the other hand, are the administrative actions, policies, and procedures that a health information custodian takes and follows to protect personal health information in the custodian's custody or control and to manage the custodian's agents in relation to the protection of that information. Technical safeguards are the technology and the policies and procedures for its use that a health information custodian implements and follows to protect electronic records of personal health information and control access to them.[62]

Each category of safeguards should contribute to a health information custodian's overall protection of the integrity, confidentiality, and availability of the personal health information, from threats, both internal and external. For example, consider the following physical, administrative, and technical safeguards that a health information custodian may put in place to protect the personal health information in the custodian's custody or control.

i)   Physical Safeguards
- Control physical access to areas in which records of personal health information are stored by locking doors and controlling access by authorized staff through such means as cipher locks or access cards.
- Store paper records of personal health information in locked filing cabinets.
- Ensure those areas in which records of personal health information are held are protected against destruction and potential damage from physical hazards, such as floods or fires.

---

61   The Act does not define these terms, although the language "physical, technical and administrative safeguards and practices" appears in the definition of the term "information practices" in *PHIPA*, s. 2. This language is similar to the language used in the CSA Privacy Code, above note 23, Principle 7, Safeguards. Principle 4.7.3 of the Code provides: "The methods of protection should include (a) physical measures, for example, locked filing cabinets and restricted access to offices; (b) organizational measures, for example, security clearances and limiting access on a "need-to-know" basis; and (c) technological measures, for example, the use of passwords and encryption."

62   These definitions draw upon the definitions that appear in the Health Insurance Reform: Security Standards; Final Rule, 45 CFR Parts 160, 162, and 164, made under the U.S. *Health Insurance Portability and Accountability Act of 1996*, Pub. L. 104-191, Title II, Subtitle F — Administrative Simplification (42 U.S.C. 1320d).

- Ensure that paper records of personal health information are not left unattended in a public environment and are not in open view of unauthorized persons when being used.
- Position a computer monitor to ensure that electronic records of personal health information cannot be viewed by a passerby, including other patients.
- Ensure that a computer is not left unattended with personal health information displayed on the screen where it may be seen by unauthorized persons.
- Organize facility space to include areas for discussion with patients out of earshot of others.
- Bolt information technology equipment in which personal health information is stored to the floor or a secure fixture.
- Implement practices and procedures governing the removal of records of personal health information and information technology off the custodian's premises.
- Require visitors to sign in upon entering the health information custodian's premises and sign out prior to leaving.
- Escort visitors while on the health information custodian's premises or specific areas of the custodian's premises.
- Follow policies and procedures to dispose of records of personal health information appropriately.
- Ensure personal health information cannot be reconstructed before media on which it was stored is reused or discarded.

ii) Administrative Safeguards
- Develop written policies and procedures governing such matters as responding to a patient's request for access to or correction of the patient's records of personal health information and faxing records of personal health information.
- Follow procedures to refer telephone requests for personal health information to agents trained to respond to such requests.
- Establish policies governing leaving voicemail messages for patients.
- Establish policies governing telephone discussions with patients and others within earshot of others.
- Administer oaths of confidentiality.
- Require security checks and other clearance procedures for agents.
- Require agreements with agents to address the protection of personal health information.
- Ensure employees and other agents are knowledgeable about the custodian's information practices, whether through training or other means.
- Develop policies about making personal health information available on a need-to-know basis.

- Regularly review records of information system activity, such as audit logs, access reports, and security incident tracking reports.
- Keep track of records accessed or removed from storage through such procedures as signing out files.
- Make the custodian's ongoing commitment to privacy and compliance with *PHIPA* clear to employees and other agents; for example, making policies on consequences of an agent's breach of the health information custodian's information practices unequivocal.
- Implement termination procedures to follow when ending an employee's employment or external user's access privileges (e.g., removal from access lists, turning in of keys, tokens, or cards that permit access).
- Establish procedures to follow in the event of a breach (e.g., internal and external reporting obligations, notifying affected patients).
- Periodically review information access privileges to ensure that they remain appropriate (e.g., subsequent to an employee's transfer to a new position).
- Create contingency plans to respond to system emergencies (e.g., data back-up plan, emergency mode operation plan).

iii)   Technical Safeguards

- Encrypt[63] personal health information and removing identifiers where appropriate.
- Encrypt backup tapes of electronic records of personal health information prior to storage.
- Require unique user identification.
- Use passwords to protect documents and directories.
- Change passwords on a regular basis.
- Implement database management to vary an agent's access to records of personal health information according to the agent's role in the custodian's operations.
- Use passwords in conjunction with screen savers that are activated after a short period of inactivity.
- Use automatic logoff capacity for information technology systems.
- Establish safeguards to protect personal health information transmitted from one place to another, such as by fax or electronic mail (e.g., sending information by electronic mail in an encrypted form).
- Install and maintain up-to-date firewalls.

---

63   The term "encryption" refers to a process that changes information into a meaning-less form through the use of a computational algorithm.

- Protect against viruses and other malicious software.
- Install patches to address software vulnerabilities.
- Create a capacity to audit activity on the health information custodian's information technology and fax systems.

The above list of potential safeguards is not exhaustive. There are many more examples, and the collection of examples will expand as health information custodians, their agents, and the public identify privacy issues and use their creativity to develop ways in which to address them. In identifying privacy issues associated with common practices, a custodian should consider whether there is an opportunity to adopt a different practice that does not give rise to the same privacy issues. In some cases, the custodian may not be able to identify alternative practices that do not result in a significant risk of a different sort, such as a risk to the quality of care that the custodian provides. In other instances, health information custodians may be surprised to discover alternative privacy protective approaches to carrying out everyday tasks. The implementation of safeguards need not be costly. Simple solutions, based on common sense, can have effective results.

b) Safeguards in Practice

It is useful to consider one example of how a health information custodian can address a privacy issue through a combination of safeguards. Arrangements for the provision of health care often occur in locations, such as reception areas, pharmacy counters, and registration desks, where patients, family members, and others are present or close by. In these areas, health information custodians are challenged to develop ways in which to ensure "acoustic privacy," which can be described as the privacy of information communicated orally, often in close proximity to others. To address this challenge, health information custodians may incorporate a blend of safeguards into their operations and facilities. Physical safeguards may include creating alcoves for private discussions and using sound-absorbing materials. Administrative safeguards may include developing and following policies governing the amount and detail of information exchanged orally within earshot of others, the use of private areas for conversations and telephone calls concerning sensitive issues, and giving patients the option to write down the nature of their visit instead of disclosing it orally. Together, the implementation of such safeguards would help enhance the acoustic privacy available to patients at a custodian's facility.

Privacy commissioners in Ontario and other jurisdictions have reported on the need to implement practical and effective safeguards. Consider the following instance, the subject of a report by Alberta's Information and Privacy

Commissioner.[64] A medical clinic that used an electronic medical record system to document patient health information and was the target of a break-in had its computers stolen. The Commissioner found that the clinic had taken reasonable steps to protect the health information. The clinic implemented their electronic medical record with defaults to automatically save health information to the data server and housed the data server in a locked office in a strategically planned location that afforded a higher level of security. The data server that stores all the health information for the clinic was not stolen. The clinic was confident that, because they only saved health information to the server and not on individual computer hard drives, the stolen computers did not contain health information. As a result of the safeguards that the clinic had put into place, this incident did not result in a breach of privacy.

Technical safeguards can also protect personal health information stored on a computer from disclosure where the computer is stolen. In an investigation arising from a stolen computer from a ministry of the government of Ontario, the Office of the Information and Privacy Commissioner's mediator considered whether the information stored on the laptop computer, which was password-protected, turned off, and equipped with the appropriate software, was disclosed. Despite the finding that such safeguards do not guarantee that an unauthorized user can never access the information, in the absence of any evidence to the contrary, the mediator was prepared to conclude that the information was not disclosed.[65]

Another report of Alberta's Information and Privacy Commissioner highlights the importance of administrative safeguards.[66] Two computers containing personal health information were stolen from the offices of a provider of home care services, which was the agent of a regional health authority. The provision of a health information directive by the regional health authority to its agent demonstrated to the Commissioner that the regional health authority reasonably complied with the requirement to maintain administrative safeguards to

---

64 Investigation Report H0283, Family Care Medical Centre (2 October 2003), online: <www.oipc.ab.ca>.

65 Privacy Complaint Report PC-020033-1, Ministry of the Attorney General (3 April 2003), online: <www.ipc.on.ca>. See also Privacy Complaint Report PC-030043-1, Ministry of Labour (23 February 2004), online: <www.ipc.on.ca>; and Privacy Complaint Report PC-030042-1, Ministry of Labour (23 February 2004), online: <www.ipc.on.ca>, where the Office of the Information and Privacy Commissioner reached similar conclusions in the case of a password-protected computer.

66 Investigation Reports H0054 & H0056, HealthWise Home Care Inc. (16 August 2002), online: <www.oipc.ab.ca>.

protect the confidentiality of the health information. However, because of the regional health authority's failure to establish policies and procedures to protect against threats or hazards to the security or integrity of health information, the Commissioner found that its overall administrative safeguards were inadequate. This finding of the Commissioner in Alberta highlights the importance of administrative safeguards to the security of health information.

5) Keeping Safeguards Current

Health information custodians must revisit their safeguards and practices regularly to ensure that they remain appropriate. Technical safeguards, in particular, may become outdated overtime as technology evolves. Health information custodians should keep abreast of developments relating to safeguards to ensure that they continue to comply with *PHIPA*, particularly the requirement to take steps that are reasonable in the circumstances to ensure that personal health information in the custodian's custody or control is protected against theft, loss, and unauthorized use or disclosure.

G. MANAGING AGENTS

1) Custodian's Responsibility for Agents

As discussed in Chapter 2, a health information custodian may employ or retain agents to assist the custodian with its functions. A custodian may permit an agent to collect, use, or disclose personal health information on behalf of the custodian where the custodian itself is authorized to do so.[67] Nevertheless, the custodian retains responsibility for information in the hands of the agent.[68] *PHIPA* prohibits an agent of a health information custodian from collecting, using, disclosing, retaining, or disposing of personal health information on the custodian's behalf unless the custodian permits the agent to do so in accordance with the Act or if the law permits or requires the agent to do so.[69] The custodian is also not permitted to allow the agent to collect, use, disclose, retain, or dispose of personal health information in a manner that is inconsistent with *PHIPA* or any other law.[70]

---

67 *PHIPA*, s. 17(1).
68 *Ibid.*
69 *PHIPA*, s. 17(2). See Chapter 2, Section B(2) for a discussion of "agents."
70 *PHIPA*, s. 17(1)(b).

2) Informing Agents

To fulfil these responsibilities, custodians and agents alike must be certain of the scope of activities in which the custodian authorizes the agent to engage on the custodian's behalf, and how the custodian may restrict and limit the agent's activities. Custodians must be clear in communications to agents to ensure that they comprehend their obligations in handling personal health information on the custodian's behalf. For example, a custodian should provide clear instructions so that agents understand when agents should obtain a patient's express consent for the custodian's disclosure of personal health information, as opposed to relying on implied consent. A custodian should also be sure that every agent is aware of the obligation to notify the custodian if personal health information that the agent handles on the custodian's behalf is lost, stolen, or accessed by unauthorized persons, in addition to the manner in which the agent must fulfil that obligation.[71] Each agent requires direction on what role that agent is permitted and expected to take with respect to all the custodian's information practices. Agents should also know how the agent may engage further agents to assist with a task involving personal health information in a manner that permits the custodian to fulfil its ongoing responsibility under *PHIPA*. The custodian need not give an agent specific direction on each collection, use, and disclosure of personal health information throughout the course of every work day, as long as sufficient general direction has been provided. Through the custodian's direction, agents must understand what they must do, what they must not do, and when they should ask for guidance.

In order to create a culture of privacy compliance, which is essential if a custodian operating a health care operation is to be able to ensure ongoing compliance with *PHIPA*, a health information custodian must communicate its expectations clearly to its agents. A custodian's messages and actions about the importance of privacy protection and maintaining the confidentiality of information must be reflected in the custodian's day-to-day operations. Once they understand the importance of their role in promoting and maintaining informational privacy, agents are more likely to conduct themselves in a manner that is consistent with the specific directions of the custodian.

There are several ways in which a custodian can achieve this goal. A custodian's contact person can play an important role in establishing a culture of privacy compliance. Key functions of the contact person are to facilitate the

---

71   This obligation on the part of an agent to notify a health information custodian arises in *PHIPA*, s. 17(3).

custodian's compliance with *PHIPA* and to ensure that agents of the custodian are appropriately informed of their duties under the Act.[72] The contact person may fulfil these duties by working with the custodian, or the management of the organization in the case of a corporate custodian, to develop the necessary directions that will apply to the agents, and then by informing the agents of the directions of the custodian, and generally of the agents' obligations to comply with the requirements of *PHIPA*. The contact person may inform the agents directly, or by arranging for others, such as managers, supervisors, or external instructors, to assist with this task. The contact person should approach this responsibility in a comprehensive manner to ensure that, regardless of the source of the information, all agents receive information appropriate to their function within the organization. The contact person should target these communications both to those agents who work on the custodian's premises and those who work elsewhere. Health information custodians should ensure that volunteers are informed of their duties, as well.

Likewise, management staff should be included in these communications co-ordinated by the contact person, so that they will understand the obligations of the custodian under the Act, and the role that managers must play in the organization for ensuring the accountability of employees and other agents with respect to their handing of personal health information. Managers play a crucial role, not just in communicating specific expectations and instructions to agents on behalf of the custodian, but also in ensuring that agents comply with directions provided, and in taking corrective action when directions are not followed. According to the Information and Privacy Commissioner, privacy obligations are part of the responsibilities of a director of a corporation. According to the Commissioner,

> [d]irectors should ensure that their knowledge about best privacy practices is current and up-to-date. … [T]here are a variety of approaches that can be taken for educating directors. For example, the board can invite privacy experts to speak at one or more of their meetings; organize a privacy workshop for directors and senior officers of their organizations, or attend one of the many privacy workshops organized by third parties.[73]

---

72   *PHIPA*, ss. 15(3)(a) & (b). Where the custodian is a natural person and does not designate a contact person, the custodian must perform the function of the contact person set out in clause (b), as discussed above in Section B(1). See *PHIPA*, s. 15(4).

73   Information and Privacy Commissioner/Ontario, *Privacy and Boards of Directors: What You Don't Know Can Hurt You* (November 2003) at 13, online: <www.ipc.on.ca>.

To the extent that the directors act as the directing mind of a corporate custodian, directors must be aware of the responsibility of the corporation for the conduct of everyone employed or retained by the corporation, directly or indirectly, for compliance with *PHIPA* with respect to personal health information within the custody or control of the corporation.

This responsibility for informing agents can be accomplished in a variety of ways. The nature of the responsibilities of the agent will help guide the custodian and contact person to determine the most appropriate method. Agents, for example, may be informed of their duties through privacy awareness training, the provision of written materials, such as a manual, and periodic privacy and security reminders. Where the custodian has many agents, the development of standard training sessions and tools, such as sets of frequently asked questions, might be useful. In other settings, the provision of written materials, in conjunction with discussions with the custodian or contact person, could be sufficient to inform an agent of his/her duties under the Act. Training and awareness sessions could be held as part of broader orientation sessions for new employees and other agents, as well as annually or at some other regular interval for existing employees and other agents to reinforce the importance of the privacy of personal health information and to address new concerns. Training should be an ongoing, evolving process that responds to developments in the law and the health information custodian's operations.

3) Agreements

Although not a general obligation under *PHIPA*, another tool that can be used to inform an agent of his or her duties under the Act is a written agreement.[74] The agreement can clearly set out an agent's responsibilities in handling personal health information. This option is particularly appealing where the agent has a relationship with the custodian that is more "remote," such as that of an external consultant or records management service provider. Agreements that address privacy issues are beneficial because they help to ensure that roles are clearly defined and privacy issues are anticipated and addressed. Parties are forced to consider the nature of the information involved in their relationship. Health information custodians may wish to develop such agreements both with respect to relationships that developed after 1 November 2004 when the

---

74   *PHIPA* Regulation, above note 19, s. 6(3)[7] requires an agreement between a health information custodian and a health information network provider, which may be an agent. See Chapter 2, Section B(3)(d)(iii) for a discussion of this requirement.

Act came into force, and relationships established prior to 1 November 2004 where no such agreement is in place.

The Information and Privacy Commissioner has developed guidelines for Ontario's provincial and municipal government institutions that rely on third parties to provide services that require access to personal information.[75] Through the guidelines, the Commissioner strongly advises institutions to consider entering into written agreements with the third parties in such situations. The guidelines outline the contents of such agreements, sometimes referred to as personal information transfer agreements, which include requirements concerning the third party's collection, use, disclosure, retention, security, and disposal of the personal information. The Commissioner advises, for example, that after the personal information has been returned to the government institution, the institution must be assured that the third party cannot reproduce it. The guidelines also provide that the institution must be satisfied that the third party is complying with the applicable information and privacy legislation. To ensure compliance, the Commissioner recommends requiring all third-party staff or sub-contractors who will have access to the personal information to sign an undertaking of confidentiality regarding personal information. Although developed for provincial and municipal government institutions governed by *FIPPA* or *MFIPPA*, it is reasonable to expect the Information and Privacy Commissioner to turn to the above guidelines and recommendations in identifying sound practices for health information custodians.

Health information custodians may consider including additional provisions in such agreements. For example, it would be prudent for a custodian to outline in the agreement the agent's obligation to notify the custodian if personal health information that the agent handles on the custodian's behalf is lost, stolen, or accessed by unauthorized persons, in addition to the manner in which the agent must fulfil that obligation.[76] Further, the health information custodian may wish to include indemnification provisions to address the situation where the third-party agent fails to comply with the agreement; termination clauses that permit the health information custodian to terminate the agreement where the third-party agent fails to comply with the requirements concerning the privacy and security of the information; and an explicit statement that the third party cannot withhold information in the event that the custodian fails to fulfil its obligations under the agreement. Consider, for

---

75 Information and Privacy Commissioner/Ontario, *How to Protect Personal Information in the Custody of a Third Party* (September 1998), online: <www.ipc.on.ca>.

76 This obligation on the part of an agent to notify a health information custodian arises in *PHIPA*, s. 17(3).

example, the Information and Privacy Commissioner's recommendations in her privacy review of the Chatham-Kent IT Transition Pilot Project.[77] The recommendations that resulted from that review included a recommendation that the party subject to the review, Smart Systems for Health,[78] seek to modify the agreement with its records management service provider to include clauses that (1) give Smart Systems for Health the right to audit or have a third-party audit conducted on the service provider's privacy policies and data storage practices as they relate to the storage of Smart Systems for Health backup tapes; and (2) stipulate that the backup tapes must be immediately returned to Smart Systems for Health in the event that the service provider goes bankrupt or is otherwise dissolved as a corporation.

H. ACCURACY OF PERSONAL HEALTH INFORMATION

1) Importance of Accurate Records of Personal Health Information

Accurate records of personal health information are essential to the effective provision of health care. In today's health care system, in which patients often receive care from multiple health care providers, accurate records take on a greater importance. Using and disclosing only accurate information helps minimize the possibility that inappropriate information may be used to make a decision about the individual to whom the information relates. Information may be inaccurate in a variety of ways. Information may be factually inaccurate, out of date, or exclude relevant information.

2) Obligations Concerning Accuracy

a) The Requirement for Accuracy

PHIPA requires a health information custodian using personal health information about a patient to take reasonable steps to ensure that the information is as

---

77   Chatham-Kent Review, above note 40..

78   The Smart Systems for Health Agency is an agency established to provide a secure province-wide information infrastructure for the storage and exchange of health information in the health sector. See *Smart Systems for Health Agency*, O. Reg. 43/02, made under the *Development Corporations Act*, R.S.O. 1990, c. D.10. The Information and Privacy Commissioner, however, prepared the report while the functions of the Agency were still being performed by the Ministry of Health and Long-Term Care, prior to the Agency becoming operational.

accurate, complete, and up-to-date as is necessary for the purposes for which it uses the information.[79] A similar requirement exists for disclosures. A health information custodian that discloses personal health information about a patient must either take reasonable steps to ensure that the information is as accurate, complete, and up-to-date as is necessary for the purposes of the disclosure that are known to the custodian at the time of the disclosure, or clearly set out for the recipient of the disclosure the limitations, if any, on the accuracy, completeness, or up-to-date character of the information.[80]

b) Accuracy Connected to Purposes

These obligations regarding the use and disclosure of personal health information include an important limitation. Through *PHIPA's* inclusion of the phrase "as is necessary for the purposes" of the use or disclosure, the accuracy, completeness, and up-to-date character of the information is tied to the purposes of the use or disclosure. As a result, the personal health information upon which a health information custodian relies need not be accurate or complete in every respect. It may be inaccurate or incomplete in a way that is not significant to the custodian because the custodian is not relying on it for a purpose relevant to the inaccuracy or omission.[81]

c) "Reasonable Steps" to Ensure Accuracy

What would constitute taking "reasonable steps" to ensure the accuracy of the personal health information?[82] To understand this obligation, consider the direction that the Office of the Information and Privacy Commissioner has provided to institutions under *FIPPA* on their obligations to ensure the accuracy of the personal information that they use and disclose.[83] According to the Assistant Commissioner,

---

79 *PHIPA*, s. 11(1).

80 *Ibid.*, s. 11(2). In the context of this provision, the term "recipient" does not refer only to persons who are not health information custodians. A recipient may be a health information custodian.

81 See also *PHIPA*, s. 55(8), which creates a standard of accuracy in the context of requests for correction of records that is consistent with the standard of accuracy described in s. 11(1).

82 See also Section C, above.

83 *FIPPA*, above note 15, s. 30(2) provides: "The head of an institution shall take reasonable steps to ensure that personal information on the records of the institution is not used unless it is accurate and up to date." Therefore, the obligations that *FIPPA* imposes on institutions are stricter, as the accuracy and up-to-date character of information is not tied to the purposes of the institution's use of the information.

The determination of whether reasonable steps have been taken hinges on the meaning of "reasonable". ... *Black's Law Dictionary* defines reasonable as:

> Fair, proper, just, moderate, suitable under the circumstances. Fit and appropriate to the end in view. ... Not immoderate or excessive, being synonymous with rational, honest, equitable, fair, suitable, moderate, tolerable.

Thus, for reasonable steps to have been taken would not have required a standard so high as to necessitate that every possible step be pursued to ensure accuracy.[84]

This statement makes it clear that, in the context of public sector privacy legislation, "reasonable steps" do not include every conceivably possible way in which to confirm the accuracy of information.

In the context of *FIPPA*, the Information and Privacy Commissioner considered a case where the Ministry of Health and Long-Term Care was aware that a physician had been convicted for fraudulently billing for health care services that were not provided.[85] The fraud conviction was sufficient to impose a responsibility on the Ministry to take steps to ensure the accuracy of the records that were found to be fraudulent, and other claims submitted by the physician during the time period covered by the fraud investigation and prosecution. The Commissioner concluded that, in some instances, it is appropriate to rely on the accuracy of information collected indirectly. However, where evidence that raises significant questions about the accuracy of the information is produced after it is collected, it might be necessary in the circumstances to take additional steps to determine the accuracy or inaccuracy of the information. These findings of the Commissioner clarify that, while steps that a health information custodian must take to ensure the accuracy of personal health information will vary from one situation to the next, a custodian must act in light of the available information. Where the circumstances suggest some inaccuracy, a custodian should take steps to verify the accuracy of the information.

d)   Advising of Limits on Accuracy

There will be cases where a health information custodian will be asked to disclose personal health information in its custody or control that is not accurate or complete for the purpose for which the recipient of the disclosure seeks the

---

84   Investigation Report I94-012M (27 September 1994), online: <www.ipc.on.ca>.
85   Interim Order PO-1881-I, Ministry of Health and Long-Term Care (20 March 2001), online: <www.ipc.on.ca>.

information. A patient may expressly instruct[86] a custodian to withhold information from a disclosure of personal health information where the information is reasonably necessary for the provision of health care to the patient. At other times, the custodian may not even be aware of the purposes for which the recipient seeks the information. In either case, the custodian will need to communicate the limitations on the information to the recipient. Such communications should be unambiguous.

In the former case, where the custodian is withholding information reasonably required for the provision of health care from a health information custodian at the express request of the patient, the custodian must notify the custodian to whom information is disclosed of that fact.[87] Simply, the custodian must indicate that, in addition to the personal health information that the custodian is disclosing, the custodian, pursuant to the express instruction of the patient, is not disclosing other information that is reasonably necessary for the provision of health care to the patient. In providing this mandatory notice, the custodian should be cautious not to disclose additional personal health information to the receiving custodian.

In the latter case, the custodian must inform the recipient of the information of the limitations on the information's accuracy, completeness, and up-to-date character.[88] The custodian should clearly indicate that the information might not be suitable for the recipient's purposes. For example, the custodian may note: "We cannot provide any assurance that the information enclosed is accurate, complete, or up-to-date for any particular purpose. Please verify this information before relying upon it. We do not assume responsibility for the consequences of any reliance on this information." It would be prudent for custodians to qualify the information that they disclose in this way where the quality of the information is at all questionable, particularly where the custodian is aware that the recipient proposes to use the information for purposes very different from those of the custodian. Again, in providing this information, the custodian should be cautious not to disclose additional personal health information, such as information about the purpose for which the custodian collected the information or the source of the information.

---

86   *PHIPA* provides patients with the right to do so pursuant to ss. 20(2), 38(1)(a), and 50(1)(e). See Chapter 5, Section F(3)(c); Chapter 7, Section G(1); and Chapter 10, Section B for a discussion of this right.

87   *PHIPA*, s. 20(3).

88   *Ibid.*, s. 11(2)(b).

I.   PLACES WHERE RECORDS ARE RETAINED

1)   Generally

Retaining records in a secure manner includes keeping them somewhere secure. Most often, a health information custodian will keep a record of personal health information at his or her place of business, such as an office, health care facility, or another place in the control of the custodian. Other times, it may be more convenient for both the patient and the custodian for the record to be kept in a place that is not in the control of the custodian. *PHIPA* addresses this issue for custodians.

2)   Records in the Patient's Home

The practice of keeping a record of personal health information in a patient's home is commonplace in the provision of community health care. Community health care often involves providing health care, such as wound management, IV therapy, and mental health support services, in a patient's home. Quite often, a number of health care practitioners record personal health information in a common record developed to ensure continuity of care. *PHIPA* recognizes the practice of keeping a record of personal health information about a patient in the patient's home. It permits a health information custodian to keep a record of personal health information about a patient in the patient's home in any reasonable manner to which the patient consents.[89] The manner in which the custodian keeps the record could, for example, involve keeping the record in an envelope out of immediate sight. However, this practice would be subject to any restrictions set out in any applicable regulation, bylaw, or published guideline under the *Regulated Health Professions Act, 1991*, an Act referred to in Schedule 1 of that Act, that is, the Health Professions Procedural Code, the *Drugless Practitioners Act*, or the *Social Work and Social Service Work Act, 1998*.[90]

3)   Records in Other Places

Just as, sometimes, it may be appropriate for a health information custodian to store records of personal health information in a patient's home, sometimes there are also sound reasons to store records of personal health information in

---

89   *PHIPA*, s. 14(1).

90   *Ibid.* See *Regulated Health Professions Act, 1991*, S.O. 1991, c. 18; *Drugless Practitioners Act*, R.S.O. 1990, c. D.18; and *Social Work and Social Service Work Act, 1998*, S.O. 1998, c. 31.

a place that is under the control of neither the patient nor the health information custodian. Under *PHIPA*, a health care practitioner may keep a record in another place where the following conditions are met:

a)   the record is kept in a reasonable manner;
b)   the patient to whom the record relates consents;
c)   the health care practitioner is permitted to keep the record in the place in accordance with a regulation, bylaw, or published guideline under the *Regulated Health Professions Act, 1991*, a health profession-specific Act referred to in Schedule 1 of that Act, the *Drugless Practitioners Act, or the Social Work and Social Service Work Act, 1998*, if the health care practitioner is a regulated health professional, such as a physician, nurse, dentist, or a registered drugless practitioner, such as a naturopath, registered social worker, or registered social service worker; and
d)   any conditions set out in the regulations are satisfied.[91]

During the public hearings concerning Bill 31, the Ontario Dental Association recommended to the Standing Committee on General Government that the Act permit dentists to use other locations, such as nursing stations and other designated centres, to store records where the dentist provides care in a setting different from the common dental office. The Association noted that this situation arises in many northern and remote communities. It argued that, because dentistry often is provided by individual practitioners on a *locum* basis in such communities, it is essential that patient records be housed in a centralized location for continuity of care by subsequent providers. According to the Association, that approach is preferable to having health information custodians remove the records to their office location for filing and safekeeping.[92]

The College of Nurses of Ontario also recognises that its members sometimes practise their profession in situations that are not conducive to traditional record storage practices. Accordingly, when more than one agency is involved in providing care in the community, for example, the College recommends that all care providers document in one health record, and that the issue of who and how the record will be retained be decided before care is provided.[93]

---

91   *PHIPA*, s. 14(2). At time of writing, no regulations have been made under this clause.
92   Ontario, Legislative Assembly, Standing Committee on General Government, *Official Report of Debates (Hansard)*, G002 (28 January 2004) at 1150 (Dr. Blake Clemes).
93   College of Nurses of Ontario, *Practices Standards: Documentation* (Toronto, Ont.: College of Nurses of Ontario, 2004) at 15, online: <www.cno.org/docs/prac/41001_documentation.pdf>.

The College of Psychologists of Ontario also takes the position that its members, when practising in an interdisciplinary setting, may use a common filing system. However, a psychologist must use appropriate care when placing records in a common file in order to ensure that his or her reports and recommendations are not misunderstood by other health care practitioners and do not include information that might, if misunderstood, be harmful.[94]

What would constitute keeping the record in "a reasonable manner"? In determining whether the manner in which a record is kept is reasonable, a health information custodian should consider such factors as the environment in which it is kept, risks to the records that have come to the custodian's attention, the nature of access to the record that the custodian requires, alternative ways in which to keep the record, and who may or should be privy to the record. For example, a high-traffic environment would make keeping the record stored in a place out of the way especially important. Similarly, where a health information custodian, and perhaps other health care practitioners, must refer to the record several times a day, it must remain accessible.

J.   RETENTION OF RECORDS OF PERSONAL HEALTH INFORMATION

1)   Requirement

A health information custodian must ensure that the records of personal health information that it has in its custody or control are retained in a secure manner and in accordance with any requirements identified in the regulations made under *PHIPA* .[95] The Act does not require a health information custodian to retain records of personal health information for a specified period of time. Obligations regarding the retention of records are found in other statutes, regulations, and policies. Generally, these obligations continue to apply, in the absence of conflicting provisions in *PHIPA* or the regulations.[96]

---

94   College of Psychologists of Ontario, *The Regulations, Standards of Professional Conduct and Guidelines of the College of Psychologists of Ontario* (Toronto: The College of Psychologists of Ontario, 2002) at 2.21, online: <www.cpo.on.ca/BylawRegStdGuide/RSPCG.pdf>.

95   *PHIPA*, s. 13(1).

96   At time of writing, no regulations made under *PHIPA* address record retention periods.

2) Identifying and Establishing Retention Periods

The rules governing the retention of records of personal health information may be specific to a particular type of health care setting or provider. Regulations made under the *Public Hospitals Act*,[97] for example, specify how long hospitals must retain records.[98] Similarly, regulations made under the *Nursing Homes Act*[99] require nursing homes to retain records for specified periods of time.[100] Regulations made under legislation that regulates the practice of a health professional, such as regulations made under the *Medicine Act, 1991*,[101] can also include requirements concerning the retention of records.[102] Some bodies that regulate health professionals, such as the College of Chiropractors and the College of Psychologists of Ontario, have issued standards of practice or standards of professional conduct that require their members to retain patient health records for specified periods of time.[103] Other obligations regarding the retention of records are specific to a particular category of records. The regulations made under the *Drug and Pharmacies Regulation Act*,[104] for instance, provide that a manager of a pharmacy must retain prescriptions that the regulations require for a period of at least six years.[105] Federal guidelines governing clinical trials require that research records be retained for a minimum of twenty-five years.[106] Custodians may be required to retain records for a specified period of time pursuant to a funding agreement with the Ministry of Health and Long-Term Care. A health information custodian must continue to comply with such requirements.

Where a health information custodian or the record is not subject to any specific records retention requirements, the custodian may follow best practices and retain the record accordingly. For example, a health information custodian may consider requirements applicable to other health care practitioners or facilities. The custodian should also consider the uses to which the record is put to ensure that it will be available when required.

---

97 R.S.O. 1990, c. P.40.
98 *Hospital Management*, R.R.O. 1990, Reg. 965, s. 20 [Reg. 965].
99 R.S.O. 1990, c. N.7.
100 *General*, R.R.O. 1990, Reg. 832, s. 90.
101 S.O. 1991, c. 30.
102 *General*, O. Reg. 114/94, s. 19.
103 See College of Chiropractors of Ontario, Record Keeping Standard of Practice, S-002, amended (30 November 30 2002), online: <www.cco.on.ca/standard_of_practice_s-002.htm>. See also above note 94.
104 R.S.O 1990, c. H.4.
105 *General*, R.R.O. 1990, Reg. 551, s. 66.
106 Part C, Division 5 of the Food and Drug Regulations C.05.012(4).

In establishing retention periods, a health information custodian may consider any medico-legal risk associated with the event to which a record relates. For example, where the record relates to a situation in which litigation has arisen in the past, a health information custodian may adjust the retention period to ensure that the record is available as evidence, if the need should arise.[107] Likewise, where the record relates to the provision of health care to a person under the age of eighteen, a health information custodian should consider retaining the record for a period of time after the person reaches the age of eighteen, even in instances in which the retention of the record for this period of time is not statutorily required. Where a health information custodian is notified of a proceeding or possible proceeding, such as an inquest, professional disciplinary hearing, or civil action, the custodian should retain records relevant to the proceeding until the final disposition of the matter.

Retention policies should recognize that records should not be kept indefinitely. A general principle of privacy is that records of personal information should not be retained longer than necessary to fulfil the identified purposes.[108] A health information custodian should track records in the custodian's custody or control to ensure that they continue to be required and have not attained their retention period. This exercise may prompt some health information custodians to revisit their current retention periods, especially where in some cases the default has been to keep records indefinitely.

3) Allowing for Access

PHIPA includes an overarching obligation with respect to a health information custodian's retention of records of personal health information. Where a patient

---

107 See *Limitations Act, 2002*, S.O. 2002, c. 24, Sch. B. A limitation period is the time period within which a person must commence a court proceeding. The *Limitations Act, 2002* establishes a basic limitation period of two years (s. 4), running from the day a claim is discovered (s. 5). A claim is discovered when the person with the claim is, or ought to be, aware of the material facts. The basic limitation period does not run while the person with the claim is unable to pursue it because of being an unrepresented minor (s. 6) or incapable person (s. 7). The Act also establishes an ultimate limitation period of fifteen years that runs from the day the act or omission on which the claim is based took place (s. 15). The ultimate limitation period does not run during the incapacity of the person with the claim, during the person's minority.

108 See, for example, CSA Privacy Code, above note 23, Principle 4.5.3. Note, *PHIPA* does not restrict the retention of records in this way, except perhaps to the extent suggested by s. 30, which limits a health information custodian's collection, use, and disclosure of personal health information to that which is necessary for the purpose of the collection, use, or disclosure, as the case may be.

has requested that a health information custodian provide access to his or her record of personal health information,[109] the custodian is required to retain the record for as long as necessary to allow the patient to exhaust any recourse that he or she may have under the Act with respect to the request.[110] The time necessary to exhaust any recourse would include the time required to make a complaint to the Information and Privacy Commissioner concerning the denial of access to the record, have the Commissioner investigate the complaint and make an order, and resolve any resulting review of the Commissioner's decision.[111] A health information custodian is guilty of an offence if the custodian disposes of a record of personal health information in the custodian's custody or control in an attempt to evade a request for access that the custodian has received.[112]

K. DISPOSAL

1) Background

The disposal of records of personal health information is an often overlooked aspect of good information practices; so much so that the media has reported on cases of inappropriate disposal of records of personal health information. In 2002, there were reports of a medical clinic leaving thousands of documents for claims for payment from the Ontario Health Insurance Plan in clear plastic garbage bags on a Toronto sidewalk.[113] The documents revealed such

---

109　See Chapter 13 for a discussion of a patient's right to request access to a record of personal health information in the custody or control of a health information custodian.

110　*PHIPA*, s. 13(2). Reg. 965, above note 98, includes a requirement for persons who operate hospitals that appears to be based on a similar policy rationale. Reg. 965, s. 20(7) requires hospitals to retain records past standard retention periods where the hospital has received notice of a court action, or of an investigation, assessment, inspection, inquest, or other inquiry relating to the records.

111　Generally, since *PHIPA*, s. 56(3) requires a patient to make a complaint to the Commissioner concerning a custodian's refusal to provide access no later than six months after the refusal, a custodian may dispose of the record shortly after six months after the refusal if no complaint is made within that time. Retention for one year after the date of the access refusal would be the safest, however, recognizing that there are certain types of possible complaints relating to access that are not covered by s. 56(3), which would therefore fall into the one-year limitation period for filing a complaint with the Commissioner in s. 56(2), (e.g., complaints about time extensions under s. 54(3), or where the custodian has refused to expedite the access request under s. 54(5)). See Chapter 15, Section B(2) for a discussion of the complaints under the Act.

112　*PHIPA*, s. 72(1)(d).

113　Karen Hill, "Personal OHIP records left on Cabbagetown sidewalk," *eye Weekly* (24 January 2002), online: eye <www.eye.net/eye/issue/issue_01.24.02/news/ohip.html>.

information as patient names, health card numbers, and diagnoses. In 2003, there were reports of ultrasound test results ending up on the back of real estate flyers delivered to Toronto homes.[114] Such incidents often arise from the failure to take simple, yet essential, steps to dispose of records properly.

2) Requirements Concerning Disposal

PHIPA requires a health information custodian to ensure that the records of personal health information in its custody or control are disposed of in a secure manner and in accordance with any requirements identified in the regulations made under the Act.[115] In the absence of guidance in the regulations, how can a health information custodian dispose of records in a "secure manner"? Given the volume of records in the hands of health information custodians, such as hospitals, the response to this question is important.

3) Disposal in Practice

Records of personal health information, regardless of the media (e.g., paper, electronic, video), must be disposed of in a manner that prevents subsequent use or reconstruction of the record. In order to determine the way in which to prevent subsequent use or reconstruction of the record, it is important to consider the record's medium. For example, a health information custodian should shred, incinerate, or pulverize paper records of personal health information to prohibit reassembling, and not simply dispose of them in the garbage or recycling bin without being destroyed. Health information custodians may physically destroy videotapes prior to their disposal. Alternatively, images on videotape can be removed by overwriting them with new images, a task most appropriately left to authorized staff on the premises.[116] On the other hand,

---

114   Interview of Ann Cavoukian, Ph.D., Information and Privacy Commissioner/Ontario by Andy Barrie (20 February 2003) on Metro Morning, CBC Radio, Toronto, online: <http://toronto.cbc.ca/regional/servlet/View?filename=to_records20030220>.

115   *PHIPA*, s. 13(1). This requirement is not new to health information custodians. See, for example, O. Reg. 544/94, made under the *Massage Therapy Act, 1991*, S.O. 1991, c. 27, s. 11(6), which provides that a member of the College of Massage Therapists must ensure that any destruction of client health records is done in such a way as to maintain client confidentiality.

116   These guidelines are based on those included in the Information and Privacy Commissioner/Ontario, "Safe and Secure Disposal Procedures for Municipal Institutions," Practices, No. 26 (September 1998), online: <www.ipc.on.ca>. Although developed for a different audience, municipal institutions governed by *MFIPPA*, the tips provide guidance to health information custodians as well.

health information custodians must delete electronic records using the appropriate technology to ensure that the records cannot be reconstructed. Merely erasing files or reformatting computer disks or computer hard drives is insufficient to protect personal health information stored there. Even by taking such steps, files remain accessible to subsequent users with minimal effort. Instead, a health information custodian may use file sanitation procedures, which involves overwriting files repeatedly. This obligation arises even where a health information custodian transfers a hard drive to another department of the custodian's operations, because providing the hard drive with accessible personal health information could result in an unauthorized use of the information.[117]

Consider the following instance, the subject of a report of Alberta's Information and Privacy Commissioner.[118] A transcriptionist worked from her home on her personal computer transcribing physicians' medical notes. When her computer stopped working, she pursued a warranty replacement. She returned the computer to the store from which she purchased it and the store provided her with a new one. Subsequently, the store sold the defective computer to a salvage company, and it was eventually purchased. When the purchaser discovered personal health information on the hard drive, he brought the matter to the attention of the media. How should the physicians have addressed these matters? The Commissioner recommended that the safeguards in place at the physician's office to protect health information should specify the disposition of computer storage components (i.e., hard drives, etc.) or portable media (i.e., tapes, diskettes, etc.) containing health information that requires exchange or disposal through destruction (i.e., physical crushing, etc.), or that the health information be permanently deleted through use of a commercial disk wiping utility. The Alberta Commissioner further recommended that agreements with agents, especially those who handle information off-site, should include specific direction related to the secure storage and disposal of health information during the course of the agreement and at the termination of the agreement.

While the term "disposes" in the definition of "information practices" would include destruction, it also includes alternative means of disposing of records of personal health information, such as by transferring them to an

---

117   For example, an unauthorized use may arise where the agent in the receiving department uses the personal health information stored on the hard drive for an unauthorized purpose.

118   Investigation Report H0252, Family Care Medical Centre (25 June 2003), online: <www.oipc.ab.ca>.

archive that complies with *PHIPA*[119] and the *PHIPA* Regulation[120] and agrees to accept the records. The restrictions and requirements with respect to such record transfers to archives are discussed in Chapter 10.

4) Policies Concerning Disposal

It is not enough for a health information custodian to be familiar with the appropriate manner in which to dispose of records of personal health information. The custodian must actually take the steps to dispose of the records appropriately. In order to ensure that this task is completed thoroughly, policies concerning the disposal of records of personal health information should form part of a custodian's information practices. For some time, boards of public hospitals have had a legal duty to determine the procedure to be followed by the hospital for the destruction of medical records and notes, charts, and other material relating to patient care or photographs of them,[121] and it is appropriate to reduce such procedures to writing to facilitate compliance.

Another report of the Alberta Information and Privacy Commissioner reinforces the importance of such documentation.[122] A television broadcaster reported that physical therapy records had been located in a field in Northeast Edmonton. The records were discovered in garbage that had been torn apart. The clinic indicated that it had a process in place to ensure that records were disposed of properly, which included shredding draft reports. However, clearly, the clinic failed to dispose of the records properly. The Commissioner found that, although the clinic's process for disposing of records was reasonable, the clinic should incorporate the process into a written policy and procedure, and train its staff.

5) Records of Disposal

Prior to disposing of records of personal health information, it is appropriate and, in some instances, legally required, for a health information custodian to create documentation that sets out such information as the names of the patients to whom the records relate and the date and manner of disposal. With such documentation, a custodian is in a better position to demonstrate that a

---

119   *PHIPA*, s. 42(3).
120   *PHIPA* Regulation, above note 19, s. 14.
121   Reg. 965, above note 98, s. 21(1).
122   Investigation Report H2001-IR-009, Lake Beaumaris Physical Therapy Ltd. (24 October 2001), online: <www.oipc.ab.ca>.

record was created for a specific patient but disposed of in a particular manner on a particular date, should those activities be the subject of inquiry. For example, when destroying records of personal health information, administrators of public hospitals in Ontario are required to create and authenticate a written statement that sets out (a) the names of the patients to whom the medical records and notes, charts, and other material relating to patient care or photographs thereof refer; and (b) the date and manner of the destruction and whether or not the destruction was carried out in accordance with the procedures determined by the board.[123] The administrators are then required to retain such statements in accordance with the bylaws of the hospital.

L. DEALING WITH A PRIVACY BREACH

1) Notice of Privacy Breach

Despite a health information custodian's best efforts and intentions, privacy breaches may occur. Agents of a health information custodian have an obligation to bring instances of theft or loss of or access by unauthorized persons to personal health information to the attention of the custodian at the first reasonable opportunity.[124] With this information, the custodian is able to fulfil its own obligations with respect to notifying patients of security breaches. A health information custodian that has custody or control of personal health information about a patient must notify the patient at the first reasonable opportunity if the information is lost, stolen, or accessed by unauthorized persons.[125]

---

123 Reg. 965, above note 98, s. 21(2).
124 *PHIPA*, s. 17(3).
125 *Ibid.*, s. 12(2). This obligation to notify the patient exists independently of the contents of the custodian's written public statement. *PHIPA*, s. 12(3) sets out an exception to this requirement. If the custodian is a researcher who collected the personal health information from another health information custodian under s. 44(1), the researcher must not notify the individual that the information was lost, stolen, or accessed by unauthorized persons unless the health information custodian under that subsection first obtains the individual's consent to having the researcher contact the individual and informs the researcher that the individual has given consent. It is necessary to distinguish unauthorized access from "access by unauthorized persons." The phrase "access by unauthorized persons" arguably does not include access by a person who is authorized to gain access. For example, if, through the use of a password, a physiotherapist has access to the personal health information of all patients on a hospital's electronic patient record system, but should only use the password to access records about patients to whom he or she provides care, he or she is "authorized" to gain

The obligation of a health information custodian to inform a patient of a security breach may also be based on the general obligation of the custodian to notify the patient of deviations from its information practices. Specifically, where a health information custodian uses or discloses personal health information about a patient, without the patient's consent, in a manner that is outside the scope of the custodian's description of its information practices, as set out in the custodian's written public statement, the custodian must inform the patient of the uses and disclosures at the first reasonable opportunity, unless the patient does not have a right of access to a record of the information under *PHIPA*.[126]

Clearly, a health information custodian should take care to notify patients of any privacy breach in a sensitive manner. A custodian has an obligation to inform the patient that the breach occurred, which presumably would include providing certain information about the nature and circumstances of the breach and the information involved in the breach. A custodian may also choose to inform the patient of steps taken to contain the breach; whether the custodian informed the Information and Privacy Commissioner of the breach; the custodian's intended next steps to deal with both the patient's particular circumstances and custodian's practices more generally; and the patient's right to make a complaint to the Commissioner.

2) Dealing with a Privacy Breach

The Office of the Information and Privacy Commissioner has provided institutions under *FIPPA* and *MFIPPA* with guidance on how best to deal with a privacy breach.[127] According to this advice, once an institution learns that a possible privacy breach has occurred, the institution should take immediate action by taking the following steps:

---

access, but access to particular records may be "unauthorized," as in the case where the physiotherapist enters the wrong patient number and briefly views another patient's record. In contrast, a member of the hospital's food services staff who intercepts the nurse's password and gains access to the system would be an "unauthorized person" as well.

126   *PHIPA*, s. 16(2). *PHIPA*, s. 52 describes exceptions to a patient's right of access to a record of personal health information about the patient in the custody or control of a health information custodian. See Chapter 13, Sections C & D for a discussion of the exclusions from and exceptions to the right of access.

127   Staff of the Information and Privacy Commissioner/Ontario, *A Privacy Breach Has Occurred — What Happens Next?* (14 September 2001), online: <www.ipc.on.ca> [*Privacy Breach Has Occurred*].

- Identify the scope of the breach and take steps to contain the damage. For example, these steps may involve retrieving hard copies of information that have been disclosed or inappropriately disposed of; determining whether the privacy breach would allow unauthorized access to an electronic information system; and changing file identification numbers.
- Ensure that appropriate staff is immediately notified of the breach.
- Immediately inform the Information and Privacy Commissioner of the privacy breach.
- Notify individuals whose personal information is the subject of the breach.[128]
- Conduct an internal investigation into the matter, report on the findings, and implement any recommendations expeditiously. The objectives of the internal investigation should include a review of the circumstances surrounding the incident, as well as the adequacy of existing policies and procedures in place to protect information.
- Address the situation on a systemic basis. In some cases, program-wide or institution-wide procedures may warrant review, such as in the case of a misguided fax transmission or inappropriate sharing of information by e-mail. Consider whether policies, procedures, and staff training is adequate.
- Try to resolve a complainant's concerns informally, at the onset of the complaint.

These suggestions may assist a health information custodian develop a strategy to follow in the event of a privacy breach. For example, a custodian's attempt to resolve a complaint could include an apology, and/or a commitment to improve the safeguards in place to protect personal health information. However, in taking these steps, health information custodians must be mindful of any limitations to this commitment. For example, it may not be appro-

---

128 The Office of the Information and Privacy Commissioner has provided health information custodians with some guidance on notifying patients of a privacy incident. See Information and Privacy Commissioner/Ontario, *PHIPA: Mediation and Other Resolutions* (31 January 2005), online: <www.ipc.on.ca>, which describes the approach that two health care facilities took to provide such notice. The Office of the Information and Privacy Commissioner indicates that a custodian may provide notification in writing, by telephone, or in person, depending on the circumstances. In the case of the two facilities, it was appropriate to notify patients of the incident at their next appointment with their health care provider. The Office of the Information and Privacy Commissioner describes the factors that made this method of notification appropriate, which include the fact that it was unlikely that the patients would have been harmed in any way by the disclosure or loss of their information. The Commissioner's office noted that this approach to notification would make the process easier, more effective, and less stressful for the patients involved.

priate for the complainant to be privy to certain reports or the deliberations of the custodian's working groups as systemic change is effected. To facilitate compliance with the strategy, the custodian should designate an agent, such as the custodian's contact person, to take action in the case of a privacy breach.

According to the Office of the Information and Privacy Commissioner, the benefits of adopting such a strategy to address possible privacy breaches include mitigating the damage by immediately preventing further inappropriate disclosures of personal information; and assuring complainants and affected persons as well as the public, the media, and the Commissioner, that the organization takes the matter, and privacy matters in general, seriously.[129] Under section 57(4)(b) of *PHIPA*, the Commissioner has discretion to refuse to review a complaint of a contravention of *PHIPA* until the complainant has addressed the complaint first to the custodian. An effective internal complaints process can also be very useful in dealing with matters in a manner that is more likely to lead to a resolution that does the least damage to a health information custodian's relationship with the person complaining.

3) Learning from a Privacy Breach

It is important for a health information custodian involved in a privacy breach to learn from that experience and take steps to prevent future breaches. In her assessment of a hospital's breach of patient privacy,[130] the Information and Privacy Commissioner suggested the following actions as elements of a reasonable approach to ensuring that the privacy breaches under review do not re-occur:

- Conduct an immediate investigation of the privacy breaches that allegedly occurred, and if necessary, take appropriate disciplinary action against the individuals who are found to have violated any privacy laws or policies.
- Review the institution's corporate policies and practices, including those relating to privacy, to determine if they can be improved.
- Put in place intensive privacy training for both new and existing staff.

As these recommendations reflect, a health information custodian that has been involved in a privacy breach should take a systemic approach in dealing with a privacy breach so as to mitigate the effects of the breach and forestall any opportunities for breaches of a similar nature in the future.

---

129 *Privacy Breach Has Occurred*, above note 127.

130 Information and Privacy Commissioner/Ontario, *Privacy Assessment: The University Health Network's Response to Recent Breaches of Patient Privacy* (30 July 2002), online: <www.ipc.on.ca>.

M. DRAFTING TIPS FOR PUBLIC PRIVACY COMMUNICATIONS

PHIPA includes a number of provisions that require health information custodians to develop communications of various sorts for patients and others. For example, the Act requires custodians to make available to the public a written statement describing matters such as the custodian's information practices.[131] *PHIPA* also permits custodians to rely on a notice of purposes of the custodian's collection, use, or disclosure of personal health information as a means to communicate these purposes to patients.[132] Such communications may be taken not simply as legal requirements, but also as opportunities for custodians to make patients knowledgeable and comfortable with their information practices by making details about such practices available or "open" in a generally understandable manner. Written documents can enhance the transparency of a health information custodian's information practices and they can help patients make decisions about the handling of their personal health information. To enhance transparency, documents must communicate information to patients effectively.

Health information custodians may consider the following drafting tips in developing notices and other "openness" documents under *PHIPA*.

1) Balance Detail with Readability

- Ensure documents fulfil the applicable requirements of *PHIPA* and the regulations.[133]
- Avoid overwhelming patients with details.

---

131 *PHIPA*, s. 16(1).

132 *Ibid.*, s. 18(6). Additional examples of communications can be found in *PHIPA*, ss. 18(2) (notice of purposes), 20(4) (disclosure to representatives of religious organizations), and 38(3) (disclosure of patient's location and status), and in the *PHIPA* Regulation, *General*, O. Reg. 329/04, s. 10(2)[2] (use and disclosure for fundraising purposes). A custodian may develop one document, or one document with multiple layers, to fulfil requirements of more than one provision in the Act. See "10 Things to Make Compliance With *PHIPA* Easier," Appendix 2. The *PHIPA* Regulation also imposes openness requirements on non-health information custodians, which require the provision or making available of specified information. See, for example, *PHIPA* Regulation, ss. 6(3)[2] (health information network providers), 13(3) (functions of a registry), 14(1)(c) (practices of an archive), and 18(2) (functions of a prescribed planning entity).

133 For example, in drafting the written statement for the public, a custodian should ensure that the statement fulfils the requirements of *PHIPA*, s. 16(1). Similarly, in drafting a notice of purposes, a custodian must ensure that it meets the requirements of *PHIPA*, s. 18(6).

- Provide enough information in documents to allow patients to decide whether or not to seek more detailed information.
- Consider layering information in multiple documents, with an increased level of detail in each layer.[134]

2) Keep It Simple

- Remember your audience.
- Avoid technical and sophisticated terminology.

3) Build on Previous Work

- Consider guidance from the Information and Privacy Commissioner.
- Consider the advice of professional governing bodies and associations.
- Build on *PIPEDA*, *FIPPA*, and *MFIPPA* compliance efforts.
- Ensure documents reflect your actual information practices.
- Avoid relying on precedents too heavily.

4) Enhance Presentation

- Recognize the importance of headings and "white space" to readability.
- Consider incorporating text into boxes.
- Consider using bullets and other symbols.
- Vary font size and styles (e.g., bold, italics).

5) Use It

- Post or make documents available in accordance with the requirements of *PHIPA* and the regulations.[135]
- Keep the contents of documents current. As information practices change, documents may require revision.
- Set a date to review the contents of documents.

---

134 See Section E(2) above for a discussion of the "layering" approach to drafting notices and similar documents.

135 For example, a custodian must make its written statement for the public available in accordance with *PHIPA*, s. 16(1). Likewise, a custodian must provide the notice regarding the use and disclosure of personal health information for fundraising purposes in accordance with the *PHIPA* Regulation, s. 10.

5 Consent

A. INTRODUCTION

The *Personal Health Information Protection Act*[1] requires a health information custodian who collects, uses, and discloses personal health information about a patient to obtain the patient's consent to do so, unless the Act permits or requires the collection, use, or disclosure *without* consent.[2]

Generally, before *PHIPA* came into force, health information custodians were comfortable with rules that require them to seek a patient's consent for the disclosure of personal health information. They were also accustomed to considering whether a law allowed them to disclose such information without consent. A variety of legislation applicable to specific categories of health information custodians include rules governing such disclosures.[3] On the other

---

1   S.O. 2004, c. 3, Sch. A. [*PHIPA*].
2   *Ibid.*, s. 29. Circumstances in which the custodian may collect, use, and disclose personal health information without consent are discussed in Chapters, 8, 9, 10, & 11.
3   For example, see the *Mental Health Act*, R.S.O. 1990, c. M.7, s. 35 [*MHA*]; the *Long-Term Care Act, 1994*, S.O. 1994, c. 26, s. 32 [*LTCA*]; *Hospital Management*, R.R.O. 1990, Reg. 965, ss. 22–23.2, made under the *Public Hospitals Act*, R.S.O. 1990, c. P.40 [*PHA*]; s. 95 of *General*, R.R.O. Reg. 832, made under the *Nursing Homes Act*, R.S.O. 1990, c. N.7 [*NHA*]. These statutes and regulations also contained a number of other provisions pertaining to consent to disclosure of patient information prior to 1 November 2004; they were repealed with the coming into force of *PHIPA*.

hand, the duty that *PHIPA* imposes on health information custodians to consider whether they require a patient's consent for the collection or use of personal health information has created, for most custodians, a new legal requirement.

A patient's consent provides sufficient authority for a custodian to collect, use, or disclose personal health information about the patient only where the collection, use, or disclosure is, to the best of the custodian's knowledge, necessary for a lawful purpose.[4]

"Consent" at issue in *PHIPA* is consent that a health information custodian needs with respect to a transaction concerning personal health information, not one that a custodian may need in order to administer *treatment*. Although this distinction may be self-evident, at times the two types of consents are confused.

Consent in *PHIPA* may be "express" or "implied," unless the Act specifically sets out that it must be express.[5] *PHIPA* defines neither the term "express" nor the term "implied." The differences between these two terms are explained further in this chapter, but it is worth noting at the outset what these phrases mean.[6] "Express consent" means a consent that is explicitly provided — either orally or in writing. "Implied consent" means a consent that a custodian concludes from a patient's action or inaction in particular circumstances. The rules governing when a health information custodian requires express consent and when a custodian may rely on an implied consent are explained below.

B. THE ELEMENTS OF CONSENT

PHIPA, Part III addresses what constitutes "consent" under the Act and what type of consent a health information custodian requires in particular circumstances.[7]

Where *PHIPA* or any other Act requires the consent of a patient for the collection, use, or disclosure of personal health information by a health information custodian, the consent must fulfil the requirements of *PHIPA*.[8] For example, if a health information custodian who is a regulated health professional requires the consent of the patient to disclose information about his or her

---

4   *PHIPA*, s. 29. The meaning of what is "necessary for a lawful purpose" and other limiting principles are outlined in Chapter 7.

5   *PHIPA*, s. 18(2).

6   See Section D below.

7   *PHIPA*, ss. 18–20. More specific rules pertaining to consent for fundraising and marketing are addressed in Part IV in ss. 32 & 33 and in *General*, O. Reg. 329/04, s. 10 [*PHIPA Regulation*].

8   *PHIPA*, s. 18(1). See further, Chapter 3, section B(2).

patient to a College within the meaning of the *Regulated Health Professions Act, 1991*[9] [*RHPA* College], that consent must meet the requirements of *PHIPA*.[10]

This general provision concerning the elements of consent does not require a health information custodian to review, as of 1 November 2004, all collections, uses, and disclosures of personal health information made with consent prior to that date and obtain new consents for ongoing collections, uses, and disclosures in all cases. The custodian may rely on the transitional provision in *PHIPA*, which provides that a consent that a patient gave the custodian before 1 November 2004 is a valid consent if it meets the requirements of the Act for consent.[11]

A consent under *PHIPA*, whether implied or express, must:

- be a consent of the individual,
- be knowledgeable,
- relate to the information, and
- not be obtained through deception or coercion.[12]

It is necessary to examine each of these elements in turn.

1) "Consent of the Individual"

The first element of a consent is that it must be "a consent of the individual," that is, a consent that the individual provides.[13] A health information custodian may presume a patient is capable of consenting to the collection, use, or disclosure of the patient's personal health information, unless it would not be reasonable to presume so in the circumstances.[14] However, if the patient is not capable, *PHIPA* provides rules for obtaining consent from someone else on the patient's behalf.[15]

2) "Knowledgeable" Consent

An important element of consent to the collection, use, or disclosure of personal health information is that the consent be "knowledgeable."[16]

---

9   S.O. 1991, c. 18 [*RHPA*].
10 See s. 85.3(4) of the Health Professions Procedural Code [*RHPA* Code] set out in Schedule 2 to the *RHPA*, *ibid*, which provides that the name of a patient who may have been sexually abused may not be disclosed to the College without the patient's consent. See further how this Act interacts with other statutes in Chapter 3, Section B(2).
11 *PHIPA*, s. 18(7).
12 *Ibid.*, s. 18(1).
13 *Ibid.*, s. 18(1)(a).
14 *Ibid.*, s. 21(4).
15 Capacity and substitute decision-making are addressed in Chapter 6.
16 *PHIPA*, s. 18(1)(b).

"Knowledgeable" consent should not be confused with "informed" consent. The criteria in *PHIPA* for consent are modelled on the *Personal Information Protection and Electronic Documents Act*[17] and mark a departure from the treatment model of "informed consent" familiar to health care providers.[18] For a consent to be "informed," the custodian would have been required to provide to the patient details about the foreseeable consequences of the decision to be made. The "informed consent" approach is cumbersome when applied to the sharing of information, especially since it would be quite difficult for the custodian to identify the "reasonably foreseeable consequences" of collections, uses,

---

17   S.C. 2000. c. 5, s. 7 [*PIPEDA*].

18   The *Health Care Consent Act, 1996*, S.O. 1996, c. 2 Sch. A, s. 11(1) [*HCCA*] provides that the following elements are required for consent to treatment:

   1. The consent must relate to the treatment.
   2. The consent must be informed.
   3. The consent must be given voluntarily.
   4. The consent must not be obtained through misrepresentation or fraud.

   For a consent to treatment to be "informed," before giving it, s. 11(2) states that (a) the person must receive the information about the matters set out in s. 11(3) that a reasonable person in the same circumstances would require in order to make a decision about the treatment; and (b) the person must receive responses to his or her requests for additional information about the following:

   1. The nature of the treatment.
   2. The expected benefits of the treatment.
   3. The material risks of the treatment.
   4. The material side effects of the treatment.
   5. Alternative courses of action.
   6. The likely consequences of not having the treatment.

   The elements of consent to treatment as set out in the *HCCA* reflect a body of law that had been developed in the context of medical malpractice suits. In essence, Bill 159, *An Act respecting personal health information and related matters* [*Personal Health Information Privacy Act, 2000*] 1st Sess., 37th Leg., Ontario, 2000 [Bill 159] imported the informed consent to treatment model familiar to health care providers. The use of the informed consent model for the collection, use, and disclosure of personal health information was criticized during the Standing Committee hearings on that Bill. For a review of contentious issues pertaining to Bill 159, see Chapter 1, Section B(5)(b). The rule for consent in Bill 159, as set out in cl. 21(3) included that it must be "informed." It specified that "'informed' means information that a reasonable person may require in the circumstances to make a decision and specified that it may include the identity of the person who will collect, use, or disclose or receive the information; the purpose of the collection, use, or disclosure; the nature and extent of the information to be collected, used, or disclosed; the reasonably foreseeable consequences of giving or withholding consent; and if the information would be used or disclosed outside Ontario, the fact that it would be so used or disclosed and that the confidentiality and privacy protection provided with respect to the information outside Ontario may be different from the protection provided in Ontario.

and disclosures of personal health information.[19] This approach also presupposes that a health information custodian would have direct contact with the patient to whom the information relates in order to discuss with the patient such reasonably foreseeable consequences, which would not always be the case.

On the other hand, "knowledgeable" consent to the collection, use, or disclosure of personal health information does not require the custodian to discuss with the patient the reasonably foreseeable consequences of the patient's decision to withhold or provide consent. *PHIPA* sets out that a consent is "knowledgeable" if it is reasonable in the circumstances for the custodian to believe that the patient knows

- the purposes of the collection, use, or disclosure, as the case may be; and
- that the patient may give or withhold the consent.[20]

Before relying on a patient's consent to a health information custodian's collection, use, or disclosure of personal health information, the health information custodian must decide whether or not it is "reasonable in the circumstances" to believe that the patient knows the purposes of the collection, use, or disclosure, as the case may be, and that the patient can give or withhold the consent.[21] Of course, a health information custodian may provide this information about the purposes and discretion to give or withhold consent orally and make a note of the discussion with the patient in the patient's record for future reference. However, the Act describes how a health information custodian can fulfil this requirement of knowledgeable consent in another way.

The Act provides that, unless it is not reasonable in the circumstances, it is reasonable to believe that a patient knows the purposes of the collection, use, or disclosure of his or her personal health information by a health information custodian if the custodian posts or makes readily available a notice describing the purposes where it is likely to come to the patient's attention, or provides the patient with such a notice.[22] Although not a requirement of the Act, such a notice should also inform the patient that the patient may give or withhold his or her consent. For a patient's consent to be knowledgeable, the patient must

---

19   See Chapter 1, quoting Daphne Jarvis at note 43.

20   *PHIPA*, s. 18(5).

21   *Ibid.*

22   *Ibid.*, s. 18(6). The option of making the notice "readily available" was added to s. 18(6) of the Act after the second reading of Bill 31, *An Act to enact and amend various Acts with respect to the protection of health information*, 1st Sess., 38th Leg., Ontario, 2003, the short title of which was the *Health Information Protection Act, 2003* [Bill 31]. Initially, s. 18(6) only referred to "posting" the notice: Bill 31, first reading, at Sch. A, cl. 18(5) (17 December 2003).

have knowledge of that discretion. According to the Information and Privacy Commissioner, examples of best practices in fulfilling these requirements may include "posting a conspicuous notice or distributing brochures that are readily available to the public describing the purposes of the collection, use and disclosure of personal health information."[23]

Accordingly, in many instances, the health information custodian may rely on a notice which is posted, such as on a wall in the reception area of a custodian's office, or which is made readily available to the patient, such as in a pamphlet, as forming a basis for a reasonable belief that the patient has knowledge of the matters set out in the notice. Whether or not it will be reasonable[24] for a custodian to come to the belief that the patient knows the purposes of the collection, use, or disclosure based on such a notice will depend on the circumstances, including how the custodian conveys information about the purposes to the patient.[25] It may not be reasonable to rely on such a poster or pamphlet if the custodian knows that the patient cannot read or see, for example, and the material is not available to the patient in an accessible format.

The Information and Privacy Commissioner has expressed her concerns about lengthy and complicated notices rife with legal jargon.[26] According to the Commissioner, such documents do not achieve their goal of informing the patient. The Commissioner encourages health information custodians to develop "short notices" to fulfil the requirements of the Act.[27] A health information custodian can keep a notice concise by "layering" its contents. For

---

23 Information and Privacy Commissioner/Ontario, *Frequently Asked Questions: Health Information Protection Act*, (Toronto, 2004) at 13, online: <www.ipc.on.ca>.

24 See discussion of "reasonable" in Chapter 4, Section C.

25 *PHIPA*, s. 18(6).

26 Dr. Ann Cavoukian has stated in "Openness and Transparency: Connecting Citizens and Government" (Notes for Remarks, Management Board Secretariat, Annual Access and Privacy Conference, Toronto, Ontario, 7 October 2004), online: <www.ipc.on.ca>:

> We have all seen notices and consent forms that are long, complicated and legalistic. If someone actually reads such a form, it is less than helpful in understanding what is being agreed to. You will probably agree with me that these kinds of forms are at best annoying, and at worst, of no value. Although in theory they are designed to inform the individual, in reality, they convey little information and are neither open nor transparent.

27 *Ibid*. The Commissioner has further remarked,

> I am committed to ensure that consent forms used by health professionals under *PHIPA* truly provide useful and understandable information to patients. These forms must reflect an open and transparent approach to informing patients. To this end, my office is participating with the Ontario Bar Association on a "short notices" working group. We will be producing a multi-layered notice that is concise, understandable and useful for both health care professionals and the public.

example, a custodian may post a brief notice kept to one page in length and provide more detailed information concerning the uses and disclosures of personal health information mentioned in the notice in other "layers," such as a brochure. In this way, the patient is not overwhelmed with particulars but can obtain full details easily if desired.[28]

A health information custodian is not required to use a notice to fulfil the Act's requirements for knowledgeable consent. In particular, where the Act permits health information custodians to assume the implied consent of patients,[29] a health information custodian can assume the knowledge of the patient in the absence of a notice or other means of communication of the purposes of the collection, use, or disclosure, as the case may be. Given the situations in which a health information custodian may collect, use, and disclose personal health information about a patient without the patient's consent[30] or by assuming the implied consent of the patient, the need to rely on a notice to communicate the purposes of a collection, use, or disclosure of personal health information may not arise very frequently. However, such instances may arise periodically, and the Information and Privacy Commissioner appears to encourage the practice of posting notices as a way to enhance the openness and transparency of health information custodians' information practices, despite the absence of a requirement to this effect in the Act. For this reason, the notice of purposes may become commonplace in health information custodians' premises.[31]

To what extent must a custodian satisfy him- or herself that a patient's consent to a disclosure of personal health information is knowledgeable, where the patient requests disclosure to a third party?[32] In the same way that the Act allows a custodian to presume a patient is capable,[33] so too, the custodian may assume that a patient knows the purpose of the disclosure. A custodian is allowed to assume the validity of a consent,[34] unless it is not reasonable in the circumstances to do so.[35] Where the patient requests a disclosure for his or her

---

28 The required written public statement may serve as notice. This is outlined in Chapter 4, Section E(3).

29 *PHIPA*, s. 20(2), and see further in Section F(3) below.

30 Collections of personal health information without consent are outlined in Chapter 8; uses in Chapter 9; and disclosures in Chapters 10 & 11.

31 As noted in Chapter 4, Section E(3), such a notice may be integrated as part of the custodian's written public statement required under s. 16.

32 As contrasted to a situation where the custodian wishes to disclose personal health information for the custodian's purposes.

33 Capacity is explained in Chapter 6, Section F.

34 *PHIPA*, s. 20(1), discussed further in Section C below.

35 *PHIPA*, ss. 20(1) and 21(4).

own purposes, it would appear to be reasonable to assume that the patient knows what those purposes are. It would not be consistent with the overall policy of the legislation of increasing the autonomy of patients to require custodians to make inquiries of patients to ensure that the patients properly understand the purposes of their requests and directions to the custodian.[36] Further, inquiries on the part of a custodian about the purpose of a disclosure can be regarded as an invasion of a patient's privacy.

3) "Relate to the Information"

A patient's consent must relate to the personal health information that is the subject of a health information custodian's collection, use, or disclosure.[37] This requirement does not mean that the consent must only pertain to the information that has already been compiled about the patient at the time the consent is given. That interpretation is not required by the text of the provision and would lead to an impractical result. Rather, it appears to mean that one cannot rely on a consent for the collection, use, or disclosure of personal health information unless the scope of the consent is broad enough to cover the information that is to be collected, used, or disclosed.

Often where a patient consents to a health information custodian's disclosure of personal health information about a patient to a third party on a regular basis, the custodian may rely on the consent that the patient provided at the time of the first disclosure. However, if the nature of the information that the custodian proposes to disclose changes in a significant way, the custodian should consider whether the consent still "relates to the information" so as to constitute a valid consent. A new consent is not necessarily required each time a health information custodian makes a fresh disclosure to the same recipient for the same purpose. Consider this example: A patient consents to her orthodontist's disclosure of her personal health information on a continuing basis to her insurer to enable the insurer to determine coverage for a series of dental procedures. In such circumstances, the orthodontist would be able to provide information to the insurer on an ongoing basis, as may be necessary, to clarify or expand on the nature of the patient's condition, the need for the treatment, and to confirm continued coverage for the service. A patient need not renew her consent for this purpose upon each visit to the orthodontist.

---

36   Of course, where the capacity of the patient is an issue, the custodian would need to probe the patient's understanding. See Chapter 6, Section F.

37   *PHIPA*, s. 18(1)(a).

PHIPA does not specifically address time limits for the validity of a patient's consent and it does not require that consent be time-limited. However, if a patient's condition changes, for example, where the patient develops a new health condition, such that the nature of the personal health information to which the patient's consent relates changes, a custodian may have to re-examine the terms of the patient's consent and consider whether the consent applies to this type of information. If the terms of the consent are comprehensive, then the health information custodian could generally rely on it to disclose personal health information that is relevant to the purpose or purposes for which the consent was provided.[38] On the other hand, where the scope of a consent is unclear and it is apparent from the circumstances in which the consent was provided that information of a particular sort was not contemplated in the provision of consent, then one could not rely on the consent to collect, use, or disclose that kind of new information.

4) "Deception or Coercion"

Consent must not be obtained by deception or coercion.[39] It must be given freely and voluntarily. A custodian must not mislead the patient into consenting with falsehoods. Based on the prohibition on "coercion" in this provision, it may be argued that "tied consents" are prohibited by *PHIPA*. If so, a custodian cannot in effect force a patient to consent by requiring the consent as a condition for providing a benefit or service that the patient desires, for example, unless the information is reasonably required to provide that benefit or service. For instance, where a pharmacist requires a patient's express consent to the pharmacist's disclosure of the patient's personal health information to a third party for the purpose of marketing goods to the patient as a condition to the pharmacist's dispensing of medication to the patient, the consent would likely be invalid. Also, where a custodian describes the purposes of a disclosure in a way that purposefully leads a patient to misunderstand the purposes of the disclosure, the patient's consent would likely be invalid as contrary to the prohibition on obtaining consent by "deception."

---

38 Of course, whether or not the custodian has the patient's consent, the custodian may not disclose more personal health information than is necessary for the purpose of the disclosure: *PHIPA*, s. 30(2). See further Chapter 7, Section C.

39 *PHIPA*, s. 18(1)(d).

C. ASSUMING THE VALIDITY OF THE CONSENT

PHIPA provides a helpful rule that allows a health information custodian who has obtained a patient's consent to a collection, use, or disclosure of personal health information, or who has received a copy of a document purporting to record the patient's consent, to assume the validity of that consent, unless it is not reasonable to assume so.[40] Consider the application of this rule to the following situation. A patient's lawyer sends the patient's psychologist a letter requesting the disclosure of information from the patient's health record. The letter is accompanied by a statement setting out the patient's consent to release the information to the lawyer, which is signed by the patient. Provided that neither the document nor the circumstances suggest that the consent is invalid or inauthentic in some way, the psychologist may disclose the information to the lawyer without having to personally confirm the patient's consent with the patient. The psychologist may assume that that consent is valid.[41]

Similarly, where a patient gives his or her physiotherapist a signed form requesting that the therapist disclose information to the patient's football coach, the physiotherapist may rely on this document as consent under the provisions of this Act to provide the patient's personal health information to the coach. The therapist does not need to create his or her own form for obtaining consent in this case.

Of course, if a health information custodian has some information that would indicate that he or she should not rely on a document purporting to record a patient's consent, the custodian could not rely on this rule. For example, if a custodian becomes aware that a patient has changed lawyers, or where the custodian believes the patient is not capable of making the decision to authorize disclosure of his or her information, it would not be reasonable to assume the validity of the consent.[42] The assumption applies "unless it is not reasonable" to make the assumption or to continue assuming.

---

40   *PHIPA*, s. 20(1).

41   The psychologist may choose to verify with the patient whether the information should be sent, and *PHIPA* in no way interferes with this.

42   Capacity is further outlined in Chapter 6, Section F.

D. "EXPRESS" AND "IMPLIED" CONSENT

The general rule in *PHIPA* is that consent to the collection, use, or disclosure may be express or implied.[43] The Act sets out when consent must be express: in all other situations, implied consent will suffice.[44]

1) What Is "Express" Consent?

PHIPA does not explain the meaning of "express" consent.[45] The Act does not require express consent to take a specific form.[46] Express consent may be given orally or in writing, but it must be a consent that the patient explicitly or positively states in some manner. For example, a patient may consent by signing a document that includes a statement of consent, by sending a letter setting out the consent, or by filling out a form and checking a box to indicate consent. Alternatively, a patient may consent by way of an oral statement, whether in the presence of the custodian or over the telephone. If consent is provided orally, it is prudent for the custodian to document the conversation as evidence of the consent.

Where a patient communicates an express consent through electronic means, such as electronic mail, the consent would be sufficient to constitute the express consent of the patient provided that the custodian could be reasonably confident that the patient sent the consent.[47] The custodian should keep a

---

43   *PHIPA*, s. 18(2).

44   Unless the Act allows the collection, use, or disclosure of personal health information without consent.

45   *PIPEDA* is similar in this regard. However, the federal Privacy Commissioner has explained the phrase "express consent" in the following way: "the organization presents an opportunity for the individual to express positive agreement to a stated purpose. Unless the individual takes action to 'opt in' to the purpose — in other words, says 'yes' to it — the organization does not assume consent." Fact Sheet "Determining the appropriate form of consent under the Personal Information Protection and Electronic Documents Act," Office of the Privacy Commissioner of Canada [OPC *PIPEDA* Fact Sheet], online: <www.privcom.gc.ca/fs-fi/02_05_d_24_e.asp>.

46   A custodian who wishes to use a specific form to obtain consent to the disclosure of personal health information that relates to the patient may develop one based on the sample consent form that has been made available on the Ministry of Health and Long-Term Care website, online: <www.health.on.ca>. A sample consent form addressing collection, use, and disclosure of personal health information is available in the Ontario Hospital Association's *Hospital Privacy Toolkit: Guide to the Ontario Personal Health Information Protection Act* (Toronto: Ontario Hospital Association, 2004) at 4.1, online: <www.oha.com>.

47   *PHIPA*, s. 20(1) appears to support such an approach.

paper copy of the consent as evidence of the consent. Professional standards of practice and institutional policies may provide custodians with further guidance on the manner and documentation of an express consent.[48]

As of 1 November 2004, Form 14 under the *Mental Health Act*, which was a consent form used in psychiatric facilities by which a patient would authorize the disclosure of his or her clinical record compiled in a psychiatric facility to a person outside of the facility, no longer exists as an approved Ministry of Health and Long-Term Care form, as the section upon which the form was based was repealed.[49] Nevertheless, a psychiatric facility would not be required to seek a new consent from the patient for the disclosure of his or her record of personal health information where a disclosure of such information to a person outside of the facility continues to be needed after 1 November 2004 and a valid, completed Form 14 pertaining to the information that is the subject of the disclosure exists on the patient's record. The psychiatric facility is entitled to rely on the validity of the consent, having regard to the consent provisions in *PHIPA*, unless it would be unreasonable to do so.[50]

2) What Is "Implied" Consent?

Like express consent, *PHIPA* does not provide guidance on the meaning of the term "implied" consent.[51]

In order for a custodian to conclude that a custodian has a patient's implied consent, the actions or inactions of the patient are crucial. A health information custodian may conclude that he or she may imply a patient's consent to the collection, use, or disclosure of personal health information about the patient in a variety of circumstances, each arising from an action or omis-

---

48   For example, the College of Massage Therapists of Ontario's guideline for its members specifies that a signed consent form authorizing the release of the patient's information be placed in the patient's file and that the consent form be dated within the last six months: "Release of Records," *Standards and Regulations: Policy* (7 July 2000), online: <www.cmto.com/regulations/release.htm>.

49   *MHA* above note 3, s. 35(3)(a) & (b) repealed as of 1 November 2004 by *PHIPA*, s. 90(6).

50   *PHIPA*, s. 20(1) and see discussion in Section C above.

51   However, the federal Privacy Commissioner has explained "implied consent" in the context of *PIPEDA*, as follows: "This covers situations where the intended use or disclosure is obvious from the context and the organization can assume with little or no risk that the individual, by providing the personal information, is aware of and consents to the intended use or disclosure. Thus, where circumstances indicate that an individual has certain understanding, knowledge, or acceptance, or certain information has been brought to the attention of an individual, consent might be implied." OPC *PIPEDA* Fact Sheet, above note 45.

sion of the patient. A patient's provision of personal health information to a custodian, for example, may suggest to the custodian that the patient consents to the custodian's collection and use of the information. A custodian may imply the patient's consent to the use of personal health information about the patient for a particular purpose where the patient provides the information to the custodian for that purpose. Similarly, a custodian may imply a patient's consent to the use or disclosure of personal health information about the patient where the patient requests a custodian to carry out an activity that would clearly require the custodian to so use or disclose the information. A patient's failure to interfere with a custodian's use or disclosure of personal health information about the patient, when provided with the opportunity to do so, may also form the basis for a custodian's conclusion that the patient implicitly consents to the use or disclosure.

For instance, where a hospital, through its agent, approaches a patient who is about to be discharged from the hospital to ask whether the patient would like to participate in a patient satisfaction survey and the patient proceeds to answer questions that are posed, the custodian may imply that the patient has given his or her consent to the collection of such information by the hospital for that purpose. The custodian would not have to ask the patient specifically whether he or she agrees to the collection of this information for the purpose of conducting the patient satisfaction survey. The custodian may imply consent from the fact that the patient answers questions about the quality of care and treatment received in the hospital, after being informed of the purpose. Similarly, where a hospital sends a patient a questionnaire after the patient's discharge, and the patient completes the questionnaire and returns it to the hospital, the hospital may imply consent for the collection of that information from the patient. Of course, implied consent, like express consent, must fulfil the requirements of the Act for consent.[52]

E. WITHDRAWAL OF CONSENT AND CONDITIONS ON CONSENT

A fundamental premise in a regime governing the collection, use, and disclosure of personal health information that requires consent is that a patient has the right to say "no," and by doing so, prohibit the action for which consent was sought. Of course, *PHIPA* also sets out specific circumstances in which collections, uses, and disclosures of personal health information may occur

---

52   *PHIPA*, s. 18(1).

without a patient's consent, and in such cases PHIPA generally does not provide the patient with the power to prevent the collection, use, or disclosure of that information.[53] Where, however, the legislation requires consent, and a patient has expressly provided such consent to a custodian or a custodian has implied such consent, the Act enables the patient to withdraw that consent.[54] A patient may withdraw both express consents and implied consents.[55]

1)   Method of Withdrawal

A patient may withdraw a consent at any time by notifying the health information custodian of the withdrawal.[56] *PHIPA* does not require such a notice to be in writing. A prudent custodian should record the exact direction received from a patient and when the withdrawal of consent came to the custodian's attention. Agents should be instructed similarly. A custodian may request that a patient confirm such a withdrawal of consent in writing. Alternatively, the custodian may document that the patient has withdrawn the consent by sending the patient a letter confirming the withdrawal. The Act, however, requires neither custodians nor patients to take such steps. Professional standards of practice or institutional policies may specify further requirements.

2)   Withdrawal Not Retroactive

PHIPA specifies that a "withdrawal of the consent shall not have retroactive effect."[57] For example, where a custodian discloses personal health information on

---

53   *PHIPA*, s. 29(b), which permits collection, use, or disclosure of personal health information without consent. In specific situations, the patient may prevent collection, use, and disclosure of personal health information for health care purposes. These are further discussed in Chapters 7 through 11.

54   *PHIPA*, s. 19(1). A substitute decision-maker may also withdraw the consent on behalf of the patient, even when it was the patient who gave the initial consent. Similarly, a patient who is capable can withdraw the consent that was originally given to the custodian on his or her behalf by a substitute decision-maker. See further discussion about the authority of a substitute decision-maker in Chapter 6, Section D.

55   The Act does not specifically require a custodian to explain to a patient the consequences of a withdrawal of consent. It should be noted that a determination of an individual's capacity includes determining whether the individual is able to appreciate the consequences of a withdrawal of consent. Where the patient's decision would result in preventing or impeding health care that is being provided to the patient, it would appear that the custodian would have some obligation to discuss the consequences of the withdrawal of the consent for the information. Not all withdrawals of consent, however, would give rise to a discussion of consequences.

56   *PHIPA*, s. 19(1).

57   *Ibid.*, s. 19(2).

the basis of a patient's consent, the patient's withdrawal of the consent does not require the custodian to retrieve the information that the custodian has already disclosed pursuant to the consent — it only means the custodian must stop disclosing the information as soon as the custodian receives notice of the withdrawal. Similarly, a withdrawal of consent can only apply to new collections of personal health information and future uses of it for the purpose for which the consent was initially obtained; it cannot apply to a health information custodian's collection or use of personal health information that has already occurred before the consent was withdrawn. It should also be noted that a withdrawal of consent to collect, use, or disclose personal health information does not affect the future uses and disclosures of that personal health information that the health information custodian is permitted to make without the patient's consent under *PHIPA*.

3) A Patient's Condition on Consent

A patient is not permitted to place a condition on his or her consent that "purports to prohibit or restrict any recording of personal health information by a health information custodian that is required by law or by established standards of professional practice or institutional practice."[58]

Therefore, for instance, an in-patient of a public hospital cannot restrict an agent of the hospital from recording a provisional diagnosis with respect to the patient in the patient's record of personal health information, as the regulations made under the *Public Hospitals Act* require hospitals to include such information in the record of an in-patient.[59] Similarly, a patient of an optometrist cannot prohibit the optometrist from recording the patient's health history in his or her record of personal health information, as the regulations made under the *Optometry Act, 1991* require the inclusion of such information in the record.[60] A patient at an independent health facility cannot prohibit the licensee of the facility from including in a patient's record of personal health information a written record of an order for an examination, test, consultation, or treatment, as the regulations made under the *Independent Health Facilities Act* require licensees to include such information in the record.[61]

However, should the patient place other kinds of conditions on the consent, the condition would generally be an effective limitation on the consent. Such con-

---

58   *Ibid.*, s. 19(2).
59   Section 19(4)(f) of Reg. 965, above note 3.
60   *General*, O. Reg. 119/94, s. 10(2)[4], made under the *Optometry Act, 1991*, S.O. 1991, c. 35.
61   *General*, O. Reg. 57/92, s. 10(2), made under the *Independent Health Facilities Act*, R.S.O. 1990, c. I.3.

ditions could include a time limit on the consent, or a restriction as to the types of uses or disclosures of the personal health information that a health information custodian could carry out pursuant to the consent. A health information custodian, however, need not act in accordance with such conditions where the custodian may collect, use, or disclose the personal health information without consent.

F. RULES FOR EXPRESS AND IMPLIED CONSENT

1) Generally

PHIPA requires consent for a health information custodian's collection and use of personal health information, unless the Act allows the collection or use without consent.[62] A health information custodian may collect and use personal health information about a patient, for most purposes, based on a patient's implied consent, if the requirements for such consent are fulfilled.[63] *PHIPA* provides further that, as a general rule, health information custodians may rely on a patient's implied consent for disclosures of personal health information as between themselves, if the requirements for such consent are fulfilled, provided that the information is being disclosed for the purpose of providing health care or assisting in the provision of health care.[64] There is no need for the patient to sign a consent form or otherwise expressly authorize a collection, use, or disclosure of personal health information by and between custodians for such a purpose.

However, as a general rule, disclosures of personal health information about a patient to other health information custodians for purposes other than the provision of health care or assisting in the provision of health care, and disclosures of personal health information for *any* purpose by a health information custodian to a person who is not a health information custodian, require the patient's express consent, unless the disclosure is specifically allowed with implied consent or without consent in *PHIPA*.[65]

---

62   *PHIPA*, s. 29.
63   *PHIPA* requires a health information custodian to obtain a patient's express consent where the collection or use of personal health information is for marketing purposes or for market research (s. 33) or for fundraising purposes where the information consists of more than the patient's name and the prescribed types of contact information (s. 32(1)). See Sections F(7) and (10) below.
64   *PHIPA*, s. 18(3).
65   A custodian may rely on an implied consent to disclose personal health information for fundraising and to religious organizations, for example, where certain conditions have been met. A pharmacy may rely on a patient's implied consent to disclose personal health information to a patient's insurer. These disclosures are discussed fur-

2) Implied Consent: Between Health Information Custodians for Health Care

A fundamental purpose of *PHIPA* is the establishment of rules "for the collection, use and disclosure of personal health information about patients that protect the confidentiality of that information and the privacy of patients with respect to that information, while facilitating the effective provision of health care."[66] *PHIPA* recognizes that, while patients are entitled to control information flow about them in the context of health care, they also want to minimize unnecessary impediments to the exchange of information necessary to obtain optimum care.

Every health information custodian may disclose personal health information about a patient to another custodian and that other custodian can collect and use the information received from the disclosing custodian on the basis of the patient's implied consent, if the purpose of the collection, use, or disclosure of personal health information is to provide health care or assist in providing health care.[67] A patient's implied consent authorizes exchanges of personal health information for health care purposes, for example, as between a psychologist and speech language pathologist; a dentist and an orthodontist; a family physician and a specialist; a hospital and a home for the aged; a social worker and a community care access centre; a medical officer of health and a laboratory; an ambulance and a psychiatric facility; the Ministry of Health and Long-Term Care and a pharmacy.

Like the definition of "health care," the phrase "for the purpose of providing health care" includes a broad range of activities.[68] The meaning of the phrase "assisting in providing health care" is somewhat less certain, though it clearly expands the scope of the activities that the phrase includes.

PHIPA does not require a health information custodian to rely on a patient's implied consent as authority for the custodian's collection, use, or disclosure of the patient's personal health information. If a custodian's practice is to request an express consent from patients for the purpose of forwarding personal health information to another health care practitioner for the provision of health care, there is no requirement in the legislation that the custodian stop

---

ther in Sections F(7), (8) & (9) below. Collections, uses, and disclosures without consent are addressed in Chapters 8 through 11.

66   *PHIPA*, s. 1(a).
67   *Ibid.*, s. 18(3).
68   *Ibid.*, s. 18(3)(b). Recall the definition of "health care" in s. 2, discussed in Chapter 2, Section B(b)(ii).

this practice. Such a practice, however, may in some situations be unwieldy and cause impediments to timely delivery of health care. The rule in *PHIPA* provides custodians with more flexibility to provide personal health information necessary for health care purposes promptly.

3) Consent and Health Care: The Assumed Implied Consent Rule for Some Health Information Custodians

a)   Generally

PHIPA provides that certain health information custodians who receive personal health information from other custodians, or from the patient or the patient's substitute decision-maker, as the case may be, are "entitled to assume" that they have implied consent for the collection, use, or disclosure of the patient's personal health information for the purpose of providing health care or assisting in the provision of health care to the patient.[69] Such a health information custodian who receives personal health information for such a purpose is entitled to make this assumption, however, only if the custodian is not aware that the patient has expressly withheld or withdrawn his or her consent.[70]

This entitlement to assume implied consent means that these health information custodians are not required to determine, in the course of providing or assisting in providing health care to a patient, whether or not the patient knows the purpose of the collection, use, or disclosure of the patient's personal health information and that the patient may give or withhold consent.

Consider this scenario. Anna has kidney failure and goes to the emergency department of her local hospital. The emergency physician arranges a consultation with a nephrologist. Anna's condition is stabilized in the hospital and, in time, Anna is discharged home. Anna knows that she will continue to need dialysis. The hospital's discharge co-ordinator contacts the community care access corporation in Anna's neighbourhood and it arranges for home dialysis.

Once discharged, Anna's family physician monitors her condition and communicates regularly with the nephrologist. The family physician regularly takes blood and urine samples and sends them to the laboratory for analysis. The laboratory receives the samples with the requisition forms from the physician and sends the results of the analyses back to the physician. After a telephone consultation with the nephrologist, the family physician discusses with Anna that her medication will need to be adjusted and then calls the pharma-

---

69   *PHIPA*, s. 20(2).
70   *Ibid.*

cy to order the medication. The pharmacy delivers the new medication to Anna's home. The community care access centre also arranges for a nurse to visit Anna regularly. The nurse keeps the family physician up-to-date on Anna's progress. The centre has also arranged for a homemaker to help Anna with her activities of daily living. The homemaker reports to the community care access corporation about the services that the homemaker has provided.

In this complex but not atypical health care situation, information is continuously and routinely required by various health information custodians to enable them to provide the best care possible to Anna.[71] In *PHIPA*, all of these custodians are entitled to assume that they have Anna's implied consent to collect personal health information from one another, use the personal health information, and disclose personal health information to one another, as long as they carry out these activities to provide health care to Anna.

b) Custodians That Can Rely on the Assumed Implied Consent Rule

The assumed implied consent rule applies only to specific categories of health information custodians as set out in *PHIPA*.[72] Generally, these are the health information custodians for which the direct provision of health care is a core business. The following types of custodians are entitled to assume an implied consent for the collection, use, or disclosure of personal health information for the purposes of providing health care or assisting in the provision of health care: health care practitioners,[73] laboratories, specimen collection centres, ambulances, pharmacies, long-term care facilities' placement co-ordinators, community care access corporations, service providers as defined in the *Long-Term Care Act, 1994*,[74] homes for special care, community health and mental health centres, programs or services, public and private hospitals, independent

---

71   The health information custodians in this scenario would need to obtain Anna's consent to the proposed health care. The personal health information that these health information custodians collect, use, or disclose is information that is necessary and ancillary to the health care proposed for Anna and, in effect, implicitly flows to support the care to which Anna has given her consent.

72   The categories of health information custodian that are entitled to assume an implied consent for the purpose of providing health care or assisting in the provision of health care are set out specifically in *PHIPA*, s. 20(2). They are those custodians described in para. 1, 2, 3, or 4 of the definition of "health information custodian" described in s. 3(1) of *PHIPA*. These same categories are referred to in *PHIPA* in ss. 20(3) and 38(1)(a).

73   Recall that "health care practitioner" is specifically defined in the Act in s. 2. The category includes all regulated health professionals, social workers, and social service workers who provide health care, and non-regulated health professionals whose primary purpose is to provide health care for payment. This category is discussed in Chapter 2, Section B.

74   Above note 3.

health facilities, and psychiatric facilities.[75] These custodians are entitled to assume the patient's implied consent for the collection, use, or disclosure of the patient's personal health information for the purposes of providing health care or assisting in the provision of health care to the patient when they receive personal health information from any health information custodian, or from the patient or the patient's substitute decision-maker. These custodians may assume a patient's implied consent to the *disclosure* of personal health information to *any* health information custodian for such health care purposes.

Those custodians who are not listed in section 20(2) are not entitled to assume a patient's implied consent. The custodians who are not listed in section 20(2) are the Minister of Health and Long-Term Care (together with the Ministry); an evaluator under the *Health Care Consent Act, 1996;*[76] or an assessor under the *Substitute Decisions Act, 1992;*[77] a medical officer of health or a board of health;[78] and any other person that is prescribed as a custodian by way of a regulation, unless the regulation specifies otherwise.[79] However, while these custodians cannot *assume* a patient's implied consent to collect, use, or disclose personal health information, they are permitted to rely on an implied consent where the elements of implied consent can be established in the circumstances.

Just as there is no time limit set out generally for the validity of a consent in *PHIPA*, there is also no time limit or time frame set out in section 20(2). A hospital may rely on this entitlement to assume implied consent, as set out in section 20(2), in order to disclose the patient's personal health information even after the patient's discharge; for example, to a community care access corporation if the corporation requires information about the patient's hospital stay to develop an appropriate plan of service for this patient in the community.

---

75   See Chapter 2 for an explanation of what is referred to by each of these types of custodians in Section B. "Long-term care facilities" includes each type of home listed in *PHIPA*, s. 3(1)4[ii].

76   Above note 18. The term "evaluator" is further explained in Chapter 2, Section B(1).

77   S.O. 1992, c. 30 [*SDA*]. The term "assessor" is further explained in Chapter 2, Section B(1).

78   See explanation of these terms in Chapter 2, Section B(1).

79   *PHIPA*, s. 73(1)(f) allows the Lieutenant Governor in Council (that is, in effect, provincial Cabinet) to make regulations "making any provision of this Act or its regulations, that applies to some but not all health information custodians, applicable to a prescribed person mentioned in paragraph 8 of the definition of 'health information custodian' in subsection 3(1) or a member of a prescribed class of persons mentioned in that paragraph." For example, the *PHIPA* Regulation adds to the s. 20(2) list of health information custodians the Ministry of Health and Long Term Care public health laboratories, each laboratory as a separate custodian: *PHIPA* Regulation, above note 7, s. 3(3).

c) Circumstances in Which the Assumption of Implied Consent Cannot Be Made

As indicated above, this permission to assume consent in these circumstances is not unconditional. Where a health information custodian that is listed in section 20(2), receives personal health information about a patient, from the patient, the patient's substitute decision-maker, or another health information custodian, and is aware that the patient has expressly withdrawn or withheld the consent for the collection, use, or disclosure of the information for the purpose of providing health or assisting in the provision of health care,[80] the health information custodian is no longer entitled to assume implied consent.[81] In this situation, the custodian must either obtain the patient's express consent for the continued use of the information for the provision of health care or stop using the information. A patient may choose to expressly withhold or withdraw the consent from only some collections, uses, or disclosures of personal health information pertaining to the provision of health care. In such cases, the patient's implied consent can be assumed only with respect to those collections, uses, or disclosures for which the patient did not withhold or withdraw consent.[82]

"Express" withholding or withdrawal of consent refers either to an oral or written communication by a patient explicitly withdrawing consent for the collection, use, or disclosure of personal health information for the provision of health care or assisting in the provision of health care. The custodian must be "aware" of the patient's express withholding or withdrawal of consent. If the custodian did not personally receive the communication, there would need to be some clear evidence of it in order for the custodian to reasonably rely on it.

i) Notice of Omitted Information

If a health information custodian discloses personal health information about the patient to another custodian for the purpose of providing or assisting in providing health care, on the basis of an *assumed* implied consent, and the disclosing custodian does not have the consent of the patient to disclose all the personal health information that the disclosing custodian considers reasonably necessary for that purpose, the disclosing custodian is required to notify the

---

80　The patient's substitute decision-maker may withdraw the consent on the patient's behalf. See the discussion about substitute decision-making in Chapter 6, Section D(2).

81　This express withdrawal or withholding of consent is sometimes referred to as the "lock box," which is not a defined term in *PHIPA*. This concept is further explained in Chapter 7, Section G.

82　This follows from *PHIPA* s. 20(2) and is evident from s. 20(3).

83　*PHIPA*, s. 20(3). Such a notification would need to be provided to any health information custodian, not just to those categories of custodians listed in *PHIPA*, s. 3(1), paras. 1, 2, 3, or 4.

receiving custodian of that fact.[83] *PHIPA* does not describe this notification in any detail. A note on the document being forwarded to the receiving custodian could stipulate that certain information about the patient that in the opinion of the disclosing custodian is reasonably necessary for health care purposes is missing from the record. The receiving custodian, having been put on notice, can take up the challenge of building a relationship of trust with the patient so that, in time, the patient may be confident in sharing with that custodian the missing information. Alternatively, the receiving custodian may collect that information as the custodian assesses the patient's condition.

4) "Circle of Care"

The selected categories of health information custodians[84] discussed above in the context of the assumed implied consent rule is sometimes referred to as being the "circle of care." "Health providers in the patient's circle of care will be able to share information and work as a team to make the best possible care decisions for that patient," the Minister of Health and Long-Term Care stated during second reading debates on *PHIPA*.[85] The phrase "circle of care" does not, however, appear in *PHIPA*.

The concept of the "circle of care" first emerged in the health information privacy context in guidelines on *PIPEDA* that Industry Canada developed for the health sector. In the questions and answers set out in the *PIPEDA* Awareness Raising Tools (PART) Initiatives for the Health Sector, the expression "circle of care" is explained as including "the individuals and activities related to the care and treatment of a patient."[86] Thus, it covers the health care providers who deliver care and services for the primary therapeutic benefit of the patient and it covers related activities such as laboratory work and professional or case consultation with other health care providers.

Use of the "circle of care" concept is unclear in the context of *PHIPA* since health information custodians and others use this phrase to mean different things, for example: It is often used as a convenient way to describe the categories of health information custodians listed in paragraphs 1 through 4 of the definition of a health information custodian in section 3(1) of the Act, which

---

84   That is, those listed in *PHIPA*, s. 20(2); see Section 3(b), above.

85   Ontario, Legislative Assembly, *Official Report of Debates (Hansard)*, 1121 (30 March 2004) at 1845 (Hon. George Smitherman).

86   Industry Canada, *PIPEDA Awareness Raising Tools (PARTs) Initiatives for the Health Sector, Questions and Answers*, see question 12, online: <http://e-com.ic.gc.ca/epic/ internet/inecic-ceac.nsf/en/h_gv00207e.html>.

have special status under provisions such as the assumed implied consent provision,[87] and under the provision allowing disclosures without consent for necessary health care where timely consent cannot be obtained.[88]

Further, the phrase "circle of care" is sometimes used more broadly, in the
context of *PHIPA*, as described by the Ministry of Health and Long-Term Care:

> The phrase "circle of care" may sometimes be used in connection with the
> term "health information custodians" more generally and in the policy reflect-
> ed in section 18(3) of *PHIPA*. Subsection 18(3) of *PHIPA* provides when con-
> sent cannot be implied, but must be express. Since the disclosure of personal
> health information for purposes other than the provision of health care is the
> focus of section 18(3), the phrase "circle of care" is sometimes used in refer-
> ence to health information custodians more generally, as the parties involved
> in providing or in assisting in the providing of health care.[89]

"Circle of care" may also refer to the custodians involved in providing
health care or assisting in providing health care to a particular patient, while
they are so engaged.

Such uses of the term "circle of care" are not inappropriate, but since the
term is not a defined term under *PHIPA* it lends itself to ambiguity and inaccurate communication of the meaning of the Act. The term tends to take on a
life of its own, one that does not necessarily correspond with what is actually
set out in the Act. For clarity, it is preferable to use the terms set out in the Act.

5) Express Consent: Health Information Custodian to Other Custodian for Non-Health Care Purposes

Exchanges of personal health information about a patient between health
information custodians that are not for the purpose of providing health care or
assisting in providing health care require the patient's express consent.[90] Circumstances requiring a patient's express consent for the disclosure of personal health information between custodians may be somewhat infrequent, given
the permissibility of relying on implied consent for disclosures of personal

---

87   *PHIPA*, s. 20(2).
88   *Ibid.*, s. 38(1)(a).
89   *Personal Health Information Protection Act, 2004: Overview for Health Information Custo-
      dians* (Toronto: Ministry of Health and Long-Term Care, 2004), question 6 at 35,
      online: <www.health.gov.on.ca>. Accordingly, the phrase is often used to address the
      general rule of implied consent between health information custodians as explained
      in Section F(2), above.
90   *PHIPA*, s. 18(3)(b).

health information for health care purposes, combined with the existence of a number of specific permissible disclosures without consent in *PHIPA*. Such disclosures of personal health information without consent sometimes apply to permit exchanges of personal health information with non-health information custodians as well as health information custodians.[91] Express consent will be required in certain circumstances, however. For example, where a health information custodian wishes to disclose personal health information about a patient to a colleague who is organizing a clinical trial relevant to the patient's condition, the custodian must seek the patient's express consent to the disclosure of the patient's name and contact information to the colleague so that he or she may contact the patient.

6) Express Consent: Health Information Custodian to a Non-Health Information Custodian

A disclosure of personal health information by a health information custodian to a non-health information custodian, even if it is for the provision of health care or for the purpose of assisting in the provision of health care, requires express consent, unless *PHIPA* permits the custodian to disclose the information without consent.[92] Such disclosures would include a disclosure by a health information custodian to the patient's insurer, lawyer, teacher, or employer. While this is the general rule, *PHIPA* includes two exceptions, allowing custodians to rely on a patient's implied consent to the custodian's collection, use, or disclosure for the purposes of fundraising and disclosure of personal health information to religious and other organizations with which the patient is affiliated.[93] One further exception to the express consent rule pertains to the disclosure of personal health information by a pharmacist to an insurer and is found in the *PHIPA* Regulation.[94]

---

91   See Chapters 10 and 11 for further discussion of permissible disclosures by health information custodians of personal health information without the patient's consent.

92   *PHIPA*, s. 18(3)(a).

93   *PHIPA*, ss. 18(4), 32, and 33.

94   *PHIPA* Regulation, above note 7, s. 1(6) and 8.

95   Another prime example of a type of health information custodian that relies on fundraising are not-for-profit long-term care facilities. Not-for-profit retirement homes, community clinics, and health services may also rely on fundraising.

7) Fundraising

Hospitals and other health care facilities[95] raise significant funds each year from private donors, many of them patients, former patients, and their families, who are grateful for the services provided, or who are, for other reasons, willing to give. As the public treasury is challenged more and more by the costs of funding an increasingly costly health care system, fundraising by health care institutions from private donors can reasonably be expected to grow, not diminish, in importance.

When Bill 31 was first introduced, it required a patient's express consent for a health information custodian's collections, uses, or disclosures of personal health information for fundraising purposes.[96] This provision was heavily criticized in the public hearings on the Bill that took place after its introduction. Hospitals, hospital foundations, the Information and Privacy Commissioner, and the Ontario Hospital Association all asserted that requiring express consent for a health information custodian's collection, use, or disclosure of personal health information for the purposes of fundraising would lead to multi-million dollar shortfalls from expected fundraising targets, for which the government would be expected to make up the difference.[97]

In the face of these strong submissions, the government amended the fundraising provisions to allow health information custodians, in addition to being able to rely on express consent, to rely on a patient's implied consent for the custodian's collection, use, or disclosure of personal health information for "the purposes of fundraising activities,"[98] where the information in question

---

96 Above note 22, Bill 31, first reading, at Sch. A, cl. 31 (17 December 2003).

97 In the Legislature during the second reading debates, a member of the Standing Committee on General Government who participated in the hearings on Bill 31, noted that with a rule requiring express consent for fundraising "fundraising efforts would essentially dry up."[Ontario, Legislative Assembly, (*Hansard*), 1139 (30 March 2004) at 2100 (Shelley Martel)]. Further, the Information and Privacy Commissioner had stated in her brief to the Standing Committee on General Government that the requirement for express consent "does not reflect the existing realities facing healthcare organizations. These organizations are heavily dependent on fundraising to meet their goals and serve the public. Requiring express consent for fundraising purposes will adversely impact their ability to raise funds." Dr. Ann Cavoukian, *Submission to the Standing Committee on General Government: Bill 31: Health Information Protection Act* (27 January 2004), online: <www.ipc.on.ca>.

98 *PHIPA*, s. 32(1). "For the purpose of fundraising activities" is a phrase that is not defined further in *PHIPA* or its regulation, although the *PHIPA* Regulation, above note 7, s. 10(2)[3] suggests that solicitations for donations addressed to the patient will be one type of fundraising activity.

consists solely of the patient's name and the prescribed types of contact information.[99] Under the regulation, the types of contact information that a custodian may collect, use, and disclose for the purpose of fundraising are

- the patient's mailing address,[100] and
- the name and mailing address of the patient's substitute decision-maker.[101]

If a health information custodian seeks to collect, use, or disclose other types of contact information for fundraising purposes, for example, where the patient prefers to be contacted by telephone or electronic mail, the patient's express consent is required. Express consent is also required for a custodian's collection, use, or disclosure of any information about the patient's state of health or receipt of health care for fundraising purposes.[102]

The *PHIPA* Regulation also sets out the method by which a health information custodian must seek a patient's implied consent for the collection, use, and disclosure of the patient's personal health information for fundraising purposes. Consent can only be implied when the hospital or other custodian

---

99 *PHIPA*, s. 32. In some cases the disclosure of a list of patient names and contact information, even where the names on the list are not explicitly identified as patients of the hospital or facility, may enable the person receiving the information to infer with some degree of confidence that the persons on the list were patients of the hospital or facility. Furthermore, where the hospital or facility is a specialized facility, for example a cancer hospital, the person receiving the information may also make inferences about the state of health of the persons in the facility. Nevertheless, the Act and regulation appear to clearly and without reservation permit the disclosure of the name and prescribed contact information on the basis of implied consent, subject only to the stipulation that (whether the disclosure or use of the information is based on implied or explicit consent) any fundraising solicitation to the individual cannot include any information about the individual's health care or state of health. Keeping in mind the purpose of this provision, which is to allow the use and disclosure of lists of patients' names and prescribed contact information by the hospital or facility for fundraising purposes, it appears that the intention was that the use and disclosure of such lists be permitted even though a person receiving the list may make certain inferences about the health care or state of health of persons on the list. It would be prudent, however, when using or disclosing such lists for fundraising purposes to ensure that the list does not explicitly identify persons on the list as patients of the hospital.

100 *PHIPA* Regulation, above note 7, s. 10(1).

101 *Ibid.*, s. 10(3). For an explanation of who may act as a substitute decision-maker for a patient, see Chapter 6, Section B.

102 See discussion below. It appears for example that a hospital in its fundraising letter to a patient cannot refer to the fact that the patient has received health care from the hospital. Such information may not be communicated back to the patient, perhaps for fear that such communications, if permitted, could expose the patient's sensitive personal health information to others.

has, at the time of patient contact, posted or otherwise made available to the patient a notice advising that, unless the patient indicates otherwise, the custodian may use and disclose the patient's name and contact information, including information about the patient's substitute decision-maker, where applicable, for fundraising purposes.[103] The notice must also provide information on how the patient can "easily opt out" from receiving any future fundraising solicitations on behalf of the custodian.[104] Only if a custodian makes such a notice available to the patient, in a manner likely to come to the patient's attention,[105] and the patient has not opted out within sixty days, may the custodian use or disclose the information for fundraising purposes.[106]

As well as setting out requirements for implied consent for fundraising, the regulation also sets out a number of restrictions and requirements that apply to all collections, uses, and disclosures of personal health information for fundraising, whether express or implied. They are as follows:

- Personal health information held by a health information custodian can only be collected, used, or disclosed for fundraising in respect of that custodian's operations, which restricts the custodian from providing the information for another custodian's or organization's fundraising purposes.[107] This restriction may have the effect of preventing the exchange of donor lists among health information custodians, but it would not impede a custodian from sharing the applicable information with its agents for fundraising on behalf of the custodian. Thus, for example, a hospital could provide the information to a hospital foundation acting as an agent of the hospital for the purpose of carrying out fundraising for the hospital.[108]

---

103   *PHIPA* Regulation, above note 7, s. 10(2)[2][i].

104   *Ibid.*

105   A similar requirement is set out in s. 18(6) of the Act. How this requirement is interpreted will depend on the circumstances. It is possible that simply posting a notice may not be sufficient for all patients, particularly where the patient would not be expected to be in the area where the notice is posted, or where the custodian knows that the patient does not understand the language in which the notice is provided.

106   *PHIPA* Regulation, above note 7, s. 10(2)[2][ii]. The custodian may not solicit a patient after the patient opts out, even if the opt-out occurs after more than sixty days. The custodian may solicit the patient after the sixty-day period, unless and until the patient opts out.

107   *PHIPA* Regulation, *ibid.*, s. 10(2)[1]. It would not appear to be reasonable to interpret the term "operations" in this context to exclude fundraising for capital needs, as more explicit language would surely have been used had it been intended to exclude such an important and common area of fundraising.

108   Even where a foundation is not acting as the agent of a hospital, the hospital may disclose the information to the foundation, but only to use the information for fundraising for the hospital, not for other hospitals or causes or for other purposes.

- The fundraising must have a charitable or philanthropic purpose, which would exclude "fundraising" efforts by for-profit organizations.[109]
- All solicitations for fundraising must provide the patient with an easy way to opt out from receiving any further solicitations.[110]
- Finally, when communicating with a patient for the purposes of fundraising, the custodian or the person fundraising on the custodian's behalf is not permitted to include in the communication any information on the patient's health care or state of health.[111] This restriction prevents explicitly referring to the fact that the person has been a patient in the facility for which the fundraising is taking place, since that is information about the patient's health care. This particular rule does not however restrict the information that may be collected, used, or disclosed for fundraising, but rather only its communication to the patient. Thus, with the patient's express consent, a custodian could use information related to the treatment or condition of the patient for fundraising purposes so long as that information is not included in any communication to the patient. A custodian may take this approach in order to direct a fundraising campaign to those patients whose health condition or treatment history make it more likely that they will contribute; for example, a campaign targeted at new mothers for donations toward the construction of a new birthing wing of a hospital.

a) Fundraising Notice

The following sample fundraising notice may give custodians who wish to rely on implied consent for the collection, use, or disclosure for fundraising purposes a starting point in developing an appropriate notice. This sample will have to be reviewed and revised to ensure that it fits all the circumstances of the custodian.

Notice to Patients Regarding Fundraising

As the cost of providing top quality health care continues to escalate, [Name of Hospital][112] relies on the generosity of donors to help meet the financial needs of the hospital, for the benefit of everyone in our community. As part of our fundraising efforts, [Name of Hospital], and/or the [Name of Hospital]

---

109 *PHIPA* Regulation, above note 7, s. 10(2)[1].
110 *Ibid.*, s. 10(2)[3].
111 *Ibid.*, s. 10(2)[4].
112 This notice is drafted for a hospital, but any custodian that operates for charitable or philanthropic purposes may rely on this type of notice, changing the references to "hospital" as appropriate.

Foundation, contacts patients of the Hospital to request that they consider making a donation to the Hospital, if they wish to do so.[113]

Unless you request otherwise, within 60 days of this notice first being made available to you, we will assume that we have your implied consent for

- [Name of Hospital] and/or the [Name of Hospital] Foundation[114] to use your name and mailing address, (and the name and mailing address of your substitute decision-maker, where applicable) to contact you to request a donation; and
- [Name of Hospital] to provide[115] this information to the [Name of Hospital] Foundation for this purpose.

You may withdraw your consent for the use of your information for these purposes by letting us know in writing, at [mailing address, fax, e-mail address] or by telephone at [provide phone number].

Rest assured that in using your information for fundraising purposes, we will

- not use any information other than your name and mailing address, (and the name and mailing address of your substitute decision-maker, where applicable) without your express consent;
- not communicate with you by any means except by regular mail without your express consent, and the material mailed to you will not refer to health care you receive or to your state of health;
- not provide any information about whether or not you donate, or the amount of any donation, to anyone involved in providing health care to you, unless you consent (e.g., if you authorize us to post a plaque recognizing your contribution); and
- stop using your information for fundraising purposes if you request us to do so.

Please let us know if you would like to be contacted in a manner other than by regular mail to your mailing address on file with [Name of Hospital].

---

113 This introductory paragraph of the notice sets the context for the solicitation. The middle paragraph forms the legally essential part of the notice.
114 Mentioning the role of the foundation here is likely not legally required in this notice, since the hospital can provide the information to a foundation that is its agent to use the information for any purpose for which the custodian is authorized to use the information: s. 37(2).

> If you have any questions about this notice, or the information practices of [Name of Hospital], please contact _____, and/or see our written public statement provided under the *Personal Health Information Protection Act, 2004*, which can be accessed at _____.

8) Religious or Other Organizational Affiliation

During the hearings on Bill 31, the Standing Committee on General Government heard from representatives of the Anglican, Evangelical, Lutheran, and Roman Catholic Churches in Ontario. They were concerned that *PHIPA* could "obstruct individual residents and patients in government-operated and funded institutions from having access to their spiritual caregivers and fellow religious community members when they need them."[116] The representatives from these churches presented two concerns: that clergy of religious communities may be denied access to members of their faith who want their presence and help, and that chaplains in these institutions may be prevented from doing their work by the provisions of *PHIPA*, or by misinterpretations of *PHIPA*.

These concerns stemmed from the fact that in the First Reading version of Bill 31, *PHIPA* did not permit a hospital or other health facility to disclose a patient's information to external representatives of religious groups without the patient's express consent.[117] Clergy who attended before the Standing Committee underlined that obtaining express consent for calls or visits from such external representatives was not possible in many instances. Further, they noted that such a requirement for express consent would change the practice of clergy contacting hospitals to enquire whether any members of their faith were admitted so that they could arrange to visit them. Traditionally, many hospitals have provided patient lists to local clergy so that the clergy could determine who from their congregation or faith community has been admitted and then arrange to visit those individuals.[118]

---

115 Where a foundation acts as an agent of a hospital, the hospital's provision of personal health information to the foundation is a use of the information and not a disclosure: *PHIPA*, s. 6(1).

116 Ontario, Legislative Assembly, Standing Committee on General Government, *Official Report of Debates (Hansard)*, G-25 (26 January 2004) at 1320 (Bishop George Elliott).

117 This fell under the general rule that requires health information custodians to obtain express consent to the disclosure of personal health information to non-health information custodians, as set out now in *PHIPA*, s. 18(3).

118 Ontario, Legislative Assembly, Standing Committee on General Government, *Official Report of Debates (Hansard)*, G-27 (26 January 2004) at 1340 (Archdeacon Harry Huskins).

Committee members noted a similar issue in the case of other organizations such as members of a Lions Club or a veterans association that volunteer in hospitals and other health facilities. The first reading version of *PHIPA* would have excluded these external volunteers from obtaining information about patients who may have appreciated their services, unless the patient provided express consent to the facility to disclose patient information to them.[119]

Both religious and secular service organizations would have been greatly challenged in obtaining the express consent of patients since they would not have had the information to know whom to contact for consent. Without a proactive initiative by health facilities in obtaining such consents, such a requirement would have effectively prevented many patients from receiving welcome supportive visits.

PHIPA was amended to allow for a health information custodian to rely on a patient's implied consent to such disclosures. Where a patient voluntarily gives a facility, such as a hospital or nursing home, information about his or her religious or other organizational affiliation, the facility may assume that it has the individual's implied consent to provide his or her name and location in the facility, to a representative of the religious or other organization, provided that the custodian has offered the patient the opportunity to withhold or withdraw the consent and the patient has not done so.[120] The facility is obliged to inform the patient of this opportunity to withhold or withdraw the patient's implied consent to such a disclosure.

A custodian that is a facility may seek information about the religious or other organizational affiliation of a patient as part of the information that a patient provides at the time of admission, and it may also provide the patient with the opportunity to withhold or withdraw his or her implied consent to the disclosure at that time. An admitting clerk, for example, can inform the patient orally about the patient's ability to choose not to consent to the facility's disclosure of the patient's information for the purpose of contacting a religious representative. Alternatively, such a custodian may provide a patient with this opportunity in writing, possibly as part of the written public statement that the custodian is required to make available.[121] If the patient does not indicate that he or she does not wish the facility to contact such a representative, after being

---

119 Ontario, Legislative Assembly, Standing Committee on General Government, *Official Report of Debates (Hansard)*, G-28 (26 January 2004) at 1340 (Jerry J. Ouellette).

120 *PHIPA*, ss. 18(4)(a) and 20(4).

121 See Chapter 4, Section E for a discussion of what may be incorporated into the written public statement.

offered the opportunity to do so, the facility may disclose to the representative the patient's name and location in the facility.

Where a patient is unconscious and the facility is not able to give the patient an opportunity to withhold or withdraw his or her consent, the facility may not disclose the patient's name and location to the applicable representative on the basis of an implied consent.[122]

Often hospitals, nursing homes, and other facilities may have programs to provide patients with spiritual care. The program may include visits from facility chaplains, for example, who may provide religious services to patients. Where the custodian has such a program in place, the custodian may use a patient's personal health information without the patient's consent for the purpose of delivering such a program. The facility may use information about the patient's religious affiliation, for example, to enable the facility's agent, such as a chaplain or other spiritual caregiver to visit the patient.[123]

Furthermore, in some situations, a facility may disclose a patient's personal health information without the patient's consent to a representative of a religious organization or other organizational affiliation much in the same way as the facility may disclose such information to others. For example, the facility may disclose information that the individual is a patient in the facility, the general health status of the patient, and the location of the patient in the facility.[124]

9) Disclosures by Pharmacists to Insurers

Along with amendments about fundraising and disclosure to religious and other organizations, the Standing Committee on General Government's review of Bill 31 after first reading led to further amendments of the express consent rule to allow health information custodians to disclose personal health information about a patient to persons who are not health information custodians, on the basis of the patient's implied consent where permitted by the regulations. Such regulations may only authorize the use of implied consent for a type of disclosure that does not include "information about an individual's state of health."[125]

---

122 The patient's substitute decision-maker, however, could consent to the custodian's disclosure to the representative on the patient's behalf.

123 *PHIPA*, s. 37(1)(c). For further discussion of uses without consent, see Chapter 9.

124 *PHIPA*, s. 38(3). A facility may disclose such information without consent, provided that the facility offers the patient the option, at the first reasonable opportunity after admission, to object to such disclosures, and the patient does not make such an objection. This provision is further explained in Chapter 10, Section E.

125 *PHIPA*, s. 18(4)(c).

A provision was included in the *PHIPA* Regulation to address a concern raised by the Ontario Pharmacists Association during the hearings about the impact of the requirement for express consent on an insurer's direct reimbursement to a pharmacist for medications and related goods and services.[126]

The *PHIPA* Regulation thus clarifies first of all, that "information about an individual's state of health" does not include information about medication or related goods or services provided by a pharmacist to a patient that the pharmacist discloses to a benefits payer where the benefits payer is asked to provide payment for the medication or related good or service.[127] Further, the regulation allows a pharmacist to disclose such information about a patient to such a payer on the basis of a patient's implied consent.[128] Where a patient ordering a prescription presents a pharmacist with specific information about drug insurance coverage, perhaps by providing a benefits card from an insurance provider, or has previously done so, then, in general, the pharmacist can infer that the patient consents to the pharmacist providing the necessary information to the insurer to provide coverage for the prescription.

10) Marketing

PHIPA does not permit health information custodians to collect, use, or disclose personal health information about a patient "for the purpose of marketing anything or for market research" unless the custodian has the patient's express consent and the custodian does so in accordance with any prescribed requirements and restrictions.[129] "Marketing" is not a defined term in the legislation. However, the *PHIPA* Regulation specifies that "marketing" does not include letters sent by physicians to their patients for the purpose of giving

---

126 The Ontario Pharmacists Association had noted that, while pharmacists could submit direct claims for reimbursement of government-funded prescriptions to the government without consent via an electronic claims network, submitting the same kind of reimbursement claim in the same way to a private insurer required express consent. See Ontario, Legislative Assembly, Standing Committee on General Government, *Official Report of Debates (Hansard)*, G-94 (27 January 2004) at 1530 (Ruth Mallon). In *PHIPA*, s.38(1)(b), government reimbursement is accommodated in a provision that allows a health information custodian to disclose personal health information without the individual's consent "in order for the Minister or another health information custodian to determine or provide funding or payment to the custodian for the provision of health care."

127 *PHIPA* Regulation, above note 7, s. 1(6).

128 *PHIPA*, s. 8.

129 *Ibid.*, s. 33. As of writing, there are no further requirements prescribed.

them the option of paying a set annual fee to the physicians for uninsured services.[130] Further, "marketing" does not include a communication by Canadian Blood Services to the public for the purpose of recruiting blood donors.[131]

During the hearings on Bill 31, the Ontario Pharmacists' Association submitted to the Standing Committee on General Government that the word "marketing" should not capture compliance and wellness programs engaged in by pharmacies.[132] Such programs cover a range of possible initiatives. Where the purpose of a pharmacist's use of a patient's personal health information is the provision of health care, the pharmacist may rely upon a patient's implied consent to use the patient's information for such a purpose. However, where the purpose of a program is not the provision of health care but has as its purpose the marketing of a device or food supplement, for example, the custodian must obtain the patient's express consent to the use of the information.

---

130 *PHIPA* Regulation, above note 7, s. 1(2)(a) specifies that "marketing" does not include a communication by a health care practitioner who provides insured services within the meaning of the *Health Insurance Act*, R.S.O. 1990, c. H.6 to a patient or a member of the patient's family or household by which the practitioner makes available to those persons an arrangement whereby they may receive ancillary uninsured services for a block fee or on the basis of a set fee for service.

131 *PHIPA* Regulation, *ibid.*, s. 1(2)(b) specifies that "marketing" does not include "a communication by the Canadian Blood Services for the purpose of recruiting donors of blood or blood products or hematopoietic progenitor cells."

132 Ontario, Legislative Assembly, Standing Committee on General Government, *Official Report of Debates (Hansard)*, G-94 (27 January 2004) at 1530 (Ruth Mallon).

6 Substitute Decision-making

A. GENERALLY

In certain situations, a patient may not be able to consent to a health information custodian's collection, use, or disclosure of personal health information about the patient. The patient may be mentally incapable,[1] or, the patient may be deceased. Alternatively, where the patient is mentally capable, but for some reason is unable or prefers not to provide consent personally, the patient may authorize another person to act on his or her behalf. In such situations where a health information custodian requires consent, be it express or implied, under the *Personal Health Information Protection Act, 2004*[2] or any other Act, the health information custodian may obtain consent from the patient's substitute decision-maker for the custodian's collection, use, or disclosure of the patient's personal health information.[3]

PHIPA defines a "substitute decision-maker" to mean, in relation to a patient, a person who is authorized under *PHIPA* to consent on behalf of the patient to the collection, use, or disclosure of personal health information about the patient.[4]

---

1   Capacity is dealt with in detail in Section F, below.
2   S.O. 2004, c. 3, Sch. 1 [*PHIPA*].
3   *PHIPA*, s. 23(1).
4   *Ibid.*, s. 5(1). The definition of "substitute decision-maker" is qualified by the words "unless the context requires otherwise." When *PHIPA* refers to a substitute decision-

The rules in *PHIPA* that enable a health information custodian to turn to another person for consent on behalf of a patient address a significant gap that exists in the *Personal Information Protection and Electronic Documents Act.*[5] While the general rule in *PIPEDA* is that an organization that is subject to that Act requires the knowledge and consent of an individual for the collection, use, or disclosure of personal information,[6] *PIPEDA* does not provide sufficient rules for obtaining consent from individuals who are incapable.[7]

PIPEDA also does not provide rules for obtaining consent for the handling of records of deceased individuals. The CSA Privacy Code, attached as Schedule 1 to *PIPEDA*, states that "consent can also be given by an authorized representative (such as a legal guardian or a person having power of attorney),"[8] but *PIPEDA* itself does not provide organizations with further rules as to who is authorized to make decisions on behalf of others. In many cases, individuals will not have legal guardians or attorneys under a power of attorney to act on their behalf.

Health care stakeholders criticized this absence of a substitute decision-making scheme in *PIPEDA* and cited this void as a critical reason as to why the *PIPEDA* rules would not be appropriate for the health sector.[9]

---

maker of an individual within the meaning of the *Health Care Consent Act, 1996*, S.O. 1996, c. 2, Sch. A [*HCCA*], the phrase means someone other than a person who is authorized to consent to the collection, use, or disclosure of the patient's personal health information. Sections 5(2), (3), & (4) of *PHIPA* deem a substitute decision-maker who is authorized to make treatment decisions, long-term care admission decisions, or personal assistance service decisions, as the case may be, under the *HCCA* as the substitute decision-maker for personal health information decisions. Accordingly, the *HCCA* substitute decision-maker has a particular role as substitute decision-maker for information decisions. This is further discussed in Section B(6)(a) below.

5 S.C. 2000, c. 5 [*PIPEDA*].

6 *Ibid.*, s. 7.

7 Interestingly, the "note" in Principle 3, Consent, of the CSA Privacy Code, Schedule 1 to *PIPEDA*, which recognizes that in some circumstances, personal information may be collected, used, or disclosed without consent because "seeking consent may be impossible or inappropriate when the individual is a minor, seriously ill, or mentally incapacitated," is not incorporated as part of *PIPEDA*: *PIPEDA*, s. 7(1).

8 CSA Privacy Code, Schedule 1 to *PIPEDA*, above note 5, at 4.3.6.

9 Mary Catherine Lindberg, Assistant Deputy Minister, Health Services Division, Ontario Ministry of Health, noted to the Standing Committee on Social Affairs, Science and Technology regarding Bill C-6, *Personal Information Protection and Electronic Documents Act*, that "[a] critical part of our [Ontario] proposed legislation is a scheme that would allow substitute consent for identified individuals who may consent to disclosure of personal health information on behalf of incapable or deceased individuals. Provisions for such a scheme are noticeably absent in Bill C-6"(2 December 1999). Online: <www.parl.gc.ca/36/2/parlbus/commbus/senate/Com-e/soci-e/05ev-e.htm?Language=E&Parl=36&Ses=2&comm_id=47>.

B. THE SUBSTITUTE DECISION-MAKING FRAMEWORK IN *PHIPA*

1) Generally

PHIPA identifies five categories of circumstances in which substitute decision-makers can exercise their powers with respect to personal health information on someone else's behalf:

- where a capable patient, who is at least sixteen years old, authorizes in writing a substitute decision-maker to make personal health information decisions on his or her behalf.[10]
- where the patient is deceased.[11]
- where other Acts confer authority on persons to act on behalf of others with respect to personal health information decisions.[12]
- where the patient is a capable child under the age of sixteen.[13]
- where the patient is mentally incapable of making his or her own information decisions.[14]

A discussion of each of these categories follows.

2) Decision-maker for the Capable Patient, Sixteen Years and Older

Where a patient is capable[15] and at least sixteen years old, anyone who is at least sixteen years old and capable[16] who the patient has authorized to act on his or her behalf may make a personal health information decision on behalf of the patient.[17] For example, where a patient has executed a continuing power of attorney for property authorizing another individual to administer his or her financial affairs that is effective even when the patient is capable, that person may make a decision concerning the patient's personal health information,

---

10   *PHIPA*, s. 23(1)[1][ii].
11   *Ibid.*, s. 23(1)[4].
12   *Ibid.*, s. 23(1)[5].
13   *Ibid.*, s. 23(1)[2].
14   *Ibid.*, s. 23(1)[3].
15   Capacity is discussed below in Section F.
16   These age and capacity requirements only apply where the person is a natural person.
17   *PHIPA*, s. 23(1)[1][ii].

where the authority of such attorney extends to such information.[18] The attorney may need to authorize the disclosure of personal health information in order to administer some aspect of the patient's financial affairs in the event of the patient's absence from Ontario, such as ensuring that accident benefits do not lapse. This category recognizes that a patient may authorize a corporate entity, such as a financial trust company, to act in respect of some of his or her information decisions; and, accordingly, this category of substitute decision-makers is not limited to natural persons. To authorize a substitute decision-maker to act on a patient's behalf with respect to personal health information, a patient must do so in writing. The permission does not need to be a formal document such as a power of attorney; a letter or form can suffice.

3) Decision-maker for the Deceased Patient

If a patient has died, the deceased patient's estate trustee or the person who has assumed responsibility for the administration of the estate, if the estate does not have an estate trustee, is authorized to give, withdraw, or withhold consent to the collection, use, or disclosure of the deceased patient's personal health information.[19]

"Estate trustee" is not defined in *PHIPA*; however, its meaning can be extrapolated from the explanation of the phrase as set out in the *Courts of Justice Act*.[20] An "estate trustee," under that Act, is an up-to-date term that includes an executor (a person who is specified in the will to carry out the wishes of the deceased individual as set out in the deceased's will), an administrator (a person who administers the estate of the deceased individual who dies without a will or where his or her will cannot be located), or an administrator with the will annexed (a person who is appointed to administer the deceased individual's estate as set out in the will, because the executors named in the will, if any, cannot be found or are unwilling or unable to act).[21]

The person "who has assumed responsibility for the administration of the estate" would include, for example, a person who has been appointed by the

---

18   *Substitute Decisions Act, 1992*, S.O. 1992, c. 30, s. 7 [SDA]. Note that a continuing power of attorney for property may only be granted by an individual who is eighteen years or older and can authorize an individual who is eighteen years or older to act on the grantor's behalf.

19   *PHIPA*, s. 23(1)[4].

20   The term is defined in *Rules of Civil Procedure*, R.R.O. 1990, Reg. 194, Rule 74.01, made under the *Courts of Justice Act*, R.S.O. 1990, c. C.43.

21   *Ibid.*

court as a "litigation administrator" to represent the interests of the deceased's estate for the purpose of a lawsuit involving the estate where there is no estate trustee.[22] Further, it appears that the phrase "who has assumed the responsibility for the administration of the estate" is intended to authorize persons who are not "estate trustees" and who do not, in fact, have a formal appointment such as that of a "litigation administrator" but who may for legitimate reasons have taken on the duty of resolving the deceased patient's financial or other affairs, such as where the value of the estate is minimal so that no court appointment of an estate trustee is pursued. This could be, for example, where a widow requires a health information custodian to provide confirmation of death to her husband's pension plan so that she may begin receiving her widow's pension. The widow, as the person who has assumed the responsibility for her husband's estate, may authorize the custodian to disclose the deceased patient's information to the pension plan.

4) Decision-maker Authorized by an Act

PHIPA allows another person whom an Act of Ontario or Canada authorizes or requires acting on behalf of a patient to make information decisions under *PHIPA*.[23] For example, under the *Drug and Pharmacies Regulation Act*, an agent of the patient is entitled to a copy of the prescription information.[24] An "agent" is not defined but would appear to mean any one who acts on behalf of the patient in presenting to or picking up from a pharmacist a prescription for the patient. The regulation under *PHIPA* clarifies that such an agent may be the patient's substitute decision-maker for the purpose of a consent for the collection, use, or disclosure of the patient's personal health information that a pharmacist requires pertaining to a patient's prescription.[25]

5) Decision-maker for a Capable Child under Sixteen

A health information custodian may obtain consent for the collection, use, and disclosure of a child's personal health information from the capable child,

---

22   *Ibid*, Rule 9.02.

23   *PHIPA*, s. 23(1)[5].

24   R.S.O. 1990, c. H.4, s. 157(1). Every person in respect of whom a prescription is presented to a pharmacist to be dispensed, unless otherwise directed by the prescriber, is entitled to have a copy of it marked as such, furnished to the person, his or her agent, or a pharmacist acting on behalf of such person or agent.

25   *General*, O. Reg. 329/04, s. 1(7) [*PHIPA* Regulation].

regardless of the child's age.[26] Where a child is less than sixteen years of age, a parent of the child or a children's aid society or other person who is lawfully entitled to give or refuse consent in place of the parent (such as a child's guardian)[27] may *also* give, withhold, or withdraw consent to the collection, use, or disclosure of the child's personal health information on the child's behalf.[28]

However, such persons may not exercise this power where the information relates to treatment about which the child has made a decision on his or her own behalf under the *Health Care Consent Act, 1996*,[29] or where the information relates to counseling in which the child has participated on his or her own under the *Child and Family Services Act*.[30] Under the *Health Care Consent Act, 1996*, a health care practitioner[31] who proposes treatment to a child obtains consent from the child, as opposed to from the parent, where the child is capable.[32] Thus, where the child makes the treatment decision, the parent is not authorized by this section in *PHIPA* to make information decisions on the child's behalf for that treatment. Where the custodian requires consent to disclose information about the treatment, the decision about the disclosure is the child's decision.

Similarly, the *Child and Family Services Act* permits a service provider[33] to provide a counseling service to a child who is twelve years of age or older with the child's consent and without the parent's consent.[34] If the service provider

---

26   *PHIPA*, s. 24(4). See discussion of capacity in Section F below.

27   In this Chapter, a reference to a "parent" includes a children's aid society or other person who is lawfully entitled to give or refuse consent in place of the parent: *PHIPA*, s. 23(1)[2]. The word does not include a parent who only has a right of access to the child: *PHIPA*, s. 23(2). If a children's aid society or other person is lawfully entitled to consent in the place of the parent, the word "parent" does not include the natural parent.

28   *PHIPA*, s. 23(1)[2].

29   *HCAA*, above note 4.

30   R.S.O. 1990, c. 11 [*CFSA*].

31   "Health care practitioner" has a narrower definition in the *HCCA* than in *PHIPA*. The definition includes a naturopath registered as a drugless therapist under the *Drugless Practitioners Act*, R.S.O. 1990, c. D.18 and most, but not all, regulated health professionals. The definition in the *HCCA* does not include a pharmacist, optician, or dental technologist. It also does not include social workers, social service workers, or unregulated health care providers. See the *HCCA*, above note 4, s. 2(1).

32   *HCCA, ibid.*, s. 10.

33   The category of "service provider" in the *CFSA*, above note 30, defined in s. 3(1) of that Act, would include some health information custodians, such as children's mental health centers. The term "service provider" here has a different meaning than in the *Long-Term Care Act, 1994*, S.O. 1994, c. 26 [*LTCA*].

34   *CFSA, ibid.*, s. 28. The section further provides: "... but if the child is less than sixteen years of age the service provider shall discuss with the child at the earliest appropriate opportunity the desirability of involving the child's parent."

provided the counseling to the child with the child's consent, then the provider (if that provider is a health information custodian) cannot rely on a parent's consent to the collection, use, or disclosure of personal health information related to the counseling where the child consented to the counseling. In these two situations,[35] where the child consented to the treatment or counseling, the health information custodian may not disclose information about the treatment or counseling, as the case may be, to the child's parent, unless the child consented to the disclosure.[36]

Aside from the circumstances to which these two exceptions apply, a health information custodian may look for authorization for the collection, use, or disclosure of personal health information about a child who is under sixteen from the child's parent, even where that child is capable. The Act does not require the custodian to seek authorization from both the parent and the child, but the Act also does not preclude the custodian from relying on both for consent.

Where there is a conflict between a capable child and the child's parent, the child's consent with respect to the information prevails.[37] *PHIPA* does not, however, require the custodian to advise the child of this option, nor is there a requirement for the custodian to canvass the views of the child. Where the custodian has the parent's consent, it will likely be the case that, in practice, the custodian would simply rely on that consent unless a contrary instruction of the capable child becomes known to the custodian.

This category of substitute decision-making does not include a parent who only has a right of access to the child.[38] In this way, *PHIPA* recognizes that decision-making with respect to a child's information rests with the custodial parent. Under the *Children's Law Reform Act*[39] a parent with only access to a child does not have an automatic right to make decisions on behalf of his or her child. The *Children's Law Reform Act* gives a person having access to the child the same right as a parent to make inquiries and to be given information

---

35 This rule, however, does not appear to apply where the child is incapable of information decisions. See Section B(6)(a) below.

36 In some situations, the health information custodian would, nonetheless, be able to disclose this personal health information without the child's consent to that parent, where a disclosure without consent provision applied to the situation, such as *PHIPA*, s. 40(1) (risk of harm). For disclosures without consent, see Chapter 10.

37 *PHIPA*, s. 23(3).

38 *Ibid.*, s. 23(2).

39 R.S.O. 1990, c. 12, s. 20(2) [*CLRA*].

as to the health, education, and welfare of the child.[40] That Act, however, does not authorize a health information custodian to disclose the child's personal health information about the child to the parent.[41] Where a parent with only a right of access to the child requires personal health information from the custodian about the child, the parent may request the custodial parent to authorize the release of such information about the child to the access parent. The access parent can enforce this request by way of court order if the custodial parent does not comply.[42]

6) Decision-maker for the Incapable Patient

a)   A Substitute Decision-maker under the *Health Care Consent Act, 1996*

Where the patient is incapable of consenting to the collection, use, or disclosure of his or her personal heath information, as the case may be,[43] the Act provides a ranked list of persons to whom the health information custodian would turn for consent to the collection, use or disclosure of the patient's personal health information on behalf of that patient under *PHIPA*.[44] However, before a health information custodian may turn to this list, the custodian must first determine whether the incapable patient has a substitute decision-maker under the *Health Care Consent Act, 1996*.[45]

Under the *Health Care Consent Act, 1996*, a substitute decision-maker makes decisions on behalf of a patient about the provision of treatment to the patient, the patient's admission to a care facility, and/or the provision of personal assistance services to the patient within a care facility.[46] These substitute decision-makers are also authorized to make decisions about information that has a connection to the decision they are responsible for under the *Health Care Consent Act, 1996*.[47] A substitute decision-maker who is making decisions on

---

40   *Ibid.*, s. 20(5).

41   Even if it is arguable that the health information custodian would be authorized to disclose to a parent who is entitled to information under the *CLRA*, the rules in *PHIPA* prevail in the event of a conflict between its provisions and those of the *CLRA*: *PHIPA*, ss. 7(2) & (3) and *PHIPA* Regulation, above note 25, s. 1(5).

42   *CLRA*, above note 39, s. 20(7).

43   See Section F below, for an explanation of how the patient is determined to be mentally incapable with respect to the collection, use, or disclosure of personal health information.

44   *PHIPA*, s. 23(1)[3], s. 26. For a discussion about the list, see next section.

45   *PHIPA*, s. 26(11).

46   *HCCA*, above note 4, s. 9 (treatment), s. 39 (admission to a care facility), and s. 56 (personal assistance services). "Care facility" is defined in s. 2(1) of the *HCCA*.

47   *PHIPA*, ss. 5(2) and 23(1)[3].

behalf of an incapable patient under the *Health Care Consent Act, 1996* is "deemed" to be a substitute decision-maker of the patient for the collection, use, and disclosure of personal health information about the patient where the collection, use, or disclosure is "necessary for, or ancillary to" a decision under that Act.[48]

Such a substitute decision-maker ranks above all other persons in the list of substitute decision-makers for an incapable patient under *PHIPA*, with respect to such a decision.[49] While the word "necessary" on its own, as a modifier, would give a narrower scope to the decision-making authority, it seems that the inclusion of the word "ancillary"[50] gives the *Health Care Consent Act, 1996* substitute decision-maker a somewhat wider scope of authority for information decisions related to the decisions for which the substitute is responsible under the *Health Care Consent Act, 1996*.

For example, where a health information custodian is treating an incapable patient, based on a substitute decision-maker's consent to a treatment plan obtained under the *Health Care Consent Act, 1996*, and requires approval for payment from the individual's insurance company for a particular service or device (such as for dental work or for prosthetics) the custodian can request the substitute decision-maker who is authorized to consent to the treatment plan to also consent to the release of information to the insurance company for the purpose of obtaining confirmation that the service or device will be paid for by the insurer.

The substitute decision-maker under the *Health Care Consent Act, 1996* would not have authority under *PHIPA* to make every information decision pertaining to the individual, as the individual may be capable of making some decisions in question on his or her own.[51] Further, the consent that the custodian

---

48   *Ibid.*, s. 5(2), (3), & (4).

49   *Ibid.*, s. 26(11). For a discussion about the list see next section. Note that a provision in the *HCCA*, above note 4, s. 44(1), specifying that authority to consent on an incapable person's behalf to his or her admission to a care facility includes authority to make decisions that are necessary and ancillary to the admission, was amended in Bill 31 by s. 84(9) of *PHIPA* to clarify that such information does not apply to personal health information within the meaning of *PHIPA* essentially because such authority has been preserved for this type of substitute decision-maker under the HCCA under s. 5(3) of *PHIPA*.

50   Meaning "supplementary; subordinate," (B.A. Garner, ed., *Black's Law Dictionary*, 8th ed. (St. Paul, Minn.: Thomson West, 2004) at 95); or "providing subsidiary support; … additional; supplementary" from Latin *ancillaris*, from *ancilla* "*maidservant*") (*Compact Oxford English Dictionary*, online: <www.askoxford.com/dictionaries/?view=uk>).

51   Note *PHIPA*, s. 21(2).

may require under *PHIPA* for a collection, use, or disclosure of a patient's personal health information may have no connection to the treatment, admission to a long-term care facility, or personal assistance service decision, for which the *Health Care Consent Act, 1996* substitute decision-maker has responsibility.

b) The List of Substitute Decision-makers

Where the incapable patient does not have a substitute decision-maker authorized to make decisions under the *Health Care Consent Act, 1996*, or where the authority of such a substitute decision-maker does not extend to the information decision at hand, the health information custodian may turn to a ranked list of persons set out in *PHIPA* for consent to the collection, use, or disclosure of the patient's personal health information on behalf of the patient.[52]

This list, in order of priority, includes the following persons:

- The patient's guardian of the person or guardian of property, if the consent relates to the guardian's authority to make a decision on behalf of the patient.[53]
- The patient's attorney for personal care or attorney for property, if the consent relates to the attorney's authority to make a decision on behalf of the patient.[54]
- The patient's representative, as appointed by the Consent and Capacity Board.[55] The representative can either be appointed on the application of the incapable patient or on the application of the person wishing to become a representative.[56]

---

52   *PHIPA*, s. 23(1)[3], s. 26.

53   *PHIPA*, s. 26(1)[1]. A guardian is a person appointed by the court to act on the patient's behalf in various respects under the provisions of the *SDA*, above note 18. That Act, in section 15, also creates statutory guardians for patients of psychiatric facilities found incapable of managing property.

54   *PHIPA*, s. 26(1)[2]. An individual may appoint an attorney for property or personal care or both in accordance with the provisions of the *SDA*, *ibid*. Where an individual, to whom personal health information relates, appointed a representative under s. 36.1 of the *Mental Health Act*, R.S.O. 1990, c. M.7 [*MHA*] with respect to clinical records compiled in the psychiatric facility, before 1 November 2004, that representative is deemed, under *PHIPA*, s. 26(8) to have the same authority as an individual in this paragraph. Sections 26(8)–)10) of *PHIPA* have implications only with respect to psychiatric facilities.

55   *PHIPA*, s. 26(1)[3]. The Consent and Capacity Board is a tribunal continued under s. 70(1) of the *HCCA*, above note 4, and it has jurisdiction to hear matters pertaining to that Act, the *MHA*, *ibid.*, the *SDA*, *ibid.*, and *PHIPA*.

56   *PHIPA*, ss. 27(1) & (2) (Board Application Forms P3 and P4 respectively). In such an application, the patient is deemed to have applied for a review of the determination of incapacity, unless the Board has determined the patient's capacity within the previous six months (*PHIPA* Regulation, above note 25, s. 10). In considering whether to appoint a representative, the Board must be satisfied that the patient to whom the per-

- The patient's spouse or partner.[57] "Spouse" is defined in *PHIPA*[58] to mean either of two persons who, (a) are married to each other, or (b) live together in a conjugal relationship outside marriage and (i) have cohabited for at least one year, (ii) are together the parents of a child, or (iii) have together entered into a cohabitation agreement under section 53 of the *Family Law Act*.[59] "Partner" means "either of two persons who have lived together for at least one year and have a close personal relationship that is of primary importance in both persons' lives."[60] The word "partner" would include, for example, two very close friends, or even two relatives, who have lived together for a year and who are not in a conjugal relationship.

- A child of the patient or the parent of the patient, a children's aid society or other person lawfully entitled to give or refuse consent in the place of the parent.[61] This category does not include a parent with only a right of access.[62] Further, if a children's aid society or other person is lawfully entitled to consent in the place of the parent, the parent may not give, withhold, or withdraw consent on the patient's behalf.

- A parent of the patient with only a right of access to the patient.[63]

- A brother or sister of the patient.[64]

---

sonal health information relates does not object to the appointment, the representative agrees to the appointment, is at least sixteen years old and is capable, and that the appointment is in the best interests of the patient. It should also be noted that the Board may, on any person's application, terminate an appointment, where, for example, the appointment is no longer in the patient's best interests or now the patient has a guardian under the *Substitute Decisions Act* or an attorney for property or for personal care, with authority to make the information decisions required on behalf of the incapable patient. Where a representative was appointed under s. 36.2 of the *Mental Health Act* that representative can continue to act on the incapable patient's behalf as if he or she were the patient's representative appointed under s. 27 of *PHIPA*: *PHIPA*, s. 28. As for all applications to the Board under *PHIPA*, the composition of the panels to hear an application, the timelines for hearings, the patient's right to counsel, and appeal rights are as those set out in the *HCCA* (*PHIPA*, s. 27(9)) (see Section M below).

57 *PHIPA*, s. 26(1)[4].
58 *Ibid.*, s. 2, definition of "spouse"; note that two persons are spouses in this definition whether or not they are of opposite sex to each other.
59 R.S.O. 1990, c. F.3.
60 *PHIPA*, s. 2, definition of "partner."
61 *Ibid.*, s. 26(1)[5].
62 *Ibid.*
63 *Ibid.*, s. 26(1)[6].
64 *Ibid.*, s. 26(1)[7].

- Any other relative.[65] A "relative" is a person related by blood, marriage, or adoption.[66]
- The Public Guardian and Trustee.[67]

c) Choosing a Substitute Decision-maker from the List

The health information custodian cannot "shop around" for a substitute decision-maker to act on behalf of an incapable patient. In locating a substitute decision-maker, *PHIPA* requires the custodian to start at the top of the list and work down until the first qualified substitute is located.[68] In order for a person to be qualified as a substitute decision-maker for an incapable patient for information decisions from this list, the person must be all of the following:

- capable;[69]
- at least sixteen years of age, or the parent of the patient to whom the information relates;
- not prohibited by a court order or a separation agreement from having access to the patient or from giving or refusing consent on the patient's behalf;
- available; and
- willing to assume the responsibility of making a decision as to whether or not to consent.[70]

A person is "available" if "it is possible, within a time that is reasonable in the circumstances, to communicate with the person and obtain a consent."[71] *PHIPA* does not explain what would be reasonable in the circumstances.[72] This will depend on the nature of the decision to be made and the timeframe in which it needs to be made. "Available" does not mean that the person must be physically present. The health information custodian may contact the appropriate substitute decision-maker by telephone, for example.

---

65   *PHIPA*, s. 26(1)[8].

66   *Ibid.*, s. 2, definition of "relative."

67   *Ibid.*, ss. 26(6) & (7). The Public Guardian and Trustee is an officer of the Legislature continued under the *Public Guardian and Trustee Act*, R.S.O. 1990, c. P.51. The Office of the Public Guardian and Trustee is part of the Family Justice Services Division of the Ministry of the Attorney General. The Public Guardian and Trustee has one Guardianship office and five regional treatment decision units. See online: <www.attorneygeneral.jus.gov.on.ca/english/family/pgt/ccntact.asp>.

68   *Ibid.*, s. 26(4) provides that "A person described in a paragraph of subsection [26]1 may consent only if no person described in an earlier paragraph meets the requirements of subsection [26]2."

69   Capacity is explained in Section F, below.

70   *PHIPA*, s. 26(2).

71   *Ibid.*, s. 26(3).

72   For a discussion of "reasonable," see Chapter 4, Section C.

Upon locating a proposed substitute decision-maker from the list, *PHIPA* "entitles" the custodian (that is, gives the custodian the right) to rely on certain assertions of the proposed substitute decision-maker, unless it is not reasonable to do so in the circumstances.[73] First of all, the custodian is entitled to rely on the assertion of the person that the person is, in fact, one of the persons in the list.[74] Further, the custodian is entitled to rely on statements by the proposed substitute decision-maker that no other person described in an earlier paragraph or of the same paragraph of the list of potential substitute decision-makers exists, or, although such a person exists, the other person is neither a guardian nor an attorney and would not object to the proposed substitute decision-maker making a decision.[75] The custodian may also rely on the assertion made by the proposed substitute decision-maker that he or she is at least sixteen years of age or the parent of the patient and is not prohibited by a court order or a separation agreement from having access to the patient or from giving or refusing consent on the patient's behalf.[76]

d) The Role of the Public Guardian and Trustee

The Public Guardian and Trustee may make a decision to consent to the collection, use, or disclosure of a patient's personal health information where two or more persons who are equally ranked disagree about whether to consent,[77] or where no other person on the list is qualified to give or refuse consent.[78] The Public Guardian and Trustee's involvement is at the discretion of that office. This approach is different from the approach taken in the *Health Care Consent Act, 1996*, where the Public Guardian and Trustee must make a decision as to whether to consent to or refuse treatment on behalf of an incapable patient where two or more persons who are equally ranked disagree or where no other person on the list is qualified.[79]

---

73 *Ibid.* See Section C below for a discussion of determining the authority of a substitute decision-maker.

74 *PHIPA*, s. 71(4)(b). See further about determining whether the person is authorized to act in Section C below.

75 *PHIPA*, ss. 26(5) and 71(4)(d). Where there is more than one person in a particular category, such as a number of brothers and sisters, one of them may be chosen as the spokesperson for the group. If the persons in the category cannot agree, the custodian may turn to the Public Guardian and Trustee for a decision: see further in Section B(6)(d).

76 *PHIPA*, ss. 26(2) and 71(4)(c).

77 *Ibid.*, s. 26(7).

78 *Ibid.*, s. 26(6).

79 *HCCA*, above note 4, ss. 20(5) & (6). The Public Guardian and Trustee is also required under the *Health Care Consent Act, 1996* to make a decision about an admission of a patient to a long-term care facility in similar circumstances (*HCCA*, s. 41).

There may be instances, therefore, where the Public Guardian and Trustee will refuse to become involved. In such cases, if there is no one else that can be found or appointed to act as the substitute decision-maker for information decisions on behalf of the incapable patient, the health information custodian will not be in a position to collect, use, or disclose that patient's personal health information, where consent is required. This result is likely to be relatively rare. First of all, the Public Guardian and Trustee would, in fact, be involved in making information decisions on behalf of a patient for whom the Public Guardian and Trustee is already deciding about treatment, placement into a care facility, or personal assistance services under the *Health Care Consent Act, 1996*, or where the Public Guardian and Trustee is a guardian or attorney of the patient under the provisions of the *Substitute Decisions Act, 1992*.[80] Further, where the Public Guardian and Trustee is not involved with the patient in such a way, and where no spouse, partner, or relative has been located, the Consent and Capacity Board could appoint a friend or caregiver as the patient's representative, if the custodian needs to obtain a consent under *PHIPA* for the collection, use, or disclosure of the patient's personal health information.[81]

C. DETERMINING WHETHER A PERSON IS AUTHORIZED TO ACT

PHIPA recognizes that a health information custodian may need to disclose some personal health information, without consent, in order to locate a substitute decision-maker. A health information custodian may disclose personal health information about a patient for the purpose of contacting a relative, friend, or potential substitute decision-maker of the patient, if the patient is

---

The involvement of the Public Guardian and Trustee for decision-making on behalf of an incapable patient with respect to personal assistance services in long term-care facilities, in the *Health Care Consent Act, 1996*, is discretionary (*HCCA*, s. 58).

80   The *Substitute Decisions Act, 1992* provides a way to appoint the Public Guardian and Trustee as a guardian of property or of person. The Public Guardian and Trustee can also be an attorney under a continuing power of attorney for property or under a power of attorney for personal care, on consent of the Public Guardian and Trustee. The Public Guardian and Trustee also has a function as statutory guardian of property for psychiatric patients found mentally incapable of managing their finances. Further, a substitute decision-maker who is authorized to make decisions under the *Health Care Consent Act, 1996* with respect to the patient is deemed to be the patient's substitute decision-maker for information decisions under *PHIPA*.

81   *PHIPA*, ss. 27(1) & (2), see further above note 56.

injured, incapacitated, or ill and unable to give consent personally.[82] Once a potential substitute decision-maker is located, the health information custodian must decide whether the custodian may rely on this person's consent for the collection, use, or disclosure of personal health information on behalf of the patient.

As set out above, there are a number of ways in which a person may be authorized to be the substitute decision-maker for a patient. In determining whether a particular person is authorized to be the substitute decision-maker for a patient, a health information custodian is entitled to rely on the accuracy of a person's assertion that he or she is entitled to act as the patient's substitute decision-maker under *PHIPA*, unless it is not reasonable to do so in the circumstances.[83] For example, where a person claiming to be the substitute decision-maker for an incapable patient presents him- or herself to the custodian where the custodian has had no connection with the patient for some time, and may not be in a position to decide whether or not the patient is, indeed, incapable, the custodian may apparently rely on the person's assertion that the patient has been determined incapable by another custodian, unless it is not reasonable to do so in the circumstances.[84]

Such an entitlement does not mean, however, that in all cases the custodian should simply proceed to rely on the person as the substitute decision-maker on the basis of a statement alone. It would be prudent to ensure that the person making the assertion records the assertion on a document that the person signs, together with relevant details; for example, the name of the custodian who determined that the patient was incapable and the date of the determination. A custodian may also choose to require the person to provide identification. These steps are not specifically required by *PHIPA*, but keeping such records will allow a custodian to provide information in support of the reasonableness and lawfulness of his or her conduct, in case, in the future, the custodian's actions based on the consent or direction of the substitute decision-maker are challenged.

---

82 *PHIPA*, s. 38(1)(c). This provision is reviewed in Chapter 10, Section D.

83 *PHIPA*, s. 71(4)(b).

84 Evidently, the custodian is entitled to rely on the assertion of a person who indicates that he or she is entitled to consent on behalf of a patient, which in the case of a substitute decision-maker for an incapable person under s. 26 would necessarily include the assertion that the patient has been determined to be incapable by a health information custodian. This entitlement to rely on the substitute decision-maker's assertion would appear to operate despite the provision in *PHIPA*, s. 21(4) that provides that a patient is presumed capable, unless it is unreasonable in the circumstances to accept the assertion.

In many situations, a person's authority to act on a patient's behalf in *PHIPA* will stem from a legal document, such as a court order for guardianship; a continuing power of attorney for property; a power of attorney for personal care; or a certificate of appointment of an estate trustee. Where a person claims to be the patient's substitute decision-maker on the basis of one of these types of documents, it would be prudent for the custodian to request to see a copy of the document as proof of authority. However, *PHIPA* does not specifically require the custodian to check the authenticity of the document provided.

Further, it would be prudent for a custodian to ask the proposed substitute decision-maker whether that person has the authority to make the decision for the collection, use, or disclosure of personal health information in question. Just because a person is the patient's guardian of property does not necessarily mean that the guardian is, in fact, authorized to make a particular information decision; this would depend on the scope of the guardian's authority as set out in the court order itself. Similarly, where the children's aid society is involved, the custodian should determine whether the society's involvement with the child is that of a parent.[85]

A custodian should exercise extra caution in a situation involving a child's parents who are separated or divorced. In this situation, requiring proof of custody of the child may be warranted. Unfortunately, a parent may claim the right to be the child's substitute decision-maker for motives unrelated to decision-making for the child's benefit.

In a situation where a patient is deceased and the estate trustee has not applied for a certificate of appointment, it may be prudent for the custodian to ask for a notarized copy of the will attesting to the fact that no one is challenging the status of this person as an estate trustee. For persons claiming to assume the responsibility for the administration of the deceased's estate, it would be reasonable for the custodian to request documentation in support of this claim, such as a letter from the person's lawyer.

Where the custodian has acted reasonably and in good faith in relying on a person's assertion that he or she is entitled to act as the patient's substitute decision-maker, *PHIPA* provides protection for the custodian from litigation in the event that the assertion is false and the person did not have the authority to consent to collect, use, or disclose the patient's information.[86] Whether or

---

85   Under the *Child and Family Services Act*, the children's aid society assumes the obligations of a parent where the child has been made a society or Crown ward (*CFSA*, above note 30, ss. 61, 62, & 63). In some cases a children's aid society may be involved in a capacity other than as parent.

86   *PHIPA*, s. 71(1).

not the custodian would be able to rely on this immunity provision will rest on the reasonableness of the custodian's actions in the circumstances with respect to the assertions made by the apparent substitute decision-maker.

D. AUTHORITY OF A SUBSTITUTE DECISION-MAKER IN *PHIPA*

In general terms, the rights and obligations that *PHIPA* confers on "individuals" — to whom this Guide refers as "patients"[87] — apply equally to substitute decision-makers.

1) Authority to Consent

Where a health information custodian requires consent for the collection, use, or disclosure of a patient's personal health information under *PHIPA*, a patient's substitute decision-maker may give, withhold, or withdraw the consent.[88] *PHIPA* also authorizes the health information custodian to turn to the patient's substitute decision-maker where the custodian requires consent for the collection, use, or disclosure of a patient's personal health information under *another* Ontario statute.[89] This authority is convenient in situations where the other Act is silent on the person to whom the custodian should turn for consent in a situation where the subject of the information is incapable.

The same obligations that a health information custodian has with respect to obtaining a valid consent from a patient apply when the custodian is obtaining the consent from a substitute decision-maker.[90] Thus, the custodian may, for example, rely on a notice describing the purposes of the collection, use, or disclosure that the custodian posts or makes readily available to the substitute decision-maker as reasonable belief that the substitute decision-maker knows the purposes of the collection, use, or disclosure of personal health informa-

---

87   See Appendix I, Glossary, for explanation of "patient."

88   *PHIPA*, s. 23(1).

89   This is based on *PHIPA*, s. 18(1), which specifically refers to any other Act, and requires that the consent be "a consent of the individual," which under *PHIPA* includes the consent of a substitute decision-maker on the individual's behalf. For a discussion on consent, see Chapter 5.

90   All the rules for consent apply equally to the substitute decision-maker. Therefore, for example, the consent must be of the substitute decision-maker, it must be knowledgeable, it must relate to the information, and it must not be obtained through deception or coercion. Consent may be express or implied, unless *PHIPA* provides that the consent must be express: see *PHIPA* s. 18 and the discussion of consent in Chapter 5.

tion, as the case may be.[91] Further, where a custodian may imply consent from a patient, the custodian may imply the consent for the collection, use, or disclosure of the patient's personal health information from the substitute decision-maker.[92] Just as some health information custodians may assume implied consent from a patient for the collection, use, or disclosure of the patient's personal health information for the purposes of providing or assisting in the provision of health care, those custodians may also assume an implied consent from the substitute decision-maker.[93]

2) Authority to Withdraw the Consent

Where a substitute decision-maker consents to the collection, use, or disclosure of a patient's personal health information, the substitute decision-maker may also withdraw the consent[94] in the manner specified in *PHIPA*. In addition, the substitute decision-maker may place a condition on the consent in the same way and to the same degree as a patient is authorized to do under the Act.[95]

Where the health information custodian initially took an action concerning the patient's personal health information with the patient's consent, the substitute decision-maker may withdraw that consent if the patient is no longer capable with respect to the information decision. Conversely, where the substitute decision-maker made a decision about the collection, use, or disclosure of the patient's personal health information, the patient can make a different decision, if the patient becomes capable of making the decision.[96]

---

91   *PHIPA*, ss. 18(5) & (6). Of course, a notice made available to the patient but not the substitute decision-maker cannot be a basis for concluding that the substitute decision-maker had knowledge of the purpose for the collection, use, or disclosure, as the case may be; and *vice versa*. The notice should also inform the individual that the individual can withdraw or withhold consent: (s. 18(5)(b)). This type of statement would also inform the substitute decision-maker in an applicable case.

92   *PHIPA*, ss. 18(2) & (3).

93   *Ibid.*, s. 20(2). See Chapter 5, Section F(3).

94   *Ibid.*, s. 23(1).

95   *Ibid.*, ss. 19(1) & (2); s. 20(2). See the discussion of withdrawal of consent and conditions on consent in Chapter 5, Section E. Note that this and the next examples in the text assume that the authority of the substitute decision-maker arises as a result of a patient's incapacity, as is often the case. Of course, it is also possible to have a substitute decision-maker acting for a capable patient, and in such a case the patient has concurrent decision-making authority. In making an information decision on behalf of the patient, the substitute decision-maker is required to take into consideration factors that are specified in *PHIPA* and outlined further in Section E below.

96   The patient may be capable at one time and incapable at another. See the discussion on capacity in Section F below.

3) Authority to Request, Give an Instruction, or Take a Step

A substitute decision-maker, who is authorized to consent on behalf of a patient to the collection, use, or disclosure of personal health information, is also authorized to make a request, give an instruction, or take a step on behalf of the patient where the Act permits or requires the patient to take such a step or other action.[97] For example, a substitute decision-maker is authorized to expressly instruct a health information custodian not to use or disclose the patient's personal health information for health care purposes.[98] Where a capable patient gives such an instruction, the substitute decision-maker may change the instruction, if that patient becomes incapable.[99] Further, a substitute decision-maker who is authorized to consent on behalf of a patient to the collection, use, or disclosure of personal health information can make an access request[100] on behalf of the patient to the patient's record of personal health information. Where the health information custodian grants the access, the substitute decision-maker also has the right to request that the record be corrected.[101]

4) Obligation of the Health Information Custodian to Notify

Since the substitute decision-maker in essence "stands in the shoes of" the patient for whom the substitute decision-maker is authorized to make decisions, where *PHIPA* requires the health information custodian to notify the patient in certain situations under the Act, it would be reasonable to conclude that where the patient is incapable and has a substitute decision-maker, the custodian should notify the substitute decision-maker, in addition to the patient. For example, a health information custodian should notify a substitute decision-maker where the custodian uses or discloses the patient's personal health information, without consent, in a manner that is outside the scope of the description of the custodian's information practices, as set out in the public written statement.[102] Further, the custodian should notify a substitute decision-maker if the patient's information is stolen, lost, or accessed by unauthorized

---

97 *PHIPA*, s. 25.

98 *Ibid.*, ss. 37(1)(a), 38(1)(a), and 50(1)(e): This express instruction is often referred to as the "lock box" and is outlined in Chapter 7.

99 See further about capacity in Section F below.

100 *PHIPA*, s. 54(1). See Chapter 13 on access to records of personal health information.

101 *Ibid.*, s. 55(1). See Chapter 14 on correction of personal health records.

102 *Ibid.*, s. 16(2). The obligations of health information custodians are outlined in Chapter 4.

103 *PHIPA*, s. 12(2).

persons.[103] Although this obligation is not set out explicitly in *PHIPA*, to interpret the provisions otherwise would run contrary to the obvious purpose of those provisions, since there would be limited value in providing such notices solely to an incapable patient who likely would not be in a position to respond to the notice.

5) Communicating with the Substitute Decision-maker

Just as the health information custodian is free to communicate with the patient, nothing in *PHIPA* prevents the custodian from communicating with the patient's substitute decision-maker. *PHIPA* allows a health information custodian to communicate a patient's personal health information to the patient where the patient has a right of access to the information, even in the absence of an access request.[104] It would be reasonable to conclude that the custodian could rely on this statement in *PHIPA* to disclose information about the patient to the substitute decision-maker. As the substitute decision-maker could also be authorized to consent to the collection, use, or disclosure of information pertaining to a deceased patient, the custodian could rely on the authority in this section of *PHIPA* to disclose information to a substitute decision-maker acting for a deceased person.

E. GUIDING THE SUBSTITUTE DECISION-MAKER

1) Factors to Consider

PHIPA guides substitute decision-makers in making decisions on behalf of capable, incapable, or deceased patients. The factors that a substitute decision-maker must consider when deciding to consent to a collection, use, or disclosure of personal health information, when withholding or withdrawing consent, or when providing an express instruction,[105] are as follows. First, a substitute decision-maker must take into consideration the wishes, values, and beliefs that the substitute decision-maker knows the capable patient holds (or the incapable or deceased patient held when capable or alive, as the case may be) and believes the patient would have wanted reflected in decisions made concerning the patient's personal health information.[106] Further, the substitute decision-maker must consider whether

---

104   *PHIPA*, s. 52(6)(b).
105   *Ibid.* Under ss. 37(1)(a), 38(1)(a), or 50(1)(e).
106   *Ibid.*, s. 24(1)(a).

- the benefits from the collection, use, or disclosure of the information outweigh the risk of negative consequences occurring as a result of the collection, use, or disclosure, as the case may be;
- the purpose for which the collection, use, or disclosure is sought can be accomplished without the collection, use, or disclosure; and
- the collection, use, or disclosure is necessary to satisfy any legal obligation.[107]

These factors are modeled on the provisions of the *Health Care Consent Act, 1996.*[108]

Unlike the approach in the *Health Care Consent Act, 1996*, however, PHIPA does not require the substitute decision-maker to strictly adhere to a patient's prior capable wishes unless it is not possible to comply with the wishes; the substitute decision-maker is required only to take the patient's prior capable wishes into *consideration*. The substitute decision-maker's final decision, however, may or may not be consistent with the patient's prior capable wishes.[109]

2) Reviewing a Decision of the Substitute Decision-maker

In the case of an incapable patient, where a health information custodian is of the view that a substitute decision-maker is not complying with the obligation to consider the factors discussed above,[110] the custodian may apply to the Con-

---

107 *PHIPA*, ss. 24(1)(b), (c), & (d). These factors were not part of the first reading version of Bill 31 (below note 111). Such factors could have been developed in regulations but, ultimately, these factors were essentially copied into *PHIPA* from Bill 159, cl. 61. The regulation-making power (as set out in Bill 31, first reading, 17 December 2003, at *PHIPA*, cl. 71(1)(k)) would have governed "the giving, withholding or withdrawing of a consent by a substitute decision-maker." The approach in *PHIPA* adopts Recommendation 13 of the Canadian Mental Health Association, Ontario Division, as submitted to the Standing Committee on General Government, 26 January 2004 and available online: <www.ontario.cmha.ca/content/reading_room/policydocuments.asp?cID=4550>.

108 The *HCCA*, above note 4, s. 21 provides that the substitute decision-maker must abide by the wishes of the incapable individual made when capable and if known to the substitute decision-maker, or if these are not known, or if it is impossible to comply with the wish, the best interests of the incapable patient as set out in that Act.

109 *HCCA, ibid.*, s. 21. Note that in the "Consent and Capacity Fact Sheets about a substitute decision-maker's role under the *Health Care Consent Act, 1996*," published by the Consent and Capacity Board with respect to an application to review a substitute decision-maker's decision, the "Board may only grant permission to depart from prior capable wishes if it is satisfied that the likely result of the proposed action is significantly better than would have been anticipated in comparable circumstances at the time the wish was expressed." The Board's fact sheets are available online: <www.ccboard.on.ca>.

110 As set out in *PHIPA*, s. 24(1), outlined in Section E(1), above.

sent and Capacity Board[111] for a determination of whether or not the substitute decision-maker has complied. The parties to such an application are the health information custodian, the incapable patient, the substitute decision-maker, and any other person whom the Board specifies.[112]

Where the Board determines that the substitute decision-maker did not comply with the requirements set out in *PHIPA*, the Board may substitute its opinion for that of the substitute decision-maker.[113] The Board may give the substitute decision-maker directions as to how to comply with the Act.[114] The Board must specify the time within which the substitute decision-maker must comply with its direction.[115] If the substitute decision-maker does not comply with the Board's direction within the time required, then the substitute decision-maker is no longer authorized to act for the patient.[116] Where the substitute decision-maker is the Public Guardian and Trustee, he or she must comply with the Board's direction.[117]

In such an application by a health information custodian to the Board, the patient is deemed to have applied for a review of his or her capacity to make the relevant decision, unless there has been such a review within the previous six months.[118]

As for all applications to the Board under *PHIPA*, the composition of the panels to hear an application, the timelines for hearings, the patient's right to counsel, and appeal rights follow the requirements set out in the *Health Care Consent Act, 1996*.[119]

---

111 *PHIPA*, s. 24(2). See note 55. After the first reading, the Standing Committee on General Government amended Bill 31, *An Act to enact and amend various Acts with respect to the protection of health information*, 1st Sess., 38th Leg., Ontario, 2003, Sch. A [Bill 31] to include this type of application to the Board, apparently on the recommendation of the Canadian Mental Health Association, Ontario Division (Recommendation 15); see *ibid.*

112 *PHIPA*, s. 24(3). Application to the Board is to be made on Form P-2 available by contacting the Board, online: <www.ccboard.on.ca>; or by phone 1-800-461-2036. Note that the form specifies that only the health information custodian or the agent authorized to make the application can bring the application.

113 *PHIPA*, s. 24(4).

114 *Ibid.*, s. 24(5).

115 *Ibid.*, s. 24(6).

116 *Ibid.*, s. 24(7). The Board has the power to deem the substitute decision-maker as not meeting the requirements of s. 26(2). See text cited by note 70 about the requirements of this section of *PHIPA*.

117 *PHIPA*, s. 24(8).

118 *PHIPA* Regulation, above note 25, s. 9.

119 *PHIPA*, s. 24(9). For ss. 73–81 of the *HCCA*, see Section H below.

3) Immunities, Offences, and Other Matters with Respect to Substitute Decision-makers

a) Immunities

A substitute decision-maker who, on behalf of a patient, gives or refuses[120] consent to a collection, use, or disclosure of personal health information about the patient; makes a request; gives an instruction; or takes a step is not liable for damages if he or she acts reasonably in the circumstances, in good faith, and in accordance with *PHIPA*.[121]

b) Offences

In connection with a health information custodian's collection, use, or disclosure of personal health information or in connection with an access to a record of personal health information, it is an offence for the substitute decision-maker to make any of the following assertions, knowing that the assertion is untrue:

- that the substitute decision-maker is entitled to consent to the collection, use, or disclosure of personal health information about the patient;[122]
- that the substitute decision-maker is at least sixteen years old or is the parent of the patient;[123]
- that the substitute decision-maker is not prohibited by a court order or separation agreement from having access to the patient;[124]
- that the substitute decision-maker believes that no other person described in an earlier paragraph or the same paragraph within the list of ranked persons allowed to make decisions on behalf of an incapable patient exists;[125] or
- that although such other person exists, the substitute decision-maker (who is present or has otherwise been contacted) believes the other person would not object to the substitute decision-maker making the decision.[126]

These offence provisions in *PHIPA* are specific to substitute decision-makers. Of course, there are other offence provisions, of a more general

---

120 The concept of "refusing" consent includes "withholding or withdrawing" consent, which are words more typically used in *PHIPA* to describe actions or inactions with respect to consent. See, for example, ss. 18(5)(b), 19(1), 20(2), and 21(1)(b).
121 *PHIPA*, s. 71(3).
122 *Ibid.*, s. 72(1)(c)(i).
123 *Ibid.*, s. 72(1)(c)(ii), referring to s. 26(2)(b).
124 *Ibid.*, s. 72(1)(c)(ii), referring to s. 26(2)(c).
125 *Ibid.*, s. 72(1)(c)(iii), referring to s. 26(5)(a).
126 *Ibid.*, s. 72(1)(c)(iii), referring to s. 26(5)(b).

nature, that could also be relevant to an action taken by a substitute decision-maker with respect to a patient's personal health information. Where a substitute decision-maker, for example, falsely asserts that a record is incorrect, such as in order to de-fraud an insurer, this constitutes an offence under *PHIPA*.[127]

c)   Other Matters

The regulation under *PHIPA* clarifies that the substitute decision-maker is not prevented from collecting, using, or disclosing the patient's health number,[128] and that the *PHIPA* restriction on recipients does not apply to personal health information the substitute decision-maker receives, in his or her capacity as substitute decision-maker, from the custodian about the patient.[129]

F. CAPACITY WITH RESPECT TO PERSONAL HEALTH INFORMATION

1) A Patient Is Presumed Capable

PHIPA provides that a patient is presumed to be capable of consenting to the collection, use, or disclosure of personal health information.[130] A health information custodian may rely on this presumption, unless the custodian has reasonable grounds to believe that the patient is incapable.[131] A custodian is not required to question whether a patient is capable of giving consent each time the custodian obtains the patient's consent to the collection, use, or disclosure

---

127   *PHIPA*, s. 72(1)(b). For a discussion of offences in *PHIPA*, see Chapter 15.

128   *PHIPA* Regulation, above note 25, s. 1(1). See further Chapter 2, Section D(4).

129   *PHIPA* Regulation, *ibid.*, s. 21(a). See further Chapter 12, Section D(1)(b).

130   *PHIPA*, s. 21(4). This provision allows the custodian simply to begin collecting information from the individual. However, once the custodian realizes that the individual may not be capable, the custodian then must take steps to decide capacity, where consent would be required with respect to the decision.

131   *PHIPA*, s. 21(5). It should be noted that where a patient's substitute decision-maker asserts that he or she has authority to make the information decision on an incapable patient's behalf, which under s. 26(1) necessarily includes the assertion that the patient has been determined by a health information custodian to be incapable, the health information custodian is evidently entitled to rely on this assertion unless it would be unreasonable to do so (*PHIPA*, s. 71(4)(b)). This suggests that where the custodian is presented with a person claiming to be the substitute decision-maker for a patient who has been determined by another custodian to be incapable, the custodian may rely on this claim unless there is reason to doubt the veracity of the substitute decision-maker's claim. Thus the custodian to whom this claim is made does not need to independently determine the patient's capacity unless the claim appears unreliable.

of personal health information. Further, this presumption in *PHIPA* permits a health information custodian, who receives a request from the patient to disclose the patient's personal health information to a third party, to presume that the patient is capable in making this request, without having to personally contact the patient to ascertain whether or not the patient is capable of authorizing the disclosure. This presumption assists the custodian in assuming the validity of the patient's consent.[132]

The custodian must, however, question the patient's capacity where it would be unreasonable to rely on this presumption, such as where the custodian is aware that the patient is very ill and unable to make decisions because of heavy reliance on medication or because the patient is suffering from extreme pain.

It is a common error to assume that *PHIPA* provides sixteen years as the "age of consent." In some contexts *PHIPA* does refer to the age of sixteen. For example, the Act provides that a patient must be at least sixteen years old to be able to authorize someone else in writing to act on the patient's behalf.[133] However, there is no "age of consent" in the Act and the presumption that a patient is capable applies to persons under the age of sixteen, as well.[134] Of course, in some cases, age can be indicative of incapacity.[135]

---

132   Under *PHIPA*, s. 20(2), the custodian who has obtained a patient's consent to a collection, use, or disclosure of the patient's personal health information or has received a document purporting to record the patient's consent is entitled to assume that the consent fulfils the requirements of *PHIPA*, unless it is not reasonable to assume so. For a discussion of this assumption of validity, see Chapter 5, Section C.

133   *PHIPA*, s. 23(1)[1][ii].

134   This is consistent with the *HCCA*, above note 4, s. 10.

135   Professor D.N. Weisstub, in his *Enquiry on Mental Competency: Final Report* (Toronto: Queen's Printer of Ontario, 1990) at 116 [Weisstub Report] conducted research indicating that "children attain their adult reasoning capacities somewhere between eleven or twelve and fourteen." His report ultimately, at 152, recommended that "young persons age 14 or above be treated as adults with respect to their decisional prerogatives, and accordingly be assessed as adults where their capacity is in question." In reviewing the case law pertaining to mental competency as existed at the time of his enquiry, Prof. Weisstub concluded, at 132, that "it would be playing legal games to pretend that the court would apply the same presumption to a child of three as to an adult. While the legal doctrine may remain unchanged, the reality is that the presumption of competence is likely to be accorded more weight in proportion to the child's age." More recently, a child's capacity to make treatment decisions has been discussed in two related cases: *Children's Aid Society of Metropolitan Toronto v. H(T)* (1995), RE1/95, 15 July 1996 (Ont. Gen. Div.) and *H(T) v. Children's Aid Society of Metropolitan Toronto* (1996), O.J. No. 2578 (Gen. Div.). TH, a thirteen-year-old Jehovah's Witness, refused to give consent to treatment using blood products to treat her aplastic anemia. TH's mother had also refused consent. The Children's Aid Society applied to court for an

Another common mistaken assumption is that a patient is incapable of making a decision about his or her personal health information if he or she suffers from mental illness. The fact that a patient is mentally ill does not mean that he or she is incapable; such a patient may still be capable of making a decision concerning his or her personal health information.[136] Also, the inability of a patient to communicate, such as because of a language barrier or speech impairment, does not make the patient incapable. Further, the fact that a patient disagrees with the custodian's judgment regarding the proper decision that the patient should be making regarding a collection, use, or disclosure of personal health information does not make the patient incapable. As emphasized by Mr. Justice Quinn in *Re Koch*: "The right knowingly to be foolish is not unimportant; the right to voluntarily assume risks is to be respected."[137]

PHIPA recognizes that a patient may be capable of consenting to the collection, use, or disclosure of some parts of the information, but incapable with respect to other parts.[138] For example, a patient may be capable of consenting to the disclosure of personal health information that consists of the patient's name and the fact that the patient has been admitted to a hospital as a patient. However, the patient may not be capable of consenting to the disclosure of the patient's entire health history. Moreover, a patient may be capable at one time, but incapable at another, and *vice versa*.[139]

---

order declaring that TH was in need of protection (under the provisions of the *Child and Family Services Act*). Counsel for the patient argued that TH was a mature minor capable of making her own treatment decisions. The court in the 1995 case concluded that there is a presumption of incapacity of a child less than sixteen years. Although this conclusion was rejected in the 1996 case, the case does underline that age is a factor that can be considered when a person's capacity is being determined.

136 The Weisstub Report, *ibid.* at 116, noted the historical failure to respect this presumption of capacity: "The tendency to conflate mental illness with lack of capacity, which occurs to an even greater extent when involuntary commitment [to a psychiatric facility] is involved, has deep historical roots, and even though changes have occurred in the law over the past twenty years, attitudes and beliefs have been slow to change. For this reason it is particularly important that autonomy and self determination be given priority when assessing individuals in this group."

137 (1997), 33 O.R. (3d) 485 at 521 (Gen. Div.), quoted with approval by the Supreme Court of Canada in *Starson v. Swayze*, [2003] 1 S.C.R. 722 at para. 76.

138 *PHIPA*, s. 21(2). This mirrors the provisions for capacity for treatment in the *HCCA*, above note 4, s. 15(1).

139 *PHIPA*, s. 21(4). A similar provision with respect to capacity for treatment is found in the *HCCA*, *ibid.*, s. 15(2). Also note that in Form P-1, Application to the Consent and Capacity Board for a Review of a Determination of Incapacity, the patient may be incapable of one of the following: a collection, use, or disclosure decision. The application to the Board is discussed in Section F(6), below.

2) The Definition of Capacity

For the purposes of *PHIPA*, in the context of consenting to a collection, use, or disclosure of personal health information, the capable patient must have both

- the ability to understand the information that is relevant to deciding whether to consent to the collection, use, or disclosure, as the case may be; and
- the ability to appreciate the reasonably foreseeable consequences of giving, not giving, withholding, or withdrawing the consent.[140]

If the patient has only the ability to understand, but cannot appreciate the consequences of a consent decision, the patient would be determined to be incapable of making a decision about his or her personal health information.

3) Who Determines Capacity?

Under *PHIPA*, the discretion to determine capacity rests with the health information custodian. In the case of a hospital, for example, the health information custodian that holds this discretion is the person who operates the hospital (i.e. the hospital corporation), as opposed to the attending physician.[141] This approach differs from the approach taken in the *Health Care Consent Act, 1996* where the opinion as to whether a patient is capable with respect to a treatment decision rests with the health care practitioner who proposes the treatment.[142] Where a custodian is not a natural person, the custodian must rely on its agents, such as physicians, psychologists, nurses, or social workers on staff with or

---

140   *PHIPA*, s. 21(1). This two-step approach to a determination of capacity has its statutory genesis in Ontario in the *Mental Health Act*, above note 54, which defined "mentally competent" as having "the ability to understand the subject-matter in respect of which consent is requested and [being] able to appreciate the consequences of giving or withholding consent: *MHA*, s. 1(1), repealed by *PHIPA*, s. 90(1). The provisions in the *Mental Health Act* that addressed findings of mental incompetence with respect to records and review rights have been repealed with the coming into force of *PHIPA* [*PHIPA*, s. 90(12), repealing ss. 36(14) & (15) of the *MHA*.] This two-step approach has been incorporated into the *HCCA*, above note 4. Under that Act, at s. 4(1), a person is capable to make a decision about a treatment, an admission to a care facility, or a personal assistance service within that facility, as the case may be, if the person (1) is able to understand the information that is relevant to making a decision about the treatment, admission, or personal assistance service, as the case may be; and (2) is able to appreciate the reasonably foreseeable consequences of a decision or lack of decision. A similar two-step analysis figures in the *Substitute Decisions Act, 1992*, above note 18 (such as at s. 47(1) pertaining to a person's capacity to give a power of attorney for personal care).
141   See discussion of "custodian" in Chapter 2, Section B(1).
142   *HCCA*, above note 4, s. 10(1).

employed by the custodian to determine the capacity of a patient and to provide a determination about the patient's capacity.[143] Even where the custodian is a natural person, the custodian's agents may be better suited to make the determination, and the custodian may delegate this task to some of them.[144]

The custodian may also disclose personal health information to another person, without the patient's consent, where information is needed to help determine the patient's capacity.[145] Where a custodian requires a second opinion about the patient's capacity, for example, or where the custodian does not have the expertise to embark on such a determination, the custodian may rely on this provision to obtain the necessary assistance. The custodian may determine incapacity by relying on a letter from the patient's family physician, for example; or the custodian may request that the patient be referred to a psychologist or psychiatrist for a more formal evaluation. In this section of *PHIPA*, the words "the custodian may disclose" refer not only to the custodian who requires a determination as to whether or not a patient is capable, but also to the custodian who was asked for an opinion to confirm the capacity of the patient. In this latter situation, the health information custodian who has been consulted would be disclosing the details of the determination back to the requesting custodian.[146]

4) Determining Capacity with Respect to Personal Health Information

Whether or not a patient is capable of consenting to the collection, use, or disclosure of his or her personal health information is a conclusion that a custodian must reach based on the legal definition as set out in *PHIPA*. "Capacity," in the context of *PHIPA*, is not a clinical condition or a diagnosis. A health information custodian would not conclude that the patient is incapable as a result of conducting a particular clinical test on the patient, such as a Mini Mental Status Examination.[147]

---

143 Note that the application forms of the Consent and Capacity Board pertaining to *PHIPA* supports this view. The forms refer to the custodian or the agent who made the determination: see, for example, Form P-2, online: <www.ccboard.on.ca>.

144 For example, in a provincially operated psychiatric facility, the "officer in charge" is the custodian. Physicians and others who provide health care to the patients would logically continue to assess the capacity of patients.

145 *PHIPA*, s. 43(1)(a).

146 *Ibid.*

147 Physicians and psychologists often use a Mini Mental Status Examination, which is a commonly used simple screening test for dementia. See, online: <www.merck.com/mrkshared/mmanual/figures/165fig1.jsp>.

Rather, a health information custodian must determine a patient's capacity, where necessary, by applying the legal test as set out in *PHIPA* to a patient's particular situation. The custodian must determine whether or not the patient has the *ability to understand* the information relevant to the decision and the *ability to appreciate* the consequences of the decision.[148]

The principles, extracted from decisions of the Consent and Capacity Board[149] and the Supreme Court of Canada in *Starson v. Swayze*,[150] may guide the health information custodian in this determination.

a) Ability to Understand the Information Relevant to the Consent

A health information custodian[151] should provide a patient with the relevant information, such as the purpose for which the custodian will collect, use, or disclose the personal health information and the identity of any persons to whom the custodian will disclose the information. By asking a patient to explain back to the custodian the information that was provided, the custodian can determine the extent to which the patient can retain, interpret, and manipulate that information.[152] This exercise can help reveal whether the patient demonstrates an ability to understand the information being discussed.[153]

---

148 *PHIPA*, s. 21(1).

149 The Consent and Capacity Board has rendered some decisions pertaining to patients' mental incompetence to consent to the disclosure of clinical records under the provisions of the *Mental Health Act*, now repealed. See above note 140. Decisions of the Consent and Capacity Board are available online at: <www.ccboard.on.ca>.

150 Above note 137. While there are no court decisions pertaining to capacity to make decisions concerning personal health information, there are a number of decisions that review the test for capacity to consent to treatment under the *HCCA*, above note 4.. In *Starson v. Swayze*, the leading case, Starson, a man with superior skills in physics, had been admitted to a psychiatric facility, on the order of the Ontario Review Board, after he was found not criminally responsible for making death threats. The Ontario Review Board ordered his detention for twelve months. Starson had been diagnosed for some years with a bipolar disorder. His attending physician proposed to treat him with various medications, to which Starson refused to give his consent. The attending physician found Starson incapable of deciding whether to reject or accept the proposed medical treatment. Starson applied to the Consent and Capacity Board for a review of the finding of incapacity. The Supreme Court of Canada overturned the Board's confirmation of his incapacity.

151 As set out above, the "health information custodian" may not make the determination, *per se*: an agent of the custodian could make the determination on the custodian's behalf.

152 According to the Supreme Court of Canada in *Starson v. Swayze*, above note 137 at para. 79, in the context of capacity to consent to treatment under the *Health Care Consent Act, 1996*, a patient must be able to understand the information about the proposed treatment relevant to making the decision. This requires the cognitive ability to process, retain, and understand the relevant information.

153 In *Re R.G. J.K.L.* 2003 CanLII 26073 (ON C.C.B.), 14 February 2003, the Consent and Capacity Board found that, although the patient knew what the record was and the

b) Ability to Appreciate the Reasonably Foreseeable Consequences of a Decision about the Consent

Further, a health information custodian must determine whether a patient can apply the relevant information discussed about the consent to the collection, use, or disclosure of personal health information, as the case may be, to his or her own situation. Can the patient weigh the foreseeable consequences of the decision?[154] Does the patient realize the consequences of the choice he or she is making? Can the patient explain the basis for the decision?[155] However, whether a patient can appreciate the consequences can only be assessed properly where the custodian has adequately informed the patient of the decision's consequences.[156] If the custodian does not provide the relevant information to

---

fact that a privacy issue was involved, she did not have the mental competency to understand key pieces of relevant information. In this case, the patient was unable to understand that she suffered from a mental illness requiring ongoing treatment, and that a plan needed to be put in place for that treatment to occur outside the hospital before she could be safely discharged. Also, she was unable to understand the fact that those charged with devising such a plan needed access to her medical record for that purpose; available online: <www.ccboard.on.ca>.

154   In *Starson v. Swayze*, above note 137 at para. 78, the Supreme Court of Canada concluded that, in the context of treatment decisions, in addition to being able to understand the information relevant to the decision, the person must be able to appreciate the reasonably foreseeable consequences of the decision or lack of one. This requires the patient to be able to apply the relevant information to his or her own circumstances, and to be able to weigh the foreseeable risks and benefits of a decision or lack thereof.

155   In *Re R.S.* 2004 CanLII 20313 (ON C.C.B.), 1 April 2004, the patient refused to sign a consent form permitting the release of information about the patient in possession of other psychiatric facilities, the Windsor Police Department, and the Windsor Probation Office to the attending physician at the London Regional Mental Health Centre. The patient felt that the information would be used against him and result in his stay in the hospital being longer. The Consent and Capacity Board concluded that this was a reasonable conclusion. The Board concluded that the patient had the ability to appreciate the consequences of giving or refusing consent, namely that without consent his physician would be unable to get information from various agencies and with consent the physician would be able to access the information; available online: <www.ccboard.on.ca>.

156   For instance, a lack of appreciation may reflect the attending physician's failure to adequately inform the patient of the decision's consequences. In the case of Professor Starson, not taking medication would lead to consequences to him with respect to future dispositions by the Ontario Review Board. But it appeared that neither of the psychiatrists who testified before the Consent and Capacity Board had discussed such possible consequences with their patient. (The Consent and Capacity Board speculated that taking medication would improve the patient's prospects before the Ontario Review Board: above note 137 at para. 101.) The Court in *Starson v. Swayze* does not explain the situation further. The Ontario Review Board has jurisdiction under the

the patient, the patient may not appreciate the consequences of his or her decision, not because of a lack of capacity but because of a lack of information. A custodian may also consider whether the decision-making is consistent with the patient's lifestyle choices and beliefs.[157] If so, this may suggest that the patient is able to make the decision, even though the decision may be inconsistent with lifestyle choices and beliefs of most people.

5) Information about a Determination of Incapacity

Where a health information custodian[158] makes a determination that a patient is incapable, the custodian is required to provide information to the incapable patient about the consequences of the determination.[159] With a determination of incapacity, the right to make some or all decisions about his or her own information is effectively taken away from the patient and is given to someone else. It is, therefore, important for the custodian to provide information to the individual so that the patient knows he or she has an opportunity to challenge the determination, either informally with the custodian or formally by way of an application to the Consent and Capacity Board.[160] The custodian is not obliged to provide such information if it is not reasonable to do so in the circumstances.[161] It

---

provisions of the *Criminal Code of Canada*, R.S.C. 1985, c. C-46 to detain patients in psychiatric facilities as well as discharge patients. This suggests that had Professor Starson been taking medication, the Review Board would possibly have allowed him to reside in a different environment. In the Court's view, a finding of incapacity is justified only if the reasons for the patient's failure to appreciate the consequences "demonstrate that the patient's mental disorder prevents him from having the ability to appreciate the foreseeable consequences of the decision," that is, not because of lack of information. See *Starson v. Swayze*, above note 137 at para. 81.

157   The Supreme Court of Canada in *Starson v. Swayze* emphasized that the best interests of the patient are irrelevant to a determination of whether or not a patient is capable of making a treatment decision. "The [Consent and Capacity] Board's sole task was to determine the patient's mental capacity," asserted Mr. Justice Major for the Court. "If Professor Starson is capable, he is fully entitled to make a decision that the Board, or other reasonable persons may perceive as foolish. The Board improperly allowed its own conception of Professor Starson's best interest to influence its finding of incapacity." *Ibid.* at para. 81.

158   That is, on its own or through its agents.

159   *PHIPA*, s. 22(2). The subsection indicates that the custodian is also obliged to provide any information that is prescribed. No such regulation exists at the time of writing. A similar requirement to provide information to an incapable patient exists in the *HCCA*, above note 4, s. 17.

160   See the next section.

161   *PHIPA*, s. 22(2).

would not be reasonable, for example, to provide such advice to a young child,[162] to a person who is in a coma, or where there is an emergency.[163]

As *PHIPA* does not specify what information a custodian must provide to a patient to fulfil the custodian's obligation to provide the patient with information about the consequences of the determination, a health information custodian has the ability to exercise significant discretion in this regard. The information may include advice to the patient that he or she has a right to a review of the finding before the Consent and Capacity Board, and information about how to make an application to the Board. It would be reasonable for the custodian to notify the patient that someone else will be making the decision about the collection, use, or disclosure of the patient's personal health information on his or her behalf.

However, in one instance, other legislation does specify what steps must be taken once a patient is determined to be incapable of consenting to the collection, use, or disclosure of personal health information. Under the *Mental Health Act*, an officer in charge of a psychiatric facility[164] is required to notify a "rights advisor" when a patient is determined incapable of consenting to a collection, use, or disclosure of personal health information. The rights advisor, in turn, is required to provide an explanation to the patient about the consequences of such determinations of incapacity.[165] Rights advice is not required in all situations.[166]

---

162 *General*, R.R.O. 1990, Reg. 741, s. 15.1(1) [Reg. 741], made under the *MHA*, above note 54, sets out that rights advice (that is, an explanation about the consequences of a finding of incapacity under *PHIPA*) is not required to be provided to a child under fourteen years of age. Providing rights advice to patients fourteen years and older, but not to younger patients, is consistent with the Weisstub Report's conclusion that children fourteen and over should be treated as adults for the purposes of capacity assessments. See above note 135. It would appear to be reasonable for the custodian to adopt a similar approach with respect to providing an explanation to patients under fourteen years of age, in general, about the consequence of a determination of incapacity in *PHIPA*.

163 For example, ss. 15.1(1) and (5) of Reg. 741, *ibid.*, provides that there is no requirement for rights advice for a patient under fourteen, where the patient is in a coma, is unconscious, is semi-conscious or is unable to communicate comprehensibly despite reasonable efforts to understand the person, or where there is an emergency.

164 An officer in charge of a psychiatric facility may be either an agent of a health information custodian (see *PHIPA*, s. 3(1)[4][i]) or a health information custodian in the case of the three government-operated psychiatric facilities (see *PHIPA*, s. 3(2)).

165 Reg. 741, above note 162, s. 15.1. Information about rights advice in psychiatric facilities can be found online: <www.ppao.gov.on.ca/ser-rig.html>.

166 See above note 163.

As most *RHPA* Colleges and the College of Social Work and Social Service Workers have already established guidelines for their members as to what kind of information their members should provide to a patient found incapable of making a decision under the *Health Care Consent Act, 1996*, they may, in time, build on these guidelines to make them useful for determinations of incapacity under *PHIPA* as well.[167] A health information custodian that is a facility may also develop its own guidelines.

6) Application to the Consent and Capacity Board

Where the health information custodian has determined that a patient is incapable of making a decision about his or her personal health information, that patient has a right to apply to the Consent and Capacity Board for a review of that determination.[168] This right, however, does not extend to a patient who already has a substitute decision-maker under the *Health Care Consent Act, 1996* where a decision about the collection, use, or disclosure of personal

---

167 For example, the Ontario College of Social Workers and Social Service Workers has published a standard of practice for social workers communicating a finding of incapacity with respect to admission to care facilities or personal assistance services. The standard sets out what the social worker should do:

- Inform the client that a substitute decision-maker will be asked to assist the client and to make final decisions on his or her behalf.
- Advise the client of his or her options if the client disagrees with the need for a substitute decision-maker or disagrees with the involvement of the present substitute. The member will assist the client if he or she expresses the wish to exercise the options. These options include applying to the Consent and Capacity Board for a review of the finding of incapacity and/or finding another substitute of the same or more senior rank.
- Help the incapable client participate as far as possible with the substitute decision-maker in planning for himself or herself.

[*Standards of Practice Handbook*, 1st ed. (Toronto: Ontario College of Social Workers and Social Service Workers, 2000) at 31, s. 1.01, online: <www.ocswssw.org>.
   The Royal College of Dental Surgeons of Ontario provides similar guidelines to its members with respect to communicating with a patient incapable of providing consent to treatment, published August 2002, online: <www.rcdso.org/pdf/guidelines/provide_consent.pdf>. See also the College of Occupational Therapists of Ontario: *Guide to the Health Care Consent and Substitute Decisions Legislation for Occupational Therapists, Practice Guidelines for Providing Information for Those Incapable* (September 1996), available online: <www.coto.org/media/documents/HCCA_Guide.PDF>.

168 *PHIPA*, s. 22(1). The application to the Board is Form P-1, available on the Board's website: <www.ccboard.on.ca>.

health information on behalf of the patient is necessary for, or ancillary to, a decision that the substitute decision-maker is authorized to make under that Act.[169] In this situation, the patient who has been found incapable of a treatment decision (for example, under the *Health Care Consent Act, 1996*) has already had an opportunity to have the finding reviewed under that Act.[170] As the information decision to be made under *PHIPA* is merely "necessary and ancillary"[171] to the treatment decision, *PHIPA* does not provide a patient with, in essence, a right to a second review of the finding of incapacity.

The parties to an application before the Board are the patient applying for the review of the determination; the health information custodian that has custody or control of the information; and all other persons whom the Board specifies.[172] Where an agent has made the determination that the patient is incapable, on the custodian's behalf, the Board may include the agent as a party.[173] The Board may confirm the determination of incapacity or it may determine that the patient is, in fact, capable.[174] If the Board confirms a determination that a patient is incapable, the patient is restricted from re-applying to the Board earlier than six months from the final disposition of the application,[175] unless there has been a material change in circumstances.[176]

For applications to the Board under *PHIPA*, the composition of the panels to hear applications, the timelines for hearings, the patient's right to counsel, and appeal rights are determined in accordance with the *Health Care Consent Act, 1996*.[177]

Where a patient makes an application to the Consent and Capacity Board for a review of a health information custodian's determination of incapacity, the custodian can rely on the determination of incapacity until such time as the

---

169 *PHIPA*, s. 22(3). See the discussion about information decisions necessary or ancillary to the decisions a substitute decision-maker is authorized to make under the *HCCA*, above note 4 and at Section B(6)(a) above.

170 *HCCA*, *ibid.*, s. 32.

171 See the discussion of "necessary and ancillary" in Section B(6)(a) above.

172 *PHIPA*, s. 22(4).

173 Consent and Capacity Board, Form P-1.

174 *PHIPA*, s. 22(5).

175 A "final disposition" would include any appeals of the Board's decision.

176 *PHIPA*, ss. 22(6) & (7). A similar right exists in the *HCCA*, above note 4, s. 32(6). Where a material change in circumstances has occurred, the Board will accept written submissions to request a new hearing. A material change in circumstances would be a situation, for example, where a patient is now taking medication and the treatment has reduced the effects of delusionary behaviour.

177 *PHIPA*, s. 22(8). Sections 73–81 under the *HCCA*, *ibid.*, apply.

Board may overturn it, and apparently may proceed to act pursuant to a substitute decision-maker's consent.[178]

G. TIPS FOR FINDING A SUBSTITUTE DECISION-MAKER FOR AN INCAPABLE PATIENT FROM THE LIST

- Go down the list from top to bottom.
- Check each category of persons described in the list.
- Stop at the first person you find on the list.
- Find out if there are any other persons in the same category.
- If there is more than one person in the category, see if the person you have contacted may speak for all.
- Ask for proof that the person is who the person says he or she is. Document their assertion and have them record or confirm the claim in writing.
- Ask yourself: is there any reason to doubt this potential substitute decision-maker is capable?
- Ask the potential substitute decision-maker:
  - Are you sixteen or older?
  - If you are under sixteen, are you the parent of the child for whom you are consenting?
  - Is there a court order or separation agreement that tells you to stay away from the patient or does not allow you to make decisions for the patient?
  - Is there no other person described in an earlier paragraph of the list or in the same paragraph in the list?
- And,
  - Even if such other person does exist, would they object to you making the decision? (Remember: if the other person is a guardian or an attor-

---

178 Although *PHIPA* does not speak to this issue specifically, one can come to this conclusion due to the absence in *PHIPA* of a specific provision that requires a delay until such time as the Board deals with a capacity determination. Contrast this approach with that taken in the *Health Care Consent Act, 1996*. In section 18 of that Act, for example, where a health care practitioner proposes treatment and finds that the patient is incapable with respect to it, treatment must not begin in circumstances where the practitioner knows an application to the Board to review the finding has been made or is about to be made . Timelines for delay are specifically set out in section 18. These timelines recognize that in some instances a patient will indicate that an application will be made but, in fact, none is made: once a timeline has passed, the practitioner should be able to clearly rely on a consent of the authorized substitute in proceeding with the treatment.

ney under a power of attorney for property or personal care, then you, the custodian, must make an effort to locate them.)

H. CONTACTS

Public Guardian and Trustee
www.attorneygeneral.jus.gov.on.ca
Toll free: 1-800-366-0335
Fax: (416) 314-2642

Psychiatric Patient Advocate Office
www.ppao.gov.on.ca
Toll free: 1-866-851-1212
Fax request for a rights advice visit: 1-866-822-2333

Consent and Capacity Board
www.ccboard.ca
Toll free: 1-800-461-2036
Fax completed forms to: (416) 924-8873

Consent and Capacity Board — Regional Offices

Toronto Phone: (416) 924-4961 Fax: (416) 924-8873	**Kingston** Phone: (613) 530-1081 Fax: (613) 530-2653
London Phone: (519) 438-7811 Fax: (519) 660-1525	**North Bay** Phone: (705) 494-8450 Fax: (705) 474-5630
Ottawa Phone: (613) 565-6368 Fax: (613) 565-9605	**Penetanguishene** Phone: (705) 733-3959 Fax: (705) 733-8268
Sudbury Phone: (705) 673-4614 Fax: (705) 673-7293	**Thunder Bay** Phone: (807) 625-0264 Fax: (807) 625-0265
Hamilton/Guelph Phone: (905) 308-9612 Fax: (905) 522-4357	

I. EXCERPT FROM THE *HEALTH CARE CONSENT ACT, 1996* PERTAINING TO APPLICATIONS TO THE CONSENT AND CAPACITY BOARD

These sections apply, with necessary modifications, to applications to the Board under *PHIPA*. See *PHIPA*, section 21(8) (application for a review of a determination of incapacity); section 27(9) (application to appoint a representative); section 24(9) (application to determine compliance by a substitute decision-maker).

Assignment of Board members to deal with applications

73. (1) The chair shall assign the members of the Board to sit alone or in panels of three or five members to deal with particular applications.

Qualifications of member sitting alone

(2) A member of the Board may be assigned to sit alone to deal with an application only if,

(a) throughout the two-year period immediately preceding the assignment, he or she has been a member of the Board or of the review board established by section 37 of the *Mental Health Act*, as it read before the day subsection 20(23) of the *Consent and Capacity Statute Law Amendment Act, 1992* came into force;

(b) he or she is a member of the Law Society of Upper Canada and has been a member of the Law Society of Upper Canada throughout the ten-year period immediately preceding the assignment;

(c) in the case of an application for a review of a finding of incapacity, he or she has experience that, in the opinion of the chair, is relevant to adjudicating capacity; and

(d) he or she meets all of the other qualifications specified by the chair under subsection 71(3).

Panel proceedings

(3) If a panel is assigned to deal with an application,

(a) the chair shall designate one member of the panel to preside over the hearing to be conducted by the panel in relation to the application; and

(b) a majority of the members of the panel constitutes a quorum.

Decision of Board

(4) If a member of the Board is assigned to sit alone to deal with an application, the decision of the member is the decision of the Board, and if a panel

is assigned to deal with an application, the decision of a majority of the members of the panel is the decision of the Board.

Disqualification

74. (1) A member of the Board shall not take part in the hearing of a matter that concerns a person who is or was the member's patient or client.

Same

(2) A member of the Board who is an officer or employee of a hospital or other facility or has a direct financial interest in such a facility shall not take part in the hearing of a matter that concerns a person who is a patient of the facility or who resides in the facility.

Application hearings

Board to fix time and place of hearing

75. (1) When the Board receives an application, it shall promptly fix a time and place for a hearing.

Hearing to begin within seven days

(2) The hearing shall begin within seven days after the day the Board receives the application, unless the parties agree to a postponement.

Decision

(3) The Board shall render its decision and provide each party or the party's counsel or agent with a copy of the decision within one day after the day the hearing ends.

Reasons

(4) If, within 30 days after the day the hearing ends, the Board receives a request from any of the parties for reasons for its decision, the Board shall, within two business days after the day the request is received, issue written reasons for its decision and provide each party or the party's counsel or agent with a copy of the reasons.

Notice of right to request reasons

(5) The Board shall advise all parties to the application that each party has a right to request reasons for the Board's decision.

Method of sending decision and reasons

(6) Despite subsection 18(1) of the *Statutory Powers Procedure Act*, the Board shall send the copy of the decision and, if reasons are required to be issued under subsection (4), the copy of the reasons,

(a) by electronic transmission;

(b) by telephone transmission of a facsimile; or

(c) by some other method that allows proof of receipt, in accordance with the tribunal's rules made under section 25.1 of the *Statutory Powers Procedure Act*.

Deemed day of receipt

(7) Despite subsection 18(3) of the *Statutory Powers Procedure Act*, if the copy is sent by electronic transmission or by telephone transmission of a facsimile, it shall be deemed to be received on the day that it was sent, unless that day is a holiday, in which case the copy shall be deemed to be received on the next day that is not a holiday.

Exception

(8) If a party that acts in good faith does not, through absence, accident, illness or other cause beyond the party's control, receive the copy until a date that is later than the deemed day of receipt, the actual date of receipt governs.

Meaning of "business day"

(9) In subsection (4), "business day" means any day other than Saturday or a holiday.

Examination of documents

76. (1) Before the hearing, the parties shall be given an opportunity to examine and copy any documentary evidence that will be produced and any report whose contents will be given in evidence.

Health record

(2) The party who is the subject of the treatment, the admission or the personal assistance service, as the case may be, and his or her counsel or agent are entitled to examine and to copy, at their own expense, any medical or other health record prepared in respect of the party, subject to subsections 35(6) and (7) of the *Mental Health Act* (withholding record of personal health information), subsections 33(2), (3) and (4) of the *Long-Term Care Act, 1994* (withholding record of personal health information) and subsections 183(2) to (6) of the *Child and Family Services Act* (withholding record of mental disorder).

Communication re subject-matter of hearing

77. (1) The member or members of the Board conducting a hearing shall not communicate about the subject-matter of the hearing directly or indirect-

ly with any party, counsel, agent or other person, unless all the parties and their counsel or agents receive notice and have an opportunity to participate.

Exception

(2) However, the member or members of the Board conducting the hearing may seek advice from an adviser independent of the parties, and in that case the nature of the advice shall be communicated to all the parties and their counsel or agents so that they may make submissions as to the law.

Only members at hearing to participate in decision

78. No member of the Board shall participate in a decision unless he or she was present throughout the hearing and heard the parties' evidence and argument.

Release of evidence

79. (1) Within a reasonable time after the final disposition of the proceeding, documents and things put in evidence at the hearing shall, on request, be released to the person who produced them.

Return of original record

(2) If an original clinical record respecting a person's care or treatment was put in evidence, it shall be returned to the place from which it was obtained as soon as possible after the final disposition of the proceeding.

Appeal

80. (1) A party to a proceeding before the Board may appeal the Board's decision to the Superior Court of Justice on a question of law or fact or both.

Time for filing notice of appeal

(2) The appellant shall serve his or her notice of appeal on the other parties and shall file it with the court, with proof of service, within seven days after he or she receives the Board's decision.

Notice to Board

(3) The appellant shall give a copy of the notice of appeal to the Board.

Record

(4) On receipt of the copy of the notice of appeal, the Board shall promptly serve the parties with the record of the proceeding before the Board, including a transcript of the oral evidence given at the hearing, and shall promptly file the record and transcript, with proof of service, with the court.

Time for filing appellant's factum

(5) Within 14 days after being served with the record and transcript, the appellant shall serve his or her factum on the other parties and shall file it, with proof of service, with the court.

Time for filing respondent's factum

(6) Within 14 days after being served with the appellant's factum, the respondent shall serve his or her factum on the other parties and shall file it, with proof of service, with the court.

Extension of time

(7) The court may extend the time for filing the notice of appeal, the appellant's factum or the respondent's factum, even after the time has expired.

Early date for appeal

(8) The court shall fix for the hearing of the appeal the earliest date that is compatible with its just disposition.

Appeal on the record, exception

(9) The court shall hear the appeal on the record, including the transcript, but may receive new or additional evidence as it considers just.

Powers of court on appeal

(10) On the appeal, the court may,

(a) exercise all the powers of the Board;

(b) substitute its opinion for that of a health practitioner, an evaluator, a substitute decision-maker or the Board;

(c) refer the matter back to the Board, with directions, for rehearing in whole or in part.

Counsel for incapable person

81. (1) If a person who is or may be incapable with respect to a treatment, admission to a care facility or a personal assistance service is a party to a proceeding before the Board and does not have legal representation,

(a) the Board may direct the Public Guardian and Trustee or the Children's Lawyer to arrange for legal representation to be provided for the person; and

(b) the person shall be deemed to have capacity to retain and instruct counsel.

Responsibility for legal fees

(2) If legal representation is provided for a person in accordance with clause (1) (a) and no certificate is issued under the *Legal Aid Services Act, 1998* in connection with the proceeding, the person is responsible for the legal fees.

Child in secure treatment program

(3) If a child who has been admitted to a secure treatment program under section 124 of the *Child and Family Services Act* is a party to a proceeding before the Board, the Children's Lawyer shall provide legal representation for the child unless the Children's Lawyer is satisfied that another person will provide legal representation for the child.

7 General Limits on Collections, Uses, and Disclosures

A. GENERALLY

The *Personal Health Information Protection Act, 2004*[1] imposes certain general limits on collection, use, and disclosure of personal health information by health information custodians. Further, the Act extends similar limits on uses and disclosures of personal health information by non-health information custodians who have received the information from a custodian.[2] These limits are often referred to as the "general limiting principles." Although the Act does not refer to the "general limiting principles," the Ministry of Health and Long-Term Care has commonly used this phrase to refer to the general limitations on personal health information described in *PHIPA*.[3]

The limits articulated in *PHIPA* are consistent with the CSA Privacy Code Principles.[4] First, the CSA Privacy Code provides that the collection of personal information must be limited to that which is necessary for the purposes identified by the organization.[5] Next, the information must be collected by fair and lawful

---

1   S.O. 2004, c. 3, Sch. A [*PHIPA*].
2   The rules for recipients are discussed in Chapter 12.
3   *Personal Health Information Protection Act, 2004: An Overview* (November 2004) at slide 16, published by the Ministry of Health and Long-Term Care, online: <www.health.gov.on.ca>.
4   Schedule 1 to *Personal Information Protection and Electronic Documents Act*, S.C. 2000, c. 5 [*PIPEDA*].

means.[6] Further, organizations must not collect personal information indiscriminately. Both the amount and the type of information that organizations collect must be limited to that which is necessary to fulfil the purposes identified.[7] *PHIPA* extends these principles not only to the collection of personal health information, but to the use and the disclosure of personal health information as well.

B. COLLECTION, USE, AND DISCLOSURE FOR A LAWFUL PURPOSE

The most fundamental limit in *PHIPA* is the rule that a health information custodian is prohibited from collecting, using, or disclosing[8] personal health information about a patient unless either the custodian has the patient's consent[9] under the Act and the collection, use, or disclosure, as the case may be, is, to the best of the custodian's knowledge, necessary for a lawful purpose,[10] or the collection, use, or disclosure is permitted or required by *PHIPA*.[11]

In other words, consent is required for all collections, uses, and disclosures of personal health information by a health information custodian unless a specific provision of *PHIPA* permits the collection, use, or disclosure.[12] Further, unless the collection, use, or disclosure of the personal health information is permitted without consent by a specific provision of *PHIPA*, it not only requires a patient's consent, but also can *only* be carried out if it is "to the best of the custodian's knowledge, necessary for a lawful purpose."

Where *PHIPA* permits a specific collection, use, or disclosure of personal health information *without* consent, this permission in *PHIPA* itself is, in essence, recognizing a "lawful purpose," and so no further modifier is necessary

---

5   *Ibid.*, Principle 4, at 4.4.

6   *Ibid.*

7   *Ibid.*, Principle 4, at 4.4.1.

8   The definitions of the terms, "collect," "use," and "disclose" are outlined in Chapter 2, Section E.

9   The requirement for consent and the kind of consent that a custodian needs in different circumstances is set out in Chapter 5. The word "patient" includes the authorized substitute decision-maker. See Chapter 6, Section D for a discussion about the authority of substitute decision-makers.

10   *PHIPA*, s. 29(1)(a).

11   *Ibid.*, s. 29(1)(b). The requirement for consent to the collection, use, or disclosure of personal health information is consistent with section 7 of *PIPEDA*, above note 4.

12   Because of the language of s. 29(b), the provisions in the Act that permit a collection, use, or disclosure of personal health information in specified circumstances are properly read as permitting such activity without consent.

in those instances. Furthermore, *PHIPA* requires a custodian to include a general description of the lawful purposes for which the custodian collects, uses, and discloses personal health information in a written statement for the public.[13]

The requirement that the collection, use, or disclosure of personal health information be necessary for a lawful purpose is a significant privacy principle. However, the "lawful purpose" requirement, in the context of the collection, use, or disclosure of personal health information with consent in *PHIPA*, is not absolute. It is modified by the phrase "to the best of the custodian's knowledge." This qualifier is particularly relevant for disclosures of personal health information with consent. It recognizes that it would not always be obvious to a health information custodian whether the purpose of the disclosure is, indeed, a lawful one or whether the disclosure is necessary for that purpose. For example, where a custodian is making the disclosure at the request of a patient, or a substitute decision-maker,[14] it is not reasonable to require the custodian to scrutinize and second-guess the patient's or the substitute decision-maker's reasons in making the request, unless some information comes to the attention of the custodian to suggest that such a disclosure would be inappropriate.[15] Indeed, a health information custodian may not even be aware of the specific purpose of the disclosure.

C. LIMITS ON COLLECTION, USE, OR DISCLOSURE OF PERSONAL HEALTH INFORMATION

1) Limits on Kind and Amount of Information

A health information custodian is prohibited from collecting, using, or disclosing personal health information if other information will serve the purpose.[16]

---

13   *PHIPA*, s. 16 (1)(a). As noted in Chapter 4, Section E, a health information custodian is required to set out in the custodian's information practices, the custodian's routine collections, uses, and disclosures of personal health information. The custodian must include a general description of the custodian's information practices in a written statement that is available to the public.

14   See above note 9 about substitute decision-makers.

15   *PHIPA*, s. 20(1). Note, however, that the custodian may challenge the substitute decision-maker's decisions with respect to the collection, use, or disclosure of the patient's personal health information by applying to the Consent and Capacity Board pursuant to s. 24(2) of the Act, to determine whether the substitute decision-maker has properly considered the factors set out in *PHIPA* when deciding on behalf of the patient. See further discussion about this in Chapter 6, Section E.

16   *PHIPA*, s. 30(1).

Such other information could include either non-identifying information or identifying information that is not personal health information.[17] For example, in using or disclosing information to carry out research, aggregate information that is not identifying information may be sufficient. A health information custodian is also prohibited from collecting, using, or disclosing more personal health information than is reasonably necessary to meet the purpose.[18] For example, where a patient asks a health information custodian to complete a form and return it to the patient's school in support of the patient's claim that the patient was too ill to write her examinations the previous week, the custodian would only need to include the relevant details of the patient's health condition on the form in support of the patient's claim. The disclosure of the patient's entire health history would not be appropriate in this situation. Both of these obligations aim at limiting the collection, use, and disclosure of personal health information to what is reasonably necessary.

2) Application of Limits Where "Reasonably Necessary"

What is, and who decides what is, "reasonably necessary"?[19] When providing health care, a health information custodian often collects extensive amounts of information about his or her patients. Information about past and present medications, family history, personal and emotional experiences, observations about family and friends, may all have significant relevance to the effective provision of health care. As noted by Mr. Justice Krever, "The nature and quantity of the information collected for the purpose of patient care depend upon the patient, the physician and the type of treatment required."[20] Although the rel-

---

17   See Chapter 2, Section C for more information on what is identifying information and what is personal health information.

18   *PHIPA*, s. 30(2). Mr. Justice Krever had recommended that health care providers limit the amount and type of information about patients they have the discretion to *disclose*. Ontario, Royal Commission of Inquiry into the Confidentiality of Health Records in Ontario, *Report of the Commission of Inquiry into the Confidentiality of Health Information* (Toronto: Queen's Printer, 1980) [*Krever Report*], vol. 2 at 294, Recommendation 56. He also stipulated that employees within the facility should use patient information on a "need to know basis" in the performance of their duties: *Krever Report*, vol. 2 at 306, Recommendation 60. *PHIPA* implements both of these recommendations.

19   For further discussion of "reasonable," see Chapter 4, Section C.

20   *Krever Report*, above note 18, vol. 2 at 282. Mr. Justice Krever went on to state there that, "Any attempt on my part to make recommendations which might limit the amount or type of information which may be collected for health-care purposes would rightly be perceived to be an interference with the practice of medicine or the provision of health care."

evance of information may not be obvious to a lay observer, a health information custodian who requires the information would understand its relevance to the proper development of a treatment plan.

PHIPA does not include an exception so as to allow custodians to disregard the general limiting principles when providing or assisting in providing health care to a patient.[21] However, the first purpose clause of *PHIPA*,[22] which states that the rules of the Act are intended not just to protect the confidentiality of information and the privacy of patients, but also "to facilitate the effective provision of health care,"[23] provides a basis for interpreting the general limitations in *PHIPA* so as to accord a large degree of deference to the judgment of health information custodians as to what is reasonably necessary in any given instance. Thus, the general limitations in *PHIPA* should not be construed in such a way as to hamper the effective delivery of health care. The Information and Privacy Commissioner has made statements that support this view. The Commissioner has emphasized that *PHIPA* does not impede the flow of information between health care professionals in order to provide health care services to patients.[24]

3) No Requirement to Collect, Use, or Disclose Where This Act Permits

Where *PHIPA* permits a health information custodian to collect, use, or disclose personal health information about a patient without consent, this does

---

21 Bill 159, *An Act respecting personal health information and related matters*, 1st Sess., 37th Leg., Ontario, 2000 [Bill 159], on the other hand, contained a broad exception to this effect. Introduced on 7 December 2000 in the Legislature, Bill 159 provided in cl. 12(9): "Nothing in this section shall be construed to restrict the collection, use, or disclosure of personal health information by a person described in one of paragraphs 1 to 4, 11 and 12 of the definition of 'health information custodian' [i.e., those custodians whose core business is the provision of or assisting in the provision of health care] in ss. 2(1) for the purpose of providing, or assisting in providing, health care to an individual."

22 *PHIPA*, s. 1(a).

23 *Ibid.*

24 In a press release, "Commissioner Takes Her Message to Ottawa Hospital," the Information and Privacy Commissioner, Dr. Ann Cavoukian stated: "While *PHIPA* builds in extensive privacy protection, it was designed not to interrupt the actual delivery of health care services." (7 December 2004), online: <http://www.ipc.on.ca>. See further, "Openness and Transparency: Connecting Citizens and Government, Notes for Remarks by Ann Cavoukian, Information and Privacy Commissioner, Management Board Secretariat" (7 October 2004), online: <http://www.ipc.on.ca>.

not mean that the custodian must, in fact, do so.[25] Custodians may exercise their discretion in collecting, using, or disclosing personal health information in such instances. Furthermore, even where the Act allows a collection, use, or disclosure without consent, the custodian may still choose to seek the patient's consent.[26] Consideration for the privacy of the patient should inform the custodian's actions with respect to the information decisions the custodian has discretion to make under *PHIPA*.[27] *PHIPA*, however, also does not relieve the custodian from a legal requirement to disclose personal health information, meaning that the fact that *PHIPA* gives a custodian permission to disclose personal health information where "permitted or required by law"[28] or for other specific purposes does not mean that the custodian has discretion not to make the disclosure where it is required by law, whether required pursuant to a statutory requirement, a court order, or other requirement.[29]

D. NON-APPLICATION OF GENERAL LIMITS WHERE REQUIREMENT TO COLLECT, USE, OR DISCLOSE

The general limits on the collection, use, or disclosure of personal health information set out in section 30 of *PHIPA* do not apply, however, where a health information custodian is required by law to collect, use, or disclose the infor-

---

25 *PHIPA*, s. 6(3)(a) only addresses disclosures of personal health information, apparently for greater certainty. *PHIPA* is silent on this point with respect to collections and uses, but where there is nothing to positively require the use or disclosure — and usually there is not — it is clear that custodians have discretion in this regard. See Chapter 10 and Chapter 11.

26 *PHIPA*, s. 6(3)(c). In this respect, professional standards of practice and codes of ethics may guide the health information custodian further.

27 Note Chapter 1, Section B(3); Chapter 3, Section A(2); and Chapter 10, Section P(3)(a).

28 *PHIPA*, s. 43(1)(h).

29 *Ibid.*, s. 6(3)(b). Where there is a legal requirement to disclose (to comply with a search warrant, for example) the custodian may pursue specific venues, such as an application to court, to challenge the requirement. In limited circumstances, *PHIPA* itself requires a health information custodian to make a disclosure of personal health information. A health information custodian is required to make a disclosure of personal health information pursuant to s. 46 (monitoring health care payments) as outlined in Chapter 10, Section Q, and in order to comply with ss. 47–48 (a disclosure of personal health information to a health data institute) as outlined in Chapter 11, Section D. A custodian and others may be required to disclose personal health information to the Information and Privacy Commissioner under certain circumstances, as set out in *PHIPA* s. 60: see Chapter 15 for more detail.

mation.[30] For instance, where a custodian is required to disclose personal health information pursuant to a search warrant, a court order, or pursuant to a statute that requires disclosure, such as the *Child and Family Services Act* under which a professional has the duty to make a report to the children's aid society where the professional believes on reasonable grounds that a child is in need of protection,[31] the custodian would continue to be required to make the disclosure. If a health information custodian is required by law to make a disclosure, the custodian is not permitted or required under *PHIPA* to refuse to make the disclosure on the grounds that non-personal health information would suffice or on the grounds that the amount of information to be disclosed is not "reasonably necessary." A health information custodian cannot rely on *PHIPA* to be relieved from the requirement to collect, use, or disclose personal health information imposed on the custodian by law.

E. LIMITS ON AGENTS

A health information custodian's use of agents to collect, use, or disclose personal health information on behalf of the custodian is discussed in detail in Chapter 2. It is important to emphasize the impact of the general limiting principles on the custodian's use of agents.

As a health information custodian has the responsibility for personal health information in the custodian's custody or control and may permit its agents to collect, use, or disclose such information on the custodian's behalf,[32] it is incumbent on the custodian to determine who within the organization should be authorized to perform those functions. Because the provision of information to an agent is considered a "use,"[33] it is subject to the general limiting principle that the use of personal health information is not permitted unless "reasonably necessary."

Not all employees and other agents of a health information custodian require access to personal health information. The need for personal health information and the amount of it that may reasonably be needed are dictated by the duties performed by each employee or other agent. A prudent health

---

30   *PHIPA*, s. 30(3). "Required by law" would include a requirement to disclose personal health information under *PHIPA*. See also above note 27. For a discussion of "required by law," see Chapter 3, Section B(3)(b).

31   *Child and Family Services Act*, R.S.O. 1990, c. C.11, s. 72.

32   *PHIPA*, s. 17(1), discussed further in Chapter 2, Section B and in Chapter 4, Section G.

33   *PHIPA*, s. 6(1).

information custodian should take some time to determine how best to put into practice this obligation to apply a "need-to-know" principle to its agents. For example, a health information custodian may retain certain records in locked cabinets or file rooms to which only certain employees have access. Where a health information custodian maintains records electronically, the custodian may configure the computer system used to gain access to the records to incorporate role-based access so that the level of access to records is determined by the job function of the person seeking access. Further, a custodian should not necessarily authorize every agent of the custodian to collect, use, or disclose personal health information for every purpose specified in *PHIPA*.[34] A health information custodian should have policies and procedures in place that describe the agents who are charged with making various types of decisions about personal health information and the circumstances in which they can make those decisions.

F.   FEES FOR COLLECTION, USE, OR DISCLOSURE OF PERSONAL HEALTH INFORMATION

1)   Fee Prohibited: Collection and Use

PHIPA prohibits a health information custodian from charging a patient or anyone else a fee for collecting or using personal health information, except as authorized by the regulations made under the Act.[35] At the time of writing, the *PHIPA* Regulation does not contain any provision authorizing fees for collecting or using personal health information, and as such *PHIPA* prohibits such fees.

2)   Fee for Disclosure: Cost Recovery

When disclosing personal health information, a health information custodian may charge a fee for the disclosure based on "reasonable cost recovery"[36] if no amount is prescribed under *PHIPA*.[37] At the time of writing, the *PHIPA* Regulation does not address fees for disclosures. Thus, a custodian has discretion

---

34   A custodian that authorizes its agents to collect, use, and disclose personal health information without appropriate limits would not be exercising its responsibility for the information under s. 17(1) of *PHIPA* and risks being held accountable for the consequences.

35   *PHIPA*, s. 35(1).

36   The Act does not specify to whom the custodian may charge the fee. "Reasonable cost recovery" in the context of access requests is reviewed in Chapter 13, Section E(2)(a).

37   *PHIPA*, s. 35(2).

to set a fee that is appropriate to the disclosure being made, taking into account such factors as the amount of staff time that is needed to assemble the personal health information requested to be disclosed, as well as photocopy charges or other charges incurred for providing information in a form suitable to the requester, such as the cost of a computer diskette, and the cost to deliver the information, such as the cost of postage or courier fees.

It would not, however, appear to be reasonable to charge a fee for disclosure of personal health information where a health information custodian is receiving payment for this service from a third party, such as, for example, a private insurer, as there would be no outstanding costs to recover in such a case. Further, it seems unlikely that a custodian would be allowed to cover more general overhead costs incurred in disclosing personal health information, like electricity charges, as such overhead costs likely would not be considered a cost related to the making of the disclosure, but rather a general operating cost that the custodian would incur even in the absence of the disclosure.

In deciding whether a fee constitutes a "reasonable cost recovery fee," health information custodians who are regulated by professional governing bodies may be guided by professional guidelines and standards of practice. Health information custodians that are facilities, such as hospitals or nursing homes, or programs and services, such as community mental health programs, may have policies in place setting out a fee schedule, but they may also turn to their voluntary associations for guidance. However, the fact that a health information custodian charged a fee consistent with such policies, guidelines, or standards is not determinative of the issue of whether a fee constitutes a "reasonable cost recovery fee." Whether the fee charged is a reasonable one is a question for the Information and Privacy Commissioner to consider and, ultimately, for the courts.

If, in the future, a regulation under the Act specifies a fee schedule, then that fee schedule would apply rather than the principle of "reasonable cost recovery," at least to those types of disclosures referred to in the regulation. Of course, a health information custodian can always exercise his or her discretion not to charge a fee for the disclosure, or to charge an amount less than what he or she is entitled to charge under *PHIPA*.

3) No Fee for a Required Disclosure

A custodian cannot charge a fee where a law requires the custodian to disclose the information; for example, where a statute mandates reporting or a court orders a disclosure.[38] Where a law compels a custodian to disclose personal health information, the custodian must comply with the requirement and is not permitted to place a condition on its compliance, like a requirement on the proposed recipient to pay for the disclosure.[39] Another Act relevant to the situation could also prohibit a charging of a fee. For example, a physician may be prohibited from charging a fee for providing a copy of a medical record to another physician in certain instances where such disclosure is a component of a publicly insured service.[40]

4) Complaint to the Commissioner about Fees

Any person can make a complaint to the Information and Privacy Commissioner about a fee that a custodian has allegedly charged in contravention of *PHIPA*, either because the fee exceeds the maximum allowed under *PHIPA*[41] or should not have been charged at all.[42] The Commissioner does not have jurisdiction to deal with a complaint that the custodian refused to exercise the discretion not to charge a fee, however, since such a refusal would not be a contravention of the Act. A professional's charging of an excessive fee may in some cases lead to discipline by the professional's regulatory body.[43] In such a

---

38 *PHIPA*, s. 6(3).

39 Under the *Health Insurance Act*, R.S.O. 1990, c. H.6, ss. 43.1(1) & (2) [*HIA*], for example, where a physician has knowledge that an ineligible person receives or attempts to receive an insured service as if he or she were an insured person, the physician must make a report to the General Manager of the Ontario Health Insurance Plan.

40 Note, section B, paragraph 1.i, General Preamble to the Physician's Schedule of Benefits, and *General*, R.R.O. 1990, Reg. 552, s. 24(1)[7], made under the *HIA*, *ibid*. A charge to the patient in certain circumstances may constitute a breach of the *Commitment to the Future of Medicare Act, 2004*, S.O. 2004, c. 5.

41 Unless and until a regulation under *PHIPA* states otherwise, the maximum fee for a disclosure is an amount based on "reasonable cost recovery."

42 This would refer to fees for collections and uses. If a fee should not have been charged for a disclosure since another Act requires the disclosure, then charging a fee under *PHIPA* as a condition of making the disclosure would apparently be a contravention of the other Act, not of *PHIPA*, so the Commissioner would appear not to have jurisdiction over such a complaint.

43 *RHPA* College regulations generally provide that it is professional misconduct for a regulated health professional to charge a fee that is "excessive" in relation to the services performed, which could include a fee for making a disclosure of the patient's personal health information. See, for example, s. 1(22) of *Professional Misconduct*, O. Reg. 858/93, made under the *Midwifery Act, 1991*, S.O. 1991, c. 31; s. 1(17) of *Professional Misconduct*, O. Reg. 681/93, made under the *Drug and Pharmacies Regulation Act*, R.S.O. 1990, c. H.4; and s. 1(20) of *Professional Misconduct*, O. Reg. 753/93, made under the *Respiratory Therapy Act, 1991*, S.O. 1991, c. 39. A similar provision exists in *Professional Misconduct*, O. Reg. 384/00, made under the *Social Work and Social Service Work Act, 1998*, S.O. 1998, c. 31, s. 2(25).

case, or otherwise, the Commissioner may decide not to review the subject matter of the complaint if satisfied that the complaint has been or could be dealt with more appropriately in another forum.[44]

G. LIMITS IN THE CONTEXT OF HEALTH CARE: THE LOCK BOX

1) Generally

As set out in Chapter 5, where a health information custodian, from the selected categories of custodians set out in section 20(2) of *PHIPA*, receives personal health information about a patient from the patient, the patient's substitute decision-maker, or another health information custodian and is aware that the patient has expressly withdrawn or withheld consent to collect, use, or disclose the information, for the purpose of providing or assisting in the providing of health care, the health information custodian is no longer entitled to assume implied consent for the collection, use, or disclosure of the personal health information, as the case may be, for that purpose.[45] This withdrawal or withholding of consent is one example of a limit that may be imposed on a health information custodian who collects, uses, or discloses personal health information in the context of providing or assisting in the providing of health care.

Further, *PHIPA* recognizes that, in some situations, a health information custodian needs to collect, use, or disclose personal health information without the patient's consent for the purpose of providing or assisting in the providing of health care to the patient.[46] However, a custodian cannot rely on these particular provisions to use and disclose personal health information, as the case may be, without consent in specific instances. If a health information custodian collected personal health information with the consent of the patient

---

44 *PHIPA*, s. 57(4)(b). The Commissioner has discretion to refuse to investigate if a College has jurisdiction over a matter: although the fact that *PHIPA* is somewhat more specific about what kind of fees are unacceptable may tend to indicate that a complaint to the Commissioner may in the end be a more appropriate forum for such a complaint.

45 *PHIPA*, s. 20(2). See the explanation of assumed implied consent in Chapter 5, Section F(3). A patient can also withdraw or withhold consent to the collection, use, or disclosure of personal health information even if s. 20(2) does not apply, but that provision applies commonly in the context of the providing of health care by many health information custodians.

46 *PHIPA*, ss. 36(1)(b), 37(1)(a), 38(1)(a), and 50(1)(e). A discussion of these provisions is set out in Chapters 8, 9, and 10.

and the patient, in giving his or her consent, expressly instructed the custodian not to use the information for any of the purposes for which it was collected, or in any specified manner for those purposes, then the custodian must honour that express instruction and not use the information in that way.[47]

Further, if a custodian collected information without consent of the patient from another source in order to provide or assist in providing health care to the patient, where it was not possible to collect reliable, accurate, and timely information directly from the patient, that patient may also provide the same type of express instruction on becoming aware of the collection.[48] The same restriction applies to disclosures of personal health information that a health information custodian proposes to make, without the patient's consent, for health care purposes to certain health information custodians.[49] If the patient expressly instructs the custodian not to make such a disclosure to those health information custodians, within Ontario, or generally for health care purposes outside Ontario,[50] the custodian is prohibited from making such a disclosure.[51]

Public hospitals are not obligated to give effect to such instructions until 1 November 2005.[52] However, they are also not prevented from complying with an express instruction in advance of 1 November 2005 if they are able to do so.[53]

---

47   *PHIPA*, s. 37(1)(a).

48   *Ibid.*, ss. 36(1)(b) and 37(1)(a).

49   *Ibid.*, s. 38(1)(a). The custodians to whom a health information custodian may disclose personal health information for health care purposes, without consent, are those described in paras. 1, 2, 3, or 4 of the definition of "health information custodian" in s. 3(1) of *PHIPA* and further described in Chapter 5, Section F(3)(b).

50   *PHIPA*, s. 50(1)(e).

51   Such an instruction, in the case of use as well as disclosure, must be from a capable patient; otherwise the patient's substitute decision-maker may express such an instruction on the patient's behalf. See further Chapter 6, Section D(3).

52   *PHIPA*, s. 31(2).

53   *Ibid.*, s. 31(3). This exemption for hospitals was included at the second clause-by-clause review of Bill 31, *An Act to enact and amend various Acts with respect to the protection of health information*, 1st Sess., 38th Leg., Ontario, 2003 [Bill 31] by the Standing Committee on General Government, as a result of concerns raised by the Ontario Hospital Association. [Ontario, Legislative Assembly, Standing Committee on General Government, *Official Report of Debates (Hansard)*, G-256 (28 April 2004) at 1630 (Kathleen O. Wynne).] The president and chief executive officer of the Ontario Hospital Association had explained to the Standing Committee, "Hospitals have told us that such a provision may in some instances seriously impair the ability of a health care provider to disclose information for purposes that may be essential to the effective delivery of health care and may thus, inadvertently, undermine the quality and safety of care to that individual." [Ontario, Legislative Assembly, Standing Committee on General Government, *Official Report of Debates (Hansard)*, G-62 (27 January 2004) at 1050 (Hilary Short).]

To the extent, however, that hospitals are included in the categories of health information custodians that are entitled to assume an implied consent from patients for the collection, use, or disclosure of personal health information when providing or assisting in the provision of health care,[54] their need to comply with a patient's express withholding or withdrawing of consent as of the day *PHIPA* came into force,[55] effectively limits the effect of the deferral.

A health information custodian, who discloses incomplete information to another custodian either because the patient has expressly withheld or withdrawn his or her consent or because the custodian has received an express instruction not to disclose certain information, must notify the receiving custodian that the custodian has been prevented from disclosing information that the custodian believes is reasonably necessary for the provision of health care to the patient.[56] If the information at issue is not, in the opinion of the disclosing health information custodian, reasonably necessary for the provision of health care to the patient, there is no obligation to "flag" that information is missing for the receiving custodian.

A similar obligation to notify the recipient that information is missing exists when a health information custodian discloses personal health information outside Ontario to any person for the purposes of health care to a patient and the patient expressly instructs the health information custodian not to make the disclosure.[57]

2) The Lock Box

The rule in *PHIPA* that enables a patient to expressly withdraw or withhold consent to the collection, use, or disclosure of personal health information for the purpose of providing or assisting in the providing of health care to that

---

54   *PHIPA*, s. 20(2).

55   1 November 2004.

56   *PHIPA*, ss. 20(3) and 38(2). The requirement to notify or flag that certain personal health information important to the delivery of health care to the patient is missing from the record of personal health information does not exist as a statutory requirement for the use of the information by agents of the health information custodian: the notice requirement pertains only to disclosures outside of the custodian. Best practices of a health information custodian could incorporate a system of notification as between agents who are accessing the patient's record in order to provide health care to the patient. See Chapter 5, Section F(3)(c)(i). How such limits affect the duty of accuracy, which includes completeness, is addressed in Chapter 4, Section H(2)(d).

57   *PHIPA*, ss. 50(1)(e) and 50(2).

58   *PHIPA*, s. 20(2).

patient,[58] and that further enables a patient to expressly state that his or her personal health information cannot be used or disclosed for health care purposes where *PHIPA* otherwise permits a use or disclosure for such a purpose,[59] has been referred to by many, including the Minister of Health and Long-Term Care, as a "lock box."[60] Like the phrase "circle of care,"[61] the expression "lock box" does not appear in *PHIPA* and is prone to misinterpretation, particularly since it suggests a control more absolute than *PHIPA* actually provides.

The idea of the "lock box" stems from a fundamental privacy principle that patients should have a degree of control over the use and disclosure of their personal health information, whether before or after they have provided it to a health care provider. Enabling a patient to expressly withdraw or withhold consent to the sharing of personal health information in the delivery of health care, or to expressly state that information cannot be used or disclosed for such a purpose, gives the patient control over information about him or her.

The "lock box" does not provide control in all circumstances. Even where a patient has "locked out" his or her information to prohibit its collection, use, or disclosure for the purpose of providing health care, a health information custodian may still use[62] and disclose that information for other purposes that *PHIPA* permits without the patient's consent, despite the "lock box."[63] The

---

59 *PHIPA*, ss. 37(1)(a), 38(1)(a), and 50(1)(e). The patient's ability to withdraw or withhold consent or to expressly prohibit a use or disclosure of information for health care purposes as set out in *PHIPA* is consistent with the *Krever Report*, above note 18, Recommendations 66, 67, 68, and 69.

60 During the second reading debates in the Legislature on Bill 31, the Minister of Health and Long-Term Care noted: "There is a provision in the bill called a lockbox, and it's a provision that perhaps doesn't enjoy universal support, but a lockbox provides that any Ontarian who so wishes to put a square, a box, a lock, a circle around any of their information to prevent its disclosure is entitled to do so. ... [I]f we have a health care system that is patient-centred, the patient, at the end of the day, has the right to determine how and when, and frankly, if their personal health information will ever or should ever be disclosed. There's a lockbox provision in this bill, and I'm particularly proud of it." [Ontario, Legislative Assembly, *Official Report of Debates (Hansard)*, 1124 (30 March 2004) at 1900 (Hon. George Smitherman).]

61 "Circle of care" is reviewed in Chapter 5, Section F(4).

62 Recall that a custodian's transfer of personal health information to its agent, or the transfer of personal health information between agents of the same custodian, is considered a "use" of the information: *PHIPA*, s. 6(1).

63 In a ruling by Manitoba's Ombudsman on a similar "lock box" provision in Manitoba's *Personal Health Information Act*, C.C.S.M., c. P33.5, (s. 22(2)(a)), the Ombudsman concluded that while a trustee (i.e., health information custodian) cannot disclose information for health care purposes if the individual has instructed the trustee not to make the disclosure, "nevertheless, in that event, it is still possible that another authorization to

"lock box" provisions generally do not override the provisions of *PHIPA* that allow uses and disclosures of personal health information without consent in certain circumstances.[64] For example, despite the "lock box," a health information custodian may use such personal health information for risk management purposes or for research conducted by the custodian, as the Act permits.[65] A health information custodian may disclose such information to find a substitute decision-maker or to determine or verify the eligibility of the patient to receive provincially-funded health care.[66] A health information custodian may also rely on the provision that allows a custodian to disclose a patient's personal health information without the patient's consent, and in the face of an express instruction to the contrary, where such a disclosure is necessary for the purpose of eliminating or reducing a significant risk of serious bodily harm to any person.[67]

When the Ministry of Health and Long-Term Care released its draft personal health information legislation for public consultation in 1997, the 1997 Draft

---

disclose without consent under section 22(2) may apply to the same information, where the individual does not have similar control." Report 2001-170: *Considering Every Ambit of Section 22(2)(a), Disclosure to Another Health Professional*, online: <www.ombudsman.mb.ca>. Also, the Ontario Hospital Association, *Hospital Privacy Toolkit: Guide to the Ontario Personal Health Information Protection Act* (Toronto: Ontario Hospital Association, September 2004) at 59 notes that a patient cannot restrict a use or disclosure that the Act otherwise permits or requires: "The Act trumps the lock box."

64 Health information custodians will need to consider additionally whether the *Canadian Charter of Rights and Freedoms*, Part I of the *Constitution Act, 1982*, being Schedule B to the *Canada Act, 1982* (U.K.), 1982, c. 11 [*Charter*], places any restrictions on such uses and disclosures, however, taking into account the express instruction or limitation on consent. See Chapter 1 and the discussion of *Charter* rights in Section B(3); Chapter 3, Section B(2); and Chapter 10, Section P(3)(a).

65 *PHIPA*, ss. 37(1)(d) and (j). For more detail about uses of personal health information without consent see Chapter 9.

66 *PHIPA*, ss. 38(1)(c) and 39(1)(a). For more detail about disclosures of personal health information without consent see Chapter 10.

67 *PHIPA*, s. 40(1). For further discussion about this provision, see Chapter 10, Section K. According to the Ministry of Health and Long-Term Care's overview of *PHIPA*, a health information custodian may rely on s. 40(1) to disclose a patient's personal health information, despite a patient's express instructions to the contrary, "since those instructions apply only in the context of the provisions in which they are referred to." See Question 7 at 36, *Personal Health Information Protection Act, 2004: An Overview for Health Information Custodians* (Toronto: Ministry of Health and Long-Term Care, August, 2004), online: <www.health.gov.on.ca>. The Information and Privacy Commissioner takes a similar approach. See *Frequently Asked Questions: Health Information Protection Act* "How does the 'lock-box work?'" Online: <www.ipc.on.ca>.

Legislation provided that health information custodians could collect, use, and disclose personal health information without consent for health care purposes. However, it also provided patients with a statutory right to block the transfer of any of their personal health information where the purpose of the disclosure was to provide or facilitate the provision of health care to the patient.[68] In the consultation paper that the Ministry released in September 2000, the Ministry proposed to remove the concept of the lock box from impending legislation, having heard from health care providers that allowing patients to "lock out" certain information could create a dangerous and, in certain circumstances, potentially life-threatening situation.[69] Bill 159, introduced that December, did not contain a lock box provision. While health care providers were generally pleased with the removal of the lock box, and the no-consent rule for the exchange of personal health information between health care providers for health care purposes,[70] the patient was left with very little control over his or her information. Privacy advocates, including the federal Privacy Commissioner and Ontario's Information and Privacy Commissioner, were critical of this deletion.[71]

---

68 Ontario, *Personal Health Information Protection Act, 1997: Draft for Consultation* (Toronto: Queen's Printer for Ontario, 1997) [1997 Draft Legislation]. In the 1997 Draft Legislation, pursuant to cl. 14(1)[4], a health information custodian could disclose personal health information without the patient's consent "for the purpose of providing, or facilitating the provision of health care to the subject of the information unless the subject has instructed the custodian in writing not to make the disclosure." Note that the disclosure for health care purposes was not limited to other health information custodians; further, the definition of "health information custodians" at that time included a broader range of persons, compared to the custodians listed in *PHIPA*, such as insurance companies: cl. 2(1) definition of "health information custodian." See Chapter 1, Section B(5)(a).

69 Ministry of Health and Long-Term Care, *Personal Health Information Privacy Legislation for the Health Sector* (Health Sector Privacy Rules) (Toronto: Queen's Printer for Ontario, 2000) at 9–10.

70 The Ontario Medical Association president at the time indicated to the Legislative Committee's Standing Committee on General Government at the hearings on Bill 159 that "We are not supportive of the lockbox ... we are frequently required to seek other opinions, consultations from specialists, where certain things are absolutely critical to the understanding of a patient and how you'll move that forward" [Ontario, Legislative Assembly, Standing Committee on General Government, *Official Report of Debates (Hansard)*, G-966 (27 February 2001) at 0920 (Dr. Albert Schumacher)].

71 The Information and Privacy Commissioner stated during the hearings on Bill 159, "From a privacy protection point of view, we think it's essential that an individual have the ability to prevent the disclosure of some sensitive information that they feel they do not want shared with other people in the health field or other fields ... I think one places information in a lockbox with the responsibility that you are making a decision that may potentially have some impact on the provision of health care services in the future, but you do that knowingly." [Ontario, Legislative Assembly, Standing Committee on General

With the rejection of the no-consent model for the collection, use, and disclosure of personal health information for health care purposes, the concept of the lock box was re-introduced into *PHIPA*.[72] While unpopular with some health care stakeholders, such as the Ontario Hospital Association[73] and the Ontario Association of Community Care Access Centres,[74] the Ontario Medical

Government, *Official Report of Debates (Hansard)*, G-829 (7 February 2001) at 1410 (Dr. Ann Cavoukian).] Also, the federal Privacy Commissioner, indicated to the Committee: "If you want to say that you're prepared to take the risk, however, infinitesimally small it may be, as an individual that you might suffer some detriment to your health by an emergency room physician not knowing that you had an abortion five years ago or whatever else it might be, that at some point in your past you were a drug addict — you name it — that is your right as a human being. That is your right as an individual." [Ontario, Legislative Assembly, Standing Committee on General Government, *Official Report of Debates (Hansard)*, G-867 (8 February 2001) at 1310 (George Radwanski).]

72   There is precedent for the inclusion of the lock box in provincial health privacy legislation. The Manitoba *Personal Health Information Act*, C.C.S.M. 2002, c. P33.5 contains a lock box. Section 22(2)(a) of that Act provides that a health care provider may disclose personal health information without the consent of the individual if the disclosure is "to a person who is providing or has provided health care to the individual, to the extent necessary to provide health care to the individual, unless the individual has instructed the trustee not to make the disclosure." Until recently, Saskatchewan's *Health Information Protection Act, 1999*, S.S. 1999, c. H-0.021 did not include a lock box. In 2003, the Act was amended to include a lock box that applies only in the context of "comprehensive health records." Section 8(1) of that Act provides that an individual has the right to prevent access to a comprehensive health record of that individual's personal health information, by providing a written direction in certain circumstances as set out in the Act. An example of a comprehensive health record is the record that may be compiled by the Saskatchewan Health Information Network (i.e., an electronic health record). The Saskatchewan legislation provides that, in the case of the comprehensive health record, the subject individual may require that the record not be disclosed to health care providers by giving a written direction to this effect. The Alberta *Health Information Act*, R.S.A. 2000, c. H-5 does not contain a lock box, *per se*, although it does include at section 58(2) a provision requiring custodians, in deciding how much health information to disclose for any purpose, to consider as an important factor any expressed wishes of the individual who is the subject of the information, together with any other factors that the custodian considers relevant.

73   See above note 53.

74   During the hearings on Bill 31, the chief executive officer of the Ontario Association of Community Care Access Centres explained to the Standing Committee on General Government: "We are concerned that an individual's choice to withhold consent for the disclosure of information that may be crucial to the delivery of appropriate health care could jeopardize their health and place health care workers at risk. Both as receivers of health information from hospitals and other providers and as providers of information to long-term care facilities and in-home service providers, we believe the disclosure of all medically necessary information to ensure appropriate treatment and placement is essential." [Ontario, Legislative Assembly, Standing Committee on General Government, *Official Report of Debates (Hansard)*, G-128 (28 January 2004) at 1430 (Dr. James Armstrong).]

Association did not object to the inclusion of the lock box in *PHIPA*. Noting in its presentation to the Standing Committee on General Government that the express consent requirement of *PIPEDA* gives patients, in effect, a right to "lock out" certain information, the Ontario Medical Association was apparently willing to accept the lock box in the Ontario legislation.[75]

How does a health information custodian implement a lock box? One challenge is to keep track of the patient's direction in this regard. Another challenge is limiting access to the excluded information where the patient allows access to the remainder of his or her personal health information. Health information custodians will need to develop information practices that allow them to meet both these challenges, and honour patient instructions to the extent required by *PHIPA*, in a manner that is consistent with the way they keep their records and use and disclose personal health information.

In practical terms, creating a "lock box" could mean the removal of certain information recorded on paper from the main record, flagging that the information has been removed, and placing it in a separate part of the file, perhaps in an opaque sleeve, to be accessed only by specified providers as set out on the sleeve. This approach relies on a great deal of trust that only those providers access the removed information, but it may be reasonable to rely on this approach, for instance, where a custodian provides its agents with clear instructions concerning acceptable access and informs its agents that the custodian will take disciplinary action against anyone who does not comply with this system. Of course, deliberate, unauthorized access of the information is an offence under *PHIPA*,[76] and could result in other repercussions such as a complaint to the Information and Privacy Commissioner.[77] A more sophisticated approach can be developed where a health information custodian retains

---

75   The Director of Health Policy with the Ontario Medical Association noted in reply to a question from a member of the Standing Committee on General Government about the Association's view that it was going to monitor the application of the lock box during the first three years of the legislation: "We know that *PIPEDA* has a lock box function and we're concerned about the substantial similarity question." [Ontario, Legislative Assembly, Standing Committee on General Government, *Official Report of Debates (Hansard)*, G-42 (26 January 2004) at 1510 (Barb LeBlanc).]

76   An agent of a custodian who deliberately accessed the information contrary to the instructions of the custodian would appear to have wilfully used the information in contravention of *PHIPA*, which is an offence under s. 72(1)(a). See the discussion of this offence, and the meaning of "wilfully" in Chapter 15, Section D.

77   *PHIPA*, s. 72(1)(a), which provides that a person is guilty of an offence if the person "wilfully collects, uses or discloses personal health information in contravention of this Act or its regulations." See the discussion of offences in Chapter 15, Section D.

records of personal health information in electronic form. Where a health information custodian maintains records of personal health information electronically, a custodian may create differential access designed to prevent certain persons or categories of persons from gaining access to certain records, parts of records, or types of information. The system could also include a reliable audit trail to create a record of users who have accessed information and when they accessed the information. In all instances, however, a health information custodian should ensure that agents understand the scope of their authority to access information.

In some circumstances, a patient's withdrawal or withholding of consent for the collection, use, or disclosure of personal health information for health care purposes or a patient's express instruction to a health information custodian not to use or disclose the patient's information for health care purposes may impact on the care that the custodian is able to provide to the patient.[78] In such circumstances, a health information custodian may sometimes choose to withdraw his or her services from the patient. *PHIPA* does not address the question of when such a withdrawal may be permitted. The custodian may be guided in this regard by professional and institutional regulations and obligations. The College of Physicians and Surgeons of Ontario, for example, has provided guidance to its members about adhering to patients' wishes in the context of *PHIPA*'s lock box provisions.[79] Although the College of Physicians and Surgeons expects physicians to respect patients' wishes, the College notes that a lack of patient information could jeopardize patient safety by preventing physicians from accurately assessing patients' health and, consequently, hindering them from providing effective, relevant medical treatment. In the College's view, patient safety should always remain paramount. In non-emergency situations, the College stipulates that physicians are not obliged to accept or treat a patient about whom they have insufficient information. The College encourages physicians to speak directly to their patients about the consequences of their decision to withhold personal health information. In a specific health encounter, a patient may very well agree to reveal information that he or she has previously withheld or expressly instructed not be disclosed. Alter-

---

78   It should also be noted that it has been well established in law that individuals have a right to refuse to consent to health treatment, even if the result leads to death: *Mallette v. Shulman* (1990), 72 O.R. (2d) 417 (C.A.); *B(N) v. Hôtel-Dieu de Québec* (1992), 86 D.L.R. (4th) 385 (Que. S.C.); *Rodriguez v. British Columbia (A.G.)*, [1993] 3 S.C.R. 519.

79   College of Physicians and Surgeons of Ontario, "Privacy Legislation," *Members' Dialogue* (November/December 2004), online: <http://www.cpso.on.ca>.

natively, the College states that physicians may be able to obtain the necessary information by taking a thorough medical history.[80]

It should be noted that *PHIPA* provides immunity from claims for damages for health information custodians who act reasonably and in good faith in the exercise or intended exercise of their powers or duties under *PHIPA*,[81] for example,

- by not providing information to another custodian, based on an express instruction of the patient or his or her substitute decision-maker;
- by not relying on information provided from another source, once becoming aware that the consent for the collection or use of the personal health information has been withdrawn or withheld;[82] or
- by making a use or disclosure of the information that is permitted under *PHIPA* without consent.

80 *Ibid.*
81 *PHIPA*, s. 71(1).
82 *Ibid.* Note, however, that this immunity does not appear to shield a custodian from the Information and Privacy Commissioner's reviews and orders, but would be a shield against a subsequent claim for damages under s. 65 for breach of *PHIPA* based on a Commissioner's order or an offence conviction. See Chapter 15, Section C(4).

Collection of Personal Health Information

A. *PHIPA*'S COLLECTION RULES: INTRODUCTION

1) Generally

Among the purposes of the *Personal Health Information Protection Act, 2004*[1] is the establishment of rules for the collection of personal health information about patients by health information custodians.[2] *PHIPA* defines the term "collect" to mean, in relation to personal health information, to gather, acquire, receive, or obtain the information by any means from any source.[3] The Act sets out the circumstances in which a health information custodian can collect personal health information about a patient, whether directly from the patient, or indirectly from another source of information.

As with the use and disclosure of personal health information, the general rule in *PHIPA* is that a health information custodian requires consent for the collection of personal health information.[4] The Act goes on to specify the

---

1   S.O. 2004, c. 3, Sch. A [*PHIPA*].
2   *PHIPA*, s. 1(a).
3   *Ibid.*, s. 2, definition of "collect." See Chapter 2, Section E(2) for a more detailed discussion of the meaning of the term "collect."
4   *PHIPA*, s. 29(a). In the context of the requirement for consent, the word "patient" includes the patient's substitute decision-maker, where the substitute is authorized to act on the patient's behalf. For further details about substitute decision-making, see Chapter 6.

circumstances in which a custodian may collect personal health information without the patient's consent.[5]

2) Change of Approach

The requirement for a health information custodian to have statutory authority to collect personal health information marks a significant change in the law.[6] Until the advent of *PHIPA*, legislation applicable in the health care sector in Ontario typically did not require health care providers to seek a patient's consent to the collection of personal health information. Health-sector-specific statutes that apply to health care providers are generally silent on rules concerning the collection of personal health information. Such legislation, however, usually addresses the disclosure of personal health information, generally requiring secrecy or confidentiality with respect to the information acquired by a person under the legislation, while permitting specific disclosures, whether with or without consent.[7] Likewise, institutions subject to the *Freedom of Information and Protection of Privacy Act*[8] or the *Municipal Freedom of Information and Protection of Privacy Act*[9] are not required to seek an individual's consent for collection of the individual's personal information.[10] Thus, health information custodians will have to adjust their practices to ensure that they consider their authority to collect personal health information.

---

5   *PHIPA*, s. 29(b).

6   This approach is consistent with the federal *Personal Information and Electronic Documents Act*, S.C. 2000, c. 5, Part 1 [*PIPEDA*], which requires consent not only for use or disclosure of personal information, but also for collection. See s. 7.

7   See, for example, the *Long-Term Care Act, 1994*, S.O. 1994, c. 26, s. 32 [*LTCA*], prior to amendments of this section by *PHIPA*, s. 89(6); the *Mental Health Act*, R.S.O. 1990, c. M.7, s. 35 [*MHA*], prior to amendment of this section by *PHIPA*, s. 90(6)–(11); and s. 22 of *Hospital Management*, R.R.O. 1990, Reg. 965, made under the *Public Hospitals Act*, R.S.O. 1990, c. P.40.

8   R.S.O. 1990, c. F.31 [*FIPPA*].

9   R.S.O. 1990, c. M.56 [*MFIPPA*].

10 *FIPPA*, above note 8, s. 38(2) provides: "No person shall collect personal information on behalf of an institution unless the collection is expressly authorized by statute, used for the purposes of law enforcement or necessary to the proper administration of a lawfully authorized activity." See also *MFIPPA*, *ibid.*, s. 28(2). Instead of requiring consent, *FIPPA* and *MFIPPA* require notice to the individual to whom the information relates of the principal purpose or purposes for which the personal information is intended to be used. See *FIPPA*, s. 39(2) and *MFIPPA*, s. 29(2). *FIPPA/MFIPPA* custodians are no longer required to provide such a notice where the information is personal health information. Instead, they are obliged to have information practices in place as set out in *PHIPA*, s. 10(1). For further discussion of these practices, see Chapter 4, Section D.

3) Personal Health Information Collected Prior to *PHIPA*

PHIPA specifically provides that the law applies to "the collection of personal health information by a health information custodian on or after the day this section comes into force."[11] Thus, *PHIPA* applies to a health information custodian's collection of personal health information after 1 November 2004, but does not regulate the collection of personal health information that occurred before 1 November 2004. *PHIPA* applies fully to any uses or disclosures of personal health information that occur after this date, however, even if the information was collected beforehand.[12]

B. DIRECT COLLECTION OF PERSONAL HEALTH INFORMATION FROM THE PATIENT

A health information custodian may collect personal health information about a patient with the patient's consent, provided that the collection, to the best of the custodian's knowledge, is for a lawful purpose.[13] Indeed, where a health information custodian collects personal health information directly from the patient to whom the information relates, the custodian may generally only do so under *PHIPA* with the patient's consent. *PHIPA* does not usually authorize a custodian's direct collection of personal health information without the consent of the patient to whom the information relates.[14]

In collecting personal health information directly from the patient to whom the information relates, *PHIPA* permits a health information custodian to rely on either the express or implied consent of the patient, unless the Act

---

11   *PHIPA*, s. 7(1)(a).

12   *Ibid.*, s. 7(1)(b). Note, however, that *PHIPA*, s. 9(1) provides that the Act does not apply to personal health information about an individual after the earlier of 120 years after the record containing the information was created and 50 years after the death of the individual, which means that the rules with respect to use and disclosure of personal health information do not apply to such old records.

13   *Ibid.*, s. 29(1)(a). See discussion in Chapter 7, Section B.

14   The exception to this principle is set out in *PHIPA*, s. 36(2), which allows a direct collection without consent where personal health information is needed for the provision of health care and it is not reasonably possible to obtain consent in a timely manner. As discussed below, this exception would apply where the patient is not capable of providing consent with respect to the collection of the information, but is able to provide certain basic information needed for the treatment.

requires express consent for the collection.[15] Where a health information custodian collects personal health information directly from a patient,[16] the custodian will usually imply the patient's consent to the collection from the patient's apparent voluntary provision of the information for a purpose that the patient apparently understands.[17] Where a health information custodian is a health care provider identified in section 20(2) of *PHIPA* and such a custodian collects personal health information directly from the patient, the custodian is entitled to assume that the custodian has the patient's implied consent to collect the information where the purpose of the collection is to provide health care or assist in providing health care to the patient, unless the custodian is aware that the patient has explicitly withheld or withdrawn the consent.[18] Because *PHIPA* gives these health care providers authority to assume patients' implied consent to the collection of their personal health information in these circumstances, *PHIPA* is not likely to change the practices of such custodians or their agents who collect information from patients directly for health care purposes.

Further, the Act clarifies the authority of a health information custodian to collect personal health information without consent directly from a patient who is incapable of consenting to the custodian's collection.[19] In some cases, a custodian will need to collect information about a patient directly from the patient to whom the information relates, even where the patient is incapable, in order to provide health care to the patient. The personal health information that a custodian would collect in some instances could be as basic as responses to such questions as: What is your name? Have you been here before? Where does it hurt? Do you take any medication? *PHIPA* permits the collection of such personal health information, even though the patient is incapable

---

15   The Act requires that the health information custodian obtain express consent for the collection of personal health information, even where it is collected directly from the patient, for the purposes of marketing or market research, and for fundraising, unless, in the case of fundraising, the requirements for implied consent are met. See *PHIPA*, ss. 33 (marketing) and 32 (fundraising) with *General*, O. Reg. 329/04, s. 10 [*PHIPA* Regulation] and discussion of these purposes in Chapter 5, Section F(7) & (10).

16   Where the patient has a substitute decision-maker authorized to act on behalf of the patient, the health information custodian may collect personal health information directly from that substitute with the substitute's consent. See below Section C(1) and generally about substitute decision-making in Chapter 6, Section D.

17   See discussion of implied consent in Chapter 5, Section D(2). This would be the case unless express consent is required. See note 15, above.

18   See discussion of *PHIPA*, s. 20(2) in Chapter 5, Section F(3).

19   Capacity is explained in Chapter 6, Section F.

of consenting to the collection of the information, provided that the collection is reasonably necessary for the provision of health care and it is not reasonably possible to obtain consent in a timely manner, such as where finding a substitute decision-maker who could consent to the collection on the incapable patient's behalf would lead to an undue delay in the provision of health care to the patient.[20] In this way, consistent with the purposes of the Act,[21] *PHIPA* recognizes that the requirement to obtain consent should not impede the timely delivery of necessary health care.

C. INDIRECT COLLECTION OF PERSONAL HEALTH INFORMATION: COLLECTING FROM OTHERS

1) Generally

PHIPA recognizes that, in a number of situations, a health information custodian collects personal health information from a source other than the patient to whom the information relates. A collection from a source other than the patient to whom the information relates is an "indirect" collection. A collection of personal health information about a patient from the patient's substitute decision-maker, however, does not appear to be an indirect collection, but rather a direct collection, as the substitute decision-maker stands in the shoes of the patient and the Act apparently treats the collection as though the custodian made the collection from the patient him- or herself.[22] *PHIPA* authorizes health information custodians to collect personal health information indirectly in specified circumstances. In fact, the Act does not impose a duty on the health information custodian to collect personal health information directly from the patient, even where the custodian is able to collect in such a manner.

2) Indirect Collection with Consent

A health information custodian may collect personal health information necessary for any lawful purpose from any source with the consent of the patient to whom the information relates.[23] The patient's consent to a custodian's indi-

---

20   *PHIPA*, s. 36(2).
21   *Ibid.*, s. 1(a).
22   *Ibid.*, ss. 23 and 25.
23   *Ibid.*, s. 36 (1)(a). Recall that the word "patient" includes the authorized substitute decision-maker.

rect collection may be express or implied, unless *PHIPA* requires express consent for the collection.[24]

3) Indirect Collection without Consent

In certain circumstances, *PHIPA* permits a health information custodian to collect personal health information indirectly without the patient's consent.[25] The circumstances in which a custodian may do so are set out below.

a) Collection for Health Care Purposes: Section 36(1)(b)

In two types of scenarios, a health information custodian may collect personal health information from any source where the collection is reasonably necessary for providing health care or assisting in providing health care and it is not reasonably possible to collect the information directly from the patient.[26]

First, it may not be reasonably possible for a health information custodian to collect personal health information directly from the patient that can reasonably be relied on as accurate.[27] Many health information custodians will be faced with such a situation frequently. A patient may not be able to provide reliable personal health information to a custodian as a result of suffering a concussion, or experiencing disorientation, for example. Alternatively, a custodian may not reasonably be able to rely on personal health information as accurate where the patient has been diagnosed with a condition that causes a loss of memory and the patient has provided the custodian with inaccurate information in the past. In other instances, the patient may not have sufficient knowledge or understanding of the questions that the custodian poses to provide the information, or may simply not have the required information.

It is significant that the standard that this provision of *PHIPA* creates is not that the information is accurate, but rather that it can "reasonably be relied on as accurate." Thus, where there is reasonable doubt about the patient's ability to provide information that can reasonably be relied upon as accurate, or where there is reasonable doubt about the accuracy of information that the

---

24   *PHIPA*, s. 18(2). See above note 15 as to when express consent is required. See further discussion about the requirements for consent in Chapter 5.

25   *Ibid.*, s. 29(b). Although *PHIPA*, s. 36(1) does not include the words "without the consent of the individual," it is clear that, with the exception of s. 36(1)(a), which explicitly refers to consent, a health information custodian may collect personal health information in the circumstances described in each clause without consent of the patient to whom the information relates.

26   *Ibid.*, s. 36(1)(b).

27   *Ibid.*, s. 36(1)(b)(i). This situation may apply whether or not the patient is capable of providing consent to the collection, use, or disclosure of personal health information.

patient provided, the custodian may rely on this provision to obtain the required information from another source.[28]

Second, it may not be reasonably possible for a health information custodian to collect the personal health information reasonably necessary for providing or assisting in providing health care directly from the patient to whom the information relates "in a timely manner."[29] These circumstances may arise, for instance, where the patient has been determined incapable, or is unconscious, and a substitute decision-maker has not yet been located.

In these situations, the health information custodian is permitted to collect personal health information about the patient from others without the patient's consent. A health information custodian will often collect the information in such instances from a family member, friend, or caregiver who attends with the patient at an appointment, or from another health care provider who provided the patient with care in the past.[30]

b) Collection by *FIPPA/MFIPPA* Health Information Custodians: Section 36(1)(c)

i) Generally

Where a health information custodian is an institution within the meaning of *FIPPA* or *MFIPPA*,[31] or is acting as part of such an institution, the custodian may collect personal health information indirectly for a purpose related to

- investigating a breach of an agreement or a contravention or an alleged contravention of the laws of Ontario or Canada,[32]
- the conduct of a proceeding or a possible proceeding,[33] or
- the statutory function of the custodian.[34]

28　The reasonableness of a custodian's reliance may also depend on the circumstances and the seriousness of the expected consequences should the information be wrongly relied on as accurate. The more serious the expected consequences of the information being wrong or incomplete, the less reasonable it would be to rely on the information without being sure that it was accurate. In this regard, if the information is not complete, the custodian cannot rely on it as being reasonably accurate.

29　*PHIPA*, s. 36(1)(b)(ii).

30　The other provider would be authorized to disclose personal health information to the custodian under *PHIPA*, s. 38(1)(a), but will also be able to assume the patient's implied consent in many such instances.

31　See Chapter 3, Section C(1).

32　*PHIPA*, s. 36(1)(c)(i).

33　*Ibid.*, s. 36(1)(c)(ii).

34　*Ibid.*, s. 36(1)(c)(iii).

These provisions essentially preserve certain existing collection authorities found in *FIPPA* and *MFIPPA* for health information custodians that are also institutions under either of those Acts, or a part of such institutions.[35] These provisions do not apply to a custodian that is not a *FIPPA/MFIPPA* institution or a part of such an institution.

A *FIPPA/MFIPPA* custodian may rely on any of these provisions as authority to collect personal health information where the purpose of the collection "relates" to the matter described in the applicable sub-clause. The Supreme Court of Canada has given the phrase "related to" a broad interpretation. The phrase has been likened to the phrase "in respect of," which, in turn, imports such meanings as "in relation to," "with reference to," or "in connection with." By contrast, the phrase "for the purpose of" implies a more narrow interpretive scope.[36]

ii)   "Investigating a Breach": Section 36(1)(c)(i)

A *FIPPA/MFIPPA* custodian may collect personal health information indirectly for a purpose related to investigating a breach of an agreement or a contravention or an alleged contravention of the laws of Ontario or Canada. The provision in *PHIPA* for *FIPPA/MFIPPA* custodians preserves the ability that such custodians had to collect personal health information indirectly in *FIPPA* and *MFIPPA*, although this clause in *PHIPA* is not identical to a parallel *FIPPA* and *MFIPPA* authority. Under *FIPPA* and *MFIPPA*, institutions are authorized to collect personal information indirectly for the purposes of "investigations or inspections that lead or could lead to a proceeding in a court or tribunal if a penalty or sanction could be imposed in those proceedings."[37]

---

35   There are some differences in wording, however, which may result in a somewhat different scope to the provisions. See Chapter 3, Section C(1)(b) for more discussion about how these provisions relate to existing provisions in *FIPPA*, above note 8, and *MFIPPA*, above note 9.

36   *Slattery (Trustee of) v. Slattery*, [1993] 3 S.C.R. 430 at paras. 20–23. In this case the Supreme Court of Canada considered the meaning of the phrase "relating to the administration or enforcement of this Act [*Income Tax Act*]." The Court held that this phrase implied a broad meaning, and that a reference to proceedings relating to the administration or enforcement of the Act encompassed other proceedings and not just proceedings brought under the *Income Tax Act*.

37   This phrase is contained in the definition of "law enforcement" in *FIPPA* and *MFIPPA*. *FIPPA* and *MFIPPA* authorize institutions subject to either of those Acts to collect personal information for the purpose of law enforcement: *FIPPA*, above note 8, s. 39(1)(g); *MFIPPA*, above note 9, s. 29(1)(g). "Law enforcement" is defined in *FIPPA* (s. 2(1)) and in *MFIPPA* (s. 2(1)) to mean (a) policing, (b) investigations or inspections that lead or could lead to a proceeding in a court or tribunal if a penalty or sanction

Under this *PHIPA* clause, a *FIPPA/MFIPPA* custodian may collect personal health information about a patient from any source for the purpose of, for example, substantiating a suspected occurrence of fraud in a situation where the custodian had entered into a funding agreement with a health care provider. A *FIPPA/MFIPPA* custodian may need to collect personal health information to prove the health care that the provider alleges has been provided has not, in fact, been rendered to the patient. Further, a *FIPPA/MFIPPA* custodian may collect personal health information to enforce compliance with standards, duties, and responsibilities set out in a statute or regulation that the *FIPPA/MFIPPA* custodian administers. This will be most relevant to the Ministry of Health and Long-Term Care, which has responsibility for a number of provincial statutes, but could be relevant to other *FIPPA/MFIPPA* custodians, such as a medical officer of health. For example, a medical officer of health may need to collect personal health information to prove that an individual continues to be infected with an agent of a virulent disease for the purpose of a motion before a judge to keep the infected individual in further detention and treatment.[38] The inclusion of the phrase "alleged contravention" in this *PHIPA* clause makes it clear that the *FIPPA/MFIPPA* custodian may collect personal health information even where the contravention has not yet been substantiated or where an investigation ultimately does not lead to the laying of a charge.

iii) The Conduct of a Proceeding: Section 36(1)(c)(ii)

Under *FIPPA* and *MFIPPA*, a *FIPPA* and *MFIPPA* institution, as the case may be, may collect personal information indirectly for the purpose of the conduct of a proceeding before a court or tribunal.[39] *PHIPA* permits a *FIPPA/MFIPPA* custodian to collect personal health information in similar circumstances, although the definition of "proceeding" in *PHIPA* is more expansive, and the purpose of the collection need only be "related to" the conduct of a proceeding or possible proceeding.[40] In *PHIPA*, the term "proceeding" is defined to include a proceeding

> held in, before or under the rules of a court, a tribunal, a commission, a justice of the peace, a coroner, committee of a College of a regulated health pro-

---

could be imposed in those proceedings, and (c) the conduct of such proceedings. Permission to collect for policing is not relevant to the *FIPPA/MFIPPA* custodians subject to *PHIPA*, since they do not perform policing functions. The part of the *FIPPA/MFIPPA* definition of "law enforcement" that relates to investigations or inspections and related proceedings may be applicable, however, to *FIPPA/MFIPPA* custodians.

38 *Health Protection and Promotion Act*, R.S.O. 1990, c. H.7, s. 35(11) [*HPPA*].

39 *FIPPA*, above note 8, s. 39(1)(f); *MFIPPA*, above note 9, s. 29(1f).

40 See note 37, above, and explanation in accompanying text.

fession, a committee of the Board of Regents under the *Drugless Practitioners Act*, a committee of the Ontario College of Social Workers and Social Service Workers, an arbitrator or a mediator.[41]

The word "proceeding" appears to encompass criminal proceedings as well.[42] A *FIPPA/MFIPPA* custodian may rely on this clause of *PHIPA* for authority to collect personal health information from a source other than a patient or his or her substitute decision-maker where, for example, the custodian requires independent evidence from others (e.g., neighbours, an employer) about the patient's state of health to prove that the patient is exaggerating his or her illness, thus to advance the custodian's position that the patient's legal claim against the custodian is without merit or overstated.[43] The clause authorizes a health information custodian to collect personal health information for the purposes of a proceeding that has not yet been commenced, or that is not even contemplated. A proceeding may merely be "possible" for the authority for collection to apply. This mirrors the *FIPPA* and *MFIPPA* provision, which permits a *FIPPA/MFIPPA* institution to collect personal information for the purpose of investigations or inspections that "could lead to" proceedings.[44]

iv) The Statutory Function of the Custodian: Section 36(1)(c)(iii)

A *FIPPA/MFIPPA* custodian may collect personal health information indirectly for a purpose related to the statutory function of the custodian.[45] This provi-

---

41   *PHIPA*, s. 2.

42   The definition of "proceeding" in *PHIPA* is not limited by words "within the jurisdiction of the Legislature" as in the *QCIPA* definition at s. 1 of that Act [*Quality of Care Information Protection Act, 2004*, S.O. 2004, c. 3, Schedule B].

43   While an indirect collection for the purposes of a proceeding or possible proceeding has been recognized in *PHIPA* for health information custodians that are institutions or a part of an institution, no similar provision exists for health information custodians generally. In a similar situation, a non-*FIPPA/MFIPPA* custodian may have to rely either on an implied consent of the patient, or possibly on s. 36(1)(h) that allows a health information custodian to collect personal health information where such a collection is permitted by law (i.e., the common law of tort where a proceeding has been commenced) in order to collect personal health information about the patient from others. Of relevance, in *Ferenczy v. MCI Medical Clinics* (2004), 70 O.R. (3d) 277 (S.C.), a case pertaining to *PIPEDA*, the Superior Court of Ontario discussed ways in which collection of personal information to aid in a person's defence could be authorized under that Act despite *PIPEDA*'s lack of clear permission to collect personal information for the purpose of a proceeding. The court noted that *PIPEDA* should be read in such a way so as not to prevent a defendant from collecting information vital for his or her defence.

44   See note 37, above.

45   *PHIPA*, s. 36(1)(c).

sion ensures the ability of a *FIPPA/MFIPPA* custodian to continue to collect personal health information as it was permitted under *FIPPA* and *MFIPPA*. For example, a medical officer of health could rely on this authority to collect personal health information from any source where such information is needed in connection with the provision of health programs and services, as mandated under the *Health Protection and Promotion Act*.[46] Under *FIPPA* and *MFIPPA*, the equivalent authority is the one that permits an institution to collect personal information, without consent, as "necessary to the proper administration of a lawfully authorized activity."[47]

The phrase "statutory function" is not defined in *PHIPA*.[48] The provision must presumably be interpreted to mean something different than "as permitted or required by law," a phrase that appears in another clause of the *PHIPA* section that authorizes indirect collections.[49] While no judicial consideration of the term "statutory function" has been reported in Canada, the bare term "function" has been the subject of such consideration. The Federal Court has defined the word "function" based on its ordinary meaning:

> Function is the act of performing and is defined as the kind of action belonging to the holder of an office; hence the function is the performance of the duties of that office. By the performance of the duties of an office, the holder thereof can be said to fulfill his function. Functions are therefore the powers and duties of an office.[50]

In general terms, therefore, a "statutory function" appears to comprise the performance of powers and duties conferred on an organization by or under an Act, whether explicitly or implicitly. It seems reasonable to conclude that so long as there is a statutory underpinning to the activities of a custodian, all collections of personal health information that are incidental to carrying out of the exercise of the statutory authority would be authorized.

Some direction for such an interpretation of this term may be taken from decisions of the Office of the Information and Privacy Commissioner under

---

46 Under the *HPPA*, above note 38, s. 5, each public health unit is required to provide a number of health programs and services, such as programs for health promotion and the control of infectious diseases.

47 *FIPPA*, above note 8, s. 38(2); *MFIPPA*, above note 9, s. 27(2).

48 The phrase is also used in *PHIPA*, s. 43(1)(e): see Chapter 10, Section P (6). Non-health information custodian recipients of personal health information are authorized to use or disclose personal health information for "the purpose of carrying out a statutory or legal duty": see *PHIPA* s. 49(1)(b) and Chapter 12, Section C(2).

49 *PHIPA*, s. 36(1)(h).

50 *Mudarth v. Canada (Minister of Public Works)* (1988), 27 C.C.E.L. 310 at para. 14 (F.C.T.D.).

FIPPA and *MFIPPA*, with respect to issues of whether or not a record is under the custody or control of an institution.[51] Critical to the Commissioner's analysis has been the Court of Appeal decision in Ontario *Criminal Code Review Board v. Hale, Inquiry Officer.*[52] In this case, the Court of Appeal upheld a Divisional Court's judgment that the backup tapes of a Criminal Code Review Board hearing, made by a court reporter whom the Board had retained, were part of the "record" that the Board was required to keep under the *Criminal Code*. This requirement in turn supported the proposition that the tapes were under the "control" of the Board for the purposes of section 10 of *FIPPA*.[53] Specifically, the Court of Appeal found that the sole purpose for creating the tapes was to fulfil the Board's "statutory mandate."[54] The court reporter had been hired specifically to fulfil the "statutory duty" of the Board.[55]

The Information and Privacy Commissioner relied on this decision in a key order made under *MFIPPA* involving the City of Kitchener.[56] In this case, the Commissioner ruled that tendering for the construction of a firehall was sufficiently related to a municipality's statutory duty to provide firefighting and fire protection services and that records of the pre-qualification screening of bidders were "closely integrated and directly connected" to the statutory function of the municipality.[57] This conclusion suggests that the term "statutory function" may be interpreted to be broad in scope and would include activities that are incidental to an explicit statutory authority. In other words, the function itself need not be expressly described in the statute but, rather, be legitimately connected to a stated statutory power. The words "related to" in the phrase "a purpose related to the statutory function of the custodian" that appears in this provision, rather than words like "necessary to," also suggest that this provision should be interpreted broadly. Of course, under the general limiting principles

---

51   See Order MO-1242, City of Kitchener (19 October 1999); Order MO-1251, Township of King (16 November 1999); Order MO-1289, Township of Edwardsburgh (31 March 2000); Order PO-1873, Ministry of the Solicitor General (19 October 1999), online: <www.ipc.on.ca>.

52   (1999), 47 O.R. (3d) 201 (C.A.) [*Hale*].

53   *FIPPA*, above note 8, s. 10(1) provides that "Every person has a right of access to a record or part of a record in the custody or under the control of a *FIPPA* institution unless, (a) the record or the part of the record falls within one of the exemptions under sections 12 to 22; or (b) the head is of the opinion on reasonable grounds that the request for access is frivolous or vexatious."

54   *Hale*, above note 52 at 209.

55   *Ibid.* at 211.

56   Order MO-1242, above note 51.

57   *Ibid.*

in *PHIPA*, a health information custodian may only collect personal health information to the extent necessary for the purpose of the collection.[58]

c) Collection for Research: Section 36(1)(d)

A health information custodian may collect personal health information from a person who is not a health information custodian where the custodian is carrying out research as allowed in *PHIPA*, unless the person is prohibited from disclosing the information to the custodian.[59]

d) Prescribed Planning Entity: Section 36(1)(e)

Where a health information custodian is a prescribed planning entity,[60] *PHIPA* permits the custodian to collect personal health information from a person who is not a health information custodian for the purposes of planning or management of the health system, as set out in the Act.[61] For example, a custodian that is a prescribed planning entity may find information from a government body (such as Statistics Canada, a non-health information custodian) useful in analysis with respect to health system planning. At the time of writing, no health information custodian is specified in the *PHIPA* Regulation as a prescribed planning entity and, consequently, no organization can rely on this provision as authority to collect personal health information.

e) Authorized by Commissioner: Section 36(1)(f)

The Information and Privacy Commissioner may authorize a health information custodian to collect personal health information in a manner other than directly from the patient to whom the information relates.[62] By providing the Commissioner with this authority, *PHIPA* recognizes that it will not always be possible for a health information custodian to collect personal health information directly from the patient to whom it relates, to obtain the patient's consent under section 36(1)(a) for the custodian's indirect collection, or to apply one of

---

58 *PHIPA*, s. 30.

59 *Ibid.*, s. 36(1)(d). The rules pertaining to research are described in Chapter 11, Section B.

60 *PHIPA*, s. 45(1). Prescribed planning entities under *PHIPA*, s. 45 are Cancer Care Ontario, the Canadian Institute for Health Information, the Institute for Clinical Evaluative Sciences, and the Pediatric Oncology Group of Ontario, as set out in *PHIPA* Regulation, above note 15, s. 18. Circumstances in which the prescribed planning entities may collect, use, and disclose personal health information is described in Chapter 11, Section E.

61 *PHIPA*, s. 36(1)(e).

62 *Ibid.*, ss. 36(1)(f) and 66(f).

the other provisions of section 36(1) to authorize a custodian's indirect collection of personal health information in circumstances where such a collection would be appropriate.

At the time of writing, the Commissioner has not issued any guidelines relating to this clause of *PHIPA*. Until any such guidelines are made available, health information custodians seeking this authorization under *PHIPA* should consider the guidelines on such applications issued by the Commissioner for the purposes of analogous applications under *FIPPA* and *MFIPPA*,[63] as the Commissioner has a similar authority to authorize institutions to collect personal information indirectly under both *FIPPA* and *MFIPPA*.[64] Adapting these guidelines to the *PHIPA* context the Commissioner is likely to consider the following questions important, at a minimum, in such applications:

- What is the purpose of the indirect collection and the proposed use of the personal health information?
- What personal health information is required to achieve the purpose?
- Could the service, program, or activity be provided without the personal health information being collected?
- Is it possible and/or practical to collect the personal health information directly from the patient to whom the personal health information relates?
- What authority under the Act does the health information custodian have to collect the personal health information?
- Is collection of the personal health information possible under another provision of the Act?
- Must the information be collected in a nominative form (i.e., with personal identifiers)?
- Can the personal health information be relied upon as accurate and complete?

The Commissioner may also request information about the source from which the custodian proposes to collect personal health information, including how the originating source collected the personal health information itself and its authority for the disclosure of such personal health information to the requesting cus-

---

63   Information and Privacy Commissioner/Ontario, *Guidelines on Applications to the Information and Privacy Commissioner/Ontario for Authorization of Indirect Collection by Institutions Covered under the Freedom of Information and Protection of Privacy Act or the Municipal Freedom of Information and Protection of Privacy Act* (2 April 1993), online: <www.ipc.on.ca>.

64   *FIPPA*, above note 8, ss. 39(1)(c) and 59(c); *MFIPPA*, above note 9, ss. 29(1)(c) and 46(c).

todian. With such information in hand, the Commissioner would be in a position to consider the privacy implications of the proposed indirect collection.

f) Where a Person Has Authority to Disclose to the Custodian: Section 36(1)(g)

i) Generally

A health information custodian is permitted to collect personal health information from a person who is permitted or required by law or by a treaty, agreement, or arrangement made under an Act of Ontario or an Act of Canada to disclose it to the custodian.[65] Each aspect of this provision is addressed below.

The scope of the phrase "permitted or required by law" is reviewed in Chapter 3. As discussed there, a fundamental theme in *PHIPA* is the preservation of existing rules set out in other legislation governing specific parts of the health sector with respect to collections, uses, and disclosures of personal health information.[66] Thus, the phrase comprises, at a minimum, other Ontario and federal statutes, and their regulations. The phrase likely comprises orders of a court or tribunal. It may also authorize a health information custodian to collect personal health information from a person who is authorized at common law to disclose it to the health information custodian.

Usually, statutes and regulations made under them will not specifically refer to "personal health information." More commonly, legislation will refer to "personal information" or "information." Where a person is authorized to disclose "personal information" or "information" to a health information custodian, the custodian may generally rely upon such a provision as authority to collect *personal health information*.[67] Further, legislation will not necessarily explicitly set out that information may be disclosed without consent, or that it may be disclosed to a particular health information custodian, but the authorization may be implicit. Where a person is authorized implicitly by legislation to disclose personal health information, the custodian may generally rely on such authority to collect the information. It may be necessary for a prudent custodian to verify with the person disclosing the personal health information to the custodian the legal basis upon which the person is making the disclosure.

---

65   *PHIPA*, s. 36(1)(g).
66   Chapter 3, Section B(3)(b).
67   "Personal health information" is a subset of "personal information." Normally, a reference to "personal information" includes "personal health information." Of course, even where a person lawfully discloses "information" to a custodian, it may be "personal health information" when collected by the custodian, and authorized under *PHIPA*, s. 36(1)(g).

b)   Where Disclosure to a Custodian Is Authorized under Legislation other than PHIPA

For example, under the *Health Protection and Promotion Act*, physicians, nurses, hospital administrators, school principals, and others are required to make a report to a medical officer of health with respect to communicable diseases.[68] As these parties are required to disclose such personal information to the medical officer of health under an Act, the *Health Protection and Promotion Act*, the medical officer of health, who is a health information custodian under *PHIPA*, is authorized to collect this information by virtue of section 36(1)(g) of *PHIPA*.[69]

A couple of other examples help to further illustrate the operation of this provision:[70]

- Under the *Ambulance Act*, the Minister of Health and Long-Term Care and an operator of an ambulance service, for instance, may disclose personal health information to each other, without the patient's consent, where the disclosure is reasonably necessary for purposes relating to the discharge or exercise by the recipient of the information of their duties or powers under the Act or its regulation.[71] Where the operator discloses personal health information to the Minister, pursuant to this provision of the *Ambulance Act*, the Minister, a health information custodian, is authorized by this clause of *PHIPA* to collect the information.
- Where an Act allows a health information custodian to "consult" with another custodian, this provision provides the custodian who is being consulted with authority to collect the needed personal health information from the consulting custodian. For example, under the *Mental Health Act*, a physician who is considering issuing or renewing a community treatment order may consult with a member of a regulated health profession or with a social worker or social service worker to determine whether the order should be issued or renewed.[72] As such, the health professionals, as health information custodians, are authorized to collect personal health information from the physician.

---

68   *HPPA*, above note 38, ss. 25–29, for example.

69   In *PHIPA* Regulation, above note 15, s. 3(2), a medical officer of health of a board of health within the meaning of the *HPPA* is prescribed as a single health information custodian with respect to the performance of his or her duties under that or any other Act.

70   While these examples pertain to statutes, it is important to keep in mind that regulations under statutes may also authorize a person to disclose personal health information to a health information custodian, in which case a custodian is authorized to collect such information pursuant to *PHIPA*, s. 36(1)(g).

71   R.S.O. 1990, c. A.19, s. 19(2)[1].

72   *MHA*, above note 7, s. 35.1(1). A community treatment order is a term used in the *MHA*. Under that Act, a physician may issue a community treatment order to provide a patient with community-based treatment or care and supervision that is less restric-

iii) *Where Disclosure to a Custodian Is Authorized under* PHIPA

Under this same provision,[73] a health information custodian is also permitted to collect personal health information from another health information custodian who is authorized to disclose the information under *PHIPA*. For example, where a health information custodian is authorized to disclose personal health information without the patient's consent for health care purposes to another custodian listed in section 38(1)(a), that receiving custodian is authorized by this clause to collect the information.[74] Further, a health information custodian may disclose personal health information to a researcher, provided the *PHIPA* conditions for research have been met.[75] Where that researcher is also a health information custodian, the custodian is permitted by this clause to collect the personal health information to conduct the research.

This provision is also relevant to consultations that may be undertaken with respect to a health information custodian's compliance with *PHIPA*. In *PHIPA*, a health information custodian may consult with a physician or psychologist for the purpose of determining whether a patient should be refused access to his or her record of personal health information on the basis that access to the record by the patient could reasonably be expected to result in a risk of serious harm to the treatment or recovery of the patient.[76] The custodian physician or psychologist, who is intended to be the receiver of the information from the referring custodian, is authorized to collect the personal health information for the purpose of the consultation, without seeking the patient's consent to the collection.[77]

---

tive to the person than being detained in a hospital environment. Such orders are for patients who suffer from serious mental disorders, who have a history of repeated hospitalizations, and who meet the *MHA* committal criteria for the completion of an application for a psychiatric assessment by a physician. The orders are also for involuntary psychiatric patients who agree to a treatment/supervision plan as a condition of their release from a psychiatric facility to the community. See:*Mental Health Act*: Brian's Law (Mental Health Legislative Reform), 2000, online: <www.health.gov.on.ca/english/public/pub/mental/treatment_order.html>.

73   *PHIPA*, s. 36(1)(g).
74   *Ibid.*, s. 38(1)(a). This clause lists the categories of health information custodians who may receive personal health information where its disclosure is reasonably necessary for the provision of health care. The list includes custodians whose core business is the provision of health care. A health information custodian may not disclose a patient's personal health information pursuant to this clause if the patient expressly instructs the custodian not to make the disclosure. See Chapter 10, Section B.
75   *PHIPA*, s. 44.
76   *Ibid.*, s. 52(5). This exemption to the right of access is described further in Chapter 13, Section D(6).
77   Again, pursuant to *PHIPA* s. 36(1)(g).

iv) *Where Disclosure to a Custodian Is Authorized Pursuant to a Treaty,*
Agreement, or Arrangement Made under a Statute

A third aspect of this provision in *PHIPA*[78] is that a health information custodian is authorized to collect personal health information that another person is permitted or required by a treaty, agreement, or arrangement made under an Act of Ontario or an Act of Canada to disclose to the custodian. For example, the Ministry of Health and Long-Term Care, as a health information custodian, is authorized to collect personal health information from the Workplace Safety and Insurance Board where the Board enters into an information sharing agreement with the Ministry as authorized under the *Workplace Safety and Insurance Act*.[79]

v) *Where Disclosure to a Custodian Is Authorized by a Law, Other than*
Legislation

A final aspect of this provision in *PHIPA*[80] is that a health information custodian is authorized to collect personal health information that another person may be authorized or required to disclose to the receiving custodian by law or legal requirement other than legislation.[81] For example, where a court orders the production of records of personal health information to a health information custodian, who is a party to a proceeding, the custodian to whom the disclosure is ordered is thereby authorized to collect the information from the person who has been ordered by the court to disclose the records.

g) Indirect Collection Authorized by Law: Section 36(1)(h)

i) *Generally*

Lastly, consistent with the rules pertaining to use[82] and disclosure,[83] the indirect collection rules in *PHIPA* authorize the health information custodian to collect personal health information indirectly without the patient's consent if the custodian is permitted or required to do so by law or by a treaty, agreement,

---

78   *PHIPA*, s. 36(1)(g).

79   *Workplace Safety and Insurance Act, 1997*, S.O. 1997, c. 16, Sch. A, s. 159 provides that for the purpose of administering that Act, the Workplace Safety and Insurance Board may enter into an agreement with a ministry under which the ministry will be allowed access to information obtained by the Board under the *Workplace Safety and Insurance Act* and the ministry will allow the Board to have access to information obtained by the ministry under statutory authority. This agreement to exchange information requires approval of the Lieutenant Governor in Council (i.e., in effect, provincial Cabinet).

80   *PHIPA*, s. 36(1)(g).

81   "Legislation" generally refers to acts or statutes enacted by the Legislature, and regulations that are made as permitted by such acts or statutes.

82   *PHIPA*, s. 37(1)(k), see Chapter 9, Section C(12).

83   *Ibid.*, s. 43(1)(h), see Chapter 10, Section P.

or arrangement made under an Act of Ontario or Canada.[84] Each aspect of this provision is addressed below. The scope of the phrase "permitted or required by law" is reviewed in Chapter 3,[85] and further outlined above.[86]

As set out above,[87] law such as statutes and regulations usually will not specifically refer to collection of "personal health information." More commonly, legislation will refer to the collection of "personal information" or "information." Furthermore, legislation may not necessarily explicitly provide that an indirect collection may occur without consent, but the authorization may be implicit. Whether the words in a particular statute authorize the indirect collection of personal health information without the consent of the patient to whom the information relates will depend on the context of the provision in question. Regulations under *PHIPA* may impose requirements and place restrictions on the collections made under this clause.[88] It should also be noted that the law may authorize a custodian's agent to collect personal health information in stated circumstances (see discussions of statutes, below). In such instances, the agent may collect personal health information as "permitted or required by law," without requiring permission of the custodian.[89]

ii) Authorized by a Statute

A health information custodian is authorized to collect personal health information where another Ontario or federal statute permits or requires that custodian to collect such information from a source other than the patient.[90] Consider the following examples of statutory provisions that authorize indirect collection.

- Pursuant to the *Health Protection and Promotion Act*, a health information custodian that is a medical officer of health may "directly or indirectly collect personal information for the purposes of this Act or for purposes related to administration of a public health program or service that is prescribed in the regulations."[91]

---

84 *PHIPA*, s. 36(1)(h).
85 Section B(3)(b).
86 See Section C (7), above.
87 *Ibid.*
88 *PHIPA*, s. 36(1)(h) provides at the outset that a collection under this clause is "subject to the requirements and restrictions, if any, that are prescribed." At the time of writing, no such regulations are in place.
89 *Ibid.*, s. 17 (2). An agent's ability may be restricted by regulation under *PHIPA*.
90 *Ibid.*, s. 36(1)(h).
91 *HPPA*, above note 38, s. 91.1. There are no purposes prescribed, but the purpose of the *HPPA* itself, referred to in this provision, is quite broad. Section 2 of the *HPPA* states that the purpose of the Act is "to provide for the organization and delivery of public health programs and services, the prevention of the spread of disease and the promotion and protection of the health of the people of Ontario."

- Under the *Independent Health Facilities Act*, the Minister of Health and Long-Term Care may directly or indirectly collect personal information, subject to such conditions as may be prescribed, "for purposes related to the administration of the *Independent Health Facilities Act*, the *Health Insurance Act*, or the *Health Care Accessibility Act* or for such other purposes as may be prescribed."[92]

- The *Mental Health Act* allows the officer in charge of a psychiatric facility to collect personal health information from any source "with or without the patient's consent" for the purposes of (a) examining, assessing, observing, or detaining the patient in accordance with that Act; or (b) complying with Part XX.1 (Mental Disorder) of the *Criminal Code* (Canada) or an order or disposition made pursuant to that Part."[93] For example, an officer in charge of a psychiatric facility is authorized, pursuant to this provision, to collect personal health information about an accused patient from a prison where the Ontario Review Board has ordered that the accused be transferred from that prison and detained at the psychiatric facility.[94]

iii) *Authorized by Regulation*

Further, the provision allowing a custodian to collect personal health information where permitted or required by law clearly incorporates authorities that

---

92   *Independent Health Facilities Act*, R.S.O. 1990, c. I.13, s. 37.1(1). The Ministry of Health and Long-Term Care is authorized to collect personal information indirectly in a number of other statutes it administers in a similar way: *Commitment to the Future of Medicare Act, 2004*, S.O. 2004, c. 5, s. 15.1; *Ontario Drug Benefit Act*, R.S.O. 1990, c. O.10, s. 13(1); *Health Insurance Act*, R.S.O. 1990, c. H.6, s. 4.1; and *Trillium Gift of Life Network Act*, R.S.O. 1990, c. H.10, s. 8.19(1). These statutes also authorize uses and disclosures of personal information without consent in the stated circumstances. Where a health information custodian is part of a *FIPPA/MFIPPA* institution, the custodian's authority to collect indirectly may also be found in a statute that speaks to the particular ministry that the custodian of which the custodian is part.

93   *MHA*, above note 7, s. 35(2). The provision also authorizes a use and a disclosure of personal health information with or without the patient's consent for these purposes. Part XX.1 (Mental Dirsorder) of the *Criminal Code*, R.S.C. 1985, c. C-46, deals with, among other matters, assessments and dispositions pertaining to accused individuals who may be unfit to stand trial for the offence they have been charged with by reason of suffering from a mental disorder or who have been found to be not criminally responsible for an offence they have been charged with by reason of suffering from a mental disorder.

94   The Ontario Review Board has jurisdiction over individuals who have been found either unfit to stand trial or not criminally responsible because of a mental disorder. It is a tribunal established pursuant to the *Criminal Code*, which requires that each province and territory must establish or designate a Review Board to oversee such accused. The role of the Board is further described online: <www.orb.on.ca>.

may be set out in regulations. For example the regulation under the *Laboratory and Specimen Collection Centre Licensing Act* authorizes laboratories to collect personal health information indirectly, from a physician outside Ontario or from an insurance company, who makes a request for an examination.[95]

Similarly, regulations under *PHIPA* itself may authorize indirect collection of personal health information in limited circumstances. Under the *PHIPA* Regulation, the Canadian Blood Services may indirectly collect personal health information about an individual who donates or attempts to donate blood or blood products, if the information is reasonably necessary to ensure the safety of the blood system and it is not reasonably possible to collect reliable information directly from the individual in a timely way.[96]

It is, therefore, important for a health information custodian to consider what provisions in regulations, and not just statutes, may provide the custodian with authority to collect personal health information indirectly without the consent of the patient to whom the information relates.

iv) *Authorized Pursuant to a Treaty, Agreement, or Arrangement Made under a Statute*

PHIPA further authorizes a health information custodian to collect personal health information indirectly where a "treaty, agreement, or arrangement made under an Act [of Ontario] or an Act of Canada" permits the indirect collection.[97] For example, under the *Ontario Drug Benefit Act*, the Minister of Health and Long-Term Care may enter into agreements to collect, use, or disclose personal information for purposes related to the administration of that Act or for such other purposes as may be prescribed by regulations under that Act.[98] Such an agreement must provide that personal information collected or disclosed under the agreement will be used only to verify the accuracy of information held or exchanged by a party to the agreement; to administer or enforce a law administered by a party to the agreement; or for a prescribed purpose.[99]

---

95   *Laboratories*, R.R.O. 1990, Reg. 682, made under the *Laboratory and Specimen Collection Centre Licensing Act*, R.S.O. 1990, c. L.1, s. 9(1.1).

96   *PHIPA* Regulation, above note 15, s. 25(1).

97   A similar phrase is found in *FIPPA* (s. 42(e)) and *MFIPPA* (s. 32(e)), in the context of the kind of disclosures a *FIPPA/MFIPPA* institution is authorized to make. Where one institution may disclose to another for this purpose, the receiving institution may collect the personal information and use it for this purpose: *FIPPA*, above note 8, ss. 39(1)(b) and 41(c); *MFIPPA*, above note 9, ss. 29(1)(b) and 31(c).

98   The *Ontario Drug Benefit Act*, R.S.O. 1990, c. O.10, s. 13(4). Regulations may prescribe conditions, although no such regulations exist at the time of writing.

99   *Ibid.*, s. 13(5).

v) Authorized by Another Law: Where Authority Not from Legislation

As outlined in Chapter 3, the provision allowing indirect collections without consent where "permitted or required by law" is not limited to authorities set out in statutes.[100] For instance, under the provisions of the *Child and Family Services Act*, where an application has been made to commit a child to secure treatment, a court may order a qualified person to perform an assessment on the child "to assist the court to determine whether the child should be committed to a secure treatment program."[101] That Act provides that the person performing an assessment must give a written report of the assessment to the court within the time specified. Where the order provides expressly or implicitly that the assessor may collect personal health information indirectly, then a health information custodian who is ordered to perform the assessment may rely on the order to collect the necessary information.

D. COLLECTION IN CONTRAVENTION OF *PHIPA*

A health information custodian that collects personal health information in contravention of *PHIPA* is not permitted to use or disclose the information unless required by law to do so.[102] The health information custodian could be compelled to disclose the personal health information acquired in contravention of *PHIPA* pursuant to a search warrant or court order, for example. Unless otherwise required by law, having collected personal health information in contravention of *PHIPA*, a health information custodian may presumably destroy the information in a secure manner.[103]

---

100   See note 66, above.

101   S.O. 1990, c. 11, s. 116.

102   *PHIPA*, s. 31(1).

103   Although *PHIPA*, s. 37(1)(f) suggests that disposing of personal health information may be considered a use, it would seem absurd to suggest that a custodian who had collected information in contravention of *PHIPA* was obligated to hold it forever. Rather, *PHIPA*, s. 37(1)(f) should be understood to simply provide greater certainty about the authority of the health information custodian to take various steps to dispose of the information. If a custodian is concerned with the lack of explicit authority to destroy the information, the custodian may choose to contact the Information and Privacy Commissioner, who has the authority under s. 61(1)(e) of *PHIPA*, following a review, to order the disposal of improperly collected information.

9

Use of Personal Health Information

A. *PHIPA*'S USE RULES: INTRODUCTION

1) Generally

Among the purposes of the *Personal Health Information Protection Act, 2004*[1] is the establishment of rules for the use of personal health information about patients by health information custodians.[2] *PHIPA* defines "use" to mean, in relation to personal health information in the custody or control of a health information custodian, to handle or deal with the information, but does not include disclosure of the information.[3] For the purposes of *PHIPA*, the provision of personal health information between a health information custodian and an agent of the custodian is a use by the custodian, and not a disclosure by the person providing the information or a collection by the person to whom the information is provided.[4] Where a custodian may use personal health information, the custodian also may provide the information to the custodian's agents, who may use the information for that purpose on behalf of the custodian.[5]

---

1   S.O. 2004, c. 3, Sch. A [*PHIPA*].
2   *PHIPA*, s. 1(a).
3   *Ibid.*, s. 2, definition of "use."
4   *Ibid.*, s. 6(1). The term "use" is further discussed in Chapter 2, Section E(3).
5   *Ibid.*, s. 37(2).

The Act sets out the circumstances in which a health information custodian may use personal health information about a patient, whether with or without the patient's consent.[6] As with the collection and disclosure of personal health information, the general rule in *PHIPA* is that a health information custodian requires consent to use personal health information.[7] The Act goes on to specify, however, the circumstances in which a custodian may use personal health information without the patient's consent.[8]

2) Change of Approach

The requirement for a health information custodian to have statutory authority to use personal health information is a change in the law in many settings. Until the advent of *PHIPA*, legislation applicable to the health care sector in Ontario typically did not require health care providers to seek consent for uses of personal health information. Further, health sector legislation generally did not specify the circumstances in which a patient's information could be used without the patient's consent.[9]

---

6   In the context of the requirement for consent, the word "patient" includes the patient's substitute decision-maker, where the substitute is authorized to act on the patient's behalf. For further details about substitute decision-making, see Chapter 6.

7   *PHIPA*, s. 29(a).

8   *Ibid.*, ss. 29(b) and 37(1).

9   Legislation pertaining to the Ministry of Health and Long-Term Care, for example, generally has authorized a "use" of personal health information, collected directly or indirectly from the individual, for specified purposes: see, for example, the *Independent Health Facilities Act*, R.S.O. 1990, c. I-13 at s. 37.1(2) [*IHFA*] and the *Ontario Drug Benefit Act*, R.S.O. 1990, c. O.10, s. 13(2) [*ODBA*]. But the information provisions in the *Long-Term Care Act, 1994*, S.O. 1994, c. 26 [*LTCA*] and the *Mental Health Act*, R.S.O. 1990, c. M.7 [*MHA*] dealt with "disclosures" and not "uses" (most of these permissible disclosure provisions have been repealed by *PHIPA*); also, professional misconduct rules under health-profession-specific statutes make it a professional misconduct for health professionals to disclose patient or client information without consent. Given that "disclosure" in some circumstances covered what is now "use" in *PHIPA*, such as where a health information custodian consults with his or her lawyer, it is not to say that there were no rules about use in those settings where legislation for disclosure of patient information existed; however, legislation was typically silent about using patient information for record keeping, improvement of services, or sharing information with the custodian's insurer or lawyer — the kinds of permissible uses without consent that are specifically set out now in *PHIPA*.

3) Use of Personal Health Information Collected Prior to *PHIPA*

PHIPA applies to a health information custodian's use of personal health information on or after the day the Act came into force, even if the custodian collected the information *before* the Act came into force.[10] Therefore, any use of personal health information that a health information custodian makes on or after 1 November 2004, even if the information was collected before that date,[11] is subject to the rules in *PHIPA*.

B. USE OF PERSONAL HEALTH INFORMATION WITH CONSENT

A health information custodian may use a patient's personal health information with the patient's consent, provided that the use, to the best of the custodian's knowledge, is for a lawful purpose.[12]

In most instances a consent from a patient for a custodian to use personal health information in a particular manner may be express or implied.[13] A health information custodian identified in section 20(2) of *PHIPA* who receives personal health information about a patient from the patient, the patient's substitute decision-maker, or another health information custodian, is entitled to assume that it has the patient's implied consent for the use of the information for the purposes of providing health care or assisting in the providing of health care, unless the custodian is aware that the patient has expressly withheld or withdrawn the consent.[14]

A custodian requires express consent, however, for the use of personal health information for the purpose of marketing or for the purpose of market research.[15] Similarly, the Act restricts reliance on implied consent for the use of personal health information for the purpose of fundraising activities. Implied consent in the fundraising context is only permitted with respect to the patient's name and prescribed contact information, provided that the custodi-

---

10   *PHIPA*, s. 7(1)(b)(i).
11   Note, however, that *PHIPA* provides that the Act does not apply to personal health information about an individual after the earlier of 120 years after the record containing the information was created and 50 years after the death of the individual: s. 9(1).
12   *PHIPA*, s. 29(1)(a). See discussion of "lawful purposes" in Chapter 7, Section B.
13   *Ibid.*, ss. 18(2) & (3). The consent rules are further explained in Chapter 5.
14   See further about s. 20(2) in Chapter 5, Section F(3).
15   *PHIPA*, s. 33 and *General*, O. Reg. 329/04, s. 1(2) [*PHIPA* Regulation].

an obtains the patient's implied consent in the manner set out in the *PHIPA* Regulation.[16]

C. PURPOSES FOR WHICH PERSONAL HEALTH INFORMATION MAY BE USED WITHOUT CONSENT

1) Generally

PHIPA authorizes a health information custodian to use personal health information that the custodian has collected for one purpose (usually for health care purposes) for certain specified secondary purposes, without requiring the custodian to obtain the patient's consent.[17] The uses of personal health information that the Act identifies as permissible without consent reflect situations where, in general, it would not be practical or reasonable to seek permission from the patient for the use or in which the use is consistent with public policy. In many cases, *PHIPA* authorizes in legislation, for the first time in Ontario, common practices in the health care sector.

Of course, a custodian is not precluded from seeking consent for any use of personal health information listed in *PHIPA* as permitted without consent, if the custodian believes that it is appropriate in the circumstances to do so. Reliance on any of the provisions that permit uses of personal health information without consent is discretionary; a health information custodian is not required to use personal health information for all purposes as set out in the Act and is not compelled to authorize any of its agents to use personal health information for such purposes. Further, where a custodian exercises discretion to use personal health information without a patient's consent for one or more of the authorized purposes, as set out in *PHIPA*, the custodian must exercise this discretion in a manner that adheres to the general limiting principles of the legislation.[18] Such discretion and limits would not apply to a situation where a law requires the custodian to use the personal health information.

---

16   *PHIPA*, s. 32 and *PHIPA* Regulation, *ibid.*, s. 10. Where implied consent is not permitted, express consent is required. See Chapter 5, Section F.

17   *PHIPA*, s. 37.

18   *Ibid.*, s. 30(1) provides that the custodian shall not use personal health information if other information will serve the purpose, and s. 30(2) provides that a custodian shall not use more personal health information than is reasonably necessary to meet the purpose.

A description of the circumstances in, and purposes for, which a health information custodian may use personal health information without a patient's consent follows.

2) For the Purpose Collected or Created and for all Functions Reasonably Necessary for That Purpose: Section 37(1)(a)

a) For the Purpose for Which Collected or Created

A health information custodian may use personal health information about a patient without the patient's consent "for the purpose for which the personal health information was collected or created."[19] For example, where a health information custodian collected personal health information from a patient, whether with or without consent, for the purpose of providing health care to the patient,[20] the custodian is authorized to use the information to provide the necessary health care to the patient, without having to obtain consent from the patient specifically for this use.

b) For all Functions Reasonably Necessary for That Purpose

As what may be regarded as an extension to the authority to use personal health information for the purpose for which the custodian collected the information, *PHIPA* permits a health information custodian to use personal health information about a patient without consent "for all functions reasonably necessary" to carry out the purpose for which the information was collected or created.[21] For example, where a health information custodian collects a patient's personal

---

19   *PHIPA*, s. 37(1)(a).

20   *Ibid.*, ss. 18, 36(1)(a) & (b).

21   *PHIPA*, s. 37(1)(a). Some information privacy statutes permit an organization to use personal information without consent for a "consistent purpose." For example, the *Freedom of Information and Protection of Privacy Act*, R.S.O. 1990, c. F.31, s. 41(b) [*FIPPA*], allows an institution to use personal information in its custody or under its control "for the purpose for which it was obtained or compiled or for a consistent purpose." The same provision appears in the *Municipal Freedom of Information and Protection of Privacy Act*, R.S.O. 1990, c. M.56, s. 31(b) [*MFIPPA*]. "Consistent purpose" is explained in these two statutes to mean a purpose for which "the individual might reasonably have expected such a use." *FIPPA*, s. 43; *MFIPPA*, s. 33. Provisions that permit a use of information for a "consistent purpose" provide a broader authority to use information than does *PHIPA*'s provision permitting a use of personal health information for the purpose of functions that are reasonably necessary for carrying out the purpose for which the information was collected. As a result of the narrower approach in *PHIPA*, *PHIPA* specifically enumerates more uses of personal health information without consent than perhaps otherwise would have been necessary had the "consistent purpose" approach been adopted.

health information for the purpose of adding the patient to a waiting list for a health care procedure, the custodian may use the information to contact the patient to inform the patient of the date of his or her appointment for the procedure. Further, in a health care facility, facility staff, such as individuals who distribute food trays, could use a patient's personal health information to ensure that a patient receives a meal that meets his or her dietary requirements.

On the other hand, where a health information custodian wishes to analyze the patient's record in order to assist the custodian in improving or maintaining the quality of the custodian's services generally, this would not be a function that could be said to be included as reasonably necessary for the provision of health care to that particular patient, and hence would not be within the scope of functions reasonably necessary to carry out the purpose for which the information was collected or created.

In interpreting the scope of the language "for all functions reasonably necessary" to carry out the purpose for which the information was collected or created, it is necessary to have regard for the other provisions in section 37 of the Act that permit a health information custodian to use personal health information without the consent of the patient to whom the information relates. It is not necessary to read this language in section 37(1)(a) so expansively as to include the other activities for which a custodian may use personal health information without consent, as set out in section 37.

c)   Exceptions

In two instances, a custodian cannot rely on this provision[22] as authority to use personal health information for the purpose for which the custodian collected or created the information.

First, where a custodian collected personal health information with the express or implied consent of the patient, and the patient, either at the time of giving his or her consent or at some later time, expressly instructed the custodian not to use the information for the purpose for which the information was collected or created or for a purpose reasonably necessary to carry out that purpose, the custodian cannot rely on this provision to use the information in a manner that is inconsistent with the patient's direction.[23] Second, if a health information

---

22   *PHIPA*, s. 37(1)(a).

23   This provision recognizes that where collections of personal health information occur with patient consent, a patient should have the ability in effect to subsequently withdraw his or her consent to uses of information that was collected with his or her consent. This provision highlights a possible constraint, which could result from a custodian requiring patient consent for collections that do not require consent. Once the custodian obtains a patent's consent for a collection of information, whether the

custodian collected personal health information indirectly without a patient's consent in order to provide health care to the patient because it was not possible to collect reliable, accurate information directly from the patient in a timely manner, the patient may expressly indicate that the information cannot be used for any or all purposes related to the purpose for which it was collected, that is, to provide health care.[24] Where the patient has a substitute decision-maker, that person may provide such an instruction on the patient's behalf.[25]

A patient's express instruction only operates to restrict a custodian's use of personal health information in these particular instances. *PHIPA* does not require a health information custodian to act in accordance with a patient's express instruction in all instances. A custodian may continue to use the information without the patient's consent pursuant to another provision of the Act that permits the custodian to use the information without the patient's consent.[26] These other provisions are discussed in greater detail below.

3) Use for a Purpose for Which Person Permitted or Required to Disclose to Custodian: Section 37(1)(b)

a) Generally

While statutes and regulations frequently contain provisions permitting persons to disclose personal health information for purposes that are considered to be appropriate, very often the authority of the recipient to use the information disclosed to it is not explicitly addressed. *PHIPA* permits a health information custodian to use a patient's personal health information for a purpose for which *PHIPA*, another Act of Ontario, or an Act of Canada permits or requires a person to disclose it to the custodian.[27] Without this type of provision, even where legislation authorized a particular disclosure of personal health information to a health information custodian, there would have been no corollary ability on the

---

consent was required by *PHIPA* or not, the custodian must subsequently honour all patient directions restricting the use of the information, unless a provision allowing the use without consent applies in the circumstances.

24 *PHIPA*, s. 37(1)(a). This limit does not apply to hospitals until 1 November 2005. See further discussion about the so-called "lock box" in Chapter 7, Section G.

25 *PHIPA*, s. 25: see Chapter 6, Section D.

26 Thus an express instruction under *PHIPA*, s. 37(1)(a) cannot restrict uses of personal health information pursuant to *PHIPA*, ss. 37(1)(b) through (k).

27 *PHIPA*, s. 37(1)(b). The reference to "another Act [of Ontario] or an Act of Canada" would also include regulations made under the relevant statutes. Note that other statutes address "personal information" or "information," not usually "personal health information." This is discussed below in Section C(12)(b).

part of the recipient custodian to use the information for that purpose, without consent, unless, of course, another clause in section 37(1) applied. Before relying on this provision to authorize a given use, a recipient custodian must ascertain that he or she has the authority to collect such information and that the disclosing custodian has authority to disclose the personal health information.[28]

b) Where *PHIPA* Permits a Disclosure

Where *PHIPA* permits a health information custodian to disclose personal health information to another custodian without the patient's consent, *PHIPA*, section 37(1)(b) permits the recipient health information custodian to use the information for the purpose for which it was disclosed. This rule applies to all of the permissible disclosures set out in *PHIPA* that a health information custodian is authorized to make with or without the patient's consent, where the recipient of the information is also a health information custodian.

For example, *PHIPA* permits a health information custodian to disclose personal health information for the purpose of a capacity assessment under the *Substitute Decisions Act, 1992*.[29] Where the person receiving this personal health information is also a health information custodian, such as an assessor, then the assessor may use the information that the disclosing custodian provided about the patient to conduct the capacity assessment, without having to obtain the patient's consent for such a use of the personal health information.[30]

c) Where Another Act of Ontario or Canada Permits or Requires Disclosure

Where another Act of Ontario or Canada permits or requires a disclosure of personal health information to a health information custodian, the custodian may use the personal health information that the custodian receives for the purpose for which it was disclosed. Consider the following examples:

- The Minister of Health and Long-Term Care, an upper-tier municipality, a local municipality, a delivery agent,[31] or a medical director[32] may disclose

---

28   The authority to collect personal health information, indirectly, is outlined in Chapter 8, Section C. For a discussion of permissible disclosures of personal health information, see Chapter 10. Further disclosures of personal health information are addressed in Chapter 11.

29   *PHIPA*, s. 43(1)(a).

30   *Ibid.* An "assessor" within the meaning of the *Substitute Decisions Act, 1992*, S.O. 1992, c. 30 [*SDA*] is listed as a health information custodian in *PHIPA*, s. 3(1)[5]. Further, the assessor would be authorized in this case to collect the personal health information pursuant to *PHIPA*, s. 36(1)(g).

31   *Ambulance Act*, R.S.O. 1990, c. A.19, s. 1(1) defines the term "delivery agent."

32   Under the *Ambulance Act, ibid.,* s. 1, a medical director means a physician designated by a base hospital as the medical director of a base hospital program. Base hospitals

personal health information to a health information custodian that operates an ambulance service where the disclosure is reasonably necessary for purposes relating to the discharge or exercise by the recipient custodian of its duties or powers under the *Ambulance Act*.[33] Where such a disclosure occurs, the recipient custodian may use the information received for such purposes.

- Under the *Mental Health Act*, an officer in charge of a psychiatric facility may disclose or transmit a patient's record of personal health information to a physician who is considering issuing or renewing a community treatment order.[34] The custodian physician who receives personal health information pursuant to this authority may use the information for the purpose of issuing or renewing the community treatment order.

4) Planning, Delivering, or Managing Own Programs or Services: Section 37(1)(c)

A health information custodian is authorized to use personal health information in the custodian's custody or control in order to

- plan or deliver the programs or services that the custodian provides or funds in whole or in part;
- allocate resources to any of such programs or services;
- evaluate or monitor any of such programs or services; and
- detect, monitor, or prevent fraud or any unauthorized receipt of services or benefits related to any of such programs or services.[35]

Of course, it must be remembered that this provision deals with uses of personal health information only. In order to *disclose* personal health information for such purposes, a health information custodian would require the consent of the patient to whom the information relates or be able to rely on a provision

---

are designated by the Minister of Health and Long-Term Care to monitor the quality of the care provided by ambulance services in the regions and districts established by the Minister and to perform such other functions as may be assigned to them by regulation (ss. 1 and 4(2)(d)).

33 *Ambulance Act, ibid.*, s. 19(2). The purposes mentioned in s. 19(2) are those relating to the provision, administration, management, operation, use, inspection, investigation, or regulation of ambulance services or to the enforcement of the *Ambulance Act* or its regulations (s. 19(3)).

34 See note 72 in Chapter 8 for an explanation of a community treatment order.

35 *PHIPA*, s. 37(1)(c).

of *PHIPA* that permits the custodian to disclose the information without the patient's consent.

A health information custodian may rely on this clause as authority to use personal health information in the custodian's custody or control as may be required to support a range of activities, including the following:[36]

- reviewing the operation of a service or program that the custodian provides or funds in whole or in part;
- record-keeping and other records management services, including transcription services;
- creating, tracking, and managing waiting times for services;
- the participation of the custodian's manager in a program delivered by the custodian to evaluate or monitor the delivery or ongoing feasibility of the program;
- discussions with the custodian's employees and other agents about health care services provided to patients within a program to determine its viability;
- comparing patient records to assess utilization of resources;
- supporting the delivery of the custodian's spiritual or religious care program;
- fulfilling the requirements of the custodian's occupational health and safety program;[37]
- complying with health surveillance protocols within the organization;[38]
- conducting an internal audit where there is a suspicion of fraud or other inappropriate use of services on the part of either a patient, or an employee, or other agent;

---

36   A custodian's provision of personal health information to a person who is not the agent of the custodian would be considered a disclosure, and thus would not be authorized by a provision in *PHIPA* that authorizes a use of personal health information. See Chapter 10 for a discussion of the provisions in *PHIPA* that permit disclosures of personal health information, which are generally narrower in scope than the provisions that permit uses of personal health information, as outlined in this chapter.

37   Pursuant to *Hospital Management*, R.R.O. 1990, O. Reg. 965 [Reg. 965], made under the *Public Hospitals Act*, R.S.O. 1990, c. P.40, s. 4(d) [PHA], a hospital occupational health and safety program must include procedures, for example, with respect to a safe and healthy work environment in the hospital, the safe use of substances, equipment, and medical devices in the hospital, the prevention of accidents to persons on the premises of the hospital — any of these types of activities could potentially require the use of personal health information.

38   For example, s. 4(e) of Reg. 965, *ibid.*, provides that such a program in a hospital includes a communicable disease surveillance program in respect of all persons carrying on activities in the hospital. A health information custodian may need to use personal health information to eliminate or reduce risks of harm.

- reviewing records of personal health information for the purpose of self-assessment as may be required by a health information custodian's *RHPA* College;[39] and
- completing a self-study as may be required for purposes of accreditation.[40]

Clearly, not all of the custodian's agents will need to use personal health information for all such activities. Who within the organization should be permitted to use information on the custodian's behalf, and the circumstances in which such use should be permitted, will require careful consideration. When making such determinations, a custodian should have careful regard to the general limiting principles of *PHIPA*.[41]

5) Risk Management, Error Management, and Quality of Care: Section 37(1)(d)

a) Generally

PHIPA authorizes a health information custodian to use personal health information about a patient for the purpose of

- risk management;
- error management;
- improving or maintaining the quality of care the custodian provides; and
- improving or maintaining the quality of any of the custodian's related programs or services.[42]

The Act clearly recognizes that generally requiring a custodian to obtain patient consent for the use of personal health information for these types of internal activities would not be reasonable. In fact, such a requirement for con-

---

39 Each *RHPA* College is required to have in place a quality assurance program, as set out in the Regulated Health Professions Code, Schedule 2 to the *Regulated Health Professions Act, 1991*, S.O. 1991, c. 18, s. 80 [*RHPA*]. One prevalent component of such a program is the requirement for self-assessment, where a member of a regulated health profession may be required to keep a portfolio or log for self-reflection. In it, the member records his or her strengths as well as areas for improvement.

40 For example, a health information custodian that operates a mental health centre and has applied for accreditation to Children's Mental Health Ontario, would be able to use its patients' personal health information as needed to complete the self-study, a prerequisite for any application for accreditation. From Frequently Asked Questions, Children's Mental Health Ontario, online: <http://www.cmho.org/Accreditation.shtml>.

41 *PHIPA*, ss. 17 and 30. See Chapter 7 for more details about the application of the general limiting principles in *PHIPA*, particularly Section E.

42 *PHIPA*, s. 37(1)(d).

sent could interfere with the ability of health information custodians to carry out many of these activities on a continual and comprehensive basis. The types of activities identified in this clause are essential components of many custodians' proper operation and delivery of health care or related programs and services.[43] These activities occur, whether or not they are expressly required by statute, in all health care organizations that provide health care. For the first time in Ontario legislation, the use of personal health information for these types of activities in the health system is specifically authorized, without the need for patient consent.[44]

b)   For Risk or Error Management or to Improve Care or Related Programs

In the health sector, the focus of risk management is the identification, reduction, and elimination of risks to patients, agents, and the public, and includes the prevention of lawsuits, other proceedings, and financial losses.[45] Risk management also includes responding to complaints and grievances.

Error management, on the other hand, is concerned with dealing with mistakes or possible mistakes. Error management encompasses activities such as preparing incident reports, conducting internal investigations, and carrying out disciplinary measures.[46]

Improving or maintaining quality of care and related services encompasses such traditional activities as utilization reviews, outcome reviews, and peer reviews.[47] These activities enable "the identification of deviant and potentially deficient and/or inordinately expensive practices of individual health care providers."[48] Where a culture of continuous quality assurance or quality

---

43   For example, see the *PHA*, above note 37, s. 34. Also see above note 39.

44   Mr. Justice Krever stressed the need for staff to have access to and use of health information for administrative purposes. See: Ontario, Royal Commission of Inquiry into the Confidentiality of Health Records in Ontario, *Report of the Commission of Inquiry into the Confidentiality of Health Information* (Toronto: Queen's Printer, 1980), vol. 1 at 300. [*Krever Report*]. See also *Re General Accident Assurance Company of Canada and Sunnybrook Hospital* (1970), 23 O.R. (2d) 513 (H.C.J.) [*Sunnybrook*].

45   See Steering Committee, *Public Hospitals Act Review*, Chapter 8, "Quality," in *Into the 21st Century, Ontario Public Hospitals* (Toronto: Publications Ontario, 1992) at 127–30.

46   *Ibid.* at 128.

47   These terms are not contained in the Act, however the draft *Personal Health Information Protection Act, 1997* provisions governing "quality improvement activities" specified that such activities included "a peer review, a utilization review, an outcome review, or a medical or other professional audit." [Ontario, *Personal Health Information Protection Act, 1997: Draft for Consultation* (Toronto: Queen's Printer for Ontario, 1997), clauses 2(1) and 18.]

48   See above note 46.

improvement prevails in an organization, all of the organization's processes are continually reviewed in the effort to establish new and better ways of providing patient treatment and care.

The types of activities that may fall into the categories of activities set out in this clause and the custodian's consequential uses of personal health information to support these activities are quite varied. Consider this range of activities that a health information custodian may need to undertake. A custodian may need to

- engage in a discussion with his or her agents about the health care that the agents have provided to a patient;
- discuss health care with agents where there is a concern about the quality of care or related services provided to the patient or where there may be a need to implement some strategies to improve the care or services of the type provided to the patient, in the future;
- assess all points of contact with patients, from how the organization deals with a patient on the telephone to timeliness of services provided to the patient;
- review records of personal health information to assess whether such information is properly collected and recorded, or review whether patient records are accessed only by authorized personnel;
- implement proper infection control measures; and
- determine when equipment and devices have been utilized, by whom, and for whom, to assess the safety and efficacy of such equipment and devices.

In practice, risk and error management activities and activities to improve care or related programs often overlap. As a result, the use of personal health information for the purpose of one such activity may overlap with the use for the purpose of another.

For any of these purposes, a health information custodian may need to involve the custodian's insurer or lawyers.[49] Where the insurer or the lawyers are agents of the custodian, such persons may use personal health information on the custodian's behalf to provide advice and other necessary support to the custodian.[50] Other types of advisors and service providers that are agents of the

---

49 A custodian remains responsible for the personal health information in its custody or control. See Chapter 4, Section G. Where a custodian may need to consult a lawyer or insurer, s. 37(1)(h) (for the purpose of a proceeding or a contemplated proceeding) may also apply. This clause also overlaps with the activities listed in s. 37(1)(b).

50 *PHIPA*, s. 37(2).

custodian and are involved in such activities may also use personal health information on the custodian's behalf to provide services to the custodian.

c)   Effect of *QCIPA* and Related Provisions

Where personal health information is prepared for or by a committee that is designated by a hospital, a long-term care facility, an independent health facility, or other authorized organization as a "quality of care committee" under the *Quality of Care Information Protection Act, 2004*,[51] the custodian must be aware of the restrictive rules pertaining to the disclosure of such information gathered in the course of work undertaken by the committee. The nature and extent of "quality of care information"[52] and the requirements and restrictions relating to its use, disclosure, and non-admissibility in proceedings is explained in Chapter 17. Not all the uses of personal health information for risk or error management or for quality of care purposes[53] will be covered by *QCIPA*, but where *QCIPA* does apply, it prevails over any provision in *PHIPA*. For example, disclosures of quality of care information as defined in *QCIPA* are only permitted where authorized by that Act.[54]

Similarly, a health information custodian who is required by his or her *RHPA* College to comply with the College's quality assurance program should be aware that information generated by the custodian in any practice reviews, self-evaluation, remedial action, and the like, in compliance with the program, is subject to the similar overriding restrictions set out in the *Regulated Health Professions Act, 1991*.[55]

6)   Educating Agents: Section 37(1)(e)

Students learning to practise a health-related profession require first-hand experience in providing or assisting in providing health care to patients, which necessarily involves having access to patient information. For instance, students who are involved in providing health care to a patient need to discuss that care and the patient's condition with their supervisors at the custodian's facility. They also need to review patients' charts in order to learn how to properly document the provision of health care, or in order to document the care that they have assisted in providing. Such practices with respect to students accessing patient information without the patient's consent are prevalent in

---

51   S.O. 2004, c. 3, Sch. B, s. 1 [*QCIPA*].

52   "Quality of care information" is defined in *QCIPA, ibid.*, s. 1.

53   That is, under s. 37(1)(c) or (d) of *PHIPA*.

54   *QCIPA*, above note 52, ss. 2 & 4(1).

55   *RHPA*, see above note 39, s. 83.1(4). See further, Chapter 17, Section I.

the health system. With some exceptions, this practice was not reflected in legislation until the coming into force of *PHIPA*.[56] Students, however, are not the only ones who may need access to patient information for educational purposes. A custodian's other agents, such as employees and professional staff, may need access to patient information, as well, where they are learning a new way of administering a procedure, for example, or where they are being trained to use equipment, such as a ventilator or MRI technology.

PHIPA specifically authorizes such uses of personal health information. Particularly, the Act allows a health information custodian to use a patient's personal health information "for the purpose of educating agents to provide health care."[57] Such permitted use includes allowing the custodian to provide personal health information to its agent for this purpose.[58] This provision also would permit a use of personal health information by a custodian and its agents in a discussion group or a medical round for teaching purposes.

To be clear, this authority to use personal health information in the context of providing education does not extend to disclosures of personal health information. Where a student, who is an agent of a health information custodian, consults with an academic supervisor who is not an agent of the custodian, for the purpose of providing health care to a patient, such a consultation is a "disclosure" of personal health information by the student to the supervisor and not a "use," and this exception to the requirement for consent does not apply. The student will usually make such a disclosure for health care purposes with the patient's implied consent to disclose personal health information for the purpose of providing health care, unless the patient has expressly stated otherwise.[59]

Similarly, where an agent of a health information custodian wishes to explain, in a manner that would reasonably be expected to identify a patient, the patient's condition and course of treatment in an educational forum that includes health professionals or students from other facilities who are not agents of that health information custodian, the patient's express consent

---

56 Note that Reg. 965, above note 38, s. 22(6)(a) allows a hospital board to permit a member of the medical, dental, midwifery, or extended class nursing staff of the hospital access to personal health information for teaching purposes. Section 32(2) of the *LTCA*, above note 9, allowed a service provider to disclose a personal record to a person for an academic pursuit (now repealed by *PHIPA*, s. 89(6)). A similar provision in the *Mental Health Act*, above note 9, s. 35(3)(f), has also been repealed by *PHIPA*, s. 90(6).

57 *PHIPA*, s. 37(1)(e).

58 *Ibid.*, s. 37(2).

59 *Ibid.*, s. 20(2).

would be required, as the explanation would involve a disclosure of personal health information to persons for a purpose other than the provision of health care. Consent, however, is not required if the information about the patient is de-identified,[60] as such information would not be "personal health information" and thus not governed by *PHIPA*.

7)   Disposal or Modification: Section 37(1)(f)

PHIPA allows a health information custodian to use personal health information for the purpose of disposing of the information.[61] Further, the Act permits the custodian to use such information in order to modify the information so as to conceal the identity of the patient to whom the information relates. Modifying information so as to conceal the identity of a patient may involve making the identity of the patient less obvious, perhaps by removing the patient's name, health number, or other identifier from a record of personal health information, or de-identifying information[62] to the point that it is no longer personal health information. A custodian must dispose of or modify personal health information "in a manner consistent with Part II";[63] that is, in a man-

---

60   See note 62, below.

61   *PHIPA*, s. 37(1)(f). The Standing Committee on General Government added the phrase "for the purpose of disposing of the information" to the clause during the first clause-by-clause review of Bill 31, *An Act to enact and amend various Acts with respect to the protection of health information*, 1st Sess., 38th Leg., Ontario, 2003, cl. 36(1)(f) [Bill 31]: Ontario, Legislative Assembly, Standing Committee on General Government, *Official Report of Debates (Hansard)*, G-215 (9 February 2004) at 1140 (Peter Fonseca). The National Association for Information Destruction submitted before the Standing Committee that, without such an addition, the custodian would be required to obtain consent from patients to allow their information to be destroyed and disposed of: Ontario, Legislative Assembly, Standing Committee on General Government, *Official Report of Debates (Hansard)*, G-109 (28 January 2004) at 1120 (Dan Steward).

62   *Ibid.*, s. 37(1)(f). *PHIPA* defines the term "de-identify," in relation to personal health information of an individual, to mean to remove any information that identifies the individual or which it is reasonably foreseeable in the circumstances could be utilized, either alone or with other information, to identify the individual. This definition is set out in s. 47(1) in the context of a health data institute's disclosure of information to the Minister of Health and Long-Term Care. The term can be used just as well outside the context of s. 47 as it is defined, in effect, in relation to the definition of the term "identifying information" in s. 4(2), so that de-identified information is by definition not personal health information. See further discussion about "identifying" information in Chapter 2, Section C(1)(d).

63   Part II of *PHIPA* — Practices to Protect Personal Health Information. Not all the provisions in Part II are relevant; the main provisions, however, have been noted.

ner that is secure,[64] that complies with any applicable regulations,[65] and that protects the information from theft, unauthorized use, or disclosure.[66]

The rationale for this privacy-protective practice is clear. Without such a provision, the custodian would arguably have had to depend on the patient's permission to de-identify the patient's record or to dispose of it. The requirement for consent might have made such information more vulnerable to a privacy breach, especially if the patient or a substitute decision-maker could not be located, thus requiring the health information custodian to keep the patient's records in identifiable form or for unnecessarily lengthy periods of time.[67] By including this provision in *PHIPA*, it is explicitly clear that a custodian may use personal health information for such purposes without the consent of the patient to whom the information relates.

8) Seeking Consent: Section 37(1)(g)

PHIPA recognizes that, sometimes, a health information custodian may need to use personal health information simply in order to contact a patient to seek the patient's consent. Where the Act requires a custodian to obtain a patient's express consent, for example, the custodian may first need to access the patient's record of personal health information in order to find the patient's address and telephone number.[68] Similarly, the custodian may use personal health information consisting of the patient's substitute decision-maker's name

---

64 *PHIPA*, s. 13(1).

65 *Ibid.* There are no regulations under *PHIPA* that specifically address the disposal of records generally; however, the *PHIPA* Regulation, above note 15, s. 6(3) sets out requirements for health information network providers, who may be agents of a health information custodian, to notify the custodian where the provider has disposed of the information other than in a manner outside its duties with a custodian, for example. See further Chapter 2, Section B(3).

66 *PHIPA*, s. 12(1).

67 If the health information custodian required consent for the disposal or destruction of personal health information, and could not obtain it, the custodian would be required to keep the record of personal health information until the earlier of 120 years after a record containing the information was created and 50 years after the death of the patient, unless the custodian would be able to transfer the personal health information to an archive under s. 42(3) if an archive willing to accept the material could be found. Disclosure to archives is further outlined in Chapter 10, Section O.

68 *PHIPA*, s. 37(1)(g). This provision was added in Committee during the first clause-by-clause review of Bill 31 on 9 February 2004; see: Ontario, Legislative Assembly, Standing Committee on General Government, *Official Report of Debates (Hansard)*, G-215 (9 February 2004) at 1140 (Peter Fonseca).

and address to contact that person.[69] A health information custodian may wish to contact a patient for the purpose of obtaining the patient's consent to a range of activities, from the patient's participating in a research study to making a donation in support of the custodian's services. The consent may or may not be a consent that is required under *PHIPA* or that relates to personal health information. This type of provision seems almost unnecessary, but without it, the custodian may have had no explicit authority to use a patient's record merely for the purpose of contacting that patient to obtain his or her consent.

9) Use in Proceedings: Section 37(1)(h)

Consider this situation. A patient sues a health information custodian and its agents for damages resulting from surgery that the patient alleges was negligently performed. Where a patient serves the health information custodian with a statement of claim, the custodian would normally be required to notify the custodian's insurer. The custodian may also need to contact a lawyer to prepare a statement of defence. Activities that would result from obtaining the statement of claim could include a review of the patient's records of personal health information and interviews with staff about the alleged events that led up to the claim for the purpose of responding to the claim.

PHIPA allows a health information custodian to use a patient's personal health information for the purpose of a proceeding or contemplated proceeding in which

- the custodian;
- an agent of the custodian; or
- a former agent of the custodian

is, or is expected to be, a party or a witness.[70]

---

69   Since *PHIPA* enables the health information custodian to obtain consent for the collection, use, or disclosure of personal health information from an authorized substitute decision-maker, it would appear that the custodian could rely on this clause of *PHIPA* to seek the substitute's consent. Effectively, the substitute decision-maker stands in the shoes of the patient, so that it appears reasonable to read the word "individual" here as including the substitute decision-maker. To read the provision otherwise would seem to frustrate the apparent intention of the clause to enable a custodian to contact the person whose consent is required for the purpose of obtaining the person's consent. For a detailed discussion of the role of the substitute decision-maker, see Chapter 6(D).

70   *PHIPA*, s. 37(1)(h). It is interesting to note that Mr. Justice Krever had recommended that this type of disclosure be clearly authorized in legislation. "Simple justice demands no less," stated Mr. Justice Krever as he recommended that, where a claim is

The personal health information may only be used, however, if it relates to, or is, a matter in issue in the proceeding or contemplated proceeding.[71] "Proceeding" is broadly defined in the Act.[72] The proceeding does not need to have been actually commenced in order for the custodian to be able to rely on this clause: it must, however, be "contemplated." The proceeding must evidently be actually and genuinely considered for this provision to apply.

Prior to the enactment of *PHIPA*, health care providers, for example, would generally have relied on the conclusion that the patient, by bringing a claim, was deemed to have authorized the provider to permit an inspection of the patient's record by its insurer or lawyer, to the extent that it was necessary to defend itself from the claim.[73] Some courts have concluded that for the purposes of litigation, in essence, the lawyer, the insurer, and the hospital are considered to form a single entity, so that the patient's medical records may be used to defend against a claim.[74] Such a use, however, was not always clearly set out in or under legislation.[75]

A custodian may rely on this provision in *PHIPA* to review relevant patient records for the purpose of preparing for an appearance, for example, at an inquest, a review before the Information and Privacy Commissioner, a mediation or an arbitration hearing, an examination for discovery, or before a com-

---

made or an action brought against a hospital by a patient or former patient in respect of the care given to that patient, the hospital board should be permitted to disclose the contents of that patient's medical record to the hospital's liability insurer and lawyers to enable them to ascertain the circumstances giving rise to the claim or action and, where appropriate, defend the hospital's position. [*Krever Report*, above note 44, vol. 2 at 324, Recommendation 61.]

71   *PHIPA*, s. 37(1)(h).

72   In *PHIPA*, s. 2, "proceeding" includes "a proceeding held in, before or under the rules of a court, a tribunal, a commission, a justice of the peace, a coroner, a committee of a College within the meaning of the *Regulated Health Professions Act, 1991*, a committee of the Board of Regents continued under the *Drugless Practitioners Act*, a committee of the Ontario College of Social Workers and Social Service Workers under the *Social Work and Social Service Work Act, 1988*, an arbitrator or a mediator."

73   See *Cook v. Ip* (1985), 22 D.L.R. (4th) 1 at 4–5 (Ont. C.A.); *Swirski v. Hachey* (1995), 132 D.L.R. (4th) 122 (B.C.S.C.).

74   *Sunnybrook*, above note 44. The courts discuss such a "use" as a "disclosure" to an advisor.

75   Note that some statutes had expressly authorized health care providers to disclose information from health records to their lawyers. For example, under s. 35(3)(e.2) of the *MHA*, above note 9, now repealed by *PHIPA*, s. 90(6), an officer in charge of a psychiatric facility could disclose a patient's clinical record to "a lawyer acting on behalf of the psychiatric facility or on behalf of any person employed in or on the staff of the facility." The *Public Hospitals Act* regulations, however, did not provide such clear authority.

mittee of a professional governing body. Sometimes, the custodian may need to review a patient's records where the actions of an agent or former agent with respect to the patient are at issue. A custodian may also use personal health information by interviewing the custodian's employees or other agents who are aware of the facts that led to the inquest, litigation, or other proceeding.[76] Further, the custodian may use personal health information to develop a statement of claim or defence, or to prepare an affidavit of documents,[77] for example.

The health information custodian may permit its agents to use the patient's personal health information, on its behalf, in the same circumstances as the custodian is authorized to by this clause.[78] For example, a custodian's agent, such as an insurer or lawyer, may use the information in support of the custodian's preparation for the proceeding or contemplated proceeding where the custodian is a party or witness or is expected to be a party or witness.[79] An agent may also use the relevant personal health information if an agent has been named, or is expected to be named, as a party, together with the custodian, or where the agent is expected to be a witness on the custodian's behalf.

Where the interests of an agent are separate from that of a health information custodian, such as where an agent is subject to discipline proceedings before a regulated governing body, or where an action has been brought against an agent, and not the custodian, *PHIPA* recognizes that agents and former agents may need access to personal health information to prepare for or defend their own interests in a proceeding. In such instances, section 37(1)(h) would not apply to permit the health information custodian to provide the agent or former agent access to personal health information, as the agent's use of the personal health information would be not on behalf of the custodian, but for the agent's own purposes; the provision of information from the custodian to the agent would thus be a disclosure and not a use.

---

76   Recall that the gathering of information by a custodian from its agents is considered a use of the custodian's information and not a collection: *PHIPA*, s. 6(1).

77   Rule 30.03 of the *Rules of Civil Procedure*, R.R.O. 1990, Reg. 194, made under the *Courts of Justice Act*, R.S.O. 1990, c. C.43, require that a party to an action shall, within ten days after the close of pleadings, serve on every other party an affidavit of documents disclosing, to the full extent of the party's knowledge, information, and belief, all documents relating to any matter in issue in the action that are or have been in the party's possession, control, or power.

78   *PHIPA*, s. 37(2). This "use" is on the health information custodian's behalf and not for the agent's own purposes.

79   The custodian could also rely on s. 37(1)(d) of *PHIPA* as authority to discuss the matter with the custodian's insurer or lawyer, for example.

However, the custodian would be able to disclose personal health information to the agent or former agent and could authorize its other agents to disclose such information to the agent or former agent for essentially the same purpose as set out in this use clause, under *PHIPA's* disclosure rules.[80] A health information custodian may rely on section 37(1)(h) to identify the relevant records needed prior to disclosing them to the agent or former agent. .

PHIPA permits an agent or former agent to whom the custodian has provided or disclosed personal health information to disclose the information received to a professional advisor, if the advisor is under a professional duty of confidentiality.[81] Therefore, the agent may disclose the personal health information that the agent receives to his or her lawyer, where the agent seeks independent advice or representation.

10) For Payment-related Purposes: Section 37(1)(i)

Where a health information custodian has provided health care to a patient, the custodian is not required to seek consent from the patient to use the patient's personal health information in order to obtain payment for either the provision of health care or related goods or services.[82] Further, a health information custodian may use a patient's personal health information for the purpose of "processing, monitoring, verifying or reimbursing claims for payment" for the provision of health care or related goods or services.[83]

This provision, in effect, provides authority for the health information custodian to retain a bookkeeper, for example, to manage the custodian's accounts for services rendered. A health information custodian could rely on this provision to send out reminder letters to patients to pay for the health care or related goods and services that the custodian provided. Further, this provision would

---

80 *PHIPA*, s. 41(1)(a) authorizes the health information custodian to disclose the personal health information to the agent or former agent, in circumstances corresponding to those set out in s. 37(1)(h) regarding uses of personal health information in proceedings.

81 *Ibid.*, s. 41(2) extends to agents who receive personal health information under s. 37(2). This provision is not limited to a disclosure to a lawyer, but could be made to other individuals who are also equally subject to a duty of confidentiality. Accountants, for example, who are subject to professional standards of practice, would fall into this category. This clause, however, would probably not apply to a union representative representing the agent employee at a grievance against a custodian, since it is unlikely that such an agent could be considered a professional advisor who has a professional duty of confidentiality with respect to the information.

82 *Ibid.*, s. 37(1)(i). "Related goods" would include such items as eyeglasses, hearing aids, medications, syringes, wheelchairs, walkers, and respirators.

83 *Ibid.*, s. 37(1)(i).

authorize the custodian to provide personal health information about a patient to a debt collection agency acting as the custodian's agent for the purposes of obtaining payment from the patient.[84]

Despite the authority to use personal health information without consent for this purpose, a custodian should not necessarily provide to an agent, such as a collection agency, in their entirety the details of the custodian's provision of services to the patient. Remember that, in *PHIPA*, personal health information about a patient could consist of the name or address of the patient linked with the name of the health care provider or the service the patient received, and the cost of the service or good provided. A health information custodian's provision of even these minimal details about the patient to a debt collection agency would be a use of the patient's personal health information. The custodian should provide the least amount of information necessary to the agency to enable the agency to carry out its task effectively, in accordance with *PHIPA*'s general limiting principles.[85]

This provision is also useful for the Ministry of Health and Long-Term Care as a health information custodian, and the largest government payer of health care and related goods and services,[86] but it can be equally useful to

---

84 During the hearings on Bill 31, above note 61, held by the Standing Committee on General Government, the Baycrest Centre for Geriatric Care argued that *PHIPA* should clearly authorize a health information custodian to share a patient's personal health information with a debt collection agency to help the custodian obtain payment from its patients [Ontario, Legislative Assembly, Standing Committee on General Government, *Official Report of Debates (Hansard)*, G-92 (27 January 2004) at 1520 (Paula Schipper)]. The first reading version of Bill 31 was amended at Committee during the clause-by-clause review of *PHIPA* to expressly add the words "obtaining payment" to cl. 36(1)(f) [now *PHIPA*, s. 37(1)(i)]: Ontario, Legislative Assembly, Standing Committee on General Government, *Official Report of Debates (Hansard)*, G-215 (9 February 2004) at 1140 (Peter Fonseca).

85 See above note 18.

86 The Ministry is responsible for the Ontario Health Insurance Plan, the Ontario Drug Benefit Plan, and the assistive devices program, for example. Note that the *Health Insurance Act*, R.S.O. 1990, c. H.6, s. 29(1) [*HIA*] provides that

Every insured person shall be deemed to have authorized his or her physician or practitioner, a hospital or health facility which provided a service to the insured person and any other prescribed person or organization to give the General Manager particulars of services provided to the insured person, (a) for the purpose of obtaining payment under the Plan for the services; (b) for the purpose of enabling the General Manager to monitor and control the delivery of insured services; (c) for the purpose of enabling the General Manager to monitor and control payments made under the Plan or otherwise for insured services; and (d) for such other purposes as may be prescribed.

other custodians such as community care access corporations, for example, which may also need to process, monitor, verify, or reimburse claims for payment with respect to services provided by their service providers.[87]

11) Use of Personal Health Information for Research: Section 37(1)(j)

PHIPA allows a health information custodian to use personal health information for the purpose of conducting research, provided the custodian has fulfilled the requirements of the Act, including preparing a research plan and obtaining the approval of a research ethics board for the research plan.[88] The requirements of this provision do not apply if another provision in the section pertaining to use of personal health information without the patient's consent applies to permit the use. For example, it is not necessary for a health information custodian to turn to the research rules set out in the Act to use personal health information where a health information custodian uses personal health information to evaluate a service provided by the custodian in accordance with section 37(1)(c).[89] *PHIPA's* requirements concerning the collection, use, and disclosure of personal health information for research purposes are explained in Chapter 11.

12) Where a Law Permits or Requires a Use: Section 37(1)(k)

a) Generally

Lastly, consistent with the rules pertaining to collection[90] and disclosure[91] of personal health information, *PHIPA* authorizes a health information custodian to use personal health information without the patient's consent if the cus-

---

PHIPA, s. 85(2) added a provision to the *HIA* to make clear that *HIA*, s. 29(1) does not apply where *PHIPA* applies, as the subject matter of s. 29(1)(b) & (c) is apparently captured in s. 37(1)(i) of *PHIPA*. Other provisions of *PHIPA* cover other aspects of s. 29(1).

87 *PHIPA*, s. 37(1)(i).

88 *Ibid.*, ss. 37(1)(j) and 37(3) provide that under s. 37(1)(j), a health information custodian may use a patient's personal health information only if the custodian prepares a research plan and has a research ethics board approve it, and for that purpose ss. 44(2)–(4) and ss. 44(6)(a)–(f) apply to the use as if it were a disclosure. See further about research in Chapter 11, Section B.

89 See Chapter 11: particularly, see the explanation of the interaction of the "use" provisions in *PHIPA* with "research" in Chapter 11, Section B(3)(b).

90 *PHIPA*, s. 36(1)(h), see Chapter 8, Section C(8).

91 *Ibid.*, s. 43(1)(h), see Chapter 10, Section P(2).

todian is permitted or required to do so by law or by a treaty, agreement, or arrangement made under an Act of Ontario or Canada.[92]

The scope of the phrase "permitted or required by law" is reviewed in Chapter 3.[93] As discussed there, a fundamental theme in *PHIPA* is the preservation of existing rules set out in other legislation governing specific parts of the health sector with respect to the collection, use, and disclosure of personal health information.[94] At a minimum, the phrase includes other Ontario and federal statutes, and their regulations. It also likely includes orders of a court or tribunal, and may include the common law. A regulation may impose requirements and place restrictions on a use of personal health information carried out pursuant to this provision.[95] Sometimes the law will directly authorize a custodian's agent to use personal health information in stated circumstances. In such instances, the agent does not require permission of the custodian to use the information as "permitted or required by law."[96]

b) Where Legislation Permits or Requires a Use

A number of statutes permit or require a health information custodian to use personal health information for purposes set out in those statutes. However, these provisions may not specifically refer to a use of personal health information by health information custodians without consent. Instead, the legislation may use different language to provide this authority. Consider the following ways in which a statute may provide a health information custodian with authority to use personal health information without a patient's consent.

- Usually statutes will not specifically refer to the use of "personal health information." More commonly, legislation will refer to the use of "personal information." The custodian may generally rely upon such a provision as authority to use personal health information, since, unless a clear contrary intention is evident, the term "personal information" can be read as including "personal health information."

---

92   *PHIPA*, s. 37(1)(k).
93   Chapter 3, Section B(3)(b).
94   Chapter 3, Section B(3)(a).
95   *PHIPA*, s. 37(1)(k) provides at the outset that a use under this clause is "subject to the requirements and restrictions, if any, that are prescribed." At the time of writing, no such regulation is in place.
96   *Ibid.*, s. 17(2). Under the *PHIPA* Regulation, above note 15, s. 7, for example, the Canadian Medical Protective Association and the Healthcare Reciprocal of Canada may use the personal health information that they receive as agents of health information custodians under s. 37(1)(d) (risk management etc.), for the purposes of systemic risk management analysis. See further in Chapter 2, Section B(2)(e).

- In other instances, legislation may not necessarily explicitly provide that a use of information may occur without consent, but the authorization may be implicit. Whether the words in a particular statute authorize the use of personal health information without the consent of the patients to whom the information relates will depend on the intent and context of the provision in question.[97]

- Moreover, where the law does not explicitly authorize a "use" of the information but simply permits or requires something that necessarily includes or entails a "use" of the information as defined in *PHIPA*, this would appear to be sufficient to conclude that the use is permitted or required by law for the purposes of *PHIPA*.[98]

- Some statutes that authorize a use of personal health information apply to only some health information custodians, while others are of general application and relevant to all health information custodians.[99]

i) Permissible Use Set Out in Statute

Where another Act applies to the health information custodian, the custodian should review its provisions, where need be, to determine whether that Act permits the custodian to use personal health information in a particular way. The following are just some examples of health-sector-specific uses of information that other legislation permits.

- A health information custodian that is a medical officer of health may use or retain personal health information for the purposes of the *Health Protection and Promotion Act* or for purposes related to the administration of a public health program or service that is prescribed in the regulations.[100]

---

97 For example, the Ministry of Health and Long-Term Care is authorized to use personal information in a number of its statutes: *HIA*, above note 86, s 4.1(2); *IHFA*, above note 9, s. 37.1(2); *Commitment to the Future of Medicare Act, 2004*, S.O. 2004, c. 5, s. 15(2). In these provisions, the words "without consent" do not appear but the use of information without consent in stated circumstances is implied.

98 This may occur, for example, where an agent of a custodian is required or permitted by law to "disclose" personal information to the custodian.

99 Some examples are set out in Section C(12)(b)(ii) below.

100 *Health Protection and Promotion Act*, R.S.O. 1990, c. H.7, s. 91.1(2) [*HPPA*]. The purpose of the *HPPA* is "to provide for the organization and delivery of public health programs and services, the prevention of the spread of disease and the promotion and protection of the health of the people of Ontario": s. 2. Regulations under that provision may place conditions on the use. As of the time of writing, no such regulations are prescribed.

- The Minister of Health and Long-Term Care may use personal information, subject to such conditions as may be prescribed, for purposes related to the administration of the *Ontario Drug Benefit Act.*[101]
- The officer in charge of a psychiatric facility[102] may use personal health information for the purposes of examining, assessing, observing, or detaining the patient in accordance with the *Mental Health Act*; or for the purpose of complying with Part XX.1 (Mental Disorder) of the *Criminal Code* or an order or disposition made pursuant to that Part.[103]

ii)   Required Use Set Out in Statute

Custodians should also review legislation applicable to their activities to determine whether an Act requires the use of personal health information in a particular way. Consider the following scenarios in which custodians are required to use personal health information. Recall that, as noted above, legislation often does not expressly permit or require health information custodians to use personal health information for a particular purpose, in the same way that legislation more frequently expressly permits or requires disclosures of personal health information.

- Under the *Independent Health Facilities Act*, every licensee (who is by definition a health information custodian) and the agents of the licensee must "co-operate fully" with an assessor carrying out an assessment of an independent health facility operated by a licensee.[104] Under that Act "co-operation" means, among other requirements, that the licensee must provide "information requested by the assessor in respect of records, including patient records, or the care of patients in the independent health facility"[105] in the "form requested by the assessor."[106] In order to "co-operate fully" as required by the *Independent Health Facilities Act*, the licensee is required to

---

101   *ODBA*, above note 9, s. 13(2).

102   In Crown-operated psychiatric facilities, the officer in charge is the health information custodian [*PHIPA*, s. 3(2)]. In facilities that are operated by a corporate board, the "officer in charge" would be an agent of the person who operates the psychiatric facility (which is the health information custodian): *PHIPA*, s. 3(1)[4][i].

103   *MHA*, above note 9, s. 35(2). Part XX.1 (Mental Disorder) of the *Criminal Code*, R.S.C. 1985, c. C-46, deals with, among other matters, assessments and dispositions pertaining to accused individuals who may be unfit to stand trial for the offence they have been charged with by reason of suffering from a mental disorder or who have been found to be not criminally responsible for an offence they have been charged with by reason of suffering from a mental disorder.

104   *IHFA*, above note 9, s. 31(2).

105   *Ibid.*, s. 31(1)(c).

106   *Ibid.*, s. 31(1)(d).

use the personal health information in order to comply with the assessor's demands, for example, by gathering and organizing the information that the assessor requires.[107]

- Similarly, under the provisions of the *Workplace Safety and Insurance Act, 1997*, a physician whom a worker selects from a roster of physicians maintained by the Workplace Safety and Insurance Board to conduct a medical assessment is required, when performing the assessment, to "consider any reports by the worker's treating health professional."[108] The health information custodian physician is thus required to use the worker's personal health information contained in these reports.

- Further, where a health information custodian is required to disclose personal health information to a health data institute under *PHIPA*, and the Minister of Health and Long-Term Care specifies the form and manner in which the custodian is required to disclose the personal health information, by implication, the custodian must use the personal health information to provide it in the form and manner required.[109]

iii) Permissible or Required Use Set Out in Regulation

Many regulations authorize health information custodians to use personal health information without the consent of the patient to whom the information relates. *PHIPA* permits a custodian to use personal health information as such regulations permit or require. Examples of such authorized uses under regulations are as follows:

- In the regulations under statutes that regulate the activities of long-term care facilities,[110] a health information custodian that is a placement co-ordinator[111] is required to keep a waiting list for each of the homes for which the co-ordinator is designated. There are detailed requirements set out in the regulations for managing the waiting list, including sorting potential candi-

---

107 Of course, providing the information to the assessor is a "disclosure" and is authorized under *PHIPA*, s. 43(1)(h).

108 S.O. 1997, c. 16, Schedule A, s. 47(5). The physician conducts a medical assessment of the worker to determine the degree of the worker's permanent impairment as a result of a work-related injury.

109 *PHIPA*, ss. 47(2) & (3). Disclosure of personal health information to a health data institute is outlined in Chapter 11, Section D.

110 *General*, R.R.O. 1990, Reg. 69, ss. 70–85, made under the *Charitable Institutions Act*, R.S.O. 1990, c. C.9; *General*, R.R.O. 1990, Reg. 637, ss. 12.5–12.50, made under the *Homes for the Aged and Rest Homes Act*, R.S.O. 1990, c. H.13; *General*, R.R.O. 1990, Reg. 832, ss. 130–54, made under the *Nursing Homes Act*, R.S.O. 1990, c. N.7.

111 *PHIPA*, 3(1)[4][ii].

dates for homes into certain categories within the waiting list, and removing candidates from the list. Keeping and managing such a waiting list, as required by the regulations, is an authorized "use" of personal health information by placement co-ordinators pursuant to *PHIPA*.

- The *PHIPA* Regulation specifically enables the Canadian Blood Services, a health information custodian, to use the personal health information of an individual who donates or attempts to donate blood or blood products for the purpose of ensuring the safety of the blood system.[112]

c) Where a Use Is Permitted Pursuant to a Treaty, Agreement, or Arrangement Made under a Statute

PHIPA authorizes a health information custodian to use personal health information where the use is permitted "by treaty, agreement or arrangement made under an Act [of Ontario] or an Act of Canada."[113] A similar phrase is found in *FIPPA* and *MFIPPA* in the context of permitted disclosures.[114] Under the *Health Insurance Act*, the Minister of Health and Long-Term Care, for example, may enter into agreements with physicians, practitioners, or health facilities to collect, use, and disclose personal information concerning insured services they provide.[115] Such an agreement must provide that personal information collected or disclosed under the agreement will be used only to verify the accuracy of information held or exchanged by a party to the agreement, to administer or enforce a law administered by a party to the agreement, or for such other purposes as may be prescribed.[116]

d) Use Permitted or Required by Law Other Than Legislation

In addition to statutes and regulations that may permit or require a health information custodian to use personal health information, other forms of law may permit or require such uses. The scope of the phrase as "permitted or required by law" likely includes an order of a court or tribunal.[117] For example, where a court orders a psychological assessment of a parent to determine whether the parent is fit to have custody of his or her child,[118] it is possible for the court also to order that the health information custodian psychologist who

---

112　*PHIPA* Regulation, above note 15, s. 25(2).
113　*PHIPA*, s. 37(1)(k).
114　*FIPPA*, above note 21, s. 42(e) and *MFIPPA*, above note 21, s. 32(e).
115　*HIA*, above note 86, s. 2(4.1).
116　*Ibid.*, s. 2(5).
117　See above note 93.
118　*Children's Law Reform Act*, R.S.O. 1990, c. C.12, s. 30(5).

will be conducting the assessment be given access to information, including the parent's personal health information, that would be relevant to the assessment. Not only would such an order authorize the custodian to collect the parent's personal health information, but also, the custodian could rely on the court order as authority to use the parent's personal health information in the custodian's custody or control in order to prepare the report for the court.

10 Disclosure of Personal Health Information

A. *PHIPA'S* DISCLOSURE RULES: INTRODUCTION

1) Generally

Among the purposes of the *Personal Health Information Protection Act, 2004*[1] is the establishment of rules for the disclosure of personal health information about patients by health information custodians.[2] *PHIPA* defines the term "disclose" to mean, in relation to personal health information in the custody or under the control of a health information custodian or a person, "to make the information available or to release it to another health information custodian or to another person, but does not include to use the information."[3]

The Act sets out the circumstances in which a health information custodian may disclose personal health information about a patient, with or without the patient's consent.[4]

---

1   S.O. 2004, c. 3, Sch. A [*PHIPA*].
2   *PHIPA*, s. 1(a).
3   *Ibid.*, s. 2 "disclose." The term "disclose" is further discussed in Chapter 2, Section E(4). As explained there, a transfer of information between a custodian and its agents, or among agents of the custodian, is a use of the information and not a disclosure.
4   In the context of the requirement for consent, the word "patient" includes the patient's substitute decision-maker, where the substitute is authorized to act on the patient's behalf. For further details about substitute decision-making, see Chapter 6.

As with the collection and use of personal health information, the general rule in *PHIPA* is that a health information custodian requires consent to disclose personal health information.[5] However, the Act goes on to specify the circumstances in which a custodian may disclose personal health information without the patient's consent.[6]

2) Disclosure of Personal Health Information Collected Prior to *PHIPA*

PHIPA applies to a health information custodian's disclosure of personal health information on or after the day the Act came into force, even if the custodian collected the information *before* the Act came into force.[7] Therefore, any disclosure of information about a patient that a health information custodian makes on or after 1 November 2004, even if the information was collected before that date, is subject to the rules in *PHIPA*.[8]

3) Where Another Law Prevents a Disclosure

Although *PHIPA* may permit a health information custodian to disclose personal health information in certain circumstances, another law may prohibit the custodian from making the disclosure. In general, where there is such a conflict between *PHIPA* or its regulations and another Act or its regulations, *PHIPA* prevails, unless *PHIPA*, its regulations, or the other Act specifically provide otherwise.[9] For example, the *Occupational Health and Safety Act* prohibits all persons from disclosing any information obtained in any medical examination, test or x-ray of a worker made or taken under that Act except in a form calculated to prevent the information from being identified with a particular person or case.[10] *PHIPA* amended that Act to make clear that the section of the *Occupational Health and Safety Act* containing this provision prevails,

---

5   *PHIPA*, s. 29(a).
6   *Ibid.*, ss. 29(b), 38–48, and 50.
7   *Ibid.*, s. 7(1)(b)(i).
8   Note, however, that *PHIPA* provides that the Act does not apply to personal health information about an individual after the earlier of 120 years after the record containing the information was created or 50 years after the death of the individual: *PHIPA*, s. 91(1).
9   *PHIPA*, s. 7(2). Such a conflict exists under *PHIPA*, s. 7(3) when it is not possible to comply with both provisions at the same time, or when *PHIPA* permits a collection, use, or disclosure that another Act prohibits: O. Reg. 329/04, s. 1(5) [*PHIPA Regulation*].
10   R.S.O. 1990, c. O.1, s. 63(1)(f) [*OHSA*].

despite anything to the contrary in *PHIPA*.[11] There are provisions in other statutes that prevail over *PHIPA*.[12] A health information custodian must be aware of other law that applies to the custodian in making disclosures of personal health information under *PHIPA* to ensure compliance with both *PHIPA* and the other law.

4) Authority to Disclose Records Obtained from Others

Where *PHIPA* permits a health information custodian to disclose a record of personal health information, whether with or without the consent of the patient to whom the information relates, the custodian may disclose the record, in the circumstances authorized by *PHIPA*, even if the custodian did not create the record. A custodian need not refer a person who seeks a disclosure of personal health information to the person who created the record. Further, *PHIPA* does not require a health information custodian to consult with the person who created a record of personal health information prior to disclosing the record.[13]

5) Disclosure and Verification of Recipient

Prior to giving a patient access to his or her record of personal health information in accordance with Part V of *PHIPA*, a health information custodian is required first to take reasonable steps to be satisfied as to the patient's identi-

---

11   *Ibid.*, s. 63(6), as amended by *PHIPA*, s. 93.

12   Further exceptions to this principle, such as those set out in *PHIPA* Regulation, above note 9, s. 5, are discussed in Chapter 3, Section B. Where a health information custodian is also subject to the *Freedom of Information and Protection and Privacy Act*, R.S.O. 1990, c. F.31 [*FIPPA*], or the *Municipal Freedom of Information and Protection of Privacy Act*, R.S.O. 1990, c. M.56 [*MFIPPA*], such a custodian must also be aware that some of the non-disclosure provisions of those Acts, such as the requirement not to disclose Cabinet records under *FIPPA*, continue to apply. These provisions are outlined in Chapter 3, Section C, Table A.

13   Where the record is only provided to the custodian on the condition that the custodian not disclose it further without permission, one can argue that since *PHIPA* permits a disclosure without reference to such a condition, a subsequent disclosure of the record is authorized without seeking further permission, where *PHIPA* permits the disclosure without consent. On the other hand, one could argue that since generally *PHIPA* only gives a custodian discretion with respect to disclosures, it is open to the custodian to agree to conditions that may constrain that disclosure. Such a condition, however, could not act as a barrier to any required disclosure. Also, since patient access is required by *PHIPA*, and not merely permitted, it is clear that such a condition cannot act as a barrier to patient access, unless the circumstances in *PHIPA*, s. 52(1)(e)(iii) apply.

ty.[14] There is no similar explicit requirement for a health information custodian to be satisfied as to a recipient's identity when the custodian discloses personal health information. However, *PHIPA* requires a custodian to take reasonable steps to ensure that personal health information in its custody or control is protected against unauthorized disclosures.[15] This requirement would apparently include an obligation to take reasonable precautions disclosing personal health information to ensure that the custodian does not erroneously provide the information or make it available to an unauthorized person. For example, a prudent health information custodian may establish processes and procedures to govern the steps the custodian and its agents should take in disclosing personal health information, including determining the types of circumstances in which the custodian or its agents should take additional steps to verify the identity of proposed recipients and the process to be followed to do so.

6) Disclosure of Personal Health Information with Consent

A health information custodian may disclose a patient's personal health information with the patient's consent, provided that the disclosure, to the best of the custodian's knowledge, is for a lawful purpose.[16] Where the custodian obtains consent from the patient for the disclosure of personal health information, the consent may be express or implied, unless the Act requires express consent.[17] A custodian may rely on a patient's implied consent for the disclosure of personal health information to another custodian for health care purposes. A health information custodian identified in section 20(2) of *PHIPA* who receives personal health information about a patient from the patient, the patient's substitute decision-maker, or another health information custodian is entitled to assume that the custodian has the patient's implied consent to disclose the information for the purposes of providing health care or assisting in providing health care to the patient, unless the custodian is aware that the patient has expressly withheld or withdrawn the consent.[18] A disclosure to a custodian for non-health care purposes or to a non-custodian for any purpose

---

14   *PHIPA*, s. 54(9).
15   *Ibid.*, s. 12(1).
16   *Ibid.*, s. 29(a). See discussion of "lawful purposes" in Chapter 7, Section B.
17   *Ibid.*, ss. 18(2) & (3). The consent rules are further explained in Chapter 5. *PHIPA* does not include a provision to state that a patient's consent to a custodian's disclosure of personal health information about the patient for the purpose of providing health care may be express, therefore it may be implied: *PHIPA*, ss. 18(2), (3), & (4).
18   See further about s. 20(2) in Chapter 5, Section F(3).

generally requires express consent.[19] The Act also sets out that a custodian requires express consent for the disclosure of personal health information for the purpose of marketing or for the purpose of market research.[20] Similarly, the Act restricts reliance on implied consent for the disclosure of personal health information to anyone for the purpose of fundraising activities. Implied consent in the fundraising context is only permitted with respect to the patient's name and prescribed contact information, where the custodian obtains the patient's implied consent in the manner set out in the regulation.[21]

7) Purposes for Which Custodian May Disclose Personal Health Information without Consent

As with the approach taken for collection and use of personal health information, *PHIPA* recognizes that, in a number of situations, obtaining a patient's consent to the disclosure of his or her personal health information for a particular purpose is not reasonably possible or would be inappropriate. The disclosures of personal health information permissible without consent in *PHIPA* reflect the Act's attempt to reconcile as much as possible patients' privacy interests, on the one hand, and the requirement to facilitate the effective provision of health care, on the other.[22] Further, certain disclosures permissible without consent reflect the need for information to fulfil compelling social objectives while maintaining appropriate safeguards and limitations.

The provisions in *PHIPA* that permit a health information custodian to disclose personal health information without the consent of the patient to whom the information relates include updated provisions from other legislation or regulations that permitted disclosures of personal health information without consent, in certain health sectors, before *PHIPA* came into force. These provisions are now applicable to all health information custodians.[23] In

---

19   See further about exceptions to the express consent rule in Chapter 5, Sections F(7), (8) & (9), such as for disclosures of limited information to religious organizations in specific circumstances under *PHIPA*, s. 20(4).

20   *PHIPA*, s. 33, and *PHIPA* Regulation, above note 9, s. 1(2). See Chapter 5, Section F(10).

21   *PHIPA*, s. 32 and *PHIPA* Regulation, *ibid.*, s. 10. Where implied consent is not permitted, express consent is required. See Chapter 5, Section F(7).

22   This dual purpose is referred to explicitly in *PHIPA*, s. 1(a).

23   For example, a number of permissible disclosures without consent have been deleted from the *Mental Health Act*, R.S.O. 1990, c. M.7 [*MHA*]; the *Long Term-Care Act, 1994*, S.O. 1994, c. 26 [*LTCA*]; the regulations under the *Public Hospitals Act*, R.S.O. 1990, c. P.40 [*PHA*]; the *Independent Health Facilities Act*, R.S.O. 1990, c. I.3 [*IHFA*]; and the three long-term care facility statutes, the *Nursing Homes Act*, R.S.O. 1990, c. N.6

other instances, the provisions in *PHIPA* are new to Ontario legislation, sometimes reflecting common law principles or a commonly accepted practice.

As already discussed,[24] it is important to note that the provisions of *PHIPA* that permit a health information custodian to disclose personal health information without the patient's consent do not require the custodian to disclose the information. Where *PHIPA* authorizes a health information custodian to disclose personal health information without the patient's consent, the custodian may exercise its discretion as to whether to disclose the personal health information in question.[25] Further, a health information custodian is generally not prevented from seeking a patient's consent for any disclosure of personal health information that the custodian may make without consent, if the custodian believes it is appropriate and practical in the circumstances to seek consent.[26] Only a specific requirement to disclose personal health information under *PHIPA*, another Act, or another legal requirement, such as a court order, can compel a custodian to disclose personal health information in any particular circumstances.[27]

Despite the general language of the provisions in *PHIPA* permitting disclosures of personal health information without consent, the provisions must all be read subject to the general limiting principles.[28] Discretionary disclosures under *PHIPA* are only permitted where necessary to meet the purpose of the disclosure and must be limited to only as much personal health information as is necessary for the purpose at hand.[29]

Disclosures of personal health information that a health information custodian is authorized to make without consent for purposes of health research and health system planning and analysis are explained in detail in Chapter 11.[30] The remaining disclosures of personal health information that *PHIPA* authorizes a health information custodian to make without the consent of the patient, to whom the information relates, are described below.

[NHA]; the *Charitable Institutions Act*, R.S.O. 1990, c. C.9 [*CIA*]; and the *Homes for the Aged and Rest Homes Act*, R.S.O. 1990, c. H.13 [*HARHA*]. Instead, a number of them have been incorporated in *PHIPA*.

24 See Chapter 7, Section C(3).

25 *PHIPA*, s. 6(3)(a).

26 *Ibid.*, s. 6(3)(c). An exception to this would be where a law requires the disclosure of personal health information.

27 *Ibid.*, s. 6(3)(b).

28 These are set out in *PHIPA*, s. 30 and are discussed in Chapter 7.

29 *Ibid.* These limits, however, do not apply where the disclosure is required: *PHIPA*, s. 30(3).

30 Chapter 11 deals with disclosure of personal health information, without consent, for health research (*PHIPA*, s. 44), to prescribed health registries (*PHIPA*, s. 39(1)(c)), to prescribed planning entities (*PHIPA*, s. 45), and to a health data institute (*PHIPA*, ss. 47–48).

B. DISCLOSURE FOR THE PROVISION OF HEALTH CARE: SECTION 38(1)(a)

In some instances, it may not be reasonably possible for a health information custodian to obtain a patient's consent to disclose the patient's personal health information. A health information custodian may disclose personal health information without the patient's consent to certain health information custodians if the disclosure is reasonably necessary for the provision of health care and it is not reasonably possible to obtain the patient's consent in a timely manner,[31] such as where the patient is not capable of consenting to the disclosure and a substitute decision-maker is not readily available.[32] The types of health information custodians to which a custodian may disclose personal health information pursuant to this provision are health care practitioners;[33] laboratories; specimen collection centres; ambulances; pharmacies; long-term care facilities; placement coordinators; community care access corporations; service providers as defined in the *Long-Term Care Act, 1994*;[34] homes for special care; community health and mental health programs or services; hospitals; independent health facilities; and psychiatric facilities.[35] A custodian who is considering relying on this provision must consider whether the circumstances in which it is applicable are present in any particular case.

A custodian cannot rely on this provision at all, however, to disclose personal health information if, in the past, the patient[36] has expressly instructed

---

31   *PHIPA*, s. 38(1)(a). This provision applies to a disclosure without consent for health care purposes that a health information custodian may make within Ontario. If a health information custodian requires to make a disclosure of a patient's personal health information for health care purposes outside Ontario, the applicable provision is *PHIPA* s. 50(1)(e), reviewed in Section S, below.

32   Capacity and the role of substitute decision-makers are outlined in Chapter 6.

33   Recall that "health care practitioner" is specifically defined in the Act in s. 2. The category includes all regulated health professionals, social workers, and social service workers who provide health care, and non-regulated health professionals whose primary purpose is to provide health care for payment. This category is discussed in Chapter 2, Section B(1)(b).

34   *LTCA*, above note 23.

35   See Chapter 2, Section B(1) for an explanation of what is referred to by each of these types of custodians. This list of custodians to whom a disclosure may be made under s. 38(1)(a) is the same list of custodians who may assume an implied consent under s. 20(2).

36   Recall that the word "patient" also includes "substitute decision-maker" where the substitute decision-maker is authorized to make a decision about the collection, use, or disclosure of the patient's personal health information on the patient's behalf. The substitute decision-maker may make an express instruction on the patient's behalf. See Chapter 6, Section D.

the custodian not to make the disclosure.[37] A patient may have given such an "express" instruction orally or in writing.[38] A health information custodian who is unable to disclose complete information to another custodian due to such an instruction must notify the receiving custodian of the fact that the record is incomplete where the disclosing custodian believes the withheld information is reasonably necessary for the provision of health care or assisting in the provision of health care to the patient.[39] Such a flag or note would not be necessary where the information (that the patient or his or her substitute decision-maker, as the case may be, does not wish disclosed) is, in the opinion of the disclosing custodian, not reasonably necessary for the purpose of the disclosure.

This provision authorizes only one category of disclosures without consent, and the express instruction referred to in it operates only in the context of this provision. Where a patient has expressly instructed a health information custodian not to make a disclosure to another custodian in accordance with this clause, the instruction does not prevent the health information custodian from disclosing the patient's personal health information in accordance with the other provisions in *PHIPA* that permit the custodian to disclose the patient's information without consent.

C. DISCLOSURE FOR FUNDING OR PAYMENT: SECTION 38(1)(b)

PHIPA permits a health information custodian to disclose a patient's personal health information to the Minister of Health and Long-Term Care or anoth-

---

37   *PHIPA*, s. 38(1)(a). The instruction is referred to as being given in the past since if it is given in the present that would simply count as a withdrawal or withholding of consent and s. 38(1)(a) would not apply. Section 38(1)(a) only applies where it is not reasonably possible to seek the patient's response and receive a response, whether affirmative or negative. It does not appear to apply where the patient simply responds negatively to the request for consent. Public hospitals are not obligated to give effect to an instruction under this clause until 1 November 2005. However, they must still comply with an express withholding or withdrawal of consent as set out in s. 20(2) of *PHIPA*. The ability to provide an express instruction under s. 38(1)(a) is part of what is often referred to as a "lock box," which is further discussed in Chapter 7.

38   Obviously, the custodian must be aware of the express instruction. If the express instruction was given orally, there would need to be some clear evidence of it, in order for the custodian to reasonably rely on it, if he or she did not personally hear it.

39   *PHIPA*, s. 38(2). The manner of notation is further reviewed in Chapter 5, Section F(3)(c)(i).

er custodian[40] so that the Minister or the other custodian may determine or provide funding or payment to that custodian for the provision of health care.[41] In this way, a custodian may disclose personal health information that the Minister or other funding custodian requires to determine the level of funding for the custodian or whether that custodian should be paid for providing health care and the amount of payment. This clause replaces a provision in the *Health Insurance Act*, for example, that deemed an insured person to have authorized his or her physician or a hospital that provided a service to the insured person to provide the General Manager of the Ontario Health Insurance Plan with particulars of the service for the purpose of obtaining payment under the Plan for the services.[42]

A health information custodian may not rely on this provision of *PHIPA* for authority to disclose personal health information to seek payment or funding from a source other than the Minister of Health and Long-Term Care or another health information custodian, such as another government body or private payer. A custodian generally requires the patient's express consent to disclose personal health information to such sources.[43] Where a non-custodian is a source of funding or payment, a health information custodian may require a patient's consent to the disclosure of personal health about the patient necessary to receive funding or payment as a condition of the custodian's provision of

---

40   The Minister of Health and Long-Term Care is a health information custodian together with the Ministry of the Minister if the context so requires. See *PHIPA*, s. 3(1)[7].Other health information custodians that provide payment or funding for the provision of health care include community care access corporations that contract with service providers to provide community services. The terms "service provider" and "community service" are both defined in the *LTCA*, above note 23: "service provider" in s. 2(1), and "community service" in s. 2(3). Such services are considered "health care" under *PHIPA*, s. 2's definition of "health care." Such service providers are health information custodians under s. 3(1)[2].

41   *PHIPA*, s. 38(1)(b). It is important to note that the payment or funding is provided to or determined in relation to the custodian who disclosed the information to the Minister or other custodian. This provision does not permit a health information custodian to disclose personal health information to the Minister or other custodian for the purpose of providing or determining funding or payment to a custodian other than the custodian who made the disclosure.

42   R.S.O. 1990, c. H.6, s. 29 [*HIA*]. This provision still exists in the *HIA*, but the section was amended by s. 85(2) of *PHIPA* to clarify that it does not apply where *PHIPA* applies. It appears to be more straightforward to consider such matters as a permitted disclosure without consent rather than a disclosure based on a "deemed" consent.

43   Patient consent, however, would not be required where another law authorizes the health information custodian to disclose such information to the payer without consent: *PHIPA*, s. 43(1)(h).

health care, in the same way and to the same extent as the custodian may require payment from the patient as a condition of providing the health care.[44]

D. DISCLOSURE TO CONTACT A RELATIVE, FRIEND, OR SUBSTITUTE DECISION-MAKER: SECTION 38(1)(c)

A health information custodian may disclose a patient's personal health information to anyone with whom it may be necessary to communicate, in order to contact the patient's relative, friend, or potential substitute decision-maker, if the patient is both incapacitated or ill and unable to give consent personally.[45] A health information custodian may not rely on this provision as authority to disclose personal health information to a relative, friend, or potential substitute decision-maker if the patient is able to give consent but has not done so. Since the name of the patient, combined with the fact that the patient is receiving health care from a health information custodian, such as a hospital, or has been injured, is personal health information, without this type of provision in *PHIPA*, typically, no contact could be made in such cases with concerned relatives or friends.[46]

Once a relative or friend has been located, a custodian's ongoing disclosure of personal health information about the patient to the relative or friend requires the patient's express consent, except where *PHIPA* authorizes the custodian to disclose personal health information without the patient's consent.[47] Of course, where the patient is incapable, consent would be required from the substitute decision-maker.[48] Nothing in *PHIPA* prevents a health information custodian from communicating with a substitute decision-maker who is authorized to make information decisions on a patient's behalf.[49] Where discussions are needed with the substitute decision-maker for treat-

---

44   A somewhat similar distinction between governmental and non-governmental payment sources is found in *PHIPA*, s. 39(1)(a), discussed in Section G, below.

45   *PHIPA*, s. 38(1)(c).

46   This clause was amended during the committee hearings on Bill 31, *An Act to enact and amend various Acts with respect to the protection of health information*, 1st Sess., 38th Leg., Ontario, 2003 [Bill 31] to recognize that a custodian may need to disclose personal health information in order to find a substitute decision-maker: Ontario, Legislative Assembly, Standing Committee on General Government, *Official Report of Debates (Hansard)*, G-259 (28 April 2004) at 1650 (Kathleen Wynne). Cl. 37(1)(c) of Sch. A of Bill 31 was amended at second reading to include the words "or potential substitute decision-maker."

47   For example, pursuant to *PHIPA*, s. 38(3).

48   See discussion about the role of the substitute decision-maker in Chapter 6, Section D.

49   *PHIPA*, s. 52(6)(a).

ment purposes, for example, such disclosures are authorized under the *Health Care Consent Act, 1996* and thus permitted under *PHIPA*.[50]

E. DISCLOSURE BY A FACILITY THAT PROVIDES HEALTH CARE: SECTION 38(3)

A health information custodian that is a facility that provides health care may disclose limited information about the location and general health status of a patient or resident in the facility, as long as the custodian first provided the patient or resident with the option, at the first reasonable opportunity after admission, to object to such disclosures.[51] The limited information that the facility may disclose is as follows:

1)   the fact that the individual is a patient or resident in the facility;
2)   the patient's or resident's general health status described as critical, poor, fair, stable, or satisfactory, or in similar terms;[52] and
3)   the location of the patient or resident in the facility.[53]

---

50   *Health Care Consent Act, 1996*, S.O. 1996, c. 2, Sch. A, ss. 22, 43, and 60 [*HCCA*]: A substitute decision-maker is entitled to receive all information required to make a decision on behalf of the incapable patient. Such a disclosure is authorized by *PHIPA*, 43(1)(h). Furthermore, under *PHIPA* a substitute decision-maker for a patient is generally entitled to access any information that the patient would have been able to access: *PHIPA*, ss. 25(1), 52, and 53.

51   *PHIPA*, s. 38(3). This provision was modified from the first reading version of *PHIPA*, where it appeared simply as a permissible disclosure of personal health information without a patient's consent: Bill 31, First Reading, Sch. A, cl. 37(3) (17 December 2003). The Standing Committee on General Government made the modification during the second clause-by-clause review of Bill 31: Ontario, Legislative Assembly, Standing Committee on General Government, *Official Report of Debates (Hansard)*, G-259 (28 April 2004) at 1650 (Kathleen Wynne).

52   "In similar terms" could include that the patient has died.

53   This reflects a recommendation of Mr. Justice Krever in the Ontario, Royal Commission of Inquiry into the Confidentiality of Health Records in Ontario, *Report of the Commission of Inquiry into the Confidentiality of Health Information* (Toronto: Queen's Printer, 1980) vol. 2 at 339, Recommendation 70 [*Krever Report*]:

That legislation permit a hospital or health-care facility to reveal the presence of a patient, his or her location and his or her general condition to any person who inquires, but only if the patient (or the patient's representative) has not objected, in writing, to this disclosure. The hospital or health-care facility shall not reveal specific information about the patient's condition or treatment unless required or permitted by law.

PHIPA does not define the phrase "facility that provides health care." Health information custodians that are facilities that provide health care appear to include such facilities as hospitals, psychiatric facilities, nursing homes, homes for special care, children's treatment centres, and drug rehabilitation centres.

Note that this provision applies only to "patients" and "residents" in a facility that provides health care. *PHIPA* does not define the terms "patient" or "resident." However, the term resident is usually used in relation to persons who have made a facility that provides health care their home, such as persons who reside in long-term care facilities. The term "patient" may refer to either patients admitted into a facility, such as a hospital, as in-patients for overnight stays of varying durations, or patients admitted into a facility as out-patients, for the purpose of out-patient procedures that last less than a da.[54] It also includes a person who is under observation, care, and treatment in a psychiatric facility.[55]

PHIPA does not describe the persons to whom a facility may disclose this information. Therefore, facilities may exercise discretion in determining whether to disclose information to any particular person pursuant to this provision. Such disclosure could be made, for example, to a patient's family members, other health information custodians, the police, the media, members of the clergy, or a florist.

It is not expected that all facilities will revise their practices to disclose such personal health information where they did not do so before *PHIPA* came into force. Custodians may consider establishing a protocol as to who within the facility should be authorized to disclose personal health information under this subsection and the circumstances in which they may disclose the information. A facility may choose to disclose only aspects of the personal health information that this provision of the Act permits a custodian to disclose, such as the fact that the patient is a patient or resident in the facility, and not disclose other aspects, such as the patient's location in the facility. Where a facility wishes to rely on this provision of *PHIPA*, the facility should ensure that it provides patients or residents with the opportunity to object to such disclosures. A facility may provide a patient or resident with this opportunity, for example, as part of the first discussion with the patient or resident after admission.

---

54 For instance, under the *Homes for the Aged and Rest Homes Act*, a "resident" means a person admitted to and lodged in a home: *HARHA*, above note 23, s. 1. Under the *Public Hospitals Act*, a "patient" means a person received and lodged in a hospital for the purpose of treatment, while an "out-patient" means a person who is received in a hospital for examination or treatment or both, but who is not admitted as a patient: *PHA*, above note 23, s. 1.

55 *MHA*, above note 23, s. 1(1).

F. DISCLOSURE ABOUT A DECEASED INDIVIDUAL: SECTION 38(4)

1) Generally

Under *PHIPA*, the individual to whom personal health information relates may be deceased.[56] A health information custodian may disclose personal health information about an individual who is, or is "reasonably suspected to be" deceased,

a) for the purpose of identifying the individual;

b) for the purpose of informing any person whom it is reasonable to inform in the circumstances of,

    i)   the fact that the individual is deceased or reasonably suspected to be deceased, and

    ii) the circumstances of death, where appropriate; or

c) to the spouse, partner, sibling or child of the individual, if the recipients of the information reasonably require the information to make decisions about their own health care or their children's health care.[57]

The meaning of the language "reasonably suspected to be" deceased is not always immediately apparent. A suspicion that an individual is deceased may be based on a variety of facts, such as the fact that the individual has been missing for some time, or the fact that the individual was last seen at the scene of an explosion or natural disaster. Usually, a lack of certainty on this point relates

---

56   *PHIPA*, s. 4 provides that "personal health information" means "identifying informa-tion about an individual ...." *PHIPA*, s. 2 defines the term "individual" so as to include a deceased individual.

57   *PHIPA*, s. 38(4). This provision in *PHIPA* is somewhat broader than the provision included in the first reading version of Bill 31, which permitted a custodian to disclose personal health information about an individual "who is deceased, or is believed to be deceased." [Bill 31. First reading, Sch. A, cl. 37(4), (17 December 2003).] The Standing Committee on General Government added the phrase "reasonably suspected to be" before the word "deceased" to allow dentists, for example, to disclose to the Canadian Police Information Centre the odontogram of an individual who has been reported to the police as being missing in circumstances that give rise to a reasonable suspicion that the person is deceased. An odontogram is a diagram indicating by tooth position missing, decayed, and filled teeth of an individual. Ontario, Legislative Assembly, Standing Committee on General Government, *Official Report of Debates (Hansard)*, G-259 (28 April 2004) at 1650 (Kathleen Wynne). The amendment appears to be a result of a request from the Ontario Dental Association: Ontario, Legislative Assem-bly, Standing Committee on General Government, *Official Report of Debates (Hansard)*, G-114 to 115 (28 January 2004) at 1150 (Frank Bevilacqua).

to uncertainty about the identity of a deceased individual. For example, the task of trying to identify a corpse presupposes the idea that the identity of the corpse is not yet known with certainty, if at all.

2) For the Purpose of Identifying the Individual

A health information custodian may disclose personal health information about an individual who is, or is "reasonably suspected to be" deceased for the purpose of identifying the individual.[58] The power to disclose personal health information about an individual for purposes of identifying the individual requires that there be reason to suspect that the individual whose information is disclosed is deceased. A dentist could not simply provide open access to dental records of all the dentist's patients to enable a match to be found with the deceased. Rather, the dentist would be able to disclose only the records of a patient or patients who were reasonably suspected to be deceased. This clause gives a health information custodian authority to disclose personal health information about an individual, where necessary, to such persons as the police, a coroner, or anyone else to whom it would be appropriate to provide information about the individual for the purpose of identifying the individual.

3) For the Purpose of Informing Any Person Whom It Is Reasonable to Inform

PHIPA permits a health information custodian to disclose personal health information about an individual who is deceased or is reasonably suspected to be deceased for the purpose of informing any person who it is reasonable to inform in the circumstances of the fact that the individual is deceased or is reasonably suspected to be deceased,[59] and the circumstances of death, where appropriate.[60]

This clause permits a disclosure not only in circumstances where the individual is known to be deceased, but also where the individual is "reasonably suspected to be deceased," reflecting the reality that certain knowledge is not always available. *PHIPA* does not describe the information that the phrase "circumstances of death" includes, but its scope will vary from situation to situation. A health information custodian should consider the extent of the information that it should disclose in informing a person about the circum-

---

58 *PHIPA*, s. 38(4)(a).
59 *Ibid.*, s. 38(4)(b)(i).
60 *Ibid.*, s. 38(4)(b)(ii).

stances of an individual's death. Like the preceding clause,[61] this clause gives a health information custodian authority to disclose such personal health information, where necessary, to any person that it is reasonable to inform, such as the police, a coroner, or relatives of the individual.[62]

In the first reading version of *PHIPA*, this provision did not permit a health information custodian to disclose personal health information without consent about a deceased patient that would reveal the "circumstances of death, where appropriate."[63] The Information and Privacy Commissioner noted that not providing a custodian with the authority to disclose such personal health information without consent could have the effect of denying family members access to timely information about the circumstances of a relative's death.[64] The clause was amended to enable a health information custodian to provide further information to family members, including, for example, how a patient died, rather than just the fact that the patient is deceased.

4) To Enable a Spouse, Partner, Sibling, or Child to Make Health Care Decisions

A custodian may disclose personal health information about an individual who is deceased or is reasonably suspected to be deceased to a spouse, partner, sibling, or child of the individual if such persons reasonably require the information to make decisions about their own health care or their children's health care. Personal health information about a deceased patient may assist the deceased patient's spouse or partner to understand, for example, the environmental risks, such as contaminated soil, present at the residence the spouse or partner shared with the deceased patient. Disclosure of personal health information about the deceased to the deceased patient's sibling or child may be significant, for example, where the deceased patient died of a heritable condition, as the information about the condition may help the sibling or child make decisions about how to monitor their own health or their children's health care needs.

In her written submission to the Standing Committee on General Government, the Information and Privacy Commissioner noted that the privacy inter-

---

61   *PHIPA*, s. 38(4)(a).

62   This is explicit in clause (b), but appears to be implicit in clause (a).

63   Bill 31, First Reading, Sch. A, cl. 37(4)(b) (17 December 2003).

64   *Submission to the Standing Committee on General Government: Bill 31: Health Information Protection Act* (Toronto: Information and Privacy Commissioner/Ontario, 2004) at 7, online: <www.ipc.on.ca>.

ests of a deceased patient should not supercede the health care needs of living family members.[65] Accordingly, the Commissioner urged the Committee to amend the Bill to remove the requirement that existed in the first reading version of *PHIPA* that, before disclosing information about a deceased patient, the custodian should have regard for the views that the patient previously expressed about such a disclosure that are known to the custodian.[66] It was not clear to the Commissioner "why the views of the deceased should be a consideration where a family member requires the personal health information to make decisions about their own health care or their children's health care."[67] The Standing Committee on General Government amended the clause to remove this condition.[68]

G. DISCLOSURE TO DETERMINE OR VERIFY ELIGIBILITY: SECTION 39(1)

A health information custodian may disclose a patient's personal health information as necessary for the purpose of determining or verifying the eligibility of the patient to receive health care or related goods, services, or benefits where they are provided under an Act of Ontario or Canada and funded in whole or in part by the government of Ontario or Canada or by a municipality.[69] The regulation under the Act clarifies that one purpose for this type of disclosure is to determine eligibility of the patient for coverage under the *Health Insurance Act* or for any other insurance or payment arrangement with respect to health care or related goods, services, or benefits that are provided under an Act of Ontario or Canada and funded by the above noted government bodies.[70]

This provision in *PHIPA* would allow, for example, a physician or a hospital to disclose a patient's personal health information to the Ministry of Health and Long-Term Care to permit the Ministry to verify that the patient is an insured person for the purposes of the Ontario Health Insurance Plan. This same provision would authorize the Ministry, as a health information custodian, to disclose per-

---

65 *Ibid.*

66 Bill 31, First Reading, Sch. A, cl. 37(4)(c) (17 December 2003). See further *Submission to the Standing Committee on General Government*, above note 64.

67 *Submission to the Standing Committee on General Government, ibid.*

68 Ontario, Legislative Assembly, Standing Committee on General Government, *Official Report of Debates (Hansard)*, G-216 (9 February 2004) at 1150 (Peter Fonseca).

69 *PHIPA*, s. 39(1)(a).

70 *PHIPA* Regulation, above note 9, s. 1(9). Thus not just eligibility to receive health care *per se* is referred to here — eligibility for insurance or other financial coverage in respect of health care is also included.

sonal health information about a patient, such as his or her health number, to a requesting custodian to confirm the patient's status under the Plan.[71]

Pharmacists could rely on this provision in a similar way to request confirmation from the Ministry as to whether or not a patient is eligible to receive financial assistance from the Ministry of Health and Long-Term Care for payment of prescriptions for medication under the *Ontario Drug Benefit Act*.[72] Likewise, a physiotherapist could disclose personal health information about a patient without the patient's consent to the Workplace Safety and Insurance Board to determine the patient's eligibility to receive payment from the Board for a health service that the physiotherapist proposes would benefit the injured worker. Despite this authority for a health information custodian to disclose personal health information without consent, in a number of such scenarios the custodian will have obtained the patient's consent for the disclosure of the patient's information. However, where the custodian did not obtain consent, the custodian may disclose personal health information without consent as this provision permits.

It should be noted that this provision in *PHIPA* does not limit a health information custodian to disclosing personal health information to the government funding source; a custodian may disclose a patient's personal health information to any person with whom it would be necessary and appropriate to share the patient's information for the purpose of determining or verifying the patient's eligibility for health care or related goods, services, or benefits, or coverage thereof. Typically, however, a custodian would disclose personal health information to the part of the federal, provincial, or municipal government that provides the funding, as that body would also be the appropriate body to determine or verify the patient's eligibility.

H. DISCLOSURE FOR AUDITING OR ACCREDITATION PURPOSES: SECTION 39(1)(b)

1) Generally

A health information custodian may disclose a patient's personal health information to a person conducting an audit, reviewing an application for accreditation, or reviewing an accreditation, if

---

71   The *HIA*, above note 42 and its regulations provide rules, for example, for who is an "insured person" and for eligibility for coverage under the Ontario Health Insurance Plan.

72   R.S.O. 1990, c. O.10 [*ODBA*].

- the audit or review relates to services provided by the custodian, and
- the person conducting the audit or accreditation review does not remove any records of personal health information from the custodian's premises.[73]

This provision contemplates that the auditor or accreditation reviewer is independent from the custodian, and not acting as an agent of the custodian. Therefore, a custodian's provision of personal health information to such a person is a disclosure of the information. By contrast, where a custodian retains a person to review the custodian's internal processes, perhaps in preparation for the external review, this type of activity involves access to personal health information and is a "use" by the custodian and its agents and not a "disclosure."[74]

Although it is sometimes suggested that auditors or accreditation reviewers should not access patient records without the consent of patients, the requirement for consent may undermine the purpose of such an activity. In order to determine whether a patient received a health service as a health information custodian claims, for example, or that records created by a health information custodian meet certain standards set by accrediting bodies, it is important for auditors and accreditation reviewers to have the power to review records on a random and representative basis at the time of the site visit.

Despite this provision's restriction on the removal of records of personal health information, *PHIPA* authorizes the removal of records off-site for audit or accreditation review purposes, if (a) the removal is authorized by or under an Act of Ontario or Canada; or (b) an agreement between the custodian and the auditor or accreditation reviewer, as the case may be, authorizes the removal and provides that the records will be held in a secure and confidential manner and will be returned when the audit or review is completed.[75]

2) Auditing

Where any level of government funds a program or service, accountability to the public requires that the government be able to determine, through audits, whether the funding was spent properly. Auditing also plays an important role in the private sector, for example, to ensure a corporation's accountability to its shareholders, or to ensure its compliance with applicable legal requirements. The need for auditors to access financial records of such programs or services

---

73   *PHIPA*, s. 39(1)(b).
74   *Ibid.*, ss. 37(1)(c) & (d) may provide authority for such a use. See further, Chapter 9, Sections C(4) & (5). Also, see discussion of "use" in Chapter 2, Section E(3).
75   *Ibid.*, s. 39(3).

is clear. However, auditors may also need to review records of personal health information to determine whether services were in fact provided and, if so, whether they were provided in an effective manner in accordance with any conditions of funding.[76]

Recent amendments to the *Auditor General Act* underline this need.[77] The amendments provide the Auditor General of Ontario[78] with the power[79] to conduct broad based value-for-money audits[80] of provincial grant recipients,[81] including public hospitals, nursing homes, and other health information custodians. In conducting such audits, the Auditor General may require access to any information that is relevant to the audit, including personal health infor-

---

76 It is interesting to note that Mr. Justice Krever had also specifically addressed the authority of a government agency to access personal health information for audit purposes: "An outright refusal to disclose a medical record to government and professional representatives who have a clear mandate to carry out in the public interest is inappropriate" (*Krever Report*, above note 53, vol. 2 at 409). He recommended that legislation authorize the disclosure of personal health information for the purposes of auditing or professional monitoring and further recommended that limits be placed on those persons who obtain information for these purposes, such as that they should be prohibited from further using or disclosing identifiable health information unless required by law or unless the information is required to relieve an emergency situation affecting the health or safety of any person. (*Krever Report*, vol. 2 at 424–25, Recommendation 79).

77 *Auditor General Act*, R.S.O. 1990, c. A.35 as amended by the *Audit Statute Law Amendment Act*, S.O. 2004, c. 17. (Amendments effective 1 April 2005) [*AGA*].

78 Formerly the Provincial Auditor.

79 *AGA*, above note 77, s. 9.1(1).

80 Such audits, referred to as "special audits" under the *Auditor General Act* include a review by the Auditor General so as to determine whether

   i)   accounts were not properly kept or public money was not fully accounted for;

   ii) essential records were not maintained or the rules and procedures applied were not sufficient to safeguard and control public property or to effectively check the assessment, collection, and proper allocation of revenue or to ensure that expenditures were made only as authorized;

   iii) money was expended other than for the purposes for which it was appropriated;

   iv) money was expended without due regard to economy and efficiency; or

   v)   where procedures could be used to measure and report on the effectiveness of programs, the procedures were not established or, in the opinion of the Auditor General, the established procedures were not satisfactory.

   AGA, *ibid.*, s. 12(2)(f). See further, s. 1 (definition of "special audit") and s. 9.1.

81 Affected grant recipients include every association, authority, board, commission, corporation, council, foundation, institution, organization, or other body, other than municipalities, that receives directly or indirectly a grant or other transfer payment from the Consolidated Revenue Fund, from an agency of the Crown, or from a Crown-controlled corporation: *AGA*, *ibid.*, ss. 1 and 9.

mation.[82] *PHIPA* allows health information custodians to disclose personal health information to the Auditor General pursuant to the *Auditor General Act*.[83]

Persons other the Auditor General may also require access to personal health information for the purpose of conducting an audit. A health information custodian may rely on section 39(1)(b) of *PHIPA*, to disclose personal health information as necessary to an auditor. For example, where an Act requires that a health information custodian submit to an audit of its activities but provides no further rules about an auditor's access to personal health information,[84] or where a custodian voluntarily submits to an audit, in the absence of any statutory requirement to do so, the custodian may disclose personal health information to the auditor in accordance with *PHIPA*.

3) Accrediting

Accreditation in the health care sector is a process whereby an external body recognizes a facility, program, or service as meeting specific standards. Accreditation

---

82   Section 12 of the *Audit Statute Law Amendment Act*, above note 77, added s. 9.1 to the *AGA*, *ibid.*, to provide authority to audit the grant recipient; s. 13 repealed and replaced s. 10 pertaining to the duty to furnish information; and s. 28 added s. 27.1 pertaining to confidentiality and retention of personal information, including medical and psychiatric records.

83   *PHIPA*, s. 43(1)(h), which allows a health information custodian to disclose personal health information without a patient's consent, where "permitted or required by law." Where the *AGA* and s. 43(1)(h) of *PHIPA* are the source of authority for the disclosure, the restrictions on removal of the information set out in *PHIPA*, ss. 39(1)(b) & (3) do not apply, but any restrictions that may be set out in the *AGA* would apply.

84   See, for example, the *Community Care Access Corporations Act, 2001*, S.O. 2001, c. 33, s. 12 which sets out requirements for audits but is silent as to an auditor's access to personal health information:

Audit

s. 12

(1) Each community care access corporation shall appoint one or more auditors licensed under the *Public Accountancy Act* to audit annually the accounts and financial transactions of the corporation.

Auditor's report

(2) Each community care access corporation shall give a copy of every auditor's report to the Minister [of Health and Long-Term Care] within six months after the end of the fiscal year to which the report relates.

Minister's audit

(3) The Minister may require that any aspect of the affairs of a community care access corporation be audited by an auditor appointed by the Minister.

is often carried out by organizations created for the purpose of assuring the public of the quality of the accredited facility, program, or service.[85] A health information custodian may disclose personal health information, in accordance with *PHIPA*, to an organization, such as the Canadian Council on Health Services Accreditation or Children's Mental Health Ontario, where such an organization applies to the activities of the custodian for the purpose of accrediting the custodian's operations.[86] An accreditation process may involve a disclosure of personal health information to the accreditation body in the course of, for instance, a site review, review of sample case files, interviews with frontline staff and managers, participation in case conferences, and observation of selected program activities.[87]

I. TO A PRESCRIBED HEALTH REGISTRY: SECTION 39(1)(c)

A health information custodian may disclose a patient's personal health information, without the patient's consent, to a person specified in a regulation made under *PHIPA* who compiles or maintains a registry of personal health information for the purposes of facilitating or improving the provision of health care or that relates to the storage or donation of body parts or bodily substances.[88] Such disclosures are described in detail in Chapter 11.

J. DISCLOSURE FOR PUBLIC HEALTH PURPOSES: SECTION 39(2)

1) The Need for Clarity

"Whatever the precise path of legislative reform, privacy, while vital, should not impede the necessary sharing between agencies and governments of informa-

---

85 Accreditation may either be permanent or may be given for a specified period of time.

86 See the accreditation program described on the Children's Mental Health Ontario website, online: <www.cmho.org/Accreditation.shtml>. Also, see further about accreditation at the Canadian Council on Health Services Accreditation website, online: <www.cchsa.ca>.

87 In his report, Mr. Justice Krever observed: "The examination of medical records is a necessary part of the accreditation process since the inquiry is concerned with the quality of all types of care administered by a hospital, as well as the adequacy of its organizational, administrative, and record-keeping procedures." He recommended "that access to confidential patient information by the official representatives of accreditation surveyors for the purpose of granting or reviewing accreditation be permitted under legislation governing hospitals." (*Krever Report*, above note 53, vol. 2 at 377–78, Recommendation 77).

88 *PHIPA*, s. 39(1)(c); *PHIPA* Regulation, above note 9, s. 13.

tion required to protect the public against an outbreak of infectious disease," urged Mr. Justice Archie Campbell in his interim report pertaining to the 2003 outbreak of SARS[89] in Ontario.[90] Whether justified or not, there was a perception among health care providers in Ontario during the SARS crisis that the law inhibited disclosures of information needed to contain and deal with the spread of this infectious disease. While it was clear that mandatory reporting provisions under the *Health Protection and Promotion Act*[91] were intended to require hospitals and long term-care facilities, for example, to report the outbreak of such a disease, the disease first had to be listed in the regulations under the *HPPA* to authorize the reporting.[92] It was also not readily apparent to health care providers, even once SARS was listed as a reportable disease, as to what information or how much information they could share and with whom to help deal with the outbreak.[93]

2) Disclosure for Public Health Purposes in *PHIPA*

To a large extent, *PHIPA* has clarified a health information custodian's authority to disclose personal health information for public health purposes. Under *PHIPA*, a health information custodian is clearly permitted to disclose personal health information about a patient to the Chief Medical Officer of Health[94] or a medical officer of health[95] if the disclosure is made for a purpose of the

---

89   SARS is the acronym used to refer to Severe Acute Respiratory Syndrome.

90   Ontario, Commission to Investigate the Introduction and Spread of SARS in Ontario, *The SARS Commission Interim Report — SARS and Public Health in Ontario* by The Honourable Mr. Justice Archie Campbell, Commissioner (Toronto: 15 April 2004) at 13 [*Interim Report*]. Online: <www.health.gov.on.ca>.

91   R.S.O. 1990, c. H.7 [*HPPA*].

92   SARS is now listed as a reportable disease in *Specification of Reportable Diseases*, O. Reg. 559/91; as a communicable disease in *Specification of Communicable Diseases*, O. Reg. 558/91; and as a virulent disease in *Specification of Virulent Diseases*, O. Reg. 95/03, all made under the *HPPA*, *ibid.*, s. 1.

93   *Interim Report*, above note 90 at 128–30.

94   The Chief Medical Officer of Health was an employee of the Ministry of Health and Long-Term Care. Recent amendments to s. 81 of the *HPPA*, above note 91, made by Bill 124, *An act to amend the Health Protection and Promotion Act*, S.O. 2004, c. 30 , 1st Session, 38th leg., Ontario, 2003 (assented to 16 December 2004), create some independence for the Chief Medical Officer of Health by providing for the appointment of the Chief Medical Officer of Health by the Lieutenant Governor in Council on the address of the Legislative Assembly, but the Chief Medical Officer of Health continues to be in the service of the Ministry of Health and Long-Term Care.

95   *HPPA*, *ibid.*, ss. 62–64 set out that a medical officer of health is appointed by the board of health, provided that he or she is a physician, possesses the qualifications set out in the regulations, and receives approval of the Minister of Health and Long-Term Care.

HPPA.[96] The purpose of the *HPPA* is "to provide for the organization and delivery of public health programs and services, the prevention of the spread of disease and the promotion and protection of the health of the people of Ontario."[97] Pursuant to this provision, any health information custodian may disclose personal health information to the Chief Medical Officer of Health or a medical officer of health for public health purposes, even in the absence of a duty to report under the *HPPA* or a request for the information.[98]

This provision of *PHIPA* enables the Chief Medical Officer of Health, as an agent of the Ministry of Health and Long-Term Care, to make a disclosure to a medical officer of health. It enables one medical officer of health, as a health information custodian, to disclose personal health information to another medical officer of health (in another health unit), or to the Chief Medical Officer of Health.

Health information custodians may make similar disclosures to public health authorities in other jurisdictions for a purpose that is "substantially sim-

---

96 *PHIPA*, s. 39(2)(a). It should be noted that this type of provision was not designed specifically as a reaction to the SARS crisis. A version of such a provision existed in all previous iterations of draft health privacy Acts. *A Consultation on the Draft of Privacy of Personal Information Act, 2002* (Toronto: Ministry of Consumer and Business Services, 2002) [*POPIA*], online: <www.cbs.gov.on.ca/mcbs/english/pdf/56XSMB.pdf>, at clause 39(1)(a) permitted a health information custodian to disclose personal health information in the same circumstances as *PHIPA*, s. 39(2)(a). Bill 159, *An Act respecting personal health information and related matters*, 1st Sess., 37th Leg., Ontario, 2000 [Bill 159], cl. 30(1)(a) allowed a health information custodian to disclose personal health information without consent to "the Chief Medical Officer of Health or a medical officer of health within the meaning of the *HPPA* [*ibid.*] or a similar public health authority established under the laws of Canada, a province other than Ontario or a territory, if the disclosure is made for the purpose of public health protection and promotion." Ontario, *Personal Health Information Protection Act, 1997: Draft for Consultation* (Toronto: Queen's Printer for Ontario, 1997) [1997 Draft Legislation] at cl. 14(1)[8] permitted a health information custodian to disclose personal health information without consent "to a public health official for the purpose of public health administration."

97 *HPPA, ibid.,* s. 2.

98 *PHIPA*, s. 39(2)(a). The breadth of this provision was noted as positive for public health. One anonymous public health official was quoted in the *Interim Report*, above note 90 at 129–30 as follows:

> The new [*Health Information*] *Protection Act 2003* allows the health information custodian to disclose — it says "may" and not "shall" — about information of an individual to the Chief Medical Officer of Health or Medical Officer of Health and is very broad. It says for the purpose of that Act. I understand that ... there has been a lot of opposition to that particular section. I think that section is great because it will help public health move quickly and collect information that it needs when faced with a situation such as SARS or another influenza pandemic; I am concerned that section is going to be wiped out in the future reiteration of the Bill.

ilar to a purpose" of the *HPPA*.[99] Therefore, a health information custodian, such as a physician, hospital, medical officer of health, or the Ministry of Health and Long-Term Care may, for example, disclose personal health information to a chief medical officer of health or a medical officer of health in another province, to a federal body, or to a person in a jurisdiction outside of Canada where necessary for health protection or promotion purposes.

Although discussed in more detail elsewhere in the Guide,[100] it is appropriate to recall here the applicability of the general limiting principles to a health information custodian's disclosure of personal health information for public health purposes. While the authority in *PHIPA* for a health information custodian to disclose personal health information for the purposes set out in the *HPPA* is seemingly broad, *PHIPA* does in fact restrict such disclosures significantly through the application of the general limiting principles. Health information custodians should ensure that they comply with these principles in disclosing personal health information under this authority.

3) Disclosures under the *Health Protection and Promotion Act*

In addition to *PHIPA's* disclosure powers related to public health,[101] provisions in the *HPPA*, including extensive mandatory reporting obligations, continue to apply to health information custodians as disclosures of personal health information that are permitted or required by law.[102]

As such, certain health care providers continue to have a duty to report to their local medical officer of health certain information about patients afflicted with diseases specified in or under the *HPPA*. These health care providers include physicians, dentists, nurses, pharmacists, optometrists, drugless practitioners (such as naturopaths), administrators of hospitals, superintendents of institutions such as nursing homes and homes for the aged, and operators of laboratories.[103]

The *HPPA* also addresses the collection, use, and disclosure of personal health information by medical officers of health and the Chief Medical Officer of Health. For instance, that Act allows a medical officer of health to collect, directly or indirectly, personal information (which would include personal

---

99 *PHIPA*, s. 39(2)(b).
100 See Chapter 7, Section C.
101 *PHIPA*, s. 39(2).
102 And therefore authorized by *PHIPA*, s. 43(1)(h).
103 See, for example, *HPPA*, above note 91, ss. 25–27 and 29.

health information) and to use it for the purposes of the *HPPA*, "or for the purposes related to administration of a public health program or service that is prescribed in the regulations [under the *HPPA*]."[104] Disclosures of such information between medical officers of health can occur for similar purposes.[105] Further, the *HPPA* provides that if the Chief Medical Officer of Health is of the opinion that a situation exists anywhere in Ontario that constitutes or may constitute a risk to the health of any persons, the Chief Medical Officer of Health may investigate the situation and take such action as the Chief Medical Officer of Health considers appropriate to prevent, eliminate, or decrease the risk.[106] For this purpose, the Chief Medical Officer of Health may exercise anywhere in Ontario any of the powers of a board of health and any of the powers of a medical officer of health.[107] Further, the Chief Medical Officer of Health may request a board of health to provide such information about the board of health and the health unit served by the board of health as the Chief Medical Officer of Health specifies. A board of health that receives such a request for information must provide the information in accordance with the request.[108]

Lastly, an exemption to the *HPPA* confidentiality provision authorizes any person to disclose the name of, or any other information that may identify, a person about whom an order or report is made in respect of a communicable disease, a reportable disease, or a virulent disease[109] where the disclosure is for the purposes of public health administration.[110] A health information custodian to whom this provision applies can rely on this *HPPA* provision as authority to disclose personal health information in the stated circumstances.[111]

---

104 *HPPA*, *ibid.*, ss. 91.1(1) & (2). These then, under *PHIPA*, would be permissible collections and uses of personal health information, without consent, authorized by another law: see *PHIPA*, ss. 36(1)(h) and 7(1)(k).

105 *HPPA*, *ibid.*, ss. 91.1(3)–(5). As mentioned, above note 102, any disclosure of personal health information permitted or required under the *HPPA* or any other law, is thereby authorized under *PHIPA*, s. 43(1)(h), further discussed below, Section P.

106 *HPPA*, *ibid.*, s. 86(1).

107 *Ibid.*, s. 86(2)(a), which presumably includes the powers under *HPPA*, s. 91.1 with respect to personal information.

108 *Ibid.*, s. 86.2. Note that the Minister may also authorize or direct the Chief Medical Officer of Health in writing to exercise any right or power or any duty that is granted to or vested in the Minister under the following sections of the *HPPA*, *ibid.*: ss. 82 (appointment of assessors), 83 (direction to board of health), 84 (power to take steps to ensure direction is carried out), and 85 (notice of failure to comply).

109 *Ibid.*, s. 39(1).

110 *Ibid.*, s. 39(2)(c).

111 *PHIPA*, ss. 43(1)(h) and 43(2).

4) Disclosures Permitted under Other Acts for Public Health Purposes

In addition to the *HPPA* and its regulations, other Acts and regulations permit or require health information custodians to disclose personal health information for public health purposes. For example, pursuant to a regulation made under the *Public Hospitals Act*, a hospital must disclose information from medical records to the Chief Medical Officer of Health, a medical officer of health, or a physician designated by the Chief Medical Officer of Health, for the purposes of the diagnosis of patients who may have contracted SARS and the investigation, prevention, treatment, and containment of SARS.[112] Pursuant to a regulation made under the *Laboratory and Specimen Collection Centre Licensing Act*, operators of laboratories also have a duty to ensure that the staff of the laboratory report certain positive laboratory findings related to communicable diseases and reportable diseases to the medical officer of health in the area from which the specimen originated.[113] Such health informaton custodians and their agents may continue to disclose personal health information as these provisions require, since *PHIPA* permits a health information custodian to disclose personal health information where another Act or a regulation authorizes the custodian to make the disclosure.[114]

K. DISCLOSURES RELATED TO RISKS: SECTION 40(1)

1) Authority in *PHIPA* to Disclose Where Significant Risk of Harm

PHIPA permits a health information custodian to disclose a patient's personal health information without consent where the custodian "believes on reasonable grounds that the disclosure is necessary for the purpose of eliminating or reducing a significant risk of serious bodily harm to a person or group of persons."[115] The regulation made under *PHIPA* creates a similar authority for an agent of a health information custodian to disclose personal health information.[116] The

---

112 *Hospital Management*, R.R.O. 1990, Reg. 965, s. 23.2 [Reg. 965], made under the *PHA*, above note 23.

113 *Laboratories*, R.R.O. 1990, Reg. 682, s. 9(1)(c).

114 *PHIPA*, s. 43(1)(h). A similar permission exists for agents of health information custodians in *PHIPA*, s. 17(2).

115 *Ibid.*, s. 40(1).

116 *PHIPA* Regulation, above note 9, s. 7(2)(i).

agent thus does not require the authorization of the custodian to disclose personal health information for this purpose.

This subsection in *PHIPA* does not create a requirement to disclose personal health information for the purpose of avoiding harm, or a "duty to warn," but rather simply provides custodians and their agents with the power to disclose personal health information where they reasonably believe the disclosure is necessary for such a purpose.[117]

2) Background on Duty to Keep Information Confidential vs. Duty to Disclose Where Risk of Harm

a) Recommendations of the *Krever Report*

This provision in *PHIPA* is consistent with the recommendations of the *Krever Report*. In the *Krever Report*, Mr. Justice Krever noted two types of situations where a health care provider may face the question of whether the provider should override his or her duty of confidentiality to a patient to eliminate or reduce a risk of serious bodily harm to a person or group of persons:

- where a request is made to the provider concerning the health of a patient in connection with a crime in progress being committed by the patient, in order to determine how best to approach the patient;[118] and
- where, in the absence of a request for the provider to disclose information, the provider may be required to act on the basis of his or her own assessment of information about a patient, such as where the provider becomes aware of a patient's commission of or intent to commit a violent act.[119]

Having identified situations such as these, Mr. Justice Krever concluded: "The absolute requirement of confidentiality without patient authorization is unworkable. The existence of discretion in hospitals and physicians to disclose health information without authorization in some situations should be permitted."[120] The *Krever Report* included a recommendation that health care providers be per-

---

117   Of course, where another law requires such a disclosure, *PHIPA* does not relieve the custodian from a legal requirement to disclose the information: *PHIPA*, ss. 6(3)(b) and 43(1)(h).

118   *Krever Report*, above note 53, vol. 2 at 426. Mr. Justice Krever described a situation where the police contacted a particular hospital in connection with an aircraft hijacking that was taking place. The police were able to obtain information from the individual's medical record and thus provide a satisfactory conclusion to the situation. There was, however, no authority in the *PHA*, above note 23, for the hospital to make such a disclosure.

119   *Krever Report*, *ibid*.

120   *Ibid.*, vol. 2 at 93.

mitted to disclose patient information to the police or others without the patient's consent where the disclosure is necessary to prevent a threatened danger.[121]

b) Jurisprudence

To a large extent, *PHIPA*'s approach to the disclosure of personal health information to eliminate or reduce a significant risk of serious bodily harm reflects the approach that the courts have developed to such disclosures.

i) *Tarasoff v. Regents of the University of California*

The first "duty to warn" case to spark significant debate in the psychiatric and psychotherapeutic communities in the United States and Canada was *Tarasoff v. Regents of the University of California*.[122] During therapy, a student at the University of California, who was being treated at the university hospital, told his psychologist that he planned to kill his former girlfriend. The therapist notified the campus police of the patient's intention. Although the police took the patient into custody, they released him on a promise that he stay away from his former girlfriend. Neither the intended victim nor her parents were notified of the threat. The patient subsequently murdered his former girlfriend. He was found not guilty by reason of insanity. In a lawsuit initiated by the victim's family, the California Supreme Court concluded that the policy favouring the protection of the confidentiality of patient/psychotherapist communications must yield to the extent to which such disclosure is essential to avert danger to others.[123] According to the court, "The protective privilege ends where the public peril begins."[124] The court concluded that the psychologist had a duty to warn the endangered person or those who could reasonably be expected to warn the person. As a result, the psychologist was held liable for failing in his legal duty in the circumstances to disclose sufficient information to provide an appropriate warning.

ii) *Smith v. Jones*

In Canada, the *Tarasoff* decision has been referred to with approval, most notably in *Smith v. Jones*,[125] a decision of the Supreme Court of Canada pertaining to when solicitor/client privilege should be set aside in the interest of protecting the safety of the public. The Court considered this issue in the context of a psychiatrist's report. An accused was charged with aggravated sexual

---

121 *Ibid.*, vol. 2 at 94, Recommendation 22.
122 131 Cal. Rptr. 14 [1976. S.C.] [*Tarasoff*].
123 *Ibid.* at 27.
124 *Ibid.*
125 [1999] 1 S.C.R. 455.

assault of a woman who engaged in prostitution. The accused's lawyer referred the accused to a psychiatrist for a forensic assessment. During the assessment, the accused described to the psychiatrist a detailed plan that included murdering a prostitute. The psychiatrist conveyed to the accused's lawyer that, in his opinion, the accused was extremely dangerous. Because the psychiatrist's report was prepared as a result of defence counsel's request for a forensic psychiatric assessment, it was subject to solicitor/client privilege.[126] When the psychiatrist learned that the information he brought to the lawyer's attention would not be revealed to the sentencing judge, the psychiatrist brought an application to the court to release him from the privilege so that he could provide to the court the details of his report.

The Supreme Court of Canada found that the safety of the public is of such importance that, in appropriate circumstances, it will warrant setting aside solicitor/client privilege.[127] The Court identified three factors to consider in determining whether solicitor/client privilege should be displaced in the circumstances: (i) Clarity: Is there a clear risk to an identifiable person or group of persons?[128] (ii) Seriousness: Is there a risk of serious bodily harm or death?[129] (iii) Imminence: Is the danger imminent?[130] The Court noted that these factors would often overlap and vary in their importance and significance. Yet, as a general rule, if the solicitor/client privilege is to be set aside, the Court must find that "there is an imminent risk of serious bodily harm or death to an identifiable person or group."[131]

---

126 For a brief explanation of solicitor/client privilege, see Chapter 3, note 85.

127 *Smith v. Jones*, above note 125 at para. 35.

128 The Court outlined the following factors, *ibid.* at para. 79: "Is there evidence of long range planning? Has a method for effecting the specific attack been suggested? Is there a prior history of violence or threats of violence? Are the prior assaults or threats of violence similar to that which was planned? If there is a history of violence, has the violence increased in severity? Is the violence directed to an identifiable person or group of persons? This is not an all-encompassing list. It is important to note, however, that as a general rule a group or person must be ascertainable."

129 The Court determined at para. 82 that the "seriousness" factor requires that "the threat be such that the intended victim is in danger of being killed or of suffering serious bodily harm ... or death." The Court noted that serious psychological harm may constitute serious bodily harm (*ibid.* at para. 83).

130 The Court stated that "the risk of serious bodily harm or death must be imminent if solicitor-client communications are to be disclosed. That is, the risk itself must be serious. The nature of the threat must be such that it creates a sense of urgency. This sense of urgency may be applicable to some time in the future. Depending on the seriousness and clarity of the threat, it will not always be necessary to impose a particular time limit on the risk." (*Ibid.* at para. 84.)

131 *Ibid.* at para. 78.

3) Guidelines and Policies for Professionals

a) Codes of Ethics

Codes of ethics for some health professionals, such as psychologists, reflect the direction of the courts in cases like *Tarasoff* and *Smith v. Jones*. The Canadian Code of Ethics for Psychologists published by the Canadian Psychological Association, for example, provides that psychologists should "do everything reasonably possible to stop or offset the consequences of actions by others when these actions are likely to cause serious physical harm or death."[132] The Code clarifies that "doing everything reasonably possible" may include reporting to appropriate authorities, such as the police; to an intended victim; to a family member; or to other persons who can intervene. The Code makes it clear that such a report could be made "even when a confidential relationship is involved."[133] Similarly, the Canadian Medical Association's Code of Ethics provides that a physician may disclose a patient's personal health information to third parties only with the patient's consent "or as provided for by law, such as when the maintenance of confidentiality would result in a significant risk of substantial harm to others or, in the case of incompetent patients, to the patients themselves."[134]

b) Policy of the College of Physicians and Surgeons of Ontario

Professional governing bodies have also considered the direction of the courts in regulating their members. Physicians are expected to comply with the Ontario College of Physicians and Surgeons' policy on a standard for the duty to inform, which provides that a physician has an obligation to notify the police if the physician forms the opinion that a patient's threats of serious violence or death are more than likely to be carried out. The policy states:

> Under the standard, a physician has an obligation to notify the police if he or she forms the clinical opinion that a patient's threats of serious violence or death are more than likely to be carried out. The factors going into the formation of this clinical judgment include: 1) the threat is directed at a person or group, 2) there is a specific plan that is concrete and capable of commission, and 3) the method for carrying out the threat is available to the one making the threat. In the appro-

---

132 *Canadian Code of Ethics for Psychologists*, 3d ed. (Ottawa: Canadian Psychological Association, 2000), Principle II, Responsible Caring, at para. II. 39, online: <www.cpa.ca/ethics2000.html>.

133 *Ibid.*

134 *CMA Code of Ethics* (Update 2004) at para. 35, online: <www.cma.ca/index.cfm/ci_id/2419/la_id/1.htm,>.

priate circumstances, the physician should also contact the intended victim of the threat. The report should include the threat, the situation, the physician's opinion and the information on which the opinion is based.[135]

The College of Physicians and Surgeons of Ontario has noted, however, that the policy does not have the power of a legislated requirement and, therefore, the policy itself cannot protect physicians from civil liability for reporting, although "case law indicates that courts do not look favorably upon civil suits against physicians who have fulfilled this obligation in good faith."[136]

4) *PHIPA* Provisions Regarding Disclosures to Avoid Harm

The provisions in *PHIPA* that permit a health information custodian or a custodian's agent to disclose personal health information where the custodian or agent believes on reasonable grounds that the disclosure is necessary for the purpose of eliminating or reducing a significant risk of serious bodily harm to a person or group of persons supports statements such as those contained in documents of professional governing bodies and associations, in that the provision authorizes the custodian or agent, as the case may be, to disclose personal health information in the circumstances described in those documents.

PHIPA, however, is different in some respects from the standards discussed above. Its key aspects can be summarized as follows:

- *PHIPA* permits a disclosure to prevent a risk of not only physical harm, but psychological harm as well.[137]
- For a custodian or agent to rely on the authority to disclose in *PHIPA*, the risk of harm does not need to be "imminent." Although it is evident from the Court's decision in *Smith v. Jones* that the qualifier "imminent" is not limited to "immediate" and can encompass a non-immediate future event,[138] the absence of this word in *PHIPA* enables the custodian or agent to rely on

---

135 *Mandatory Reporting*, Policy #10-00, (March, 2001), online: <www.cpso.on.ca/Policies/mandatory.htm>.

136 *Ibid.*

137 In *R. v. McCraw*, [1991] 3 S.C.R. 72, in the context of s. 264.1(1)(a) of the *Criminal Code of Canada*, R.S.C. 1985, c. C-46 [*Criminal Code*], which makes it an offence to threaten to "cause death or serious bodily harm," the Court at 81 defined "serious bodily harm" as "any hurt or injury, whether physical or psychological, that interferes in a substantial way with the physical or psychological integrity, health or well-being of the complainant." The Court concluded that "there can be no doubt that psychological harm may often be more pervasive and permanent in its effect than any physical harm."

138 *Smith v. Jones*, above note 125.

the authority more comfortably in the face of an urgent situation that is not necessarily immediate, but nonetheless critical to address. The focus of the language in *PHIPA* is not when a harm is expected to arise, but on the likelihood and seriousness of the harm, and whether the disclosure is "necessary" to reduce or eliminate the risk.[139]

- The authority to disclose in *PHIPA* is not limited to disclosures to police; it authorizes disclosure to others as well, such as potential victims.

- The authority to disclose in *PHIPA* does not require that the person or group to whom the risk of harm relates be identifiable. For instance, if a patient makes a credible[140] threat to kill the next person who comes through a certain door, or someone who the patient will choose at random, *PHIPA* authorizes a health information custodian's disclosure to the police in order to stop the person.

- *PHIPA* permits a health information custodian or an agent of a custodian to disclose personal health information for the purpose of eliminating or reducing a significant risk of serious bodily harm to "a person." As *PHIPA* does not discuss the identity of the person to whom the risk of harm relates, it appears that the person may be the patient to whom the information relates; that is, a custodian or agent may disclose a patient's personal health information to protect the patient from harm to him- or herself.[141] A custodian or agent would appear to be able to rely on this provision to disclose personal health information about a patient without the patient's consent, for example, to facilitate the patient's admission to a psychiatric facility where the patient is apparently suffering from a mental disorder and may

---

139 If a disclosure is in fact necessary to reduce or eliminate a significant risk of serious bodily harm, then it is hard to see the relevance of the question of whether the risk of harm is imminent or not. Of course the less imminent the harm, the harder it will be to establish that the disclosure is necessary to address it.

140 *PHIPA* requires that a custodian believe on reasonable grounds that the disclosure is necessary for the purpose of eliminating or reducing a significant risk of serious bodily harm to a person or group of persons. This standard would appear to require that the disclosing custodian have reasonable grounds for believing that the threat poses a significant risk of this type. A threat that is not credible would generally not create sufficient grounds for making such a disclosure.

141 Causing harm to oneself would also appear to fall within the concept of "serious bodily harm" as evident from *Conway v. Fleming*, [1996] O.J. No. 1242, (Gen. Div.), upheld in (1999), 173 D.L.R. (4th) 372 (Ont. Div. Ct.), leave to appeal to C.A. denied, 12 July 1999, which deals with the power to restrain certain persons to prevent serious bodily harm to themselves. A similar power to impose restraint exists at common law, and for hospitals under the *Patient Restraints Minimization Act, 2001*, S.O. 2001, c. 16, s. 6.

cause either "serious bodily harm" or "serious physical impairment" to him-
or herself, as defined in the *Mental Health Act.*[142]

- Finally, *PHIPA* provides protection from liability to custodians and agents
  who exercise their judgment in good faith and reasonably in the circumstances and disclose personal health information[143] or refrain from so disclosing[144] for the purpose of eliminating or reducing a significant risk of
  serious bodily harm.

5) Relationship of Harm Disclosures to "Lock Box"

In the context of discussions of *PHIPA's* "lock box" provisions, the Ministry of
Health and Long-Term Care's material, the Ontario Hospital Association's *Hospital Privacy Toolkit*, and the Information and Privacy Commissioner's educational materials all note that where a patient expressly instructs a health
information custodian not to disclose his or her personal health information for
the purpose of providing health care to the individual, as permitted under certain provisions of *PHIPA*, the custodian may nevertheless disclose the information pursuant to section 40(1) of *PHIPA* where the custodian believes on
reasonable grounds that the disclosure is necessary to eliminate or reduce a significant risk of serious bodily harm to any person.[145] As noted in the discussion
of the "lock-box" provisions,[146] an express withholding or withdrawal of consent,[147] or an express instruction[148] does not limit uses and disclosures that
PHIPA permits a custodian to make in certain circumstances without a patient's
consent, such as a disclosure to avoid harm in accordance with section 40(1).[149]

---

142 *MHA*, above note 23, for example, ss. 15, 16, and 20.
143 *PHIPA*, s. 71(1)(a). Of course, this immunity provision does not pertain just to a dis-
     closure made pursuant to s. 40(1).
144 *Ibid.*, s. 71(1)(b).
145 See the *Hospital Privacy Toolkit: Guide to the Ontario Personal Health Information Protection
     Act* (Toronto: Ontario Hospital Association, 2004) at 59 [*OHA Privacy Toolkit*], online:
     <www.oha.com>. See *Personal Health Information Protection Act, 2004: An Overview for
     Health Information Custodians* (Toronto: Ministry of Health and Long-Term Care, 2004),
     question 7 at 36 [*Overview*], online: <www.health.gov.on.ca>. See, further, the Information
     and Privacy Commissioner/Ontario, *Frequently Asked Questions: Health Information Pro-
     tection Act*, "How does the 'lock-box' work?" Online: <www.ipc.on.ca>.
146 See Chapter 7, Section G.
147 Such an express withholding or withdrawal of consent applies in the context of the
     assumed implied consent under *PHIPA*, s. 20(2).
148 A patient has the ability to make such express instructions under *PHIPA*, ss. 37(1)(a),
     38(1)(a), and 50(1)(e).
149 The *OHA Privacy Toolkit*, the Information and Privacy Commissioner's *Frequently
     Asked Questions: Health Information Protection Act*, and the Ministry of Health and

6) Mandatory Reporting of Gunshot Wounds

Bill 110, *An Act to require the disclosure of information to police respecting persons being treated for gunshot wounds*, was introduced in the Legislature for first reading on 23 June 2004.[150] If passed into law, the Act would impose an obligation on public hospitals and prescribed health care facilities to report information to police when treating a patient for a gunshot wound. A hospital or other prescribed facility would be required to disclose to the police the fact that a person is being treated for such a wound, the person's name, if known, and the name and location of the facility.[151] The hospital or other health care facility would be

---

Long-Term Care's *Overview*, above note 145, do not specifically address the issue of a health information custodian's disclosure of personal health information to another custodian pursuant to *PHIPA*, s. 40(1) for the purpose of eliminating a risk of harm to a patient by providing health care to the patient, where the patient has expressly instructed the custodian not to disclose his or her personal health information to another custodian for this very purpose, as permitted by *PHIPA*, ss. 20(2) and 38(1)(a). As to how *PHIPA*, s. 40(1) will be read in such circumstances in relation to an express instruction that a patient gives in accordance with these provisions may be the subject of varying interpretations based on such matters as the rules of statutory interpretation, custodians should monitor additional guidance that the Commissioner may provide on this issue in the future, as well as direction from professional governing bodies and the courts. In addition to possible issues of the proper interpretation of the provisions of *PHIPA* in this regard, there may also be questions about whether the *Canadian Charter of Rights and Freedoms*, Part I of the *Constitution Act, 1982*, being Schedule B to the *Canada Act, 1982* (U.K.), 1982, c. 11 [*Charter*] would prohibit or lead to an interpretation that would prohibit a disclosure under *PHIPA*, s. 40(1) for the purpose of avoiding harm to the patient where that patient him- or herself had specifically instructed that the disclosure not be made. See Chapter 3, Section B(2).

150 Bill 110, 1st Sess., 38th Leg., Ontario, 2004 [Bill 110]. Order for second reading discharged pursuant to Standing Order 72(a) and order referred to the Standing Committee on Justice Policy, 14 December 2004. Bill 110 was reviewed in Committee on 2–3 March 2005, and it was reported as amended to the Legislature on 9 March 2005. At the time of writing, the Bill has been ordered for second reading. The Bill as amended by Committee adds a provision to enable the government, by way of regulation, to add to the meaning of "facility" a clinic that provides health care services, as well as a medical doctor's office.

In introducing the Bill, the Minister of Community Safety and Correctional Services noted in the Legislature that forty-five American states have some form of similar legislation: Ontario, Legislative Assembly, *Official Report of Debates (Hansard)*, 3175 (23 June 2004) at 1350 (Hon. Monte Kwinter). The Ontario Medical Association on Emergency Medicine had called for such legislation in its position statement. H. Ovens, H. Morrison, A. Drummond, B. Borgundvaag, OMA Section of Emergency Medicine Position Statement, *The Case for Mandatory Reporting of Gunshot Wounds in the Emergency Department* (November 2003), online at <www.oma.org/pcomm/omr/nov/03gunshot.htm>.

151 Bill 110, *ibid.*, cl. 2(1).

required to disclose the information orally as soon as is it was "reasonably prac-ticable to do so without interfering with the person's treatment or disrupting the regular activities of the facility."[152] The Act, which if passed would create the first legislation of its kind in Canada,[153] would impose the obligation to report even where the gunshot wound was the result of an accident or a suicide attempt.

Bill 110 includes a provision that states, "Nothing in this Act shall prevent a facility from disclosing information to a municipal or regional police force of the Ontario Provincial Police that the facility is otherwise by law permitted or authorized to disclose."[154] Therefore, the duty to make the report would build on the disclosures of personal health information permitted in *PHIPA* and does not replace, for example, the provision in *PHIPA* that authorizes a health information custodian to disclose personal health information for the purpose of eliminating or reducing a significant risk of serious bodily harm to a person or group of persons. The disclosure that a facility would be required to make under Bill 110, if passed, would be authorized under *PHIPA*.[155]

At the time of the *Krever Report*, Mr. Justice Krever did not support such mandatory reporting and specifically recommended that legislation not address this issue.[156] In opposition to such provisions, he noted that persons in need of care might be deterred from seeking care if they believe that physi-cians, hospitals, and other health care providers were obliged to disclose confi-dential health information to the police.[157] He did, however, recommend that, where a senior official of a hospital or health care facility or a physician believes, on reasonable grounds, that a patient has been a victim or the perpe-trator of a crime, he or she should be *permitted* to so inform the police without the patient's authorization.[158]

---

152 Bill 110, *ibid.*, cl. 2(2).

153 Ontario, Legislative Assembly, *Official Report of Debates (Hansard)*, 3175 (23 June 2004) at 1350 (Hon. Monte Kwinter).

154 Bill 110, above note 150, cl. 3.

155 *PHIPA*, s. 43(1)(h) discussed below in Section P.

156 *Krever Report*, above note 53, vol. 2 at 92, Recommendation 21.

157 *Ibid.* This is the same concern that was raised in the Legislature when Bill 110 was introduced: Ontario, Legislative Assembly, *Official Report of Debates (Hansard)*, 3178 (23 June 2004) at 1420 (Peter Kormos), where a member of the legislature noted that this type of law would be a disincentive to seek treatment.

158 *Krever Report*, *ibid.*, vol. 2 at 94, Recommendation 24.

L. DISCLOSURES RELATED TO CARE OR CUSTODY: SECTIONS 40(2) & (3)

1) Arrangements for the Provision of Health Care

A health information custodian may disclose personal health information about a patient:

- to the head of a penal or other custodial institution[159] in which the patient is being lawfully detained,[160] or
- to the officer in charge[161] of a psychiatric facility[162] in which the patient is being lawfully detained,[163]

in order to assist the institution or facility in making a decision concerning arrangements for the provision of health care to the patient.[164]

---

159 The scope of the phrase "penal or other custodial institution" appears to be clarified in *PHIPA*, s. 40(3) and would appear to include a federal prison, a provincial correctional facility, and a facility for temporary or secure custody for young offenders. *PHIPA*, s. 40(3)(b) refers to the placement of individuals into custody or detention, conditional release or discharge, or actual release or discharge "under Part IV of the *Child and Family Services Act*, the *Mental Health Act*, the *Ministry of Correctional Services Act*, the *Corrections and Conditional Release Act (Canada)*, Part XX.1 of the *Criminal Code (Canada)*, the *Prisons and Reformatories Act (Canada)* or the *Youth Criminal Justice Act (Canada)*." However, the application of *PHIPA*, s. 40(3)(a) may be read more broadly to include detention or "lock-up" facilities established under the *Police Services Act*, R.S.O. 1990, c. P.15. Under s. 16.1 of that Act,

> Subject to the approval of the Ontario Civilian Commission on Police Services, the council of every local municipality may establish, maintain and regulate detention facilities for the detention and imprisonment of persons sentenced to imprisonment therein for not more than 10 days, and of persons detained for examination on a charge of having committed any offence, or for transfer to any correctional institution for trial, or in the execution of any sentence, and such persons may be lawfully received and so detained in the detention facilities.

160 *PHIPA*, s. 40(2).
161 *MHA*, above note 23, s. 1(1) defines the "officer in charge" of a psychiatric facility to mean "the officer who is responsible for the administration and management of a psychiatric facility."
162 *MHA, ibid.*, s. 1(1) defines the term "psychiatric facility" to mean "a facility for the observation, care and treatment of persons suffering from a mental disorder, and designated as such by the Minister [of Health and Long-Term Care]."
163 *PHIPA*, s. 40(2). This provision does not apply to a voluntary patient of a psychiatric facility.
164 *Ibid.*, ss. 40(2) & (3)(a). The Standing Committee on General Government added s. 40(3)(a) to *PHIPA* during the clause-by-clause review of Bill 31, held after the first reading: Ontario, Legislative Assembly, Standing Committee on General Government, *Official Report of Debates (Hansard)*, G-218 (9 February 2004) at 1320 (Peter Fonseca).

This provision in *PHIPA* reflects the intermediary role that such institutions and facilities sometimes fulfil in the provision of health care to individuals who they detain. In many instances, such institutions and facilities must make arrangements so that the detained individual can receive health care. To make decisions concerning those arrangements, such institutions and facilities require personal health information about the individual from a health information custodian. Depending on the individual in question and his or her state of health, in some instances, the institution or facility will require significant amounts of personal health information about a patient in order to make the appropriate arrangements.

For example, where a patient who is charged with an offence or has been convicted of an offence is transferred from a hospital to a correctional institution, the hospital may disclose relevant personal health information about the patient to the head of the institution, such as the superintendent, so that the institution may make appropriate arrangements for the provision of health care to the patient after the transfer. Such information could include, for instance, information about a patient's epilepsy, including when the patient is prone to seizure and the medication the patient requires to control his or her condition; the fact that a patient is pregnant and information about the care the patient requires throughout the pregnancy, such as prenatal visits, nutritional information, and the likelihood of premature labour; the fact that a patient is prone to asthma attack in certain circumstances and how the patient controls his or her asthma; or the fact that the patient suffers from depression and requires particular counselling.

Recall that communications about a patient between a health care practitioner who is an employee of a custodial institution and an employee who is the head of the institution constitutes a *disclosure* of personal health information by a health information custodian to a non-custodian.[165] Sections 40(2) and 40(3)(a) of *PHIPA*, therefore, permit an employee health care practitioner, such as a nurse working within a health unit of a correctional institution, to disclose an inmate's personal health information to the head of the institution, such as the institution's superintendent, so that the head may make a decision about arranging for diagnostic tests, such as an x-ray, for the inmate patient.

It is important to note that these provisions of *PHIPA* authorize a health information custodian to disclose personal health information about a patient for the purpose of assisting the custodial institution or a psychiatric facility in making a decision about the *arrangements* to have appropriate health care available to the patient. Despite a health information custodian's disclosure of personal health

---

165   See Chapter 2, Section B(1)(b)(iii).

information about a patient to a such an institution or officer in charge without the patient's consent, other law addresses the patient's right to give or withhold consent to the proposed health care.[166]

2) Placement into Custody, etc.

A health information custodian may disclose personal health information about a patient to the head of a penal or other custodial institution where the patient is being lawfully detained or to the officer in charge of a psychiatric facility in order to assist the institution or facility in making a decision abut the placement of the patient into custody, detention, release, conditional release, discharge, or conditional discharge[167] under Part IV of the *Child and Family Services Act*,[168] the *Mental Health Act*,[169] the *Ministry of Correctional Services Act*,[170] the *Corrections and Conditional Release Act*,[171] Part XX.1 of the *Criminal Code*,[172] the *Prisons and Reformatories Act*,[173] or the *Youth Criminal Justice Act*.[174]

166　The rules for obtaining consent to treatment are governed, generally, in Ontario by the *HCCA*, above note 50.

167　*PHIPA*, ss. 40(2) & (3)(b).

168　R.S.O. 1990, c. C.11 [*CFSA*]. Part IV of the *Child and Family Services Act* addresses programs and services for young offenders (individuals between twelve and seventeen) including temporary detention and secure custody arrangements for such offenders.

169　*MHA*, above note 23. The *Mental Health Act* addresses, among other matters, the observation, care, and treatment of patients suffering from a mental disorder, including involuntary patients.

170　R.S.O. 1990, c. M.22. [*MCSA*]. The *Ministry of Correctional Services Act* regulates the custody, detention, and arrangements for release of inmates under the provincial corrections system.

171　S.C. 2002, c. 20. The *Corrections and Conditional Release Act* regulates matters pertaining to the federal correctional system, including custody detention and arrangements for release of inmates convicted of a federal offence.

172　See above note 137. Part XX.1 of the *Criminal Code* deals with, among other matters, assessments and dispositions pertaining to accused individuals who may be unfit to stand trial for the offence they have been charged with by reason of suffering from a mental disorder or who have been found to be not criminally responsible for an offence they have been charged with by reason of suffering from a mental disorder. Such individuals frequently end up being detained and observed in a provincial psychiatric facility.

173　R.S.C. 1985, c. P-20. The *Prisons and Reformatories Act* addresses such matters as the reception and transfer of prisoners from one prison to another, an earned remission program for prisoners, and the temporary absence program for prisoners under the federal corrections system.

174　S.C. 2002, c. 1. The *Youth Criminal Justice Act* addresses all matters pertaining to individuals between twelve and seventeen who have been charged with an offence under the *Criminal Code* or have been convicted of such an offence, including placement of such individuals into custody, assessment, detention, disposition for release, etc.

PHIPA does not define the term "placement." Decisions about the placement of an individual would include, for example, decisions about the appropriate location of the individual within the institution or facility. A custodial institution may require personal health information about an inmate from a health information custodian, for example, to ensure that the inmate is placed within the institution in a location that appropriately meets the inmate's health needs, such as placement near a defibrillator for an inmate with a cardiac condition, or placement that provides safe custody with close supervision for an inmate with suicidal tendencies.

Decisions about the "placement" of an individual also encompass, for example, consideration as to whether an individual is ready to be moved from a more secure part of the institution or facility to a less secure unit, discharged from an institution or facility, or placed on parole, and what conditions should be imposed upon that individual, if any. "Placement" would also include possible transfers to another institution or facility under the legislation referred to above.[175]

M. DISCLOSURE FOR PROCEEDINGS: SECTION 41

1) Generally

a) Context of *PHIPA* Provisions on Disclosure for Proceedings

PHIPA contains provisions allowing a health information custodian to disclose personal health information for the purposes of a "proceeding" under certain circumstances. Before addressing the details of each of these provisions, it is important to understand the legal context of the provisions generally.

The term "proceeding" is broadly defined in *PHIPA* to include "a proceeding held in, before or under the rules of a court, a tribunal, a commission, a justice of the peace, a committee of a College within the meaning of the *Regulated Health Professions Act, 1991*, a committee of the Board of Regents continued under the *Drugless Practitioners Act*, a committee of the *Ontario College of Social Workers and Social Service Work Act, 1998*, an arbitrator or a mediator."[176]

There is a vast body of law, apart from *PHIPA*, which specifically addresses the production of documents and the admissibility of evidence in the types of proceedings referred to in this definition, which includes civil lawsuits, criminal proceedings, and proceedings before various administrative tri-

---

175   As listed in s. 40(3)(b).
176   *PHIPA*, s. 2.

bunals, including the Information and Privacy Commissioner. As discussed in more detail in Chapter 3,[177] *PHIPA* provides that nothing in the Act is to be construed to interfere with the following:

- any legal privilege;[178]
- the law of evidence or information otherwise available by law to a party or a witness in a proceeding;[179] or
- the power of a court or a tribunal to compel a witness to testify or to compel the production of a document.[180]

Therefore, *PHIPA* does not attempt to legislate extensively in this area. It merely provides some supplementary rules and a framework in which disclosures for the purpose of proceedings may occur. *PHIPA* differs in this respect to Bill 159, which created a sweeping statutory privilege for personal health information, under which most custodians and their agents were prohibited, subject to a number of broad exceptions, from disclosing personal health information in a proceeding without the patient's consent or a court's order that the disclosure was essential in the interests of justice.[181] *PHIPA*, in contrast, does not create a new statutory privilege or new requirements for the introduction of evidence but, rather, relies on common law privileges and rules that are already in place. It is important to read the provisions allowing disclosures for proceedings with this broader legal context in mind. A prudent custodian should take a cautious approach in disclosing personal health information pursuant to the provisions in *PHIPA* that allow disclosures for the purposes of proceedings.

---

177 Chapter 3, Section B(3)(c).

178 *PHIPA*, s. 9(2)(b).

179 *Ibid.*, s. 9(2)(c).

180 *Ibid.*, s. 9(2)(d). Also of relevance in the context of disclosure of personal health information in proceedings, are those clauses in this section providing that nothing in *PHIPA* shall be construed to interfere with (a) anything in connection with a subrogated claim or a potential subrogated claim; (b) the regulatory activities of a College under the *Regulated Health Professions Act, 1991*, S.O. 1991, c. 18 [*RHPA*], the College under the *Social Work and Social Service Work Act, 1998*, S.O. 1998, c. 31 [*SWSSWA*], or the Board under the *Drugless Practitioners Act*, R.S.O. 1990, c. D.18 [*DPA*]; and (c) any provision of any Act of Ontario or Canada or any court order, if the provision or order, as the case may be, prohibits a person from making information public or from publishing information.

181 Bill 159, above note 96, cl. 34(4). The provisions in Bill 159 were based on provisions in the *MHA*, above note 23, and the *LTCA*, above note 23, and would have superseded those provisions. *POPIA*, above note 96 s. 42, contained similar provisions that would have applied only to "personal mental health information," as defined in that draft.

b)   Interaction with Other Legislation

In some cases, other provincial legislation that prevails[182] over *PHIPA* provides that personal health information may not be disclosed unless the requirements of that legislation are followed first. For instance, Bill 31 amended the *Mental Health Act*, the *Long-Term Care Act, 1994*, and the *Child and Family Services Act* to provide that, in the event of a conflict, the provisions of those Acts pertaining to the disclosure of records of personal health information pursuant to a summons or a similar requirement and a disclosure of information in respect of a patient in a proceeding prevail over *PHIPA*.[183]

Further, where the *Criminal Code*[184] or any other federal legislation provides rules about the disclosure of personal health information, these rules prevail over the provisions of *PHIPA* if it is not possible to comply with both the federal legislation and *PHIPA*.[185] For example, the provisions of Part VIII of the *Criminal Code* that set out that no record[186] shall be disclosed to an accused charged with a sexual offence set out in that portion of the *Code*,

---

182   *PHIPA*, s. 7(2) provides that in the event of a conflict between a provision of *PHIPA* or its regulations and a provision of any other Act or its regulations, *PHIPA* and its regulations prevail unless *PHIPA*, its regulations, or the other Act specifically provide otherwise. Section 7(3) sets out that there is no conflict unless it is not possible to comply with both *PHIPA* and its regulations and any other Act or its regulations. Section 1(5) of the *PHIPA* Regulation, above note 9, stipulates further that for the purposes of *PHIPA*, s. 7(3), if *PHIPA* or its regulations provides that an action, including a collection, use, or disclosure, may be taken, and another Act or regulation provides that it may not be taken, then "it is not possible to comply with both" and the *PHIPA* provision would therefore prevail unless the other Act provided that it applied despite *PHIPA*.

183   *MHA*, above note 23, s. 34.1, amended by *PHIPA*, s. 90(5); *LTCA*, above note 23, s. 35.1, amended by *PHIPA*, s. 89(13); *CFSA*, above note 168, s. 183 (6.1), amended by *PHIPA*, s. 78(8). Generally, these Acts require that a record of personal health information be disclosed pursuant to a summons, order, direction, or similar requirement unless a disclosure is likely to result in harm to the treatment of the patient or harm to someone else, in which case the court or body must determine whether the disclosure is essential in the interests of justice. The *Mental Health Act* and the *Long-Term Care Act, 1994* further provide that no person shall disclose in a proceeding in any court or before any body any information in respect of a patient, unless the patient (or the patient's substitute decision-maker) has consented or the court has determined that the disclosure is essential in the interests of justice: *MHA*, above note 23, s. 35(9); *LTCA*, above note 23, s. 35.

184   *Criminal Code*, above note 137.

185   See the discussion of the general principle governing the interaction of federal and provincial legislation in Chapter 3, Section D(4)(a).

186   The *Criminal Code*, above note 137, in s. 278.1 defines a "record" for the purposes of ss. 278.2 to 278.9 of the *Criminal Code* to mean "any form of record that contains personal information for which there is a reasonable expectation of privacy" and includes, medical, psychiatric, and therapeutic records. Part VIII — Offences against the Person, *Criminal Code*, at ss. 278.1–278.91 set out rules for the production of such records to an accused.

unless the procedure, as specified in the *Code*, is followed, applies to a health information custodian's disclosure of personal health information in such a proceeding. Such requirements apply to a health information custodian's disclosure of personal health information despite anything in *PHIPA* that may appear to permit a disclosure in a criminal proceeding without conditions.

Even where *PHIPA* prevails over other legislation that would otherwise prohibit the disclosure or requires certain steps to be followed prior to the disclosure of information,[187] the custodian may nevertheless exercise discretion to refrain from making the disclosure, or to impose conditions on the disclosure.

c) Common Law Privileges and Rules of Evidence

Where other legislation does not prohibit or place conditions on a disclosure of personal health information in a proceeding or, where it does, but does not prevail over *PHIPA* in the event of a conflict, a health information custodian must nonetheless be mindful of the provisions in *PHIPA* that stipulate that nothing in *PHIPA* must be construed to interfere with any legal privilege[188] or the law of evidence or information otherwise available by law to a party or a witness in a proceeding.[189]

Therefore, the issue of whether or not a health information custodian should disclose personal health information in a proceeding and how much information the custodian should disclose, continues to be subject to the rules of common law privilege, which has been held to apply, on a case by case basis, to patient information in the hands of a health care provider.[190] An example of the application of the common law privilege in the health care context can be found in the case of *A.M. v. Ryan*,[191] in which the Supreme Court of Canada provided some indication of the application of common law privilege to the production and disclosure of records of personal health information in a civil action, in a manner that "guard[s] against the injustice of cloaking the truth" while at the same time "ensures the highest degree of confidentiality and the least damage to the protected [therapist/patient] relationship."[192] In that case,

---

187 See, for example, the *Workplace Safety and Insurance Act, 1997*, S.O. 1997, c. 16, Sch. A, s. 134(6), which provides that the Appeals Tribunal will not allow a disclosure of information by a particular health professional before the tribunal in certain circumstances without the written consent of the parties to the proceeding. FSee discussion in Section M(1)(c), below.

188 *PHIPA*, s. 9(2)(b).

189 *Ibid.*, s. 9(2)(c).

190 This type of privilege is described in greater detail in Chapter 3, Section B(3)(c).

191 [1997] 1 S.C.R. 157.

192 *Ibid.* at para. 33.

psychiatric counseling records were held to be subject to common law privilege. The Court applied the privilege so as to permit limited disclosure of the records for the purpose of the proceeding only to the defendant's lawyer, while denying access to the defendant, and imposing conditions to ensure that the information would remain confidential.[193]

d) *Charter* Limitations

As discussed in Chapter 1, although the *Charter*[194] includes no explicit right to privacy, courts have turned to the *Charter* in support of such a right.[195] In *A.M. v. Ryan*, for example, the Supreme Court of Canada applied "*Charter* values" to its interpretation and application of common law privilege to the circumstances of that case.[196] According to the Court, of particular relevance to a consideration of a common law privilege are the provisions of the *Charter* that provide the right of each person "to be secure against unreasonable search or seizure" under section 8 and the right of every person to "the equal protection and equal benefit of the law without discrimination" under section 15.[197] Health information custodians should be mindful that the *Charter* may also be directly relevant to disclosures under *PHIPA* in certain circumstances, including the

---

193   In *A.M. v. Ryan, ibid.*, Dr. Ryan, a psychiatrist who sexually assaulted his patient, M, sought production of records and notes compiled about M by another psychiatrist, Dr. P, who treated M's mental health condition subsequent to the assault, in the context of an action for damages that M had brought against Dr. Ryan. When required to produce the records, Dr. P agreed to disclose M's medical record but claimed that her therapy notes were privileged. On appeal to the British Columbia Court of Appeal, the court had ordered disclosure of Dr. P's reporting letters and notes recording discussions between her and M. The disclosure that the court ordered was subject to several conditions, including that inspection be confined to Dr. Ryan's solicitors and expert witnesses and that any person who saw the documents should not disclose their contents to anyone not entitled to inspect them [at para. 11]. Ultimately, on M's appeal to the Supreme Court of Canada, Madam Justice McLachlin, for the majority, concluded that the order of the Court of Appeal was appropriate. The Supreme Court of Canada underlined that where justice requires that communications between a health care provider and his or her patient be disclosed, the court should consider qualifying the disclosure by imposing limits aimed at permitting the opponent to have the access justice requires while preserving the confidential nature of the documents to the greatest degree possible [at para. 37].

194   See above note 149.

195   See Chapter 1, Section B(3).

196   *A.M. v. Ryan*, above note 191 at paras. 22 & 23.

197   *Ibid.* at para. 30. As noted in Chapter 1, Section B(3), the courts have also focused on section 7 of the *Charter*, which guarantees the right "to life, liberty and the security of the person and the right not to be deprived thereof except in accordance with the principles of fundamental justice," in the discussion of privacy rights.

circumstances described in the *PHIPA* provisions that authorize disclosures of personal health information for proceedings, which should be interpreted and applied in a reasonable manner that is consistent with the *Charter*.[198]

e)   General Limiting Principles

In addition to any limits that legislation, the *Charter*, or the common law may impose on disclosures of personal health information, the general limiting principles with which a health information custodian must comply in deciding whether or not to disclose personal health information and the amount of disclosure that would be appropriate to make in the circumstances are also important.[199]

Now that the broader context of the provisions that permit a health information custodian to disclose personal health information for proceedings is established, each of the particular provisions that authorize such disclosures may be examined in detail.

2)   For the Purpose of Complying with an Order or Similar Requirement

PHIPA provides that a health information custodian may disclose personal health information, whether or not a custodian is, or is expected to be, a party in a proceeding for the purpose of complying with

- a summons, order, or similar requirement issued in a proceeding by a person having jurisdiction to compel the production of information;[200] or
- a procedural rule that relates to the production of information in a proceeding.[201]

In some respects, section 41(1)(d) of in *PHIPA* overlaps with section 41(1)(a), discussed above.[202] It may also overlap with section 43(1)(h), which authorizes a custodian to disclose personal health information if "permitted or required by law."[203] In the context of *FIPPA* and *MFIPPA*, the Information and Privacy Commissioner has interpreted the phrase "for the purpose of complying" to apply only where the disclosure is required.[204]

---

198 See Chapter 3, Section B(2) for further elaboration.
199 *PHIPA*, s. 30, discussed in Chapter 7, Section C.
200 *Ibid.*, s. 41(1)(d)(i).
201 *Ibid.*, s. 41(1)(d) (ii).
202 See Section M(3).
203 Discussed in Section P(2) below.
204 See Section P(2)(a), below note 302.

a) Pursuant to a Summons, Order, or Similar Requirement Issued in a Proceeding

When served with a summons, order, or similar requirement issued in a proceeding for the production of information, a health information custodian should ascertain the precise information that is subject to the summons, order, or similar requirement, as the case may be, as well as to whom and when the custodian must disclose the information. A summons to witness will usually direct a custodian to attend to answer questions before the person having jurisdiction to compel the production of the information, such as a presiding judge in a civil action or the Information and Privacy Commissioner in the case of a review,[205] and to bring the records of personal health information pertinent to the matter. It is important for the custodian to review the documentation received, and the legal provisions on which it is based, and to obtain appropriate advice, where necessary, to be clear about the custodian's obligations pursuant to the requirement. In determining how to comply with the requirement, the custodian should consider whether the disclosure is inconsistent with the other legal requirements discussed above, such as whether the information is subject to a legal privilege.[206]

As set out above, other legislation, such as the *Criminal Code*, the *Mental Health Act*, the *Long-Term Care Act, 1994*, and the *Child and Family Services Act*, may specifically set out steps that a health information custodian must take or criteria that must be fulfilled in order for the custodian to be authorized to disclose personal health information pursuant to such a summons, order, or similar requirement.[207] Even where specific steps are not required by a statute or regulation, a professional governing body may have further direction for its members. For example, the "Code of Ethics and Standards of Practice" of the College of Social Workers and Social Service Workers requires College members who are served with a formal notice or summons to produce client records before a court and who are of the opinion that disclosure would be detrimental to the client to advocate for non-disclosure of the records to the court, whether by themselves, or through legal counsel.[208] It may be prudent for a

---

205 *PHIPA*, ss. 59(2) and (12).

206 How the disclosure should be challenged depends on the context. Appropriate advice should be obtained where necessary, given the seriousness of a refusal to comply with a summons, order, or similar requirement.

207 For a discussion of Part VIII of the *Criminal Code*, see above note 186 and accompanying text. For discussion of the relevant provisions in the key provincial statutes, see above note 183 and accompanying text.

208 See s. 4.3.7 of the *Code of Ethics and Standards of Practice*, 1st ed. (Toronto: College of Social Workers and Social Service Workers, 2000), online: <www.ocswssw.org/index.asp>.

custodian to advise the patient whose information is at issue, if it is practical to do so, that his or her records have been summoned, as such notification may provide an opportunity for the patient to find an avenue to object to the production of his or her records in the proceeding.[209] *PHIPA*, however, does not require a custodian to take such a step.

b) Pursuant to a Procedural Rule

Particular procedural rules that relate to the production of information in a proceeding are common. For instance, some criminal proceedings require specific steps to be taken in a situation where an accused charged with a sexual offence requires production of a patient's records.[210] Detailed rules for civil proceedings are set out in the Ontario *Rules of Civil Procedure*, including rules that require the disclosure of information, including personal health information, in such actions. For example, the *Rules of Civil Procedure* set out rules for the discovery of documents[211] and the examination of witnesses, including expert witnesses.[212] Various tribunals, boards, commissions, and similar bodies have procedural rules that address production of information in their proceedings.[213] Where such rules require a custodian, whether as a party in a proceeding or a non-party witness, to produce personal health information, the custodian is authorized to do so pursuant to this clause in *PHIPA*, subject to the possible overriding exceptions, such as where the information is subject to a legal privilege, or where other legislation prevails over *PHIPA*, as discussed above.

3) For the Purpose of a Proceeding or Contemplated Proceeding

Even where a health information custodian is not required to disclose personal health information pursuant to a summons, order, or similar requirement, or a procedural rule applicable in the proceeding, *PHIPA* allows a custodian to make certain disclosures of personal health information for the purpose of a proceeding or contemplated proceeding in which

---

209 Alternatively, the patient might be willing to consent to the disclosure, or to a partial disclosure that would be sufficient in the circumstances.

210 See above note 186.

211 *Rules of Civil Procedure*, R.R.O. 1990, Reg. 194, Rule 30 [*Rules of Civil Procedure*], made under the *Courts of Justice Act*, R.S.O. 1990, c. C.43 [*CJA*].

212 *Ibid.*, Rule 53.

213 Procedural rules under a variety of legislation may be relevant, such as the *Statutory Powers Procedures Act*, R.S.O. 1990, c. S.22; the *Coroners Act*, R.S.O. 1990, c. 37; the *Arbitrations Act, 1991*, S.O. 1991, c. 17; and the *Public Inquiries Act*, R.S.O. 1990, c. P.41. Note that the Information and Privacy Commissioner has the power to make rules of procedure the Commissioner considers necessary: *PHIPA*, s. 59(1).

- the custodian, or
- the custodian's agent or former agent

is, or is expected to be, a party or witness. A health information custodian may only disclose personal health information under this provision, however, if the information "relates to or is a matter in issue" in the proceeding or contemplated proceeding.[214] Regulations under *PHIPA* may set out further requirements and restrictions on such disclosures.[215] A proceeding need not have been actually commenced in order for the custodian to be able to rely on this clause; it must, however, be "contemplated." The proceeding must evidently be actually and genuinely considered for this provision to apply.

Consider these situations. An orthodontist wishes to submit a description of the health services provided to a patient in a mediation in order to help settle a dispute over payment. An operator of a nursing home discloses personal health information to its insurer[216] to determine whether or not to settle a claim pertaining to a resident's allegation of negligence against the home. An ambulance attendant provides an eyewitness account to the prosecutor about a motor vehicle accident, including information about the state of the patient who the attendant transported to hospital from the scene of the accident. A patient's lawyer requests the patient's treating psychiatrist to provide a report to the lawyer about the state of the mental health of the lawyer's client to advance the client's case in a lawsuit.

PHIPA recognizes that health information custodians and their agents are often called upon to provide expert testimony or eyewitness accounts, in advance of or in preparation for a proceeding. In a prosecution it may be appropriate for a health information custodian to disclose such information to the prosecutor or to the accused's lawyer in preparation for the case. In a civil action, the plaintiff or the defendant, as the case may be, may seek to rely on a health information custodian or its agents for information about the subject matter of the action.

As set out in Chapter 9,[217] the interests of an agent may be separate from that of a health information custodian. This may be the case, for example,

---

214 *PHIPA*, s. 41(1)(a).

215 At the time of writing, no regulations have been prescribed under this provision.

216 The custodian may decide who its agents are. An insurance company may or may not be the custodian's agent. If an insurer is the custodian's agent, *PHIPA* provides a similar authority in the use section to enable the custodian to provide personal health information to the insurer: *PHIPA*, s. 37(1)(h).

217 See Section C(9), above.

where an agent is subject to discipline proceedings. *PHIPA* permits a custodian to disclose personal health information to an agent or former agent for the purpose of a proceeding or contemplated proceeding in which the agent or former agent is, or is expected to be, a party or a witness.[218] Where an agent or former agent receives personal health information under this clause in *PHIPA* for the purposes of a proceeding or contemplated proceeding, the agent or former agent is authorized to share this information with his or her professional advisor, if the advisor is under a professional duty of confidentiality, so that the advisor may provide the agent or former agent with advice or representation.[219]

Disclosures under this provision, however, are subject to all the restrictions discussed above,[220] such as common law privilege. Custodians should exercise caution in disclosing personal health information that may be subject to a privilege or for other reasons be subject to legal restrictions on its disclosure. A prudent custodian will limit its reliance on section 41(1)(a) of *PHIPA*, and leave more complex disclosures to be subject to section 41(1)(d), thus permitting a court or tribunal conducting the proceeding to determine any questions of legal privilege or other legal restrictions that may apply to the personal health information.

4) To a Litigation Guardian or Legal Representative

a) For the Purpose of Having the Person Appointed as a Litigation Guardian or Legal Representative

A health information custodian may disclose personal health information to a proposed litigation guardian or legal representative of the patient for the purpose of having the person appointed as such.[221]

Under the Ontario *Rules of Civil Procedure*,[222] an individual who is a "party under a disability"[223] requires a "litigation guardian" to conduct a civil proceeding on the individual's behalf. Unless there is some other proper person willing and able to act as litigation guardian, an individual's litigation guardian will

---

218 *PHIPA*, s. 41(1)(a).

219 *Ibid.*, s. 41(2). See note 81 and accompanying text in Chapter 9 for an explanation of "an advisor under a professional duty of confidentiality."

220 In Section M(1), above.

221 *PHIPA*, s. 41(1)(b).

222 *Rules of Civil Procedure*, above note 211, Rule 7, "Parties under Disability."

223 This phrase refers to a minor or an adult who is mentally incapable: *ibid.*, r. 7.04. An individual is a "minor" in Ontario if the individual is under eighteen years of age: *Age of Majority and Accountability Act*, R.S.O. 1990, c. A.7 s. 1.

be the Children's Lawyer[224] in the case of a minor,[225] or the Public Guardian and Trustee[226] in the case of a mentally incapable adult.[227] Court appointment of a litigation guardian is not required in order for such a person to commence a proceeding on behalf of an individual under disability.[228] However, such an appointment is generally required in order for a person to act as a litigation guardian for a defendant or respondent to a proceeding.[229]

A "litigation guardian" for a mentally incapable adult may also act on behalf of the adult where the adult is not a party in a proceeding, but requires separate representation in a proceeding, such as where the individual has an interest in an estate or trust. In the case of a minor who is not a party but requires representation because his or her interests may be affected by the proceeding, such as in the case of child protection proceedings or a dispute over custody involving the child, this function is usually performed by a court-appointed "legal representative" who is either the Children's Lawyer, or some other proper person who is willing and able to act as the individual's "legal representative."[230] Accordingly, the term "legal representative of the individual" in this clause of *PHIPA* does not necessarily mean the patient's lawyer; rather, the term means someone who intends to be officially appointed to represent the patient's interests in litigation.

A proposed litigation guardian or legal representative may require personal health information from a health information custodian about an individual, for example, so that the proposed guardian or representative may establish to the court that the individual is mentally incapable. Prior to disclosing personal health information under this clause, a health information custodian should require clear documentation from the requester to be satisfied that personal health information about the patient is required to facilitate such an appointment.

b) To a Litigation Guardian or Legal Representative to Participate in a Proceeding

PHIPA permits a health information custodian to disclose personal health information to a litigation guardian or legal representative who is authorized

---

224 See below Section P(6)(c) for an explanation of the Children's Lawyer.
225 See above note 218.
226 See below Section P(6)(b) for an explanation of the Public Guardian and Trustee.
227 *Rules of Civil Procedure*, above note 211, R. 7.04.
228 *Ibid.*, R. 7.02.
229 *Ibid.*, R. 7.03.
230 *Ibid.*, R. 7.04.

under the Ontario *Rules of Civil Procedure*,[231] or by a court order,[232] to commence, defend, or continue a proceeding on behalf of the patient or to represent the patient in a proceeding.[233]

For example, in a lawsuit pertaining to a motor vehicle accident, a litigation guardian may require access to records of personal health information about the patient whom the guardian is representing, in order to assess the nature and costs of the treatments needed by the patient who suffered injuries in the accident, so that the guardian may advance the patient's position in the lawsuit.

A health information custodian may exercise its discretion, however, and not rely on this clause in *PHIPA* to disclose personal health information to a litigation guardian or legal representative. For example, where a health information custodian is a party adverse in interest to a patient in a proceeding, nothing in this clause compels the custodian to disclose information about the patient to the patient's litigation guardian or legal representative in this situation absent an order or other legal requirement to do so.

N. DISCLOSURE OR TRANSFER TO A SUCCESSOR: SECTIONS 42(1) & (2)

1) Disclosure to a Potential Successor

PHIPA permits a health information custodian to disclose personal health information to a potential successor of the custodian, for the purpose of allowing the potential successor to assess and evaluate the operations of the custodian.[234] The *PHIPA* Regulation clarifies that the terms "potential successor" and "successor,"

---

231 *Ibid.*, Rule 7, "Parties under Disability."

232 For example, *Family Law Rules*, O. Reg. 114/99, Rule 4, made under the *Courts of Justice Act*, above note 211, where a court may authorize a person to represent a special party if the person is appropriate for the task and willing to act as representative. If there is no appropriate person willing to act as a special party's representative, the court may authorize the Children's Lawyer or the Public Guardian and Trustee to act as representative. A "special party" means, in R. 2, s. 2(2) of this regulation, a party who is a child or who is or appears to be mentally incapable for the purposes of the *Substitute Decisions Act, 1992*, S.O. 1992, c. 30 [*SDA*] but does not include a child in a custody, access, child protection, adoption or child support case.

233 *PHIPA*, s. 41(1)(c).

234 *Ibid.*, s. 42(1). During the public hearings on Bill 31, the Ontario Chiropractic Association noted that *PHIPA* did not expressly allow a health information custodian to provide a potential purchaser of the custodian's practice access to records of the practice as necessary prior to its sale. The Association submitted that

as these terms appear in section 42, mean a successor or potential successor that is a health information custodian or that will become a health information custodian if it becomes the successor.[235] In other words, the provisions for a transfer of records to a successor appear to apply only if the custodian's practice or operation is being taken over by a person who will be qualified to run it as a going concern. For example, a physiotherapist who intends to retire may disclose the records of personal health information of his or her patients to another physiotherapist who is considering purchasing the retiring physiotherapist's practice. This provision pertaining to a transfer does not provide authority for a disclosure or transfer of records to a person who is not a health information custodian or who will not subsequently operate as a custodian if the person becomes the successor.

Before any personal health information can be disclosed, the potential successor must first enter into an agreement with the custodian to keep the information confidential and secure and not to retain any of the information longer than is necessary for the purpose of the assessment or evaluation, in the event the parties do not complete the transfer.[236]

2) Transfer to a Successor with Notice

Once the potential successor becomes the actual successor of the custodian, the custodian may then transfer the records of personal health information relating to the practice or operations to the successor if the custodian makes reasonable efforts to give notice to the individuals to whom the records relate before trans-

---

Continuity of health care in Ontario remains heavily dependent on the ability of established chiropractors, physicians and other practitioners to transfer their practices to their successors at an appropriate market value. For many, the equity built into the practice is a key component of their retirement plans. Unless the prospective buyers, who are regulated health professionals, have the ability to review the health records, it will not be possible to establish the size and nature of a private health care practice.

[Ontario, Legislative Assembly, Standing Committee on General Government, *Official Report of Debates (Hansard)*, G-182 (5 February 2004) at 1150 (Dr. Bob Haig).] The Standing Committee on General Government amended the Bill at the second clause-by-clause review of Bill 31 to permit a health information custodian who is planning to sell or otherwise transfer his or her practice (or its operations, in the case of a hospital or long-term care facility, for example) to disclose patient records relating to the practice or operations to a potential successor to allow that potential successor to assess and evaluate the practice or operations: Ontario, Legislative Assembly, Standing Committee on General Government, *Official Report of Debates (Hansard)*, G-259 (28 April 2004) at 1650 (Kathleen Wynne).

235   *PHIPA* Regulation, above note 9, s. 1(10).

236   *PHIPA*, s. 42(1).

ferring the records, or if that is not reasonably possible, as soon as possible after transferring the records.[237] For example, an optician may notify his or her patients by mail that he or she will be moving his or her practice to another city and that he or she intends to transfer his or her records to another optician who will continue to practise from the optician's former place of business. Similarly, a health facility that is being closed or merged with another may transfer its records to another facility if the notice requirement is satisfied.

In some instances, it will be reasonably possible for a health information custodian to give notice to the patients to whom the records of personal health information relate on an individual basis. For example, a massage therapist who has been operating a practice for a short period of time may not have any difficulty in providing such notice to each patient, for example, by telephoning the patients or sending notices by mail. In such cases, contacting patients in these ways would involve the custodian making "reasonable efforts" to notify the patients of the transfer. In other instances, such as where a hospital is subject to closure, providing notice may involve notifying tens of thousands of patients. *PHIPA* does not require a health information custodian to provide notice to each patient on an individual basis.

A custodian may provide notice under *PHIPA* in a number of ways: by way of a letter to a patient,[238] by way of a notice posted in the custodian's office, or in the case of a larger custodian, by way of a notice posted in areas where there is significant patient contact, such as the admissions or emergency departments of a public hospital. In some situations, a general notice in a newspaper might be most reasonable, particularly where the records in question that are to be transferred were created many years ago.

Policies of professional governing bodies may provide further guidelines as to what steps must be taken with respect to records of personal health information on or before the transfer of such records to a successor. For example, guidelines published by the Royal College of Dental Surgeons of Ontario provide that a dentist's letter to patients explaining the transfer to a successor should point out that a copy of the patient record will be transferred to any dentist that the patient chooses, should the patient provide that instruction.[239]

---

237 *PHIPA*, s. 42(2).

238 Although individualized notice is in many ways preferable, it also raises a concern that the patient's personal health information may be exposed inadvertently to others who may gain access to the notice in one way or another. Custodians should consider this issue in determining what type of notice is appropriate in the circumstances.

239 *Guidelines: Change of Practice Ownership* (Toronto: Royal College of Dental Surgeons of Ontario, 2002), online: <www.rcdso.org/pdf/guidelines/change_practice.pdf>.

A health information custodian does not cease to be a health information custodian with respect to a record of personal health information until complete custody and control of the record, where applicable, passes to another person who is legally authorized to hold the record.[240] As a result, a health information custodian does not cease to be a custodian if the custodian ceases to provide health care but continues to retain records at the custodian's residence, for example.[241]

Where a custodian dies, the estate trustee[242] of the deceased custodian or the person who has assumed responsibility for the administration of the deceased custodian's estate, if the estate does not have an estate trustee, is deemed under the Act to be the health information custodian of the records of the deceased custodian, until such time as the custody and control of the records passes to another person who is legally authorized to hold the records. In this situation, the estate trustee or person who is responsible for the administration of the estate is obliged to fulfill the requirements with respect to transfers as set out in the Act.[243]

O. TRANSFER TO AN ARCHIVE: SECTION 42(3)

1) Transferring Records of Personal Health Information to an Archive

A health information custodian that is permitted to retain records[244] may do so only in a manner that is secure[245] and consistent with any specific professional standards[246] or rules under other legislation.[247] The custodian may retain

---

240 *PHIPA*, s. 3(11).

241 Once the person has become a health information custodian by virtue of *PHIPA*, s. 3(12), or in any other manner, then the person is bound by *PHIPA*, s. 3(11) and cannot simply resign the custodian function.

242 The estate trustee was in the past referred to either as an executor or an administrator of the estate, for example.

243 *PHIPA*, s. 3(12).

244 *PHIPA* does not require custodians to destroy records after a certain amount of time or when certain conditions are met. This contrasts with the *Personal Information Protection and Electronic Documents Act*, S.C. 2000, c. 5, Schedule 1, s. 4.5.3 [*PIPEDA*], which provides that personal information that is no longer required to fulfil the purpose(s) for which it was collected should be destroyed, erased, or made anonymous. *PHIPA* regulations may address minimum and maximum retention periods, but at the time of writing, none do so.

245 *PHIPA*, s. 13(1).

246 *Ibid.*, s. 9(2)(e).

247 *Ibid.*, ss. 7(2) & (3).

records in its own archives or records retention facility, or may contract this out to an agent to do so on behalf of the custodian, subject to the *PHIPA* rules governing agents.[248] Whether the custodian holds records itself, or another person acting on behalf of the custodian holds the records, the custodian is fully responsible for the records under *PHIPA*.[249]

The continuance of a health information custodian's duties with respect to records of personal health information[250] raises the question of how a health information custodian can divest itself of the responsibility for records.[251] Methods by which a custodian can discharge such responsibility include disposing of a record in a manner that destroys the information contained in the record,[252] or transferring complete custody and control of the record to a successor of the custodian, as discussed in the preceding section.[253] Further, a health information custodian may transfer complete custody and control of a record of personal health information to an archive that is not acting as an agent of the custodian.[254] Where a health information custodian wishes to divest itself of responsibility for records of personal health information, but destruction of the records is not appropriate and the custodian has no successor who is willing to take the records, the only option may be to transfer the records to an eligible archive independent of the custodian.

A custodian may transfer records to the Archives of Ontario,[255] or to an archive prescribed in a regulation under *PHIPA*.[256] Any such transfer requires the agreement of the receiving archives, meaning that the records cannot sim-

---

248 *PHIPA*, s. 17.

249 *Ibid.*, s. 17(1).

250 As noted at the end of Section N above.

251 Once a person becomes a health information custodian, the person cannot simply walk away from the accompanying responsibilities without either properly disposing of the records or transferring full custody and control of the records to another person in a manner authorized by law: *PHIPA*, s. 3(11).

252 This method for a health information custodian to relieve itself of responsibility is not referred to explicitly as such in the Act, but s. 37(1)(f) of *PHIPA* allows a custodian to use a record for the purpose of disposing of the information or for the purpose of de-identifying it. Once the information no longer identifies a patient, then it is no longer personal health information and hence no longer covered by the Act. Note that a health information custodian may be prevented or restricted from disposing of a record by rules of the professional governing body that applies to the custodian, or by the retention rule set out in s. 13(2) of *PHIPA*. At the time of writing, there are no regulations under s. 13(1) of *PHIPA* about the retention of records.

253 Under *PHIPA*, s. 42(2).

254 Under *ibid.*, s. 42(3).

255 *Ibid.*, s. 42(3)(a).

256 *Ibid.*, s. 42(3)(b).

ply be handed off to archives without the active acceptance by the archive of the records.[257] As the Archives of Ontario, which is established under the *Archives Act*,[258] primarily serves provincial governmental bodies, it will not be available to take records from most custodians.[259]

Under the regulations, broad classes of archives other than the Archives of Ontario are authorized to accept transfers of personal health information. To be eligible to receive such transfers of personal health information, an archive must

- meet the description set out in *PHIPA*, which is that its functions "include the collection and preservation of records of historical or archival importance";[260]
- have in place reasonable measures to ensure the security of the records;[261]
- have in place a policy that allows patients whose records of personal health information the archive holds to have reasonable access to their records;[262]

---

257 *PHIPA*, s. 42(3). This does not however appear to require a contract or written agreement.

258 R.S.O. 1990, c. A.27.

259 The Archives of Ontario also has a mandate to pursue "the discovery, collection and preservation of material having any bearing upon the history of Ontario," "the collecting of municipal, school and church records," and other general objects set out in s. 5 of the *Archives Act*, but these generally may not be applied in practice to extend to most bulk collections of health records from health information custodians.

260 *PHIPA*, s. 42(3)(b). Furthermore, the custodian's transfer of the records to the archive must be made for the purpose of that function.

261 *PHIPA* Regulation, above note 9, s. 14(1)(a). The standard set out here parallels the standard that health information custodians are required to meet under s. 12 of *PHIPA*. This clause of the regulation requires that the person must have "in place reasonable measures to ensure that personal health information in the person's custody or control is protected against theft, loss and unauthorized use or disclosure and to ensure that the records containing the information are protected against unauthorized copying, modification or disposal."

262 *PHIPA* Regulation, *ibid.*, s. 14(1)(b). What constitutes "reasonable access" is not defined. Presumably, if the access policy of the archive mirrored that set out in Part V of *PHIPA*, it would be considered reasonable by *PHIPA* standards, but the language "reasonable access" may provide more latitude for archives and allow them to retain existing access policies or to have policies that are less elaborate than that set out in *PHIPA*. One significant difference from the *PHIPA* access scheme is that the Information and Privacy Commissioner does not have oversight over requests for access to records of personal health information held by an archive, since refusals of reasonable access are not a contravention of *PHIPA* by the archive, but may instead have the result that the archive does not comply with the Regulation and is obligated under s. 14(2) of the Regulation to transfer the records instead to a compliant archive. However, the Commissioner does have the power to deal with complaints that the archive is in contravention of the *PHIPA* Regulation by, for example, failing to transfer the records that it holds to a compliant archive as required by s. 14(2) of the regulation in the event that the archive ceasesg to comply with the requirements of s. 14(1) of the Regulation.

- make publicly available a written statement that identifies the mandate and "organizational links and affiliations" of the archive[263] that describes the information practices[264] of the archive, and that sets out how a patient may obtain access to the patient's record with the archive[265] and how anyone can make a complaint to the archive and to the Information and Privacy Commissioner;[266] and
- register with the Commissioner the archive's intention to act as an archive for personal health information under *PHIPA*, and provide the Commissioner with the publicly available written statement and any further information reasonably requested by the Commissioner.[267]

An archive that fulfils all of these requirements is eligible to receive transfers of records from health information custodians under *PHIPA*.[268] However, if the archive ceases to comply with any of the above requirements, it is required to immediately transfer the records that it received under *PHIPA* to an archive that does comply, or to the Archives of Ontario.[269]

Persons who are not health information custodians and who received personal health information from a health information custodian, whether pursuant to a patient's consent or under any of the provisions of *PHIPA* that permit disclosure of personal health information without patient consent, are also authorized to transfer any records containing personal health informa-

---

263 *PHIPA* Regulation, *ibid.*, s. 14(1)(c)(iii). These terms are not further defined, but appear to require a very general description of the role of the archive, and by and for whom the archive is operated.

264 *PHIPA* Regulation, *ibid.*, s. 14(1)(c)(i). This term is defined in the Act, s. 2, specifically in relation to health information custodians, but the intention is apparently to have a similar concept apply here, since no further definition of this distinctive term is provided.

265 *PHIPA* Regulation, *ibid.*, s. 14(1)(c)(ii). See above note 248.

266 *PHIPA* Regulation, *ibid.*, s. 14(1)(c)(iv). This appears to require the archive to have a policy in place for dealing with complaints about how it carries out its functions.

267 *PHIPA* Regulation, *ibid.*, s. 14(1)(d).

268 Section 42(3)(b) of *PHIPA* authorizes a health information custodian to transfer personal health information to an archive that meets such prescribed criteria "in the prescribed circumstances." The *PHIPA* Regulation, *ibid.*, provides that "a health information custodian may transfer records of personal health information" to such an archive without limitations on the circumstances, thus apparently indicating that any circumstances are to be considered "prescribed circumstances" for the purposes of s. 43(3)(b).

269 *PHIPA* Regulation, *ibid.*, s. 14(2). Once again, this can only be done with the agreement of the proposed accepting archive.

tion, including the health number,[270] to the Archives of Ontario or an archive meeting the criteria discussed above.[271]

An archive receiving a transfer of a record of personal health information under either *PHIPA* or its regulation is authorized to collect any health number that may be contained in the records being transferred.[272]

2) Subsequent Uses and Disclosures of Personal Health Information Held by an Archive

An archive that is not a health information custodian that receives a transfer of records of personal health information from a health information custodian[273] is generally[274] subject to the "recipient rules" under *PHIPA*.[275] The general effect of the recipient rules is that such a recipient is not permitted to use or disclose the personal health information except for the purpose for which the custodian was allowed to disclose it to the recipient,[276] or where the recipient needs to use or disclose the information for the purpose of carrying out a statutory or legal duty.[277] The ability of an archive that is subject to this rule to use and disclose personal health information under this rule is limited, since the purpose of the disclosure was for "the collection and preservation of records of

---

270 Health numbers are specifically mentioned since non-health information custodians require specific authorization to disclose health numbers, under *PHIPA*, s. 34(3), while health information custodians can disclose the health number together with other personal health information where authorized to disclose personal health information.

271 *PHIPA* Regulation, above note 9, s. 14(3). Again, this can only be done with the agreement of the proposed accepting archive. Without this provision, *PHIPA*, s. 49(1) may restrict such disclosures.

272 *PHIPA* Regulation, *ibid.*, s. 14(4)(a).

273 Under *PHIPA*, s. 42(3)(b). This does not apply to records transferred to an archive under *PHIPA* Regulation, *ibid.*, ss. 14(2) & (3) since s. 49 applies only to personal health information that was received directly from a health information custodian.

274 An exception to this rule is that an archive that is subject to *FIPPA/MFIPPA*, including the Archives of Ontario and presumably any municipal archive, is not subject to the recipient rules: *PHIPA*, s. 49(5).

275 The recipient rules are set out in s. 49 and apply to anyone other than a *FIPPA/MFIPPA* institution that receives personal health information from a health information custodian.

276 *PHIPA*, s. 49(1)(a). Where a health information custodian disclosed the information to the recipient prior to *PHIPA* coming into force, when custodians were therefore not authorized by *PHIPA* to make disclosures, the *PHIPA* Regulation provides that the recipient may use and disclose the information for the purpose for which it was originally disclosed to the recipient: *PHIPA* Regulation, above note 9, s. 20.

277 *PHIPA*, s. 49(1)(b).

historical or archival importance."[278] Authorizing the use and disclosure of information for this purpose does not clearly authorize much in the way of ongoing uses and disclosures.[279]

Under the *PHIPA* Regulation, however, each personal health information archive[280] is specifically authorized to use and disclose personal health information, including health numbers, for research purposes as if it were a health information custodian.[281] Further details on the requirements for using and disclosing personal health information for research is set out in Chapter 11.[282] The essential requirement in *PHIPA* for the use and disclosure of personal health information without consent of the patients to whom the information relates is that the research plan of the archive or researcher, as the case may be, be approved by a research ethics board that complies with the requirements of the Act and the regulation.[283] Alternatively, a health information custodian may use or disclose personal health information for the purpose of carrying out research without the approval of the research ethics board pursuant to the valid consent of the patients to whom the information relates,[284] or under special transitional provisions, where applicable.[285] The provision allowing uses and disclosures pursuant to a valid patient consent generally provides a person who is not a health information custodian and who receives personal health information from a custodian with an additional authority for uses and disclosures of personal health information not just for research, but for any other purpose, provided valid consent is obtained.[286]

---

278 This is the language in s. 42(3)(b).

279 This provision may arguably give authority to provide the information back to the health information custodian, in case the custodian needs the information to be returned, though that would appear to be permitted in any case under s. 1(3) of the *PHIPA* Regulation, above note 9, that permits personal health information to be provided back to the person who initially provided it. It may arguably provide authority to disclose the information to patients or health care providers who need it for the ongoing treatment of the patient. Disclosure of patient information back to the patient is apparently authorized under s. 14(1)(b) of the *PHIPA* Regulation, and also under s. 21(1)(b) of that regulation since the patient necessarily consents to any disclosure of the personal health information requested by the patient.

280 That is, an archive of the class prescribed under *PHIPA*, s. 42(3)(b). This provision in the *PHIPA* Regulation does not apply to the Archives of Ontario, which continues to be subject to *FIPPA* with respect to uses and disclosures of the information for research purposes.

281 *PHIPA* Regulation, above note 9, ss. 14(4) & (5).

282 See Chapter 11, Section B below.

283 *PHIPA*, s. 44(1).

284 *PHIPA* Regulation, above note 9, s. 21(1)(b).

285 *PHIPA*, s. 44(8) or (12).

286 *PHIPA* Regulation, above note 9, s. 21(1)(b).

An archive that has received records of personal health information under *PHIPA* or the *PHIPA* Regulation is also permitted to disclose this information to a prescribed planning entity[287] or a health data institute[288] as if the archive were a health information custodian.[289]

P. DISCLOSURES RELATED TO OTHER ACTS: SECTION 43

1) Generally

PHIPA complements a variety of existing legal frameworks that relate to health information custodians and personal health information.[290] A number of the provisions that reflect this complementary approach are set out in section 43 of the Act. The disclosures that this section permits can be divided into two categories. The first category includes disclosures of personal health information related to other Acts or laws generally, such as

- disclosures permitted or required by law;[291] and
- disclosures to legally authorized investigators.[292]

The second category of disclosures that this section permits relates to specific contexts, and includes disclosures:

- for the purpose of determining, assessing, or confirming a patient's capacity;[293]
- to a professional governing body for administration and enforcement activities for which it is statutorily responsible;[294]
- for the statutory functions of specific entities related to children and vulnerable adults;[295] and
- by *FIPPA/MFIPPA* custodians under certain specific sections of *FIPPA* or *MFIPPA*.[296]

Each of these categories of permitted disclosures will be discussed in turn.

---

287 Under *PHIPA*, s. 45.
288 Under *ibid.*, s. 47.
289 *PHIPA* Regulation, above note 9, s. 14(4)(c). See Chapter 11, Sections D & E, for more details about the rules applicable to these types of disclosures.
290 This theme is identified and explored in Chapter 3, Section B(3).
291 *PHIPA*, s. 43(1)(h).
292 *Ibid.*, s. 43(1)(g).
293 *Ibid.*, s. 43(1)(a).
294 *Ibid.*, ss. 43(1)(b), (c), & (d).
295 *Ibid.*, s. 43(1)(e).
296 *Ibid.*, s. 43(1)(f).

2) Where Permitted or Required by Law: Section 43(1)(h)

a) Generally

Consistent with the rules pertaining to the collection[297] and use[298] of personal health information, *PHIPA* authorizes a health information custodian to disclose personal health information without the patient's consent if the custodian is permitted or required to do so by law or by a treaty, agreement, or arrangement made under an Act of Ontario or an Act of Canada.[299]

The scope of the phrase "permitted or required by law" is reviewed in Chapter 3.[300] As discussed there,[301] a fundamental theme in *PHIPA* is the preservation of existing rules set out in other legislation covering specific parts of the health sector for collections, uses, and disclosures of personal health information. Thus, the phrase comprises, at a minimum, other Ontario and federal statutes, and their regulations. It also likely comprises orders of a court or tribunal. Further, it may authorize a health information custodian to disclose personal health information where such a disclosure is authorized at common law. The inclusion of the word "permitted" with the word "required" expands the scope of the authorities that this provision includes considerably.[302] Regulations made under *PHIPA* may impose requirements and place restrictions on disclosures made under this clause.[303]

---

297 *PHIPA*, s. 36(1)(h), see Chapter 8, Section C(8).

298 *Ibid.*, s. 37(1)(k), see Chapter 9, Section C(12).

299 *Ibid.*, s. 43(1)(h).

300 Chapter 3, Section B(3)(b).

301 *Ibid.*, Section B(3)(a).

302 Other privacy legislation does not authorize disclosures "permitted by law." Under *FIPPA* and *MFIPPA*, the institution is permitted to disclose personal information without the individual's consent in order to "*comply* with an Act of the Legislature or an Act of Parliament or a treaty, agreement or arrangement thereunder.": *FIPPA*, above note 12, s. 42(e); *MFIPPA*, above note 12, s. 32(e). In the view of the Ontario Information and Privacy Commissioner, legislation must impose an express duty to disclose information at issue in order to satisfy the requirement that the disclosure "complies" with the Act in question. See, for example, Order PC-990033, Ministry of Consumer and Commercial Relations (20 December 2000), online: <www.ipc.on.ca>. *PIPEDA*, above note 244, s. 7(3)(i) allows an organization to disclose personal information without the individual's knowledge or consent where such disclosure is "required by law." This clause has been interpreted by the Ontario Superior Court to include the rules of court and at trial: *Ferenczy v. MCI Medical Clinics* (2004), 70 O.R. (3d) 277 at para. 33 (S.C.).

303 *PHIPA*, s. 43(1)(h) provides at the outset that a disclosure under this clause is "subject to the requirements and restrictions, if any, that are prescribed." At the time of writing there are no such regulations in place.

Sometimes, another Act or regulation that applies to a health information custodian specifies that the custodian is required to keep information secret or confidential, unless authorized by that particular Act or regulation to disclose the information. Such an Act or regulation then usually enumerates exceptions to this requirement of secrecy. *PHIPA* explicitly interprets these exceptions as permissible disclosures, in accordance with the apparent legislative intention behind such provisions. Where such a secrecy provision applies to a health information custodian, the health information custodian is authorized to disclose personal health information in the circumstances as set out in the exceptions.[304] It is also important to note that the law, such as a number of the statutes that are listed below, may directly authorize a custodian's agents to disclose personal health information in stated circumstances. In such instances, an agent holding personal health information in the course of carrying out its duties for a health information custodian does not require permission of the custodian to disclose the information that the agent is directly "permitted or required by law" to disclose.[305]

b)   Where Another Statute Permits or Requires a Disclosure

A number of statutes permit or require a health information custodian to disclose personal health information for purposes set out in those statutes. Usually, statutes will not specifically refer to disclosure of "personal health information." More commonly, legislation will refer to the disclosure of "personal information" or "information."[306] Further, legislation will not necessarily explicitly set out that information may be disclosed without consent, but the authorization may be implicit. Moreover, some statutes that authorize disclosure of personal health information apply to only some health information cus-

---

304   *PHIPA*, s. 43(2): This section provides that for the purpose of s. 43(1)(h), if an Act of Ontario, an Act of Canada, or a regulation made under any of those Acts specifically provides that information is exempt, under stated circumstances, from a confidentiality or secrecy requirement, that provision shall be deemed to permit the disclosure of the information in stated circumstances. For example, see the *HPPA*, above note 91, s. 39(1). This is consistent with the apparent policy of the legislation that *PHIPA* prevails over other legislation, as discussed in Chapter 3, Secion A(2).

305   *PHIPA*, s. 17(2). An agent's ability to do so may be restricted by a regulation under *PHIPA*. At the time of writing there are no such regulations in place.

306   For example, the Ministry of Health and Long-Term Care is authorized to disclose personal information in a number of its statutes: *HIA*, above note 42, ss. 4.1(3) & (4); *IHFA*, above note 23, ss. 37.1(3)–(7); and *Commitment to the Future of Medicare Act, 2004*, S.O. 2004, c. 5, ss. 15(3)–(5). Unless a clear contrary intention is evident in the context, the term "personal information" includes "personal health information."

todians, while others are of general application and as such are relevant to all health information custodians. Whether the words in a particular statute authorize the disclosure of personal health information without consent will depend on the intent and context of the specific provision in question.

i) Permissible Disclosure Pursuant to Another Act

If a proposed disclosure does not appear to be authorized in other disclosure provisions of *PHIPA*, a health information custodian should review legislation that applies to the custodian to determine whether that legislation would authorize the disclosure in question. The following are some examples of health sector-specific disclosures of information that are permitted in other Acts.

- A health information custodian that operates an ambulance service may disclose personal health information to one of an upper-tier municipality, a local municipality, and a delivery agent;[307] as well as to a medical director,[308] where the disclosure is reasonably necessary for purposes relating to the discharge or exercise by the recipients of the information of their duties or powers under the *Ambulance Act*.[309]
- A health information custodian that is a "service provider" within the meaning of the *Long-Term Care Act, 1994*,[310] is permitted to disclose a record of personal health information to the Minister of Health and Long-Term Care to enable the Minister to

---

307 A "delivery agent" under the *Ambulance Act*, R.S.O. 1990, c. A.19, s. 1(1) means an organization designated as such by the Minister of Health and Long-Term Care under ss. 6.7 or 6.10 of that Act. Generally, the delivery agent will be an upper-tier municipality or a local municipality, (both terms defined in that Act), but it can also be an agency, board, or commission established by the province. If the Minister does not designate a delivery agent for certain areas, the Minister may be deemed to be the delivery agent.

308 Under s. 1 of the *Ambulance Act, ibid.*, a medical director means a physician designated by a base hospital as the medical director of a base hospital program. Base hospitals are designated by the Minister of Health and Long-Term Care to monitor the quality of the care provided by ambulance services in the regions and districts established by the Minister and perform such other functions as may be assigned to them by regulation (ss. 1 and 4(2)(d)).

309 *Ambulance Act, ibid.*, s. 19(2). The purposes are further set out in s. 19(2) as relating to the provision, administration, management, operation, use, inspection, investigation, or regulation of ambulance services or to the enforcement of the *Ambulance Act* or its regulations.

310 *LTCA*, above note 23, s. 2. See Chapter 2, Section B(1)(a)(ii), for an explanation of the term "service provider."

1. ensure compliance with that Act, its regulations, or an agreement made under the Act for the provision of community services[311] or a term or condition imposed by the Minister under that Act;

2. monitor and evaluate community services provided by service providers;

3. monitor and assess the health, safety, and well-being of persons applying for or receiving community services;

4. enforce the right to which the Minister is subrogated under the Act;[312] and

5. comply with federal-provincial cost-sharing requirements.[313]

- An officer in charge of a psychiatric facility[314] may disclose personal health information about a patient to anyone for the purposes of examining, assessing, observing, or detaining the patient in accordance with the *Mental Health Act*.[315]

ii) Required Disclosure Pursuant to Another Act

A number of statutes require a health information custodian to disclose personal health information. *PHIPA* does not interfere with a requirement to disclose personal health information imposed on a health information custodian by another Act.[316] The following are examples of the kinds of required disclosures that can be found in other legislation.[317]

- Pursuant to the federal *Aeronautics Act*, where a physician or an optometrist believes on reasonable grounds that a patient who is a flight crew member, an air traffic controller, or other holder of a Canadian aviation document

---

311 *LTCA, ibid.*, s. 4(c). See Chapter 2, Section B(1)(a)(ii), for an explanation of the term "community service."

312 *LTCA, ibid.*, s. 59.5.

313 *Ibid.*, s. 32, which permits a service provider to disclose a record of personal health information to the Minister of Health and Long-Term Care to enable the Minister to exercise a power under s. 64 of that Act.

314 An "officer in charge" is a defined term in the *Mental Health Act* and means the officer who is responsible for the administration and management of a psychiatric facility: *MHA*, above note 23, s. 1(1). In the three Crown-operated psychiatric facilities, the officer in charge is the health information custodian: *PHIPA*, s. 3(2). In psychiatric facilities that are operated by a corporate board, the "officer in charge" would be an agent of the person who operates the psychiatric facility (which is the health information custodian): *PHIPA*, s. 3(1)[4][i].

315 *MHA*, above note 23, s. 35(2).

316 *PHIPA*, s. 6(3)(b) provides that a provision permitting a health information custodian to disclose personal health information without the consent of the individual does not relieve the custodian from a legal requirement to disclose the information.

317 Additional examples are identified in the *OHA Privacy Toolkit*, above note 145, Tab 4 at 60–62.

that imposes standards of medical or optometric fitness, the practitioner must, if in his or her opinion the patient has a medical or optometric condition that is likely to constitute a hazard to aviation safety, inform a designated medical advisor of the opinion and the reasons on which the opinion is based.[318]

- Under the *Child and Family Services Act*, any person who believes on reasonable grounds that a child is or may be in need of protection shall forthwith report the belief and the information upon which it is based to a children's aid society.[319] Further, any person who in the course of his or her official or professional duties, has reasonable grounds to suspect that a child is or may be suffering or may have suffered abuse, must report to a children's aid society the suspicion and the information upon which that suspicion is based.[320]

- The *Coroners Act* requires every person who has reason to believe that a deceased person died (1) as a result of violence, misadventure, negligence, misconduct, or malpractice; (2) by unfair means; (3) during pregnancy or following pregnancy; (4) suddenly and unexpectedly; (5) from disease or sickness for which he or she has not been treated by a legally qualified medical practitioner; (6) from any cause other than disease; or (7) under circumstances that may require investigation, to immediately report the facts and circumstances to a coroner or a police officer.[321]

- As outlined in Section J above, many health information custodians have statutory obligations to report cases of various diseases to a medical officer of health, as set out in the *Health Protection and Promotion Act*.[322]

- Pursuant to the provisions of the *Highway Traffic Act*, a physician and an optometrist must report to the Registrar of Motor Vehicles the name, address, and medical condition of a person sixteen years of age or older who, in the opinion of the practitioner, is suffering from a condition that makes it dangerous for the person to operate a motor vehicle.[323]

---

318 *Aeronautics Act*, R.S.C. 1985, c. A-2, s. 6.5.

319 *CFSA*, above note 168, s. 27(2).

320 *Ibid.*, s. 72(3). Section 72(9) of the *CFSA* explicitly clarifies that this obligation prevails over *PHIPA*, but even without this provision the disclosure would still be required by virtue of *PHIPA*, s. 43(1)(h).

321 *Coroners Act*, R.S.O. 1990, c. C.37, s. 10.

322 *HPPA*, above note 91, ss. 25–34: Health information custodians to whom these provisions apply include physicians, chiropractors, dentists, nurses, pharmacists, optometrists, naturopaths, and medical laboratory operators. An administrator of a hospital and a superintendent of an institution also have certain reporting obligations under that Act.

323 *Highway Traffic Act*, R.S.O. 1990, c. H.8, s. 203 (physician), s. 204 (optometrist).

- Under the *Nursing Homes Act*, any person who has reasonable grounds to suspect that a resident of a nursing home has suffered or may suffer harm as a result of unlawful conduct, improper or incompetent treatment or care, or neglect must immediately report the suspicion and the information upon which it was based to the Director of Nursing Homes.[324]
- Under the provisions of the *Workplace Safety and Insurance Act, 1997*, every health care practitioner[325] who provides health care to a worker claiming benefits under the insurance plan or who is consulted with respect to his or her health care must promptly give the Workplace Safety and Insurance Board such information relating to the worker as the Board may require.[326] Further, every hospital or health facility that provides health care to a worker claiming benefits under the insurance plan has a comparable duty.[327]

c) Where a Disclosure Is Permitted or Required by Regulation

Section 43(1)(h) also pertains to regulations under Acts that permit or require a health information custodian to disclose personal health information.[328] Examples of such authorized disclosures under regulations include the following:

- Regulations under the three long-term care facility statutes continue to enable such facilities to disclose residents' information to persons appointed by the Director of Nursing Homes for the purpose of assessing and classifying residents to determine the level of care required by them, and for the purpose of determining and planning for the care that may be required, in the future, by such residents.[329]
- Pursuant to regulations under the *Ministry of Correctional Services Act*,[330] a "health care professional," who is a physician or a nurse[331] must immediately report to the superintendent of the correctional facility whenever an

---

324 *NHA*, above note 23, s. 25. The Director of Nursing Homes is an employee of the Ministry of Health and Long-Term Care.

325 In the *Workplace Safety and Insurance Act, 1997*, S.O. 1997, c. 16, Sch. A, s. 2 [*WSIA*], a health care practitioner means a member of the college of a health profession as defined in the *RHPA*, above note 180, a drugless practitioner regulated under the *DPA*, above note 180, or a social worker.

326 *WSIA*, ibid., s. 37(1).

327 *Ibid.*, s. 37(2).

328 See Chapter 3, Section B(3)(b).

329 *General*, R.R.O. 1990, Reg. 69, made under the *CIA*, above note 23, s. 29(4); *General*, R.R.O. 1990, Reg. 637, made under the *HARHA*, above note 23, s. 2(4); *General*, R.R.O. 1990, Reg. 832, made under the *NHA*, above note 23, s. 95(2).

330 *MCSA*, above note 170.

331 *General*, R.R.O. 1990, Reg. 778, s. 1, definition of "health care professional."

inmate is seriously ill.[332] Further, when an inmate is injured, a health care professional must make a written report to the superintendent about the nature of the injury and the treatment provided.[333] A health care professional who examines an inmate who claims to be unable to work because of illness or disability and is of the opinion that the inmate is unfit to work, must immediately report the fact to the superintendent.[334]

- Pursuant to regulations under the *Mental Health Act*,[335] the officer in charge of a psychiatric facility must notify a rights advisor[336] about a patient where a community treatment order pertaining to the patient has been issued, where a patient has been found incapable to make a treatment decision under the *Health Care Consent Act, 1996*,[337] or where a patient has been determined incapable of consenting to a collection, use, or disclosure of personal health information, in the circumstances set out in those regulations.[338]

- Further, the regulations made under the *Mental Health Act* provide for communications between a police officer and a psychiatric facility's staff in circumstances where the police officer brings a person to the facility. Pursuant to those regulations, an officer in charge of a psychiatric facility or his or her delegate must ensure that a decision is made as soon as is reasonably possible as to whether the facility will take custody of such a person. For the purpose of making this decision, the regulations require that facility staff consult

---

332 *Ibid.*, s. 4(3). Although the physician or nurse may be an employee within the facility, in the circumstances, such a physician or nurse, as a health information custodian, would be disclosing personal health information to the superintendent of the facility, a non-health information custodian.

333 *Ibid.*, s. 4(4).

334 *Ibid.*, s. 4(5). *PHIPA* further permits a health information custodian to disclose personal health information to a superintendent of a correctional facility to assist the facility to make a decision concerning arrangements for the provision of health care to the inmate, for example. See further discussion about *PHIPA*, ss. 40(2) & (3) in Section L above.

335 See above note 23.

336 A rights advisor is a person who has successfully completed a training program to provide rights advice and has been designated to perform this function by a psychiatric facility or the Minister of Health and Long-Term Care.

337 See above note 50.

338 *General*, R.R.O. Reg. 741, ss. 14.3, 15, & 15.1. Other obligations are set out in the statute itself, such as the requirement that an officer in charge notify a rights advisor where a patient has been involuntarily admitted to the psychiatric facility: *MHA*, above note 23, s. 38(1). For more information about functions of rights advisors, see *Personal Health Information Protection Act, 2004 and Rights Advice under the Mental Health Act and its Regulations*, online: <www.health.gov.on.ca/english/providers/legislation/priv_legislation/advice_under_mentalhealth3.pdf>.

with the police officer, communicate to the police officer any delay in making the decision, and promptly inform the police officer of the decision.[339]

- Pursuant to the regulations made under the *Public Hospitals Act*,[340] a public hospital, when requested to do so by the Minister of Health and Long-Term Care, must provide information (1) from records of personal health information, including x-ray films, to Cancer Care Ontario; (2) from records of personal health information to a person for purposes of information and data collection, organization, and analysis; and(3) from records of personal health information to a physician assessor appointed by the Ministry of Health and Long-Term Care, for the purposes of evaluating applications to the Underserviced Area Program.[341]

- The regulation made under *PHIPA* also authorizes health information custodians to disclose personal health information in certain circumstances. For example, the *PHIPA* Regulation permits the Canadian Blood Services to disclose personal health information about a deceased individual who has received blood or blood products to the individual's relative or estate trustee for the purpose of determining eligibility for compensation.[342]

d) Where a Disclosure Is Permitted or Required by Law Other Than Legislation

As set out in Chapter 3, the scope of the phrase as "permitted or required by law" is not entirely certain.[343] In addition to authorizing a health information custodian to disclose personal health information as authorized under Ontario and federal statutes (including their regulations), the phrase would likely authorize a health information custodian to disclose personal health information pursuant to an order of a court or tribunal.[344] It may also authorize disclosures of personal health information where they are authorized at common law. However, given the scope of the disclosures permitted by other provisions of *PHIPA* — for example, to avoid

---

339   Reg. 741, *ibid.*, s. 7.2.

340   See above note 23.

341   Reg. 965, above note 112, s. 23, made under the *PHA*, *ibid.* The Underserviced Area Program of the Ministry of Health and Long-Term Care provides incentives to health care professionals to locate their practices in a part of Ontario that has been designated as in need of recruitment and retention of professionals. Under the program, communities apply for the designation and are eligible if they meet specific criteria, online: <www.health.gov.on.ca/english/providers/program/uap/about/designation.html>.

342   *PHIPA* Regulation, above note 9, s. 25(5). This provision of the regulation appears to be made under *PHIPA*, s. 73(1)(n).

343   Chapter 3, Section B(3)(b).

344   Although, the provisions of *PHIPA*, s. 41(1) would also be of relevance. See Section M above.

harm, for the purposes of a proceeding, and where permitted by other legislation — there may not be many practical implications to this possibility.[345]

e) Where a Disclosure Is Made Pursuant to a Treaty, Agreement, or Arrangement Made Under an Act

PHIPA permits a health information custodian to disclose personal health information where the disclosure is permitted "by a treaty, agreement or arrangement made under an Act [of Ontario] or an Act of Canada."[346] For example, under the *Ministry of Health and Long-Term Care Act*, the Minister of Health and Long-Term Care "may enter into agreements for the provision of health services and equipment required therefor and for the payment of remuneration for such health services on a basis other than fee for service."[347] Where the Minister enters into such an agreement with a health information custodian, it would appear that if such an agreement authorized the health information custodian to disclose personal health information to the Minister or other person, the custodian could rely on this authority in *PHIPA* to disclose the information.[348]

3) To a Person Carrying Out a Legally Authorized Inspection, Investigation, or Similar Procedure: Section 43(1)(g)

a) Generally

A health information custodian may disclose personal health information to a person carrying out an inspection, investigation, or similar procedure that is authorized by a warrant, by or under *PHIPA*, or by or under an Act of Ontario or Canada in order to comply with the warrant or to facilitate the inspection, investigation, or similar procedure.[349]

As indicated in previous chapters,[350] the *Charter* may also be relevant to a custodian's disclosures of personal health information pursuant to a statutory

---

345 See the discussion of "duty to warn" in Section K above. Note *Ferenczy v. MCI Medical Clinics*, above note 302, where the court gave a broad interpretation to the provision in *PIPEDA*, above note 244, that permits an organization to disclose personal information as "required by law."

346 *PHIPA*, s. 43(1)(h). A similar phrase is found in *FIPPA*, above note 12, s. 42(e) and *MFIPPA*, above note 12, s. 32(e).

347 R.S.O. 1990, c. M.26, s. 6.

348 Another example of such an agreement is that authorized under the *Nursing Homes Act*, above note 23, as explained in Chapter 3, Section B(3)(b).

349 *PHIPA*, s. 43(1)(g). The permission to disclose personal health information without a patient's consent in these circumstances may become subject to requirements and restrictions as set out in regulations: *PHIPA*, s. 43(1)(g). At the time of writing, no regulations have been prescribed under this section.

350 Chapter 1, Section B(3) and Chapter 3, Section B(2).

requirement or power , particularly when the disclosure is to or by a government or investigative body. Where a health information custodian discloses records of personal health information, in which a patient has a reasonable expectation of privacy, to a government or investigative body, or where such a body requires a custodian to disclose such records, the body's collection of the records may amount to an unreasonable search or seizure contrary to section 8 of the *Charter*,[351] particularly where the custodian collected the information for another purpose, such as the provision of health care. Evidence obtained by a government or other investigative body in violation of the *Charter* may be excluded from a proceeding and other remedies may apply.[352] Due to these significant consequences, health information custodians and such bodies must consider the *Charter* in disclosing or seeking the disclosure of personal health information in connection with inspections, investigations, and similar procedures.

b) Inspection, Investigation, or Similar Procedure Authorized by a Warrant

PHIPA authorizes a health information custodian to disclose a patient's personal health information "for the purpose of complying with" a warrant.[353] A justice of the peace[354] may issue a warrant to a police officer or an official who is authorized to act upon the warrant either under federal[355] or provincial[356]

---

351 Section 8 of the *Charter*, above note 149, provides: "Everyone has the right to be secure against unreasonable search or seizure." In *R. v. Dersch*, [1993] 3 S.C.R. 768, where the police requested a hospital to provide the results of a blood alcohol test done on a highway accident victim for medical reasons, the Supreme Court of Canada held this to be an unreasonable search, and the information was excluded from evidence at the proceeding.

352 The *Charter, ibid.*, provides, regarding remedies for violation:

> 24. (1) Anyone whose rights or freedoms, as guaranteed by this *Charter*, have been infringed or denied may apply to a court of competent jurisdiction to obtain such remedy as the court considers appropriate and just in the circumstances.
>
> (2) Where, in proceedings under subsection (1), a court concludes that evidence was obtained in a manner that infringed or denied any rights or freedoms guaranteed by this *Charter*, the evidence shall be excluded if it is established that, having regard to all the circumstances, the admission of it in the proceedings would bring the administration of justice into disrepute.

353 *PHIPA*, s. 43(1)(g). In the context of *PHIPA*, a "warrant" refers to a search warrant (as opposed to a warrant for committal of a person, for example).

354 Or provincial court judge (as per *Criminal Code*, above note 137, definition in s. 2 "justice").

355 Under the *Criminal Code, ibid.*, s. 487, a justice may issue a search warrant where there are reasonable grounds to believe that an offence under the *Criminal Code* or any other Act of Parliament has been or is suspected to have been committed.

356 *Provincial Offences Act*, R.S.O. 1990, c. P.33, s. 158, which allows a justice to issue a warrant to allow a person named in the warrant to search premises for "anything upon or in respect of which an offence has been or is suspected to have been commit-

jurisdiction, as the case may be. A warrant may authorize the holder of the warrant to enter premises and to seize records and other tangible property as set out in the warrant. Where the custodian objects to complying with a warrant, the custodian may need to pursue judicial remedies to quash it.

A health information custodian who is served with a warrant should review the scope of the warrant to determine what exact records of personal health information the custodian must disclose. A warrant in itself does not authorize a health information custodian to disclose personal health information orally. However, to the extent the language of this provision in *PHIPA* also allows a disclosure "for the purpose of facilitating the investigation," it would appear to authorize a custodian to communicate orally with an investigator about the subject matter of the warrant. Such communication, however, is discretionary.

c) Inspection under *PHIPA*

Under *PHIPA*, the Information and Privacy Commissioner may conduct a review pertaining to a contravention or alleged contravention of the legislation.[357] As described more comprehensively in Chapter 15, in conducting a review the Commissioner and her agents have certain powers.[358] For example, subject to certain exceptions and limitations, the Commissioner may, without a warrant or court order, enter and inspect premises, demand production of documents, and inquire into all information and information practices of a health information custodian.[359] Before entering a dwelling, the Commissioner requires the consent of the occupier or a search warrant.[360] The Commissioner has power to summon any person to appear and compel him or her to give oral or written evidence.[361]

Subject to the limitations referred to below, a health information custodian is generally permitted to disclose personal health information to the Information and Privacy Commissioner and her agents for the purpose of such reviews, whether or not the Commissioner exercises the formal powers to enter and inspect premises or to compel a person to produce documents or written or oral evidence.[362]

However, there are limits on the Commissioner's access to personal health information, and, as such, a health information custodian may not disclose

---

ted; or anything that there is reasonable ground to believe will afford evidence as to the commission of an offence."

357 *PHIPA*, ss. 56 and 58.
358 Chapter 15, Section B(5)(c).
359 *PHIPA*, s. 60(2).
360 *Ibid.*, s. 60(3).
361 *Ibid.*, s. 60(12).
362 *Ibid.*, s. 43(1)(g).

personal health information to the Commissioner or her agents until such time as the Commissioner first fulfils the requirements of the legislation.[363] Particularly, prior to disclosing personal health information to the Commissioner or her agents, a health information custodian must be satisfied that the Commissioner has obtained the consent of the patient to whom the personal health information relates or the custodian must have received a statement from the Commissioner to the effect that the Commissioner reasonably requires access to the personal health information in question in order to conduct the review and that the public interest in carrying out the review justifies dispensing with obtaining the patient's consent in the circumstances.[364]

d)   Inspections, Investigations, and Similar Procedures, without a Warrant

As set out above, the Information and Privacy Commissioner has been granted authority by a statute to search and seize records of personal health information without a warrant and to interview individuals. Such statutory authority is not unusual for other officials with regulatory or oversight powers. Powers are often set out in health sector statutes to enable an official to ensure compliance with the statutory regime to which a health information custodian or agent of the custodian may be subject. For example, the *Health Insurance Act* gives an inspector under that Act the power to inspect and receive information from health records or from notes, charts, or other material relating to patient care.[365] An inspector has the power to interview a physician or practitioner and members of his or her staff on matters that relate to the provision of insured services.[366] Similarly, an operator and administrator of every hospital, health facility, and other health care facility in which insured services are provided are required to co-operate fully with an inspector and must ensure that employees also co-operate fully.[367] Section 43 (1)(g) of *PHIPA* authorizes a health information custodian to disclose personal health information as required by these provisions of the *Health Insurance Act* and more generally for the purpose of facilitating such an inspection under that Act.[368]

---

363   *PHIPA*, s. 60(13). This is further discussed in Chapter 15, Section B(5)(c)(iv). Another limitation is that the Commissioner may not require access to, or production of, quality of care and quality assurance information, as discussed in Chapter 15, Section B(5)(c)(vi).

364   *Ibid.*

365   *HIA*, above note 42, ss. 40.1(1)[5] and [7].

366   *Ibid.*, s. 40.1(1)[1].

367   *Ibid.*, s. 40.2(4).

368   *PHIPA*, s. 43(1)(g). Where the disclosures of personal health information are permitted or required by the *HIA*, above note 42, they are also permitted under *PHIPA*, s. 43(1)(h).

Other examples of where a statute or a regulation under a statute provides authority for an inspector or investigator to access records of personal health information and interview individuals, in the absence of a warrant[369] include inspections by assessors and inspectors under the *Independent Health Facilities Act;*[370] investigations undertaken by investigators under the provisions of the Health Professions Procedural Code;[371] and inspections of a service provider undertaken by program supervisors under the provisions of the *Long-Term Care Act, 1994.*[372]

PHIPA also authorizes a health information custodian to disclose personal health information in the context of statutory inspections, investigations, or similar procedures that may go beyond the health sector, or apply to only parts of the health sector and parts of other sectors. Examples include

- Disclosures to a coroner under the *Coroners Act.*[373] A coroner may enter and inspect any place where a dead body is and any place from which the coroner has reasonable grounds for believing the body was removed.[374] In so doing, a coroner may inspect and extract information from any records or writings relating to the deceased.[375] A person must not knowingly obstruct or interfere with, or attempt to do so, or refuse to furnish information to a coroner in the performance of his or her duties in connection with an investigation.[376]
- Disclosures to the Auditor General of Ontario, in the course of audits under the *Auditor General Act,*[377] which, as of 1 April 2005,[378] includes the power of the Auditor General to conduct broad based value-for-money audits[379] of provincial grant recipients,[380] including public hospitals, nursing homes, and others.

---

369 Unless the premises to be entered are a dwelling; in which case, generally, statutes require that a warrant authorize the entry.

370 *IHFA*, above note 23, ss. 30–32.

371 *RHPA*, above note 180; Health Professions Procedural Code, Schedule 2 to the *RHPA*, ss. 76–78 [*RHPA* Code].

372 *LTCA*, above note 23, s. 62.

373 Above note 213, s. 16.

374 *Ibid.*, s. 16(1).

375 *Ibid.*, s. 16(2).

376 *Ibid.*, s. 16(6).

377 *AGA*, above note 80.

378 *Ibid.*, s. 9.1(1).

379 See explanation of "special audits" in the *AGA* in Section H (note 80 and accompanying text).

380 Affected grant recipients include every association, authority, board, commission, corporation, council, foundation, institution, organization, or other body, other than municipalities, that receives directly or indirectly a grant or other transfer payment from the Consolidated Revenue Fund, from an agency of the Crown or from a Crown controlled corporation: *AGA*, above note 77, ss. 1 and 9.

• Disclosures to Ontario's provincial Ombudsman, who has the power to conduct investigations of provincial governmental organizations,[381] such as the Ministry of Health and Long-Term Care, in the course of such an investigation.[382]

Generally, these types of statutory provisions do not leave room for a health information custodian to exercise his or her discretion with respect to how much personal health information is reasonable to disclose, as the disclosure of information is typically required by the Act. However, to the extent the language of this *PHIPA* provision also allows a disclosure "for the purpose of facilitating the inspection, investigation or similar procedure," which may go beyond what is actually required by law, a custodian's disclosure is discretionary and the custodian should limit the amount of information to that which is necessary for the purpose of the disclosure.[383]

4) Disclosure for the Purpose of Determining, Assessing, or Confirming Capacity: Section 43(1)(a)

A health information custodian may disclose personal health information about a patient for the purposes of determining, assessing, or confirming capacity under the *Health Care Consent Act, 1996*,[384] the *Substitute Decisions Act, 1992*,[385] or *PHIPA*.[386] In brief, the types of capacity determinations at issue are as follows.

---

381 *Ombudsman Act*, R.S.O. 1990, c. O.6, ss. 1 and 14(1), and see *Ontario (Ombudsman) v. Ontario (Health Disciplines Board)* (1979), 26 O.R. (2d) 105 (C.A.), in which Morden J.A. established an approach to interpreting the term "governmental organization" in the *Ombudsman Act*.

382 *PHIPA* also made an amendment to s. 19 of the *Ombudsman Act*, ibid., to make it clear that anyone subject to *PHIPA* or *FIPPA*, above note 12, is not prevented by anything in those Acts from providing the information to the Ombudsman when required to do so under ss. 19(1) or (2) of the *Ombudsman Act*: *PHIPA*, s. 94. This amendment also clarifies the Ombudsman's investigative powers with respect to all institutions under *FIPPA* whether or not they are health information custodians under *PHIPA*. In addition to ensuring that *PHIPA* and the *Ombudsman Act* function harmoniously, this amendment appears to clarify any uncertainties that may have arisen about the Ombudsman's investigative powers over all *FIPPA* institutions when s. 42(m) of *FIPPA*, which expressly authorized disclosures by such institutions to the Ombudsman, was repealed by the *Municipal Freedom of Information Statute Law Amendment Act, 1989*, S.O. 1989, c. 64, s. 3(17).

383 See limits on disclosure of personal health information outlined in Chapter 7, Section C.

384 See above note 50.

385 See above note 232.

386 *PHIPA*, s. 43(1)(a).

- Under the *Health Care Consent Act, 1996,* before a treatment is administered to a patient, a health care practitioner who proposes the treatment must obtain consent from the capable patient, or the patient's substitute decision-maker if the patient is, in the opinion of the health care practitioner, incapable of making the treatment decision.[387] A "health care practitioner" is defined differently from *PHIPA* in that Act and includes most regulated health professionals except for pharmacists, opticians, and dental technologists.[388] A health care practitioner within the meaning of the *Health Care Consent Act, 1996,* may be a health information custodian, if not acting as agent of another custodian.[389]

- Further, under the *Health Care Consent Act, 1996,* an evaluator determines whether an individual is capable of making a decision about his or her admission to a care facility[390] and may further determine whether an individual is capable of making a decision about a personal assistance service in a care facility.[391] An "evaluator" is a defined term and includes social workers and a number of regulated health professionals.[392] Such an evaluator may be a health information custodian under *PHIPA,* if not acting as an agent of another custodian.[393]

- Under the *Substitute Decisions Act, 1992,* assessors assess an individual's capacity for a number of purposes under that Act, such as to determine whether the individual is capable of executing a continuing power of attorney for property[394] or a power of attorney for personal care,[395] or whether the

---

387 *HCCA*, above note 50, s. 10(1). A "substitute decision-maker" in the *HCCA* has a particular definition.

388 *Ibid.,* s. 2(1).

389 *PHIPA*, ss. 3(1)[5] and 3(3)[1].

390 *HCCA*, above note 50, ss. 40(1) and 2(1). A "care facility" means (a) an approved home for the aged, as defined in the *CIA*, above note 23; (b) a home or joint home, as defined in the *HARHA*, above note 23; (c) a nursing home, as defined in the *NHA*, above note 23; or (d) a facility prescribed by the *HCCA* regulations as a care facility.

391 *HCCA, ibid.,* s. 57(1). "Personal assistance service" is a defined term in that Act, see s. 2(1) of the *HCCA.* The term generally includes activities of daily living, such as dressing, eating, and walking.

392 *HCCA, ibid.,* s. 2(1). An evaluator may be an audiologist, a speech-language pathologist, a nurse, an occupational therapist, a physician, a physiotherapist, or a psychologist. Pursuant to section 1 of *Evaluators*, O. Reg. 104/96, made under the *HCCA*, an evaluator also includes a social worker who is a member of the Ontario College of Social Workers and Social Service Workers. Such individuals may evaluate a patient's capacity to decide about admission to a care facility or personal assistance services in such a facility.

393 *PHIPA*, ss. 3(1)[5] and 3(3)[1].

394 *SDA*, above note 232, s. 8(1).

395 *Ibid.,* s. 47(1).

Public Guardian and Trustee should become the patient's statutory guardian.[396] An assessor is a defined term.[397] Under the *Substitute Decisions Act, 1992*, a person is qualified to perform assessments of capacity if he or she is a physician, psychologist, social worker or social service worker, occupational therapist, or nurse, has completed a training course for assessors, and is covered by specified provincial liability insurance.[398] Such an assessor may be a health information custodian under *PHIPA*, if not acting as an agent of another custodian.[399]

- Under *PHIPA*, the responsibility for determining a patient's capacity to consent to the collection, use, or disclosure of personal health information by a health information custodian rests with the health information custodian. A custodian's agent may perform this task.[400]

This clause provides authority for a health information custodian to disclose personal health information either in a situation where the custodian or the custodian's agent is conducting the capacity determination, assessment, or confirmation or where the custodian or the custodian's agent is facilitating someone else's determination, assessment, or confirmation of a patient's capacity.

As discussed in Chapter 6, where a custodian is not a natural person, the custodian must rely on its agents to determine patients' capacity.[401] Even where the custodian is a natural person, the custodian may delegate this task to an agent, who may be a regular employee of the custodian, or may be a person contracted specifically for this purpose.[402] Where agents of the custodian consult each other or the custodian about a patient's capacity, the agents and custodian "use" personal health information and do not "disclose" the information. Furthermore, a custodian or the custodian's agent "uses" personal health information when he or she reviews a patient's health record in the custody or control of the custodian for the purpose of making a determination about the patient's capacity.[403] In either situation, section 43(1)(a) of *PHIPA* is not relevant.

---

396   *Ibid.*, s. 16. A "statutory guardian" may be appointed under the *SDA, ibid.*, where an individual, who is a patient in a psychiatric facility, for example, is incapable of managing property.

397   "Assessor" under the *SDA, ibid.*, s. 1, is a member of a class of persons who are designated by the regulations as being qualified to do assessments of capacity.

398   *Capacity Assessment*, O. Reg. 293/96, made under the *SDA, ibid.*, s. 1(1).

399   *PHIPA*, ss. 3(1)[5] and 3(3)[1].

400   *PHIPA*, s. 22 (1). See Chapter 6, Section F(3).

401   See Chapter 6, Section F(3).

402   *HCCA*, above note 50, s. 57(1).

403   *PHIPA*, s. 37(1)(c).

Where a health information custodian wishes to consult with another health information custodian about a patient's capacity, however, the custodian seeking the consultation would need to "disclose" the patient's personal health information to the other custodian. Section 43(1)(a) of *PHIPA* authorizes this type of disclosure.[404] It appears that this provision permits both the consulting custodian and the consulted custodian to disclose to each other personal health information as necessary for the purpose of determining, assessing, or confirming capacity. Consider the following. A health information custodian who receives a written consent from a patient permitting the custodian to disclose the patient's personal health information to a third party may wish to seek confirmation from the patient's family physician that the patient is capable of consenting. A similar situation arises where a substitute decision-maker provides a custodian with consent to disclose the patient's personal health information and the custodian wishes to make inquiries from another custodian, such as the patient's nursing home, as to the patient's capacity. Inquiries about a particular patient's capacity may involve, unavoidably, the disclosure of certain personal health information about the patient. A health information custodian's disclosure of personal health information in these circumstances is authorized by this provision of *PHIPA*.

Disclosures of personal health information authorized under this clause do not appear to be limited to those made to health information custodians. Thus, an assessor whom an applicant for a guardianship order[405] has asked to assess an individual's capacity for the purpose of commencing such an application may rely on this provision of *PHIPA* for authority to provide the applicant with results of the assessment.

5) Disclosure to a Professional Governing Body: Section 43(1)(b), (c), & (d)

PHIPA recognizes the need for health information custodians and their agents to disclose personal health information to a professional governing body that is authorized by legislation to regulate the practice of a profession in the pub-

---

404 A health information custodian's collection of personal health information from a disclosing custodian is authorized under s. 36(1)(g) of *PHIPA*. Use of the personal health information is authorized under ss. 37(1)(a) & (b).

405 Such as pursuant to s. 55 of the *SDA*, above note 385, (application to the court to appoint a guardian of the person).

lic interest.[406] First, *PHIPA* provides[407] that nothing in *PHIPA* should be construed to interfere with the regulatory activities of a College under the *Regulated Health Professions Act, 1991*,[408] the College of Social Workers and Social Service Workers,[409] or the Board of Regents under the *Drugless Practitioners Act*.[410] The Standing Committee on General Government added this provision during the clause-by-clause review of Bill 31 in response to the College's concerns that one of the unintended consequences of the new health information privacy bill may be that some health information custodians or their agents may use the legislation to thwart the statutory mandate of these professional governing bodies.[411]

Second, *PHIPA* further provides that a health information custodian may disclose personal health information to the following bodies:

---

406 Section 3(1) of the *Social Work and Social Service Work Act, 1998*, above note 180, provides that in carrying out its objects, the College's primary duty is to serve and protect the public interest. The provisions of the *RHPA* Code, above note 371, apply to each of the twenty-one regulated health profession Colleges. Section 3(2) of the Code states that "In carrying out its objects, the College has a duty to serve and protect the public interest." Perhaps because it is an older statute, the *DPA*, above note 180, does not expressly contain such a duty.

407 *PHIPA*, s. 9(2).

408 Above note 180.

409 *SWSSWA*, above note 180, s. 2.

410 *DPA*, above note 180, s. 2.

411 This issue dominated the first half of the hearings on Bill 31 before the Standing Committee on General Government. The Director of Investigations and Hearings for the College of Medical Laboratory Technologists of Ontario summarized the College's concern as follows: "The creativity of defence counsel is sometimes endless. So in any area where there is a lack of clarity, colleges potentially face defences from members and their counsel that *HIPA* [i.e., *PHIPA*] was in fact intended to provide them with a shield from the college's powers to inquire into their practices or into their records, or frankly, it might be argued that it blocks the college from using information that comes to their attention." Ontario, Legislative Assembly, Standing Committee on General Government, *Official Report of Debates (Hansard)*, G-50 to G-52 (26 January 2004) at 1620 (Christina Langlois). All of the other Colleges that presented at the hearings articulated a similar concern: the College of Medical Radiation Technologists of Ontario, the Royal College of Dental Surgeons of Ontario, the College of Physicians and Surgeons of Ontario, and the Ontario College of Social Workers and Social Service Workers. The Federation of Health Regulatory Colleges, which represents most of the regulated health profession Colleges also noted this issue: see Ontario, Legislative Assembly, Standing Committee on General Government, *Official Report of Debates (Hansard)*, (26–28 January 2004). Further, the Information and Privacy Commissioner noted that "Clearly, this Bill is not intended, nor should it, serve as a shield in any way in the context of a disciplinary action.": Ontario, Legislative Assembly, Standing Committee on General Government, *Official Report of Debates (Hansard)*, G-59 (27 January 2004) at 1020 (Dr. Ann Cavoukian).

- a College within the meaning of the *Regulated Health Professions Act, 1991* for the purposes of the administration or enforcement of that Act, or any of the profession-specific Acts listed in Schedule 1 to the *Regulated Health Professions Act, 1991* or the *Drug and Pharmacies Regulation Act;*[412]
- the Board of Regents under the *Drugless Practitioners Act* for the purpose of the administration or enforcement of that Act;[413] and
- the Ontario College of Social Workers and Social Service Workers for the purpose of the administration or enforcement of the *Social Work and Social Service Work Act, 1998.*[414]

A custodian's agent also has authority, independent of the health information custodian, to disclose personal health information for these purposes.[415] Therefore, an agent does not require a custodian's authorization to make a disclosure to a professional governing body for such purposes.

The mandate of such professional governing bodies is to regulate the practice of their members by

- developing, establishing, and maintaining standards of qualifications for membership;
- developing, establishing, and maintaining programs and standards of practice to assure the quality of the practice of the profession;
- developing, establishing, and maintaining standards of knowledge and skill and promoting continuing competence among members;
- issuing certificates of registration to members and renewing, amending, suspending, canceling, revoking, and reinstating those certificates;
- establishing and enforcing professional standards and ethical standards; and
- receiving and investigating complaints against members and dealing with issues of professional misconduct, incompetency, and incapacity.[416]

---

412 *PHIPA*, s. 43(1)(b). Twenty-three health professions in Ontario are regulated by twenty-one Colleges. Schedule 1 to the *Regulated Health Professions Act*, above note 180, lists the following regulated health professions: audiology; speech-language pathology; chiropody (and podiatry); chiropractic; dental hygiene; dental technology; dentistry; denturism; dietetics; massage therapy; medical laboratory technology; medical radiation technology; medicine; midwifery; nursing (including nurse practitioners); occupational therapy; opticianry; optometry; pharmacy; physiotherapy; psychology; and respiratory therapy. The *Drug and Pharmacies Regulations Act*, R.S.O. 1990, c. H.4 [*DPRA*], regulates pharmacies and the compounding, dispensing, and selling of drugs

413 *PHIPA*, s. 43(1)(c): The Board of Regents regulates professions such as naturopaths.

414 *Ibid.*, s. 43(1)(d).

415 *PHIPA* Regulation, above note 9, s. 7(2)[ii].

416 This is a summary of objects of *RHPA* Colleges as outlined in the *RHPA* Code, above note 406, s. 3(1) and the *SWSSWA*, above note 180, s. 3(2). The *Drugless Practitioners*

In order to fulfil such a mandate, professional governing bodies are authorized to perform certain administrative and enforcement functions under their respective statutes. To perform such functions professional governing bodies often require access to personal health information, such as information that relates to health care that a member provided to a patient. Clearly, where one of these Acts permits or requires a health information custodian to disclose personal health information to a professional governing body, *PHIPA* permits the custodian to do so, as *PHIPA* allows a custodian to disclose personal health information as permitted or required by law.[417] Similarly, *PHIPA* permits a custodian's agent, independently of the custodian, to make such a disclosure in the case where a law permits or requires the agent to make such a disclosure.[418] But the additional provisions in *PHIPA* that authorize a health information custodian and an agent to disclose personal health information to such professional governing bodies "for the purpose of the administration or enforcement" of the relevant regulatory legislation[419] also clarify that a custodian and an agent may disclose personal health information for such purposes, even if the relevant legislation does not include specific authority for such disclosures.

The phrase "for the purpose of administration or enforcement" of an Act, as it appears in sections 43(1)(b), (c), and (d), is not defined in *PHIPA*. The provisions must presumably be interpreted to authorize disclosures of personal health information that are not addressed by other provisions in *PHIPA*, such as provisions that permit a custodian to disclose personal health information

---

Act does not contain such objects, but the mandate of the Board of Regents is generally comparable, as set out in the regulation-making authorities of that legislation: *DPA*, above note 180, s. 6. Under the *RHPA* Code one of the objects of every *RHPA* College is "to administer the health profession Act, this Code and the *Regulated Health Professions Act, 1991* as it relates to the profession:" *RHPA* Code, above note 371, s. 3(1)[7].

417 *PHIPA*, s. 43(1)(h). For example, this provision of *PHIPA* preserves the duty that a member has to report to a College a reasonable belief that another member of the same or different College has sexually abused a patient as set out in s. 85.1(1) of the *RHPA* Code, *ibid*. A similar provision is found in the *SWSSWA*, above note 180, s. 43. A custodian is also permitted to disclose personal health information to an investigator conducting an investigation on behalf of a professional governing body, pursuant to *PHIPA*, s. 43(1)(g).

418 *PHIPA*, s. 17(2).

419 *Ibid*., s. 43(1)(b), (c), & (d). Also, under *PHIPA*, s. 50(1)(c) a health information custodian may disclose personal health information in similar circumstances to professional bodies outside Ontario that perform functions comparable to that of the professional regulatory bodies referred to in *PHIPA*, ss. 43(1)(b), (c), or (d). See further about a custodian's authority to disclose personal health information outside Ontario, below Section S.

for the purpose of a proceeding,[420] "as permitted or required by law,"[421] or to a person carrying out an investigation that is authorized under an Act.[422] Likewise, the phrase should be interpreted, evidently, to refer to something other than the carrying out of "statutory functions," a phrase that appears in another clause of section 43(1).[423]

The phrase "for the purpose of administration or enforcement" of an Act does not appear to have been judicially considered in the context of other legislation, although the Supreme Court of Canada has considered the phrase "*relating to* the administration or enforcement" of an Act, in *Slattery (Trustee of) v. Slattery*, as discussed in Chapter 8.[424] Some guidance in interpreting this phrase may be taken from jurisprudence that has addressed the words within the phrase. The Supreme Court of Canada has interpreted the word "administration" broadly "to encompass all conduct engaged in by a governmental authority in furtherance of governmental policy, business or otherwise."[425] While the jurisprudence does not analyze the meaning of the word "administration" in the sense of the administration of an Act, it seems reasonable to conclude that the word "administration" refers to the application or the carrying out of an authority granted to a body under a statute. The "administration" of an Act can thus be interpreted to include a wide range of activities addressed in the Act.

The word "enforcement," on the other hand, may require a more restrictive interpretation, tied to requirements in the Act with which persons must comply, especially where relevant legislation already provides an enforcement mechanism.[426] However, since a disclosure pursuant to sections 43(1)(b), (c) or (d) need be only for the purpose of either the administration or enforcement of the statute, the phrase can nevertheless be interpreted broadly.

---

420 *PHIPA*, ss. 41(1)(a) and (d).
421 *PHIPA*, s. 43(1)(h).
422 *Ibid.*, s. 43(1)(g).
423 *Ibid.*, s. 43(1)(e). For a discussion of "statutory function" see below Section P(6) and Chapter 8, Section C(3)(d).
424 *Slattery (Trustee of) v. Slattery*, [1993] 3 S.C.R. 430 at paras. 20–23. See Chapter 8, Section C(3)(a).
425 *B.C. Development Corp. v. Friedmann*, [1984] 2 S.C.R. 447.
426 This is more relevant to the *RHPA* Code, above note 371, and the *SWSSWA*, above note 180 as they both set out powers for investigation, for example. In regulations under the *DPA*, above note 180, the Board of Regents may appoint an inspector for the purpose of investigating a complaint, but, unlike under the *RHPA* Code and the *SWSSWA*, the inspector is not granted powers to access information for the purpose of the investigation.

In general, it would be reasonable for a health information custodian to give these clauses in *PHIPA* a liberal interpretation, noting, of course, that the clauses only permit a custodian to disclose personal health information to professional governing bodies for such purposes, but do not require a custodian to make such disclosures.

Given this background, it is useful to consider the application of authority in *PHIPA* for a health information custodian and an agent of a custodian to disclose personal health information to particular situations. For example, a health information custodian and an agent of a custodian may wish to make a complaint to, or file a report with, the relevant professional governing body about the conduct, competence, or capacity of a member of the profession. Sometimes, this type of complaint or report entails disclosing information of a general nature about the care provided by the member without identifying a particular patient. In other cases, specific information, including personal health information, about a particular patient and situation will be required, in order to deal with a complaint relating to the specific incident, for example. While the *RHPA* Code and the *Social Work and Social Service Work Act, 1998* provide that a complaint filed with the Registrar of the relevant professional governing body about the conduct or actions of a member must be investigated by a panel of the Complaints Committee, they do not specifically permit health care practitioners to disclose any information to the Registrar to make a complaint.[427] Further, where a complaint relates to the way in which a member keeps records, a professional governing body may need to review several patient charts to determine whether the member's standard of practice falls below the standard of practice for the profession. A complaint to a professional governing body of this nature would not require the consent of each patient whose records of personal health information are at issue. Requiring a professional governing body to obtain patient consent, a warrant, or a summons[428] each time the body needs access to personal health information seems con-

---

427 *RHPA* Code, *ibid.*, s. 25.1; *SWSSWA, ibid.*, s. 24.
428 Reg. 965, above note 112, s. 22(3), made under the *PHA*, above note 23, enables the Registrar of the College of Physicians and Surgeons of Ontario to inspect and receive information from medical records or from notes, charts, and other material relating to patient care. The Registrar can also interview medical and other staff about the admission, treatment, care, conduct, control, and discharge of patients or any class of patients, as well as the general management of the hospital insofar as it relates to the hospitalization of a patient or patients whose care and treatment are being investigated by the College. In the *Krever Report*, Mr. Justice Krever had recommended that other health professional governing bodies be equally authorized to obtain such access. See *Krever Report*, above note 53, vol. 2 at 361, Recommendation 74.

trary to the apparent policy intent of legislation applicable to such profession-al governing bodies, namely, that such bodies should be able to act swiftly and effectively in regulating their members in the public interest.

In other instances, independent of a complaint about a member's activities, a professional governing body may require a member to participate in a review program.[429] In order to review the member's practice effectively, a representative from the professional governing body may need to examine patient charts or observe the member's treatment of his or her patients. Without the authority set out in *PHIPA* for a custodian to disclose personal health information to a pro-fessional governing body for such administrative and enforcement purposes, *PHIPA* may have impeded such access to personal health information. These examples illustrate some types of situations in which a health information cus-todian may rely on the authority in *PHIPA* to disclose personal health informa-tion to a professional governing body for the purposes of the administration or enforcement of relevant regulatory legislation.

It should be noted that the professional governing bodies themselves are generally subject to secrecy provisions.[430] Further, professional governing bod-ies who receive personal health information from a health information custo-dian are bound by certain "recipient" restrictions under *PHIPA* that prohibit them from using or disclosing the information except

- as permitted or required by law;
- for the purpose for which the custodian disclosed the information to the body; or
- for the purpose of carrying out a statutory or legal duty.[431]

6) For the Statutory Functions of the Public Guardian and Trustee and Other Entities: Section 43(1)(e)

a) Generally

PHIPA permits a health information custodian to disclose personal health information to certain specified statutorily authorized officers or bodies, so

---

429 See, for example, *General*, O. Reg. 114/94, made under the *Medicine Act, 1991*, S.O. 1991, c. 30, s. 29, which provides for physician review programs.

430 *RHPA*, above note 180, s. 36, which applies to every person engaged in the adminis-tration of the *RHPA*; a health profession Act; or the *DPRA*, above note 412. The *SWSSWA*, above note 180, s. 50 has a similarly broad confidentiality provision; the *DPA*, above note 180, however, does not address confidentiality requirements for any person tasked with the administration or enforcement of the Act.

431 *PHIPA*, s. 49(1). See Chapter 12, Section C(2).

that such officers or bodies may carry out their "statutory functions."[432] These officers and bodies are as follows:

- the Public Guardian and Trustee;
- the Children's Lawyer;
- a children's aid society;
- a Residential Placement Advisory Committee established under section 34(2) of the *Child and Family Services Act*; and
- the Registrar of Adoption Information appointed under section 163(1) of the *Child and Family Services Act*.

As explained in Chapter 8, the term "statutory function" may be interpreted to be broad in scope and would include activities that are incidental to an explicit statutory authority. The function itself need not be expressly described in the statute, but rather, must be legitimately connected to a stated statutory power.[433]

Further, such statutorily authorized officers or bodies who receive personal health information from a health information custodian are also bound by certain "recipient" restrictions under *PHIPA*, which prohibit them from using or disclosing the information except in the following circumstances:

- as permitted or required by law;
- for the purpose for which the custodian disclosed the information to the body; or
- for the purpose of carrying out a statutory or legal duty.[434]

b)   Disclosure to the Public Guardian and Trustee

A health information custodian may disclose personal health information to the Public Guardian and Trustee (PGT) so that he or she may carry out his or her statutory functions.[435] The Lieutenant Governor in Council (effectively Cab-

---

432   *PHIPA*, s. 43(1)(e).

433   Chapter 8, Section C(3)(d). It should be noted that in s. 36(1)(c)(iii), a *FIPPA/MFIPPA* custodian may collect personal health information without the individual's consent for a purpose related to the statutory function. The purpose as stated in s. 43(1)(e), on the other hand, is somewhat narrower as it is not qualified by the word "related."

434   *PHIPA*, s. 49(1). See Chapter 12.

435   *Ibid.*, s. 43(1)(e). Although not stated explicitly in *PHIPA*, where *PHIPA* permits a disclosure to the PGT, the disclosure may apparently be made to any of the staff of the Office of the PGT, as the function of the Public Guardian and Trustee is supported by a staff of hundreds. A health information custodian and its agents may communicate with any staff person who is fulfilling an official function for that Office.

inet) appoints an individual to the Office of the Public Guardian and Trustee, pursuant to the *Public Guardian and Trustee Act*.[436]

The PGT has responsibilities under several statutes, including the *Public Guardian and Trustee Act*,[437] the *Crown Estates Administration Act*,[438] and the *Substitute Decisions Act, 1992*.[439] The following are some examples of the kinds of statutory functions the PGT undertakes.

The PGT has a statutory role in administering estates of Ontario residents or property owners who have died without a will and without known next of kin in Ontario.[440] The PGT may be a litigation guardian or a legal representative for an incapable adult, under the *Rules of Civil Procedure*, or may need to be appointed as such.[441] Under the *Substitute Decisions Act, 1992*, the PGT may be appointed as a statutory guardian of property for a patient of a psychiatric facility, a guardian of property or of personal care, or an attorney for property or personal care in certain circumstances.[442] Further, the PGT has a substitute decision-making function under the *Health Care Consent Act, 1996* and *PHIPA*.[443] The PGT also has a statutory duty to investigate an allegation that, as a result of an individual's incapacity to manage property or personal care, as

---

436 R.S.O. 1990, c. P.51, s. 1(1) [*PGTA*].

437 *Ibid.*

438 R.S.O. 1990, c. 47 [*CEAA*].

439 *SDA*, above note 385.

440 Under the *CEAA*, above note 438, the PGT may apply to court to administer an estate where a resident of Ontario or a person who had property in Ontario died without a will or the person's executor or estate trustee has died or become incapable, there are no next of kin living in Ontario or the next of kin are minors or mentally incapable adults and the value of the estate is more than $5,000: from *Estate Administration: The Role of the Public Guardian and Trustee*, online: <www.attorneygeneral.jus.gov.on.ca/english/family/pgt/estatesadmin.pdf>.

441 For further discussion about the role of a "litigation guardian" and "legal representative," see Section M(4) above. Note that a health information custodian may disclose personal health information so that the PGT can become an individual's guardian or legal representative pursuant to *PHIPA*, s. 41(1)(b). A custodian may also disclose personal health information to the PGT so that the PGT may commence, defend, or continue a proceeding on behalf of an individual: *PHIPA*, s. 41(1)(c).

442 *SDA*, above note 385, s. 16; *MHA*, above note 23, s. 57.

443 For example, under the *HCCA* the PGT is required to be the substitute decision-maker of last resort for treatment decisions and for decisions pertaining to admissions to care facilities on behalf of individuals found incapable of such decisions and for whom no other substitute has been located. Under *PHIPA*, the role of the PGT as substitute decision-maker of last resort is discretionary on the part of that office: *HCCA*, above note 50, ss. 20(5) & (6) (treatment) and 41 (admissions); *PHIPA*, ss. 26(6) & (7).

the case may be, the individual is suffering or may suffer serious adverse effects, and may therefore need a court-appointed guardian.[444]

A health information custodian may disclose relevant and necessary personal health information to the PGT to support any such statutory functions of that office. For example, a health information custodian may need to communicate with the PGT about a patient for whom the PGT is a statutory guardian. Or, the health information custodian may wish to alert the PGT of a concern that, as a result of a patient's incapacity, the patient is suffering serious adverse effects.[445] An agent of a custodian is also explicitly permitted to disclose personal health information to the PGT, independent of any permission from the custodian, so that the PGT may carry out its statutory functions.[446]

The personal health information that is the subject of the custodian's disclosure will typically relate to the person for whom the PGT is a guardian or for whom the PGT takes or intends to take on another particular role (like that of a substitute decision-maker), but it may also relate to another person, such as where another patient is taking advantage of an individual's vulnerability, or where the capacity of an attorney for personal care who is acting on behalf of a patient is questionable.

c) Disclosure to the Children's Lawyer

A health information custodian may disclose personal health information to the Children's Lawyer so that he or she may carry out his or her statutory functions.[447] Under the *Courts of Justice Act*, the Lieutenant Governor in Council (effectively Cabinet) appoints an individual to the Office of the Children's Lawyer, on the rec-

---

444 *SDA*, above note 385, ss. 27 and 62. The PGT has power to enter premises (s. 82) and access records (s. 83) for the purpose of such an investigation. The *Mental Health Act* continues to provide that an officer in charge of a psychiatric facility must disclose a record of personal health information to a person entitled to have access to the record under s. 83 of the *Substitute Decisions Act, 1992*: *MHA*, above note 23, s. 35(4.1). However, discretionary provisions that authorized health care providers to disclose patient information to the PGT to facilitate an investigation under s. 83 of the *SDA*, above note 385, in, for example, the *LTCA*, the *MHA*, and regulations under the *PHA*, above note 23, have been repealed, as they were apparently unnecessary as a result of *PHIPA*, s. 43(1)(e).

445 See *ibid.*

446 *PHIPA* Regulation, above note 9, s. 7(2)(iii).

447 *PHIPA*, s. 43(1)(e). Although not stated explicitly in *PHIPA*, where *PHIPA* permits a disclosure to the Children's Lawyer, the disclosure may apparently be made to any of the staff of the Office of the Children's Lawyer, as the function of the Children's Lawyer is supported by a staff of lawyers, clinical investigators, and others who are in the service of the Children's Lawyer. A health information custodian and its agents may communicate with any staff person who is fulfilling an official function for that Office.

ommendation of the Attorney General.[448] Under that Act, the Children's Lawyer serves as litigation guardian of a minor under eighteen years of age or an unborn person, who is a party to a proceeding when required to do so by an Act or by court rules.[449] This role is most common in civil proceedings involving property rights, such as proceedings involving estate and trust matters, claims for support under the *Succession Law Reform Act*, division of property claims under the *Family Law Act*, or court actions for damages for personal injury.[450]

Further, at the request of a court, the Children's Lawyer may also act as the legal representative of a minor or unborn person who is not a party to a proceeding.[451] For example, a court may request the appointment of an independent legal representative for a child when the court believes a lawyer for a child is necessary to represent the child's interest in a child protection proceeding or where the court requires independent information about the interests, needs, and wishes of the child in a proceeding about child custody and access.

A health information custodian may disclose relevant and necessary personal health information to the Children's Lawyer to support any such statutory functions. The personal health information that is the subject of the custodian's disclosure may relate to the child who the Children's Lawyer represents, or to another person. For example, the Children's Lawyer may need to discuss the health of the child or of a parent with a health information custodian to advise the court in a custody and access matter where the parents cannot resolve the dispute.

d) Disclosure to the Children's Aid Society

A health information custodian may disclose personal health information to a children's aid society so that it may carry out its statutory functions.[452] An agent of a custodian is also authorized to make such a disclosure to a children's aid society and does not require the custodian's authorization to do so.[453] A children's aid society is not created by statute, but is a type of "service provider" under the *Child and Family Services Act*.[454] Its functions, set out in that Act, are to

---

448 *CJA*, above note 211, s. 89(1).
449 *Ibid.*, s. 89(3). See further about the role of a litigation guardian above, Section M(4).
450 These functions are summarized on the website of the Ministry of the Attorney General pertaining to the Children's Lawyer, "More About What We Do," online: <www.attorneygeneral.jus.gov.on.ca/english/family/ocl>.
451 *CJA*, above note 211, s. 89(3.1). See further about the role of a legal representative above, Section M(4).
452 *PHIPA*, s. 43(1)(e).
453 *PHIPA* Regulation, above note 9, s. 7(2)(iii).
454 *CFSA*, above note 168, s. 3(1) definitions of "service provider" and "society."

- investigate allegations or evidence that children who are under the age of sixteen years or are in the society's care or under its supervision may be in need of protection;
- protect, where necessary, children who are under the age of sixteen years or are in the society's care or under its supervision;
- provide guidance, counselling, and other services to families for protecting children or for the prevention of circumstances requiring the protection of children;
- provide care for children assigned or committed to its care under the *Child and Family Services Act*;
- supervise children assigned to its supervision under the *Child and Family Services Act*;
- place children for adoption; and
- perform any other duties given to it by the *Child and Family Services Act* or another Act.[455]

Health information custodians, their agents, and others are sometimes required by various provisions of the *Child and Family Services Act* to disclose certain information to a children's aid society, and those reporting requirements continue to apply.[456] In addition to these specific required disclosures, custodians and their agents may disclose personal health information to a children's aid society as necessary in order for the society to perform any of its above noted statutory functions, ranging from child abuse investigations, to arranging adoptions, to acting as a ward in respect of a child.

Children's aid societies themselves are not health information custodians, so the health care practitioners who are employed or retained by a society to provide health care are individual custodians in their own right.[457] As such, any transfer of information from such a health care practitioner to the society is a disclosure[458] and requires patient consent if not authorized by *PHIPA* without consent.[459] Section 43(1)(e) of *PHIPA*, however, appears to provide such authorization any time the disclosure is reasonably necessary[460] for the purpose of

---

455   *Ibid.*, s. 15(3).

456   *PHIPA*, s. 43(1)(h); *PHIPA* Regulation, above note 9, s. 5(1), and see Chapter 3, Section B(2).

457   They are not excepted from being custodians under *PHIPA*, s. 3(3). See Chapter 2, Section B(1)(b)(iii) for more detail and for practical guidance.

458   Even the health care practitioner simply making the information available to the society would be considered a disclosure. See definition of "disclose" in *PHIPA*, s. 2.

459   *PHIPA*, s. 29.

460   *Ibid.*, s. 30.

allowing the children's aid society to perform any of its statutory functions. The personal health information that is the subject of the custodian's disclosure will typically relate to the child in whom the children's aid society has an interest, but may relate to another person, such as a parent of the child in question.

It should be noted that in addition to the general "recipient rule" that applies to all recipients of personal health information,[461] the *PHIPA* Regulation specifically provides that the limit on the extent of personal health information that a recipient can use or disclose does not apply to a children's aid society or any person providing services on behalf of or on the request of a children's aid society.[462]

e) Disclosure to a Residential Placement Advisory Committee

A health information custodian may disclose personal health information to a Residential Placement Advisory Committee so that it may carry out its statutory functions.[463] A Residential Placement Advisory Committee is established under the *Child and Family Services Act*[464] by the Minister of Children and Youth Services to advise and assist parents, children, and service providers with respect to the availability and appropriateness of, and alternatives to, residential services.[465] For example, a child may need to be placed in a setting away from his or her own home where the parent of the child is temporarily unable to care adequately for a child,[466] and the committee may advise as to the suitability of a residential placement for the child.

The committee conducts reviews of every residential placement in an institution where a child is placed within its territorial jurisdiction, if the placement is intended to last ninety days or more.[467] It also reviews every residential placement of a child who is twelve years of age or older and who objects to the placement, regardless of the duration of the placement.[468] Further, the commit-

---

461 *PHIPA*, s. 49(1).

462 *PHIPA* Regulation, above note 9, s. 22(b). See discussion of this in Chapter 12, Section D.

463 *PHIPA*, s. 43(1)(e).

464 *CFSA*, above note 168, s. 34(2): The composition of the committee is set out in the Act. The Minister of Children and Youth Services specifies the territorial jurisdiction of each committee.

465 *Ibid.*, s. 34(4). "Residential service" is defined in the *CFSA*, *ibid.*, s. 3(1) to mean "boarding, lodging and associated supervisory, sheltered or group care provided for a child away from the home of the child's parent, and 'residential care' and 'residential placement' have corresponding meanings." "Service Providers" is a defined term as well, and includes the children's aid societies.

466 *Ibid.*, s. 29.

467 *Ibid.*, s. 34(6)(a).

tee is required to review an existing or proposed residential placement of a child that the Minister of Children and Youth Services refers to the committee.[469] The committee also has powers to review an existing or proposed residential placement of a child, on any person's request or on its own initiative.[470]

The *Child and Family Services Act* describes the committee's review as "informal."[471] The committee may interview the child and members of the child's family, any persons engaged in providing services, and "other persons who may have an interest in the matter or may have information that would assist the advisory committee."[472] The committee may also examine documents and reports that are presented to the committee.[473] In its review, the committee must consider the matters that are specified in the *Child and Family Services Act*, such as the special needs of the child, if any, and whether the placement is appropriate for the child.[474]

A health information custodian may disclose to the committee personal health information that is reasonably necessary for the committee to perform any such statutory functions. For instance, where there is an issue about the health of the child, or health care required or received by the child in a given residential placement that the committee is reviewing, a custodian with necessary information may disclose it to the committee in accordance with this provision. The personal health information that is the subject of the custodian's disclosure will typically relate to the child whose residential placement is in question, but may relate to another person.

f)   Disclosure to the Registrar of Adoption Information

Under the provisions of the *Child and Family Services Act*, the Minister of Children and Youth Services appoints an employee of the Ministry as the Registrar of Adoption Information.[475] The Registrar's statutory duties include

- maintaining the Adoption Disclosure Register;[476]

---

468 *Ibid.*, s. 34(6)((b).
469 *Ibid.*, s. 34(6)(c).
470 *Ibid.*, s. 34(7).
471 *Ibid.*, s. 34(8).
472 *Ibid.*
473 *Ibid.*
474 *Ibid.*, s. 34(9).
475 *CFSA*, above note 168, s. 163(1).
476 The Register is established in s. 167 of the *CFSA*, *ibid.*, and is a voluntary register for the parties to an adoption The confidentiality requirements of adoption information under the *CFSA*, ss. 165 and 168(3) prevail over any permitted disclosures in *PHIPA*: *PHIPA* Regulation, above note 9, s. 5(1).

- ensuring that counselling is provided to persons who receive identifying information from the Registrar;[477]
- ensuring that counselling is made available to persons who receive non-identifying information from the Registrar, who are or may wish to be named in the register, or who are concerned that they may be affected by the disclosure of identifying information;[478] and
- having searches conducted at the request of adopted pesons who have attained eighteen years of age.[479]

A health information custodian may disclose personal health information to the Registrar of Adoption Information so that the Registrar may carry out such statutory functions.[480] For example, a custodian may disclose personal health information to the Registrar of Adoption Information where necessary to show that a person who wishes to receive identifying information about an adoption has received the counseling that the *Child and Family Services Act* requires.

7) Disclosures Relevant to *FIPPA/MFIPPA* Custodians: Section 43(1)(f)

Where a health information custodian is also subject to *FIPPA* or *MFIPPA*, the custodian may continue to rely on certain provisions in those Acts that permit the disclosure of personal information without consent.[481] These provisions permit a disclosure of personal information

- for the purpose for which the information was obtained or compiled or for a consistent purpose;[482]
- to a *FIPPA* or *MFIPPA* institution or a law enforcement agency in Canada to aid an investigation undertaken with a view to a law enforcement proceeding or from which a law enforcement proceeding is likely to result;[483]

---

477 *CFSA, ibid.*, s. 167(5).
478 *Ibid.*, ss. 166(6) and 170(4).
479 *Ibid.*, s. 169.
480 *PHIPA*, s. 43(1)(e).
481 *Ibid.*, s. 43(1)(f).
482 *FIPPA*, above note 12, s. 42(c),*MFIPPA*, above note 12, s. 32(c).
483 *FIPPA, ibid.*, s. 42(g); *MFIPPA, ibid.*, s. 32(g). "Law enforcement" is defined in those statutes (at s. 2(1) in both statutes) to mean (a) policing, (b) investigations or inspections that lead or could lead to a proceeding in a court or tribunal if a penalty or sanction could be imposed in those proceedings, and (c) the conduct of such proceedings. See the discusion in Section P(3) about disclosure of personal health information for investigations.

- to the government of Canada in order to facilitate the auditing of shared cost programs;[484] and
- in the case of a custodian that is subject to *MFIPPA*, also to the government of Ontario in order to facilitate the auditing of shared cost programs.[485]

This authority in *PHIPA* to disclose personal health information in these circumstances would appear to apply to custodians that are *FIPPA/MFIPPA* institutions, part of such an institution, or acting for or on behalf of such an institution.[486] Therefore, a health information custodian that is an employee or other agent of a *FIPPA* or *MFIPPA* institution, such as a nurse employed in a correctional facility operated by the Ministry of Community Safety and Correctional Services, or a psychologist retained by a school board, would appear to be able to rely on this provision to disclose personal health information in such circumstances.

Q. DISCLOSURES REQUIRED BY *PHIPA*: SECTION 46

Although, in general, *PHIPA* only permits a health information custodian to disclose personal health information, *PHIPA* requires a health information custodian to disclose personal health information in certain limited circumstances. For example, section 47 of *PHIPA* requires a health information custodian to disclose personal health information to a health data institute in specified circumstances.[487] One additional provision in *PHIPA* requires a health information custodian to disclose personal health information.[488] On the request of the Minister of Health and Long-Term Care, a health information custodian must disclose personal health information to the Minister for the purpose of monitoring or verifying claims for payment for health care funded in whole or in part by the Ministry of Health and Long-Term Care or for goods used for such health care.[489] For example, at the request of the Minister, a custodian may be required to disclose personal health information to

---

484 *FIPPA, ibid.,* s. 42(n); *MFIPPA, ibid.,* s. 32(l).

485 *MFIPPA, ibid.,* s. 32(l).

486 Under *PHIPA,* s. 43(1)(f) these provisions apply if the custodian on whose behalf the disclosure is made is subject to *FIPPA* or *MFIPPA*. This would appear to include a part of a *FIPPA* or *MFIPPA* institution or a person acting for or on behalf of the institution, who would be bound to observe the restrictions imposed under the applicable one of those Acts.

487 See Chapter 11, Section D.

488 Note, however, that when another Act requires a disclosure, that requirement continues to be effective: *PHIPA,* ss. 6(3)(b), 43(1)(g), & (h).

489 *PHIPA,* s. 46(1).

Disclosure of Personal Health Information **433**

the General Manager of the Ontario Health Insurance Plan, as agent of the Minister of Health and Long-Term Care, to establish that the custodian provided health care for which the custodian claimed payment from the Ontario Health Insurance Plan.[490]

Where the Minister collects personal health information from a health information custodian pursuant to such a request, the Minister may disclose the information to any person for the purpose of monitoring or verifying the claims for payment for such health care or for goods used for that health care, if the disclosure is reasonably necessary for that purpose.[491]

R. DISCLOSURES TO POLICE: GENERAL GUIDANCE

1) Generally

How a health information custodian should respond to a police officer who appears at the custodian's door seeking information about a patient is a problem as prevalent today as it was in the late 1970s, at the time of the *Krever Report*. Indeed, allegations of inappropriate disclosures of confidential personal information to the Ontario Provincial Police by health care providers such as hospitals and the Ontario Health Insurance Plan were the main impetus for the Royal Commission of Inquiry into the Confidentiality of Health Information that led to the *Krever Report*.[492] Health information custodians and their agents sometimes feel pressured to co-operate with the police, perhaps under the threat or assumption that they will be charged with obstructing a police officer if they do not do so. It is clear, however, in law, that a health information custodian is not required to disclose patient information to police unless the law actually requires such a disclosure.[493]

---

490 It should also be noted that ss. 29(1)(b) & (c) of the *HIA* provide that every insured person shall be deemed to have authorized his or her physician or practitioner, a hospital, or health facility that provided a service to the insured person and any other prescribed person or organization to give the General Manager [of the Ontario Health Insurance Plan] particulars of services provided to the insured person, ... (b) for the purpose of enabling the General Manager to monitor and control the delivery of insured services; and (c) for the purpose of enabling the General Manager to monitor and control payments made under the Plan or otherwise for insured services. With the coming into force of *PHIPA*, these clauses do not apply where *PHIPA* applies: *HIA*, above note 42, s. 29(3).

491 *PHIPA*, s. 46(2).

492 *Krever Report*, above note 53, vol. I at 1.

493 *PHIPA*, ss. 29 and 6(3)(a).

2) Authorities before *PHIPA*

Before *PHIPA* came into force, generally, a health care provider's disclosure of a record of personal health information to police was authorized in very narrow circumstances. A health record could have been disclosed to police with consent of the patient to whom the record related or pursuant to a warrant. A warrant pertains to records and other things; that is, something tangible that can be seized. It does not authorize oral communications with police, such as a discussion that provides police with information enabling them to establish reasonable and probable grounds that evidence that relates to an offence is located at the custodian's, or other's, premises, for the purposes of obtaining a warrant. A health care provider, however, could have been authorized to provide information orally pursuant to a summons to witness, where a provider was required to make an appearance in court. A court proceeding, however, typically occurs well after the need for the information by police first arises.

Alternatively, a disclosure of patient information to police may have been authorized under a statute. For example, under the provisions of the *Coroners Act*, every person who has reason to believe that a deceased person died as a result of violence must immediately notify a coroner or a police officer of the facts and circumstances relating to the death.[494] Institutions subject to *FIPPA* or *MFIPPA*, such as the Ministry of Health and Long-Term Care could have also relied on provisions in those Acts that permit the disclosure of personal information to a law enforcement agency to aid in an investigation.[495] Finally, the common law "duty to warn" factors could have been applied in certain circumstances to justify a health care provider's disclosure of a patient's information to police.[496]

3) Authorities under *PHIPA*

a) Preservation of Authorities Pre-*PHIPA*

PHIPA preserves a custodian's ability to make the types of disclosures to the police discussed above, as permitted before *PHIPA* came into force. A health information custodian may continue to disclose personal health information about a patient to the police:

---

494   *Coroners Act*, above note 213, s. 10(1). Such a disclosure is thereby authorized under *PHIPA*, s. 43(1)(h).

495   *FIPPA*, above note 12, s. 42(g); *MFIPPA*, above note 12, s. 32(g).

496   See above Section K about the common law "duty to warn."

- with the express consent of the patient;[497]
- pursuant to a warrant;[498]
- for a proceeding;[499]
- to a law enforcement agency to aid in an investigation where the custodian is subject to *FIPPA* or *MFIPPA*;[500] and
- where permitted or required by law.[501]

b)   Other Authorities under *PHIPA*

Under *PHIPA*, a health information custodian may lawfully communicate with the police without the patient's consent in a number of situations that were not explicitly set out in legislation before *PHIPA* came into force.[502] In the majority of cases, where *PHIPA* permits a disclosure of personal health information, the Act does not refer to a specific recipient. A police officer may be one of several potential lawful recipients of personal health information, in either oral or recorded form, under *PHIPA*. A list of the most relevant of these permissible disclosure provisions, where the recipient could be the police, follows.

A custodian may disclose personal health information to the police:

- for the purpose of contacting a relative, friend, or potential substitute decision-maker of the patient, if the patient is injured, incapacitated, or ill and unable to give consent personally to the disclosure of personal health information;[503]
- where the information is limited to the fact that a patient is in the facility, the patient's general health status described in general terms, and the location of the patient in the facility. This permission to disclose applies only to health information custodians that are facilities, such as hospitals, psychiatric facilities, and nursing homes. A custodian may not rely on this clause as authority for a disclosure where the patient has objected to the disclosure,

---

497   *PHIPA*, s. 18(3)(a). See Chapter 5, Section F.

498   *Ibid.*, ss. 43(1)(g) & (h). See Section P(3) above.

499   *Ibid.*, ss. 41(1)(a) and (d). See Section M. Disclosures in proceedings are subject to limitations arising from legal privileges and restrictions which arise outside of *PHIPA*, as outlined in Section P(3) above.

500   *PHIPA*, s. 43(1)(f). See Section P(3) above.

501   *Ibid.*, s. 43(1)(h). The common law "duty to warn" is likely captured here in this list, as health information custodians apparently continue to be required to disclose patient information where the common law requires such a disclosure. See above Section K. However, *PHIPA* itself gives a health information custodian discretion, rather than imposing a requirement, to disclose personal health information for the purpose of eliminating or reducing a significant risk of serious bodily harm to any person.

502   The provisions noted here have been discussed elsewhere in this chapter.

503   *PHIPA*, s. 38(1)(c). See Section D above.

and the patient must be given the opportunity to object at the first reasonable opportunity after admission to the facility;[504]

- about a deceased individual or a person reasonably suspected to be deceased in order to identify the individual or, where reasonable in the circumstances, to inform the police of the fact of death and the circumstances of death;[505]
- where there are reasonable grounds to believe that the disclosure is necessary for the purpose of eliminating or reducing a significant risk of serious bodily harm to a person or group of persons;[506] and
- for the purpose of complying with a warrant or facilitating an investigation where the police are carrying out an investigation that is authorized by the warrant or by or under an Act of Ontario or Canada.[507]

In these situations, unless other prevailing legal requirements or privileges dictate otherwise,[508] a health information custodian may make, or may permit the custodian's agents to make, the necessary disclosure of personal health information to the police. It would be prudent for a custodian to have a policy and procedures in place governing disclosures of personal health information by the custodian and its agents to the police in the circumstances described in *PHIPA*. The policy and procedures could specify such matters as the conditions under which such disclosures, oral or recorded, will be made, when contact should be made with a legal or other advisor to discuss whether a disclosure should be made, and what documentation should be required of the police.

In a number of situations, a health information custodian's agent will have an obligation, independent of the custodian, to respond to a police inquiry. For example, an agent would have such an obligation where a law requires the agent to make such a disclosure,[509] or where the agent determines there are reasonable grounds to believe that a disclosure to the police is necessary for the purpose of eliminating or reducing a significant risk of serious bodily harm to a person or group of persons.[510]

It should be emphasized that, while the Act permits communications with the police in the circumstances noted above, *PHIPA* does not require a custodian to disclose personal health information to the police in such circum-

---

504   *PHIPA*, s. 38(3). See Section E above.

505   *Ibid.*, s. 38(4)(a), (b). See Section F above.

506   *Ibid.*, s. 40(1). See Section K above.

507   *Ibid.*, s. 43(1)(g). See Section P(3) above.

508   See Sections M(1)(c), (d), and P(3)(a), and Chapter 3, Section B(2).

509   *PHIPA*, s. 17(2), which authorizes the agent to disclose personal health information where the agent is "permitted or required by law."

510   *PHIPA* Regulation, above note 9, s. 7(2)(i).

stances, unless a law other than *PHIPA* requires the disclosure.[511] A law may require a custodian to disclose personal health information, for instance, in circumstances where a custodian must comply with a warrant, another statute places a mandatory duty on the health information custodian to report personal health information to the police,[512] or where the custodian is legally compelled to produce records or testify in court.[513]

c)   Obstructing the Police

What happens if a health information custodian or an agent of a custodian does not provide personal health information to the police, as requested? Under the *Criminal Code*, for example, while there is an obligation not to interfere with an activity of a police officer, there is no duty, generally, to actively assist the police. The relevant clause of the *Criminal Code* provides that it is an offence to resist or wilfully obstruct a public officer or peace officer in the execution of his or her duty or any person lawfully acting in aid of such an officer.[514] The word "wilfully" connotes an intention to bring about a prohibited result. In the context of this section "wilful" has been held to mean not only intentional acts, but also "something which is done without lawful excuse."[515] Where a police officer demands personal health information from a health information custodian or the custodian's agent, but there is no legal requirement to disclose the information in such a circumstance, and so the custodian declines to provide the information to the police, there would appear to be no basis upon which a charge of obstructing the police could be made.[516]

---

511   *PHIPA*, s. 6(3)(a).

512   See, for example, *Coroners Act*, above note 213, s. 10(1), where any person who has reason to believe that a deceased person died as a result of malpractice or during pregnancy, for example, must immediately notify a coroner or a police officer. Further, Bill 110, above note 150, if passed, would place a requirement on public hospitals and prescribed health facilities to make reports about certain patients afflicted with a gunshot wound to the police. See discussion of Bill 110 in Section K(6).

513   Where a law requires a disclosure, there may be remedies available to the custodian to challenge the requirement, where the custodian is concerned about making the disclosure, such as an application to court to quash a warrant, for example. This is further discussed in note 29 and accompanying text in Chapter 7, Section C(3); and above in Sections P(3) & M.

514   *Criminal Code*, above note 137, s. 129(a).

515   *Rice v. Connolly*, [1966] 2 Q.B. 414, referred to in *R. v. Buzzanga* (1979), 49 C.C.C. (2d) 369 (Ont. C.A.). This may not be the case if the custodian purposefully deceives or actively interferes with the police investigation.

516   *PHIPA*, s. 6(3)(a) is clear in specifying that a provision of the Act that permits a health information custodian to disclose personal health information about an individual without the consent of the individual "does not require the custodian to disclose it unless required to do so by law."

S. DISCLOSURES OUTSIDE ONTARIO: SECTION 50

PHIPA specifically addresses the disclosures of personal health information that a health information custodian in Ontario may make to a person in a jurisdiction outside Ontario. Generally, the purposes for which a custodian may disclose personal health information to a person outside Ontario are the same purposes for which the custodian may disclose such information within Ontario. However, *PHIPA* authorizes a custodian to make disclosures of personal health information outside Ontario for additional purposes.

The provisions in *PHIPA* that allow health information custodians to disclose personal health information with or without consent are generally not explicitly limited to disclosures that health information custodian may make within Ontario.[517] However, certain types of disclosures that a custodian is authorized to make under Part IV of *PHIPA* may not apply to disclosures to a person outside Ontario by virtue of the terms in which they are authorized:

- The provisions allowing one health information custodian to disclose personal health information to another custodian for the purpose of providing health care to a patient, whether authorized by way of an assumed implied consent[518] or authorized without consent where consent cannot be obtained in a timely way,[519] do not apply to disclosures that a health information custodian may make to a non-health information custodian, which requires explicit consent.[520]
- The provisions allowing for disclosures to a statutory body in Ontario, like the Public Guardian and Trustee,[521] apply only to disclosures to that body and not to bodies performing analogous roles outside Ontario.

When a health information custodian operates outside Ontario, generally the law of Ontario will not apply to the custodian's activities outside Ontario. When the custodian is in Ontario, but provides personal health information to an agent outside Ontario, or to an agent in Ontario who subsequently takes the

---

517   As discussed further below, *PHIPA*, s. 50 provides that disclosures of personal health information outside Ontario by a health information custodian are only permitted if they are made in accordance with s. 50, though one of the ways in which a custodian may comply with s. 50 is if the disclosure is permitted by a provision elsewhere in Part IV of the Act: *PHIPA*, s. 50(1)(b).

518   Under *PHIPA*, s. 20(2).

519   *Ibid.*, s. 38(1)(a).

520   *Ibid.*, s. 18(3)(a).

521   *Ibid.*, s. 43(1)(e).

information outside Ontario, it appears that the provisions of the Act that govern a custodian's responsibility for agents[522] continue to apply to the custodian with respect to the agent's activities.[523]

As noted above, given the limitations inherent in some of the disclosure provisions under *PHIPA*, it was apparently considered necessary to explicitly allow disclosures outside Ontario in specific circumstances, some of which go beyond the scope of what is permitted in Ontario. Under *PHIPA*, disclosures outside Ontario of personal health information by a health information custodian are permitted *only if* they fall into one or more of the following categories:

- disclosures pursuant to the patient's consent;[524]
- disclosures permitted by the Act; that is, where the terms of a provision of *PHIPA* allow a disclosure in unrestricted terms that can apply to a disclosure outside Ontario;[525]
- disclosures to a person who performs functions comparable to the functions of certain persons in Ontario to whom disclosure is permitted without consent, such as

  − the head of a penal or other custodial institution or of a psychiatric facility in another jurisdiction for the purpose of making a decision about

---

522 *PHIPA*, s. 17(1).

523 It is not clear to what extent the provisions governing the agent's responsibilities, that is, *PHIPA*, ss. 17(2) & (3), would be directly applicable to the agent when the agent is operating outside Ontario. A prudent custodian dealing with agents who are outside Ontario, or who may leave Ontario, or who send the information outside Ontario in the course of their duties, should have appropriate contractual provisions in place to ensure that the custodian continues to meet its obligation under s. 17(1) to be responsible for the information in its custody or control, which includes being in the custody or control of its agents in the course of the agency, and to ensure that it only permits its agents to use, retain, or disclose the information in accordance with the restrictions in s. 17(2).

524 *PHIPA*, s. 50(1)(a). These disclosures are permitted under the Act but need to be mentioned here since s. 50(1) allows disclosures outside Ontario "only if" one of the lettered clauses under that subsection apply.

525 *Ibid.*, s. 50(1)(b). Where a *PHIPA* provision does not mention specifically who the intended recipient of the personal health information may be, or where the intended recipient is specified in *PHIPA* but from the context of the provision it is evident that the recipient could be either within or outside Ontario, a custodian may rely on such a provision to disclose the information outside Ontario, in the appropriate circumstances. For example, this clause authorizes a health information custodian to disclose personal health information about a deceased patient, as set out in *PHIPA*, s. 38(4), to a person outside Ontario in the circumstances set out in s. 38(4). Similarly, s. 50(1)(b) authorizes a health information custodian to disclose personal health information as authorized under s. 40(1) (risk of harm).

the appropriate placement of the patient, or to make arrangements for the provision of health care,[526]

- an organization outside Ontario performing statutory functions analogous to those performed by the Public Guardian and Trustee, the Children's Lawyer, a children's aid society, or the Registrar of Adoption Information in Ontario,[527]
- a licensing or regulatory body governing a class of health care providers;[528]

• disclosures that are reasonably necessary for the provision of health care, unless the patient has instructed the custodian not to disclose the information;[529]

• disclosures that are reasonably necessary for the administration of payments in connection with the provision of health care to the patient or for contractual or legal requirements in that connection;[530]

• disclosures by a health information custodian that is a prescribed planning entity and is prescribed under *PHIPA* to another provincial or territorial government regarding health care provided in Ontario to a resident of that

---

526 *PHIPA*, s. 50(1)(c). This provision refers to *PHIPA*, s. 40(2) to describe such a person in charge of such facilities.

527 *Ibid.*, s. 50(1)(c). This provision refers to *PHIPA*, s. 43(1)(e), to describe such organizations.

528 *Ibid.*, s. 50(1)(c). This provision refers to *PHIPA*, ss. 43(1)(b), (c), & (d) to describe such bodies, which refer respectively to a College within the meaning of the *RHPA*, above note 180; the Board of Regents under the *DPA*, above note 180, and a College, as defined in the *SWSSWA*, above note 180. This would appear to allow, for example, a health professions regulatory body outside Ontario to be advised where one of its members was found to be guilty of professional incompetence in Ontario. (Such notification may not always need to include personal health information, however.)

529 *PHIPA*, s. 50(1)(e). Where a patient has instructed a custodian not to disclose personal health information about him or her for the provision of health care to the patient, the custodian may still disclose that information for other purposes that this subsection permits without the patient's consent. Furthermore, as in other contexts in the Act where this type of provision is found, if due to such an express instruction a custodian is prevented from disclosing all personal health information that the custodian considers reasonably necessary to disclose for the provision of health care to the patient, the disclosing custodian must notify the receiving person of that fact: *PHIPA*, s. 50(2). Public hospitals are exempted from this obligation to notify until 1 November 2005: *PHIPA*, s. 31(2). See further, Chapter 7, Section G.

530 *PHIPA*, s. 50(1)(f). This appears to be broader than the authority to disclose personal health information within Ontario for this purpose, perhaps with the aim of ensuring that health care provided outside Ontario is not impeded by restrictions on providing information for the purposes of facilitating payment for the services.

province or territory, for the purposes of health planning or health administration;[531] and

- disclosures by the Canadian Institute for Health Information[532] to another provincial or territorial government regarding health care provided in Ontario to a resident of that province or territory, for the purposes of health planning or health administration.[533]

A health information custodian is not required to make any disclosures set out in this section of *PHIPA*, though of course other applicable law may require such a disclosure.[534] In appropriate circumstances, a custodian may choose to impose conditions[535] on disclosures to be made outside Ontario. For example, a custodian may require a recipient outside Ontario to have in place the administrative, technical, and physical safeguards that are appropriate in the circumstances to ensure the security, accuracy, and integrity of the information.[536]

531 *PHIPA*, s. 50(1)(d). At the time of writing no prescribed health entity is listed as a health information custodian so this clause is not operational.

532 The Canadian Institute for Health Information is discussed further in Chapter 11, Section E.

533 *PHIPA* Regulation, above note 9, s. 18(7). Note that *PHIPA*, s. 50(1)(d) does not apply since although the Canadian Institute for Health Information is a prescribed planning entity, as discussed in Chapter 11, it is not a health information custodian.

534 *PHIPA*, ss. 6(3)(a) & (b).

535 A health information custodian may impose such conditions by way of confidentiality agreements, for example.

536 Custodians disclosing personal health information outside Ontario would have been required to ensure that the recipient had such safeguards in place under the terms of the 1997 Draft Legislation, above note 96, s. 21. This provision was not incorporated into *PHIPA*, perhaps because it is not appropriate in all circumstances, such as when the disclosure is necessary for health care and the custodian is, practically speaking, unable to exercise such control in the circumstances. Even a requirement like that in Bill 159, above note 96, s. 37, that for disclosures of personal health information outside Ontario, the custodian must believe on reasonable grounds that the person receiving the information will take appropriate steps to preserve its confidentiality, would be too onerous in such situations since the information may be required and the custodian may not be in the position to harbour such a belief.

11 Health Research and Health System Planning and Analysis

A. GENERALLY

It is clear that the collection, use, and disclosure of personal health information is crucially important for the provision of health care. However, there is also widespread recognition that personal health information is essential for a number of secondary uses of great importance, including health research and health system planning and analysis. Most recently, the First Ministers noted the need for such secondary uses as part of their ten-year plan to strengthen health care.[1] The First Ministers recognized the need to collect meaningful health information to assess progress made in achieving improvements in the health care system, such as reduced wait times. This recognition built on comments included in the report of the Commission on the Future of Health Care in Canada, which highlighted the importance of better information sharing systems to government and provider accountability to Canadians.[2] The Information and Privacy

---

1   Office of the Prime Minister, News Release, "A 10-year Plan to Strengthen Health Care" (16 September 2004), online: <www.pm.gc.ca/eng/news.asp?category=1&id=260> [10-year plan].

2   According to the report, "If we are to build a better health system, we need a better information sharing system so that all governments and all providers can be accountable to Canadians." Canada, Commission on the Future of Health Care in Canada, *Building on Values: The Future of Health Care in Canada* (Ottawa: The Commission, 2002) at xix. See also Chapter 3 of the report.

Commissioner has also acknowledged that activities like health research are vital to the development of new treatments and cures for diseases.[3]

It is not always possible to carry out health research and health system planning and analysis on the basis of de-identified information. Identifiers are often necessary to link various records of personal health information about a patient. Health research often requires accessing records from many custodians, such as hospitals, laboratories, and physicians. Linking permits the study of relationships between certain health determinants and health status. Linking also permits the tracking of patients over time in order to study the evolution of certain diseases after long latent periods or to assess patients' progress over the continuum of health care.

The *Personal Health Information Protection Act, 2004*[4] reflects the importance of health research and health system planning by allowing limited use and disclosure of personal health information for such secondary purposes in a manner that also protects the privacy of the patients whose information is the subject of the use or disclosure. This balance is accomplished with the involvement of such bodies as the Information and Privacy Commissioner, research ethics boards, prescribed health registries, health data institutes, and prescribed planning entities. This chapter explains the roles of such bodies in the context of health research and health system planning and analysis.

B. RESEARCH

1) Background

PHIPA includes special rules concerning the use and disclosure of personal health information for research purposes. These special rules reflect the importance of health research in the steady improvement in health care capabilities, which benefit us all. The research rules in the Act reflect an effort to harmonize as much as possible the protection of the privacy of personal health information with the public interest served by health research.[5]

---

3   Information and Privacy Commissioner/Ontario, *Frequently Asked Questions: Health Information Protection Act* (13 August 2004), online: <www.ipc.on.ca>. See the question: "Why do we need a health privacy law in Ontario?"

4   S.O. 2004, c. 3, Sch. A [*PHIPA*].

5   It is interesting to note that *PHIPA's* requirements with respect to a health information custodian's use and disclosure of personal health information for the purpose of carrying out research are largely consistent with recommendations in the *Krever Report*: Ontario, Royal Commission of Inquiry into the Confidentiality of Health

2) Application of Requirements Related to Research

a) Application of Requirements to De-identified Information

Health information custodians and researchers should remember that the research rules found in *PHIPA* do not apply to the use and disclosure of information that is not personal health information within the meaning of the Act. Therefore, the research rules do not apply to a health information custodian's disclosure of aggregate or statistical information that is not personal health information, such as information that has been de-identified.[6] The definition of the term "personal health information" is important in this context.[7]

b) Application of Requirements Where Consent Is Obtained

Likewise, health information custodians and researchers should keep in mind that the research rules found in *PHIPA* only apply to situations in which a health information custodian uses or discloses personal health information for the purpose of carrying out research without the consent of the patients to whom the information relates.[8] It is not necessary for health information custodians to comply with the research rules set out in the Act where the use or disclosure occurs with the consent of the patients to whom the information relates. Consent is an alternative authority for the collection, use, and disclosure of personal health information for the purpose of carrying out research.[9] A health information custodian may use a patient's name and contact informa-

---

Records in Ontario, *Report of the Commission of Inquiry into the Confidentiality of Health Information* (Toronto: Queen's Printer, 1980) vol. 3 at 51, Recommendation 94.

6   *PHIPA*, s. 47(1) defines the term "de-identify" to mean "in relation to personal health information of an individual, [which] means to remove any information that identifies the individual or for which it is reasonably foreseeable in the circumstances that it could be utilized, either alone or with other information, to identify the individual" and "de-identification" has a corresponding meaning. Although defined in the context of the Act's rules for the Minister's directed disclosures of personal health information to a health data institute, the term "de-identify" is useful more generally to communicate in a precise way the idea of modifying personal health information so that it is no longer personal health information. See Chapter 2, Section C(1)(d) for a discussion of de-identified information.

7   See Chapter 2, Section C for a detailed discussion of what constitutes "personal health information."

8   *PHIPA*, ss. 18(2) & (3). A health information custodian who discloses personal health information about a patient to a researcher for the purpose of research may rely on the patient's express consent to make the disclosure. A custodian may collect and use personal health information about a patient for the purpose of research, however, on the basis of the patient's express or implied consent.

9   *Ibid.*, s. 29.

tion for the purpose of seeking the patient's consent.[10] Where a custodian relies on a patient's consent to use and disclose personal health information for the purpose of carrying out research, the custodian may choose to follow some of the research rules found in the Act as a matter of practice, but it is not required to do so. For example, a health information custodian may choose to enter into an agreement with the researcher, even where not required by law.

c) Application of Other Rules Concerning Research

Health information custodians and researchers should be aware that the research provisions in *PHIPA* do not replace all other requirements, policies, and guidelines concerning research applicable to a health information custodian's collection, use, and disclosure of personal health information for the purpose of carrying out research. For example, the researcher may also be required to fulfil any applicable requirements of the *Tri-Council Policy Statement: Ethical Conduct for Research Involving Humans*,[11] the Food and Drug Regulations,[12] and/or the *International Conference on Harmonization — Good Clinical Practice Guidelines.*[13]

As discussed above in Chapter 2, *PHIPA*'s definition of "personal health information" does not include any reference to blood, tissue, or other samples from humans as types of personal health information, and an analysis of the definition strongly suggests that samples do not constitute personal health information for the purposes of the Act.[14] As a result, *PHIPA* does not govern a health information custodian's collection, use, or provision of such samples for the purpose of carrying out research.

From a practical perspective, however, research ethics boards will likely consider health information custodians' use of such samples when asked to approve a research plan that involves the use or disclosure of personal health informa-

---

10 *PHIPA*, s. 37(1)(j). A custodian, however, cannot disclose the information to a researcher who is not an agent of the custodian for the purpose of the researcher obtaining consent.

11 Medical Research Council of Canada, Natural Sciences and Engineering Research Council of Canada, Social Sciences and Humanities Research Council of Canada, *Tri-Council Policy Statement: Ethical Conduct for Research Involving Humans* (Ottawa: June 2003), online: <www.ncehr-cnerh.org/english/code_2> [TCPS]. The Councils consider funding, or continued funding, only to individuals and institutions that certify compliance with this policy regarding research involving human subjects.

12 *Food and Drug Regulations*, C.R.C., c. 870, Part C, Division 5 (Drugs for Clinical Trials Involving Human Subjects) [*Food and Drug Regulations*].

13 International Conference on Harmonization of Technical Requirements for the Registration of Pharmaceuticals for Human Use, 1997, *Good Clinical Practice: Consolidated Guidelines* (Ottawa: Minister of Public Works and Government Services, 1997), online: <www.ncehr-cnerh.org/english/gcp>.

14 See Chapter 2, Section C for a more detailed discussion of this issue.

tion together with a sample, particularly where the approval of the research ethics board is required for such use or disclosure, whether under other legislation, or as a matter of organizational policy. Therefore, despite the fact that the use and disclosure of such samples falls outside the scope of *PHIPA*, research ethics boards will often take the inclusion of a sample with personal health information into consideration in determining whether to approve a research plan and in enumerating the conditions to which its approval is subject.

d) Application of Requirements in Other Legislation

The introduction of requirements concerning the use and disclosure of personal health information for the purpose of carrying out research is new to many settings. Some health information custodians are unaccustomed to statutory requirements governing their use and disclosure of personal health information for the purpose of carrying out research,[15] while others are more accustomed to the need to turn their minds to such statutory requirements concerning research.[16] *PHIPA* makes it clear that, where an Act other than *PHIPA* permits a health information custodian to disclose personal health information to a researcher for the purpose of conducting research, the custodian and researcher are required to comply with *PHIPA's* research-related rules.[17] For example, the *Cancer Act* refers to the disclosure of information respecting a case of cancer for the purpose of enabling Cancer Care Ontario to carry out medical research.[18] When a custodian wishes to disclose personal health information to Cancer Care Ontario for the purpose of enabling Cancer Care Ontario to carry out research without the express consent of the patient to whom the information

---

15 For example, there were no statutory requirements specific to research carried out by community mental health centres. Likewise, although *Professional Misconduct*, O. Reg. 856/93, s. 1(2)(b), made under the *Medicine Act*, S.O. 1991, c. 30 [Reg. 856], provides that it is not professional misconduct for a physician to give information about a patient, including access to the patient's records, to a person for the purpose of research or health administration or planning if the physician reasonably believes that the person will take reasonable steps to protect the identity of the patient, the regulation does not set out a process and requirements for such disclosures.

16 Prior to *PHIPA* coming into force, the *Long-Term Care Act, 1994*, S.O. 1994, c. 26, s. 32(2)(g) provided persons governed by that Act with direction concerning the disclosure of personal health information for the purpose of research. *PHIPA*, s. 89(6) repealed this provision of the *Long-Term Care Act, 1994*.

17 *PHIPA*, s. 44(9).

18 R.S.O. 1990, c. 1, s. 7(1). Although this provision does not explicitly refer to the disclosure of personal health information, s. 7(2) clarifies that the Act contemplates the disclosure of information to Cancer Care Ontario. Some such provisions have been repealed: see *PHIPA*, s. 90(6) concerning s. 35(3)(f) of the *Mental Health Act*, R.S.O. 1990, c. M.7.

relates, the health information custodian and Cancer Care Ontario must ensure compliance with the research rules set out in *PHIPA*.

e) Application to Personal Information

In some instances, a researcher may submit a research plan for a health information custodian's disclosure of both personal health information and personal information that does not constitute personal health information. Where the custodian is also an institution under the *Freedom of Information and Protection of Privacy Act* or the *Municipal Freedom of Information and Protection of Privacy Act*, the research-related rules of *PHIPA* apply to the entire disclosure to the researcher and those two other Acts do not apply.[19] This provision is consistent with the policy thrust of the provision of *PHIPA* concerning mixed records.[20]

3) What Is "Research"?

a) Definition

PHIPA defines the term "research" to mean a systematic investigation designed to develop or establish principles, facts, or generalizable[21] knowledge, or any combination of them, and includes the development, testing, and evaluation of research.[22] This definition draws upon other definitions of research. For example, the definition is similar to the definition of research included in the *Tri-Council Policy Statement: Ethical Conduct for Research Involving Humans*.[23]

---

19 *PHIPA*, s. 44(7). Both the *Freedom of Information and Protection of Privacy Act*, R.S.O. 1990, c. F.31, s. 2 [*FIPPA*] and the *Municipal Freedom of Information and Protection of Privacy Act*, R.S.O. 1990, c. M.56, s. 2(1) [*MFIPPA*] define the term "institution."

20 *PHIPA*, s. 4(3). See Chapter 2, Section C(1)(e), for a discussion of the concept of "mixed records."

21 Although not defined in the Act, knowledge may be "generalizable" when it contributes to the knowledge regarding health that is generally accessible through standard searches of academic literature. Further, where the knowledge to be developed by an investigation is applicable to groups beyond the group being studied, it may be considered "generalizable." A patient whose information is the subject of the investigation may or may not benefit directly from the investigation, but a larger group is expected to gain from the knowledge developed by the investigation. See Johns Hopkins Medicine Institutional Review Boards, *Definition of Research as it Applies to Clinical Practice, Quality Improvement/Quality Assurance, and Public Health Activities* (Baltimore, Maryland: February 2004), online: <http://irb.jhmi.edu/Guidelines/QI_QA.html>. See also Alberta Research Ethics Community Consensus Initiative, *Draft Recommendations for Ethics Screening and Review of Research, Program Evaluation, and Quality Assurance or Quality Improvement* (Edmonton, Alberta: 10 May 2004) [Ethics Screening Recommendations].

22 *PHIPA*, s. 2.

23 TCPS, above note 11 in Article 1.1.a. defines "research" as "a systematic investigation to establish facts, principles or generalizable knowledge."

b)   "Research" and Other Investigations

PHIPA permits health information custodians to use personal health information without the consent of the patient to whom the information relates "for
the purpose of activities to improve or maintain the quality of care or to
improve or maintain the quality of any related programs or services of the custodian."[24] The Act also permits a health information custodian to use personal
health information to plan or evaluate services that the custodian provides.[25] It
is not necessary for a health information custodian to turn to the research rules
set out in the Act to use personal health information where a health information custodian uses personal health information for such purposes.[26] Although
the Act does not include interpretative guidance about the scope of these provisions, quality improvement programs often have as their purpose the
improvement or assessment of service delivery. Where the purpose of the
investigation is to justify the introduction, continuation, elimination, or significant modification of a health service, then the investigation may be service
planning or evaluation.[27]

4) Collection of Personal Health Information for Research

What is a health information custodian's[28] authority to collect personal health
information for the purpose of carrying out research? The response to this
question depends on the source of the information.

---

24   *PHIPA*, s. 37(1)(d). TCPS, *ibid.*, in Article 1.1(d) also provides that quality assurance
     studies, performance reviews, or testing within normal educational requirements
     should not be subject to research ethics board review for the purpose of the TCPS.
     Studies related directly to assessing the performance of an organization or its employ-
     ees or students, within the mandate of the organization or according to the terms and
     conditions of employment or training, should also not be subject to research ethics
     board review for the purposes of the TCPS. However, performance reviews or studies
     that contain an element of research in addition to assessment may need ethics review
     under the TCPS.
25   *PHIPA*, s. 37(1)(c).
26   *Ibid.*, s. 37(1)(j) provides that a health information custodian may use personal health
     information without the consent of the patient to whom the information for research
     relates, conducted by the custodian in accordance with *PHIPA's* research rules
     "unless another clause of this subsection applies."
27   Ethics Screening Recommendations, above note 21.
28   *PHIPA* does not address the authority for a researcher who is not a health informa-
     tion custodian to collect personal health information for the purpose of carrying out
     research, as it is beyond the scope of the Act's focus on the activities of health infor-
     mation custodians. Other legislation may speak to this issue, however (e.g., *Personal
     Information Protection and Electronic Documents Act*, S.C. 2000, c. 5 [*PIPEDA*]).

a) From a Health Information Custodian

Where a health information custodian collects personal health information from another custodian, such as the Ministry of Health and Long-Term Care or a hospital, for the purpose of carrying out research, *PHIPA* authorizes the researcher custodian to collect the information in any case where the disclosing custodian is permitted to disclose it, provided that the disclosing custodian acted in accordance with the research rules of the Act[29] in making the disclosure.[30] Alternatively, a health information custodian may collect personal health information from a custodian who may disclose the information for the purpose of carrying out research with the consent of the patient to whom the information relates.[31]

b) From a Non-Health Information Custodian

In other instances, a health information custodian may collect personal health information from a person who is not a health information custodian for the purpose of carrying out research. For example, a health information custodian may collect personal health information for the purpose of carrying out research from a government body, such as Statistics Canada, a registry of personal health information that is not a health information custodian, or a weight-management service provider.[32] The source of the information may be within or outside Ontario. In such instances, the custodian can rely on the provision of *PHIPA* that permits a health information custodian to collect personal health information from a person who is not a health information custodian for the purpose of carrying out research that is conducted in accordance with the research rules of the Act, provided that the person is not prohibited by law from disclosing the information to the custodian.[33] Alternatively, the researcher custodian may collect the information with the consent of the patient to whom the information relates.[34]

---

29 The research rules pertaining to disclosures of personal health information by health information custodians are primarily found in *PHIPA*, s. 44.

30 *PHIPA*, s. 36(1)(g).

31 A combination of *PHIPA*, ss. 29, 36(1)(a), and 36(1)(g) would apply, depending on the extent of the consent.

32 Section 2(1) in *General*, O. Reg. 329/04 [*PHIPA* Regulation] clarifies that persons who provide such services are not health information custodians.

33 *PHIPA*, s. 36(1)(d) provides that a health information custodian may collect personal health information from a person who is not a health information custodian for the purpose of research carried out in accordance with *PHIPA*'s research rules. Such collections are only authorized under this provision where the research is conducted in accordance with the research provisions of *PHIPA*, which generally require the researcher to develop a research plan and obtain a research ethics board's approval of the plan.

34 A combination of *PHIPA*, ss. 29 and/or 36(1)(a) would apply, depending on the circumstances (e.g., whether the custodian collected the information directly).

5) Use of Personal Health Information for Research

Of course, a health information custodian may have collected personal health information for one purpose, such as the provision of health care, but may then wish to use it for the secondary purpose of carrying out research, or to provide it to an agent[35] for that purpose. In such instances, no authority is required for the custodian to collect the information for the purpose of carrying out research, as it was collected for another purpose. The custodian, however, requires authority to use the information for this purpose. The health information custodian's use is permitted provided that the custodian follows the applicable research rules in *PHIPA*.[36] The custodian is required to prepare a research plan and obtain approval of the plan from the research ethics board. The custodian is also required to comply with certain requirements set out in the Act.[37] These requirements, which also apply where a health information custodian discloses personal health information to a researcher, are described in detail below.

6) Disclosure of Personal Health Information for Research

a) Power to Disclose Personal Health Information

As mentioned above, *PHIPA* permits a health information custodian to use and disclose personal health information for research purposes without the consent of the patients to whom the information relates provided that the requirements of the Act are fulfilled.

A health information custodian may disclose personal health information to a researcher for research purposes if the researcher enters into a research agreement with the custodian[38] and submits to the custodian:

i)   an application in writing;[39]

ii)   a research plan;[40] and

---

35   Recall that a custodian's provision of personal health information to an agent is a use of the information and not a disclosure: *PHIPA*, s. 6(1). An agent may use personal health information on a custodian's behalf where the custodian is permitted to use the information: *PHIPA*, s. 17(1). See Chapter 2, Section B(2) for a discussion of agents.

36   *PHIPA*, ss. 37(1)(j) and 37(3). *PHIPA*, s. 37(4) provides that if a research plan proposes that a *FIPPA/MFIPPA* custodian use personal health information, together with personal information within the meaning of *FIPPA/MFIPPA* that is not personal health information, ss. 37(1)(j) and 37(3) of *PHIPA* apply to the use of the personal health information, and *FIPPA/MFIPPA* do not apply.

37   *PHIPA*, s. 37(3).

38   *Ibid.*, ss. 44(1)(b) and 44(5).

39   The Act does not identify additional requirements for the application and the *PHIPA* Regulation does not prescribe a form.

40   See Section B(6)(b) below.

iii) a copy of the decision of a research ethics board approving the research plan.[41]

Like most other disclosures of personal health information that the Act permits to occur without consent of the patients to whom the information relates, a health information custodian's disclosure to a researcher is at the discretion of the health information custodian; the custodian is not required to make the disclosure. The health information custodian must consider whether it wishes to make the disclosure, even where the researcher has fulfilled all the requirements of the Act.

Some health information custodians may be concerned about exercising this discretion to disclose personal health information to researchers. When approached by a researcher with an application, research plan, and copy of a research ethics board's approval, how does a health information custodian know whether the research ethics board was properly constituted? Is the custodian required to confirm the composition of the research ethics board? How can a custodian be certain that the approval is authentic? As with many other requirements applicable to health information custodians, the custodian should act reasonably. Custodians who disclose personal health information to a researcher in good faith and reasonably,[42] in the circumstances, are protected by the immunity provisions in *PHIPA*.[43] Where the health information custodian receives documentation from the researcher that does not suggest impropriety, the custodian is not required to probe further. However, where the documentation is unusual in some regard or the research ethics board is not one with which the custodian is familiar, it may be reasonable to expect the custodian to pose questions to the researcher to ensure compliance with the Act. The custodian may consider requesting documentation from the research ethics board attesting that, for example, that the composition of the board fulfilled the requirements of the Act.[44]

b) Research Plans

The requirements for research plans are set out in *PHIPA* and the regulation made under *PHIPA*.[45] Research plans must be in writing and must set out the following matters:

---

41   *PHIPA*, s. 44(1)(a).

42   For a discussion of the meaning of "reasonable" in the context of a health information custodian's actions, see Chapter 4.

43   *PHIPA*, s. 71(1). See Chapter 15 for a discussion of *PHIPA*, s. 71(1).

44   Such an attestation is required in the context of the *Food and Drug Regulations*, above note 12.

45   *PHIPA*, s. 44(2) and *PHIPA* Regulation, above note 32, s. 16. There is no prescribed form for research plans.

1. *The affiliation of each person involved in the research.*[46]

    For example, the researcher may indicate whether the researcher is conducting the research on behalf of an organization, or with the support of an organization.

2. *A description of the research proposed to be conducted, and the duration of the research.*[47]

    This aspect of the research plan will likely be the most detailed and lengthy. The description of the research should be thorough, so as to permit the members of the research ethics board to understand the research and the role of the personal health information in the research.

3. *The nature and objectives of the research, and the public or scientific benefit of the research that the researcher anticipates.*[48]

    This aspect of the proposal may overlap with the description of the research proposed to be conducted. The researcher should provide detailed information to support a conclusion that the research will result in public or scientific benefits. Such information may include information concerning other research that the researcher or others have carried out.

4. *A description of the personal health information required and the potential sources.*[49]

    For the purposes of clarity, it is appropriate that the researcher describe each data element sought. The researcher should describe the potential sources of the personal health information with similar specificity (e.g., particular hospitals, physicians in a specific geographic area).

5. *A description of how the personal health information will be used in the research; and, if it will be linked to other information, a description of the other information as well as how the linkage will be done.*[50]

    The researcher may propose to link the personal health information to other information, perhaps already in the possession of the researcher, or not sought from a health information custodian. Typically, to link a record of personal health information to another record of information, the records must share a common data element that is unique. When dealing with personal health information, researchers and others often use a

---

46   *PHIPA*, s. 44(2)(a).
47   *PHIPA* Regulation, above note 32, s. 16(1).
48   *PHIPA*, s. 44(2)(b).
49   *PHIPA* Regulation, above note 32, s. 16(2).
50   *Ibid.*, s. 16(3).

patient's health number to link two or more records of personal health information. Information about such linkages is important to a research ethics board's assessment of the privacy implications of the research.

In addition to a description of any linkages, in describing how the personal health information will be used in the research, the researcher should discuss such matters as the nature of the proposed analysis of the information.

6. *An explanation as to why the research cannot reasonably be accomplished without the personal health information and, if it is to be linked to other information, an explanation as to why this linkage is required.*[51]
It may be possible for the researcher to carry out the research with less personal health information than he or she is seeking to use or have disclosed. Alternatively, it may be possible for the researcher to carry out the research without personal health information by using de-identified information.[52]

Identifiers, however, may be necessary to link various records of personal health information about a patient. Linking, for example, permits the tracking of patients over time in order to study the development of diseases or to assess patients' progress over the continuum of health care. Once the linkage is complete, the information can often be de-identified such that re-identification is not possible.

7. *An explanation as to why consent to the disclosure of the personal health information is not being sought from the individuals to whom the information relates.*[53]
The researcher should fulfil this requirement on the assumption that consent will be necessary unless shown otherwise. Unless there is a reason why obtaining consent would be impractical, it generally would be reasonable to require patients' consent to the disclosure of their personal health information for the purpose of research. The researcher should discuss such matters as the number of patients whose personal health information is sought, difficulties in contacting patients for their consent, and whether the patients have passed away since the custodian collected their personal health information. The need to have information from a complete group of patients, without omissions or effective self-selection on the

---

51 *Ibid.*, s. 16(4).
52 Researchers and health information custodians should keep in mind *PHIPA*, s. 30, which sets out the general limiting principles of the Act, as they apply to a health information custodian's collection, use, and disclosure of personal health information. See Chapter 7.
53 *PHIPA* Regulation, above note 32, s. 16(5).

basis of refusals to consent, may also be a basis for showing that consent should not be required in certain circumstances.

8. *A description of the reasonably foreseeable harms and benefits that may arise from the use of the personal health information and how the researchers intend to address those harms.*[54]
   To be clear, the description relates to harms "that may arise from the use of the personal health information." Other possible harms, such as those related to a patient's participation in a clinical trial, are not the subject of this description. Reasonably foreseeable harms may include a risk of further disclosure of a patient's personal health information, or a risk of concern or anxiety on the part of patients to whom the information relates about the security of their personal health information. Benefits, on the other hand, may include improved delivery of health services or treatments as a consequence of the research based on personal health information that can be relied on as valid, complete, and accurate.

9. *A description of all persons who will have access to the information, why their access is necessary, their roles in relation to the research, and their related qualifications.*[55]
   Some research involves many investigators, while other research involves only a few or even just one. *PHIPA* and its regulation do not require the researcher to include the names of all such persons. The description may describe a category of persons where these persons share the same roles and qualifications. In describing why such persons require access to the personal health information, a researcher should consider whether any such person may carry out their work as part of the research with information that is not personal health information, such as de-identified health information.

10. *The safeguards that the researcher will impose to protect the confidentiality and security of the personal health information, including an estimate of how long information will be retained in an identifiable form and why.*[56]
    Once a researcher has personal health information in his or her custody, the researcher must not disclose the information except in accordance with *PHIPA*.[57] To ensure that the researcher does not disclose the information in an unauthorized manner, even unintentionally, the researcher should impose safeguards to protect the confidentiality and security of the

---

54   *Ibid.*, s. 16(6).
55   *Ibid.*, s. 16(7).
56   *Ibid.*, s. 16(8).
57   *PHIPA*, s. 44(6)(d).

personal health information. Such safeguards may include physical, technical, and administrative safeguards, such as confidentiality agreements with persons who will have access to the information, password protected databases, and secure premises on which to carry out the research.[58]

As a matter of good practice, researchers should work from de-identified health information as much as possible. Working with de-identified health information helps researchers reduce the risk of unauthorized access to the information. Researchers may conceal the identity of the patients to whom the personal health information relates by assigning a unique identifier to a patient and removing all other identifiers from data sets that relate to that patient. A researcher may use a computer to construct algorithms that generate such unique identifiers for patients.

11. *Information as to how and when the personal health information will be disposed of or returned to the health information custodian.*[59]
     Appropriate disposal of personal health information is an essential aspect of the security of personal health information. Like health information custodians, researchers must take appropriate steps to dispose of personal health information in a manner that prevents subsequent use or reconstruction of the record.[60]

12. *The funding source of the research.*[61]
     The information that the researcher provides to fulfil this requirement should reflect all funding sources, whether the source(s) operate in the public or private sector, or on a for-profit or not-for-profit basis.

13. *Whether the researcher has applied for the approval of another research ethics board, and if so, the response to or status of the application.*[62]
     In addition to this basic information about applications before other research ethics boards, the researcher may wish to include how the application before the other research ethics board may have differed from the application before the current research ethics board. For example, the application may have dealt with a request for different categories or amounts of personal health information.

---

58 See Chpat er 4, Section F(4) for additional examples of physical, technical, and administrative safeguards.
59 *PHIPA* Regulation, above note 32, s. 16(9).
60 See Chapter 4, Section K for a discussion of the appropriate disposal of personal health information.
61 *PHIPA* Regulation, above note 32, s. 16(10).
62 *Ibid.*, s. 16(11).

14. *Whether the researcher's interest in the disclosure of the personal health information or the performance of the research would likely result in an actual or perceived conflict of interest with other duties of the researcher.*[63]

A conflict of interest may arise, for example, between the researcher's planned research and the researcher's duties to another party, such as a funding source for the research that would have a clear interest in the results of the research.

c) Research Ethics Boards

i) Role

Many health information custodians are familiar with the role of research ethics boards in the conduct of research. *PHIPA* focuses on one particular role for research ethics boards: the approval of research plans from an informational privacy perspective. The research plans that require the approval of a research ethics board under the Act are those research plans of a researcher (a) who seeks to have a health information custodian disclose personal health information to him or her without the consent of the patients to whom the information relates; or (b) who is a health information custodian[64] seeking to use personal health information in his or her custody or control for the purpose of carrying out research without the consent of the patients to whom the information relates.

ii) Composition

In *PHIPA*, the term "research ethics board" is defined to mean a board of persons that is established for the purpose of approving research plans under section 44 and that meets the requirements enumerated in the regulation.[65] The regulation made under the Act sets out additional requirements.[66] In many respects, these criteria align with those identified for research ethics boards in the *Tri-Council Policy Statement: Ethical Conduct for Research Involving Humans.*[67] A research ethics board must have at least five members, including

---

63 *Ibid.*, s. 16(12).

64 Also, *PHIPA* Regulation, *ibid.* ss. 18(3) and 13(4) provide that a prescribed planning entity and a prescribed health registry may use personal health information for the purpose of carrying out research as if they were a health information custodian for the purposes of ss. 37(1)(j) and 37(3) of *PHIPA*. See Sections C and E below for a discussion of prescribed health registries and prescribed planning entities.

65 *PHIPA*, s. 2.

66 *PHIPA* Regulation, above note 32, s. 15.

67 TCPS, above note 11.

- at least one member with no affiliation with the person or persons that established the research ethics board;[68]
- at least one member knowledgeable in research ethics, either as a result of formal training in research ethics, or practical or academic experience in research ethics;[69]
- at least two members with expertise in the methods or in the areas of the research being considered;[70] and
- at least one member knowledgeable in considering privacy issues.[71]

A research ethics board may only act with respect to a proposal to approve a research plan where there is no conflict of interest existing or likely to be perceived[72] between its duty under the Act in considering whether to approve research plans and any participating board member's personal interest in the disclosure of the personal health information or the performance of the research.[73] To help determine whether a situation gives rise to a conflict of interest, a research ethics board may consider whether a third party would question the ability of the member to make a proper decision due to the member's possible consideration of private interests. Alternatively, a research ethics board may consider whether the public would lose faith in the integrity of the research ethics board's review process if it had accurate knowledge about the situation.[74] Therefore, for example, a research ethics board could not approve a research plan where a member of the research ethics board would benefit from the board's approval of the research plan through his or her association with the researcher, perhaps by a monetary gain that is expected to arise as a result of the member's investment in the proposed research.

PHIPA does not set out limitations on the researchers from whom any given research ethics boards can accept and approve research plans. This is a

---

68   This member may represent the community to which the research relates, for example, or the community in which the person that established the research ethics board is located.

69   Examples of such persons may include bioethicists and scholars of research ethics.

70   For example, for epidemiological research, an epidemiologist may fulfil this membership requirement.

71   The language used to describe this member is not very specific. Persons who may fulfil this role on a research ethics board include a privacy officer or a lawyer whose practice includes privacy law.

72   As stated in the TCPS, above note 11, in Section 4, Conflict of Interest, "The appearance of a conflict may in some cases be as damaging as a real conflict."

73   *PHIPA* Regulation, above note 32, s. 15(2).

74   TCPS, above note 11, in Section 4, Conflict of Interest, includes this guidance to help research ethics boards identify conflicts of interest concerning researchers. Research ethics boards are accustomed to such considerations.

matter that is left up to researchers and research ethics boards. A researcher may approach the research ethics board of the health information custodian from which the researcher seeks a disclosure of personal health information. For example, a researcher seeking a disclosure of personal health information from a large teaching hospital in Toronto may seek the approval of the research ethics board in place at the hospital. It is also possible that several health information custodians with similar interests, perhaps custodians from the same part of the health sector, such as the long-term care sector, may work together to establish one research ethics board for a group of custodians in that sector.[75] Alternatively, a group of entities that researchers often approach for disclosures of personal health information may establish a research ethics board together to address their particular needs.[76] However, in other instances, there will be no research ethics board in place at the health information custodian from which the researcher seeks the information. In such cases, the researcher will need to seek the approval of a research ethics board in place at another health information custodian, or may seek the approval of a research ethics board not affiliated with a health information custodian.

iii) Considerations

When deciding whether or not to approve a research plan that a researcher submits to it, a research ethics board must consider the matters that it considers relevant, including the following:

- whether the objectives of the research can reasonably be accomplished without using the personal health information that is to be disclosed;[77]
- whether, at the time the research is conducted, adequate safeguards will be in place to protect the privacy of the patients whose personal health information is being disclosed and to preserve the confidentiality of the information;[78]

---

75   There is precedent for this approach for research ethics boards more generally. For example, in the context of scientific and ethical review for multi-centre oncology trials, the Ontario Cancer Research Ethics Board may act as the Board of Record for multiple institutions. See <www.ocrn.on.ca/ethics_HowItWorks.htm>.

76   An existing research ethics board that was established for purposes other than to approve research plans under *PHIPA* can also review research plans under *PHIPA* provided that it complies with the requirements set out in the Act.

77   *PHIPA*, s. 44(3)(a). If the objectives can be accomplished in this way, then the disclosure may also be restricted under s. 30.

78   *Ibid.*, s. 44(3)(b). Consider the administrative, physical, and technical safeguards that health information custodians are required to have in place. See Section B(6)(b), above for a discussion of safeguards, which must be detailed in research plans.

- whether the public interest will be served both in conducting the research and in protecting the privacy of the patients whose personal health information is being disclosed;[79] and
- whether obtaining the consent of the patients whose personal health information is being disclosed would be impractical.[80]

---

79   *PHIPA*, s. 44(3)(c). *PHIPA* does not provide research ethics boards with guidance on what factors to evaluate in considering this issue. However, Alberta's *Health Information Act*, S.A. 1999, c. H-4.8, which includes a similar requirement, enumerates certain considerations that may provide research ethics boards under *PHIPA* with guidance. Under that legislation, in assessing whether the proposed research is of sufficient importance to the public interest to clearly outweigh the interest in protecting the privacy of the individuals involved, the review body must consider the extent to which the research contributes to the following: identification, prevention, or treatment of illness or disease; scientific understanding relating to health; promotion and protection of the health of individuals and communities; improved delivery of health services; or improvements in health system management. In her submission to the Standing Committee on General Government on *PHIPA*, as Bill 31, *An Act to enact and amend various Acts with respect to the protection of health information*, 1st Sess., 38th Leg., Ontario, 2003 [Bill 31], the Information and Privacy Commissioner identified such criteria for the purpose of including them in *PHIPA*. See *Submission to the Standing Committee on General Government: Bill 31: Health Information Protection Act* (Toronto: Information and Privacy Commissioner/Ontario, 2004) at 7, online: <www.ipc.on.ca> [*Submission to the Standing Committee on General Government: Bill 31*].

80   *PHIPA*, s. 44(3)(d). *PHIPA* Regulation, above note 32, s. 16(5) provides that research plans must include an explanation as to why consent of the individuals to whom the information relates is not being sought for the disclosure of the information. See Section B(6)(b), above. *PHIPA* does not provide research ethics boards with guidance in considering whether obtaining the consent of the individuals whose personal health information is being disclosed would be impractical. The Information and Privacy Commissioner's submission to the Standing Committee on General Government on Bill 31, however, recommended that research ethics boards be required to consider certain factors, including the number of people involved in the research; the proportion of individuals who are likely to have moved or died since the information was originally collected; the risk of introducing potential bias into the research, if consent is required; the risk of creating additional threats to privacy by having to link personal health information with other information in order to contact individuals to seek their consent; the risk of inflicting psychological, social, or other harm by contacting individuals in certain circumstances; the difficulty of contacting individuals; and whether the additional resources needed to obtain consent will impose an undue hardship on the organization. See *Submission to the Standing Committee on General Government: Bill 31, ibid.* at 7. The Information and Privacy Commissioner noted in her submission that the factors that she identified in the submission were borrowed from the work of the Canadian Institutes of Health Research (CIHR). See Canadian Institutes of Health Research, *Recommendations for the Interpretation and Application of the Personal Information Protection and Electronic Documents Act (S.C. 2000, c. 5) in the Health Research Context* (Ottawa: 30 November 2001), online, <www.cihr-irsc.gc.ca>, in which CIHR outlined a number of criteria to be considered when assessing the practicality of obtaining consent.

PHIPA does not restrict research ethics boards to consider only the matters identified in the Act. A research ethics board has the power to consider matters that it considers to be relevant.[81] For example, although not specifically identified as matters that a research ethics board must consider, the Act suggests, by requiring such information to be included in the research plan, that it would be appropriate for the research ethics board to consider any conflicts of interest arising from the researcher's interest in the performance of the research. Similarly, as *PHIPA* requires a researcher to explain why consent to the disclosure of the personal health information is not being sought from the patients to whom the information relates, it is reasonable to expect a research ethics board to consider this explanation.[82]

iv) Approval

After reviewing a research plan that a researcher has submitted to it, a research ethics board is required to provide to the researcher a decision in writing,[83] with reasons, setting out whether the board approves the plan, and whether the approval is subject to any conditions, which must be specified in the decision.[84] Conditions to which a research ethics board may make an approval subject might include requiring the researcher to refrain from linking certain information, or a requirement to report back to the research ethics board on a particular aspect of the research.

---

81   *PHIPA*, s. 44(3).

82   In her submission to the Standing Committee on General Government on Bill 31, the Information and Privacy Commissioner submitted that *PHIPA* should include a requirement for a research ethics board to consider whether consent should be required before personal health information is used or disclosed for research purposes. According to the Commissioner, in assessing whether the research should be permitted without consent, the research ethics board should consider the purposes for which the personal health information will be used. The Commissioner noted that it may not be necessary to require a researcher to obtain consent if the personal health information is only needed for the purpose of linking or matching information across time and/or sources, provided that certain safeguards are in place, including the de-identification of the information. The *PHIPA* Regulation does not include these details. See *Submission to the Standing Committee on General Government: Bill 31*, above note 79.

83   Although not a requirement set out in *PHIPA*, it is prudent for a research ethics board to retain records concerning its reviews of research plans to support its decision-making.

84   *PHIPA*, s. 44(4).

d) Requirements for Researchers

PHIPA includes several requirements with which researchers to whom health information custodians disclose personal health information without consent for research must comply.[85] A researcher must

- comply with the conditions, if any, specified by the research ethics board in respect of the research plan;
- use the information only for the purposes set out in the research plan as approved by the research ethics board;[86]
- not publish the information in a form that could reasonably enable a person to ascertain the identity of a patient;[87]
- not disclose the information except as required by law, subject to the exceptions and additional requirements, if any, that are set out in the regulations;[88]
- not make contact or attempt to make contact with the patients to whom the information relates, directly or indirectly, unless the custodian first obtains the patients' consent to being contacted;[89]
- notify the custodian immediately in writing if the researcher becomes aware of any breach of any requirements imposed on the researcher or the required research agreement;[90] and

---

85   *PHIPA*, s. 44(6). Sections 44(6)(a) to (f) also apply to a custodian who uses personal health information without consent of the individual to whom the information relates: *PHIPA*, s. 37(3).

86   For this reason, the research plan should describe the purposes in sufficient detail so as make the limitations on the use of the information clear.

87   Although it does specifically refer to "de-identified information," it appears that this clause refers to such information, as defined in *PHIPA*, s. 47(1).

88   This restriction applies to researchers, despite the recipient rule set out in *PHIPA*, s. 49(1). See B(6)(f) below for a discussion of disclosures by researchers. However, *PHIPA* does not prohibit the health information custodian who disclosed the information to the researcher from restricting the researcher's disclosures to only those required by law.

89   In her submission to the Ministry of Consumer and Business Services, the Information and Privacy Commissioner stated: "... where the researcher proposes to contact individuals directly or indirectly, the consent of the individual should be obtained by the custodian before disclosure." The Commissioner made this comment in response to the provision in draft legislation that indicated that a researcher could contact a person whose information was the subject of research with the written consent of the custodian who disclosed the information to the researcher. See *Submission to the Ministry of Consumer and Business Services: Consultation Draft of the Privacy of Personal Information Act, 2002* (Toronto: Information and Privacy Commissioner/Ontario, 2002), online <www.ipc.on.ca>. *PHIPA*, s. 37(1)(g) permits a health information custodian to use personal health information about an individual for the purpose of seeking the individual's consent, when the personal health information is limited to the individual's name and contact information.

90   *PHIPA*, s. 12(3) provides that where a health information custodian is a researcher who has received personal health information from another health information custo-

- comply with the research agreement entered into by the researcher and the health information custodian.[91]

e)   Agreement

In addition to the requirements discussed above, a health information custodian disclosing personal health information for research purposes must also enter into an agreement with the researcher.[92] The agreement must bind the researcher to comply with the conditions and restrictions, if any, that the custodian imposes relating to the use, security, disclosure, return, or disposal of the information; for example, provisions that address the health information custodian's monitoring of the researcher's activities through on-site visits and reports and establish a process by which the researcher would advise the custodian of unauthorized access to the personal health information.[93]

f)   Disclosure by Researcher

The regulation made under *PHIPA* provides that, despite the prohibition on a researcher's disclosure of personal health information collected from a health information custodian for the purpose of carrying out research, a researcher may disclose the information to

- a prescribed planning entity;
- to a prescribed health registry; or
- to another researcher.[94]

However, such a disclosure is permitted only where the disclosure is either (i) part of a research plan approved by a research ethics board under the Act; or (ii) necessary for the purpose of verifying or validating the information or the research.[95] As prescribed planning entities and prescribed health registries, as

---

dian under section 44(1) of the Act, and the information is lost, stolen, or accessed by unauthorized persons, the researcher shall not notify the individual of the loss, theft, or unauthorized access unless the health information custodian who disclosed the information to the researcher first obtains the individual's consent to being contacted by the researcher.

91   As a result of this provision, a researcher's failure to comply with a research agreement with a health information custodian is both a breach of the agreement and a breach of the *PHIPA*.

92   *PHIPA*, ss. 44(1)(b) and 44(5). A research agreement is also required under *FIPPA*. See Form 1 under *General*, R.R.O. 1990, Reg. 460, made under *FIPPA*. The requirements set out in *PHIPA* build on that form.

93   *PHIPA*, s. 44(5).

94   *PHIPA* Regulation, above note 32, s. 17.

95   *Ibid.*

well as some researchers, may hold comprehensive information, a disclosure of personal health information by a researcher to such a person or organization may be useful for the purpose of verifying or validating information where the integrity of the researcher's information is questionable, and the disclosure would serve to ensure confidence in the integrity of the information.

g) Health Numbers

Researchers have various powers to collect, use, and disclose health numbers, despite the general restrictions set out in *PHIPA* with respect to this issue.[96] Chapter 2 includes an in-depth discussion of the powers that researchers have to collect, use, and disclose health numbers.

7) Addressing Non-Compliance

What should a health information custodian do if it becomes aware that a researcher to whom it disclosed personal health information is not complying with the requirements of *PHIPA* and/or the agreement between the health information custodian and the researcher? The Act does not specifically require the custodian to take steps with respect to information that is not in the custody or control of the custodian. Nevertheless, it would be appropriate for the custodian to take steps to stop the inappropriate actions. First, of course, informal discussions and correspondence between the researcher and the health information custodian may lead to a resolution of the issue. If such steps do not lead to a satisfactory resolution, the custodian may have recourse to the courts for a remedy under the agreement that it has with the researcher. On a more practical level, the custodian can inform or make a complaint to the Information and Privacy Commissioner about the researcher's non-compliance with the Act. Note that non-compliance with the research agreement would constitute non-compliance with *PHIPA*, as well.[97] The custodian may also notify patients whose personal health information was involved in the non-compliance of the situation, who may themselves take steps to address the non-compliance, including making a complaint to the Commissioner.[98] Where the research involves the health information custodian's ongoing disclosure of personal health information to the researcher, and the researcher refuses to comply with *PHIPA* or the research agreement, the custodian should cease making disclosures of the information, whether permanently or until such

---

96   *PHIPA*, s. 34.
97   *Ibid.*, s. 44(6)(g).
98   See Chapter 4, Section L for a discussion of how to deal with a privacy breach.

time as the health information custodian is satisfied that the researcher is able to and will comply with the requirements of the Act and the agreement.

Where a researcher is also a health information custodian, unless the custodian received the personal health information from another custodian without the consent of the patients to whom the information relates in accordance with the Act,[99] the researcher custodian must notify the patient at the first reasonable opportunity if personal health information in the researcher custodian's custody or control that relates to the patient is stolen, lost, or accessed by unauthorized persons, even if the theft, loss, or access arose in the context of the researcher custodian's research work.[100]

8) Research and Other Jurisdictions

By including special rules for research involving researchers and/or information from outside Ontario, *PHIPA* recognizes that health research crosses provincial and national borders, whether by the disclosure of information or researchers crossing borders.

a)   Information from Outside Ontario

A custodian may use or disclose personal health information that originates wholly or in part outside Ontario for research purposes if the research has received the prescribed approval of a body outside Ontario that has the function of approving research and the requirements set out in the regulations are met.[101] At the time of writing, the regulations do not describe any approval from a body outside Ontario that is recognized for this purpose.[102] Until such regulations may be in place, the Act does not recognize a role for approvals of research from outside Ontario, except to the extent that they comply with the regular provisions of *PHIPA* and its regulation regarding research. Thus at present, health information custodians may use or disclose personal health information that originates wholly or in part outside Ontario by complying with the general rules in *PHIPA* that govern a health information custodian's use or disclosure of personal health information for research purposes, as discussed above.

---

99   *PHIPA*, s. 12(3).

100   *Ibid.*, s. 12(2).

101   *Ibid.*, s. 44(10).

102   Such a regulation could, for example, provide that an approval of one of the six designated research ethics boards under Alberta's *Health Information Act*, above note 79, would be sufficient under this section, and, if so, a health information custodian that has custody of personal health information originating in whole or in part from the province of Alberta may use the information to carry out research in Ontario where the research was approved by such a body.

b) Researcher Outside Ontario

Where a health information custodian collects personal health information about a patient in Ontario, and the custodian has custody or control of that information in Ontario, the custodian may disclose that information to a researcher outside of Ontario, provided that the custodian and the researcher comply with the rules in *PHIPA* that govern a health information custodian's disclosure of personal health information for research purposes generally.[103]

9) Transition Rules

a) Research Commenced prior to 1 November 2004

It would have been problematic had the research rules in *PHIPA* applied retroactively or without a sufficient transition period to the uses and disclosures of personal health information by health information custodians for research purposes that commenced prior to 1 November 2004. A transition period was required to permit custodians and researchers sufficient time to take steps to ensure that their research-related practices comply with the Act, without needing to stop their activities in the meantime.

i) Disclosure

PHIPA permits a health information custodian that lawfully[104] disclosed personal health information to a researcher for the purpose of carrying out research in the three-year period prior to 1 November 2004, when *PHIPA* came into force, to continue to do so for the purposes of that research until 1 November 2007.[105] By the end of this three-year period, the health information custodian should ensure that the custodian and the researcher take any necessary additional steps to comply with the requirements of the Act before disclosing additional information to the researcher. Typically this will involve ensuring that the researcher has developed a research plan that meets the requirements of the Act and receives the approval of a properly constituted research ethics board, and establishing or amending a research agreement. Of

---

103 *PHIPA*, s. 50(1)(b).

104 "Lawfully" means not contrary to law. For example, Reg. 856, above note 15, s. 1(2)(b) provides that it is not professional misconduct for a physician to give information about a patient, including access to the patient's records, to a person for the purpose of research or health administration or planning if the physician reasonably believes that the person will take reasonable steps to protect the identity of the patient, where the regulation does not set out a process and requirements for such disclosures.

105 *PHIPA*, s. 44(12). It is interesting to note that the first reading version of Bill 31, above note 79, only provided for a one-year transition period. The Bill was amended after the first reading.

course, the Act does not interfere with a custodian and researcher who wish to fulfil the requirements prior to that date.

ii)   Use

PHIPA includes a similar three-year transition period for a health information custodian's use of personal health information for the purpose of conducting research. A health information custodian that lawfully[106] used personal health information for the purpose of conducting research in the three-year period before 1 November 2004 can continue to use personal health information for the purposes of that same research until 1 November 2007.[107] By that latter date, the custodian must ensure compliance with the Act's research rules, including the development of a research plan that is approved by a research ethics board. Again, a custodian may wish to fulfil these requirements before 1 November 2007.

b)   Disclosure by an Institution under *FIPPA* or *MFIPPA*

PHIPA includes a special transition provision for *FIPPA/MFIPPA* custodians, in recognition of the fact that those Acts already contain research provisions. *FIPPA* permits an institution, a term defined in that Act, to include ministries of the government of Ontario and other designated bodies in the public sector,[108] to disclose personal information for a research purpose in certain circumstances.[109] A similar provision is found in *MFIPPA*.[110] *PHIPA* permits a *FIPPA/MFIPPA* custodian to continue to disclose personal health information to a researcher if, prior to 1 November 2004, the researcher entered into a research agreement in respect of

---

106 The word "lawfully" does not mean more than not contrary to law. See, for example, prior to 1 November 2004, *Hospital Management*, R.R.O. 1990, Reg. 965, s. 22(6), made under the *Public Hospitals Act*, R.S.O. 1990, c. P.40, which provided that a board may permit a member of the medical, dental, midwifery, or extended class nursing staff to have access to patient records for scientific research that has been approved by the medical advisory committee.

107 *PHIPA*, s. 44(13).

108 *FIPPA*, above note 19, s. 2.

109 *FIPPA*, *ibid.*, s. 21(1)(e) provides:

The disclosure of personal information is permitted for a research purpose where,

(i)   the disclosure is consistent with the conditions or reasonable expectations of disclosure under which the personal information was provided, collected or obtained,

(ii) the research purpose for which the disclosure is to be made cannot be reasonably accomplished unless the information is provided in individually identifiable form, and

(iii) the person who is to receive the record has agreed to comply with the conditions relating to security and confidentiality prescribed by the regulations.

110 *MFIPPA*, above note 19, s. 14(1).

the disclosure under either of those Acts.[111] *FIPPA/MFIPPA* custodians can rely on this grandfathering authority for disclosures after 1 November 2004 until the agreement expires or the parties choose to terminate the agreement.

C. PRESCRIBED HEALTH REGISTRIES

1) Generally

One of the goals of the First Ministers' ten-year plan to strengthen health care is reducing wait times in priority areas such as cancer treatment, cardiac care, diagnostic imaging, joint replacements, and sight restoration.[112] Registries of personal health information can play an important role in achieving this goal by connecting patients in need of health care to health care providers.

PHIPA permits a health information custodian to disclose personal health information about a patient, without the consent of the patient, to a prescribed health registry; that is, a person identified in the regulations made under the Act who compiles or maintains a registry of personal health information for the purposes of facilitating or improving the provision of health care or for a purpose relating to the storage or donation of body parts or bodily substances.[113] A prescribed planning entity may also disclose personal health information without the consent of the patient to whom the information relates to a prescribed health registry as if it were a health information custodian.[114] Similarly, a researcher may disclose personal health information that he or she receives without patient consent for research purposes to a prescribed health registry, provided that the disclosure is part of a research plan approved in accordance with research rules set out in section 44 of the Act, or the disclosure is necessary for the purpose of verifying or validating the information or research.[115]

2) Who Is a Prescribed Health Registry?

a) General Characteristics

While *PHIPA* does not define the term "registry," it is important to examine in some detail a few aspects of the provision that provides for a health information custodian's disclosure to a prescribed health registry.

---

111 *PHIPA*, s. 44(8).
112 10-year plan, above note 1.
113 *PHIPA*, s. 39(1)(c).
114 *PHIPA* Regulation, above note 32, s. 18(4).
115 *Ibid.*, s. 17.

First, this provision of the Act describes, in general terms, the purposes of the registries: facilitating or improving the provision of health care or carrying out functions relating to the donation or storage of body parts or bodily substances.[116] A registry that does not have these types of functions would fall outside the scope of this provision.

This provision of the Act also makes it clear that in order to be prescribed, a "person" must compile or maintain the registry. The term "person" is defined to include a partnership, association, or other entity, but would also include a natural person and corporation.[117] Thus, the name of a registry cannot be identified alone in the regulations, without identifying the "person" who compiled or maintained it, such as a hospital or other corporation. A person who compiles or maintains a registry of personal health information of this type may or may not be a health information custodian. It should not be assumed that such persons are health information custodians unless the Act or the regulations identifies them as such.[118] Where the person who compiles or maintains the registry is a health information custodian, such as where the person that compiles or maintains the registry also operates a laboratory, the person is still not a health information custodian with respect to its registry work unless the registry is an integral part of the person's work as a custodian or the regulations made under the Act designate the person as a custodian for such purposes.[119] In the case of such a designation, the person who compiles or maintains the registry would be a separate health information custodian from the custodian that operates the laboratory.[120] Where the prescribed health registry is not a health information custodian but receives personal health information from a health information custodian, the registry is subject to the recipient rules set out in the Act.[121]

---

116 It is interesting to note the evolution of this provision from the first to second reading of Bill 31, above note 79. Clause 38(1)(c) of Schedule A to Bill 31 at first reading provided: "Subject to the requirements and restrictions, if any, that are prescribed, a health information custodian may disclose personal health information about an individual … (c) to a prescribed person who compiles or maintains a registry of personal health information that relates to a specific disease or condition or that relates to the storage or donation of body parts or bodily substances or a prescribed class of such persons."

117 *PHIPA*, s. 2. The *Interpretation Act*, R.S.O. 1990, c. I.11, s. 29(1) provides that in every Act, unless the context otherwise requires, "person" includes a corporation.

118 In *PHIPA*, s. 3(1), or in a regulation made under *PHIPA*, s. 3(1)[8].

119 *PHIPA* Regulation, above note 32, s. 3(1)[8].

120 *PHIPA*, s. 3(5), subject to a single health information custodian designation under s. 3(8).

121 *Ibid.*, s. 49. These rules restrict subsequent uses and disclosures of personal health information by persons who are not health information custodians but receive personal health information from a custodian. See Chapter 12.

Finally, this provision of the Act relates to a health information custodian's disclosure of "personal health information" to a registry of "personal health information." Therefore, a person who compiles a registry of information that is not personal health information, such as de-identified[122] information, would not be identified in the regulations for this purpose.

As noted in the introduction, these registries are referred to in this Guide as "prescribed health registries."

b) Identifying Registries

The Minister of Health and Long-Term Care's Notice of Proposed Regulations[123] included a request that provides some insight into the government's decision-making process concerning which health registries the regulation prescribes. The Minister requested that persons who wished to be prescribed for this purpose provide information in response to the following questions:

1. Do the objects of the Registry include the collection of personal health information for the purpose of facilitating or improving the provision of health care, or the storage or donation of body parts or bodily substances? Please give details.
2. Under what legal authority does the Registry currently collect, use, and/or disclose personal health information, and how will that change when the *Personal Health Information Protection Act, 2004* comes into force?
3. Is the Registry located and operating in Ontario for the benefit of the people of Ontario?
4. Was the Registry established pursuant to a request or direction of the government of Ontario?
5. Can the Registry function without being prescribed under section 39(1)(c) of the *Personal Health Information Protection Act, 2004*? Can the functions of the Registry be performed without personal health information? Why is consent not being obtained?
6. What is the past and current performance of the Registry in respect to appropriate secure and privacy-protective information practices?
7. Have any views been expressed by the Information and Privacy Commissioner regarding the Registry?

The criteria identified in the Minister's notice suggest that, in order to be allowed to receive disclosures of personal health information from health information custodians without consent, the registry must demonstrate that it

---

122 See Chapter 2, Section C(1)(d) for a discussion of de-identified information.

has eligible objects, as described above, that cannot be properly carried out without being able to receive personal health information without patient consent, and that it is able to protect the information so that patient privacy is not at risk. A prescribed health registry must outline not only its impact on the improvement of the provision of health care and benefit to the people of Ontario, but also whether the registry can operate without personal health information and how its information practices protect the personal health information.

c)   Prescribed Health Registries

The regulation made under *PHIPA* permits health information custodians to disclose personal health information without consent to the following prescribed health registries:

- Cardiac Care Network of Ontario in respect of its registry of cardiac services;[124]
- INSCYTE (Information System for Cytology etc.) Corporation in respect of CytoBase;[125]
- London Health Sciences Centre in respect of the Ontario Joint Replacement Registry;[126] and
- Canadian Stroke Network in respect of the Canadian Stroke Registry.[127]

3)   Options for Health Registries Not Prescribed

The questions enumerated in the Minister's notice also recognize that other options exist for health registries that are not identified in the regulation. First, a health information custodian may disclose personal health information about a patient to a registry with the consent of the patient. Depending on the circumstances, the patient's consent may be express or implied.[128] By providing the health information custodian with information to distribute to patients from whom consent would be sought, the registry could assist the custodian in fulfilling the requirements of knowledgeable consent.

As another alternative for health registries that are not identified in the regulation, a health information custodian could disclose to the registry infor-

---

123   O. Gaz. 2004.I.1548.

124   See <www.ccn.on.ca>.

125   See <www.inscyte.org> for information about INSCYTE.

126   See <www.ojrr.ca> for information about the Ontario Joint Replacement Registry.

127   See <www.canadianstrokenetwork.ca> for information about the Canadian Stroke Network.

128   *PHIPA*, ss. 18(2) & (3). Implied consent is appropriate in instances where the disclosure is to a health information custodian for the purpose of providing health care.

mation that is not personal health information.[129] In some instances, de-identified information may be sufficient for the purposes of a registry's success. It is always important to remember that health information custodians must not disclose personal health information if other information will serve the purpose of the disclosure.[130]

4) Requirements for Prescribed Health Registries

a) Information Practices

Prescribed health registries must put in place practices and procedures to protect the privacy of the patients whose personal health information they receive, and to maintain the confidentiality of the information.[131] Such practices and procedures may include administrative, technical, and physical safeguards, such as procedures to secure the premises from which to operate the registry and regular privacy training for staff.[132] As registries in the twenty-first century will inevitably be computer-based, technical safeguards should form a significant component of a prescribed health registry's safeguards.

b) Approval of the Information and Privacy Commissioner

PHIPA requires that a prescribed health registry's practices and procedures to safeguard privacy and confidentiality be approved by the Information and Privacy Commissioner.[133] However, the practices and procedures do not require such approval until 1 November 2005. *PHIPA's* incorporation of a specific responsibility for the Information and Privacy Commissioner with respect to prescribed health registries, which typically will not be health information custodians,[134] constitutes an important privacy protection in the Act.

c) Description of Functions

Prescribed health registries must make publicly available a plain language description of the functions of the registry, including a summary of the practices and procedures approved by the Commissioner.[135] This plain language descrip-

---

129 See also Chapter 2, Section C(1)(d) for a discussion of de-identified information.

130 *PHIPA*, s. 30(1).

131 *PHIPA* Regulation, above note 32, s. 13(2). Prescribed health registries may wish to refer to the obligations of health information custodians with respect to a written public statement, as set in *PHIPA*, s. 16, for guidance on preparing such a description.

132 See Chapter 4, Section F(4), for a discussion of safeguards that health information custodians may wish to put into place, many of which would be appropriate for prescribed health registries, as well.

133 *PHIPA* Regulation, above note 32, s. 13(2).

134 At time of writing, no prescribed health registries are health information custodians.

135 *PHIPA* Regulation, above note 32, s. 13(3).

tion should serve as a useful tool to communicate the work of the registry to patients, as well as health information custodians, and to foster confidence in the registry's ability to undertake its work in a privacy-protective manner.

5) Powers to Collect, Use, and Disclose Personal Health Information

a) Collection

A prescribed health registry that is not a health information custodian may collect personal health information that a custodian discloses to the registry under section 39(1)(c) of *PHIPA*.[136] Where a prescribed health registry is a health information custodian, the registry may rely on various provisions in the Act for authority to collect personal health information from a health information custodian that discloses the information to the registry for the registry's work.[137]

b) Use

A prescribed health registry, whether or not it is a health information custodian, may use personal health information that it collects for that purpose.[138] Further, prescribed health registries may use personal health information for the purpose of carrying out research without the consent of the patients to whom the information relates in the same way that a health information custodian is permitted to do so; that is, with research ethics board approval of a research plan, etc.[139]

c) Disclosure

Where a prescribed health registry is not a health information custodian, the registry is a recipient for the purposes of *PHIPA*.[140] Such a prescribed health registry that collects personal health information from health information custodians may disclose the information as permitted or required by law and for the purpose of carrying out a statutory or legal duty, as other recipients may do so.[141] Such a registry may also disclose personal health information that it collects from a health information custodian for the purpose of its registry work

---

136   *PHIPA*, s. 39(4).

137   For example, *PHIPA*, s. 36(1)(g).

138   *PHIPA*, ss. 37(1)(a) and 49(1)(a), respectively.

139   *PHIPA* Regulation, above note 32, s. 13(4). Prescribed health registries are permitted to use personal health information as though they are health information custodians for the purposes of ss. 37(1)(j) and 37(3) of the Act.

140   See Chapter 12.

141   *PHIPA*, s. 49(1).

of facilitating or improving the provision of health care or of carrying out activities related to the storage or donation of body parts or bodily substances.[142]

PHIPA also provides prescribed health registries with the power to disclose personal health information, subject to the applicable restrictions, to a researcher; a prescribed planning entity; and a health data institute pursuant to section 47 of the Act.[143] Although prescribed health registries are typically not health information custodians, the requirements applicable to health information custodians in disclosing personal health information to such bodies apply to these registries as though they were health information custodians. For example, a prescribed health registry must enter into an agreement with a researcher to whom it disclosed personal health information for the purpose of carrying out research described in a research plan and approved by a research ethics board, as required by the Act.[144]

d) Health Numbers

Prescribed health registries have various powers to collect, use, and disclose health numbers, despite the restrictions on such collections, uses, and disclosures set out in *PHIPA*.[145] Chapter 2 includes an in-depth discussion of the powers that prescribed health registries have to collect, use, and disclose health numbers.

6) Disclosing Personal Health Information to Prescribed Health Registries

PHIPA does not impose any specific requirements on health information custodians that disclose personal health information to prescribed health registries. *PHIPA*, for example, does not require a health information custodian to enter into an agreement with a prescribed health registry in making a disclosure to the registry. Even without such specific requirements, health information custodians should consider what information they may require from a prescribed health registry in exercising their discretion to disclose personal health information. At a minimum, a custodian may require confirmation from the registry that it meets all the requirements relevant to authorizing such a disclosure to the registry by the custodian. Also, a custodian may request a copy of the registry's plain language description of its functions and information practices,[146] in addition to

---

142 *PHIPA*, s. 49(1).
143 *PHIPA* Regulation, above note 32, s. 13(5).
144 *PHIPA*, s. 44(5).
145 *Ibid.*, s. 34.
146 *PHIPA* Regulation, above note 32, s. 13(3).

information concerning the status of the Commissioner's approval of the entity's privacy practices and procedures.[147] Further, a health information custodian may request documentation describing the personal health information that the prescribed planning entity seeks from the custodian.

D. HEALTH DATA INSTITUTE

1) Background

The *Ministry of Health and Long-Term Care Act* describes the functions of the Minister, as head of the Ministry, to include responsibility for the development, co-ordination, and maintenance of comprehensive health services and a balanced and integrated system of hospitals, nursing homes, laboratories, ambulances, and other health facilities in Ontario.[148] In order to fulfil these functions effectively, the Ministry requires information about the health system and the persons who rely on that system. For the same reasons that identifying information is required in the context of research, it is required for the analysis that is needed for system planning and co-ordination. Achieving consensus on the parameters of the Ministry's ability to access personal health information, however, was a challenge in Ontario. The provisions in Bill 159[149] that required health information custodians to disclose personal health information directly to the Minister of Health and Long-Term Care for health system planning-related purposes, rather than having the information sent first to a health data institute for analysis and de-identification of the information, was one of the mostly strongly opposed aspects of that Bill.[150]

---

147 *Ibid.*, s. 13(2).
148 R.S.O. 1990, c. M.26, s. 6(1)[3].
149 Bill 159, *An Act respecting personal health information and related matters*, 1st Sess., 37th Leg., Ontario, 2000 [Bill 159].
150 The Ontario Medical Association (OMA) objected strongly to what was called the "directed disclosure" provision in the Bill, which would have empowered the Minister of Health and Long-Term Care to compel health care providers to disclose information from patient charts directly to the Minister for the purposes of planning and management of the health system. See Ontario Medical Association, News Release, "OMA Calls for Fundamental Changes to Bill 159" (27 February 2001), online <www.oma.org>, in which the OMA criticized the Bill, arguing that patients' charts are not needed for planning and management of the health care system. See also *Submission to the Standing Committee on General Government: Bill 159, Personal Health Information Protection Act, 2000* (Toronto: Information and Privacy Commissioner/Ontario, 2001) online: <www.ipc.on.ca>. See Chapter 1 for further discussion of such concerns with Bill 159.

Can this work be accomplished without identifying information? *PHIPA* suggests that, with the involvement of what the Act terms a "health data institute" this will be possible, at least in some instances. As a result of the introduction of the health data institute in *PHIPA*, in her submission to the Standing Committee on General Government, the Information and Privacy Commissioner identified the use of the health data institute to limit the government's need to access personal health information for the purpose of health system analysis as one of the significant improvements of *PHIPA* over previous legislative initiatives in Ontario.[151]

2) Required Disclosures to the Minister

Under *PHIPA*, a health information custodian must disclose personal health information, without the consent of the patients to whom the information relates, upon the request of the Minister of Health and Long-Term Care, to a health data institute for analysis with respect to the management, evaluation, or monitoring of the allocation of resources to or planning for all or part of the health system, including the delivery of services.[152] The health data institute is responsible for performing the analysis requested by the Minister, linking as necessary with other data as the Minister requires,[153] de-identifying the information,[154] and providing the results of the analysis and linking (generally consisting of only de-identified information) to the Minister or to the persons that the Minister approves.[155] The Act defines the term "de-identify" to mean, "in relation to the personal health information of an individual, to remove any information that identifies the individual or for which it is reasonably foresee-

---

151 *Submission to the Standing Committee on General Government: Bill 31*, above note 79. It is interesting to note that the role developed for a health data institute in Ontario is unique to health information privacy legislation in Canada.

152 *PHIPA*, s. 47(2). At the time of writing, the Minister of Health and Long-Term Care had not announced any approved health data institutes. *PHIPA*, s. 47(16) provides that if the Minister lawfully required the disclosure of personal health information for such a purpose in the eighteen months prior to 1 November 2004, s. 47 does not apply with respect to a disclosure the Minister requires for a substantially similar purpose until 1 November 2005. However, where the Minister requires a disclosure for such a substantially similar purpose after 1 November 2004, the Minister must notify the Information and Privacy Commissioner within the later of the time of requiring the disclosure and ninety days after 1 November 2004: *PHIPA*, s. 47(17).

153 *PHIPA*, s. 47(15)(b).

154 *Ibid.*, s. 47(15)(c).

155 *Ibid.*, s. 47(15)(d).

able in the circumstances that it could be utilized, either alone or with other information, to identify the individual."[156]

3) Preconditions to Requiring Disclosure to the Minister

This requirement for health information custodians to disclose personal health information to the Minister of Health and Long-Term Care, one of only two such requirements in *PHIPA*,[157] arises only when the Minister fulfils the necessary preconditions.[158] First, the Minister must submit a proposal regarding the disclosure to the Information and Privacy Commissioner.[159] Within thirty days of receiving the proposal, the Commissioner must review and may comment in writing on the proposal.[160] The Commissioner's review must include a consideration of the public interest in conducting the analysis, and the privacy interests of the patients to whom the personal health information that is the subject of the Minister's request relates.[161] The Minister is required to consider the comments of the Commissioner and may choose to amend the proposal based on the Commissioner's comments.[162] The Minister may choose to disclose to the health data institute other personal health information for the purposes of analysis and linking that the Minister requires, provided that the Minister's proposal incorporates such a disclosure.[163] Once these requirements have been fulfilled, the Minister may request a health information custodian to make the disclosure of personal health information, in the form and manner and at the time specified,[164] to the health data institute identified in the proposal, and the custodian that receives such a request is obligated to comply.

---

156   *PHIPA*, s. 47(1). This definition reflects the other side of the coin of the definition of "identifying information": *PHIPA*, s. 4(2).

157   The other instance being that described in *PHIPA*, s. 46(1), which deals with a health information custodian's disclosure of personal health information to the Minister for the purpose of verifying claims for payment.

158   *PHIPA*, s. 47(2).

159   *Ibid.*, s. 47(4). Section 47(5) provides that the proposal must identify a health data institute to which the personal health information would be disclosed, in addition to any prescribed matters. At the time of writing, the regulation does not identify any additional matters.

160   *Ibid.*, s. 47(6).

161   *Ibid.*, s. 47(7).

162   *Ibid.*, s. 47(8). The Minister, however, is not required to change the proposal.

163   *Ibid.*, s. 47(14).

164   *Ibid.*, s. 47(3).

4) Requirements for a Health Data Institute

PHIPA enumerates a series of requirements for a health data institute, which it must meet before it is eligible to receive disclosures of personal health information from health information custodians under the Act. The corporate objects of a health data institute must include performing data analysis of personal health information, linking the information with other information, and de-identifying the information for the Minister of Health and Long-Term Care.[165] A health data institute must have in place practices and procedures to protect the privacy of patients whose personal health information it receives and to maintain the confidentiality of the information.[166] The Commissioner must approve these practices and procedures prior to the Minister's approval of the health data institute,[167] reviewing them every three years thereafter to advise the Minister whether the health data institute continues to fulfil the requirements of the Act.[168]

A health data institute that receives personal health information as part of a disclosure directed by the Minister under sections 47(2) or (14) must

a) follow the practices and procedures concerning privacy and confidentiality approved by the Commissioner;[169]

b) not disclose the information to the Minister or to the persons that the Minister approves except in de-identified form;[170] and

c) not disclose to any persons the information, even in de-identified form, or any information derived from the information.[171]

5) Withdrawal of Approval of Health Data Institute

The failure of a health data institute to fulfil its obligations under *PHIPA* has serious consequences. Where a health data institute fails to continue to meet the requirements of the Act, or it fails to carry out its objects, the Minister must

---

165 *PHIPA*, s. 47(9)(a).

166 *Ibid.*, s. 47(9)(b).

167 *Ibid.*

168 *Ibid.*, s. 47(10).

169 *Ibid.*, s. 47(15)(a). To contravene this provision is an offence under s. 72(1)(f). See Chapter 15, Section D, for details about offences.

170 *Ibid.*, s. 47(15)(e). To contravene this provision is an offence under s. 72(1)(f). See Chapter 15, Section D, for details about offences.

171 *Ibid.*, s. 47(15)(f). To contravene this provision is an offence under s. 72(1)(f). See Chapter 15, Section D, for details about offences.

withdraw the approval of the health data institute, unless the Minister obliges the institute to take immediate steps to satisfy the Minister that it will meet the requirements or carry out the objects.[172] If the Minister withdraws the approval of a health data institute, the health data institute is prohibited from making further use or disclosure of any personal health information that a health information custodian has disclosed to it as a health data institute pursuant to the provisions of the Act or of any information derived from that personal health information.[173] In such a case, the health data institute is required to comply with the written directions of the Minister with respect to such information that the Commissioner has approved in writing.[174] Given the approval process that the Act establishes for health data institutes, one should hope the Minister's withdrawal of the approval of a health data institute will be an exceptional event.

6) Where the Ministry Requires Personal Health Information

Although, typically, de-identified information will be sufficient, *PHIPA* accommodates situations where the Ministry of Health and Long-Term Care will require personal health information, and not just de-identified information, from health information custodians to fulfil its health system planning and management-related functions. A health data institute to which a health information custodian has disclosed personal health information under section 47 of the Act, must, upon the request of the Minister, disclose the information to the Minister or another person approved by the Minister if both the Minister and the Information and Privacy Commissioner are of the opinion that it is in the public interest to request the disclosure.[175] First, the Minister must submit to the Commissioner a detailed proposal for such a disclosure.[176] The proposal must include the following:

---

172   *PHIPA*, s. 47(11).

173   *Ibid.*, s. 47(12)(a).

174   *Ibid.*, s. 47(12)(b). Similarly, if a health data institute ceases to exist, the persons holding the information that the institute received under s. 47(2) and held when it ceased to exist must comply with the written directions of the Minister that the Commissioner has approved in writing: *PHIPA*, s. 47(13). Section 47(18) provides that the Minister is not required to hold a hearing or to afford any person an opportunity for a hearing before making a decision under s. 47.

175   *Ibid.*, s. 48(1). *PHIPA* does not provide details about the identity of persons that the Minister may approve for such purposes. Presumably, the Minister would want to ensure, prior to approval, that the person had appropriate safeguards in place to protect the privacy and security of the information.

176   *Ibid.*, s. 48(3).

a) a statement as to why the disclosure is reasonably required in the public interest and why the disclosure under section 47, which results in the disclosure of only de-identified information to the Minister, was insufficient to meet the public interest;

b) the extent of the identifiers[177] that the Minister proposes be part of the information disclosed and a statement as to why the use of those identifiers is reasonably required for the purpose of the disclosure;

c) a copy of all proposals and comments previously made or received under section 47 of the Act in respect of the information, if any; and

d) all other information that the Information and Privacy Commissioner requires.[178]

Even with the Commissioner's approval, the personal health information that a health data institute discloses to the Minister cannot include notes of personal health information about a patient that are recorded by a health information custodian and that document the contents of conversations during a private counseling session, or a group, joint, or family counselling session, or any other information that is specified in the regulations.[179] Prior to the health data institute's disclosure of the personal health information, the Information and Privacy Commissioner must provide an approval of the disclosure, which may be subject to any limitations and conditions that the Commissioner believes are appropriate.[180] The Act does not describe the nature of such limitations and conditions, but they may, for example, require the Ministry to implement special safeguards to protect the privacy and confidentiality of the personal health information prior to the health data institute's disclosure of the information to the Ministry.

---

177 *PHIPA* does not define the term "identifier." The term identifier is used to refer to a data element that identifies an individual. The removal of all identifiers results in de-identified information. The health number is a common identifier in the health sector. The social insurance number is another identifier, along with name, date of birth, and address. Unique identifiers are considered most useful in undertaking the linkage of records of personal health information, as they result in the most accurate linkages.

178 *PHIPA*, s. 48(4).

179 *Ibid.*, s. 48(2). At the time of writing, the *PHIPA* Regulation does not specify additional information.

180 *PHIPA*, ss. 48(3) and 48(5).

7) Alternatives to Use of Health Data Institute

Provisions in other legislation and regulations provide the Minister of Health and Long-Term Care with the power to require health information custodians to disclose personal health information to the Ministry, in the absence of the involvement of a health data institute.[181] These provisions continue to apply to health information custodians. Such provisions do not conflict with *PHIPA*, as the Act provides that a health information custodian may disclose personal health information where permitted or required by law.[182]

Similarly, where the Ministry collects personal health information for one purpose, such as reimbursing claims for payment for the provision of health care, the Ministry, as a health information custodian, may use the information to plan or deliver programs or services that the Ministry funds.[183] It can also use the information to allocate resources to such programs or services and evaluate and monitor their progress.[184] Pre-existing databases containing personal health information are useful sources of information for monitoring and evaluating the performance of the health care system and the effectiveness of new health programs.

As well, the Act does not prohibit the Minister from asking a health information custodian to disclose information that is not personal health information to the Minister for such purposes, as *PHIPA* does not govern the disclosure of information that is not personal health information, such as de-identified information.[185] In this way, the Ministry has different options open to it to meets its obligations in the planning and management of the health system.

---

181 For example, see the *Independent Health Facilities Act*, R.S.O. 1990, c. I.3, s. 37.2(1), which provides that, at the request of the Minister-appointed Director of independent health facilities, a licensee must submit information to the Director and disclose information to persons specified by the Director for purposes related to the administration of the *Independent Health Facilities Act* or the *Health Insurance Act*, R.S.O. 1990, c. H.6 or for other prescribed purposes. See also the *Health Insurance Act*, s. 37(1), which requires physicians to provide the General Manager with such information, including personal information, as may be prescribed for purposes related to the administration of the *Health Insurance Act*, the *Health Care Accessibility Act*, or the *Independent Health Facilities Act*.

182 *PHIPA*, s. 43(1)(h). See Chapter 10 for a discussion of s. 43(1)(h).

183 *Ibid.*, s. 37(1)(c). See Chapter 9 for a discussion of s. 37(1)(c).

184 *Ibid.*

185 Of course, such a request may raise an issue about the source of the resources required to de-identify the information.

8) Limitations on Role

A health data institute is not responsible for managing the Ministry of Health and Long-Term Care's disclosures of de-identified information. The Ministry remains responsible for the disclosure of de-identified health information to parties that use such information for research and other purposes. A health data institute does not have a role in such disclosures of information by the Ministry.

9) Health Numbers

Health data institutes have various powers to collect, use, and disclose health numbers, despite the limitations that *PHIPA* places on such collections, uses, and disclosures.[186] Chapter 2 includes an in-depth discussion of these powers.

E. PRESCRIBED PLANNING ENTITIES UNDER SECTION 45

1) Generally

PHIPA makes it clear that the Ministry of Health and Long-Term Care is not the only party involved in analysis with respect to the planning and management of the health system. For many years, several organizations have played a significant role in such activities, complementing the work of the Ministry. Such organizations undertake essential work ranging from reporting on patient utilization of emergency department services to tracking survival rates for heart transplants.[187] Health information custodians have become accustomed to meeting the information requirements of such organizations. Section 45 of the Act creates a scheme whereby health information custodians can disclose personal health information to such entities to permit them to continue to carry out their work in a manner that recognizes the importance of informational privacy.[188]

2) Disclosure to a Prescribed Planning Entity

A health information custodian may disclose personal health information, without the consent of the patients to whom the information relates, to a prescribed

---

186 *PHIPA*, s. 34.

187 The Institute for Clinical Evaluative Sciences and the Canadian Institutes for Health Research have undertaken such work, for example.

188 The first reading version of Bill 31, above note 79, did not provide health information custodians with authority to disclose personal health information to such organizations. The concept of disclosures to "prescribed entities" was included in the Bill at second reading.

planning entity (referred to in *PHIPA* as a "prescribed entity") "for the purpose of analysis or compiling statistical information with respect to the management of, evaluation or monitoring of, the allocation of resources to or planning for all or part of the health system, including the delivery of services."[189]

3) Restrictions on Information Disclosed to a Prescribed Planning Entity

PHIPA includes restrictions on the type of personal health information that a health information custodian may disclose to a prescribed planning entity pursuant to this provision of the Act. A health information custodian may not disclose to a prescribed planning entity for the purposes of this provision notes of personal health information about a patient that are recorded by a health information custodian and that document the contents of conversations during a private counselling session or a group, joint, or family counselling session.[190]

4) Prescribed Planning Entities

The *PHIPA* Regulation identifies four prescribed planning entities, including any registries maintained within the entity:[191]

- Cancer Care Ontario (CCO);[192]
- Canadian Institute for Health Information (CIHI);[193]
- Institute for Clinical Evaluative Sciences (ICES);[194] and
- Pediatric Oncology Group of Ontario (POGO).[195]

---

189   *PHIPA*, s. 45(1).

190   *Ibid.*, s. 45(2)(a). The regulations made under *PHIPA* may identify additional types of information that a health information custodian may not disclose to a prescribed planning entity for these purposes of the Act.

191   *PHIPA* Regulation, above note 32, s. 18(1). By including a reference to registries that prescribed entities may maintain, this provision makes it clear that custodians may disclose personal health information to prescribed planning entities in connection with the work of the prescribed planning entity related to the registry, even though the registry itself is not prescribed under *PHIPA*, s. 39(1)(c).

192   CCO is continued under the *Cancer Act*, R.S.O. 1990, c. C.1.

193   In September 1992, federal, provincial, and territorial ministers of health approved the creation of CIHI. CIHI's mandate was established jointly by federal and provincial/territorial ministers of health, and includes the co-ordination of the development and maintenance of a comprehensive and integrated approach to health information for Canada; and the co-ordination of the provision of accurate and timely data and information required for establishing sound health policy, and effectively managing the Canadian health system. See <www.cihi.ca>.

194   See <www.ices.on.ca>.

195   See <www.pogo.on.ca>.

The work of these entities predates *PHIPA* and is familiar to many. The First Ministers' ten-year plan to strengthen health care, for example, assigned the role of reporting on progress on wait times across jurisdictions to the Canadian Institute for Health Information.[196]

5) Requirements for a Prescribed Planning Entity

a) Information Practices
Before a health information custodian discloses personal health information to a prescribed planning entity for the purposes of section 45 of *PHIPA*, the prescribed planning entity must demonstrate that it has practices and procedures in place to protect the privacy of patients whose personal health information it receives and to maintain the confidentiality of the information.[197]

b) Approval of the Information and Privacy Commissioner
The information practices and procedures of a prescribed planning entity require the approval of the Information and Privacy Commissioner.[198] Every three years from the date of the approval, the Commissioner is required to review the practices and procedures of the prescribed planning entity. The Commissioner must advise a health information custodian disclosing personal health information to a prescribed planning entity for the purposes of section 45 of *PHIPA* whether the practices and procedures of the prescribed planning entity continues to meet the Commissioner's approval.[199] As a prescribed planning entity may not be a health information custodian,[200] this role for the Information and Privacy Commissioner in reviewing and approving the practices and procedures of prescribed planning entities constitutes an important additional privacy-protective element of the Act.

c) Description of Functions
The prescribed planning entity is required to make publicly available a plain language description of the functions of the entity, including a summary of its practices and procedures regarding the protection of privacy and confidentiality.[201]

---

196 10-year plan, above note 1.

197 *PHIPA*, s. 45(3)(a).

198 *Ibid.*, s. 45(3)(b). However, health information custodians can make disclosures until 31 October 2005 in the absence of the Commissioner's approval. This one-year delay for this requirement gives the Commissioner and the prescribed planning entities the opportunity to develop and undergo the approval process.

199 *Ibid.*, s. 45(4).

200 At time of writing, no prescribed planning entities are health information custodians.

201 *PHIPA* Regulation, above note 32, s. 18(2). Prescribed planning entities may wish to refer to the obligations of health information custodians with respect to a written public statement, as set in *PHIPA*, s. 16, for guidance on preparing such a description.

6) Powers to Collect, Use, and Disclose Personal Health Information

a) Collection

PHIPA explicitly gives a prescribed planning entity that is not a health information custodian the authority to collect the personal health information that a health information custodian discloses to it under section 45.[202] Further, authority is given to a prescribed planning entity that is a health information custodian to collect personal health information for the purposes described in section 45 of the Act from a person who is not a custodian.[203] Where the prescribed planning entity is a health information custodian, the entity may rely on various provisions in *PHIPA* for authority to collect personal health information from a health information custodian that discloses it to the entity for the entity's work under section 45.[204]

b) Use

A prescribed planning entity may use the personal health information that it collects from a health information custodian as a prescribed planning entity for the purposes for which it received the information.[205] Further, a prescribed planning entity may use personal health information for the purpose of carrying out research as if it were a health information custodian, provided that it follows the research requirements in *PHIPA* applicable to health information custodians.[206]

c) Disclosure

PHIPA prohibits a prescribed planning entity from disclosing personal health information except as required by law, subject to any exceptions set out in the regulation.[207] The regulation provides that a prescribed planning entity may disclose personal health information, in the same way that a health information custodian may make such disclosures under the Act, to

- a prescribed health registry;
- a researcher;
- another prescribed planning entity; and

---

202 *PHIPA*, s. 45(5).
203 *Ibid.*, s. 36(1)(e).
204 For example, *PHIPA*, s. 36(1)(g).
205 *Ibid.*, s. 45(6).
206 *PHIPA* Regulation, above note 32, s. 18(3).
207 *PHIPA*, s. 45(6).

- a health data institute.[208]

A prescribed planning entity may also disclose personal health information that it receives as a prescribed planning entity to a governmental institution of Ontario or Canada, where permitted or required by law or by a treaty, agreement, or arrangement made under an Act of Ontario or an Act of Canada.[209] Finally, a prescribed planning entity may disclose the information that it receives as such an entity to a health information custodian who provided the information, whether directly or indirectly, whether or not the information has been manipulated or altered, provided that the information does not contain any additional identifying information.[210] For example, a prescribed planning entity may disclose to a hospital personal health information in a tabular form where the hospital disclosed the information to the prescribed planning entity through the provision of copies of laboratory reports. Similarly, the prescribed planning entity can disclose the personal health information in this way even if another custodian acted as an intermediary and disclosed the information to the prescribed planning entity.

d) Health Numbers

Prescribed planning entities have various powers to collect, use, and disclose health numbers. Chapter 2 includes an in-depth discussion of these powers.

7) Disclosing Personal Health Information to a Prescribed Planning Entity

What duties does a health information custodian have in disclosing personal health information to a prescribed planning entity? *PHIPA* does not impose any specific requirements on custodians that disclose personal health information to prescribed planning entities. *PHIPA*, for example, does not require a health information custodian to enter into an agreement with a prescribed planning entity in making a disclosure to the entity. Despite the absence of specific requirements from the Act, custodians will need to determine what information they may require from a prescribed planning entity in exercising their

---

208 *PHIPA* Regulation, above note 32, s. 18(4).

209 *Ibid.*, s. 18(6). Further, *PHIPA* Regulation, s. 18(7) provides that the Canadian Institute for Health Information, as a prescribed planning entity, may disclose personal health information about a patient to a person outside Ontario where (a) the disclosure is for the purpose of health planning or administration; (b) the information relates to health care provided in Ontario to a person who is a resident of another province or territory of Canada; and (c) the disclosure is made to the government of that province or territory.

discretion to disclose personal health information. At a minimum, a custodian being requested to disclose to a prescribed planning entity may wish to seek written confirmation from the entity that it is fully complying with all the requirements necessary to authorize the disclosure. Also, a custodian may request a copy of the entity's plain language description of its information practices,[211] in addition to information concerning the status of the Commissioner's approval of the entity's privacy practices and procedures.[212] Further, a health information custodian may request brief documentation outlining the information that the prescribed planning entity seeks from the custodian.

8) Prescribed Planning Entities Distinguished from Health Data Institutes

The work of prescribed planning entities is to be distinguished from that of a health data institute, as described above. Prescribed planning entities have greater discretion and scope with regard to the use and disclosure of the information disclosed to them by health information custodians, provided that it is for the purposes described in section 45(1) of *PHIPA* or for the purposes permitted by the regulations, such as research. With this greater discretion, a prescribed planning entity is able to set an agenda in a manner not open to a health data institute. The role of the health data institute is a technical one that focuses on the analysis and de-identification of data prior to its delivery to the Minister. Its role is also one-sided, in that it does not provide services with respect to personal health information that the Minister wishes to disclose, but only with respect to information that the Minister seeks. The Act does not suggest a policy-setting role for the health data institute, but leaves such activities to the Ministry of Health and Long-Term Care.

---

210 *Ibid.*, s. 18(5).
211 *Ibid.*, s. 18(2).
212 *PHIPA*, s. 45(4).

12 Rules for Recipients of Personal Health Information from Health Information Custodians

A. GENERALLY

As we have seen thus far, the *Personal Health Information Protection Act, 2004*[1] primarily regulates the collection, use, and disclosure of personal health information by health information custodians — a defined group of persons, largely within the health care sector, known to collect, use, and disclose personal health information regularly. Unlike one of Ontario's earlier attempts to develop privacy legislation, *PHIPA* does not attempt to regulate actions with respect to personal health information in every context.[2] However, the Act's reach extends beyond health information custodians to regulate the activities of other persons as well. These persons include a person who is not a health information custodian to whom a health information custodian discloses personal health information, commonly referred to as a "recipient."[3] The examples of

---

1   S.O. 2004, c. 3, Sch. A [*PHIPA*].
2   Compare this approach to the approach reflected in the draft *Privacy of Personal Information Act, 2002*. The draft Act was developed to regulate personal information, including personal health information, across the entire private sector and the health sector. See Ontario, *A Consultation on the Draft Privacy of Personal Information Act, 2002* (Toronto: Ministry of Consumer and Business Services, 2002) [*POPIA*], online: <www.cbs.gov.on.ca/mcbs/english/pdf/56XSMB>. See Chapter 1, Section (B)(5)(d) for a discussion of *POPIA*.
3   *PHIPA* uses the term "recipient" in the heading for s. 49(1) to refer to such persons.

recipients that most readily come to mind include employers, insurers, and researchers. The Act's recipient rules apply to a recipient's use and disclosure of personal health information, even if the recipient received the information before 1 November 2004, the day on which the Act came into force.[4]

B.   IDENTIFYING RECIPIENTS

1)   Who Is a Recipient?

A person is subject to the recipient rules only for personal health information that a health information custodian disclosed directly to the person. The term "disclose" is defined in *PHIPA* to mean to make the information available or release it to another person.[5] There are many obvious examples of such disclosures. A dental surgeon discloses personal health information about a patient to an insurer in the course of seeking payment from the insurer for treatment provided to the patient. A physiotherapist discloses personal health information about an athlete to the athlete's coaches and trainer. A nurse practitioner discloses personal health information about a child to a children's aid society in the course of fulfilling reporting requirements concerning children in need of protection under the *Child and Family Services Act*.[6] Health information custodians disclose personal health information to recipients everyday, whether with consent or, as permitted by *PHIPA*, without consent.

2)   Who Is Not a Recipient?

a)   Agent

An agent of a health information custodian is not considered a "recipient" of a disclosure of personal health information from the health information custodian, as the provision of personal health information by a custodian to its agent

---

4   *PHIPA*, s. 7(1)(b)(ii). See also *General*, O. Reg. 329/04, s. 20 [*PHIPA* Regulation].

5   *PHIPA*, s. 2. See Chapter 2, Section E(4), for a discussion of the term "disclose." The rules imposed by *PHIPA*, s. 49 on recipients obviously apply only where the recipient has actually received the information in question. Where the custodian has merely made the information available to the recipient, which falls within the definition of "disclose" for the purposes of the rules relating to collection, use, and disclosure, but the "recipient" has not received the information in some form, then the restrictions set by s. 49 on subsequent uses and disclosures of the information by the recipient do not apply, because the information never actually reached the hands of the "recipient."

6   *Child and Family Services Act*, R.S.O. 1990, c. C.11, s. 72 [*CFSA*].

is considered a "use" of the information rather than a disclosure by the custodian or a collection by the agent.[7]

b) Person Performing the Work of a Custodian

A health information custodian who receives personal health information from another health information custodian is governed by the rules in the rest of Part IV of *PHIPA*, but is not covered by the recipient rules. A person who is a health information custodian is not a "recipient" covered by the recipient rules in the Act when it performs the powers, duties, or work of a custodian.

However, it is possible for a person who is otherwise a health information custodian to be subject to the recipient rules where the person is not performing the powers, duties, or work of a custodian. For example, a corporation may operate a hospital and be a health information custodian for that work. The same corporation may also maintain a registry of personal health information, independently from the operation of the hospital. Unless the corporation is in some way in the Act or the regulations deemed to be a health information custodian in relation to its work in maintaining the registry, it is not a health information custodian in relation to that work. Therefore, where it receives personal health information from a health information custodian in relation to its work in maintaining the registry, it is not a health information custodian and is subject to the recipient rules in the Act.

How does this principle apply where the person receiving personal health information from a health information custodian is a health information custodian, but is also an agent of a non-custodian? Consider the example of a psychologist's disclosure of personal health information about a patient to a nurse, who provides health care, and works on behalf of the patient's employer. Clearly, where the psychologist disclosed the personal health information directly to the employer's management staff, the employer would be a recipient of the information and subject to *PHIPA's* recipient rules. Where the psychologist discloses the personal health information to the nurse, the nurse is not governed by the recipient rules, as the nurse is a health information custodian. However, the nurse's provision of the information to the employer would be a disclosure under *PHIPA*, and the nurse would need to make the disclosure in accordance with the Act.[8] Further, the nurse's disclosure of the infor-

---

7   *PHIPA*, s. 6(1). See Chapter 2, Section (B)(2) for a discussion of the rules applicable to the activities of agents.

8   Under *PHIPA*, s. 6(1), the principle that internal organizational transfers of information are uses rather than disclosures applies only to transfers within a health information custodian's organization; that is, between a custodian and its agent or among the

mation to the employer would be a disclosure of personal health information by a health information custodian to a person who is not a custodian, and the employer would be subject to the recipient rules for this information.[9] Therefore, the result is the same whether the employer receives the personal health information directly from the psychologist, or indirectly from the psychologist through the nurse. In both cases, the employer receives personal health information from a health information custodian and is bound by the recipient rules for the information.

c)   Non-Health Information Custodian Collecting Directly from Individual or Other Non-Health Information Custodian

The recipient rules apply only where a person who is not a health information custodian receives a disclosure of personal health information directly from a custodian or an agent of the custodian. The rules do not apply where the non-custodian receives personal health information directly from the individual to whom the information relates. Likewise, the recipient rules do not apply where the non-custodian receives personal health information from any other person who is neither a health information custodian nor an agent of a custodian.

Consider the following situation. An employee injures his shoulder and cannot perform his job at the automobile manufacturing plant where he works. He visits his family physician, who provides the employee with a letter confirming the employee's inability to perform his job for the next month. The employee provides the letter to his employer when he visits the manufacturing plant for a meeting to discuss accommodation of his injury. *PHIPA* would not regulate how the employer could subsequently use and disclose that personal health information. The employer did not receive the personal health information from the physician, but from the employee. Therefore, the employer is not

---

agents of a custodian. When a custodian provides personal health information in its custody or control to a non-custodian who is not the agent of the custodian, the provision of the information is considered a disclosure. See also *PHIPA*, s. 2, definitions of "use" and "disclose."

9   It may be argued that, depending on the circumstances, the nurse is merely acting as the agent of the employer in accepting the information, and the employer does not ever take custody or control of the information on the nurse's behalf but only on behalf of the custodian. If this can be established in a particular situation, based on the arrangement between the employer and the nurse, and based on the interpretation of "custody and control" under *PHIPA*, then the transfer of information may be considered a transfer from the psychologist to the employer, and the nurse acts merely as a conduit. In such a scenario, the result would be the same; that is, the employer would be bound by the recipient rules for the information received from the psychologist.

subject to the recipient rules. In this way, the Act may treat the use and disclosure of the same information in different ways, depending on the source of the information.

C. THE RECIPIENT RULES

1) Generally

Although the restrictions on the activities of recipients are not as detailed as the rules for collection, use, and disclosure applicable to health information custodians, they are both significant and broad in their application. They suggest a distinction in policy between health information custodians and other persons. Unlike health information custodians, who are given broad discretion under *PHIPA* to determine appropriate secondary uses and disclosures of personal health information in their custody or under their control without the consent of the individual to whom the information relates, the Act does not give recipients the same discretion.

2) Restriction on Purposes for Use and Disclosure

The main restriction that *PHIPA* imposes on recipients is that, subject to the exceptions and additional requirements set out in the regulations made under the Act, and except as permitted or required by law, a recipient cannot use or disclose the personal health information that the recipient receives from a health information custodian for any purpose other than the purpose for which the custodian disclosed the information under the Act, or for the purpose of carrying out a statutory or legal duty.[10] It is necessary to consider a number of aspects of this rule in detail, including the exceptions to the rule.

a) For the Purpose for Which Personal Health Information Was Disclosed

This provision permits a recipient to use or disclose personal health information that it received from a health information custodian for "the purpose for which the custodian disclosed the information under the Act." How should this language be interpreted? It is prudent to interpret this language narrowly, but reasonably. Often the purpose will be stated either explicitly by the custodian in disclosing the information, or in the request to the custodian that prompted the disclosure. Where the purpose was not explicitly stated, it may

---

10   *PHIPA*, s. 49(1).

be inferred from the circumstances. Identifying the custodian's authority to make the disclosure, or the nature of the consent that authorized the disclosure, may assist in determining the purpose of the disclosure. In some cases, there will be room for interpretation. A purpose may be interpreted narrowly or broadly. Obviously, the intention behind the inclusion of this language in *PHIPA* is to impose restrictions; therefore, in general, it would not be reasonable to interpret it in an open-ended manner so as to describe the purpose of the disclosure by the custodian as being "so that the recipient would use the information." One must interpret the purpose of the disclosure having in mind the apparent purpose of this provision; that is, to protect patients against unjustified and unrelated subsequent disclosures of the information, while not frustrating the purposes of the disclosure to the non-custodian. As such, it is probable that a recipient may use or disclose the information for purposes directly ancillary to the specific purpose of the disclosure, such that the recipient's use or disclosure is not frustrated.

The regulation also provides some guidance by limiting the scope of this authority. Recipients must not rely on this provision of the Act to disclose personal health information where the disclosure is otherwise prohibited by law.[11] For example, the *Occupational Health and Safety Act* includes a general prohibition on the disclosure of any information obtained in any medical examination of a worker made under that Act unless it is in a form that prevents the information from being identified with a particular person or case, except as required by law and as permitted in the regulations made under that Act.[12] Similarly, the *Workplace Safety and Insurance Act, 1997* prohibits employers from disclosing an employee's personal health information contained in a functional abilities form completed by a physician except in limited circumstances related to assisting the employer to return the employee to work.[13] These prohibitions will continue to prohibit a recipient from disclosing personal health information, even if the disclosure is for a purpose for which a health information custodian disclosed the information to the recipient.

Consider the following situation. A health information custodian, a dental surgeon, discloses personal health information about a patient to the patient's employer for the purpose of approving the employee's leave of absence. Would *PHIPA* permit the employer to then disclose the information to the employee's

---

11   *PHIPA* Regulation, above note 4, s. 21(3).

12   *Occupational Health and Safety Act*, R.S.O. 1990, c. O.1, s. 63(1)(f) [*OHSA*]. *OHSA*, s. 63(6) specifically provides that s. 63 prevails over *PHIPA*.

13   *Workplace Safety and Insurance Act, 1997*, S.O. 1997, c. 16, Sch. A, s. 37(4) [*WSIA*].

insurer? Where the employer disclosed the information to the insurer to determine and provide the employee with benefits during the employee's leave of absence, it can be argued that the employer's disclosure of the personal health information to the insurer is permitted under the Act as a disclosure made for "the purpose for which the custodian disclosed the information under the Act."[14] One reaches the same conclusion when considering the following example. A physician discloses personal health information about a patient to the patient's employer for the purpose of addressing a claim under the *Workplace Safety and Insurance Act*. The employer may use the information for the purpose of addressing the claim.

The recipient rules apply to personal health information whether the recipient received it before or after 1 November 2004, the date on which *PHIPA* came into force. For information disclosed to the recipient before that date, there would appear to be no "purpose for which the custodian was authorized to disclose the information under this Act,"[15] since *PHIPA* did not authorize any disclosures before it came into force. Where a recipient holds personal health information received from a custodian before *PHIPA* came into force, the *PHIPA* Regulation permits the recipient to use or disclose the information for the purpose for which it was disclosed to the recipient, except where the use or disclosure is otherwise prohibited by law.[16]

b) "Permitted or Required by Law" and "Legal Duty"

PHIPA also permits a recipient's subsequent use or disclosure of the personal health information that the recipient received from a health information custodian where "permitted or required by law" or to fulfil a "legal duty."[17] Common law duties, that is, those not set out in legislation or regulations, but

---

14   In the context of Ontario's municipal public sector privacy legislation, the Office of the Information and Privacy Commissioner had the opportunity to consider an individual's complaint concerning her employer's disclosure of medical information to an insurance company. The Assistant Commissioner found the employer's disclosure of medical information about the employee to an insurance company to have been disclosed by the employer for "a consistent purpose"; that is, for the purpose of determining the compensation benefits due to the employee. See Investigation Report I93-016M (25 May 1994), online: <www.ipc.on.ca>. This investigation report may be indicative of the approach that the Information and Privacy Commissioner may take in interpreting a recipient's authority to disclose for "the purpose for which the custodian disclosed the information under the Act" in *PHIPA*.

15   *PHIPA*, s. 49(1)(a).

16   *PHIPA* Regulation, above note 4, s. 20.

17   See Chapter 3 for a discussion of the language "permitted or required by law," which appears in a number of provisions in *PHIPA*.

identified by courts in case law, may require a recipient to use or disclose the information. In addition, a court order, search warrant, or similar legal requirement may require a recipient to use or disclose personal health information that it received from a health information custodian.

Recipients can also use or disclose the personal health information where other legislation permits or requires the recipient to use or disclose the information. Such other legislation could include legislation that governs a particular category of recipients. For example, under the *Workplace Safety and Insurance Act, 1997*, employers are required to notify the Workplace Safety and Insurance Board within three days after learning of an accident to a worker employed by the employer if the accident necessitates health care or results in the worker not being able to earn full wages. The employer is required to give the Board such other information as the Board may require from time to time in connection with the accident.[18] Therefore, regardless of whether the employer received such information from the worker or from a health information custodian, such as the worker's physician, the employer is required to disclose the information, which would include personal health information, to the Board. *PHIPA's* recipient rules would permit the employer to make this disclosure of personal health information.

Alternatively, such other legislation could include legislation of more general application, such as the federal *Personal Information Protection and Electronic Documents Act*.[19] *PIPEDA* applies to an organization that collects, uses, or discloses personal information in the course of a commercial activity.[20] Where *PIPEDA* permits an organization to which *PIPEDA* applies to disclose personal information for a particular purpose without the knowledge or consent of the patient to whom the information relates,[21] the disclosure would be "permitted by law" for the purposes of *PHIPA*.

The regulation made under *PHIPA* also makes it clear that the requirements for recipients do not apply to prevent a person who received personal health information from a health information custodian from using or disclosing the information pursuant to a valid consent of the individual to whom the information relates.[22] In other words, if the individual consents, the recipient can use or disclose the information for any lawful purpose.

---

18   *WSIA*, above note 13, ss. 21(1) & (2).
19   S.C. 2000, c. 5 [*PIPEDA*].
20   *Ibid.*, s. 4(1)(a).
21   *Ibid.*, s. 7(3).
22   *PHIPA* Regulation, above note 4, s. 21(1)(b). However, the consent rules in *PHIPA*, as discussed in Chapter 5 do not regulate the requirements for an individual's consent to a non-

c) "Statutory Duty"

A recipient may use or disclose personal health information for the purpose of carrying out a "statutory duty." As both phrases appear in the provision, the language "for the purpose of carrying out a statutory duty" must be interpreted to mean something different than "where required by law." A recipient's disclosure of personal health information "for the purpose of carrying out a statutory duty" may be understood as a disclosure made by a recipient to fulfil the recipient's statutory function where the legislation does not specifically provide that the recipient must make the disclosure. Instead, the disclosure contributes to the recipient's fulfillment of its statutory duty. For example, the statutory functions of a children's aid society include investigating allegations that children may be in need of protection, and providing counselling and other services to families for the prevention of circumstances requiring the protection of children.[23] Therefore, a children's aid society to which a health information custodian, such as a psychologist, discloses personal health information for the purpose of notifying the society that a child is in need of protection may first use that information to investigate whether the child is in need of protection, but then, having determined that the child is not in need of protection, it may also use the information to provide the child and his or her family with counselling to prevent circumstances that would require the protection of the child.

D. EXCLUSIONS FROM AND EXCEPTIONS TO RECIPIENT RULES

1) Exclusions and Exceptions for Categories of Persons

In limited circumstances, the requirements for recipients do not apply to certain persons.[24]

a) Institutions under Public Sector Privacy Legislation

Institutions within the meaning of the *Freedom of Information and Protection of Privacy Act*[25] or the *Municipal Freedom of Information and Protection of Privacy*

health information custodian's use or disclosure of personal health information, since *PHIPA*, s. 18(1) refers only to consent for the collection, use, or disclosure of personal health information by a health information custodian, not by non-custodian recipients.

23   *CFSA*, above note 6, s. 15(3).

24   For a summary of the exceptions to and exclusions from the rules applicable to recipients, see Table A at the end of this chapter.

25   R.S.O. 1990, c. F.31 [*FIPPA*].

Act,[26] such as ministries of the government of Ontario, school boards, and municipalities, may continue to use and disclose information as permitted by those Acts.[27] Similarly, the requirements for recipients do not apply to a person employed by or acting for an institution within the meaning of *FIPPA* or *MFIPPA*, to the extent that the person is acting within the scope of one of those Acts.[28] For example, the Registrar of Motor Vehicles, an agent of the Ministry of Transportation, which is an institution under *FIPPA*, collects personal health information from an optometrist who reports the name and clinical condition of a person who suffers from an eye condition that makes it dangerous for the person to operate a motor vehicle, as required by the *Highway Traffic Act*.[29] The Registrar's use and disclosure of that information is not subject to *PHIPA's* recipient rules.

b)   Individual to Whom Information Relates and Substitute Decision-maker

The regulation made under *PHIPA* also excludes a patient or substitute decision-maker of a patient from the requirements for recipients in respect of personal health information about the patient.[30] Therefore, when a person receives personal health information about him or herself from a health information custodian, the person is not restricted, in the name of his or her own privacy, from freely using or disclosing the information. Perhaps this exception can be understood without being explicitly clarified in the regulation, since, generally, the Act operates on the premise that an individual or an individual's substitute decision-maker is free to make decisions about the individual's personal health information.

c)   Payment Providers: Disclosures to Pharmacists

Another exception to the requirements for recipients in *PHIPA* arises in the context of disclosures to pharmacists. A person who is not a health information custodian and who provides coverage for payment to or on behalf of individuals in respect of medications or related goods or services may, where a claim is made to the person through a pharmacist for such a payment to or on behalf of an individual, disclose personal health information about the individ-

---

26   R.S.O. 1990, c. M.56 [*MFIPPA*].

27   *PHIPA*, 49(5), which provides, except as prescribed, that s. 49 does not apply to an institution within the meaning of *FIPPA* or *MFIPPA* that is not a health information custodian.

28   *PHIPA* Regulation, above note 4, s. 23(1).

29   R.S.O. 1990, c. H.8, s. 204(1).

30   *PHIPA* Regulation, above note 4, s. 21(1)(a).

ual to the pharmacist to assist the pharmacist in advising the individual or providing health care to the individual.[31] This exception to the requirements for recipients in the Act would permit a health insurer, upon receiving a claim for coverage for medication prescribed to an individual, to inform the pharmacy of any other medications for which the individual claimed coverage where there is a possibility of a dangerous interaction. Such disclosures are an important part of patient safety initiatives involving health insurers and pharmacies.

d) Researchers

Researchers to whom health information custodians disclose personal health information without the consent of the patients to whom the information relates are restricted to using the information only for the purposes set out in the approved research plan.[32] Further, requirements concerning the researcher's disclosure of the information are narrower than the powers to disclose included in the recipient rules. Subject to the exceptions in the regulations made under *PHIPA*, a researcher must not disclose the information except pursuant to any regulations made under the Act and as required by law, such as a statutory requirement, court order, or search warrant.[33] This narrower restriction applicable to researchers, instead of the somewhat broader restrictions in the general recipient rules,[34] reflects the expectation that researchers may have access to a broad range of personal health information to use for approved research, but are not expected to use or disclose the information further except as required in very limited circumstances.

e) Prescribed Health Registries

PHIPA permits a health information custodian to disclose personal health information to a prescribed health registry; that is, a person identified in the regulations who maintains a registry of personal health information, for purposes of improving the provision of health care, or that relates to the storage or donation of body parts or bodily substances.[35] Where the prescribed health registry is not a health information custodian, it is a recipient and is subject to the restrictions on recipients. Despite these restrictions, the regulation made under the Act makes it clear that prescribed health registries can disclose the

---

31 *Ibid.*, s. 21(2).
32 *PHIPA*, s. 44(6)(b).
33 *Ibid.*, s. 44(6)(d). See Chapter 11, Section B for a discussion of the obligations of researchers.
34 See the words "despite subsection 49(1)" in *PHIPA*, s. 44(6)(d).
35 *Ibid.*, s. 39(1)(c); *PHIPA* Regulation, above note 4, s. 13(1).

information that they receive as recipients in certain circumstances, including those related to the research and planning of the health system.[36]

f) Prescribed Planning Entities

PHIPA also imposes specific requirements on prescribed planning entities identified in the regulation made under section 45 of the Act, such as the Canadian Institute for Health Information and Cancer Care Ontario, to which health information custodians can disclose personal health information for the purpose of analysis with respect to the management or planning of the health system.[37] The general recipient rules do not apply to such entities.[38] Subject to the exceptions set out in the regulation, prescribed planning entities, when receiving personal health information from health information custodians pursuant to section 45(1), are subject to the narrower restriction that they must not use the information except for the purpose for which it was received and must not disclose it except as required by law.[39] However, the regulation made under the Act permits prescribed planning entities to disclose personal health information that they receive from health information custodians as prescribed planning entities in the circumstances set out in the regulation, which include, for example, circumstances related to research.[40]

g) Health Data Institutes

A health information custodian must disclose personal health information, without the consent of the individuals to whom the information relates, upon the request of the Minister of Health and Long-Term Care, to a health data institute for analysis with respect to the management or planning of the health system.[41] By receiving this personal health information from health information custodians, the health data institute becomes a recipient. *PHIPA* includes specific requirements for this category of recipients. A health data institute that receives personal health information as a consequence of the Minister's request to health information custodians is prohibited from disclosing the information or information derived from the information, even in de-identified form, to persons other than the Minister or persons approved by the Min-

---

36   *PHIPA* Regulation, *ibid.*, ss. 13(4) & (5). For a discussion of prescribed health registries, see Chapter 11, Section C.

37   *PHIPA*, s. 45(1); *PHIPA* Regulation, *ibid.*, s. 18(1).

38   *PHIPA*, s. 45(6).

39   *Ibid.*

40   *PHIPA* Regulation, above note 4, ss. 18(3), (4), (5), (6), & (7). For a discussion of prescribed planning entities, see Chapter 11, Section E.

41   *PHIPA*, s. 47(2).

ister.[42] This specific restriction on a health data institute's disclosure of personal health information, and even information derived from such information, applies despite the more general restrictions on recipients' disclosures of personal health information.[43]

h) Archives

PHIPA permits health information custodians to transfer records of personal health information to the Archives of Ontario or an archive identified in the regulations for the purposes of collecting and preserving records of historical or archival importance.[44] The Archives of Ontario is an institution under *FIPPA*,[45] and some other archives that register with the Information and Privacy Commissioner to be eligible for such transfers may be institutions under *MFIPPA*. Any archives that are institutions under those statutes are not subject to the recipient rules for the records.[46] Archives that are not institutions under one of those Acts are subject to the recipient rules. However, the regulation sets out certain exceptions to the recipient rules that allow archives to use and disclose personal health information transferred to them under *PHIPA* or its regulations for research purposes with research ethics board approval in accordance with *PHIPA*.[47] An archive is also required to provide the patients to whom the information relates with reasonable access to their own records of personal health information.[48]

i) Information and Privacy Commissioner

As a person who is not a health information custodian but receives personal health information from health information custodians in the course of carrying out powers and duties under *PHIPA*, the Information and Privacy Commissioner is captured by the recipient rule. However, this result does not impose any practical restrictions on the Commissioner. Any uses and disclosures of personal health information by the Commissioner generally would be

---

42 *PHIPA*, s. 47(15)(f). See Chapter 11, Section D for a discussion of the requirements pertaining to a health information custodian's disclosure of personal health information to a health data institute.

43 *PHIPA* Regulation, above note 4, s. 21(3).

44 *PHIPA*, s. 42(3). See Chapter 10, Section O for a discussion of the transfer of information to archives.

45 *General*, R.R.O. 1990, Reg. 460, made under *FIPPA*, above note 25.

46 *PHIPA*, s. 49(5). See Section D(1)(a), above for a discussion of the exclusion applicable to such institutions.

47 *PHIPA* Regulation, above note 4, s. 14(4). See Chapter 10, Section O for a discussion of the transfer of information to archives.

48 *PHIPA* Regulation, *ibid.*, s. 14(1)(b).

for the purposes of carrying out a statutory or legal duty,[49] and the rule limiting uses and disclosures to what is reasonably necessary[50] is already part of the rules under the Act that apply specifically to the Commissioner.[51]

2) Exception for Transfers to Archives

Just as health information custodians are permitted under *PHIPA* to transfer records of personal health information to an archive that meets the requirements set out in the regulation, so any non-custodian recipients of personal health information from a custodian are also permitted under the regulation to transfer records of personal health information to the same class of archives.[52] In the absence of a provision that provides this authority to transfer records, recipients may have experienced difficulty divesting themselves of the records of personal health information that they have received from a health information custodian, short of destroying them.

E. LIMITATIONS ON USE AND DISCLOSURE

1) General Limiting Principles

As discussed above, *PHIPA* includes certain prohibitions commonly referred to as the general limiting principles.[53] These prohibitions are included to limit the type of information and the amount of personal health information that a health information custodian may use and disclose.[54] Similar restrictions are imposed on recipients of personal health information from health information custodians. Where a recipient can use and disclose personal health information that a health information custodian disclosed to the recipient, the recipient must not use or disclose more of the information than is reasonably necessary to meet the purpose of the use or disclosure.[55]

---

49 *PHIPA*, ss. 49(1) and 68(3).
50 *Ibid.*, s. 49(2).
51 *Ibid.*, s. 68(2).
52 *PHIPA* Regulation, above note 4, s. 14(3). See Chapter 10, Section O for a discussion of the transfer of information to archives. See also Chapter 11, Section B for a discussion of *PHIPA*'s research rules.
53 See Chapter 7 for a discussion of the general limiting principles applicable to health information custodians.
54 *PHIPA*, s. 30.
55 *Ibid.*, s. 49(2).

As with the general limitations imposed on health information custodians, how much information is practically required to meet the purpose of a particular use or disclosure will depend on the circumstances. Again, it is a question of assessing the amount of information required for the proper fulfilment of the recipient's duties. Before disclosing an employee's entire record containing personal health information received from a custodian, for example, an employer must consider the purpose for which the recipient is seeking the information and the surrounding circumstances. Based on that information, the employer would be required to determine whether disclosure of all the information from the custodian would be necessary or if a part of the information would suffice.

2) Exclusions from and Exceptions to General Limiting Principles

a) "Required by Law"

There is an exception to this prohibition concerning the amount of personal health information that a recipient may use or disclose, however. This prohibition does not apply to the recipient's use or disclosure of the information where the use or disclosure is required by law.[56] A recipient required by law to use or disclose personal health information does not have the discretion to restrict the use or disclosure by concluding that a lesser amount of personal health information is "reasonably necessary" to meet the purpose of the use or disclosure. Further, the recipient may use or disclose whatever information, including personal health information, is necessary to meet the requirements. An example of such a disclosure that is required by law can be found in the *Child and Family Services Act*.[57] That Act requires a person who performs professional duties involving children, including early childhood educators and youth workers, to disclose information about a child in need of protection to a children's aid society.[58] *PHIPA* would not interfere with this statutory duty to disclose so as to limit the information that the early childhood educator or youth worker could disclose, even where some or all of the information was personal health information that the early childhood educator or youth worker received from a health information custodian. As a result of this exception to the general limiting principles, the early childhood educator or youth worker

---

56   *PHIPA*, s. 49(2). See Chapter 3, Section B(3)(b) for a more detailed discussion of the language "required by law."

57   *CFSA*, above note 6.

58   *Ibid.*, s. 72.

would not be required, or even permitted, to apply the general limiting principles so as to withhold from disclosure some, or all, of the information concerning the child in need of protection.

b) Statutory Bodies and Other Persons

Similarly, this prohibition does not apply to professional governing bodies, including a College under the *Regulated Health Professions Act, 1991*, the Ontario College of Social Workers and Social Service Workers, the Board under the *Drugless Practitioners Act*, a children's aid society or any person providing services on behalf of or on the request of a children's aid society, or a foster parent.[59] These exemptions help ensure that *PHIPA* does not restrict these bodies and persons in such a manner that they could be impeded from performing their important responsibilities aimed at the protection of the public and children.

F. CUSTODIANS AS RECIPIENTS OF EMPLOYEE HEALTH INFORMATION

As discussed earlier, "personal health information" does not include identifying information contained in a health information custodian's record if the identifying information contained in the record relates primarily to employees or other agents of the custodian, and the record is maintained primarily for a purpose other than the provision of health care to the employees or other agents.[60] In short, the term "personal health information" does not include information about a custodian's employees and other agents, except where the information relates to the custodian's provision of health care to the employee or agent.

Nevertheless, health information custodians are not left unregulated with respect to this information about their employees and other agents. Rather, they are treated as non-health information custodian recipients when they act as employers. In this way, health information custodians are treated like other employers when acting in the capacity of employer.[61] This provision does not apply to *FIPPA/MFIPPA* custodians, however.[62]

---

59   *PHIPA* Regulation, above note 4, s. 22.
60   *PHIPA*, s. 4(4). See Chapter 2, Section C(1) for a discussion of the meaning of the term "personal health information."
61   The policy rationale for treating employers that are health information custodians like other employers uniformly may be because of the absence of a basis to distinguish employers that are health information custodians from other employers.
62   *PHIPA* Regulation, above note 4, s. 23(2) provides that s. 49(3) of the Act does not apply to an institution that is a health information custodian within the meaning of *FIPPA* or *MFIPPA*.

As is the case for a person who is not a health information custodian but receives personal health information from a custodian, the Act restricts a custodian's use and disclosure of personal health information about its employee or other agent where the custodian receives the information from another custodian for a purpose other than the provision of health care to the employee or other agent. Such a collection would arise, for example, where a hospital, in its capacity as employer, receives a note from a physician confirming that a nurse employed by the hospital was absent from work for a few days due to illness. Except as permitted or required by law and subject to the regulations,[63] if a health information custodian discloses personal health information about an employee or agent of another custodian to that custodian for a purpose other than the provision of health care to the employee or other agent, the receiving custodian must not use or disclose the information for any purpose other than the purpose for which the disclosing custodian was authorized to disclose the information under the Act; or the purpose of carrying out a statutory or legal duty.[64] The general limiting principles also continue to apply to such uses and disclosures. The receiving custodian must not use or disclose more information than is reasonably necessary to meet the purpose of the use or disclosure.[65]

G. HEALTH NUMBER

For the purposes of *PHIPA*, the health number is a particular kind of personal health information.[66] The collection, use, and disclosure of health numbers by persons who are not health information custodians are restricted to the purposes and circumstances specified in the Act.[67] These purposes and circumstances are discussed in Chapter 2.[68] The restrictions on the collection, use, or disclosure of a health number by a person who is not a health information custodian apply regardless of whether the person receives the health number from a health information custodian, another person who is not a health information custodian, or directly from the individual to whom the number relates. It is necessary to keep the restrictions concerning the use and disclosure of health numbers in mind when considering the effect of the recipient rules,

---

63 At time of writing, there were no such exceptions set out in the *PHIPA* Regulation.
64 *PHIPA*, s. 49(3)(a).
65 *Ibid.*, s. 49(3)(b).
66 *Ibid.*, s. 4(1)(f).
67 *Ibid.*, ss. 34(2) & (3).
68 Chapter 2 includes a discussion of who and what the Act covers, and includes a discussion of the rules in the Act specific to health numbers.

however, since these health number restrictions on persons who are not health information custodians supercede the general rules about a recipient's use and disclosure of personal health information.[69] Therefore, although a recipient may be able to disclose certain personal health information as permitted by law, the health number would not be part of the information the Act permits a recipient to disclose if the purposes and circumstances of the disclosure were not among those specified in the provisions of the Act or regulations specifically referring to health numbers.[70] Such restrictions on the disclosure of health numbers are new. The *Health Cards and Numbers and Control Act, 1991*,[71] legislation repealed by *PHIPA*, did not address the disclosure of health numbers, only their collection and use.

H. IMPLICATIONS

1) Jurisdiction of Information and Privacy Commissioner

The jurisdiction of the Information and Privacy Commissioner extends to conducting investigations and making binding orders, based on complaints received by the Commissioner or on reviews commenced on the Commissioner's own initiative, with respect to any circumstances in which there are reasonable grounds to believe that any person contravened or is about to contravene any provision of *PHIPA* or the regulations.[72] Thus, the Commissioner has jurisdiction to review allegations that a recipient has illegally used or disclosed personal health information it collected from a health information custodian, in contravention of the recipient rules set out in the Act and regulations.

2) Offences

PHIPA makes the wilful use or disclosure of personal health information by any person in contravention of the Act an offence.[73] Therefore, a recipient who wilfully discloses personal health information in contravention of the Act is guilty of an offence. Similarly, a recipient who collects, uses, or discloses health numbers in contravention of the restrictions in the Act on these activities is

---

69   *PHIPA*, s. 34(2).
70   *Ibid.*, s. 34(3).
71   S.O. 1991, c. 1, repealed by *PHIPA*, s. 82.
72   *PHIPA*, ss. 56(1) and 58(1).
73   *Ibid.*, s. 72(1)(a).

also guilty of an offence.[74] On conviction, persons guilty of such offences are liable to significant fines of up to $50,000 for individuals and $250,000 for corporations.[75]

3) Damages

Where a recipient is subject to a final order of the Commissioner or is convicted of an offence, and any relevant appeals are exhausted, the recipient may also be liable to pay damages to the person affected by the conduct that gave to rise the order or conviction.[76] Recipients who are subject to a claim for damages are protected by the immunity provisions in *PHIPA* where they have acted reasonably and in good faith in the circumstances.[77]

I.   RECIPIENT'S REVIEW OF INFORMATION PRACTICES

Faced with these new restrictions on the use and disclosure of any personal health information received directly from health information custodians, recipients should consider the sources of the personal health information that they collect, and the role (or potential role) for direct collections of personal health information in their operations. Collecting information directly from the individual is generally regarded as preferable from a privacy perspective, and has the added attraction that the information will not then be subject to the recipient rules in *PHIPA*.[78] Recipients should conduct a review of legislation and regulations that regulate their operations to determine what authority they may provide for the use and disclosure of personal health information that health information custodians disclose to them. Having conducted such a review, recipients should consider the impact of *PHIPA* on secondary uses and disclosures of personal health information that they commonly make. In the past, recipients may have relied on personal health information disclosed to them by health information custodians for the purposes of, for example, mar-

---

74   *PHIPA*, s. 72(1)(f).

75   For a more detailed discussion of offences under *PHIPA*, see Chapter 15, Section D.

76   *PHIPA*, s. 65.

77   *Ibid.*, s. 71(1). See Chapter 15, Section C(4) for a discussion of this immunity provision.

78   However, the restrictions on health numbers would continue to apply, regardless of whether the recipient received the information from the individual to whom the information relates, a health information custodian, or any other person.

keting and research. As recipients subject to the Act, they should evaluate whether such secondary uses of information can continue, and what steps they must take before they can proceed to undertake them, such as ensuring that the individual's consent is on file for any subsequent uses or disclosures of the information.

Table A: Summary of Exclusions from and Exceptions to Recipient Rules[79]

Exclusions from and Exceptions to *PHIPA*, Section 49(1)	Exclusions from and Exceptions to *PHIPA*, Section 49(2)
Basic Rule: A person who is not a health information custodian and to whom a health information custodian discloses personal health information shall not use or disclose the information.	**Basic Rule:** A person who is not a health information custodian and to whom a custodian discloses personal health information shall not use or disclose more of the information than is reasonably necessary to meet the purpose of the use or disclosure, as the case may be.
• *PHIPA*, s. 49(1): may use and disclose for purpose for which custodian disclosed the information	• *PHIPA*, s. 49(2): where use or disclosure is required by law
• *PHIPA*, s. 49(1): may use and disclose for purpose of carrying out statutory or legal duty	• *PHIPA* Regulation, s. 22(a): does not apply to professional governing bodies
• *PHIPA*, s. 49(1): may use or disclose as permitted or required by law	• *PHIPA* Regulation, s. 22(b): does not apply to a children's aid society or any person providing services on behalf of or on the request of a children's aid society
• *PHIPA* Regulation, s. 14(3): may transfer records containing personal health information to Archives of Ontario or archives that fulfill requirements of s. 14(1) of *PHIPA* Regulation	• *PHIPA* Regulation, s. 22(c): does not apply to a foster parent
• *PHIPA*, s. 49(5): does not apply to institutions within the meaning of *Freedom of Information and Protection of Privacy Act* and *Municipal Freedom of Information and Protection of Privacy Act*	
• *PHIPA* Regulation, s. 23(1): does not apply to a person employed by or acting for institution within the meaning of *Freedom of Information and Protection of Privacy Act* and *Municipal Freedom of Information and Protection of Privacy Act* when acting in scope of one of those Acts	

---

79   This table does not include special rules applicable to the use and disclosure of health numbers. See Chapter 2 for a detailed discussion of the rules applicable to persons who are not health information custodians when using and disclosing health numbers.

Exclusions from and Exceptions to *PHIPA*, Section 49(1)	Exclusions from and Exceptions to *PHIPA*, Section 49(2)
• *PHIPA* Regulation, s. 21(1)(a): may disclose to individual to whom information relates	
• *PHIPA* Regulation, s. 21(1)(a): may disclose to substitute decision-maker of individual to whom information relates	
• *PHIPA* Regulation, s. 21(1)(b): may use or disclose pursuant to a valid consent	
• *PHIPA* Regulation, s. 21(2): payment providers may disclose to pharmacists to assist pharmacists in providing health care	
• *PHIPA*, ss. 44(6)(b) and 44(6)(d); *PHIPA* Regulation, s. 17: uses and disclosures particular to researchers	
• *PHIPA* Regulation, ss. 13(4) & (5): uses and disclosures particular to prescribed health registries	
• *PHIPA*, s. 45(6); *PHIPA* Regulation, ss. 18(3), 18(4), 18(5), 18(6), & 18(7): uses and disclosures particular to prescribed planning entities	
• *PHIPA* Regulation, ss. 14(4) and 14(1)(b): disclosures particular to Archives of Ontario or archives that fulfil requirements of s. 14(1) of *PHIPA* Regulation	
• *PHIPA* Regulation, s. 21(3): shall not disclose the personal health information where the disclosure is otherwise prohibited	

13 Patient's Right of Access to Records of Personal Health Information

A. RIGHT OF ACCESS: BACKGROUND

1) Access as a Fundamental Privacy Right

An individual's ability to see the information that an organization has compiled about the individual and require its correction is a cornerstone of fair information practices. Principle 9 of the CSA Privacy Code articulates this fundamental rule: "Upon request, an individual shall be informed of the existence, use, and disclosure of his or her personal information and shall be given access to that information."[1]

The *Personal Information Protection and Electronic Documents Act*[2] incorporates Principle 9 of the CSA Privacy Code and sets out a procedure for individuals to obtain access to their personal information held by organizations subject to *PIPEDA*.[3] Industry Canada has indicated that the provision of the right of access to one's information is one of the key factors in determining

---

[1]   CSA Privacy Code 4.9, Principle 9, Individual Access. "CSA Privacy Code" is the term commonly used to refer to the Code incorporated in Schedule 1 of *PIPEDA*, below note 2, which is officially entitled "Principles Set Out in the National Standard of Canada Entitled Model Code for the Protection of Personal Information, CAN/CSA-Q830-96."

[2]   S.C. 2000, c. 5. [*PIPEDA*].

[3]   *Ibid.*, ss. 8–10 and s. 4.9 of Schedule 1.

whether provincial privacy of personal information legislation is substantially similar to *PIPEDA*, so as to justify an order dispensing with compliance with *PIPEDA* for those organizations covered by the provincial legislation.[4]

2) The Supreme Court of Canada's Position on a Patient's Right of Access

Canadian courts have clearly held that patients have a right of access to information about themselves, subject to limited exceptions. In 1992, the Supreme Court of Canada in *McInerney v. MacDonald*,[5] held unanimously that patients have such a right based on physicians' fiduciary obligations to their patients. The patient, Mrs. MacDonald, had requested the contents of her complete medical file from Dr. McInerney. Dr. McInerney gave Mrs. MacDonald copies of all reports and medical records she had prepared herself, but refused to provide copies of reports she had received from other physicians, stating that those reports were the property of the other physicians and that it would be unethical for her to release them. Mr. Justice La Forest, for the Court, held that the ownership of the tangible records lies with the person that compiles them. However, "the patient is entitled to reasonable access to examine and copy the records, provided that the patient pays a legitimate fee for the preparation and reproduction of the information."[6] The Court noted that the patient confides sensitive information to the doctor and has an interest in what happens to that information. In sharing information with the physician, the patient entrusts this information to the physician. The trust-like beneficial interest that the patient has in the information gives rise to a right of access and the physician has a corresponding obligation to provide the information. The patient's right of access applies both to information produced by the attending physician and to information contained in the patient's medical record produced by other physicians.[7]

3) Right of Access in Other Ontario Legislation

Well before the landmark decision in *McInerney v. MacDonald*, psychiatric patients in Ontario's psychiatric facilities already had a legislated right to

---

4   Notice (Department of Industry), "Personal Information Protection and Electronic Documents Act, Process for the Determination of 'Substantially Similar' Provincial Legislation by the Governor in Council," C. Gaz. (3 August 2002), online: <http://canadagazette.gc.ca/partI/2002/20020803/html/notice-e.html#i10>.

5   [1992] 2 S.C.R. 138 [*McInerney*].

6   *Ibid.* at 159.

7   *Ibid.* at 152.

access their clinical records. Amendments made in 1986 to the *Mental Health Act* provided that a "mentally competent" psychiatric patient, which included an out-patient and former patient, had a right to examine and copy his or her clinical record, at his or her own expense.[8]

The procedure set out in the *Mental Health Act* was replicated in the *Long-Term Care Act, 1994* for clients' personal health records in the custody or control of service providers, but the *Long-Term Care Act, 1994* also extended the right of access to all patients, whether or not they were "mentally competent."[9]

Since 1988, the *Freedom of Information and Protection of Privacy Act*[10] has provided a mechanism for individuals to obtain access to information about themselves held by government institutions.[11] In 1992, with the coming into force of the *Municipal Freedom of Information and Protection of Privacy Act*,[12] the procedure for obtaining access to records extended to municipal homes for the aged and, in time, ambulance services as well as to public health units.

4) Codifying the Right of Access in Most Health Care Settings

Although the Supreme Court of Canada decision in *McInerney v. MacDonald* established a patient's clear right of access to his or her own health records, without clear procedural rules in place, and a practical and inexpensive means of enforcement,[13] it was often difficult for patients to exercise their rights. The *Personal Health Information Protection Act, 2004*[14] codifies the common law right of access and sets out a uniform procedure by which patients may obtain access to records of their own personal health information virtually anywhere in the

---

8   *Mental Health Act*, R.S.O. 1990, c. M.7 [*MHA*]; see ss. 35(1) and 36(1). Repealed by ss. 90(6) and 90(12), respectively, of the *Personal Health Information Protection Act, 2004*, S.O. 2004, c. 3, Sch. A [*PHIPA*]. In s. 1(1), the *MHA* defined "mentally competent" as "having the ability to understand the subject-matter in respect of which consent is requested and able to appreciate the consequences of giving or withholding consent." Repealed by *PHIPA*, s. 90(1).

9   *Long-Term Care Act, 1994*, S.O. 1994, c. 26, s. 36 [*LTCA*]. Now repealed by *PHIPA*, s. 89(14).

10   R.S.O. 1990, c. F.31 [*FIPPA*].

11   *Ibid.*, ss. 10 and 21.

12   R.S.O. 1990, c. M.56 [*MFIPPA*].

13   Enforcing the common law right of access requires the use of the courts, which can be very expensive and time consuming, meaning that it is effectively out of the reach of most patients in ordinary circumstances.

14   S.O. 2004, c. 3, Sch. A [*PHIPA*].

health care system.[15] As a result of *PHIPA*, the access rules in the *Mental Health Act* and the *Long-Term Care Act, 1994*, referred to above, have been repealed.[16]

B. RIGHT OF ACCESS IN *PHIPA*

One of the purposes of *PHIPA* is "to provide individuals with a right of access to personal health information about themselves, subject to limited and specific exceptions set out in this Act."[17]

Part V of the Act sets out the rules governing a patient's access to his or her records of personal health information.[18] Under *PHIPA*, a patient has a right of access to a record of personal health information about the patient that is in the custody or under the control of a health information custodian unless one of the exclusions or exceptions set out in the Act apply. The right extends to the patient, whether or not the custodian has determined that the patient is incapable of consenting to the collection, use, or disclosure of the patient's personal health information.[19] Further, a substitute decision-maker may take steps to exercise this right on the patient's behalf.[20]

---

15 In fact, one of the most contentious proposals in Mr. Justice Krever's *Report of the Commission of Inquiry into the Confidentiality of Health Information* (Toronto: Queen's Printer, 1980) [*Krever Report*] was that individuals should have a right of access to information in their health records: Ontario, Legislative Assembly, Standing Committee on General Government, *Official Report of Debates (Hansard)*, G-809 (7 February 2001) at 1020 (Gilbert Sharpe). See further, *Krever Report*, vol. 2, Recommendations 82–85.

16 *PHIPA*, s. 90(12), repealing s. 36 of the *MHA*, above note 8; and *PHIPA*, s. 89(14), repealing s. 36 of the *LTCA*, above note 9.

17 *PHIPA*, s. 1(b).

18 *Ibid.*, ss. 51–54: where the patient who has a right of access to his or her personal health record also has a right to require correction or amendment of that record, which is outlined in Chapter 14. If a patient made a request for access to his or her clinical record under the *MHA* immediately before 1 November 2004, the rules under that Act continue to apply to the request, and not the new *PHIPA* rules. For new access requests after 1 November 2004, the *PHIPA* rules apply. The situation is the same for access requests made by patients for records held by service providers under the *LTCA*, above note 9, prior to 1 November 2004. See above note 16. Similarly, access requests under *FIPPA* or *MFIPPA* made before 1 November 2004, continue to be governed by those Acts until the request is answered and all associated appeal rights are exhausted (*PHIPA*, s. 8(5)).

19 For a discussion of capacity, see Chapter 6, Section F.

20 See Chapter 6, Section D(3).

1) Right of Access Applies to a Patient's "Record of Personal Health Information"

a) A Record and Its Location

A patient's right of access applies to a record of personal health information that is in the custody or under the control of a health information custodian.[21]

The right of access in *PHIPA* applies to a patient's "personal health information," which includes all identifying information about the patient, whether or not generally related to the individual's health, such as the patient's income information, that is together in the same record with health-related identifying information.[22]

PHIPA defines the term "record" to mean "a record of information in any form or in any medium, whether in written, printed, photographic or electronic form or otherwise, but [which] does not include a computer program or other mechanism that can produce a record."[23] Health information custodians, therefore, create records on a variety of media, and a patient's right of access can extend to each of them.

A record may be organized and located in one place on the custodian's premises, such as a health records department. However, a record of personal health information about a patient may be located in various places throughout a facility or institution; for example, where there is a chart about the patient on the floor where the patient is being treated, and a record of previous admissions about that patient is situated in a central filing location or in the institution's archives. Alternatively, a record may be located off-site, such as when data processing occurs at a location separate from the custodian's premises. A record of personal health information may remain in the custody or control of a health information custodian, even where the custodian's agent holds it.

b) A Record Dedicated Primarily to the Patient

Where a record is "a record that is dedicated primarily to personal health information about the [patient] requesting access,"[24] such as, for example, a patient

---

21   *PHIPA* s. 52(1). See Chapter 2, Section B(1)(e), for a detailed discussion of "custody or control" and Section C(1)(b) of that chapter for a discussion of "record."

22   Note the Act's inclusion of "mixed records" in the definition of "personal health information." Identifying information that is not health-related information nevertheless constitutes personal health information for the purposes of the Act where it is found in a record that contains health-related identifying information. Both health-related and non-health-related information is thus captured in the definition of a record of personal health information. See Chapter 2, Section C(1)(g).

23   *PHIPA*, s. 2.

24   *Ibid.*, s. 52(3).

chart, the right to request access applies to the entire record compiled about the patient, even if the record contains information about others in it, such as family history or information about caregivers, unless a specific exception or exclusion applies.

It is evident that the phrase "a record that is dedicated primarily to personal health information about the [patient] requesting access" was meant to be interpreted narrowly as referring to records such as a patient's health record, in which the patient would be justified in being able to access all information in the record, including information about third parties. Clearly, access to such information would be justified where it is found in a patient's health record or dedicated patient file, since the patient should be able to see everything in his or her "own" record. Where the record is not a record *dedicated* to the patient, even though the record may contain information about the patient, it should generally not be considered "a record that is dedicated primarily to personal health information about the [patient] requesting access."

c) A Record That Is *Not* Dedicated Primarily to the Patient

In many instances, recorded information about a patient will be contained in a record that is not dedicated primarily to a particular patient, but involves a number of patients. Examples of these "non-dedicated" records include a Ministry of Health and Long-Term Care database on insured persons, or a dentist's accounts-payable database on the dentist's patients. In such cases, a patient only has a right of access to the information in the record that pertains to the patient, where that information can "reasonably be severed from the record" for the purpose of providing access.[25]

This means a patient could request access to his or her health care practitioner's appointment book, for example, but would only be able to obtain access to the entry that pertains to him or her; the patient could not see information about the practitioner's other patients.

2) Who Can Request Access?

A patient's right of access under *PHIPA* belongs to the patient to whom the record relates.[26] The rules in *PHIPA* do not extend to permit third persons to access information about them that happens to be in the patient's record. For

---

25 *PHIPA*, s. 52(3). In some cases, the information will be so inextricably intertwined with information about other patients or clients or other matters that it would not be reasonable for the custodian to sever the record for the purpose of providing access.

26 A patient's authorized substitute decision-maker may exercise this right on the patient's behalf in the same way as a patient may do so. See above note 20.

example, Part V does not provide a nurse with a right of access to information about her that is an incident report on the patient. Further, Part V does not provide a husband with a right of access to information about him that is contained in his wife's medical record.[27]

3) The Right of Access Where the Custodian Works for a Non-Custodian *FIPPA* or *MFIPPA* Institution

Where a health information custodian is employed by or in the service of a *FIPPA* or *MFIPPA* institution (such as a psychologist who works for a school board or a nurse who works in a provincially-operated correctional facility) and a patient has a right of access to information compiled about him or her by such a health information custodian by way of an access request under *FIPPA* or *MFIPPA*, as the case may be, Part V of *PHIPA* does not apply to the patient's request for access to the record.[28] In such circumstances, the patient should be directed to make his or her request to the custodian's institution in accordance with *FIPPA* or *MFIPPA*, as the case may be.[29]

---

27 This is clarified in the regulations. Section 24(3) of the *General*, O. Reg. 329/04 [*PHIPA* Regulation] provides that "Part V does not apply to entitle a person to a right of access to information about the person that is contained in a record that is dedicated primarily to the personal health information of another person." Although Part V does not extend the right of access to third parties, such persons may continue to have a right of access under the relevant public access to information and privacy statutes, if the health information custodian is employed by or in the service of a *FIPPA* or *MFIPPA* institution, or if the health information custodian is also subject to either of those Acts as an institution, for non-personal health information: see *PHIPA*, ss. 8(4), 51(3), and 52(3).

28 *PHIPA*, s. 51(3).

29 This exception to the access provisions in *PHIPA* applies when a health information custodian is an "agent" of a *FIPPA/MFIPPA* institution that is not a custodian. The term "agent" is used in s. 51(3) with respect to the institution that is not a health information custodian, despite the fact that "agent" is defined only in relation to health information custodians. *PHIPA's* access rules, however, apply to *FIPPA/MFIPPA* custodians. The language used to describe a health information custodian acting as an agent of a *FIPPA* or *MFIPPA* institution in this provision does not include a *FIPPA/MFIPPA* custodian. For example, where a municipality operates a home for the aged, the health information custodian is actually the person who operates the home for the aged, which is the municipality itself for the home (*PHIPA*, s. 3(1)[4][ii]). In this case, the custodian is not an "agent" of the institution (the municipality) within the meaning of s. 51(3). This is due to the fact that it seems unlikely that the municipality as operator of the facility can be considered the "agent" of the municipality as a *MFIPPA* institution. The analysis for a municipally operated ambulance service would appear to be the same. This provision does not exclude from a patient's right of access a right of access to records in the custody or control of a *FIPPA/MFIPPA* custodian.

4) Triggering the Procedures: The Written Access Request

A patient exercises his or her right of access to his or her record of personal health information in *PHIPA* by way of a written request to the health information custodian.[30] A written request may be made electronically.[31]

PHIPA's formal process for requesting access to a record of personal health information does not preclude a health information custodian from communicating with his or her patient, and nothing in *PHIPA* precludes a custodian from providing the patient with information about him- or herself in the absence of a written access request. In fact, the Act specifies that where a patient has a right of access, a health information custodian can grant the patient access to a record, with or without an oral request from the patient, and can communicate with the patient or his or her substitute decision-maker.[32] Typically, if a health information custodian's practice includes open communication with patients, and the custodian makes health records readily available to them when requested, patients are not likely to resort to the more formal access process that is set out in Part V.

Though a health information custodian may provide a patient with access to his or her record of personal health information in response to an oral request[33] or in the absence of a request, only a written request invokes the rights and requirements set out in *PHIPA*.

Each custodian must have a contact person for accepting and responding to such requests, although the patient is not explicitly required by *PHIPA* to submit the request to the contact person. A custodian should have a process in place to deal promptly with requests for access that patients make to persons within the custodian's organization other than the contact person.[34]

---

30 *PHIPA*, s. 53(1).
31 Section 6(1) of the *Electronic Commerce Act, 2000*, S.O. 2000, c. 17, provides:

> A legal requirement that a person provide information or a document in writing to another person is satisfied by the provision of the information or document in an electronic form that is,
>
> (a) accessible by the other person so as to be usable for subsequent reference; and
> (b) capable of being retained by the other person.
>
> Subsection 1(1) defines "electronic" to include created, recorded, transmitted, or stored in digital form or in other intangible form by electronic, magnetic, or optical means or by any other means that has capabilities for creation, recording, transmission, or storage similar to those means.

32 *PHIPA*, ss. 52(6)(a) & (b).
33 *Ibid.*, s. 52(6).
34 *Ibid.*, s. 15(3)(d). See Chapter 4, Section B for a further discussion of the "contact person." The Act does not require the written access request to be submitted to the con-

a)   No "Form" for Request

Other than requiring it to be in writing, *PHIPA* does not specify the format for the access request. The patient, for example, may provide a letter or a direction to the custodian. The custodian may wish to create a simple application form to be used by the custodian's patients that would be helpful to the custodian in finding the requested information. In order to be able to answer the request effectively, a health information custodian should obtain as much detail about the record that is the subject of the patient's request as is practical. The written access request must contain enough information to enable the custodian to identify and locate the record "with reasonable efforts."[35] If the request does not contain sufficient detail, the health information custodian must offer assistance to the person requesting access to reformulate the request.[36]

C.   EXCLUSIONS: INFORMATION TO WHICH PART V DOES NOT APPLY

The provisions in *PHIPA* that provide a patient with a right of access to his or her record of personal health information do not apply to records that contain any of four categories of information, as set out in the Act,[37] and as described below.

This might mean, strictly speaking, that if a record subject to a patient's request for access contains information of the excluded type, the custodian is not obliged to tell the patient that the custodian refuses to grant access, as the procedure for access, including the custodian's notification of the patient, does not apply to such information. On the other hand, even if *PHIPA* does not apply to a particular record, the custodian may still be required under section 54(1)(c) to respond that the custodian is refusing the request, as the custodian is entitled to do.[38] Whatever interpretation is ultimately accepted, it appears that a prudent custodian should still respond to the requestor indicating that the custodian is refusing the request. This would avoid an assumption by the

---

tact person, however, access requests to the custodian may come through various agents of the custodian.

35   *PHIPA*, s. 53(2): for a discussion of "reasonable," see Chapter 4, Section C.
36   *Ibid.*, s. 53(3).
37   *Ibid.*, s. 51(1).
38   *Ibid.*, s. 54(1) arguably appears to apply to every "request" for access to personal health information under Part V. Section 51(1) on its face excludes "records" but not "requests."

patient that the custodian ignored the request and provides the custodian with assurance that the custodian complied with *PHIPA*. Of course, a custodian may be able to sever information to which the patient does not have a right of access from other personal health information to which the patient does have a right of access in accordance with the procedures set out in Part V and, if so, the patient continues to have a right of access to the severed information.[39]

Especially given the fact that the Commissioner may still be asked to review complaints that the custodian is contravening the Act by not granting access to information over which there is a disagreement about whether it falls within the terms of these exclusions, or whether a severance was or could have been appropriately made, it would likely be prudent for a custodian to respond to such a request in the normal manner. This approach would generally be preferable from a "client service" point of view as well.

The Act excludes from a patient's right of access those records that contain the following four types of information.

1) Quality of Care Information

"Quality of care information" is defined in the *Quality of Care Information Protection Act, 2004*[40] as information prepared by or for a quality of care committee designated under that Act, or that relates solely or primarily to the quality of care functions of such a committee.[41] Certain kinds of information are excluded from the scope of quality of care information, such as information in patient health records, and facts recorded in incident reports.[42] What "quality of care information" encompasses is discussed in detail in Chapter 17.

QCIPA prohibits the disclosure of "quality of care information" except as permitted by that Act.[43] This prohibition exists despite *PHIPA*.[44] Consistent with this special protection for quality of care information in *QCIPA*, a patient's right of access to a record of personal health information does not apply to quality of care information.[45] A health information custodian has no discretion to provide quality of care information to a patient.

A patient to whom a custodian refuses access to a record because it contains quality of care information may make a complaint to the Information and

---

39 *PHIPA*, s. 51(2).
40 S.O. 2004, c. 3, Sch. B [*QCIPA*].
41 *Ibid.*, s. 1, definition of "quality of care information."
42 *Ibid.*
43 *Ibid.*, s. 4. See Chapter 17.
44 *Ibid.*
45 *PHIPA*, s. 51(1)(a).

Privacy Commissioner. However, there is no exception set out in *QCIPA* that would permit a disclosure of quality of care information to the Commissioner for the purpose of investigating a complaint. The blanket prohibition in *QCIPA* on any admission of quality of care information as evidence in proceedings also applies to proceedings of the Information and Privacy Commissioner.[46] Therefore, it can be argued that, where a custodian takes the position that information in its possession is quality of care information, the custodian would be prohibited from disclosing it to the Information and Privacy Commissioner, and the Commissioner would not have the ability to view the information for any purpose, even to determine whether or not it is actually "quality of care information."[47]

2) Information That Is Part of a Quality Assurance Program

For underlying reasons similar to the exclusion of quality of care information, a patient's right of access to a record of personal health information does not apply to personal health information collected or created by a health information custodian for the purpose of complying with the requirements of a quality assurance program within the meaning of the Health Professions Procedural Code.[48]

The *RHPA* Code defines "quality assurance program" as "a program to assure the quality of the practice of the profession and to promote continuing competence among the members."[49] Each *RHPA* College is required to establish its own quality assurance program through regulations.[50] The program has various components, some of which may require a regulated health professional to self-evaluate his or her practice or skills.[51] Information generated by a health information custodian in compliance with such a program is protected

---

46   The definition of proceeding in *QCIPA*, s. 1 includes a proceeding before a "commission."

47   The courts may at some point be faced with the issue of how to allow challenges to whether information is in fact "quality of care information," given the difficulty that quality of care information under *QCIPA* is totally shielded from being disclosed or admitted in any proceeding within the jurisdiction of the Ontario Legislature.

48   [*RHPA* Code], Sch. 2 to the *Regulated Health Professions Act, 1991*, S.O. 1991, c. 18 [*RHPA*]. See also *PHIPA*, s. 51(1)(b).

49   *RHPA* Code, *ibid.*, s. 1(1).

50   *Ibid.*, s. 80.

51   For example, see ss. 16–23 of *General*, O. Reg. 218/94, made under the *Dental Hygiene Act, 1991*, S.O. 1991, c. 22 and further about the requirements of the College of Dental Hygienists of Ontario's quality assurance program, online: <www.cdho.org/quality_qar.htm>. Also, note the Royal College of Dental Surgeons of Ontario website with respect to its quality assurance program, online: <www.rcdso.org/quality_4html>.

from most disclosures outside of the quality assurance program and cannot be disclosed in most proceedings.[52]

The *RHPA* Code prohibits the disclosure of "quality assurance information," which includes information prepared by a member of a regulated health profession in compliance with the requirements of the quality assurance program, except as may be permitted by the *Regulated Health Professions Act, 1991*,[53] the *RHPA* Code, a health profession Act, or regulations or bylaws made under the *Regulated Health Professions Act, 1991* or a health profession Act.[54] This prohibition applies despite *PHIPA*. A health information custodian has no discretion to provide quality assurance information to a patient. Consistent with this prohibition on the disclosure of quality assurance information in the *RHPA* Code, a patient's right of access to a record of personal health information does not apply to information that is contained in material that a health information custodian has prepared for the purpose of complying with the requirements of the quality assurance program. The prohibition also applies to the Commissioner who is not permitted access to such "quality assurance information."[55]

A patient to whom a custodian refuses access to a record because it contains quality assurance information may make a complaint to the Information and Privacy Commissioner. However, there is no exception set out in the *RHPA* Code that would permit a disclosure of quality assurance information to the Commissioner for the purpose of investigating a complaint. The prohibition in the *RHPA* Code on admission of quality assurance information as evidence in most proceedings also applies to proceedings of the Information and Privacy Commissioner.[56] Therefore, just as in the previous category, it can be argued that where a custodian takes the position that information in its possession is quality assurance information, the custodian would be prohibited from disclosing it to the Commissioner, and the Commissioner would not have the ability to view the information, even to determine whether or not it is actually "quality assurance information."

---

52 "Proceeding" in the *RHPA* Code is defined differently from a proceeding in *PHIPA*: see Chapter 17 on *QCIPA*.

53 See above note 48.

54 *Ibid.*, s. 83.1(4). The *RHPA* Code was amended by *QCIPA*, above note 40, s. 11.

55 *QCIPA*, *ibid.*, s. 11(2), amending Sch. 2 to the *RHPA*, above note 48. A new s. 83.1(4) provides that "Despite the *PHIPA, 2004*, no person shall disclose quality assurance information except as permitted by the *Regulated Health Professions Act, 1991* including, this Code or an Act named in Schedule 1 to that Act or regulations or bylaws made under the *Regulated Health Professions Act, 1991* or under an Act named in Schedule 1 to that Act."

56 The definition of proceeding in the Code, s. 83.1 is broad and includes a proceeding before a "commission."

3) Raw Data from Standardized Psychological Tests or Assessments

Testing materials and assessment tools that are used by psychologists in assessing patients are not subject to *PHIPA*, as such materials and tools are not "personal health information."[57] However, questions and other testing materials linked to a patient's responses to an examining psychologist are personal health information. Of course, even separated from the testing material, the raw unscaled scores and the patient's responses to test questions or stimuli are also "personal health information."

A patient's right of access under Part V of the Act does not apply to a record that contains "raw data from standardized psychological tests or assessments."[58] Therefore a custodian may, but is not required to, refuse to provide a patient access to this type of information. During the hearings before the Standing Committee on General Government on Bill 31,[59] the Hospital Psychology Association of Ontario succinctly explained the need to exclude such information from a patient's right of access:

> If the answers were known for all the questions on an IQ test and could simply be memorized, it would certainly impact the ability to use those tests in the future. Those tests take years to develop and are tested on tens of thousands of people before they're employed. If they go into the public domain, it seriously damages their validity.[60]

Therefore, to preserve the test's usefulness, the Act excludes such personal health information from a patient's right of access. Further, a patient's access to the questions and answers the patient provided may skew results of future assessments of the patient. The Act does not exclude from a patient's right of access the patient's aggregate scores on such tests. And, the patient does have a right of access to a summary report prepared by the psychologist.[61]

---

57   See the discussion of "personal health information" in Chapter 2, Section C.

58   *PHIPA*, s. 51(1)(c).

59   *An Act to enact and amend various Acts with respect to the protection of health information*, 1st Sess., 38th Leg., Ontario, 2003 [Bill 31].

60   Ontario, Legislative Assembly, Standing Committee on General Government, *Official Report of Debates (Hansard)*, G-171 (5 February 2004) at 1030 (Dr. Ian Nicholson).

61   This right of access is itself subject to certain exceptions as set out further in Section D below.

4) Personal Health Information of the Prescribed Type in the Custody or under the Control of a Prescribed Class or Classes of Health Information Custodian

The fourth category of personal health information that *PHIPA* excludes from a patient's right of access to records of personal health information is that which is set out in regulations.[62] The *PHIPA* Regulation excludes the following types of records.

a) Research

The regulation under *PHIPA* provides that Part V does not apply to personal health information that a health information custodian researcher uses solely for the purposes of research, where the research is conducted in accordance with a research plan approved under *PHIPA*.[63] The research rules in *PHIPA* apply where, without the consent of the patients to whom the information relates, a health information custodian uses personal health information for research purposes or discloses personal health information to a researcher for the purpose of carrying out research.[64] This exclusion from a patient's right of access reflects the fact that patients retain a right of access to such information in the hands of the health information custodian who disclosed it to the researcher. Where the health information custodian uses personal health information solely for research purposes, such that the research records are kept separate from the patient's health record and are not used, for example, for health care purposes, the patient does not have a right of access to the research records, though nevertheless retaining a right of access to the health record. The researcher is not the most appropriate source of information for the access request.[65] The researcher custodian generally has discretion to provide this information to the patient despite this provision, however.

---

62 *PHIPA*, s. 51(1)(d). See *PHIPA* Regulation, above note 27, s. 24.

63 *Ibid.*, s. 24(1). This clause applies to research that is conducted in accordance with a research plan approved under *PHIPA* s. 44(4) (research ethics board in Ontario) or s. 44(10)(b) (research that has received prescribed approval from a body outside Ontario that has the function of approving research; no such regulation exists at the time of writing).

64 *PHIPA* provides that a health information custodian may use or disclose personal health information for research purposes, without the consent of the patient to whom the information relates, provided that the rules as set out in *PHIPA* are followed. For example, there should be in place a research plan that has been approved by a research ethics board and, in the case of a disclosure, an agreement should exist between the custodian and the researcher. See Chapter 11, Section B.

65 Where a health information custodian collects personal health information directly from a patient for research, the patient would consent to the collection, and the use of

b) Laboratories

In certain circumstances, the regulation further excludes a patient's right of access to personal health information that is in the custody or control of a laboratory[66] in respect of a test requested by a health care practitioner for the purpose of providing health care to the patient. This exclusion arises where the patient already has a right of access to the information through the health care practitioner, or will have such a right when the laboratory provides the information to the practitioner and the health care practitioner has not directed the laboratory to provide the information directly to the patient.[67] This exclusion from the right of access preserves the practice pertaining to laboratory results that existed prior to 1 November 2004. Patients are accustomed to accessing laboratory test results through the health care practitioner who requested the test, and not directly from the laboratory.[68] This provision of *PHIPA* does not prohibit a laboratory from providing the patient with direct access to this information, however, even without a direction to do so from a health care practitioner, if it decides in its discretion to do so.[69]

---

the information would not be conducted in accordance with a research plan approved under *PHIPA*. Therefore, this exclusion from a patient's right of access would not apply. In addition, a health information custodian who, without the consent of the patients to whom the information relates, uses personal health information for the purpose of research in accordance with the Act's research rules, generally could not rely on this exclusion from a patient's right of access where the custodian also uses that information for the purpose for which it was collected, such as the provision of health care, and not "solely for the purposes of research."

66   A "laboratory" means (a) a laboratory or a specimen collection centre as defined in s. 5 of the *Laboratory and Specimen Collection Centre Licensing Act*, R.S.O. 1990, c. L.1; or (b) a laboratory operated by a ministry of the Crown in right of Ontario. See *PHIPA* Regulation, above note 27, s. 24(2).

67   *PHIPA* Regulation, *ibid.*, s. 24(1)[2].

68   Although, it should be noted that *Professional Misconduct*, O. Reg. 752/93, made under the *Medical Laboratory Technology Act, 1991*, S.O. 1991, c. 28, s. 1(25) states that it is professional misconduct for a medical laboratory technologist to fail "to provide, when requested, within a reasonable length of time, to a patient or the patient's authorized representative a copy of a patient's laboratory record, unless the member believes on reasonable grounds, that providing the copy may result in harm to the patient or to another person."

69   Under *Laboratories*, R.R.O. 1990, Reg. 682, s. 9 (1)(b), made under the *Laboratory and Specimen Collection Centre Licensing Act*, above note 66, the laboratory is required to "report the results of a test directly to the person who requested it," which would not include the patient, but this does not appear to prohibit the provision of the information to the patient.

D. EXEMPTIONS TO THE RIGHT OF ACCESS

The exclusions discussed above are situations where the patient would not have a right of access at all to recorded information of the described type. In these cases, Part V of *PHIPA* simply does not apply.

Even where Part V applies, there are situations in which a health information custodian can refuse the patient access to a record of personal health information. These exceptions to the right of access in *PHIPA* build on the common law as set out in *McInerney v. MacDonald*.[70] In that case, La Forest J. noted that a patient's right of access is not absolute. La Forest J. stated that the fiduciary relationship imposes an obligation on the part of the physician to act in the best interests of the patient. If a physician reasonably believes it is not in the best interests of the patient to inspect the medical records, the physician may consider it necessary to deny the patient access to the information.[71] Further, the exceptions in *PHIPA* build on certain exceptions to the right of access found in *FIPPA*, *MFIPPA*, and *PIPEDA*.[72]

1) Legal Privilege

First of all, the patient does not have a right of access to a record that is subject to a legal privilege[73] that restricts its disclosure.[74] Personal health information that is subject to solicitor/client privilege, for example, may be withheld from the patient, even if the information is about the patient. The term "legal privilege" is expansive, covering a number of legally recognized privileges, such as solicitor/client privilege, litigation privilege, and settlement privilege. This exception would apply, for example, to letters the health information custodian has received from its lawyer setting out legal advice with respect to aspects of the custodian's relationship with a particular patient. In the case of solicitor/client privilege, the custodian who receives the legal advice may, however, waive the privilege. Where the custodian waives the privilege for a document, the custodian may then provide the record to the patient requesting access to the record. Where the custodian is a party or a witness in a litigation or other proceeding, and receives an access request from a patient for informa-

---

70   *McInerney*, above note 5.

71   *Ibid.* at 154.

72   *FIPPA*, above note 10, s. 49; *MFIPPA*, above note 12, s. 38; *PIPEDA*, above note 2, s. 9.

73   See the discussion about privilege in Chapter 3, Section B(3)(c), and, in particular, note 85 in that chapter.

74   Secion 52(1)(a).

tion that pertains to such litigation or proceeding, it is prudent to seek legal advice before responding to the request.

2) Court Order or Another Act

Next, *PHIPA* excepts from a patient's right of access information that another Act of Ontario or Canada or a court order prohibits disclosing to the patient.[75] For example, where a court orders under the *Mental Health Act* or the *Child and Family Services Act* that the record not be disclosed to the patient, the patient cannot gain access to this record under *PHIPA*.[76] The custodian has no discretion to provide such information to the requesting patient where it is contrary to law or a court order.

3) Proceedings

If the information in the record was collected or created primarily in anticipation of or for use in a proceeding,[77] and the proceeding has not been completed, the patient does not have access to this information until such time as all appeals or processes pertaining to the proceeding have been concluded.[78]

This exception appears to some extent to be a codification of litigation privilege and would apply, for example, to witness statements forwarded to the custodian for review by its lawyer for the purpose of preparing for a defence in a lawsuit.[79] Though it is not stated in *PHIPA*, there may be a fair argument that the custodian, or the other person or persons who are entitled to the privilege, may waive the privilege, and in doing so the custodian may be permitted to provide access to the record to the patient.

Even where a proceeding and any associated appeals and process have been "concluded," and this exception to the patient's right of access no longer applies, the custodian may deny the patient access to the record on the basis of another

---

75 Section 52(1)(b).

76 *MHA*, above note 8, s. 35(7); *Child and Family Services Act*, R.S.O. 1990, c. C.11, s. 183 [*CFSA*].

77 Note the broad definition of "proceeding" in s. 2. The word includes a proceeding "held in, before or under the rules of a court, a tribunal, a commission, a justice of the peace, a coroner, committee of a College of a regulated health profession, a committee of the Board of Regents under the *Drugless Practitioners Act*, a committee of the Ontario College of Social Workers and Social Service Workers, an arbitrator or a mediator."

78 *PHIPA*, s. 52(1)(c).

79 This category, in some respects, overlaps with that described in ss. 52(1)(a), (b), and (d).

ground in the Act, if applicable; such as, where the record is subject to a legal privilege that restricts disclosure, or a court order precludes the disclosure.[80]

4) Inspection, Investigation, or Similar Procedure

The patient does not have a right of access to information that was

- collected or created in the course of an inspection, investigation, or similar procedure authorized by law, such as an assessment performed by an assessor under the *Independent Health Facilities Act*;[81] or
- undertaken for the purpose of the detection, monitoring, or prevention of a person's receiving or attempting to receive a service or benefit, to which the person is not entitled under a program operated by the Minister of Health and Long-Term Care, or a payment for such a service or benefit.[82]

This exception, similar to the exception concerning information created for use in a proceeding, only applies until such time as all proceedings, appeals, or processes resulting from this activity have been concluded.[83]

This category of exceptions would apply to information that the custodian creates or compiles in response to an inspection, investigation, or similar procedure. This category is particularly relevant to the Ministry of Health and Long-Term Care as a custodian of personal health information that has been collected in the course of monitoring fraudulent activities or in the course of investigations, inspections, and assessments conducted to ensure compliance with Ministry of Health and Long-Term Care legislation. Once again, as with the previous exception, it is arguable that this exception to the right of access is in essence a privilege that may be waived.

5) Exemptions for *FIPPA/MFIPPA* Custodians

Specific exemptions to a patient's access rights apply to *FIPPA/MFIPPA* custodians, such as the Ministry of Health and Long-Term Care, a medical officer of health, and an ambulance service or a home for the aged operated by a municipality. In these situations, these types of custodians can also rely on certain provisions found in *FIPPA* and *MFIPPA*, as the case may be, to deny a

---

80   Of course, this applies to all the exceptions from the right of access. They each provide a separate and independent ground for refusing access.

81   R.S.O. 1990, c. I.13.

82   *PHIPA*, s. 52(1)(d)(i).

83   *Ibid.*, s. 52(1)(d)(ii).

patient access to his or her record.[84] It should be noted that, to the extent the relevant provision in *FIPPA* or *MFIPPA* imposes a mandatory exemption from the access right, the custodian will be obligated to refuse access, but where the *FIPPA* or *MFIPPA* provisions provide for a discretionary ground for refusing access, the custodian has discretion under this provision of *PHIPA* whether the custodian will provide access or not.[85] This category of exemption is not relevant to the vast number of custodians who are not themselves institutions or a part of institutions under *FIPPA* or *MFIPPA*.

6) Risk of Serious Harm

PHIPA provides that a patient does not have a right of access to a record of personal health information where such access can reasonably be expected to result in a risk of serious harm to the treatment or recovery of the individual or a risk of serious bodily harm to the individual or another person.[86]

---

84   Under *PHIPA*, s. 52(1)(f) a custodian subject to *FIPPA*, above note 10, can refuse to give access under the grounds set out in *FIPPA*, s. 49(a), (c), or (e). Those provisions provide essentially as described below. For further detail, see Chapter 3, Table A.

- *FIPPA*, s. 49(a) provides that a head of an institution can refuse to disclose to the individual to whom the information relates personal information where access is required to be refused under that Act; for example, because the record is a Cabinet record, advice to the Minister, or would reveal a trade secret, or scientific, technical, commercial, or labour relations information supplied in confidence to the institution by a third party. A "head" of an institution is a defined term in *FIPPA*, s. 2(1) and means, for example, in the case of a provincial ministry, the Minister of the ministry.
- *FIPPA*, s. 49(c) provides that a head of an institution may refuse access to a record that is evaluative or opinion material compiled solely for the purpose of determining suitability, eligibility, or qualifications for employment, or for the awarding of government contracts and other benefits where the disclosure would reveal the identity of a source who furnished information to the institution in circumstances where it may reasonably have been assumed that the identity of the source would be held in confidence.
- *FIPPA*, s. 49(e) provides that a head of an institution may refuse access to a record that is a correctional record where the disclosure could reasonably be expected to reveal information supplied in confidence.

Similar types of exemptions exist in *MFIPPA*, s. 38(a) and (c). These exemptions apply to a custodian subject to *MFIPPA*, above note 12: *PHIPA*, s. 52(1)(f).

85   This is evident from the use of the word "would" rather than "could" in s. 52(1)(f)(ii). Only if the custodian "would" refuse access under *FIPPA*, *ibid.* or *MFIPPA*, *ibid.*, either because the exemption was mandatory or because the custodian would choose to rely on a discretionary exemption, is the custodian obligated to refuse access under this provision in *PHIPA*.

86   *PHIPA*, s. 52(e)(i).

This exception to the right of access reflects the view articulated by the Supreme Court of Canada in *McInerney v. MacDonald,* where La Forest J. concluded that "non-disclosure may be warranted if there is a real potential for harm either to the patient or third party."[87] This exemption also builds on exemptions that existed in the *Mental Health Act* and in the *Long-Term Care Act, 1994.*[88]

Section 52(e)(i) of *PHIPA* differs from the *PIPEDA* exemption that allows a denial of access to a record about the individual if providing such access would likely reveal personal information about a third party.[89] The *PIPEDA* exemption does not apply if the individual needs the information because an individual's life, health, or security is threatened.[90] The *PIPEDA* exemption does not recognize that providing access to the individual could also, at times, pose a danger to the treatment or recovery of the individual or even cause harm to that individual.

The risk of serious harm described in *PHIPA* does not need to be imminent. As with the provisions allowing a health information custodian to disclose personal health information to avoid a significant risk of serious bodily harm, the focus of this language is not on the question of how soon the harm would be expected to arise, but rather on the likelihood and seriousness of the harm.[91] If the custodian provides a patient with access to the patient's record, would such access reasonably be expected to lead to the types of harm described in this provision? If so, access must be denied. Of course, the less imminent the expected harm, the more difficult it will be for the custodian to establish that there is a reasonable expectation that the harm will be caused by granting access, but once again the primary point is not the imminence in

---

87 *McInerney,* above note 5 at 157.

88 Under the provisions of the *MHA,* access to the clinical record could be denied if the disclosure of the clinical record would likely result in (a) serious harm to the treatment or recovery of the patient while in treatment at the psychiatric facility; or (b) serious physical harm or serious emotional harm to another person [*MHA,* above note 8, s. 36(6), now repealed by *PHIPA,* s. 90(12)]). Similarly, the *LTCA* provided that access could be denied if giving the individual access to a specific part or any part of the personal record would likely result in "serious physical or serious emotional harm to the person or another person" [*LTCA,* above note 9, s. 36(6), now repealed by *PHIPA,* s. 89(14)]. Unlike *PHIPA,* where a health information custodian may rely on a broader range of exclusions or exemptions, the exemptions in these two statutes were the only exemptions allowed to the right of access.

89 *PIPEDA,* above note 2, s. 9(1).

90 *Ibid.,* s. 9(2).

91 For a detailed discussion of *PHIPA,* s. 40(1), which authorizes a health information custodian to disclose personal health information where the custodian "believes on reasonable grounds that the disclosure is necessary for the purpose of eliminating or reducing a significant risk of serious bodily harm to a person or group of persons," see Chapter 10, Section K.

itself but the likelihood of the harm. The harm that may arise is not limited to physical harm, but can pertain to psychological harm as well.[92]

It is for the custodian to make the judgment whether in the circumstances it appears that granting access would reasonably be expected to result in the risk of harm referred to in section 52(e)(i) of *PHIPA*. Before deciding to refuse a patient access to a record of personal health information pursuant to this provision, a health information custodian may consult with a physician or a psychologist, even if they are not associated with the custodian.[93] In addition, a health information custodian can, in the course of answering an access request, involve its own agents as necessary for that purpose.[94] But once the custodian decides that there is indeed such a reasonable expectation of harm, then the custodian has no discretion to provide access.

7) Protecting the Privacy of Others

a) Where Person Was Required by Law to Disclose to Custodian

Two exceptions to the right of access serve to protect the privacy of third parties.[95] A patient does not have a right of access to information in his or her record of personal health information that "could reasonably be expected to lead to the identification of a person who was required by law to provide information in the record to the custodian."[96] For example, where a medical officer of health receives a report from a physician about a patient with a reportable disease, as the physician is required to provide under the *Health Protection and Promotion Act*, that patient does not have a right to access the information in the hands of the medical officer of health that would lead to the identification

---

92   *R. v. McCraw*, [1991] 3 S.C.R. 72 at 81. The Court defined "serious bodily harm" for the purposes of s. 264.1(1)(a) of the *Criminal Code*, R.S. 1985, c. C-46, which makes it an offence to threaten to "cause death or serious bodily harm" as "any hurt or injury, whether physical or psychological, that interferes in a substantial way with the physical or psychological integrity, health or well-being of the complainant."

93   *PHIPA*, s. 52(5). The word "consult" implies a two-way communication. And so, for this purpose, the requesting health information custodian and the psychologist or physician could reveal personal health information about the patient to each other for the purpose of the consultation.

94   This involves a use of personal health information within the custodian's organization, rather than a disclosure to an outsider, and in many circumstances would be authorized under *PHIPA*, s. 37(2). The custodian is obviously permitted to consider the requester's information to decide whether access should be granted, so the custodian can provide the information to its own agent for that same purpose.

95   It should be remembered that the definition of "personal health information" does include identifying information about third parties such as family members (s. 4(1)(a)).

96   *PHIPA*, s. 52(1)(e)(ii).

of that physician.[97] As a result of the inclusion of the words "reasonably be expected," this exception to the right of access is not limited to the name of the person who made the report. The exception encompasses all information that, if revealed to the patient, would reasonably be expected to reveal the identity of the person who was required to report the information. Where the custodian determines that this exception from the access right applies, the custodian is not permitted to provide the patient with access.

b)   Where Person Provided Information in Confidence to Custodian

A patient does not have a right of access to information that "could reasonably be expected to lead to the identification of a person who provided information in the record to the custodian explicitly or implicitly in confidence if the custodian considers it appropriate in the circumstances that the name of the person be kept confidential."[98] A physician, for example, could rely on this exception to withhold the name of a family member who provided information about the patient. However, in some instances, deleting the name alone may not be enough to protect the identity of the individual. As in the case of information about a person who was required by law to provide information, this exception to the right of access extends to information that could "reasonably be expected" to lead to the identification of the person. However, the custodian must exercise its discretion to determine whether withholding this information is "appropriate in the circumstances." If the custodian decides that withholding the information is not appropriate, it may provide access.

In cases where the disclosure of third party information is in issue, the health information custodian should also consider whether another exception, such as the risk of harm exception, applies to the information that is the subject of the request for access.[99]

8)   Mandatory Refusal of Access

As indicated in the context of the discussion above about each of the exceptions to the right of access, a health information custodian has discretion when

---

97   Such as the duty to report set out in the *Health Protection and Promotion Act*, R.S.O. 1990, c. H.7, s. 25 [*HPPA*], where a physician, chiropractor, dentist, nurse, optometrist, and naturopath all have a duty to report that a patient has or may have a "reportable disease" to the medical officer of health. "Reportable" diseases are set out in s. 1 of *Specification of Reportable Diseases*, O. Reg. 559/91, made under the *HPPA* and include, for example, Acquired Immunodeficiency Syndrome (AIDS), diphtheria, food poisoning, hepatitis, and syphilis.

98   *PHIPA*, s. 52(1)(e)(iii).

99   *Ibid.*, s. 52(1)(e)(i).

deciding whether some of the exceptions apply in the circumstances. For example, when deciding whether information provided in confidence should be withheld from the patient, the custodian has discretion to determine whether withholding the information is "appropriate." With other exceptions, for example the exception to the right of access where access is prohibited by another Act or a court order, the custodian has no discretion to provide access to the record.

When a custodian has discretion, it should keep in mind that, as pointed out by La Forest J. in *McInerney v. MacDonald*, the discretion to withhold information should not be exercised without careful consideration.[100]

Where one of the exceptions to access applies, whether it applies automatically because the custodian has no discretion, or whether the custodian exercises its discretion and determines that one of the discretionary exceptions applies, then the custodian is required to deny access.[101]

9) Severing the Record

Even where one of the exemptions applies to part of a record, the custodian must provide access to any part of the record that can reasonably be severed from the part containing the information to which an exemption applies.[102] A record can be severed, for example, by photocopying the original, blotting out the information subject to the exception, such as with a white-out or ink, and providing the patient with the blotted-out photocopies.

10) Frivolous and Vexatious, or Made in Bad Faith

In addition to these specific exceptions upon which the health information custodian can rely on to refuse access, a health information custodian may refuse to grant a patient access if the custodian believes on reasonable grounds that a request is frivolous or vexatious or is made in bad faith.[103] The custodian need not believe the request is all three of these things to rely on this provision.

To understand when a request may be "frivolous or vexatious," a custodian may consider the interpretation of this language in the context of *FIPPA* and *MFIPPA*. While *FIPPA* and *MFIPPA* contain provisions allowing institu-

---

100   *McInerney*, above note 5 at 154.
101   This is clear from the language in ss. 54(1)(c) & (d). See the discussion in Section E(3)(e)(iii) below about communicating such refusals.
102   *PHIPA*, s. 52(2).
103   *Ibid.*, s. 53(6).

tions governed by those Acts to refuse an access request on the basis that it is "frivolous or vexatious,"[104] the regulations under those Acts essentially define a "frivolous or vexatious" request to mean *either* that the request is part of a "pattern of conduct that amounts to an abuse of the right of access or would interfere with the operations of the institution" or the request is "made in bad faith or for a purpose other than to obtain access."[105]

As no similar definition of "frivolous or vexatious" exists in *PHIPA* or its regulations, a health information custodian is not required to interpret the phrase "frivolous or vexatious" in *PHIPA*. Nevertheless, the approach taken in *FIPPA* and *MFIPPA*, in addition to the Information and Privacy Commissioner's interpretation of this phrase, may provide health information custodians with guidance in denying a patient access to personal health information on the basis of this provision.[106] As such, a custodian, in responding to access requests, may consider whether a patient's request amounts to an abuse of the right of access, interferes with the custodian's operations, or is made for a purpose other than to obtain access. Further, a custodian may consider the number of requests for access that the patient has made and whether the patient makes requests in an attempt to revisit an issue that the custodian has addressed in the past.

---

104 *FIPPA*, above note 10, s. 27.1; *MFIPPA*, above note 12, s. 20.1.
105 Section 5.1 of *General*, Reg. 460, made under *FIPPA*, *ibid.*; s. 5.1 of *General*, Reg. 823, made under *MFIPPA*, *ibid.* These provisions were added in 1996. Prior to 1996, the Commissioner exercised an implied discretion to control abuse of process and occasionally exercised power to restrict a requester's right to make unlimited access requests where, for example, the volume of requests was high in a short amount of time and there was evidence that the requests were being pursued for the purpose of posing a nuisance to institutions: Order M-618, London Police Services Board (18 October 1995), upheld in *Riley v. Ontario (Information and Privacy Commissioner)* (1999), Toronto Doc. 59/96 (Ont. Div. Ct.), online: <www.ipc.on.ca>.
106 Several orders provide guidance as to the Commissioner's approach. Order MO-1488, City of Vaughan (20 November 2001) reviews a number of Commissioner decisions interpreting the power to refuse frivolous or vexatious access requests. Factors include whether the number of requests are excessive by reasonable standards; whether the requests are overly broad and varied in scope or unusually detailed or repetitive; whether the requests are being used for a nuisance value or with the intent to harass. Order M-850, Town of Midland (24 October 1996) indicated that the power to refuse requests on this ground should not be exercised lightly; online: <www.ipc.on.ca>. For a discussion of the application of the provision of *PHIPA*, s. 57(4)(e), which allows the Commissioner to refuse to review a complaint on the ground that it is frivolous or vexatious or made in bad faith, see Chapter 15, Section B(3).

11) Plan of Service under the *Long-Term Care Act, 1994*

Despite any of these exemptions, a health information custodian must always grant the patient access to his or her plan of service.[107] A plan of service means a plan of service developed or revised by an "approved agency" under section 22 of the *Long-Term Care Act, 1994*.[108] Approved agencies include community care access corporations and other community service providers approved by the Minister of Health and Long-Term Care.[109] Each approved agency is required to develop a plan of service for each person whom it determines to be eligible to receive services.[110] The plan of service sets out what community services the patient will receive, when the patient will receive them, and who will provide them. The approved agency reviews and updates a patient's plan of service, for example, when the patient's needs for community services change.

E. PROCESSING THE ACCESS REQUEST

1) Satisfying Yourself as to the Patient's Identity

Before making a record of personal health information available to a patient or his or her substitute decision-maker, a health information custodian must first take "reasonable steps" to be satisfied as to the individual's identity.[111] In many instances, such as where a health information custodian has been treating a patient for a number of years and the patient makes an access request in person, the custodian will not need to take steps out of the ordinary. In other cases, "reasonable steps" could include asking for photo identification, or a copy of the power of attorney document, where a substitute decision-maker,

---

107 *PHIPA*, s. 52(4). This provision apparently comes from the now-repealed s. 36(14) of the *LTCA*, above note 9, which provided that an approved agency shall not apply to the Review Board for authority to authorize an approved agency's refusal to give a person access to his or her plan of service. Section 22(1) of the *LTCA* provides that when a person applies to an approved agency for any of the community services that the agency provides or arranges, the agency shall (a) assess the person's requirements; (b) determine the person's eligibility for the services that the person requires; and (c) for each person who is determined to be eligible, develop a plan of service that sets out the amount of each service to be provided to the person. Section 22(2)(b) requires that the plan be revised if necessary when the person's requirements change.

108 *LTCA, ibid.*

109 *Ibid.*, s. 5(1).

110 *Ibid.*, s. 22.

111 *PHIPA*, s. 54(9).

who claims to be authorized by such a document, makes a request for access on a patient's behalf.

The requirement to take reasonable steps does not require a health information custodian to verify the authenticity or validity of the document provided to the custodian, unless there is reason to doubt it. A custodian is entitled to rely on the accuracy of an assertion made by a person that he or she is authorized to request access to a record of personal health information, or is a substitute decision-maker of the patient, unless it is not reasonable in the circumstances to do so.[112] Where the custodian is faced with an indication that the document may be false, the custodian should require additional information to satisfy itself of the patient or substitute decision-maker's identity.

No action or other proceeding for damages may be instituted against a custodian for providing access to someone who asserts that he or she has authority to request access, if the custodian acts in good faith and reasonably in the circumstances.[113]

2) Charging a Fee for Access

Consistent with the principle originally established by the Supreme Court of Canada's decision in *McInerney v. MacDonald*, *PHIPA* provides that a health information custodian may charge a fee for making the record available, or for providing a copy to a patient.[114] However, the custodian must first give the patient an estimate of the fee.[115] In cases where the fee may be routine, such as for copies of ultrasound printouts, it may be sufficient for a health information custodian to post a notice of the fee in a public area.

a) "Reasonable Cost Recovery"
The amount of the fee cannot exceed the amount of "reasonable cost recovery," or the amount prescribed by regulation, if any.[116] At the time of writing, the

---

112 *PHIPA*, s. 71(4)(a): "Unless it is not reasonable to do so in the circumstances, a person is entitled to rely on the accuracy of an assertion made by another person, in connection with a collection, use, or disclosure of, or access to, the information under this Act, to the effect that the other person, (a) is a person who is authorized to request access to a record of personal health information under section 53."

113 *Ibid.*, s. 71(1).

114 *McInerney*, above note 5 at 159, where La Forest J. stipulated that the patient "is entitled to reasonable access to examine and copy the records, provided the patient pays a legitimate fee for the preparation and reproduction of the information."

115 *PHIPA*, s. 54(10).

116 The access provisions in the *LTCA*, repealed with the coming into force of *PHIPA*, did not permit a fee to be charged to the individual for examining or copying his or her

PHIPA Regulation does not address fees for access. Thus, a custodian has discretion to set a fee, taking into account factors such as the amount of staff time that is needed to assemble the personal health information requested, as well as photocopy charges or charges incurred for providing information in a form suitable to the requester, such as the costs of a computer diskette and delivery services (i.e., postage or courier).

Can a custodian charge a patient for time spent explaining a record or for supervising access to the record to ensure that it is not in any way altered by the requester? If it is reasonably necessary to supervise the requester or to explain the record, it could be argued that this is all part of making the record available to the requester, and so a charge may be levied, but it is not entirely clear.[117]

In deciding whether a fee constitutes a "reasonable cost recovery fee," health information custodians who are regulated by professional governing bodies may be guided by professional guidelines and standards of practice. Health information custodians that are facilities, such as hospitals or nursing homes, or programs and services such as community mental health programs, may have policies in place setting out a fee schedule, but they may also turn to their voluntary associations for guidance. *FIPPA/MFIPPA* custodians may be guided by regulations under those Acts that address fees for access to records generally, even though those Acts generally will not apply to access requests for personal health information processed by such custodians, since *PHIPA* now applies instead. For example, the regulation made under *FIPPA* sets out in detail the fees that government institutions, such as the Ministry of Health and Long-Term Care, may charge for such matters as photocopies, computer printouts, and manual searches of records.[118]

---

personal record (see s. 36(15) of the *LTCA*, above note 9, now repealed by *PHIPA*, s. 90(12)). The *MHA*, above note 8, was silent on this issue. CSA Privacy Code, Sch. 1 to *PIPEDA*, above note 2, Principle 9, Access, 4.9.4 provides that access requests should be processed at "a minimal or no cost to the individual."

117 *PHIPA*, s. 54(1)(a).

118 *General*, R.R.O. 1990, Reg. 460, s. 6.1, made under *FIPPA*, above note 10, sets out how much an institution may charge an individual to access personal information about the individual: 1) For photocopies and computer printouts, twenty cents per page. 2) For floppy disks, $10 for each disk. 3) For developing a computer program or other method of producing the personal information requested from a machine-readable record, $15 for each fifteen minutes spent by any person. 4) The costs, including computer costs, that the institution incurs in locating, retrieving, processing, and copying the personal information requested if those costs are specified in an invoice that the institution has received. The same provision exists in s. 6.1 of *General*, R.R.O. 1990, Reg. 823, made under *MFIPPA*, above note 12.

However, the fact that a health information custodian charged a fee consistent with such policies or guidelines is not determinative of the issue of whether a fee constitutes a "reasonable cost recovery fee." Whether the fee charged is a reasonable one is a question for the Information and Privacy Commissioner to consider; and, ultimately, the courts.

b) Waiver of the Fee

PHIPA provides a health information custodian with the discretion to waive a fee for a patient's access to personal health information. A health information custodian may waive a fee if, in the opinion of the custodian, it is "fair and equitable to do so."[119] Since the waiver is discretionary, a patient may not complain to the Information and Privacy Commissioner about a custodian's refusal to waive a fee.[120]

c) Complaint about an Excessive Fee

A patient who makes a request to a health information custodian for access to a record of personal health information may complain about a fee that exceeds the amount of "reasonable cost recovery," or the amount set by the regulations, if any, to the Information and Privacy Commissioner.[121] A professional's charging of an excessive fee may in some cases constitute professional misconduct and lead to discipline by the professional's regulatory body.[122] The Commissioner may decide not to review the subject matter of the complaint if satisfied that the complaint has been or could be dealt with more appropriately in another forum.[123]

Further, where there is a legal requirement apart from *PHIPA* for a health information custodian to disclose information or provide access, a fee may not be charged under *PHIPA* since the custodian cannot make its compliance with the legal requirement conditional on payment of a fee.

---

119   *PHIPA*, s. 54(12).

120   *Ibid.*, s. 56(1).

121   See further Chapter 15.

122   *RHPA* College regulations generally provide that it is professional misconduct for a regulated health professional to charge a fee that is "excessive" in relation to the services performed. See, for example, *Professional Misconduct*, O. Reg. 858/93, s. 1(22), made under the *Midwifery Act, 1991*, S.O. 1991, c. 31; s. 1(17) of *Professional Misconduct*, O. Reg. 681/93, made under the *Drug and Pharmacies Regulation Act*, R.S.O. 1990, c. H.4; s. 1(20) of *Professional Misconduct*, O. Reg. 753/93, made under the *Respiratory Therapy Act, 1991*, S.O. 1991, c. 39. A similar provision exists in s. 2(25) of O. Reg. 384/00, made under the *Social Work and Social Service Work Act, 1998*, S.O. 1998, c. 31.

123   The Commissioner has discretion to refuse to investigate if a professional governing body has jurisdiction over a matter: see *PHIPA*, s. 57(4)(b), although the fact that *PHIPA* is a little more specific about what kind of fees are unacceptable may tend to indicate that a complaint to the Commissioner may in the end be a more appropriate forum for such a complaint.

3) Response Time for Access Requests

a) The Thirty-day Rule

In general, a health information custodian must respond to a written access request within thirty days of receiving the request.[124] However, the custodian can extend the time period for providing access up to an additional thirty days, as long as the health information custodian notifies the patient of the extension within the initial thirty-day time period.[125] In identifying the date by which the custodian must respond to the access request, the custodian should count both the day on which the custodian received the request and the last day of the time period; that is, the thirtieth day.

As *PHIPA* does not include a definition of the term "day," it would appear that the thirty -day period or sixty-day period for responding to a patient's request for access is calculated on a calendar day basis, subject to the provisions of the *Interpretation Act* to allow for the thirtieth or sixtieth day falling on a holiday.[126]

Although consistent with the time periods set out in *PIPEDA*,[127] the time periods for responding to a patient's written request for access in *PHIPA* differ from the shorter time periods that existed for a patient's request for access under Ontario health sector legislation. Both the *Mental Health Act* and the *Long-Term Care Act, 1994* required facilities subject to those Acts to respond to a patient's request for access within seven days.[128] In Ontario public sector access to information and privacy legislation, the timeframes are longer. Under *FIPPA* and *MFIPPA*, an institution has thirty days to respond to a request for access to records in the custody or control of the institution, with an ability to extend the period of time in which to respond.[129]

b) Timelines under *PHIPA* and a Fee Estimate

As mentioned above, prior to charging a patient a fee for access to a record of personal health information, a health information custodian must provide the

---

124   *PHIPA*, s. 54(2).

125   *Ibid.*, s. 54(3).

126   The *Interpretation Act*, R.S.O. 1990, c. I.11 states that "where the time limited by an Act for a proceeding or for the doing of any thing under its provisions expires or falls upon a holiday, the time so limited extends to and the thing may be done on the day next following that is not a holiday": s. 28(g). A "holiday" includes Sunday, all other statutory or other public holidays, and, when any holiday, except Remembrance Day falls on a Sunday, the day next following is deemed to be a holiday: s. 29(1).

127   *PIPEDA*, above note 2, ss. 8(3) & (4).

128   *MHA*, above note 8, s. 36(4), now repealed by *PHIPA*, s. 90(12); *LTCA*, above note 9, s. 36(3), now repealed by *PHIPA*, s. 89(14).

129   *FIPPA*, above note 10, ss. 26 & 27; *MFIPPA*, above note 12, ss. 19 & 20. *FIPPA* and *MFIPPA* do not set time limits for extensions.

patient with an estimate of the fee.[130] *PHIPA*, however, does not speak to a patient's response upon the notice of the fee estimate. As a result, it is not clear that the custodian may wait for a response from the patient before processing the request. In many instances, the absence of a response from the patient will be of no consequence to the custodian, as the custodian may, for example, both collect the fee and provide the patient with access on the patient's arrival at the custodian's premises. In other instances, a custodian may hesitate to process the request in the absence of a response from the patient, such as when the fee is a substantial amount of money and the custodian must takes steps to retrieve records stored off-site.

It does not appear that *PHIPA* allows the "clock to stop ticking" for timelines set out in the Act for granting the request while waiting for a patient's response to the fee estimate. This is also the case under *FIPPA*. However, under *FIPPA*, the Information and Privacy Commissioner has concluded that timelines are essentially suspended until the custodian is advised by the requester to continue proceeding with the request.[131] Where the fee is not substantial, or where processing the request will not give rise to significant costs, it would be prudent for a health information custodian to process the request for access prior to the patient's confirmation of his or her intention to pay the fee. In other cases, pending clarification of this issue, a custodian may wish to indicate, when providing a fee estimate, that the custodian will await the patient's further instructions whether to proceed or not in light of the fee estimate.

c) Reasons for Extension, and Notice Thereof

Where a health information custodian requires more than thirty days to respond to a patient's request for access, the custodian must notify the patient in writing. The notice must set out the length of the extension and explain why the custodian needs more than thirty days to respond to the request.[132] *PHIPA* does not require a custodian to provide the notice in a specific format. The Act permits a health information custodian to extend the deadline for access for two reasons:

- First, an extension is permitted if responding within thirty days would "unreasonably interfere" with the health information custodian's operations because the records contain numerous pieces of information or a lengthy search is required to locate them.[133]

---

130   *PHIPA*, s. 54(10).

131   Order 81, Ministry of Labour (26 July 1989), online: <www.ipc.on.ca>; an order of the first Information and Privacy Commissioner, Sidney Linden, that is cited frequently.

132   *PHIPA*, s. 54(4).

133   *Ibid.*, s. 54(3)(a).

- Secondly, an extension is allowed if the time required to undertake consultations necessary to reply to the request would make it "not reasonably practical" to reply within thirty days of receiving it.[134] A health information custodian could rely on this reason for an extension, for example, where a custodian needs to consult a physician or psychologist about denying a patient access to a record on the basis that access would result in a risk of serious harm to the treatment of the patient, and more than thirty days is necessary to make arrangements for such a consultation.[135]

The time periods set out in *PHIPA* for a health information custodian's response to a patient's request for access to a record are the maximum allowed. Nothing in the Act, however, precludes a custodian from responding within a shorter time period.[136] It is good practice to respond to a request as quickly as possible.

d)   Expedited Access

Perhaps to recognize the fact that *PHIPA* has lengthened the period of time that a health information custodian has to respond to a patient's request for access in comparison to the time periods in place in some parts of the health sector prior to 1 November 2004, *PHIPA* also provides for "expedited access" to permit a patient to specify a shorter response time. Where a patient satisfies a health information custodian that he or she needs the record on an "urgent basis" within a period of time less than thirty days, the health information custodian is required to comply with this request if the custodian is "reasonably able to give the required response within that time period."[137] A patient may make a complaint to the Information and Privacy Commissioner where a health information custodian refuses or fails to respond to a request for expedited access in such circumstances.[138]

Furthermore, nothing in Part V of *PHIPA* relieves a health information custodian from a legal duty to provide personal health information in an appropriate manner as necessary for the provision of health care to the patient.[139] This provision emphasizes that procedures set out in Part V should

---

134   *PHIPA*, s. 54(3)(b).

135   *Ibid.*, s. 52(1)(e)(i) and s. 52(5). See Section D(6) below.

136   Note that *PIPEDA*, above note 2, s. 8(3) requires that "An organization shall respond to a request with due diligence and in any case not later than thirty days after receipt of the request" unless a further extension is made.

137   *PHIPA*, s. 54(5).

138   See Chapter 15, Section B(2).

139   *PHIPA*, s. 52(7). *RHPA* College regulations generally provide that it is professional misconduct for a regulated health professional to fail, without "reasonable cause, to provide a

not be used to justify delays in providing a patient with information necessary to the patient's care. A health information custodian should keep this provision in mind in interpreting its obligations to respond to patients' requests for access to records of personal health information.[140]

e) Responses of a Health Information Custodian to a Written Request for Access

i)   *Providing Access to the Record*

If a health information custodian retrieves a record and no exceptions or exclusions apply to the patient's right to request access, the custodian must make the record available to the patient for examination and, upon request, provide a copy of the record.[141] If "reasonably practical," upon the patient's request, the custodian must also provide to the patient an explanation of any term, code, or abbreviation used in the record.[142] Unlike *PIPEDA*, which requires that the form of the information provided or made available to the patient be generally understandable,[143] there is no such duty specified in *PHIPA*. Nor is the custodian required to explain the contents of the record, although such a require-

---

report or certificate relating to an assessment or treatment performed by the member, within a reasonable time after a client or his or her authorized representative has requested such a report or certificate." See, for example, s. 1(24) of *Professional Misconduct*, O. Reg. 203/00, made under the *Dietetics Act, 1991*, S.O. 1991, c. 26. A similar obligation is set out in s. 1(29) of *Professional Misconduct*, O. Reg. 853/93, made under the *Dentistry Act, 1991*, S.O. 1991, c. 24 with respect to access to a patient record or radiograph.

140   Due to the language of this provision, existing duties are preserved, but no duty is being imposed under *PHIPA*, thus this provision cannot be "contravened" so as to be the basis of a complaint to the Information and Privacy Commissioner.

141   *PHIPA*, s. 54(1)(a).

142   *Ibid.*, s. 54(1)(a). *FIPPA*, above note 10, s. 41(4) and *MFIPPA*, above note 12, s. 37(3) provide that, where access to personal information is given, the head shall ensure that the personal information is provided to the individual in "a comprehensible form."

143   Section 4.9.4 of Schedule 1 of *PIPEDA*, above note 2, provides that the requested information shall be provided or made available" in a form that is generally understandable." For example, "if the organization uses abbreviations or codes to record information, an explanation shall be provided." *PIPEDA*, s. 10 also deals specifically with sensory disability:

> [The] organization shall give access to personal information in an alternative format to an individual with a sensory disability who has a right of access to personal information under this Part and who requests that it be transmitted in the alternative format if (a) a version of the information already exists in that format; or (b) its conversion into that format is reasonable and necessary in order for the individual to be able to exercise rights under this Part.

ment may be specified by a professional governing body or by policy of the custodian.[144]

Making the record "available" to a patient means giving the patient an opportunity to view the record. To ensure that a patient does not tamper with or alter a record, a health information custodian may supervise a patient viewing a record. Of course, even after viewing the record, a patient may still request a copy of the record, and the custodian must comply with this request.[145]

ii) The Record Does Not Exist or Cannot Be Found

If the custodian concludes that a record either does not exist or cannot be found, the custodian is required to give the patient requesting the record a written notice explaining that, after a reasonable search, the custodian has concluded that the record either does not exist or cannot be found.[146] The issue of whether a custodian conducted a "reasonable search" may be the subject of a complaint to the Information and Privacy Commissioner. As set out above, when making a written access request, the patient must provide the custodian with sufficient detail to enable the custodian to identify and locate the record.[147] Thus, to a large degree, whether a reasonable search has been conducted will depend on the nature of the record requested and the level of detail provided. It would be reasonable for the custodian to search for the record in the records department where current files are kept. It may be reasonable to search for the record in storage, if the patient identifies the period of time in which the record was created or compiled. Where the custodian is a facility with a number of departments, it may be prudent to search several departments, depending on the nature of the record.

iii) Access to the Record Is Refused: Written Notice as a Response

If a custodian locates a record but determines that an exemption applies, the custodian must give the patient a written notice explaining that the request is being refused, either in whole or in part.[148] In the notice, the custodian must inform the patient that he or she is entitled to make a complaint about the

---

144 This contrasts with the *LTCA* that required the personal record or copy of it to "be given to the person for examination in readable form" (*LTCA*, above note 9, s. 36(15), now repealed by *PHIPA*, s. 89(14)). Also, there was a duty to provide an explanation of the plan of service (*LTCA*, s. 36(2), now repealed by *PHIPA*, s. 89(14)). There was no such duty for the examination by a patient of his or her clinical record in the *MHA*, above note 8.

145 For which there may be a charge levied for photocopying.

146 *PHIPA*, s. 54(1)(b).

147 *Ibid.*, s. 53(2).

148 *Ibid.*, ss. 54(1)(c) & (d). And see the discussion above in Section D(8).

refusal to the Information and Privacy Commissioner.[149] Usually, the custodian must include a reason for the refusal as well.[150]

However, a health information custodian is not required to provide a reason for the refusal where the custodian denies access because the record pertains to "ongoing proceedings," "ongoing investigations," or "risk of harm."[151] Indeed, for these three categories of exemptions, the custodian is not required to inform the patient requesting access to the record that such a record even exists. On the contrary, the custodian is required to provide a written notice to the patient "refusing to confirm or deny the existence of any record subject to any of those provisions."[152] The rationale for requiring the custodian to provide such a response is that, in some instances, such as where a third party supplies information in confidence, the circumstances may be such that providing a reason for refusing access would have the same potential for a negative outcome as the provision of access to the record.[153]

PHIPA does not require health information custodians to provide such notices in a specific format.

iv) Failure to Respond: Deemed Refusal

If a health information custodian fails to provide a patient with any response within the thirty-day time limit, or before the end of an extension or abridged time period, *PHIPA* deems the health information custodian to have refused the patient's request for access.[154]

f) Consequences of a Refusal

If a custodian refuses or is deemed to have refused a patient's request for access, whether in whole or in part, the patient is entitled to make a complaint about the refusal to the Information and Privacy Commissioner.[155] A patient

---

149   *PHIPA*, ss. 54(1)(c) & (d).

150   *Ibid.*, s. 54(1)(c).

151   This short form of addressing these exemptions is taken from the Ministry of Health and Long-Term Care Overview of the *Personal Health Information Protection Act, 2004* (August 2004), online: <www.health.on.ca>. "Ongoing proceedings" refers to *PHIPA*, s. 52(1)(c); "ongoing investigations" refers to *PHIPA*, s. 52(1)(d); and "risk of harm" exemptions refers to *PHIPA*, s. 52(1)(e), exemptions to the right of access. Each category is explained in greater detail in Section D above.

152   *PHIPA*, s. 54(1)(d).

153   *Ibid.*

154   *Ibid.*, s. 54(7).

155   *Ibid.*, s. 54(8). The rules in *PHIPA* now apply to psychiatric facilities as set out in the *MHA*, above note 8, and service providers as defined in the *LTCA*, above note 9. In both statutes, the onus was on the attending physician (in the case of a psychiatric facility) or service provider, as the case may be, to make an application to the Consent

must make a complaint about a refusal or a deemed refusal to the Commissioner within six months[156] from the date on which the health information custodian refuses or is deemed to have refused the request.[157] In such a complaint, consistent with the Supreme Court of Canada decision in *McInerney v. MacDonald,* the burden of proof to justify the refusal rests on the health information custodian.[158] The Commissioner has the power to make an order directing the health information custodian about whom a complaint was made to grant the patient access to the record.[159] Although a patient cannot appeal the decision of the Commissioner concerning a complaint about a health information custodian's response to a request for access, the patient may apply to the Divisional Court for judicial review of the Commissioner's decision.[160]

---

and Capacity Board for permission to deny access to all or part of the patient's clinical record or client's personal health record, as the case may be. A decision of the Board could be appealed to the Superior Court of Justice on a question of law or fact or both (*MHA,* s. 48(1); *LTCA,* s. 36(10.1)). These provisions no longer apply to patients' access to their records, as the access provisions in those statutes have been repealed by *PHIPA,* ss. 89(14) and 90(12). The Consent and Capacity Board is a tribunal continued under s. 70(1) of the *Health Care Consent Act, 1996,* S.O. 1990, c. 2, Sch. A and has jurisdiction to hear matters pertaining to that Act, the *MHA,* the *Substitute Decisions Act, 1992,* S.O. 1992, c. 30, and *PHIPA.*

156 *Interpretation Act,* above note 126, s. 29(1): "month" means a calendar month.

157 *PHIPA,* s. 56(3). For further rules of enforcement by the Information and Privacy Commissioner see Chapter 15. The Information and Privacy Commissioner has developed an "Access/Correction Complaint Form" to accept such complaints, online: <www.ipc.on.ca>.

158 *PHIPA,* s. 54(8). As stated by La Forest, J. in *McInerney,* above note 5 at para. 39: "The onus is on the physician to justify a denial of access."

159 *PHIPA,* s. 61(1)(a).

160 *Ibid.,* s. 62(1).

14 Correction of Personal Health Information Records

A. RIGHT OF CORRECTION: BACKGROUND

Under the *Personal Health Information Protection Act, 2004*,[1] a patient has a right to require that a record of inaccurate or incomplete personal health information about him- or herself be corrected or amended, subject to some specific exceptions.[2] The subject matter of the correction may be major or minor in nature: the right extends equally to matters large and small, provided that it is significant enough to affect the purpose for which the custodian uses the information.[3] The provision of this right is set out as one of the purposes of the Act.[4] Where the patient has a substitute decision-maker authorized to act on his or her behalf under *PHIPA*, the substitute decision-maker may take the steps to correct the patient's record on behalf of the patient.[5]

The rules for correction in *PHIPA* build on Principle 9 of the CSA Privacy Code, incorporated in Schedule 1 of the *Personal Information Protection and Electronic Documents Act*,[6] which specifies that "an individual shall be able to chal-

---

1   S.O. 2004, c. 3, Sch. A [*PHIPA*].
2   *Ibid.*, s. 55(1).
3   *Ibid.*, s. 55(8).
4   *Ibid.*, s. 1(c).
5   *Ibid.*, s. 25(1). See Chapter 6, Section D.
6   S.C. 2000, c. 5. [*PIPEDA*].

lenge the accuracy and completeness of the information and have it amended as appropriate."[7]

A patient may ask to see his or her record for a variety of reasons. The patient may wish to see whether the information, in his or her view, is accurate. An error in a patient's health record can lead to compounded errors in treatment or in the evaluation of benefits, for example. A legislated right of correction, thus, goes hand in hand with a right of access.

Legislated rules to provide individuals with a way to correct or amend their record exist in the *Freedom of Information and Protection of Privacy Act*[8] and the *Municipal Freedom of Information and Protection of Privacy Act*.[9] Psychiatric patients have had a legislated right to request correction of their clinical records under the provisions of the *Mental Health Act*[10] since 1986 and clients of services under the *Long-Term Care Act, 1994*[11] have had such a right since that Act came into force in 1994.[12]

B. RIGHT OF CORRECTION IN *PHIPA*

1) Correction of Record outside of a Request under *PHIPA*

PHIPA specifies that, where appropriate, a custodian can simply correct a record based on an oral request.[13] For example, a patient, in the course of informally reviewing his or her record before the custodian, may indicate to the custodian that information in the record is incorrect, and the custodian may correct the record at that moment. In such cases, the procedure set out in *PHIPA* for cor-

---

7   *Ibid.*, CSA Privacy Code, Principle 9. There are no further procedures set out for correction in *PIPEDA*. Section 4.9.5 of Principle 9 does provide that when an individual "successfully demonstrates the inaccuracy or incompleteness of personal information, the organization shall amend the information as required." The amendment could involve correction, deletion, or addition of information. This depends on the nature of the information challenged.

8   R.S.O. 1990, c. F.31, s. 47(2) [*FIPPA*].

9   R.S.O. 1990, c. M.56, s. 36(2) [*MFIPPA*].

10 R.S.O. 1990, c. M.7, s. 36(13) (repealed by *PHIPA*, s. 90(14)) [*MHA*].

11 S.O. 1994, c. 26 [*LTCA*].

12 *Ibid.*, s. 37 (repealed by *PHIPA*, s. 89(12)). It should be noted that the right in the *MHA*, above note 10, extended only to "mentally competent" patients. In the *LTCA*, *ibid.*, the right pertained to the mentally capable as well as incapable patient. *PHIPA* extends the right to every patient, irrespective of capacity. The capacity determination in *PHIPA* applies to collections, uses, and disclosures of personal health information and not to the right of access.

13 *PHIPA*, s. 55(2).

rections does not apply. Furthermore, there is a general duty in *PHIPA* for a health information custodian to keep personal health information records it uses as accurate, complete, and up-to-date as necessary for the purposes for which the custodian uses the information, and a custodian must fulfil this obligation even absent a request to correct the record on the part of the patient.[14]

2) Where No Right to Correct

In the formal correction process set out in *PHIPA*, a patient has a right to request correction of his or her record of personal health information only where the health information custodian has granted that patient access to the record.[15] If the custodian has refused or is deemed to have refused an access request, there is no right to require the correction of the information to which access was refused.[16]

3) The Written Request

For *PHIPA's* procedural requirements to apply to a request for correction, the patient must set out the request in writing.[17] In the same way that the custodian's contact person would respond to an access request, the custodian's contact person would respond to the request for correction.[18] Similar to a request for access, there is no prescribed form in *PHIPA* for a request for correction. A patient can provide a letter of request, for example, or a note. A custodian may develop its own form for the purpose of accepting requests for correction. A custodian must also be satisfied as to the patient's or the substitute decision-maker's identity (where the substitute decision-maker is taking the step to request correction on the patient's behalf) prior to responding to a written request to correct.[19]

---

14   *PHIPA*, ss. 11(1) & (2). Accuracy of records is further explained in Chapter 4, Section H.
15   *Ibid.*, s. 55(1). This is no different from the right that existed in the *Mental Health Act* and *Long-Term Care Act, 1994*: *MHA*, above note 10, s. 36(13), repealed by *PHIPA*, s. 90(12); *LTCA*, above note 11, s. 37(1), repealed by *PHIPA*, s. 89(15).
16   In such a case, however, the patient could complain to the Commissioner that the custodian was in contravention of the accuracy obligation under s. 11, and the Commissioner would have the power, if the complaint were substantiated, to order remedial steps, which might include a correction. Also, recall *PHIPA*, s. 55(2), which states that nothing in Part V prevents the custodian from responding to an oral request for correction — which means that this is irrespective of whether or not the record would have been denied to the patient had a written access request been made.
17   This request may be sent out electronically. See further note 31, Chapter 13.
18   *PHIPA*, s. 15(1)(d).
19   *Ibid.*, s. 54(9). This is discussed in Chapter 13, Section E(1).

4) Right to Correct Where the Record Is "Inaccurate or Incomplete"

A patient's right to have a record of personal health information corrected aris-es in *PHIPA* if the patient believes that the record is inaccurate or incomplete for the purposes for which the custodian uses the information.[20] This limita-tion means that there is no statutory right under *PHIPA* to correct information in every instance; rather, the issue of inaccuracy or incompleteness is tied to the particular purpose or purposes for which the custodian collects or uses the information.[21]

For example, if the custodian collects information for the purpose of pro-viding health care to a patient, and in the course of collecting such information has improperly recorded the patient's occupation, but this information is not relevant to the care the patient is obtaining from the custodian, there would apparently be no right to require the custodian to correct that information. If, however, the patient's occupation is relevant to the kind of health care that the patient requires (such as where the occupation involves standing all day and this information would have an impact on the kind of physiotherapy the patient requires), then this type of information would be subject to correction under the provisions of the Act.

5) Duty on the Patient to Show Record Incomplete or Inaccurate

In order for the requested correction to be granted, it is up to the patient to show, to the satisfaction of the custodian, that the record is incomplete or inac-curate for the purposes for which the custodian uses the information.[22] With-out evidence from the patient making the assertion that it is inaccurate, the custodian may not be in a position to assess the appropriateness of the pro-posed correction. In some instances, it will be easy for a patient to fulfil this requirement. For example, a patient may provide a custodian with his or her health card as evidence of the patient's health number where an incorrect

---

20   In the context of describing the right to request correction, *PHIPA*, s. 55(1) refers to "the purposes for which the custodian has collected or used the information." Howev-er, it is evident from s. 55(8), which describes the actual right to have the information corrected, that the right is limited to making the information correct and complete for "the purposes for which the custodian uses the information."

21   Especially in the context of ensuring that information is "complete" it is essential to refer to the purpose, otherwise the provision is without clear limitation. See further Chapter 4, Section G.

22   *PHIPA*, s. 55(8).

health number is recorded in the patient's record. In other cases, however, it will be more difficult for a patient to fulfil this requirement of satisfying the custodian of the inaccuracy or incompleteness of the record. For example, a patient who feels laboratory test results are incorrect may need new test results to substantiate the assertion.

Furthermore, the obligation is on the patient to provide the custodian with the information that would enable the custodian to correct the record; that is, to provide the correct information.[23] In some cases, of course, it is possible that information may be identified as inaccurate without having accurate information to replace it, and in such a case the custodian may have an obligation simply to identify the information as inaccurate.

6) Circumstances Where No Duty to Correct

The health information custodian has no duty under *PHIPA* to correct a record if the record was not originally created by the custodian and the custodian does not have "sufficient knowledge, expertise and authority" to correct it.[24] There is also no duty to correct the information if the information subject to the request is a "professional opinion or observation" that the custodian or any other custodian has made in good faith about the patient.[25] For example, a medical diagnosis made by the custodian physician or another physician that is in the patient's record is not subject to the correction requirement under the Act if it is made in good faith.

C. PROCEDURE

1) The Thirty-day Rule and Extending the Time

The time periods for responding to a request for correction are the same as those set out for an access request.[26] Upon receiving a written request to cor-

---

23 *Ibid.*
24 *Ibid.*, s. 59(9)(a). All three elements are required. In other words, if the custodian lacks the necessary knowledge or lacks the necessary authority or lacks the necessary expertise to make the correction, the custodian is not obliged to do so.
25 *Ibid.*, s. 55(9)(b).
26 See Chapter 13, Section E(3). As noted, *PIPEDA* does not provide specific timelines for correction. See above note 7. The *Mental Health Act*, above note 10, did not set out any timelines for correction. The *Long-Term Care Act, 1994* provided that the request to correct had to be fulfilled within thirty days of the request and the service provider had to give a notice to the patient if the correction was being refused, as well as rea-

rect a record, a health information custodian must respond to the patient "as soon as possible in the circumstances" and no later than thirty days after receiving a request.[27] However, in some instances, the custodian can extend the time period to respond up to an additional thirty days, thus totaling up to sixty days, as long as the health information custodian notifies the patient of the extension within the initial thirty-day time period.[28]

The custodian may extend the deadline for replying to the request for a period of not more than thirty more days in two circumstances:

- First, if replying to the request within thirty days would "unreasonably interfere with the activities of the custodian" the custodian can extend the deadline.[29] This means that the custodian is not obliged to give priority to answering correction requests within thirty days to such an extent that it compromises the timely provision of health care to the custodian's patients. This provision is particularly relevant to sole practitioners or group practices, but may not be as relevant in an institutional setting with staff dedicated to the custodian's information management functions.
- Second, an extension is permitted if "the time required to undertake the consultations necessary to reply to the request within thirty days would make it not reasonably practical to reply within that time."[30] For example, a custodian may need to seek advice about the correction of a very old or very large and complex record.

As with the timelines associated with requests for access, the custodian should count both the day on which the custodian received the request and the last day of the time period; that is, the thirtieth day. The patient's request for correction should be calculated on a calendar day basis, subject to the provisions of the *Interpretation Act* to allow for the thirtieth or sixtieth day falling on a holiday.[31]

---

sons for the refusal: *LTCA*, above note 11, s. 37(2), repealed by *PHIPA*, s. 89(14) . There are no timelines for correction set out in *FIPPA*, above note 8 (see s. 47(2)) and *MFIPPA*, above note 9 (see s. 36(2)).

27   *PHIPA*, s. 55(3)(a).
28   *Ibid.*, ss. 55(3) & (4)(a).
29   *Ibid.*, s. 55(3)(a).
30   *Ibid.*, s. 55(3)(b).
31   R.S.O., 1990, c. I.11, ss. 28(g) and 29(1). See further about timelines in Chapter 13, Section E(3) and note 126.

2) Notice of Extension

The notice of extension of the period of time that the custodian will require to reply to the request for correction must be in writing and must set out the length of the extension and the reason for it.[32] *PHIPA* does not require a specific format for the notice.

3) Where the Matter Is Urgent

Unlike the access provisions, the correction provisions have no specific reference to an expedited process where a correction may be needed in a quicker manner. Of course, the patient may request informally that the matter be treated expeditiously where urgent, but *PHIPA* does not obligate the custodian to agree to such requests, so there is no recourse to the Commissioner from a custodian's refusal to expedite the handling of a correction request.

However, as in the procedures set out for access requests, the time periods set out in *PHIPA* are the maximum allowed in normal circumstances.[33] Nothing in the Act, however, precludes the custodian from responding within a shorter time period. As a matter of good practice, a custodian should respond to a request for correction as quickly as possible.

4) Responding to the Patient by Written Notice

The formal procedure of *PHIPA* requires that the custodian respond to the patient by "written notice" indicating that the custodian either grants or refuses the request.[34] Again, there is no prescribed notice in the Act. The custodian can create the form of the written notice to suit the custodian's practice.

5) Failure to Respond: Deemed Refusal

If the custodian fails to respond in the time allowed for answering the request, this is deemed to be a refusal of the request.[35] In this case, the patient has a right to take certain steps, such as requiring a statement of disagreement to be attached to the record.[36]

---

32 *PHIPA*, s. 55(4)(a).
33 *Ibid.*, ss. 54(2) & (3).
34 *Ibid.*, s. 55(3)
35 *Ibid.*, s. 55(5).
36 See, below, Section D about the statement of disagreement.

6) Fees Associated with Corrections

As discussed in Chapter 13, under *PHIPA* a health information custodian may charge a patient for the provision of access to a record of personal health information.[37] However, the Act does not include a power for a custodian to charge a patient a fee for making a request for correction, the correction of a record, or for complying with the requirement to notify third parties of the corrected information.[38]

7) Frivolous, Vexatious, or Made in Bad Faith Requests

There may be situations where a patient repeatedly, and with no reasonable justification, asks that his or her record be corrected. In such circumstances, where the custodian believes that the request is any one of "frivolous or vexatious or made in bad faith," the custodian may refuse to grant the request.[39] The custodian need not believe the request is all three of these things. If this type of situation exists, the custodian must provide the patient with a notice that sets out the reasons for the refusal and that states that the patient is entitled to make a complaint about the refusal to the Information and Privacy Commissioner.[40] A health information custodian should be cautious in refusing the correction of a record of personal health information on the basis that the request is frivolous, vexatious, or made in bad faith.

8) Granting the Request for Correction

Where the custodian grants a request for a correction of a record of personal health information, the legislation specifies the manner in which the correction must be made.[41] *PHIPA* does not permit the inaccurate information to be deleted, because the information that requires correction could be required for litigation purposes, as evidence that a custodian has relied on inaccurate information in treating a patient, for example. Each method of correction in

---

37 Chapter 13, Section E(2).
38 This is evident from the fact that s. 55 imposes the duty to correct, notify third parties, attach a statement of disagreement, etc., without any provision allowing it to be made conditional on the payment of a fee. A custodian does not have the power to make compliance with s. 55 conditional on the patient paying a fee to the custodian.
39 *PHIPA*, s. 55(6). See discussion of frivolous or vexatious or made in bad faith in Chapter 13, Section D(10).
40 *Ibid.*, s. 55(6). For further discussion about complaints to the Information and Privacy Commissioner, see Chapter 15.
41 *Ibid.*, s. 55(10).

PHIPA ends with the correct information being provided, while the incorrect information still being accessible, but held in such a manner that it is known to be incorrect.

a) Manner of Correction

Where possible, the health information custodian must make the correction by recording the correct information in the record, and striking out the incorrect information without obliterating it.[42] For example, a custodian may simply draw a line through the incorrect information and note the new information.

Where it is not possible to correct the record in this way, *PHIPA* provides custodians with other alternatives. The custodian may make the correction by

- labeling the information as inaccurate,
- severing the incorrect information from the record,
- storing the inaccurate information separately from the record, and
- maintaining a link in the record that enables a person to trace the incorrect information.[43]

A custodian who retains records of personal health information electronically may find this method of correction appropriate for its systems. For example, a file retained in "read-only" electronic format may be severed from the larger collection of a patient's records, labeled as inaccurate, and stored separately.

If the custodian cannot record the correct information in the record by either of these two methods, the Act permits the custodian to make the correction by "ensuring that there is a practical system in place" to inform a person who accesses the record that the information in the record is incorrect and to direct the person to the correct information.[44] A custodian who retains records of personal health information on microfiche, for example, could include a notice of incorrect information in the envelope in which the microfiche is kept, directing people reading the records to also check another place, such as a binder, for notes about corrections made to information contained on the microfiche.

b) Notice to the Patient of the Correction

In every case, the custodian must give the patient notice of what steps the custodian has taken in response to the patient's request for correction.[45] *PHIPA*

---

42 *PHIPA*, s. 55(10)(a)(i)(A).
43 *Ibid.*, s. 55(10)(a)(i)(B).
44 *Ibid.*, s. 55(10)(a)(ii).
45 *Ibid.*, s. 55(10)(b).

does not stipulate that this notice must be in writing. Thus, it appears that the custodian may give the patient notice orally. From a practical perspective, a custodian may include this information in the required written notice of the custodian's granting of the request for correction.[46] In either case, it is prudent for the custodian to retain a record of the steps the custodian has taken in response to the patient's request and the timing of those steps, in the event that the custodian's conduct becomes the subject of a complaint to the Information and Privacy Commissioner.

c) Notice to Others of the Requested Correction

On the request of the patient, the custodian must also give a written notice of the requested correction to persons to whom the custodian has, in the past, disclosed the incorrect information.[47] This obligation is not absolute.[48] A health information custodian must fulfil this requirement "to the extent reasonably possible."[49] Where, for example, a custodian no longer has access to current contact information for such a person, despite the custodian's efforts to find this information, this notification obligation may not apply.

Further, a health information custodian is not required to notify persons to whom the custodian has in the past disclosed the incorrect information "if the correction cannot reasonably be expected to have an effect on the ongoing provision of health care or other benefits"[50] to the patient. In practice, therefore, if the patient's information is incorrect, but a recipient of that information is no longer treating the patient, the custodian may have no obligation to inform that person of the requested correction. Although patients may request health information custodians to take a broader approach to notifying third parties of the requested correction, and custodians may agree to do so, *PHIPA* does not require custodians to comply with such a request where the correction is not expected to have practical relevance for the patient.

---

46   *PHIPA*, s. 55(3).

47   A similar obligation is set out in CSA Privacy Code, Sch. 1 to *PIPEDA*, Principle 9-4.9.5: "Where appropriate, the amended information shall be transmitted to third parties having access to the information in question." *FIPPA*, above note 8 (s. 47(2)(c)) and *MFIPPA*, above note 9 (s. 36(2)(c)) also require that any person or body to whom the personal information has been disclosed within the year before the time a correction is requested be notified of the correction. The *MHA*, above note 10 and the *LTCA*, above note 11, contained similar provisions.

48   By contrast, this obligation is absolute in *FIPPA*, *ibid.*, *MFIPPA*, *ibid.*, as well as in the now-repealed provisions of the *MHA*, *ibid.* and the *LTCA*, *ibid.*

49   *PHIPA*, s. 55(10)(c). In *PIPEDA*, the requirement is to be complied with "where appropriate." See above note 47.

50   *PHIPA*, s. 55(10)(c).

D. STATEMENT OF DISAGREEMENT

1) Notice to the Patient Where There Is a Refusal

If a health information custodian refuses to correct a record, the custodian must give the patient requesting the correction a written notice and reasons for the refusal.[51] *PHIPA* does not prescribe a form for this detailed notice. However, the notice must inform the patient that he or she

- is entitled to prepare a concise statement of disagreement setting out the correction the health information custodian has refused to make;[52]
- can require the custodian to attach the statement of disagreement to the patient's record of personal health information;[53]
- can require the custodian to disclose the statement of disagreement in the future whenever the custodian discloses information to which the statement relates;[54]
- can require the custodian to make all reasonable efforts to disclose the statement of disagreement to any person who would have received a notice of the correction if the custodian had granted the request (unless the correction would not reasonably be expected to have an effect on the ongoing provision of health care or other benefits to the patient);[55] and

---

51   *PHIPA*, s. 55(11).

52   *Ibid.*, s. 55(11)(a). This compares with CSA Privacy Code, Sch. 1 to *PIPEDA*, s. 4.9.6, which provides that "when a challenge is not resolved to the satisfaction of the individual, the substance of the unresolved challenge shall be recorded by the organization."

53   *PHIPA*, s. 55(11)(b). *FIPPA*, above note 8 (s. 47(2)(b)) and *MFIPPA*, above note 9, (s. 36(2)(b)) require that a statement of disagreement be attached to the information reflecting any correction that was requested but not made. A similar requirement existed in the *MHA*, above note 10. In the *LTCA*, above note 11, the statement of disagreement that was required to be attached to the record also had to contain an explanation from the service provider as to why the correction was not being made. The service provider was required to attach the statement of disagreement within ten days after receiving the request for the attachment.

54   *PHIPA*, s. 55(11)(b).

55   *Ibid.*, ss. 55(10)(c) and 55(11)(c). CSA Privacy Code, Sch. 1 to *PIPEDA*, s. 4.9.6 provides that "when appropriate, the existence of the unresolved challenge shall be transmitted to third parties having access to the information in question." *FIPPA*, above note 8 (s. 47(2)(c)) and *MFIPPA*, above note 9 (s. 36(2)(c)) require that any person or body to whom the personal information has been disclosed within the year before the time a statement of disagreement is required be notified of the statement of disagreement. A similar provision existed in the *MHA*, above note 10. The *LTCA*, above note 11, required that within thirty days of the patient's request for distribution of a notice of the statement of disagreement, the service provider was required to notify all those

- has a right to make a complaint about the refusal to make the correction to the Information and Privacy Commissioner.[56]

Even in the absence of such notification by the custodian (for example, where there has been a deemed refusal of a correction request, or where the custodian decides that the request is frivolous or vexatious) the patient is entitled to proceed as though the custodian provided such a notice and exercise the rights referred to in such a notice, as listed above.[57]

2) Concise Statement of Disagreement

PHIPA does not define the word "concise" in connection with the statement of disagreement.[58] The length of the statement will vary from situation to situation. The length may depend on the extent of the information to be corrected and the extent of the information that the patient needs to include in the record to provide what the patient considers to be the correct information. Health information custodians may indicate their expectations of the length of the statement to patients, though patients may dispute it. Under *PHIPA*, a regulation could be developed, in time, to explain what is meant by "concise."[59] In the absence of a regulation, it is up to the custodian, and ultimately the Information and Privacy Commissioner and the courts, to determine what length is acceptable in the circumstances.

If the patient prepares such a statement of disagreement, and the custodian attaches it to the patient's record, the attached statement becomes part of the patient's record of personal health information with the custodian.[60]

---

who received the patient's information within the year preceding the attachment to the personal record of the statement of disagreement.

56 *PHIPA*, s. 55(11)(d). See Section D, below and further about enforcement of the legislation in Chapter 15.

57 *PHIPA*, s. 55(12).

58 *Ibid.*, s. 55(11)(a). Some other jurisdictions provide more guidance. For example, Alberta's *Health Information Act*, R.S.A. 2000, c. H-5, s. 14(1)(b) provides that the statement should be five hundred words or less. The Ontario draft *Privacy of Personal Information Act, 2002*, which was the subject of a public consultation, restricted the length of the statement of disagreement to five hundred words or the prescribed length, if any: cl. 62(12). See Ontario, *A Consultation on the Draft Privacy of Personal Information Act, 2002* (Toronto: Ministry of Consumer and Business Services, 2002) [*POPIA*], online: <www.cbs.gov.on.ca/mcbs/english/pdf/56XSMB>.

59 *PHIPA*, s. 73(1)(e).

60 *Ibid.*, s. 55(11)(b).

3) The Custodian's Duty to Provide the Statement of Disagreement to Others

Where a patient first prepares a statement of disagreement and requests the custodian to attach it to the patient's personal health record, and then requests the custodian to disclose the statement whenever the custodian discloses information to which the statement relates, or requests that the custodian make all reasonable efforts to disclose the statement to any person who would have received the notice if the request had been granted, the custodian has a duty to comply with the request.[61]

The consequence of non-compliance is that a complaint could be made by anyone about the custodian's inaction to the Information and Privacy Commissioner.[62]

4) Fees Associated with Statements of Disagreements

As discussed in Chapter 13, under *PHIPA* a health information custodian may charge a patient for the provision of access to a record of personal health information.[63] However, the Act does not include a power for a custodian to charge a fee for attaching a statement of disagreement to a record. Further, a fee cannot be charged for fulfilling the obligation of disclosing the statement of disagreement to third parties of the information in question.[64]

E. THE PATIENT'S RIGHT TO COMPLAIN

Where a custodian has refused a request for correction, in whole or in part, or there has been a deemed refusal, the patient has a right to make a complaint about this to the Information and Privacy Commissioner under Part VI of *PHIPA*. The Act sets out that the patient has six months from the time of the refusal or deemed refusal to make a complaint to the Commissioner and that

---

61 *PHIPA*, s. 55(13).

62 *Ibid.*, s. 56(1).

63 Chapter 13, Section E(2).

64 This is apparent from the fact that ss. 55(11) & (12) impose the duty on the custodian to attach the statement of disagreement, provide it with any related disclosure, and make all reasonable efforts to disclose it to previous recipients of the information, without any provision allowing such a statement to be made conditional on the payment of a fee. A custodian does not have the power to make compliance with these provisions conditional on the payment of a fee to the custodian.

the complaint must be in writing.[65] The Commissioner has the power to order the custodian to make the requested correction.[66] Neither the patient nor the custodian can appeal the decision of the Commissioner concerning a complaint about a health information custodian's response to a request for correction, but both have a right to apply to the Divisional Court for judicial review of the Commissioner's decision.[67]

However, where the issue pertains not to the actual or deemed refusal of a request for correction, but rather to the manner in which a correction was made (whether to the statement of disagreement or to the notification of others of either the correction or the statement of disagreement) the patient may make a complaint to the Commissioner anytime within one year after the matter came to the patient's attention.[68] Orders made with respect to such complaints can be appealed to the Divisional Court on a question of law.[69] The provisions and processes for reviews by the Information and Privacy Commissioner are discussed in more detail in Chapter 15.

---

65   *PHIPA*, s. 56(3). The Information and Privacy Commissioner has published a form to be used for complaints about access and corrections, online: <www.ipc.on.ca>.

66   *Ibid.*, s. 61(1)(b).

67   *Ibid.*, s. 64(4).

68   *Ibid.*, s. 56(2). Unlike the six-month timeframe for complaints about refusals of correction requests, the Commissioner has discretion to extend the one-year period if satisfied that doing so would not prejudice any person.

69   *Ibid.*, s. 62(1).

15 The Enforcement of *PHIPA*

A. TYPES OF ENFORCEMENT UNDER *PHIPA*

Health information custodians and others who are not in compliance with the *Personal Health Information Protection Act, 2004,*[1] or who are alleged to have breached the legislation or the regulation, risk becoming the object of enforcement action. There are several formal legal ways of enforcing *PHIPA* and obtaining redress for breaches of the legislation, including the following:

- a review by the Information and Privacy Commissioner, whether on the basis of a complaint or on the initiative of the Commissioner, who has the power to make enforceable orders;
- a court action for damages for breach of the legislation; and
- a prosecution for an offence under the Act.

Each of these processes is considered in detail below.

---

1   S.O. 2004, c. 3, Sch. A [*PHIPA*].

B. COMMISSIONER'S REVIEW

1) Background on the Commissioner and the Legislation

The Ontario Information and Privacy Commissioner,[2] referred to in *PHIPA* simply as "the Commissioner," is the main enforcement body under *PHIPA*.

The Office of the Information and Privacy Commissioner was created under the *Freedom of Information and Protection of Privacy Act*,[3] in 1988 as the oversight body when Ontario's first public sector privacy legislation came into force. When Ontario's municipal sector was added to Ontario's public sector freedom of information and protection of privacy legislative regime on 1 January 1991 with the coming into force of the *Municipal Freedom of Information and Protection of Privacy Act*,[4] the oversight powers of the Information and Privacy Commissioner were extended accordingly. Since then, the office has developed considerable experience in interpreting privacy law and has been a consistent advocate for the importance of protecting privacy in both the public and private sectors. The Commissioner is an independent officer of the Ontario Legislature, not reporting to any Minister.[5] The Commissioner continues to be governed by the general provisions of *FIPPA*, as amended by *PHIPA*, for *PHIPA* matters within the Commissioner's jurisdiction.[6] Among those general provisions are provisions that require the Commissioner to report to the Legislature annually on her activities under *FIPPA*, *MFIPPA*, and *PHIPA*.[7]

For some time, the Commissioner has been critical of the extent of her powers under *FIPPA* and *MFIPPA* to investigate and make orders in connection with complaints about the privacy practices of institutions subject to *FIPPA* and *MFIPPA*.[8] Those Acts contain a power for the Commissioner to

---

2 Serving as Ontario's Information and Privacy Commissioner since 1998, Dr. Ann Cavoukian (Ph.D., Psychology) was re-appointed in May 2004 for a further term of five years.

3 S.O. 1987, c. 25, subsequently R.S.O. 1990, c. F.31, s. 4 [*FIPPA*].

4 S.O. 1989, c. 63, subsequently R.S.O. 1990, c. M.56 [*MFIPPA*].

5 *FIPPA*, above note 3, s. 4(1). The Commissioner is appointed by the Lieutenant Governor in Council on the basis of approval by the Legislature (s. 4(2)) for a five-year renewable term (s. 4(3)).

6 This would include *FIPPA*, *ibid.*, ss. 4–9, and 58, as amended by *PHIPA*, s. 81.

7 *FIPPA*, *ibid.*, s. 58.

8 Information and Privacy Commissioner, *A Special Report to the Legislative Assembly of Ontario on the Disclosure of Personal Information by the Province of Ontario Savings Office, Ministry of Finance* (26 April 2000) [POSO Report]; see especially the Addendum entitled "Powers Necessary to Conduct a Proper Investigation." The POSO Report arose out of a review conducted by the Commissioner in 2000 based on a

conduct "inquiries," which include the powers to enter and inspect premises,[9] require the production of records,[10] and summon and examine persons under oath.[11] The Commissioner's powers to conduct inquiries, however, apply only to "appeals" from a decision of an institution concerning an access request or a correction request.[12] The Commissioner does not have any similar investigative powers under *FIPPA* or *MFIPPA* to review complaints about the information practices of institutions subject to those Acts.[13] Furthermore, *FIPPA* and *MFIPPA* provide the Commissioner with powers to order effective remedies for access and correction matters.[14] Regarding other types of complaints, however, the Acts provide the Commissioner only with the power to order an institution to cease information practices that contravene the Acts or to destroy information collected in contravention of the Acts.[15] Apart from the powers to order these particular remedies, the Commissioner is otherwise limited to making assessments about compliance, and recommendations on the infor-

---

news reporter's information that in 1997 the Ontario government provided personal information about POSO customers, including account information, to a private financial consultant and private market research firm to analyze prospects for a possible privatization of POSO and to survey POSO account holders to determine their reactions. Ultimately the Commissioner determined that the disclosure of personal information by the government in those circumstances was not in accordance with *FIPPA*. The issue of relevance here was that the Commissioner reported that a number of government officials whose input was expected to be relevant refused to co-operate with the investigation, and that her office lacked the powers to require their co-operation. The Addendum to the Report focused on this issue and recommended amending *FIPPA* and *MFIPPA* to provide improved investigative powers. As noted in the Report, the same types of recommendations for enhanced powers had been made to and accepted by the Standing Committee on the Legislative Assembly in 1991 and 1994 during the three-year reviews of *FIPPA* and *MFIPPA* respectively, though the Acts were not amended in accordance with the recommendations.

9   *FIPPA, ibid.,* s. 52(4); *MFIPPA, ibid.,* s. 41(4).

10   *FIPPA,* above note 3, ss. 52(4) & (7); *MFIPPA,* above note 4, ss. 41(4) & (7).

11   *FIPPA, ibid.,* s. 52(8); *MFIPPA, ibid.,* s. 41(8).

12   *FIPPA, ibid.,* ss. 50(1) & 52(1); *MFIPPA, ibid.,* ss. 39(1) & 41(1).

13   In fact, there appears to be little formal recognition of the Commissioner's role with respect to such complaints; rather, the ability to deal with such matters is largely seen as being implicit in the Commissioner's powers to assess compliance with *FIPPA* and *MFIPPA* and to make recommendations on the practices of particular institutions: *FIPPA, ibid.,* ss. 58(2)(b) & (c), and see page iv in the Addendum to the POSO Report.

14   *FIPPA, ibid.,* s. 54; *MFIPPA,* above note 4, s. 43.

15   *FIPPA, ibid.,* s. 59(b); *MFIPPA, ibid.,* s. 46(b). This order power, however, does not appear to have any enforcement mechanism. Improvement of the order powers in *FIPPA* and *MFIPPA* was one of the key elements recommended by the Commissioner in Appendix E to the Addendum to the POSO Report.

mation practices, of institutions whose activities the Commissioner has examined.[16]

The Ontario Information and Privacy Commissioner's limited powers under *FIPPA* and *MFIPPA* contrast to some extent with the powers assigned to the federal Privacy Commissioner under the *Personal Information Protection and Electronic Documents Act*.[17] Under *PIPEDA*, the federal Privacy Commissioner has fairly strong investigative powers, including the powers to summon and examine persons under oath,[18] enter and inspect premises,[19] and require the production of documents or things.[20] The federal Commissioner does not have an order-making power, however, being more like an ombudsman in that respect. While the federal Commissioner may make findings and recommendations,[21] order-making is left to the federal court, which has the power following a report from the Commissioner to order the organization to correct its information practices to comply with *PIPEDA*,[22] to publish a notice of actions taken to correct its information practices,[23] and to pay damages, including damages for "any humiliation that the complainant has suffered."[24]

The Commissioner's powers in Bill 159[25] for dealing with complaints largely mirrored the scheme of *FIPPA* and *MFIPPA*, with its limitations.[26] Under Bill 159, the Commissioner would have had powers to enter and inspect premises,[27]

---

16 *FIPPA, ibid.*, ss. 58(2)(b) & (c).
17 S.C. 2000, c. 5 [*PIPEDA*].
18 *Ibid.*, s. 12(1)(a).
19 *Ibid.*, s. 12(1)(d). The power of entry does not apply to dwellings, however.
20 *Ibid.*, ss. 12(1)(a) and (f).
21 *Ibid.*, s. 13(1)(a).
22 *Ibid.*, s. 16(a).
23 *Ibid.*, s. 16(b).
24 *Ibid.*, s. 16(c).
25 Bill 159, *An Act respecting personal health information and related matters*, 1st Sess., 37th Leg., Ontario, 2000, the short title of which was the *Personal Health Information Protection Act, 2000* [Bill 159]. See Chapter 1, Section B(5)(b) for a general discussion of Bill 159.
26 The Commissioner made this point in her submission to the Standing Committee on General Government on Bill 159, stating "this same weak oversight framework [from *FIPPA* and *MFIPPA*] is essentially being replicated in Bill 159." She stated further: "The provisions of Bill 159 are totally inadequate and fail to provide Ontarians with a robust oversight over their most sensitive personal information": Ontario, Legislative Assembly, Standing Committee on General Government, *Official Report of Debates (Hansard)*, G-828 (7 February 2001). And see Ontario Information and Privacy Commissioner, "Speaking Notes for a Presentation to the Standing Committee on General Government, Bill 159: *Personal Health Information Protection Act, 2000*" (7 February 2001) at 8 [Speaking Notes]. Online: <www.ipc.on.ca/userfiles/page_attachments/PHIPA-spk-01.pdf>.

require the production of records,[28] and summon and examine persons under oath.[29] But these powers would only have applied to complaints about the patient's right of access and correction,[30] not to complaints about a custodian's collection, use, or disclosure of personal health information or other non-compliance issues.[31] Furthermore, though the Commissioner would have had sufficient order-making powers to address access and correction matters,[32] the Commissioner's order-making powers for complaints about other matters were limited to ordering a custodian to cease collecting or dispose of records collected in contravention of the Act.[33] Not surprisingly, the Commissioner was quite critical of Bill 159's proposed approach to the Commissioner's investigation and order-making powers.[34]

PHIPA addresses these concerns by providing the Commissioner with full investigation and order-making powers for the entire range of matters that she has the power to review relating to alleged contraventions of *PHIPA*. These powers are described in more detail further below.

PHIPA also contains provisions setting out the Commissioner's general powers under the Act, including the power to

- conduct related research and public education;[35]
- receive representations from the public about the functioning of *PHIPA*;[36]
- comment on a health information custodian's information practices where requested to do so by the custodian;[37]

---

27 Bill 159, above note 25, cl. 69(4).

28 *Ibid.*, cl. 69(4)(c).

29 *Ibid.*, cl. 69(12).

30 *Ibid.*, cl. 69(1).

31 Furthermore, the Commissioner's review of such complaints would be required to be conducted in accordance with a procedure prescribed by the regulations: Bill 159, *ibid.*, cl. 68(13).

32 *Ibid.*, cls. 71(1) & (2).

33 *Ibid.*, cl. 68(14)(b).

34 See Chapter 1, Section B(5)(b), on the Commissioner's reaction to Bill 159. The lack of adequate powers for the Commissioner was one of the "major areas of concern" she identified: Ontario, Legislative Assembly, Standing Committee on General Government, *Official Report of Debates (Hansard)*, G-828 (7 February 2001), and see Ontario Information and Privacy Commissioner, Speaking Notes, above note 26 at 3–4 and 7–8.

35 *PHIPA*, ss. 66(a) & (b).

36 *Ibid.*, s. 66(c).

37 *Ibid.*, s. 66(d). Health information custodians may wish to request the Commissioner's input when faced with difficult issues in the development of information practices that comply with the Act and are reasonable. It should be noted, however, that the Commissioner is not obligated to respond to such requests. If the Commissioner does respond, he or she will have to exercise caution to do so in a manner that does not prejudice the Commissioner's ability to adjudicate future complaints fairly.

- assist in investigations conducted by the federal Privacy Commissioner or similar officer;[38] and
- authorize indirect collections of personal health information by a health information custodian.[39]

PHIPA authorizes but does not require the Commissioner to perform any or all of the functions listed above.

In addition to the general powers set out above, the Commissioner has a specific role under *PHIPA* in several matters already discussed in preceding chapters, including the following:

- reviewing and approving the privacy practices and procedures of a prescribed planning entity,[40] a health data institute,[41] or a prescribed health registry;[42]
- reviewing and approving proposals by the Minister of Health and Long-Term Care to require a health data institute to disclose personal health information to the Minister in the public interest subject to the terms, conditions, and limitations specified by the Commissioner;[43] and
- receiving registrations by archives that intend to act as recipients of personal health information from health information custodians and others under *PHIPA*.[44]

Under the amendments that *PHIPA* made to *FIPPA*,[45] the Commissioner may appoint an Assistant Commissioner for Personal Health Information, referred

---

38   *PHIPA*, s. 66(e). This section appears to allow the Commissioner to accept a delegation from the federal Privacy Commissioner or similar federal official to assist in conducting investigations relating to federal privacy matters. Thus the Commissioner and his or her office could be involved in investigating federal privacy matters. However, this power may not be of great practical value where someone complains about a privacy breach by an organization that is covered by both *PHIPA* and the federal *PIPE-DA*, since under s. 66(e) the Commissioner is not allowed to use information collected in the course of a *PHIPA* review in the context of a federal investigation. Therefore the Commissioner may not be able in a practical manner to act as the investigator conducting a single investigation on both federal and provincial aspects of the complaint.

39   *PHIPA*, s. 66(f), as contemplated by s. 36(1)(f). See further discussion of this in Chapter 8.

40   *PHIPA*, ss. 45(3) & (4). See also Chapter 11.

41   *Ibid.*, s. 47(9)(b). See also Chapter 11.

42   *General*, O. Reg. 329/04, s. 13(2) [*PHIPA* Regulation]. See also Chapter 11.

43   *PHIPA*, s. 48.

44   *Ibid.*, s. 42(3)(b) and *PHIPA* Regulation, above note 42, s. 14(1)(d). See further discussion about disclosure to archives in Chapter 10, Section O.

45   *PHIPA*, s. 81(1); *FIPPA*, above note 3, s. 4(4).

to in *PHIPA* simply as "the Assistant Commissioner,"[46] to assist in exercising the Commissioner's powers and responsibilities under *PHIPA*.[47]

2) Type of Commissioner's Review

The Commissioner has jurisdiction to conduct a review of any person's compliance with *PHIPA*, whether resulting from a complaint or initiated by the Commissioner.

a) Complaints to Commissioner

Any person may make a complaint to the Commissioner where the person has reasonable grounds to believe that another person has contravened or is about to contravene a provision of *PHIPA* or its regulations.[48] No fee is required for making a complaint to the Commissioner.[49] In the case of a complaint, it is not the Commissioner who must have reasonable grounds, but the person making the complaint, though in practice the Commissioner will have to decide if there is an appropriate basis for the review.[50]

b) Self-initiated Review

As an alternative to a complaint-initiated review, the Commissioner may commence a review on her own initiative where the Commissioner has reasonable grounds to believe that another person has contravened or is about to contravene a provision of *PHIPA* or its regulations.[51] This may be prompted by the Commissioner's reading media reports about activities that involve contraven-

---

46   *PHIPA*, s. 2, definition of "Assistant Commissioner."

47   The Commissioner has appointed Ken Anderson as the first Assistant Commissioner for Personal Health Information.

48   *PHIPA*, s. 56(1).

49   The IPC submission on Bill 159 stated: "Subsection 68(2) states that an individual who makes a complaint to the Commissioner must pay the fee prescribed by the regulations. However, it is our view that individuals should not be charged a fee for making a complaint, as this could present an unreasonable barrier to the Commissioner's processes. The charging of a fee to complain seems particularly inappropriate in cases where the individual is seeking redress for an alleged invasion of privacy." Ontario Information and Privacy Commissioner, Speaking Notes, above note 26 at 3–4 and 7–8.

50   The Commissioner also has the power under s. 57(4) to decline to conduct a review for any reason that he or she considers appropriate, including that the person complained about has already responded adequately to the complaint.

51   *PHIPA*, s. 58(1). Unlike the Commissioner's recommendation in the context of the Bill 159 hearings and the POSO Report, above note 8, *PHIPA* does not provide the Commissioner with an "audit" power; that is, the power to conduct a review where there are no reasonable grounds to believe that the subject of the review has contravened or is about to contravene *PHIPA*.

tions of the legislation, or by the Commissioner's receiving anonymous reports of violations of the Act. The Commissioner is not obligated to initiate a review, however, even if faced with clear evidence of a contravention of *PHIPA*.

c) Types of Matters That May Be Reviewed

The Commissioner's jurisdiction is broad, allowing him or her to conduct a review of virtually any type of alleged violation of *PHIPA*. Because of the extensive application of the provisions relating to recipients of personal health information from a health information custodian, and the provisions regulating the collection, use, and disclosure of the health number, the Commissioner's jurisdiction extends significantly into the Ontario private sector. The health sector is most affected because the obligations of the health sector are the primary focus of the legislation, but anyone who receives personal health information from a health information custodian, or who deals with a health number, is also covered to some extent and is therefore subject to the jurisdiction of the Commissioner. Examples of the types of matters that the Commissioner may investigate include

- a health information custodian collecting, using, or disclosing personal health information without proper authority, or otherwise breaching the Act;[52]
- a breach by an agent of a health information custodian of its obligations under the Act;[53]
- "recipients" (i.e., persons or organizations that are not health information custodians and that receive personal health information from a health information custodian) using or disclosing the information in violation of the restrictions set out in section 49;[54]

---

[52]   Authority for collections, uses, or disclosures by a health information custodian is dealt with primarily in Part IV of *PHIPA*. A custodian's contravention of any other parts of the Act (e.g., any of the "Practices to Protect Personal Health Information" set out in Part II) are also contraventions that the Commissioner may review. The Ministry of Health and Long-Term Care is a health information custodian and is also subject to the Commissioner's review and orders for any contraventions of the Act, with the exception of alleged contraventions of s. 74 (relating to public consultation before making regulations, a legislative matter, which is subject to different enforcement principles). See the discussion on this in Chapter 16.

[53]   An agent's obligations are set out mainly in s. 17 of the Act and are discussed in Chapter 2, Section B(2) and Chapter 4, Section G.

[54]   Such recipients include a wide range of possible persons, including prescribed health registries under s. 39(1)(c), prescribed entities under s. 45(1), etc., as long as they are not health information custodians: see Chapter 12. Due to *PHIPA*, s. 49(5), such recipients would not include institutions under *FIPPA* or *MFIPPA* that are not health information custodians, but the Commissioner has jurisdiction over these institutions with respect to their compliance with *FIPPA* or *MFIPPA*.

- anyone collecting, using, or disclosing a health number contrary to section 34;
- researchers breaching their confidentiality obligations;[55]
- a breach by a health data institute of its obligations;[56] and
- a breach of the special rules imposed under *PHIPA* on persons supplying electronic goods or services to health information custodians.[57]

In addition to the Commissioner's general power to review contraventions of *PHIPA*, the Commissioner also has specific powers in the Act to deal with complaints from a patient or his or her substitute decision-maker about a health information custodian's refusal to grant access to or correction of the patient's record of personal health information. The Commissioner's powers and procedural rules for complaints about access and correction refusals are slightly different from the rules and powers for other complaints under *PHIPA*.[58]

3) Commissioner's Discretion to Refuse to Review

Though the Commissioner's jurisdiction is broad, so is the Commissioner's discretion to refuse to review, or discontinue the review, of any complaint.[59] The Commissioner may do so for any reason she considers proper; by way of guidance, *PHIPA* also provides an itemized list of specific examples of reasons that the Commissioner can use in his or her discretion to refuse or discontinue a review. These reasons include the following:

- the complaint has already received an adequate response;[60]

---

55 *PHIPA*, s. 44(6).

56 *Ibid.*, s. 47. For example, a health data institute might breach its duty under s. 47(15) to disclose only de-identified information to the Minister of Health and Long-Term Care, and not to disclose any personal health information to the Minister or others without specific approval by the Commissioner under s. 48.

57 *Ibid.*, s. 10(4); *PHIPA* Regulation, above note 42, ss. 6(1) and/or (3).

58 The Commissioner's powers are set out in s. 54(8)for access requests and ss. 55(7) and (12) for correction requests. These provisions appear to overlap with the general complaint provisions under s. 56, although access and correction matters do have some special provisions that apply, such as a shorter and stricter time (six months) for making a complaint under s. 56(3), compared with the one-year period with discretion to extend it allowed under s. 56(2). Also, complaints about refusals of access and correction are not subject to the appeal provisions: s. 62(1) does not apply to orders under ss. 61(1)(a) & (b). The Commissioner has also indicated an intention to use somewhat different procedures for these different types of complaints. These provisions are discussed further in the text.

59 *PHIPA*, s. 57(4).

60 *Ibid.*, s. 57(4)(a).

- another procedure is a more appropriate forum for addressing the complaint; for example, where the custodian has an internal complaint process that the patient should try first, or where the patient has made a complaint to a professional governing body;[61]
- a delay occurred in making the complaint, of a nature that would in the circumstances of the complaint likely cause unacceptable prejudice; for example, if certain important witnesses or documents were no longer reasonably available to allow the person complained of to answer the complaint;[62]
- the complainant does not have a sufficient personal interest in the subject matter of the complaint;[63] for example, where the complaint relates to an action that primarily affects another person and that other person is reasonably able to make a complaint on his or her own behalf but does not do so; or
- the complaint was made in bad faith or was frivolous or vexatious.[64]

---

61   *PHIPA*, s. 57(4)(b). This includes the possibility that the complainant should use another process *before* coming to the Commissioner. It also includes the possibility that the complainant should use another process *instead of* coming to the Commissioner. These two possibilities can be construed from the words "initially or completely." An example may be where the complainant could pursue the matter as a complaint of professional misconduct to a College or a Board or Regents, as the case may be, about a member under a health-profession-specific Act, the *Social Work and Social Service Work Act, 1998*, S.O. 1998, c. 31, or the *Drugless Practitioners Act*, R.S.O. 1990, c. D.18, as the case may be.

62   *PHIPA*, s. 57(4)(c).

63   *Ibid.*, s. 57(4)(d). This is especially relevant since the provision allowing for a complaint, s. 56(1), does not limit complaints to those who are personally affected by the subject matter of the complaint.

64   *Ibid.*, s. 57(4)(e). The terms "frivolous or vexatious" have been used in *FIPPA* and *MFIPPA* since 1996 in relation to access requests, but are further defined by the regulations under those Acts as applying to an access request that is believed on reasonable grounds to be "part of a pattern of conduct that amounts to an abuse of the right of access or would interfere with the operations of the institution; or ... made in bad faith or for a purpose other than to obtain access": *General*, R.R.O. 1990, Reg. 460, s. 5.1, made under *FIPPA*, above note 3; *General*, R.R.O. 1990, Reg. 823, s. 5.1, made under *MFIPPA*, above note 4. These elaborations and the interpretation of them in individual cases by the Commissioner may be of limited assistance in interpreting this provision of *PHIPA*, though since the context here is the making of a complaint rather than making an access request, and since the regulations under *FIPPA* and *MFIPPA* do not apply here, these regulations and cases may not be considered entirely authoritative. See also Chapter 13, Section D(10) regarding a similar provision in the context of *PHIPA's* access provisions.
       Prior to 1996, the Commissioner exercised an implied discretion to control abuse of process, and occasionally exercised power to restrict a requester's right to make unlimited access requests, for example where the high volume of requests in a short amount of time combined with evidence that the requests were being pursued for the purpose of posing a nuisance to institutions: IPC Order M-618, London Police Services Board (18 October 1995), online: <www.ipc.on.ca>, upheld in *Riley v. Ontario*

Where the Commissioner exercises his or her discretion to refuse to review a complaint, the Commissioner is required to notify the complainant of the reasons for the refusal.[65]

4) The Preliminary Complaint Process

a) Custodian's Internal Complaints Process

As noted in Chapter 4, every health information custodian is required to make publicly available a written statement about the custodian's information practices, including a description of how to make a complaint to the custodian and how to make a complaint to the Commissioner under *PHIPA*.[66] A custodian who is successful in communicating to its patients about its internal complaints process, and in encouraging them to use that process when dissatisfied with personal health information issues being handled by the custodian, will gain an opportunity to remedy problems at an early stage, when it is easier to do so, and avoid as much as possible the prospect of external review. But where a patient is unwilling for some reason to use the custodian's internal complaints process, or where that process does not resolve the matter, a complaint to the Commissioner may result.

The Act does not require that a person access or exhaust the custodian's internal complaints process before complaining to the Commissioner. However, the Commissioner does have discretion to inquire whether the complainant has used the custodian's internal complaints process,[67] and to require that the complaint be dealt with initially through the custodian's own process before becoming the subject of a Commissioner's review.[68] This response may be appropriate

---

(*Information and Privacy Commissioner*) (1999), Toronto Doc. 59/96 (Ont. Div. Ct.), also accessible on the IPC website.

    IPC Order MO-1488, City of Vaughan (26 November 2001), online: <www.ipc.on.ca> reviews a number of Commissioner decisions interpreting the power to refuse frivolous or vexatious access requests. Factors include whether the number of requests is excessive by reasonable standards; whether the requests are overly broad and varied in scope or unusually detailed, or repetitive; whether they are being used for a nuisance value or with the intent to harass.

    IPC Order M-850, Town of Midland (24 October 1996), online: <www.ipc.on.ca> indicated that the power to refuse requests on this ground should not be exercised lightly. One can expect that the Commissioner will be slow to dismiss complaints on this ground, especially since the Commissioner has considerable discretion to refuse to investigate complaints on the other grounds set out here in s. 57(4).

65 *PHIPA*, s. 57(5).
66 *Ibid.*, s. 16(1)(d). See Chapter 4, Section E.
67 This discretion is set out in *PHIPA*, s. 57(1)(a).
68 This discretion is set out in *PHIPA*, s. 57(4)(b) and applies to all types of complaints, including complaints about a refusal to grant access or make a correction.

where the custodian has a credible and effective internal complaints procedure, and where delaying a review of the matter would not cause undue prejudice.

b)   Timeframes for Making Complaint

A complaint to the Commissioner must be in writing and must be made within one year of the time the complainant became aware, or should have become aware, of the matter in question.[69] The Commissioner has discretion to extend the one-year time limit, where appropriate, as long as the Commissioner is satisfied that the extension would "not result in any prejudice to any person."[70] Although this extension is at the discretion of the Commissioner, the standard to be met (i.e., *no* prejudice to *any* person) sets a fairly high and apparently absolute standard. It will be interesting to see if the Commissioner will interpret this provision to allow any balancing of the complainant's interest in pursuing the complaint against any prejudice that allowing the extension would cause.

Complaints about refusals of access and correction requests are subject to a time limit of six months from the time of the refusal, and the Commissioner has no discretion to extend this time limit.[71] It is arguable, however, that access and correction matters that may not fall within the scope of the sections specifically referenced in section 56(3) are subject to the one-year time limit. An example of such an issue may be where the health information custodian provides access to a record but does not provide the explanation required in section 54(1)(a), or where the custodian refused to assist the complainant in reformulating a faulty request as required under section 53(3). It may also be possible that a complaint about the refusal of a correction request could be re-framed as a complaint about contravention of the accuracy obligations set out in section 11 of *PHIPA* so as to try to take advantage of the longer time allowed for making a complaint.

c)   Preliminary Steps by Commissioner

From the time the complaint is received, the Commissioner may inform the health information custodian or other person complained about (the "respondent") of the complaint.[72] At that time, the Commissioner may seek feedback from the respondent in order to quickly assess whether a review is warranted. In addition, the respondent may try to settle or resolve the matter without

---

69   *PHIPA*, s. 56(2)(a).

70   *Ibid.*, s. 56(2)(b).

71   *Ibid.*, s. 56(3).

72   *Ibid.*, s. 57(1). It can be expected that the Commissioner will typically inform the respondent of the complaint at this stage, unless a review seems clearly not warranted, since the Commissioner's office has indicated an intention of trying to resolve as many complaints as possible at an early stage without the need for a formal review. See note 77, below.

becoming the subject of a formal review by the Commissioner. The Commissioner is not obligated to inform the respondent of the complaint, however, until the Commissioner commences a formal review.[73]

Anytime after receiving a complaint, and before launching a formal review, the Commissioner is empowered under *PHIPA* to conduct preliminary inquiries on what other means the complainant may be using or may have used to address the complaint.[74] At this stage the Commissioner may also require the respondent to try to settle the matter directly with the complainant, or to authorize a mediator to work with the parties to attempt to reach a settlement.[75] However, any information related to such settlement attempts will be considered privileged and cannot be referenced later in the context of a formal review that may be subsequently initiated by the Commissioner.[76] The Commissioner has indicated that she intends to stress the use of mediation and alternative dispute resolution methods in an attempt to resolve complaints at an early stage.[77] The Commissioner has identified the intake stage and the mediation stage as the two distinct stages of processing a complaint prior to the actual review.[78]

5) The Review Process

a) Notice Requirement

If the Commissioner decides to initiate a formal review, whether self-initiated or in response to a complaint, the Commissioner must inform the respondent.[79]

b) Procedure for Review

The Commissioner's review is conducted in accordance with the requirements and powers set out in *PHIPA*, which the Commissioner may supplement with the Commissioner's own rules of procedure.[80]

---

73 *PHIPA*, s. 57(6).

74 *Ibid.*, s. 57(1)(a).

75 *Ibid.*, ss. 57(1)(b) & (c).

76 *Ibid.*, s. 57(2).

77 In "IPC's Complaint Process under *PHIPA*," *IPC Perspectives*, 13:2 (Fall 2004) at 6, the Commission sets out its position as follows: "Where possible, the IPC prefers to resolve complaints informally, through mediation or other means. If necessary, the IPC may use its broad order-making powers to resolve the issues. Mediation is always the IPC's preferred method of resolving complaints." [*IPC Perspectives*]

78 Information and Privacy Commissioner/Ontario, *Personal Health Information Protection Act: The Role of the IPC* (21 September 2004), slides for Toronto presentation, Slide 13.

79 *PHIPA*, ss. 57(6) & 58(2).

80 *Ibid.*, s. 59(1). At the time of writing, there are no such formal rules of procedure. Watch the Commissioner's website, online: <www.ipc.on.ca> for further developments.

The Commissioner's office has outlined the processes that it will use in addressing complaints:[81]

- In the case of access and correction complaints, the complaint goes from intake screening to mediation, and then to an adjudicator to review, consider written or oral representations, and make a binding order.[82] Of course not all complaints are expected to complete this process.
- There is a somewhat more involved process for other types of complaints, which would mostly relate to the collection, use, or disclosure of personal health information. After intake screening and mediation, such complaints are assigned to an investigator who conducts a review, and seeks written representations from the parties.[83] In the course of the review, the investigator provides the parties with a draft order, on which the parties may comment. A formal order may follow.[84]

The Commissioner has posted flow charts of both of these processes on the Commissioner's website.[85]

The provisions of the *Statutory Powers Procedure Act*[86] do not apply to the review.[87] Nor does the *Ombudsman Act*[88] apply to any matter that is or could be the subject of a Commissioner's review.[89] In carrying out the review, the Commissioner may accept as evidence whatever information the Commissioner believes is relevant and is not limited to evidence that would be acceptable to a court.[90] Of

---

81   See *IPC Perspectives*, above note 77.

82   *Ibid.*

83   The fact that an "investigator" handles the matter rather than an "adjudicator" suggests that such a review may involve an investigation that goes beyond seeking representations from the parties.

84   See *IPC Perspectives*, above note 77.

85   The process for access and correction reviews is set out, online: <www.ipc.on.ca/scripts/index_.asp?action=31&P_ID=15569&N_ID=1&PT_ID=11105&U_ID=0>.The process for other reviews is set out, online: <www.ipc.on.ca/scripts/index_.asp?action=31&P_ID=15571&N_ID=1&PT_ID=11105&U_ID=0>.

86   R.S.O. 1990, c. S.22.

87   *PHIPA*, s. 59(1).

88   R.S.O. 1990, c. O.6.

89   *PHIPA*, s. 56(4). Thus, for example, complainants with issues about Ministry of Health and Long-Term Care compliance with *PHIPA* must address their complaints to the Commissioner. Most health information custodians are not subject to the *Ombudsman Act*, however, which applies only to provincial "governmental organizations": *Ombudsman Act, ibid.*, s. 1. See *Re Ombudsman and Health Disciplines Board of Ontario* (1979), 26 O.R. (2d) 105 (C.A.) for guidance on the interpretation of the term "governmental organization" in this context.

90   *PHIPA*, s. 59(2).

course, to the extent that *PHIPA* does not explicitly address any procedural matters, the Commissioner will also be bound by common law principles of procedural fairness.[91]

c)   Investigative Powers

Typically, the Commissioner can be expected to conduct reviews by simply requesting that the respondent provide information, and receiving and reviewing the information that the respondent provides.[92] However, to back up the force of such requests, the Commissioner also has full formal investigative powers under *PHIPA*.[93]

i)   Delegation of Investigative Powers

The Commissioner may delegate her investigative powers under *PHIPA* to one or more of the Commissioner's officers or employees.[94] As discussed above, the Commissioner apparently intends to have intake officers, mediators, adjudicators, and investigators processing complaints on her behalf.[95] A person exercising such delegated powers on behalf of the Commissioner is required, on request, to produce the relevant certificate of the delegation.[96] Almost always, it can be expected that investigative powers will be exercised by the Commissioner's staff members rather than by the Commissioner personally. However, certain investigative powers, specifically those relating to the Commissioner's power to allow her staff to access a person's personal health information without consent, can be exercised only by the Commissioner or Assistant Commissioner.[97] For ease of reference however, the following discussion speaks of the Commissioner exercising all investigative powers.

ii)   Power to Compel Documents, Things, and Testimony

The Commissioner has the power to compel the production of any relevant documents or things.[98] The Commissioner's demand for documents must be

---

91   *Martineau v. Matsqui Institution (No. 2)*, [1980] 1 S.C.R. 602 and see S. Blake, *Administrative Law in Canada*, 3d ed. (Toronto: Butterworths, 2001) at 12–14 [Blake].

92   This is generally the most efficient and least intrusive way for the Commissioner to function. The preference for such an approach also reflects resource issues, and the fact that the Commissioner does not have regional offices.

93   As noted above in Section B(1) of this chapter, the full powers provided under *PHIPA* contrast with the more limited investigative powers that would have been provided under Bill 159.

94   *PHIPA*, s. 67(1).

95   Section B(4)(c) below.

96   *PHIPA*, s. 60(21).

97   *Ibid.*, s. 60(14).

98   *Ibid.*, s. 60(2).

in writing and describe what is required to be produced.[99] The Commissioner may make copies of such documents on the premises that the Commissioner has entered, on paying a reasonable cost recovery fee.[100] Except for documents required for a person's current health care, the Commissioner may remove the documents from premises that the Comissioner has entered upon giving a written receipt, for the purpose of making copies or further inspecting them.[101] In inspecting documents on premises entered by the Commissioner, he or she may use the computer system there and require any necessary assistance to access and read computer-readable records.[102]

The Commissioner is also empowered to summon persons, and to require questions to be answered under oath or affirmation.[103]

A person is not allowed to obstruct the Commissioner or to provide any false or misleading information to the Commissioner.[104]

iii)   Power to Inspect Premises

In conducting a review, the Commissioner has the power to enter and inspect premises without a warrant or court order where (a) the Commissioner has reasonable grounds to believe that the respondent is using the premises for a purpose related to the subject matter of the review, and (b) the premises contain relevant records. The power to enter the premises is contingent on both conditions being met. It is apparently not enough that the premises contain a relevant record. There must also be reason to think that the premises are being used by the respondent for a purpose related to the matter under review.

This power to enter premises without a warrant does not apply where the premises are a dwelling place,[105] or where the Commissioner has reasonable grounds to believe an offence has been committed by any person,[106] including an offence under *PHIPA*.[107] In such cases a warrant will be required.[108]

---

99   *PHIPA*, s. 60(7).

100   *Ibid.*, s. 60(2)(e).

101   *Ibid.*, s. 60(9).

102   *Ibid.*, ss. 60(2)(d) and (8).

103   *Ibid.*, s. 60(12).

104   *Ibid.*, s. 60(6).

105   The general power of entry without a warrant is set out in *PHIPA*, s. 60(1). Provisions with respect to dwelling places are set out in ss. 60(3) & (4). In such a case the Commissioner may, in the case of a review under s. 57 (i.e., a complaint-driven review, as distinct from a self-initiated review under s. 58) seek a search warrant from a justice of the peace that will authorize a search of the premises.

106   *PHIPA*, s. 60(1)(c).

107   Typically the offence provisions require more than that a contravention of *PHIPA* be shown — the contravention must be wilful. See Section D below for more detail. The Commissioner apparently may enter premises to investigate such a contravention with-

iv)   *Restricted Power to Inspect Health Records without Consent*

A novel feature of the Commissioner's investigative powers in *PHIPA* is the restriction that the Commissioner may not access personal health information about any person without that person's consent, unless the Commissioner determines that it is necessary to do so and follows the procedures set out in the Act.[109] Before accessing personal health information without consent, the Commissioner must provide a statement to that effect (i.e., that her access to the information without the person's consent is reasonably necesary) to the holder of the record, together with reasons, and any restrictions or conditions that the Commissioner believes are appropriate.[110] Only the Commissioner or

---

out a warrant provided the Commissioner does not have reasonable grounds to believe that the contravention was committed wilfully, since if the Commissioner did have such grounds then he or she would have reasonable grounds to believe that an offence had been committed, and would require a warrant to enter. Where the offence does not require showing a mental element, as for instance with the offence under s. 72(1)(f) for breaching the health number provisions (so that mere contravention of the provision is considered an offence) then it would appear that the Commissioner will not be able to enter premises to investigate such contraventions without a warrant.

108   *PHIPA* does not contain specific provisions for obtaining a warrant. Where required, a warrant may be sought under s. 158 of the *Provincial Offences Act*, R.S.O. 1990, c. P.33, which allows a justice (i.e., a provincial judge or justice of the peace) to issue a warrant to allow a person named in the warrant to search premises for "anything upon or in respect of which an offence has been or is suspected to have been committed; or anything that there is reasonable ground to believe will afford evidence as to the commission of an offence." The warrant may only be issued where the justice is satisfied by information provided under oath that there are reasonable grounds to believe that such a thing is on the premises. When any item is seized under the warrant it must be returned to the court for further direction under s. 159 of that Act. Under s. 160 of that Act, a special procedure is required when seizing a document for which solicitor/client privilege is claimed.

109   Section 60(13). In the first reading version of *PHIPA*, the Commissioner was required to obtain a warrant from a justice of the peace in every case where the Commissioner sought to inspect a record of personal health information of an individual without consent. Though the Commissioner supported the Bill in most respects, this requirement was the prime focus of her critical comments on aspects of the Bill made at public hearings on Bill 31. She stated there: "No other jurisdiction in Canada or elsewhere, no other commissioner, is subject to this limitation, and I am quite frankly baffled by this requirement in the bill. ... It would cripple us in terms of our ability to conduct effective reviews and investigations." (Ontario, Legislative Assembly, Standing Committee on General Government, *Official Report of Debates (Hansard)*, (27 January 2004.) Assistant Commissioner Ken Anderson at the same committee hearing argued that allowing the Commissioner to have greater access than was proposed to personal health information would not offend the *Canadian Charter of Rights and Freedoms*, enacted as Part I of the *Constitution Act, 1982*, being Schedule B to the *Canada Act, 1982* (U.K.), 1982, c. 11 [*Charter*]. The government subsequently substantially amended the provisions to allow the Commissioner to authorize such investigations him- or herself, as described in the text.

110   *PHIPA*, s. 60(13)(b).

Assistant Commissioner may make such a determination[111] and approve the reasons to be set out in the statement.[112] This process, under which the Commissioner or Assistant Commissioner is required to issue his or her staff[113] an authorization to access personal health information without patient consent, may create an opportunity for the holder of the record to inform the patient whose personal health information is to be accessed, and enable that patient to challenge in court the Commissioner's intrusion into his or her health information, possibly on constitutional grounds.[114]

v)   Authority for Complying with Commissioner's Requirements

Where the Commissioner requires access to personal health information without the patient's consent under the provisions described above, a health information custodian subject to the Commissioner's requirement for the information can disclose it to the Commissioner without the patient's consent.[115] A non-health information custodian may disclose the personal health information in such circumstances under an exception to the recipient rules.[116]

vi)   Commissioner Not to Access Quality of Care and Quality Assurance Information

The Commissioner does not have the power, however, to require access to "quality of care information" as defined in the *Quality of Care Information Protection Act, 2004*[117] with or without patient consent. As discussed in more detail in Chapter 17,

---

111   *PHIPA*, s. 60(13)(a).

112   *Ibid.*, s. 60(14).

113   While only the Commissioner or Assistant Commissioner may make a determination under s. 60(13)(a) and approve the reasons to be set out in the statement, typically it is Commission staff and not the Commissioner or Assistant Commissioner who will conduct the actual inspection.

114   The holder of the record may also be able to challenge the intrusion in court, but the privacy interests of the holder of the information would typically be less clear and compelling than the privacy interests of the patient. See Chapter 1, Section B(3), for a brief discussion of the impact of the *Charter*, above note 109, on privacy obligations and entitlements. To the extent that a provision of any legislation or regulation is found to be inconsistent with the *Charter*, that provision would be "of no force or effect" under s. 52(1) of the *Constitution Act, 1982*, of which the *Charter* is a part. See Chapter 3, Section B(2) for more information.

115   This is under the authority of s. 43(1)(g). This provision allowing disclosure to the Commissioner and other official inspectors or investigators is "subject to the requirements and restrictions, if any, that are prescribed" by regulation, but no such requirements or restrictions have been prescribed at the time of writing.

116   *PHIPA*, s. 49(1) provides restrictions on non-health information custodians who received information from a custodian, but allows disclosures where "permitted or required by law." See Chapter 12.

117   S.O. 2004, c. 3, Sch. B [*QCIPA*].

QCIPA provides that quality of care information may not be disclosed except as permitted under that Act.[118] Furthermore, where there is a conflict between *QCIPA* and any other Act, including *PHIPA*, the terms of *QCIPA* prevail.[119] Based on these provisions it would appear that the Commissioner is not empowered to summon, examine, or have access to quality of care information. Furthermore, a health information custodian or any other person is not permitted to make quality of care information available to the Commissioner and, indeed, to do so may be considered an offence under *QCIPA*.[120] This will pose a significant limitation on the Commissioner's power to investigate certain types of issues, particularly refusals of a health information custodian to provide a patient with access to his or her personal health information on the grounds that it is quality of care information.[121]

For similar reasons, the Commissioner will not be able to require access to, or even be permitted to access, quality assurance information, which is information collected or created by a health information custodian for the purpose of complying with the requirements of a quality assurance program within the meaning of the Health Professions Procedural Code, Schedule 2 to the *Regulated Health Professions Act, 1991*.[122] There is no exception set out in the Code that would permit a disclosure of quality assurance information to the Commissioner for the purpose of investigating a complaint. The prohibition in the Code on

---

118 *Ibid.*, s. 4(1).

119 *Ibid.*, s. 2; *PHIPA*, s. 7(4).

120 *QCIPA, ibid.*, ss. 4 and 7(1).

121 As discussed above in Chapter 13, Section C(1), Part V of *PHIPA*, providing for patient access and correction of records of his or her personal health information, does not apply to quality of care information, (s. 51(1)(a)), though the patient has a right to access that part of a record of his or her personal health information that can reasonably be severed from the quality of care information (s. 51(2)). The restriction on the Commissioner's access to quality of care information may result in practical limitations on the Commissioner's ability to determine whether information that is claimed to be quality of care information indeed qualifies as such. Note that in Bill 159, cl. 68(1), the Commissioner was specifically prevented from dealing with complaints "with respect to what constitutes quality of care information." That provision was not included in *PHIPA*, but the effect of the restrictions on quality of care information may in the end have a similar effect. It is likely that ultimately the courts may develop a process for dealing with disputes about what is and is not quality of care information, and the Commissioner may be able to use that process where appropriate.

122 S.O. 1991, c. 18 [*RHPA*]. What is "quality assurance information" is discussed in more detail in Chapter 17, Secction I. Section 11(2) of *QCIPA*, amending Schedule 2 to the *RHPA*, added a new s. 83.1(4), which provides that "Despite the *Personal Health Information Protection Act, 2004*, no person shall disclose quality assurance information except as permitted by the *Regulated Health Professions Act, 1991* including this Code or an Act named in Schedule 1 to that Act or regulations or bylaws made under the *Regulated Health Professions Act, 1991* or under an Act named in Schedule 1 to that Act."

admission of quality assurance information as evidence in most proceedings also applies to proceedings of the Information and Privacy Commissioner.[123]

vii) General Limitations on Commissioner's Collection, Use, and Disclosure of Personal Health Information

Just as *PHIPA* imposes on health information custodians general limitations on their powers to collect, use, and disclose personal health information,[124] similarly the Commissioner's power to collect, use, retain, and disclose personal health information is limited under the Act to what is reasonably necessary to allow her to carry out her functions.[125] Furthermore, the Commissioner is not permitted to collect, use, or retain personal health information if other information would serve the purpose.[126] This principle may act to some extent as a constraint, though probably not an onerous one, on the Commissioner's powers.

The Commissioner's power to disclose any information coming to her in her role as Commissioner is also limited. She is not permitted to disclose any such information except where the disclosure is needed for the purpose of her exercising her functions; to a regulatory body with oversight power over a person being reviewed; or in connection with the prosecution of certain offences.[127] The Commissioner must take every reasonable precaution to conduct the proceedings so as to prevent the disclosure of any personal health information to anyone who would not be entitled to access it under the Act.[128] Such precautions may include conducting hearings that are closed to the public or receiving representations in private.[129]

d) Commissioner's Immunities

The Commissioner and her staff are immune from being compelled to provide in any "proceeding of a judicial nature" any evidence or testimony concerning

---

123 The definition of proceeding in the Code at s. 83.1 is broad and includes a proceeding before a "commission."

124 For example, *PHIPA* limits health information custodians' collections, uses, and disclosures of personal health information to what is necessary for a lawful purpose or is otherwise authorized by law: ss. 29–30. See Chapter 7.

125 *PHIPA*, s. 68(2). These provisions were also introduced subsequent to public hearings on the initial text of Bill 31 as introduced on 17 December 2003. While these provisions are unusual when compared to health privacy legislation in other jurisdictions, precedent for these provisions can be found in recent amendments to Ontario's *Auditor General Act*: S.O. 2004, c. 17, s. 28, adding s. 27.2 to the *Auditor General Act*, R.S.O. 1990, c. A-35.

126 *PHIPA*, s. 68(1).

127 *Ibid.*, s. 68(3), and see (4), (5), & (6).

128 *Ibid.*, s. 68(5).

129 A court dealing with a damages claim under s. 65 or a prosecution under the Act is obligated to take similar precautions: s. 68(5).

anything that they know from their official duties.[130] Furthermore the Commissioner and her staff are immune from any court action, or any other proceeding for damages, for any good faith acts or omissions in the course of their duties.[131]

e) The Right to Make Submissions

The Commissioner must provide any affected person, including the complainant and the respondent, with the opportunity to make written or oral[132] representations to the Commissioner about the matter being reviewed.[133] Such persons are also entitled to be represented by counsel.[134] The Commissioner has discretion to allow any person to have access to such representations, but not where doing so would reveal personal health information that is, or is claimed to be, exempt from access under *PHIPA*[135]

f) Remedial Powers

i) Orders

The Commissioner has broad powers under *PHIPA* to order a wide range of remedies.[136] After completing a review, the Commissioner may make an order:

- ordering a custodian to grant access, in the case of a complaint about the refusal or deemed refusal of an access request;[137]
- ordering a custodian to make a correction, in the case of a complaint about the refusal or deemed refusal of a correction request;[138]
- directing any person whose activities were the subject of a review to perform a duty under the Act or regulations;[139]

---

130 *PHIPA*, s. 68(6).
131 *Ibid.*, s. 69. Interestingly, the Commissioner is not held to a standard of having acted "reasonably in the circumstances" before being able to rely on the immunity, in contrast to the Act's general immunities under s. 71.
132 The multiple possible forms of the representations is suggested by the language used in s. 60(20).
133 *PHIPA*, s. 60(18).
134 *Ibid.*, s. 60(19).
135 *Ibid.*, s. 60(20), and see s. 68(5).
136 See discussion above in Section B(1), on the Commissioner's narrower order-making powers under *FIPPA*, *MFIPPA*, and Bill 159.
137 *PHIPA*, s. 61(1)(a).
138 *Ibid.*, s. 61(1)(b).
139 *Ibid.*, s. 61(c). This provision and the two that follow are notable since they apply to anyone whose activities were the subject of a review, which could be a health information custodian, an agent of a custodian (*PHIPA*, s. 17), a researcher (*PHIPA*, s. 44), a person supplying electronic goods or services to a custodian (*PHIPA*, s. 10(4)), an archive (*PHIPA*, s. 42(3)), or other recipient of personal health information from a custodian (*PHIPA*, s. 49): all of whom may have duties under the Act or the regulations, depending on the circumstances.

- directing any person whose activities were the subject of a review to cease or refrain from collecting, using, or disclosing personal health information in contravention of the Act, regulations, or an agreement[140] made under the Act;[141]
- directing any person to dispose[142] of records collected, used, or disclosed in contravention of the Act, regulations, or an agreement made under the Act, where the disposal of the record would not reasonably be expected to adversely affect the health care of any person;[143]
- directing a health information custodian whose activities were the subject of a review to change, cease, or implement a specific information practice[144] specified by the Commissioner in order to achieve compliance with the Act and its regulations;[145] and
- directing the agent of a health information custodian to take or refrain from taking a specific action, but only where the Commissioner also orders the health information custodian to take or refrain from taking that same specific action.[146]

The Commissioner can include related terms and conditions in any of the orders described above, as the Commissioner deems appropriate, to achieve the purposes of the Act.[147]

The Commissioner may rescind or vary an order, or make an additional order, at any time based on significant new facts coming to the attention of the Commissioner or a material change in circumstances.[148]

---

140   This could be a research agreement under s. 44(5), for example.

141   *PHIPA*, s. 61(1)(d).

142   The term "dispose" appears to include "destroy," so that the Commissioner could evidently make an order that such records be destroyed in appropriate circumstances. In the event that the records were not to be destroyed, the Commissioner could order that the disposal be conducted in a secure manner. Section 61(2) gives authority for such additional terms and conditions.

143   *PHIPA*, s. 61(1)(e).

144   The term "information practice" is defined very broadly in s. 2 of the Act to include any of the custodian's policies on the collection, use, or disclosure of personal health information, and the administrative, technical, and physical safeguards and practices that are used to hold and protect the information.

145   *PHIPA*, ss. 61(1)(f) & (g).

146   *Ibid.*, s. 61(1)(h).

147   *Ibid.*, s. 61(2).

148   *Ibid.*, ss. 64(1) & (2). Such a change or new order can be made even if the original order has been filed with the court for enforcement. Presumably, though, the original order may no longer be enforced at that point, at least to the extent it is inconsistent with the new order. The rules governing appeal rights, and who is entitled to a copy of the order and reasons, are the same as for original orders and are discussed below.

ii)   Comments and Recommendations

As well as making orders, the Commissioner is specifically authorized to make comments and recommendations relating to the privacy aspects of the matter being reviewed.[149] In some cases, this may be the only remedy that the Commissioner invokes.[150] In other cases, comments and recommendations may supplement one or more remedial orders of the Commissioner.

iii)   Notice of Orders, etc.

The Commissioner must provide a copy of the Commissioner's order, together with reasons for the order, or any comments and recommendations, to

- the complainant (if applicable) and the respondent;[151]
- all other persons to whom the order is directed;[152]
- the applicable body or bodies that are legally entitled to regulate or review the activities of the health information custodian involved, if any;[153] and
- any other person the Commissioner considers appropriate.

iv)   Publication of Orders, etc.

The Commissioner is authorized to provide a copy of the Commissioner's comments, recommendations, or order to, among others, "any ... person whom the Commissioner considers appropriate," which would appear to include members of the media, and may include the public generally.[154] Though the matter is not

---

149   *PHIPA*, s. 61(1)(i).

150   The Commissioner has indicated that she will use her "order-making power ... as a last resort": Commissioner's slides, above note 78, Slide 11.

151   *PHIPA*, ss. 61(3)(a) & (b).

152   *Ibid.*, s. 61(3)(c). This may include agents of the respondent, for example.

153   *Ibid.*, s. 61(3)(d). For example, if a physician is subject to an order, the Commissioner is required to provide a copy of the order to the College of Physicians and Surgeons of Ontario. Not all health information custodians have such a regulatory body, however. Where the person directed by the order is not a health information custodian, due to the operation of the rule in s. 3(3)[1] (which states that health-care-providing custodians who are agents of another custodian will not be considered a custodian under the Act) it is not clear that the Commissioner is obligated to provide the order to the person's regulatory body, though the Commissioner has discretion to do so under s. 61(3)(e), which allows the Commissioner to provide a copy of her order to any other person she considers appropriate. Further, where the custodian is an independent health facility or a nursing home, for example, the IPC would notify the Ministry of Health and Long-Term Care, which regulates such entities.

154   *PHIPA*, s. 61(3)(e). Under s. 66(b) the Commissioner is authorized to "provide information concerning the Commissioner's ... activities." On the other hand, under s. 68(3) the Commissioner and the Commissioner's staff are restricted in disclosing any information that comes to their knowledge in the course of exercising functions under the Act, except for the purpose of exercising those functions, etc.

perfectly clear, it appears that the Commissioner has the power to make public the orders, comments, and recommendations related to the Commissioner's reviews, which may, in many cases, enhance the effectiveness of the order, comment, or recommendation, as the case may be. Publicizing the Commissioner's orders may also enable others who have been impacted by the circumstances out of which the order arose to take steps to protect their interests.

The Commissioner has indicated that she will be treating her orders as "public documents" and will make them available on the Commissioner's website.[155] She has also indicated that her "investigation reports" will be made public.[156] This statement appears to refer to the fact that not just the order, but also the reasons and accompanying factual findings will be made public.

According to the Commissioner, her office is planning to "name names," in other words "publicly identifying custodians" who are the subject of an order.[157] However, she has stated that this will not be done:

- during the first year of the operation of *PHIPA* that is, for orders made before 1 November 2005;[158] or
- where identifying the custodian would reveal the identity of the complainant.[159]

6) Appeals

If the Commissioner makes an order affecting a health information custodian or any other person, that custodian or person may appeal the order to court, except in the case of orders to give a patient access to a record or to correct a patient record.[160] There is also no appeal from the Commissioner's decision not to make an order, whether the matter complained of related to access, correction, or any other issue of compliance with *PHIPA*. A person need only be

155   Information and Privacy Commissioner/Ontario, above note 78, Slide 15. The IPC website is found online: <www.ipc.com>.

156   *Ibid.*, Slide 16.

157   *Ibid.*

158   *Ibid.* Presumably the one-year grace period will apply to orders made in the first year rather than to orders made relating to complaints filed in the first year, since the latter approach would be hard to administer and would lead to inconsistent practices with the publication of orders made at the same time for complaints made at different times.

159   *Ibid.* Presumably this would nevertheless be allowed where the complainant consented to be identified, or to assume the risk of being identified.

160   *PHIPA*, ss. 62(1) and 64(4). It is interesting to note that the initial version of Bill 31 introduced on 1 December 2003, unlike earlier versions of health privacy legislation in Ontario, had no provision for appeal from any decisions of the Commissioner under the Act. Bill 159, s. 72, provided for a right of appeal on questions of law even on matters of access and correction.

"affected" by the order to have a right to appeal, which arguably does not require that the person was a party to the Commissioner's review or was named in the order.[161]

The appeal is limited to "questions of law," which means that the Commissioner's findings of fact in a given case will not be able to be challenged on appeal unless they are so unreasonable as to suggest that the Commissioner was acting outside the scope of the Commissioner's proper powers.[162] Findings of fact, as distinct from interpretations of the law, do not have force as precedents, so there is little compelling rationale to provide appeals from findings of fact, unless there was some fundamental unfairness in the process through which the findings of fact were made — in which case, it would generally be considered appealable as a question of law.

In conducting the appeal, the court is authorized to take any steps that it deems appropriate to ensure the non-disclosure of any personal health information.[163]

7) Judicial Review

While the Commissioner's orders to give a patient access to a record or to correct a patient record, and the Commissioner's decisions not to make an order in any case, are not subject to any statutory right of appeal, they can still be challenged by way of judicial review.[164] Judicial review involves asking the court to exercise its inherent power to prevent statutory powers being used in a manner that is outside the scope of the legislation.[165] A court may intervene in this way where, for example, the body exercising the statutory powers attempted to do something that it had no power to do,[166] where the body's decision was clearly

---

161 Blake, above note 91 at 147: "Some statutes state that any person 'directly affected' or 'aggrieved' by the tribunal's decision may appeal. Such a provision permits appeals by persons who were not parties before the tribunal, but can show adverse effect." See cases cited there. This may arguably allow representative organizations to pursue appeals on behalf of others.

162 *PHIPA*, ss. 62(1) and 64(4). "An appeal provision restricted to questions of law only, suggests that the legislator intended to give deference to the decisions of the tribunal": Blake, *ibid.* at 191.

163 *PHIPA*, s. 62(3).

164 In Ontario, the procedures for judicial reviews are set out in the *Judicial Review Procedure Act*, R.S.O. 1990, c. J.1 [*JRPA*].

165 *TransCanada Pipelines Ltd. v. Beardmore (Township)* (2000), 186 D.L.R. (4th) 403 at 446–48 (Ont. C.A.), leave to appeal to S.C.C. refused [2000] S.C.C.A. No. 264.

166 *Syndicat des Employés de Production du Québec et de l'Acadie v. Canada (Labour Relations Board)* (1984), 14 D.L.R. (4th) 457 at 478–80 (S.C.C.).

unreasonable (for example, not supported by evidence),[167] or where the body's process was fundamentally and manifestly unfair.[168] In a judicial review, a court is likely to show significant deference to a decision-maker like the Commissioner who will be developing expertise in the application of *PHIPA* and will be interpreting and applying a complex regulatory framework in the public interest.[169] As such it may often be difficult to challenge the Commissioner's orders on complaints about access and correction, and the Commissioner's decisions not to issue an order in a given case.[170]

8) Enforcement of Commissioner's Orders

Once a Commissioner's order becomes final, which occurs when all rights of appeal have been exhausted or have expired, the order can be filed with a court office of the Superior Court of Justice.[171] When filed it can be enforced like an order of that court, which ultimately involves allowing force or penal sanctions to bear to ensure that persons subject to the order comply with it.

9) How to Contact the Commissioner

As indicated in Chapter 1, additional information about the Information and Privacy Commissioner and the role of that office with respect to *PHIPA*, along with some basic explanatory material relating to *PHIPA*, can be found at <www.ipc.on.ca>. This website also contains much information about the Commissioner's role under *FIPPA* and *MFIPPA*, including decisions of the Commissioner under those Acts. Where *PHIPA* contains terms that are similar to those set out in *FIPPA* or *MFIPPA*, the Commissioner's decisions under the corresponding provisions in *FIPPA* and *MFIPPA* may be helpful in interpret-

---

167 *JRPA*, above note 164, s. 3(3).

168 *Bezeau v. Ontario Institute for Studies in Education* (1982), 36 O.R. (2d) 577 (Div. Ct.).

169 Blake, above note 91 at 188. This deference may be limited to matters on which the Commissioner has developed a special expertise, and may not extend to matters on which courts are considered to be equally if not more conversant; for example, questions of what constitutes solicitor/client privilege: *Ontario (Ministry of Community and Social Services) v. Ontario (Information and Privacy Commissioner)* (2004), 70 O.R. (3d) 680 (Div. Ct.).

170 Since *PHIPA* does not obligate the Commissioner to make an order in any case, even where it is clear that the Act has been contravened, it may be difficult to convince a court to intervene in the Commissioner's decision not to make an order, but it appears possible for the court to do so; for example, where the process for arriving at the decision was clearly unfair.

171 *PHIPA*, s. 63.

ing the provisions of *PHIPA*. The Commissioner has committed to publishing copies of her orders under *PHIPA* in much the same manner, and these will eventually provide a further resource for interpreting and applying the Act. The Commissioner's website also contains complaint forms and flow charts describing the processes that the office uses for processing complaints.[172]

Persons wishing to contact the Commissioner for any reason, whether to lodge a complaint or to consult the Commissioner on any matter under *PHIPA*, may contact the Commissioner or a member of her staff at 2 Bloor St. East, Suite 1400, Toronto, Ontario M4W 1A8, telephone: 416-326-3333, fax: 416-325-9195.

C. ACTION FOR DAMAGES FOR BREACH OF THE LEGISLATION

1) Background on Damages Provisions

Earlier drafts of Ontario health privacy legislation[173] contained no specific provisions providing for an award of damages in case of a breach of the legislation. Nevertheless, except where an immunity provided otherwise, persons suffering damages from privacy breaches in violation of the legislation would sometimes have been able to sue for damages based on general common law (judge-made) legal principles (e.g., based on the principle that anyone causing damage to another person through negligence or intentional conduct can be held liable to compensate the person for the damage caused, or based on breach of fiduciary duty).[174]

---

172 A flow chart outlining the access/correction complaint procedure is accessible online: <www.ipc.on.ca>. A flow chart outlining the collection, use, and disclosure complaint procedure is also accessible there.

173 Ontario, *The Draft Personal Health Information Protection Act, 1997* (Toronto: Ministry of Health, 1997) and Bill 159, above note 25. A provision for damages was first set out in the draft *Privacy of Personal Information Act, 2002*, discussed in Chapter 1, Section B(5)(d). See Ontario, *A Consultation on the Draft Privacy of Personal Information Act, 2002* (Toronto: Ministry of Consumer and Business Services, 2002), online: <www.cbs.gov.on.ca/mcbs/english/pdf/56XSMB>.

174 Whether or not a legal claim can be based on "invasion of privacy," which has been questioned absent a statutory basis, disclosures of information in breach of a fiduciary duty or in breach of a duty of care to avoid foreseeably harming certain other persons may give rise to a duty to compensate for damages so caused. See, for example, *Haskett v. Trans Union of Canada Inc.*, [2001] O.J. No 4949 (S.C.J.), reversed on other grounds (2003), 63 O.R. (3d) 577 (C.A.). The fact that damages are caused by a release of information rather than by other causes does not mean that traditional legal grounds to claim compensation will not be applicable, depending on the facts of the case and the relationship of the parties.

A possible reason for including an express damages provision in the legislation may be for the purposes of helping to achieve "substantial similarity" with the federal private sector privacy legislation, *PIPEDA*.[175] Under *PIPEDA*, following a final report of the federal Privacy Commissioner with respect to a complaint under that Act, the Federal Court is given the power on an application to "award damages to [a] complainant, including damages for any humiliation that the complainant has suffered."[176] This would not be a particularly compelling reason, however, since Industry Canada's official statement of the criteria on which it focuses in deciding the issue of substantial similarity mentions the importance of "an independent and effective oversight and redress mechanism with powers to investigate" but does not single out the availability of damages as an especially relevant factor.[177]

2) Statutory Right to Seek Compensation

Patients whose privacy rights have been infringed may in certain instances seek compensation for damages that they allege were caused by the privacy breach.

In addition to existing common law rights to seek compensation for damages, *PHIPA* creates a statutory right to seek damages "for actual harm that the person has suffered" as a result of a contravention of the Act or its regulations.[178]

Such a statutory right to claim damages requires that the defendant first be either convicted of an offence under the Act, or be subject to a final order of the Commissioner, and that any associated right of appeal with respect to the conviction or the Commissioner's order be exhausted or have expired.[179]

---

175 See Chapter 3 for a discussion of why it is important that *PHIPA* be "substantially similar" to *PIPEDA*, so that the federal Cabinet is able to make an order exempting those subject to *PHIPA* from complying with *PIPEDA* for collections, uses, and disclosures of personal health information within the province.

176 *PIPEDA*, above note 17, s. 16(c).

177 Industry Canada, Process for the Determination of "Substantially Similar" Provincial Legislation by the Governor in Council, C. Gaz. (3 August 2002), online: <http://canadagazette.gc.ca/partI/2002/20020803/html/notice-e.html#i10>.

178 *PHIPA*, s. 65(1). It remains to be seen whether and to what extent the existence of a statutory right to damages here may be interpreted as a limitation on common law rights to damages outside the statute.

179 *Ibid.*, ss. 65(1) & (2). Given these requirements, it is probably reasonable to assume that the courts will generally not be open to allowing the re-litigation of the underlying conviction or final order of the Commissioner for which appeal rights have been exhausted, absent unusual circumstances that may justify it.

3) Limitations on Statutory Right to Compensation

A breach of privacy rights (for example, by improperly transferring electronic records so that a large number of sensitive records are exposed to unauthorized persons) may cause damages to a large number of people that are difficult to evaluate (like embarrassment). With a wrong click of a mouse, the potential is there for large damages claims. It appears that the *PHIPA* damages provisions incorporate several significant limitations on damages claims that will help to protect health information custodians against difficult-to-defend open-ended damages claims:

- First, damages are only payable for "actual harm that the person has suffered" as a result of a contravention or offence.[180] The apparent intention is to exclude claims for open-ended potential future damages that may result from the contravention or offence after the court makes its award of damages.
- Second, damages for "mental anguish" are capped at $10,000[181] and are only payable at all if the court determines that the harm was caused by a contravention or offence that "the defendants engaged in willfully[182] or recklessly."[183]

4) Immunities from Damages Claims

In addition to these limitations, *PHIPA* contains immunity provisions that apply to all types of legal proceedings for damages (i.e., proceedings in which monetary compensation is sought), but not for other types of proceedings (e.g., disciplinary proceedings or reviews by the Commissioner).[184] These immunity

---

180 *PHIPA*, ss. 65(1) & (2). It is notable that in s. 65(1), the language of the section does not appear to require that the contravention on which the damages claim is based necessarily be the subject of the Commissioner's order mentioned in the section, though one might argue that this is implicit. Further in s. 65(2), the damages need only flow from "conduct that gave rise to the offence" in respect of which the conviction was made, which is arguably broader than the conduct that actually constituted the offence.

181 This apparently means $10,000 per person. The legislation does not explicitly say this, but it would likely be considered unreasonable and arbitrary to interpret it so that regardless of the number of affected parties involved in the proceeding, the $10,000 would have to be divided among them all. Such an interpretation would also cause an unnecessary pressure to manipulate proceedings as plaintiffs would seek to carry out separate proceedings and defendants would seek to consolidate proceedings.

182 See the discussion below in Section D(2)(a) about the meaning of the term "wilfully."

183 *PHIPA*, s. 65(3). This limitation mirrors the policy and language in s. 41(1)(b) of the Ontario *Human Rights Code*, R.S.O. 1990, c. H-19.

184 *PHIPA*, s. 71(1).

provisions appear to provide a shield not just against the statutory right to damages set out in the Act, as described above, but also any other action or proceeding for damages. *PHIPA* provides that an action or proceeding for damages cannot be undertaken against a health information custodian or any other person for acts or omissions, in the course of exercising powers or duties under the Act, that were both made in good faith and were reasonable in the circumstances.[185]

A further specific immunity from damages is provided for persons acting as the substitute decision-maker of a patient, provided that they were acting in good faith, reasonably in the circumstances, and in compliance with the Act.[186]

D. PROSECUTION FOR OFFENCES UNDER THE ACT

1) Offences as a Secondary Form of Enforcement under *PHIPA*

The offence provisions of *PHIPA* offer an alternative means of enforcing the obligations set out under the Act, as distinct from a Commissioner's review. Whether or not the Commissioner has reviewed allegations of a contravention of the Act, the matter can be the subject of a prosecution if it comes within the scope of the offences listed in the Act.

The Attorney General of Ontario, not the Information and Privacy Commissioner, is responsible under the Act for prosecuting offences. No person other than the Attorney General or his or her agent is authorized to commence a prosecution.[187] The Commissioner is authorized, however, to provide information about an apparent offence to the Attorney General,[188] so it is possible that a Commissioner's review could lead to a prosecution in certain circum-

---

185 For a discussion of the meaning of "reasonable," see Chapter 4, Section C.

186 *PHIPA*, s. 71(3). The addition of the requirement that the person be acting in compliance with the Act, which is not mentioned in the general immunities in s. 71(1) may in some cases make it difficult for a substitute decision-maker to rely on the immunity in subs. (3). It appears arguable that they may rely on subs. (1) also, without this limitation, though it could also be argued that since subs. (3) is specifically for substitute decision-makers, this shows that subs. (1) was not intended to apply to substitute decision-makers.

187 Under s. 72(5). As such, private prosecution of offences is not an option under this Act.

188 *PHIPA*, s. 68(3)(d).

189 The Commissioner is also authorized under s. 68(3) to disclose information necessary for the prosecution of a perjury offence related to a Commissioner's review, and to disclose whatever information the Commissioner believes is justified to a body that regulates the health information custodian that was subject to the Commissioner's attention.

stances.[189] The Attorney General can also rely on other sources of information in considering a prosecution.

It can be expected, for the following reasons, that the prosecution of offences will likely not be used often as a means of enforcing *PHIPA*:

- Though Ontario's *FIPPA* and *MFIPPA* both contain offence provisions,[190] supplementing the Commissioner's limited ability to conduct investigations and make orders under those Acts, there is evidently no reported decision on any offence ever having been prosecuted under either of those Acts.
- Furthermore, the offence provisions in *PHIPA* typically set a much higher threshold for a conviction (e.g., wilful and/or knowing contravention)[191] than the Commissioner's order-making powers, which need only be based on a finding of contravention of *PHIPA*. This threshold will make prosecutions more difficult to pursue than Commissioner reviews.
- Prosecutions do not have an enforcement official like the Commissioner who is provided with a budget directed at *PHIPA* enforcement. Rather, prosecutions are conducted by the Ontario Attorney General[192] who has responsibility for prosecutions under a wide range of provincial statutes.

2) What Are the Offences under *PHIPA*?

Not every contravention of the Act is an offence. Nevertheless, the offence provisions are quite broad.

a) Records Management Offences

A number of offences of particular interest to health information custodians are those that relate to the custodian's record management practices.

The broadest category of offence applicable to health information custodians and their agents under *PHIPA* is "wilfully" collecting, using, or disclosing personal health information in contravention of the Act or the regulations.[193] In

---

It should be noted that, as mentioned above, the Commissioner is not entitled to inspect premises without a warrant where the Commissioner has reasonable grounds to believe that an offence has been committed, including an offence under this Act, and this may affect the Commissioner's ability to obtain information about the commission of an offence under the Act.

190 *FIPPA*, above note 3, s. 61 and *MFIPPA*, above note 4, s. 48 contain a number of offence provisions similar to some of those found in *PHIPA*. Prosecutions under *FIPPA* and *MFIPPA* require the consent of the Attorney General. The maximum fine is $5,000.

191 See the discussion of the substantive offences, set out below.

192 *PHIPA*, s. 72(5).

193 *Ibid.*, s. 72(1)(a).

addition to being a contravention of the Act or regulations, the collection, use, or disclosure in question must have been "wilful." The Supreme Court of Canada has indicated that the requirement that an act be committed "wilfully" in order to constitute an offence means that a high degree of knowledge and intention must be shown in order to secure a conviction:

> The word "wilfully" [in a section of the *Criminal Code* dealing with wilfully failing or refusing to comply with a probation order] is perhaps the archetypal word to denote a *mens rea* [guilty intention] requirement. It stresses intention in relationship to the achievement of a purpose. It can be contrasted with lesser forms of guilty knowledge, such as "'negligently" or even "'recklessly." In short, the use of the word "'wilfully" denotes a legislative concern for a relatively high level of *mens rea* requiring those subject to the probation orders to have formed the intention to breach its terms and to have had that purpose in mind while doing so.[194]

On the other hand, it has been acknowledged that

> The word "wilfully" has not been uniformly interpreted and its meaning to some extent depends on the context in which it is used. Its primary meaning is "intentionally," but it is also used to mean "recklessly" .... The word "wilfully" has, however, also been held to mean no more than that the accused's act is done intentionally and not accidentally.[195]

Thus at a minimum, the word "wilfully" would require that the collection, use, or disclosure in question was conducted intentionally (e.g., was not a case of accidentally making information available to a person who should not have received it). A mistake of fact may arguably be a defence (e.g., where the accused disclosed to a person who he or she mistakenly thought was a person who would be entitled under *PHIPA* to receive the disclosure). It seems less likely, however, that the fact that the person disclosing information did not know that it was contrary to *PHIPA* would be considered a defence.[196]

---

194 *R. v. Docherty*, [1989] 2 S.C.R. 941 at 949–50. The Court in *Docherty* even went so far as to suggest that the requirement to show wilfulness in that case created an exception to the general statutory principle that ignorance of the law is not an excuse for committing an offence, but this would likely not apply beyond cases like *Docherty* where the offence of wilfully breaching parole related to the commission of another substantive offence by the accused.

195 *R. v. Buzzanga* (1979), 101 D.L.R. (3d) 488 at 498 (Ont. C.A.).

196 See above note 194. The *Provincial Offences Act*, above note 108, s. 41 provides that ignorance of the law by the person who commits the offence is not a valid excuse.

Another records management offence is disposing of a record of personal health information with the intent to evade an access request.[197] It will be important for a health information custodian to instruct its employees and other agents that disposing of a record of personal health information is not an appropriate response to a patient's access request and is, in fact, an offence under *PHIPA*.

A closely related offence prevents a custodian from disposing of information that is the subject of an access request. This offence arises where a custodian contravenes the provision requiring that, where a request for access to personal health information is made to a health information custodian, the custodian retain the requested information for as long as is necessary to allow the requestor to exhaust any recourse that he or she may have with respect to the request (i.e., until the request and any resulting appeals are completed or the time for doing so has passed).[198] "Wilfully" contravening this obligation by disposing of a record is a distinct offence under the Act.[199]

Also, whether or not an access request has been made, wilfully disposing of personal health information in a manner that is not secure or not in accordance with any prescribed standards is an offence.[200] It would likely be an offence under this provision, for example, to deliberately put paper records of personal health information out in regular garbage without first shredding them.

b)   Dishonesty Offences

A further category of offence relates primarily to persons who falsely claim to be entitled to request access or correction, or to consent with respect to personal health information. It is an offence for a person to make an assertion, knowing it to be untrue, that

- the person is entitled to consent on behalf of the individual with respect to personal health information;[201]

---

197   *PHIPA*, s. 72(1)(d).

198   *Ibid.*, s. 13(2).

199   *Ibid.*, s. 72(1)(e). Once again there appears to be some overlap between ss. 72(1)(d) & (e), as (d) relates to 13(2). There may be some uncertainty as to the meaning of the word "disposes" in this context. Given the apparent intention of the section, it would seem capable of referring to any act of putting the record outside the control and custody of the health information custodian, whether by destroying it or transferring it to another person.

200   *Ibid.*, s. 72(1)(e) combined with s. 13(1).

201   *Ibid.*, s. 72(1)(c)(i). This could be where the person impersonates the patient, or where the person falsely claims to be the substitute decision-maker of the patient.

- the person fulfils certain specific requirements of acting as a substitute decision-maker of the patient,[202] that is,
  - that the person is at least sixteen years of age or is the parent of the patient;[203]
  - that the person is not prohibited by a court order or separation agreement from having access to the patient, typically where the patient is the person's child;[204]
  - that the person is not prohibited by a court order or separation agreement from acting as a substitute decision-maker for the patient;[205]
  - that the person believes that there is no higher ranking substitute decision-maker, since in that case the higher ranking substitute decision-maker would have to be approached first;[206] or
  - that the person believes that, although there is a higher ranking substitute decision-maker, that higher ranking substitute decision-maker would not object to the person acting as substitute decision-maker instead in the circumstances.[207]
- the person is entitled to access a record of personal health information under the access provisions of *PHIPA*, which may include an assertion that the person is the substitute decision-maker of the patient to whom the record relates;[208] or

---

202 *PHIPA*, s. 72(1)(c)(ii).

203 *Ibid.*, s. 26(2)(b). Given the fact that a person must be under sixteen to be convicted as a principal party to this offence, it is not likely to be the subject of prosecutions.

204 *Ibid.*, s. 26(2)(c). If contrary to the person's assertion, the person is prohibited by the court order or separation agreement from having access to the patient, then he or she is not permitted to act as the substitute decision-maker for that patient.

205 *Ibid.* If contrary to the person's assertion, the person is prohibited by the court order or separation agreement from acting as a substitute decision-maker for the patient, then he or she is therefore not permitted to act as the substitute decision-maker.

206 *Ibid.*, s. 72(1)(c)(iii), referring to s. 26(5)(a).

207 *Ibid.*, referring to s. 26(5)(b). It may be challenging to prove that the person did not hold this belief, though it could be done by showing that the person knew or believed that the higher ranking substitute decision-maker would in fact object.

208 *Ibid.*, s. 72(1)(c)(iv). Note that clauses (b) and (c)(iv) appear to overlap for access requests, with slightly different formulations, that may capture somewhat different scenarios. It would seem that (c)(iv) would include all the scenarios under (b), but that (b), even limited in its applications to access requests only, may contain additional scenarios; for example, where the person requests the access knowing he or she is not entitled but without actually making any specific false assertion to that effect.

- the person is entitled to request correction to the record under the Act, which once again may include an assertion that the person is the substitute decision-maker of the patient to whom the record relates.[209]

c) Health Data Institute Offences

Another type of offence under *PHIPA* relates to the functioning of the health data institute. Such an institute is approved by Ontario's Minister of Health and Long-Term Care under the Act[210] as the trusted organization that receives disclosures of personal health information that are directed by the Minister from anywhere in the health sector for the purposes of analysis.[211] It is an offence for this organization to

- deviate from the privacy practices approved for the organization by the Commissioner;[212]
- disclose any personal health information to the Minister of Health and Long-Term Care or any other person at the request of the Minister;[213] and
- disclose any personal health information, or even any de-identified derivatives of the personal health information it received in its role as health data institute, to any person except the Minister of Health and Long-Term Care or another person approved by the Minister.[214]

d) Health Number Offences

A further type of offence under *PHIPA*,[215] relating to the unauthorized collection, use, and disclosure of health numbers, continues an offence provision previously found in the *Health Cards and Numbers Control Act, 1991*.[216] It is an

---

209 *PHIPA*, s. 72(1)(b). Again, this language is broad enough to include where the person requests the correction knowing he or she is not entitled to do so, but without actually making any specific false assertion that he or she is so entitled.

210 *Ibid.*, s. 47(9).

211 See Chapter 11, Section D, for a discussion of the role and obligations of a health data institute under *PHIPA*.

212 *PHIPA*, s. 72(1)(f), in reference to s. 47(15)(a). This appears to set quite a strict standard for this organization, which is perhaps not surprising given its intended functions.

213 *Ibid.*, in reference to s. 47(15)(e). Of course this would not be an offence where the disclosure was approved by the Commissioner under *PHIPA*, s. 48.

214 *Ibid.*, in reference to s. 47(15)(f).

215 *Ibid.*, in reference to ss. 34(2), (3), & (4).

216 S.O. 1991, c. 1, s. 3(1) [HCNCA]. That provision made it an offence to require the production of a person's health card or collect or use another person's health number. It appears that there are no reported cases of prosecutions under that Act. Despite the fact that this offence is not new, it is notable since everyone in the province of Ontario will be capable of committing this offence, even without particularly sinister intentions.

offence for any person who is not a health information custodian, and not acting on behalf of a custodian,[217] to collect or use any person's health number except as permitted in the exceptions under section 34(2).[218] Unlike most of the other offences described in the Act, no "wilfulness" or element of knowledge or bad intention is explicitly required. Based on judicially established principles for classifying and interpreting offence provisions, this type of offence would likely be considered a "strict liability" offence, meaning that, although it is not necessary for the prosecution to prove any bad intention in order to secure a conviction, a person accused of such an offence can avoid conviction by proving that the person took reasonable care in the circumstances not to commit the offence.[219] A collection of a health number may possibly take place quite innocently when a person receives a document that includes the health number, even though the person has not requested that the health number be provided, and may not even be aware that it is in the document.[220]

Disclosing the health number by a non-health information custodian except pursuant to an exception set out in the regulations is also an offence,

---

217 *PHIPA* Regulation, above note 42, s. 1(8). The individual whose health number it is, and the individual's substitute decision-maker, are also outside the scope of the restrictions, under this same provision.

218 The exceptions set out there include allowing collections and uses of a health number by a non-health information custodian only:

   (a) for purposes related to the provision of provincially funded health resources to that other person;

   (b) for the purposes for which a health information custodian has disclosed the number to the person;

   (c) if the person is the governing body of health care practitioners who provide provincially funded health resources and is collecting or using health numbers for purposes related to its duties or powers; or

   (d) if the person is prescribed and is collecting or using the health number, as the case may be, for purposes related to health administration, health planning, health research, or epidemiological studies.

   Note that the power to make exceptions by regulation in (d) is significantly constrained.

219 The principles of strict liability offences were discussed in detail by the Supreme Court of Canada in *R. v. Sault Ste. Marie*, [1978] 2 S.C.R. 1299 at 1325. There is an interpretive presumption that regulatory offences that do not specify a mental element are strict liability offences with a defence of due diligence available, rather than "absolute liability" offences, which require no mental element and which allow no defence of due diligence. The potentially large size of the fine for a violation tends to reinforce the presumption that an accused may rely on a defence that he or she took reasonable care in the circumstances.

220 The *PHIPA* Regulation, above note 42, contains a number of provisions, however, that create exceptions to the prohibitions set out in s. 34. For further discussion about health numbers, see Chapter 2, Section D.

and may also happen inadvertently as part of the disclosure of other information that happens to contain the health number.[221] Where a collection or disclosure of a health number takes place without the knowledge of the person making the collection or disclosure, because the health number is, unknown to the person, contained in other documents, then the person may argue that this lack of knowledge was reasonable in the circumstances, and hence did not constitute an offence. This argument could be strengthened if the person could say that he or she had checked the documents in some way first, or had received assurances from the party supplying the documents that no health number was contained in the documents.[222]

Finally, one further offence involving health numbers is for any person to require the production of an individual's health card except for the provision by the person of provincially-funded health services or goods to the individual.[223]

e) Offences Related to Commissioner Process

Several offences relate to the obligation to co-operate with the Commissioner in the exercise of his or her powers. It is an offence to wilfully obstruct the Commissioner or the Commissioner's staff members in the performance of their functions.[224] Wilfully making a false statement to mislead the Commissioner or the Commissioner's staff is also an offence,[225] as is wilfully failing to comply with an order of the Commissioner.[226]

f) "Whistleblowing" and the Offence of Retaliation

Finally, it is an offence for anyone to contravene the provision[227] that prohibits anyone from retaliating against another person for complying with *PHIPA* or

---

221   *PHIPA*, s. 72(1)(f), referring to s. 34(3). Disclosures were not covered by the offence provisions in the *HCNCA*, above note 216.

222   This suggests that it may be prudent when collecting documents to ask the person supplying the information if any health numbers may be contained in the material.

223   *PHIPA*, s. 72(1)(f), referring to s. 34(4). This type of offence also has no requirements for wilfulness, but it appears not to be difficult to avoid committing this offence inadvertently. An example of what seems to be meant to be prohibited: in 2001 the Toronto media reported about a night club requiring that prospective patrons provide as identification, and allow to be scanned, their Ontario health card (*Toronto Star* (12 November 2001) A1 and 19, B2). This appears to be prohibited under *PHIPA*, and punishable as an offence.

224   *PHIPA*, s. 72(1)(g).

225   *Ibid.*, s. 72(1)(h).

226   *Ibid.*, s. 72(1)(i). This applies also to wilfully failing to comply with the order of a person known to be acting under the authority of the Commissioner, who makes an order under the Commissioner's authority. See above Section D(2)(a) for a discussion of the meaning of the term "wilfully."

227   *Ibid.*, s. 70.

for "whistleblowing."[228] Typically, this kind of offence would be committed by an employer against an employee, but it is not limited to those circumstances. Instead, the provision prohibits anyone from dismissing, suspending, demoting, disciplining, harassing, or otherwise disadvantaging any other person for any one of a number of specific reasons. The reasons include the following:

- the person has disclosed information to the Commissioner about a contravention or anticipated contravention of the Act or its regulations;[229]
- the person has done something to prevent a contravention of the Act by someone else, or has stated an intention of doing so;[230] or
- the person has refused to do something that would contravene the Act or the regulations, or has stated an intention of doing so.[231]

In each case, however, *PHIPA* only prohibits taking negative action against the person if the person carrying out the acts described above was "acting in good faith and on the basis of reasonable belief."[232] It would be very risky for a health information custodian to rely in advance on this qualification to justify retaliating against an employee who has blown the whistle on the employer or taken another action protected by the above provisions; that is, for the custodian to argue that retaliation was not prohibited in the circumstances since the employee was not "acting in good faith and on the basis of reasonable belief."[233] However, it is possible that, after the fact, when faced with an allegation of contravening this section, particularly when it is being dealt with as an offence rather than as a Commissioner's review or action for damages,[234] the health information custodian may try to argue that the employee was not acting in good faith, or was not acting on the basis of reasonable belief. If this can be

---

228 *PHIPA*, s. 72(1)(j).

229 *Ibid.*, s. 70(a).

230 *Ibid.*, s. 70(b).

231 *Ibid.*, s. 70(c).

232 *Ibid.*, ss. 70(a), (b), & (c).

233 Given the purpose of the provision, to protect employees who whistleblow on wrongdoing or who insist on complying with the Act, it is likely that these exceptions will be read narrowly, possibly so as to apply only to cases where the employee is clearly motivated entirely by malevolence, or where the employee's whistleblowing was essentially a fabrication, or in comparable types of cases.

234 The commission of an offence must be proven in court beyond a reasonable doubt, while findings to support a Commissioner's order or a court order for damages need only be proven on the balance of probabilities (i.e., more likely than not that is what happened).

established, then there is no contravention of the non-retaliation provisions of section 70 and there is, therefore, also no offence.

3) Parties to an Offence

The person who carries out the prohibited act referred to in the offence provisions discussed above, with the intention or knowledge, if any, set out in those offence provisions, is liable for committing the offence.[235]

Under the *Provincial Offences Act*, there are a number of other less straightforward situations in which a person would be guilty of an offence, as set out below.

- A person who "does or omits to do anything for the purpose of aiding any person to commit" the offence is liable as a party to the offence.[236] This would include those knowingly assisting with or facilitating the offence.[237]
- A person who "abets any person in committing" the offence would be a party to the offence.[238] This would include anyone who instigated or encouraged another person to commit the offence.[239]
- Where two or more persons form a common intention to carry out an unlawful purpose together, both are liable for any offence that either commits in the course of carrying out the unlawful purpose where they knew or should have known that the offence was a probable consequence of carrying out the unlawful purpose.[240]
- A person who counsels or procures another to commit the offence is considered a party to that offence, if it is actually committed, and is also party to any other offence that was committed by the other that the person should have realized was a probable consequence of the counseling or procuring.[241]

---

235 *Provincial Offences Act*, above note 108, s. 77(1)(a).

236 *Ibid.*, s. 77(1)(b).

237 John P. Allen, *Defending Provincial Offences Cases in Ontario, 2003* (Toronto: Carswell, 2003) at 53. The mere failure of a person to stop or attempt to stop the commission of the offence, however, will not usually be enough on which to base a conviction (*R. v. Dunlop* (1979), 47 C.C.C. (2d) 93 at 111 (S.C.C.)), unless *PHIPA*, s. 72(3) applied, or unless the person otherwise had the authority or responsibility to stop the offence but knowingly refrained from doing so: *R. v. Halmo* (1941), 76 C.C.C. 116 (Ont. C.A.); and *R. v. Nixon* (1990), 57 C.C.C. (3d) 97 (B.C.C.A.). Note the use of the word "omits" in the *Provincial Offences Act*, above note 108, s. 77(1)(b). See K. Roach, *Criminal Law*, 3d ed. (Toronto: Irwin Law, 2004) at 129–31.

238 *Provincial Offences Act*, *ibid.*, s. 77(1)(c).

239 *R. v. Greyeyes* (1997), 116 C.C.C. (3d) 334 at 344 (S.C.C.).

240 *Provincial Offences Act*, above note 108, s. 77(2).

241 *Ibid.*, s. 78.

PHIPA also provides for the liability of board members, officers, and other agents or employees of a corporation for offences committed by the corporation in certain circumstances. Such persons may be found to be a party to an offence (i.e., guilty of an offence), where the corporation committed the offence, whether or not the corporation itself was actually charged or convicted;[242] where the person either authorized the offence or had the authority and knowledge to prevent the offence but knowingly refrained from doing so.[243] A person who is a principal, officer, agent, or employee of an operation other than a corporation may also apparently be considered to have "aided" in the commission of the offence, and hence be a party to the offence, if the person knew the type of offence that was planned and had the power and authority to prevent the offence from occurring but knowingly refrained from doing so.[244]

4) Procedures for Prosecutions

Additional provisions regarding provincial offences, including the offences set out in both *PHIPA* and *QCIPA*, are set out in the *Provincial Offences Act*. A detailed discussion of the provisions of the *Provincial Offences Act* is beyond the scope of this book. Specific legal advice and assistance should be obtained by anyone charged with an offence under either *PHIPA* or *QCIPA*. Several points from the *Provincial Offences Act* are noteworthy:

- A proceeding to prosecute an offence cannot be commenced after six months from the time the offence under *PHIPA* or *QCIPA* was alleged to have been committed.[245]
- Ignorance of the law by the person who commits the offence is not a valid excuse.[246]
- There are two procedures set out for commencing a prosecution of provincial offences other than parking infractions under the *Provincial Offences Act*. A proceeding can be commenced by a "certificate of offence," and the

---

242 The corporation itself may not be charged or convicted for various reasons. If the corporation were not convicted, it would apparently have to be demonstrated beyond a reasonable doubt that the corporation committed the offence, before the corporation's board member, officer, agent, or employee could be convicted under this provision.

243 *PHIPA*, s. 72(3).

244 See notes 236 and 237, above.

245 *Provincial Offences Act*, above note 108, s. 76(1).

246 *Ibid.*, s. 81. See discussion above regarding "wilfully," in Section D(2)(a) of this chapter, however, for a possible exception.

defendant issued with a ticket,[247] where a set fine of $500 or less has been established for the offence.[248] Given the high maximum fines set out in *PHIPA* and *QCIPA*, it seems unlikely that this process would ever be used for such offences. More likely, offences under *PHIPA* and *QCIPA* will be prosecuted under the provisions of the *Provincial Offences Act* applying to more serious offences[249] under which a sworn statement (an "information") is provided to a justice, who then must determine if there are reasonable and probable grounds for the charges, in which case a summons or arrest warrant is issued.[250] The applicable appeal rights vary with each of these two prosecution procedures.[251]

5) Penalties

If found guilty of an offence, an individual can be fined up to $50,000. A convicted corporation or defendant that is an organization can be fined up to $250,000.

---

247 The ticket is officially known as an "offence notice" or "summons." This procedure is set out in Part 1 of the *Provincial Offences Act, ibid.*

248 Ministry of the Attorney General, POA Transfer Project, *Handbook for POA Prosecutors* (Toronto, 2001) at 5.

249 Part III of the *Provincial Offences Act*, above note 108.

250 *Ibid.*, ss. 23–24.

251 *Ibid.*, ss. 116–39.

16 *PHIPA*: Regulation-making Powers

A. *PHIPA*'S SOLUTION TO THE "REGULATION PROBLEM"

As with many laws passed by the Legislature, the *Personal Health Information Protection Act, 2004*[1] includes provisions that allow the Lieutenant Governor in Council, acting on the direction of the Cabinet of the Ontario government,[2] to make regulations on certain matters connected with the Act.[3] *PHIPA*, like other Acts, was enacted by way of a bill that was approved through an elaborate public process in the Legislature, in which there were various opportunities for open debate.[4] Regulations are also laws, but rather than being made directly by the Legislature, they are made under powers delegated by the Legislature, usually to the provincial Cabinet, and sometimes, as in the case of certain regula-

---

1   S.O. 2004, c. 3, Sch. A [*PHIPA*].
2   In other words, the regulation is made by the Lieutenant Governor, but practically speaking the Cabinet has control over how the Lieutenant Governor exercises the power, including the timing and content of any regulation. For the rest of this chapter, we will speak in more informal terms of such regulations being made by Cabinet.
3   *PHIPA*, s. 73.
4   Every bill must pass through three votes of approval by the Legislature (termed first, second, and third readings of the bill), and there is a possibility of public committee hearings and consideration of the bill at least at two stages in the process. See Ontario Legislative Library, *How a Government Bill Becomes Law* (2001), online: <www.ontla.on.ca/library/billsresources/govbill.pdf>.

tion-making powers under the *Quality of Care Information Protection Act, 2004,*[5] to a specific Minister of the government. Regulations may be based on consultation with affected groups, but generally speaking there is no requirement that regulations be made public until after they are approved and are ready to come into force.

As noted in Chapter 1, a focus of the criticism of Bill 159 was the extent of its regulation-making powers. The Information and Privacy Commissioner of Ontario, for example, stated: "In almost every part of the legislation, key issues are left to be addressed in the regulations, leaving far too much to be decided at a later date in a non-public forum."[6]

On one hand, the broad scope of this complex legislation, covering not just the whole health sector but also containing provisions of broad general application, necessitates a power to make regulations so that the Act can be fine-tuned on an ongoing basis, in a manner that protects privacy appropriately without causing undue dislocations to existing processes and activities. The power to make regulations is common to a wide range of legislation and allows the government to modify a law relatively quickly as needed to respond to emerging circumstances and stakeholder concerns. It also permits the government to address certain details and technical matters that require regular updating to remain appropriate.[7] The legislative process for bills, though open to more public scrutiny, is also typically very much slower.

On the other hand, for the sake of democratic public accountability, the power of the executive branch of government to make law by regulations, outside the transparent democratic processes of the Legislature, should be kept as narrow as possible.

Perhaps due to the newness, complexity, and comprehensive scope of *PHIPA*, it was apparently not feasible to substantially limit the scope of regulation-making powers from what had been set out in past iterations of the legislation over the years.[8] *PHIPA* attempted to meet the criticisms around the broad scope of its regulation powers not so much by narrowing the scope of those powers, but rather by providing for a mandatory public consultation

---

5   S.O. 2004, c. 3, Sch. B, s. 9(2) [QCIPA].
6   Ontario Legislative Assembly, Standing Committee on General Government, *Official Report of Debates (Hansard)*, G-827 (7 February 2001) at 1400.
7   The amount of fees, for example, is often left to regulation.
8   All past drafts of Ontario's health privacy legislation as it evolved over the years, as discussed in Chapter 1, Section B(5), had broad powers to make regulations similar in scope to *PHIPA*.

process for regulations under the Act.[9] The mandatory public consultation process for regulations will allow those with an interest in *PHIPA* to have input into the content of the regulations under the Act before they are finalized and become law.

It is important that those affected by *PHIPA* understand the Act's regulation-making powers, and the process by which such regulations are made. This understanding can help enable the effective participation of affected persons by ensuring that, as much as possible, *PHIPA*, as interpreted and constrained by its regulations, appropriately reflects the needs of both stakeholders and the public.

B. OUTLINE OF *PHIPA* REGULATION-MAKING POWERS

PHIPA, in its current form, continues to contain broad regulation-making powers, including the powers for the Lieutenant Governor in Council to make regulations:

- including[10] or excluding[11] any persons or classes of persons from the category of "health information custodian" to whom the Act applies;
- including or excluding any type of information from the definition of "personal health information" in section 4(1) of the Act;[12]

---

9   *PHIPA's* mandatory consultation provisions relating to the regulations were loosely based on provisions of the *Environmental Bill of Rights, 1993*, S.O 1993, c. 28, and were subsequently substantially adopted in the *Commitment to the Future of Medicare Act, 2004*, S.O. 2004, c. 5, ss. 7 and 35.

10 *PHIPA*, s. 3(1)[8]. Note that under *PHIPA*, s. 73(1)(f), when a person is prescribed as a health information custodian under this provision, the regulation may also specify another section of the Act that will apply to such custodians in addition to the custodians that the section already explicitly applies to. For example, if a person is prescribed as a health information custodian, a regulation could provide that the person should be treated as if included in the list of types of custodians (sometimes referred to as custodians who are part of the "circle of care") set out in ss. 20(2) & (3) and 38(1) of the Act: this has been done under *General*, O. Reg. 329/04, s. 3(3) [*PHIPA* Regulation], for public health laboratories operated by the Ministry of Health and Long-Term Care.

11 *PHIPA*, s. 73(1)(c).

12 *Ibid.*, s. 73(1)(d). It should be noted that this power may not make the definition of "personal health information" entirely changeable, since the power to include or exclude from the definition only pertains to s. 4(1), and not to the entirety of s. 4; so, for instance, it cannot alter the exclusion of employee and agent information set out in s. 4(4). Section 4 of the *PHIPA* Regulation, above note 10, may be an example of this power being used.

- defining any word or expression used in the Act that has not already been defined;[13]
- specifying information practices that a health information custodian must follow,[14] including any special rules for electronic information practices;[15]
- setting requirements that apply to a health information custodian's use of employees or other agents to handle personal health information on behalf of the custodian;[16]
- setting requirements that apply to everyone (whether or not they are an agent of the health information custodian) who supplies a custodian with goods or services for the purpose of facilitating the use of electronic information;[17]
- putting additional restrictions on any collection, use, or disclosure of personal health information by any person under the Act;[18]
- creating additional exceptions to the restrictions that apply to recipients of personal health information from a health information custodian;[19]
- resolving conflicts between *PHIPA* and any other legislation;[20] and
- "respecting any matter necessary or advisable to carry out effectively the purposes of this Act."[21]

The legislation contains numerous other specific regulation-making powers,[22] but those listed above are the most significant general powers.

---

13 *PHIPA*, s. 73(1)(e). Note that where a term is otherwise defined in the Act, it may be possible to define a term or expression that is used in the definition of that previously defined term, as a way of potentially adjusting the meaning of the already-defined term.

14 *Ibid.*, ss. 73(1)(g) and 10(1). "Information practices" is defined in the Act as meaning any policy of a health information custodian for actions in relation to personal health information, including policies for the routine collection, use, disclosure, modification, retention, and disposal of personal health information, and policies about administrative, technical, and physical safeguards with respect to that information: s. 2, definition of "information practices." For more information on information practices, see Chapter 4, Section D.

15 *Ibid.*, ss. 73(1)(h) and 10(3) clarify that such regulations can include specific requirements related to electronic information.

16 *Ibid.*, ss. 73(1)(i) and 17(1)(c).

17 *Ibid.*, ss. 10(4) and 73(1)(a). Section 6 of the *PHIPA* Regulation, above note 10, appears to be largely based on the exercise of this power.

18 *Ibid.*, s. 73(1)(k).

19 *Ibid.*, ss. 49(1) and 73(1)(a).

20 *Ibid.*, ss. 7(2) and 73(1)(a).

21 *Ibid.*, s. 73(1)(p). Though this power sounds broad, powers of this type have not been interpreted broadly by the courts: J.M. Keyes, *Executive Legislation* (Toronto: Butterworths, 1992) at 193ff. See, for example, *Steve Dart Co. v. Canada (Board of Arbitration)* (1974), 46 D.L.R. (3d) 745 (F.C.T.D.)

22 Under *PHIPA*, s. 73(1)(a) there is power to make a regulation anywhere where the Act refers to something being specified by regulation, for example as in s. 7(2), or being "prescribed."

C. *PHIPA*'S MANDATORY PUBLIC CONSULTATION PROVISIONS

As discussed above, concerns about the breadth of the regulation-making powers under *PHIPA* were addressed to some extent by instituting a mandatory public consultation process on the regulations made under the Act.

Under *PHIPA*, before the Lieutenant Governor in Council makes a regulation, the Minister of Health and Long-Term Care must first publish a notice of the proposed regulation in the *Ontario Gazette*,[23] and by any other means the Minister deems appropriate,[24] allowing a minimum sixty-day period for public comment. The notice must contain:

- the text of the proposed regulation, together with a description of it,[25]
- the time period to be allowed for providing comments,[26]
- how and where to provide the comments,[27]
- a description of any other applicable opportunities to make public comment,[28]
- a statement of where and when people may view written information about the proposed regulation,[29] and
- any other information required to be provided by the regulation[30] or that the Minister considers it appropriate to provide.[31]

The Minister may shorten the consultation period,[32] or dispense with it altogether,[33] where the Minister is of the opinion that urgency requires it, or where the regulation in question is of a minor or technical nature, or merely clarifies the intention or operation of the Act or the regulations. The Minister is

---

23   *PHIPA*, s. 74(1).

24   For the first *PHIPA* regulations the Minister also provided the notice on the public website of the Ministry of Health and Long-Term Care and in the *Ontario Gazette* (3 July 2004) vol. 137-27 at 1548, online: <www.ontariogazette.gov.on.ca/mbs/Gazette/ Gazette.nsf/Main/C55931AF70373F0085256EC5006931F3/$FILE/137-27.pdf>. Consultation on the draft regulations began on 3 July 2004, and concluded on 3 September 2004.

25   *PHIPA*, s. 74(2)(a).

26   *Ibid.*, s. 74(2)(b).

27   *Ibid.*

28   *Ibid.*, s. 74(2)(c). This might, for instance, refer to public hearings to be conducted on the proposed regulation, though such hearings are not required to be held.

29   *Ibid.*, s. 74(2)(d).

30   *Ibid.*, s. 74(2)(e). This refers to previously existing regulations under *PHIPA*. Such additional information will not need to be provided until there is such a regulation, and any such regulation will first be subject to public comment under these provisions (unless the Minister decides to dispense with the consultation).

31   *Ibid.*, s. 74(2)(f).

32   *Ibid.*, s. 74(4).

33   *Ibid.*, s. 74(6).

required to give public notice any time the the Minister shortens or dispenses with the consultation.[34]

If the Minister dispenses with the Act's consultation period, the regulations would then be made in the regular manner; that is, by the Lieutenant Governor in Council (Cabinet) without a requirement for any formal consultation. Where the consultation is dispensed with specifically on the ground of urgency,[35] the resulting regulation made without public consultation must be identified as a "temporary regulation," and it automatically expires two years after it comes into force.[36] Within this two-year period, the Minister has an opportunity to conduct a consultation in accordance with the Act on a permanent regulation to replace the temporary one, with or without changes to the temporary regulation.

When the consultation takes place, the Minister is required to consider whatever comments and submissions were received on the proposed regulation.[37] When the period for public comments comes to an end, the Minister is required to report to the Lieutenant Governor in Council (Cabinet) on what, if any, changes to the proposed regulation the Minister considers appropriate.[38] This report is not required to be made public.[39]

After the Minister has provided his or her report, the Lieutenant Governor in Council may actually make the regulation. The final regulation may include any changes from the proposed regulation that the Lieutenant Governor in Council considers appropriate, whether or not the changes are mentioned in the Minister's report.[40] In other words, Cabinet has the final say in what goes into the regulation, not the Minister. It should be noted that, because of this, there is no legal obligation to consult on any new provisions included in the

---

34 Where public consultation is being dispensed with, notice is required under *PHIPA*, s. 74(7)(b) and must be published in the *Ontario Gazette* and by all other means that the Minister considers appropriate: s. 74(9). Where the period for consultation is simply being reduced, the notice of the shorter period will be part of the notice of the proposed regulation under s. 74(1)(a), though it does not explicitly require that the Minister specify the ground for shortening the period of consultation.

35 Under *PHIPA*, s. 74(6)(a).

36 *Ibid.*, s. 74(10). No such provisions apply where the consultation is dispensed with on grounds other than urgency or where the consultation period is merely shortened rather than being altogether dispensed with.

37 *Ibid.*, s. 74(1)(d). The Minister is not required to consider submissions that were not received within the consultation period, but may do so if the Minister is able.

38 *Ibid.*

39 In fact, it appears that s. 12 of the *Freedom of Information and Protection of Privacy Act*, R.S.O. 1990, c. F.31 requires that it be kept confidential, as a Cabinet record, unless Cabinet decides otherwise.

40 *PHIPA*, s. 74(5).

regulation that were not part of the proposed regulation that was the subject of consultation. Such new provisions may be extensive in some cases.[41]

In cases where it is alleged that the Minister or Lieutenant Governor in Council has in some way contravened the mandatory consultation provisions,[42] there is very limited legal recourse available. Both the courts and the Commissioner are expressly prohibited from reviewing acts, omissions, or decisions of the Minister or Lieutenant Governor in Council with respect to public consultation on regulations.[43] This prohibition is subject to the qualification that a person does have a right to apply to court for judicial review where the Minster has not taken a step required by these provisions,[44] provided that the application is made within the timeframes set out in *PHIPA*.[45]

D. *QCIPA*'S MANDATORY PUBLIC CONSULTATION PROVISIONS

In *QCIPA* there is a substantially identical requirement for public consultation on regulations.[46] The main differences between the *PHIPA* and the *QCIPA* regulations provisions are as follows:

---

41 Where the Lieutenant Governor in Council determines that it is appropriate in the circumstances, perhaps based on submissions received during the consultation, any or all of the content of the proposed regulation can be replaced, without any legal requirement for a new consultation. It appears that the Legislature intended that there only be political and not legal accountability for proceeding in this manner.

42 *PHIPA*, s. 74.

43 *Ibid.*, s. 74(11).

44 *Ibid.*, s. 74(12). This provision, which resembles s. 118 of the *Environmental Bill of Rights, 1993*, S.O 1993, c. 28, was added to *PHIPA* following second reading of Bill 31, *An Act to enact and amend various Acts with respect to the protection of health information*, 1st Sess., 38th Leg., Ontario, 2003, apparently in response to criticism of the lack of such a provision by MPP Shelley Martel during the proceedings of the Standing Committee on General Government on 26 January 2004 and then again on 9 February 2004. It should be noted that for constitutional reasons a statute is not capable of entirely ousting the right to apply to a court for judicial review, so the addition of this provision may not add much of substance. Courts can be expected to exercise their powers to judicially review legislative functions quite sparingly, unless there is a clear and fundamental breach of procedural requirements.

45 Under *PHIPA*, s. 74(13) the application for judicial review must be made within twenty-one days of the *Ontario Gazette's* publication of the Minister's notice of the proposed regulation or the Minister's notice of dispensing with the consultation. Under s. 5 of the *Judicial Review Procedure Act*, R.S.O. 1990, c. J.1, however, despite this time limit in *PHIPA* (and *QCIPA*), "the court may extend the time for making the application, either before or after expiration of the time so limited, on such terms as it considers proper, where it is satisfied that there are apparent grounds for relief and that no substantial prejudice or hardship will result to any person affected by reason of the delay."

46 *QCIPA*, above note 5, s. 10.

- due to the brevity of *QCIPA*, the regulation powers are much less lengthy, though they can also quite significantly affect the scope of that Act;[47] and
- in *QCIPA* some of the regulation-making powers are given to the Minister of Health and Long-Term Care and not to the Lieutenant Governor in Council,[48] and the requirement for public consultation does not apply to the Minister's regulations.[49]

E. WHEN DOES REGULATION COME INTO FORCE?

Unless otherwise specified in the regulation, a regulation made under either *PHIPA* or *QCIPA* comes into force when the Ministry of Health and Long-Term Care files it with the Registrar of Regulations.[50] A regulation is published in the *Ontario Gazette* about three weeks after it is filed.[51] Until a regulation is published, it is not effective against a person who has not had actual notice of the regulation.[52]

F. WHAT THE PROCESS MEANS TO THOSE AFFECTED

Given the complexity of the legislation, especially *PHIPA* (but also *QCIPA* to a somewhat lesser degree), it can be expected that there will be a fairly regular ongoing need to amend or create new regulations. Those affected by either or both of these Acts should keep in mind the powers set out in the regulations that might be able to address any difficulties related to the legislation, and they should watch for periodic public consultations on regulations either as a way of putting forward proposed regulations to address any such apparent difficulties, or as a means of participating in the regulation-making process to ensure that regulations are drafted in such a way as to enhance, or at least not unduly interfere with, "the effective provision of health care," the facilitation of which is a prime purpose of *PHIPA*.[53] Some practical tips for effectively participating in the regulation-making process under *PHIPA* and *QCIPA* are set out below.

---

47 See Chapter 17, Section H.

48 *Ibid.*

49 *QCIPA*, s. 10(1) refers only to the Lieutenant Governor in Council. As a matter of practice though, the Ministry of Health and Long-Term Care's first consultation on draft regulations under Bill 31, above note 44, included draft Minister's regulations as well as draft Lieutenant Governor in Council regulations in the consultation. This was apparently not legally required, however, under *QCIPA*.

50 *Regulations Act*, R.S.O. 1990, c. R.21, s. 3.

51 *Ibid.*, s. 5(1). The *Ontario Gazette* is published weekly on Saturdays.

52 *Ibid.*, s. 5(3).

53 As set out in *PHIPA*, s. 1(a).

G. TEN PRACTICAL TIPS FOR PARTICIPATING EFFECTIVELY IN THE REGULATION-MAKING PROCESS

1. Don't wait to be asked. If you know of a need that should be addressed by the regulations, let the Ministry of Health and Long-Term Care (Ministry) know about it, so that your proposed regulation may potentially be part of any draft regulation published for consultation.

2. Keep an eye out for draft regulations in the *Ontario Gazette* or published on the health care provider's health information privacy page of the Ministry's website.[54] If it is not practical to keep track of developments yourself, make sure that your professional or institutional organizations do so.

3. Read the proposed regulations carefully, including any explanatory material provided by the Ministry and your professional or institutional organizations.

4. Determine if any changes should be made to the proposed regulations. At the same time, if you want a provision of the proposed regulations to be passed without changes, consider communicating your support for the provision, describing why it is appropriate.

5. Co-ordinate your possible response with others who may be similarly situated.

6. If changes to the draft regulations appear to be needed, communicate with the Ministry as early as possible. It will likely be advantageous to provide a response, even if it has to be in draft form, to the Ministry well before the deadline for making submissions. Keep in mind that formal governmental decision-making processes may take significant time, and that numerous submissions may require consideration.

7. Be clear about describing any problems you see, giving concrete examples where possible.

8. Be specific about proposing a solution.

9. Where possible propose several options for fixing the problem, identifying a preferred option where applicable. Think it through, and try to address possible objections.

10. Consider inquiring whether the Ministry has any additional information relevant to your issues, or possible concerns about the approach you are thinking of suggesting, so that you can tailor your submission to be as persuasive as possible.

---

54   See <www.health.gov.on.ca>. When using the Ministry website, be sure to access the information designated for "health care providers" as it is more extensive (based on current practice) than information provided for a broader audience.

17 Quality of Care Information Protection

A. BACKGROUND

1) What Is *QCIPA*?

As mentioned in Chapter 1, Bill 31 enacted two free-standing pieces of legislation: the *Personal Health Information Protection Act, 2004*[1] and the *Quality of Care Information Protection Act, 2004*,[2] the latter being the subject of this chapter.

Since *QCIPA* came into force on 1 November 2004,[3] Ontario for the first time has a broad legislative framework under which activities to improve the quality of health care are effectively encouraged by ensuring that the information provided or generated by health care professionals in the course of such activities[4] will be shielded from disclosures in proceedings and beyond, subject to specific limitations and exceptions.

---

1 S.O. 2004, c. 3, Sch. A [*PHIPA*].
2 S.O. 2004, c. 3, Sch. B [*QCIPA*].
3 Under *QCIPA*, *ibid.*, s. 12, all the substantive provisions of *QCIPA* came into force on 1 November 2004. *PHIPA* came into force at the same time. As with *PHIPA*, the provisions requiring public consultation on the regulations came into effect from the time of Royal Assent, 20 May 2004, to allow the consultation process for the regulations to be conducted, in order to be able to have regulations ready when the substantive provisions of the Act came into force.
4 The term "health care practitioner" is not used here since it is not a defined term in *QCIPA*, but rather in *PHIPA*.

2) Rationale for Quality of Care Information Protection

"To err is human," and there is no exception to this principle in the health care system. Recently published material has emphasized that errors in the delivery of health care, often with serious consequences, may be more common than many people would have suspected. A recent well-publicized Canadian study found that adverse events (unintended injuries and complications) arose in 7.5 percent of Canadian hospital admissions.[5] The study found that 37 percent of these adverse events were preventable and over 20 percent of the adverse events resulted in death, causing about 37,000 deaths per year.[6] And, of course, even in more typical cases where there is no "error" or adverse event, improvements in the quality of health care being provided can be expected to lead to better outcomes.

Once an error has occurred in the provision of health care, it is not always possible to reverse the effects of the error in the individual case. What is often possible, however, is to try to fix the problem that caused the error to occur in the first place, so the likelihood of further errors can be reduced, thus improving the future quality of care of other patients. To do this, it is necessary to accurately identify all the conditions that contributed to the error occurring. A crucial challenge here is that the conditions and factors that led to the error are often known only by the health professionals who were involved in the error. Yet they may be reluctant to divulge this information for fear that it will be used against them.

Although the effects of an error made in the delivery of health care may not be reversible, it may be possible and legally and morally appropriate to have the party at fault compensate the party who experienced the adverse effect, or that person's estate or dependents. The fact that substantial compensation may be at stake, combined with the fact that fault and causation are often disputed gray areas, makes the issue of shielding quality of care information one that requires a fine policy balance. Enough information must be shielded to encourage participation in quality of care reviews, while not shielding information where doing so would interfere with a patient's existing right to seek compensation through litigation for the adverse effects of medical errors in appropriate cases.

Health Minister George Smitherman described the purposes of *QCIPA* as follows:

---

5   Baker *et al.*, "The Canadian Adverse Effects Study: The Incidence of Adverse Events Among Hospital Patients in Canada," (2004) 170: 11 CMAJ 1678.

6   *Ibid.*

The ... government is particularly aware of the need to encourage health professionals to share information and hold open discussions that can lead to improved patient care and safety. That's why Bill 31 has been drafted with protections for quality-of-care information generated by hospital committees that deal with quality improvement.

When a medical error occurs in a hospital or other health care setting, open disclosure and discussion of the facts surrounding the incident are absolutely critical. Without this, the institution will not be able to analyze the root cause or gaps that led to the incident and frankly to direct appropriate measures to make sure it doesn't happen again. ...

This legal protection for quality-of-care information is available only if the facts of a medical incident are recorded in the patient's file. The information provided to the quality-of-care committee and the opinions of committee members would be shielded from disclosure in legal proceedings as well as most other disclosures outside the hospital. In this way, we have carefully balanced the need to promote quality care with the need to ensure accountability.[7]

3) Recommendations for Quality of Care Information Protection

Quality of care information protection has been recommended over the years in the course of significant reviews of the health care system. Two examples are particularly noteworthy in the development of *QCIPA*.

In 1990, University of Toronto President Robert Prichard[8] presented a report that became known as "the Prichard Report."[9] In the report Prichard, with the support of a distinguished advisory committee representing health, legal, and government sectors, recommended to Canada's federal, provincial, and territorial deputy ministers of health "that a broad evidentiary protection be extended to safeguard health care institutions and health care professionals against the use of the results of their post-incident inquiries in personal injury claims in order to encourage the widest and most vigorous possible pursuit of these matters," and that "this privilege in civil litigation should extend to the results of quality assurance, risk management, and peer review processes."[10]

---

7   Ontario, Legislative Assembly, Standing Committee on General Government, *Official Report of Debates (Hansard)*, G-7–G-8 (26 January 2004) at 1020.
8   Formerly Dean of the University of Toronto Faculty of Law.
9   *Liability and Compensation in Health Care, A Report to the Conference of Deputy Ministers of Health of the Federal/Provincial/Territorial Review on Liability and Compensation Issues in Health Care* (Toronto: University of Toronto Press, 1990) [Prichard Report].

He identified the issue of such privilege as "the most prominent legal issue" with respect to efforts to increase the implementation and effectiveness of quality of care improvement processes.[11] After reviewing the need to balance the competing objectives of promoting effective quality of care reviews and of allowing injured parties to access the information they need to secure compensation, Prichard concluded that "given the central importance of injury avoidance" it is appropriate to promote quality assurance and peer review initiatives by instituting an evidentiary privilege, but that the privilege should be designed to interfere as little as possible with "the access to justice interests of individual patients."[12]

Two years later, the Steering Committee of the *Public Hospitals Act* Review, commissioned in 1989 by Ontario Health Minister Elinor Caplan, presented its report to a subsequent Ontario Health Minister, Frances Lankin.[13] The report included three significant recommendations concerning the protection of quality of care information:

- that a legislative privilege be instituted "mak[ing] all records and proceedings of a hospital's Quality Improvement Committee, including analyses and reports prepared for the committee and statements made at committee meetings [not including patient records[14]], inadmissible in legal proceedings";[15]
- that persons participating in such reviews be granted immunity from testifying about "any aspect of the quality improvement activities of these committees"[16] and from any associated liability for good-faith involvement in the committee's activities;[17] and
- that all proceedings and records of quality improvement activities undertaken by or for the Quality Improvement Committee be treated as confidential and not used in investigations, credentialing, or disciplinary actions.[18]

---

10   *Ibid.* at 27, Recommendation 38.

11   *Ibid.*, Appendix A, Health Care Liability and Compensation Review Working Paper at 339.

12   *Ibid.*, Appendix A, Health Care Liability and Compensation Review Working Paper at 342.

13   *Into the 21st Century: Ontario Public Hospitals, Report of the Steering Committee, Public Hospitals Act Review* (Toronto: Ontario Ministry of Health, 1992) at 139.

14   *Ibid.* at 139.

15   *Ibid.*, Recommendation 8.05 at 139.

16   *Ibid.*, Recommendation 8.06 at 139.

17   *Ibid.*, Recommendation 8.07 at 140.

18   *Ibid.*, Recommendation 8.08 at 140.

4) Quality of Care Information Protection in Other Contexts

Past versions of Ontario privacy legislation in draft or bill form have also contained such provisions.[19]

All other provinces have instituted legislation that shields the information divulged by health professionals involved in discussions about improving patient care from disclosure in legal proceedings. Generally speaking, the protections only apply to disclosures in proceedings, and they are typically found in each province's *Evidence Act*, but there are a variety of different types of provisions across the country.[20]

---

19   The protections first appeared in legislative form in Ontario in s. 18 of the draft *Personal Health Information Privacy Act, 1997*, a Draft discussed in Chapter 1 that was published for public consultation in the fall of 1997. The 1997 Draft Legislation provided briefly that "quality improvement information is not admissible in evidence in an inquest or a civil proceeding in a court" and is not compellable. This shielded information, other than a patient record, produced by or for a quality improvement committee of a regulated health profession, a hospital, or other prescribed health facility. "Quality improvement activities" included a "quality assurance program undertaken by a College within the meaning of the *Regulated Health Professions Act, 1991*, S.O. 1991, c. 18 [*RHPA*], a peer review, a utilization review, an outcome review or a medical or other professional audit." Disclosures outside of proceedings were not addressed.

Ontario's Bill 159, *An Act respecting personal health information and related matters*, 1st Sess., 37th Leg., Ontario, 2000 (*Personal Health Information Protection Act, 2000*) [Bill 159] contained similar provisions on quality of care information in Part VII of that Bill, though as with the 1997 Draft Legislation the provisions there did not restrict disclosures outside the context of proceedings. Further, Bill 159 did not address the quality improvement activities covered under the quality assurance program undertaken by an *RHPA* College, as amendments to provide such a shield had been made to the Regulated Health Professions Code, Schedule 2 of the *RHPA*, that same year.

As noted in Chapter 1, Section B(5)(d), in 2002 the Ontario Ministry of Consumer and Business Services conducted a public consultation of draft private sector privacy legislation, the draft *Privacy of Personal Information Act, 2002*. For the first time, this legislation put forward the quality of care information protections as a separate Act, with the same title as the current Act, *QCIPA*, (to have been enacted as a schedule attached to the bill containing the privacy legislation). The provisions of this draft legislation were very similar to *QCIPA* as it is today. Disclosures outside proceedings were to be regulated, though the exclusions to what counted as quality of care information were not as extensive as in today's *QCIPA*.

20   Other Canadian jurisdictions provide legislative protections of some kind for at least some types of quality of care information. Highlights are as follows:
- In Alberta information on "quality assurance activities" carried out by hospitals, nursing homes, etc., as health services and health care providers is protected from disclosure in proceedings. Original patient records are not covered: *Alberta Evidence Act*, R.S.A. 2000, c. A-18, s. 9.
- British Columbia has among the most comprehensive provisions in Canada other than Ontario, though the provisions are primarily focused on hospitals. Informa-

5) Legal Privilege

To the extent that such legislative provisions do not exist or are not applicable, it may be possible in certain circumstances to rely on legal privilege as a means of shielding information, generated in the course of activities to improve the quality of care, from being disclosed in a legal proceeding.[21] A legal privilege is a judicially recognized exception to the general rule that all relevant information may be required to be produced in a legal proceeding.[22]

---

tion associated with specified committees are shielded from disclosure in proceedings (not including professional competence proceedings). Like *QCIPA*, the B.C. provisions, though contained in that province's *Evidence Act*, R.S.B.C. 1996, c. 124, s. 51, also regulate disclosures beyond proceedings.

- The Manitoba provisions are similar to Nova Scotia, as set out below: *Evidence Act*, C.C.S.M., c. E.150, s. 9.
- In New Brunswick, the protection is limited to hospitals but goes beyond committees, and protects all information for the dominant purpose of medical education or improving medical/hospital care or practice, including opinions provided about critical incidents. Patient and required hospital records are excluded. Privilege review functions of a medical advisory committee are excluded: *Evidence Act*, s. 43.3: R.S.N.B. 1973, c. E-11, as amended by S.N.B. 1987, c. 19, s. 1 and 1999, c. 38, s. 1.
- In Newfoundland and Labrador, information associated with specified committees including a provincial perinatal committee, and hospital and nursing home quality assurance and peer review committees is shielded from disclosures in legal proceedings. Original patient records are not covered: *Evidence Act*, R.S.N.L. 1990, c. E.16, s. 8.1.
- In Nova Scotia, information from specified hospital committees, or other Minister-approved committees, relating to education or improving medical or hospital care or practice is shielded from disclosures in a proceeding. Original patient records are not covered: *Evidence Act*, R.S.N.S. 1989, c. 154, s. 60.
- In Prince Edward Island, only peer assessments are covered: *Medical Act*, R.S.P.E.I. 1988, c. M.5, s. 38.7.
- Quebec requires health care institutions to establish a risk and quality management committee that is responsible for identifying risks, and for analyzing the cause of incidents and accidents so as to recommend preventative measures. Information provided to such a committee in the course of its functions is not admissible in a proceeding, and the minutes of such a committee are confidential. See *An Act respecting Health Services and Social Services*, R.S.Q., c. S-4.2, ss. 183.1–183.4.
- In Saskatchewan, information from hospital "quality assurance committees" is protected, with exclusions similar to those contained in *QCIPA* (e.g. for facts, patient care records, and legally required records): *Saskatchewan Evidence Act*, R.S.S. 1978, c. S-16, s. 35, as amended by S.S. 1989–90, c. 57, s. 3.

21 The concept of legal privilege is complex, and it is beyond the scope of this work to go beyond a cursory general description. If a significant issue of legal privilege arises, it will generally be necessary to seek legal guidance.

22 *Dictionary of Canadian Law*, 3d. ed. (Toronto: Carswell, 2004) at 994.

The best known type of legal privilege is solicitor/client privilege, which entitles a person to refuse to disclose information about communications to or from a lawyer for the purpose of receiving legal assistance. If a lawyer is not involved, however, this type of privilege would generally not apply. Another type of privilege is litigation privilege, under which a person who prepares a document in anticipation of litigation may refuse to disclose it. This type of privilege may not apply to a document, however, until the prospect of litigation for a matter becomes an operative factor. Where applicable, these types of privilege, particularly solicitor/client privilege, can provide some certainty about the shielding of information. However, these types of privilege will not apply to a broad range of quality of care improvement activities.

At common law, courts have also developed a type of privilege that may shield information from disclosure where the information was prepared with an expectation of confidentiality, and the court determines that it is appropriate in the circumstances to shield the information from disclosure.[23] However, such protections are only applied by the court after the fact on a case-by-case basis.[24] The case-by-case nature of this type of privilege makes it incapable of providing the optimum confidence to participants in quality of care improvement efforts that the information they provide will be shielded from disclosure.

Despite the limited role that judicially established legal privileges can play in the context of shielding information concerning quality of care improvement processes from disclosure in proceedings, such privileges may continue to play a role in circumstances where for one reason or another *QCIPA* does not apply. For example, where no properly designated quality of care committee is involved, information provided by a health care provider for the purposes of improving quality of care may still be shielded from disclosure in a proceeding

---

23   For example see *Steep (Litigation Guardian of) v. Scott* (2002), 62 O.R. (3d) 173 (S.C.J.) in which quality assurance reports and peer review evaluations undertaken after events of alleged malpractice were held to be privileged under the common law, in accordance with the "Wigmore test" adopted by the Supreme Court of Canada in *Slavutych v. Baker*, [1976] 1 S.C.R. 254. The four required criteria for such privilege to apply are that (1) the communications in question originated with an expectation of confidentiality, (2) the confidentiality was essential to the task at hand, (3) the task requiring the confidential communication was an essential task from the point of view of the public interest, and (4) the damage in disclosing such information would be greater than the damage in maintaining the information as privileged.

24   This type of privilege has been described as "case-by-case privilege," since information is presumed not privileged until the four-step analysis adopted in *Slavutych v. Baker*, referred to in the previous note, is conducted and shows that the privilege is required in the circumstances: *R. v. Gruenke*, [1991] 3 S.C.R. 263.

if it is covered by one of the types of privilege mentioned above. A detailed discussion of such privileges is beyond the scope of this work, however.

B. THE RELATIONSHIP OF *QCIPA* AND *PHIPA*

Since *PHIPA* and *QCIPA* were enacted in the same Ontario bill, and have a history of mutual development, it is not surprising that their relationship to each other is confused. It is important to remember that *PHIPA* and *QCIPA* are quite distinct statutes, though they overlap to some degree.

PHIPA is about protecting patient privacy in a manner consistent with the effective provision of health care. *QCIPA*, on the other hand, is about fostering frank discussions about the provision of health care among health care professionals to determine what may have gone wrong and how quality of care can be improved or maintained in a facility. *QCIPA* achieves this goal by shielding information given to a quality of care committee for these purposes from being disclosed in legal proceedings or outside the organization to which it relates.[25]

To understand this distinction in practice, it is important to understand the difference between personal health information and quality of care information.

Personal health information is identifiable information about a patient, generally relating in some way to the patient's health or health care. (See Chapter 2, Section C for full details of the definition of personal health information.) *PHIPA* protects personal health information.

In contrast, *QCIPA* protects quality of care information. Quality of care information is not necessarily personal health information or even personal information, though it is clear that quality of care information may include personal health information. Subject to some specific exceptions, quality of care information, whether or not it identifies any individual, is information that is collected by or prepared for a quality of care committee for the sole or primary purpose of assisting the committee in carrying out its functions, or that relates solely or primarily to any activity that a quality of care committee carries on as part of its functions. This term covers anonymous statistical information collected by such a committee. The concept of quality of care information is discussed in greater detail below in Section D. To understand what quality of care information includes, it is first necessary to understand what a quality of care committee is.

---

25   The precise nature of the restrictions on disclosure will be reviewed at length below. See the statement of the Health Minister quoted in Section A(2) above.

C. QUALITY OF CARE COMMITTEES

1) What Is a Quality of Care Committee?

The concept of a "quality of care committee"[26] is key to the operation of *QCIPA*, since without a quality of care committee in place none of the protections provided by the Act apply. To put it another way, without a quality of care committee there is no quality of care information. If information is discussed without any connection to a quality of care committee, even for the purposes of improving the quality of care, the protections provided in *QCIPA* will not apply.[27]

To be a quality of care committee, the committee must meet several criteria set out in the definition of quality of care committee.[28]

First and foremost, a committee can only be a quality of care committee if it has a quality of care function. The way this requirement is stated in the Act is that a function of the committee must be "to carry on activities for the purpose of studying, assessing or evaluating the provision of health care with a view to improving or maintaining the quality of the health care or the level of skill, knowledge and competence of the persons who provide the health care."[29] This provision includes a very broad range of functions.[30]

It is notable that the quality of care functions of the committee need not be the committee's sole or primary functions.[31] The committee is treated as a quality of care committee only for its quality of care functions, however. A multi-purpose committee will receive quality of care protection only for its quality of care

---

26 In the discussion that follows, we often refer to this kind of committee simply as "a committee."

27 As noted above in Section A(5), in such cases the common law privilege may apply depending on the circumstances. "Quality of care information" is not limited, however, to information produced by or discussed by a quality of care committee. Information that is prepared for a quality of care committee is also quality of care information, as discussed in more detail below.

28 *QCIPA*, above note 2, s. 1.

29 *Ibid.*, s. 1, clause (c) of definition of "quality of care committee."

30 This description of quality of care functions appears to include all the matters covered in the definition of quality of care "committee" in cl. 40 of Bill 159 (*PHIPA*, 2000), except that the definition there was more detailed, for example, explicitly referring to the education of health care providers as a quality of care purpose. The definition there concluded with the clarification that quality of care purpose includes "quality assurance, error and risk management, peer review, ethics review, utilization review, outcome review or a medical or other professional audit." The description in *QCIPA* seems general enough to cover all these functions without having to explicitly list them, and possibly risk unintentionally excluding certain types of quality of care review that are not in the list.

functions, not for the other functions it carries out. The *QCIPA* General Regulation,[32] which provides in effect that only information related to the quality of care functions of the committee will receive protection as quality of care information, necessitates this interpretation.

Second, the committee must meet the prescribed requirements.[33] Under the regulations, there are two such requirements.

- The first requirement under the regulations is that the quality of care committee must first be formally designated in writing as a quality of care committee by the organization that is establishing the committee or that is approving it to perform quality of care functions.[34] A formal designation must be made before any of the information relating to the committee in question will be subject to the protections under the Act. If there is no formal designation in place, then the Act will not apply. Once a formal designation is made, however, information that was previously held by the committee (before its formal designation) for quality of care purposes may be disclosed to the committee in its new formal role as quality of care committee pursuant to section 3, and would then arguably be subject to the protections in *QCIPA*, provided that the information is of continuing relevance to the ongoing quality of care functions of the committee.[35] This suggests that when establishing a quality of care committee, one should ensure that

---

31 The provision in the draft Minister's regulation, "Notice of Minister of Health and Long-Term Care, Notice of Proposed Regulations," *Personal Health Information Protection Act, 2004*, and the *Quality of Care Information Protection Act, 2004*, Ontario Gazette (3 July 2004), which would have restricted quality of care committees to performing only (or primarily) quality of care functions was omitted from the regulations that were finalized. The draft *QCIPA* Minister's regulation, s. 3, included the following two requirements that were removed from the Minister's regulation as finalized, O. Reg. 297/04, below note 34:

> 3. The committee must be established, appointed or approved for the sole or primary purpose of improving or maintaining the quality of the health care or the level of skill, knowledge, and competence of the persons who provide the health care.
>
> 4. The committee may not be engaged in any function required under a statute other than the *Independent Health Facilities Act* or the *Laboratory and Specimen Collection Centre Licensing Act*.

The omission of these two provisions evidently confirms that a committee may qualify as a quality of care committee even if it performs functions other than quality of care functions, and even though its quality of care functions may be carried out under other legislation.

32 *General*, O. Reg. 330/04, s. 4, made under *QCIPA* [Reg. 330].

33 *QCIPA*, above note 2, clause (b) of definition of "quality of care committee" in s. 1.

34 *Quality of Care Committee*, O. Reg. 297/04, s. 3(1) [Reg. 297].

any such *relevant* information from prior to the designation of the committee is disclosed to the committee.

- The second prescribed requirement is that the terms of reference of the committee and the written designation be made publicly available.[36]

Finally, a quality of care committee can only be established by an organization that is eligible under the Act to start such a committee.[37]

2) Organizations That Can Designate a Quality of Care Committee

Only the types of organizations described or named in *QCIPA* or the *QCIPA* Minister's regulation (Regulation 297) are entitled to start a quality of care committee that can benefit from the provisions of *QCIPA*.

First, certain organizations that provide health care are authorized to designate such a committee. These are as follows:

- a "health facility," which is defined to mean a public hospital under the *Public Hospitals Act*, a private hospital under the *Private Hospitals Act*, a psychiatric facility governed by the *Mental Health Act*, an "institution" under the *Mental Hospitals Act*, or an independent health facility under the *Independent Health Facilities Act*;[38]
- a prescribed entity that provides health care,[39] which under the regulations includes long-term care facilities[40] and licensed medical laboratories and specimen collection centres.[41]

Second, the regulations may prescribe a health oversight body that may designate a quality of care committee. *QCIPA* describes this as a prescribed entity

---

35   As required under clauses (a) and (b) of the definition of "quality of care information" in s. 1.

36   Reg. 297, above note 34, s. 3(2).

37   *QCIPA*, above note 2, clause (a) of definition of "quality of care committee" in s. 1.

38   *Ibid.*, s. 1, clause (a)(i) of definition of "quality of care committee," and definition of "health facility."

39   *Ibid.*, s. 1, clause (a)(ii) of definition of "quality of care committee."

40   Reg. 297, above note 34, ss. 1 (1)–(3). Long-term care facilities eligible under the regulation to designate a quality of care committee include nursing homes under the *Nursing Homes Act*, R.S.O. 1990, c. N.7; approved charitable homes for the aged under the *Charitable Institutions Act*, R.S.O. 1990, c. C.9; and homes under the *Homes for the Aged and Rest Homes Act*, R.S.O. 1990, c. H.13.

41   Reg. 297, above note 34, s. 1 (4). This refers to laboratories and specimen collection centres as defined in s. 5 of the *Laboratory and Specimen Collection Centre Licensing Act*, R.S.O. 1990, c. L.1.

that "carries on activities for the purpose of improving or maintaining the quality of care provided by a health facility, a health care provider or a class of health facility or health care provider."[42] This refers to an entity that does not necessarily itself provide health care but that carries on activities aimed at improving the quality of care provided by one or more health facilities or among some group or class of health care providers. The regulations have designated the Ontario Medical Association, in respect of its activities concerning the services of licensed medical laboratories and specimen collection centres, as one such body.[43]

3) How to Designate a Quality of Care Committee

The committee may be a pre-existing committee, or it may be newly established for the purpose of being a quality of care committee under *QCIPA*. One of the purposes of the committee must be improving or maintaining the quality of the health care or the level of skill, knowledge, and competence of the persons who provide the health care.[44]

A committee is permitted to act as a quality of care committee even if it is engaged in a function required under another statute.[45] For instance, a medical advisory committee[46] established under the *Public Hospitals Act* is eligible to be designated as a quality of care committee under *QCIPA*, though information

---

42   *QCIPA*, s. 1, clause (a)(iii) of definition of "quality of care committee." The term "health oversight body" is not used in *QCIPA*, however.

43   Reg. 297, above note 34, s. 2(1). To monitor the proficiency of medical laboratories under the *Laboratory and Specimen Collection Centre Licensing Act*, above note 41, the Ministry of Health and Long-Term Care funds the Quality Management Program — Laboratory Services (QMP-LS), operated by the Ontario Medical Association (OMA). See Ontario Health Insurance Program, *Resource Manual for Physicians 2003*, Section 6.10 Laboratory Services, online: <www.health.gov.on.ca/english/providers/pub/ohip/physmanual/pm_sec_6/6-29.html>. It is this program that is evidently being referred to in the regulation.

44   *QCIPA*, s. 1, clause (c) of definition of "quality of care committee."

45   See note 31 above.

46   Public hospitals are required to establish a medical advisory committee under s. 35 of the *Public Hospitals Act*, R.S.O. 1990, c. P.40. Such committees perform a number of functions under that legislation, for example making recommendations on appointments to the medical staff of the hospital under s. 37 of that Act. Some but not all of the functions of a medical advisory committee will likely be considered quality of care functions for the purposes of *QCIPA*. For example, under *Hospital Management*, R.R.O. 1990, Reg. 965, s. 7(2)(v) [Reg. 965], made under the *Public Hospitals Act*, one of the functions of the medical advisory committee is to make recommendations to the hospital board on the quality of care provided in the hospital by medical staff and other specified health care professionals in the hospital. This function appears to be clearly a quality of care function for the purposes of *QCIPA*.

that relates to the committee's functions that are not quality of care functions[47] will not be treated as quality of care information.[48]

Though a multi-purpose quality of care committee is permitted under *QCIPA*, there will be special practical difficulties in maintaining such a committee in accordance with *QCIPA* and its regulations. The quality of care functions must be carefully kept separate from other functions of the committee for two important reasons.

First, information can only be protected as quality of care information where it has been collected or prepared solely or primarily for, or relates solely or primarily to, the quality of care functions of the committee, and not other committee functions. Therefore, allowing a multi-function committee to operate as a quality of care committee raises the possibility that information will not be protected as quality of care information if it is seen as being significantly related to the non-quality of care functions of the committee.[49]

Second, exposures of the quality of care information to persons who are associated with the multi-purpose quality of care committee only for its non-quality of care functions may be treated as a prohibited disclosure under the Act.[50]

The risks and difficulties associated with the need to separate the functions of the committee in this manner suggest that it may be simpler and less risky in most cases simply to have a separate, dedicated quality of care committee. This is especially so when one considers that a committee that is not a quality of care committee may be delegated with quality of care functions by a quality of care committee, thus reducing the practical need to designate multi-purpose committees as quality of care committees.[51]

Whether it is a new or pre-existing committee, the committee must be formally "established, appointed or approved" by a body that is authorized to do so, as described above.[52] For instance, in the case of a hospital, this would be done through a resolution of the board, or by a person or persons authorized to do so by the board. The regulations require that the designation be in writing,[53] and the Committee's activities are not protected until such a designation is made, and is made publicly available.[54]

---

47 As described in clause (c) of the definition of "quality of care committee" in s. 1.
48 Reg. 330, above note 32, s. 4.
49 See discussion in Section D(1), below.
50 See discussion in Section F(1), below.
51 See Section F(1), below.
52 *QCIPA*, above note 2, s. 1, clause (a) of definition of "quality of care committee."
53 Reg. 297, above note 34, s. 3(1).
54 *Ibid.*, s. 3(2).

QCIPA does not require that any organization listed or described in *QCIPA* or the regulations establish or designate a quality of care committee. But in the absence of such a committee being designated, the restrictions set out in the Act simply do not apply.

Nor does *QCIPA* require that only one quality of care committee can be established. A health facility or other body eligible to designate a quality of care committee may therefore establish more than one committee.

Absent special considerations, health facilities and other bodies eligible to designate a quality of care committee likely will want to take advantage of the provisions of the Act by designating at least one such committee.

Then the immediate practical question arises: which committee or committees should be designated as a quality of care committee? Furthermore, to what extent can the existing committees of the institution be used, or is it necessary to create one or more new committees?

It will be important, before making these determinations, to review the existing quality of care mechanisms in the institution, as they exist and operate both on paper and in practice. Ultimately, any decisions about the design or structure of the quality of care committee will need to balance the convenience of preserving existing institutional committee/organizational structures relating to quality of care with the need to fulfil the requirements of the legislation in a practical manner.

Although each institution must make a judgment based on its unique circumstance, several practical considerations may weigh against having multiple committees within one facility, bearing in mind that multiple committees will generally only be designated as quality of care committees based on the expectation that they will be performing other functions at the same time:

- First, while the restrictions on disclosures may enhance certain aspects of the committee's work, these restrictions may render certain activities difficult for the committee to accomplish. Therefore careful consideration should be given, before designating a committee as a quality of care committee, as to whether the application of all the restrictions in the legislation will be compatible with the work of the committee.[55] The restrictions on the

---

55 For example, before designating a medical advisory committee of a hospital as a quality of care committee, consideration should be given to how the committee will be able to perform all its functions required under the *Public Hospitals Act* or the regulations thereunder, including, for example, s. 7(2)(b) of Reg. 965, above note 46 which requires that the committee "supervise the practice of medicine, dentistry, midwifery and extended class nursing in the hospital," or s. 7(4) of that regulation, which requires the medical advisory committee to report to the medical staff of the hospital at each regularly scheduled meeting of the medical staff. See the discussion of medical advisory committee in Section C(3) above.

disclosure of quality of care information cannot be waived by the committee or the organization, so if the information may be needed for the purposes of discipline or dismissal, for example, which may ultimately involve a proceeding, the committee collecting or generating that information should not be designated as a quality of care committee.

- Second, it may be preferable from the point of view of maintaining the maximum flexibility combined with strong organizational control to have one central, senior quality of care committee designated, which can then delegate functions as it deems appropriate to other committees or individuals within the facility.
- Third, as noted, designating multiple quality of care committees tends to go together with relying on multi-purpose quality of care committees, often in an attempt to apply the provisions of *QCIPA* to a pre-existing committee structure within the hospital or institution. Multi-purpose quality of care committees have special considerations and challenges, as discussed above.[56]

While it is not required by *QCIPA*, it may be good practice for a health care organization covered by *QCIPA*, and perhaps even if not covered, to appoint a person who will take lead responsibility within the organization for managing and co-ordinating all quality of care matters arising within the organization.[57] It is also important to see that the organization has practices in place so that quality of care issues are referred to a committee in the appropriate manner, to ensure that quality of care reviews are conducted as necessary and in a manner so that the reviews will be subject as appropriate to *QCIPA's* protections.[58]

D. QUALITY OF CARE INFORMATION

1) What Is "Quality of Care Information"?

Under *QCIPA*, only quality of care information is shielded from disclosure. Quality of care information includes only information that was collected by or prepared for a quality of care committee for the sole or primary purpose of assisting the committee in carrying out its functions, or that relates solely or primarily to any activity that a quality of care committee carries on as part of

---

56 See Section C(3) above.

57 This is recommended in the Ontario Hospital Association's *Quality of Care Information Protection Act Toolkit* (Toronto: Ontario Hospital Association, 2004) at 20. See <www.oha.com>

its quality of care functions.[59] The information need not actually have come from the committee in order to be protected as quality of care information. It is enough that it was "prepared for" the committee as long as the sole or primary purpose of the preparation of the information was to assist the committee in fulfilling its quality of care function.[60]

The requirement that the information be collected or prepared "for the sole or primary purpose" of assisting the committee in carrying out its quality of care functions should be easy to meet where the sole or primary mandate of the committee is carrying out quality of care functions. Where the committee is involved in other significant functions, however, and the information relates largely to those other functions, then it would not be considered quality of care information.[61]

Quality of care information, as defined in the Act, is not limited to recorded information. Thus, for example, information discussed by or with a quality of care committee may be considered quality of care information even if it is never reduced to writing.

2) What Is Excluded from "Quality of Care Information"?

The definition of quality of care information also contains certain exclusions, which are dealt with below in turn.

a) Patient Record

Quality of care information does not include "information contained in a record that is maintained for the purpose of providing health care to an individual." Thus, for example, information contained in a patient's hospital chart, or in a nursing home resident's record of care, would not be considered to be quality of care information.[62] The scope of this exclusion includes but also

---

58   *Ibid.* at 20–28.

59   QCIPA, above note 2, s. 1, definition of "quality of care information," clauses (a) and (b). Also see s. 4 of Reg. 297, above note 34, which makes it clear that information relating to the committee's non-quality of care functions is not considered quality of care information.

60   QCIPA, *ibid.*, s. 1, definition of "quality of care information," clause (a).

61   This is an important consideration, since, as discussed above, the regulation appears to allow a committee with significant purposes other than quality of care purposes to be eligible to be considered a quality of care committee. See note 31 above. If information relates primarily to that non-quality of care purpose it would not be considered quality of care information. This consideration suggests the advantage of ensuring, as much as possible, that quality of care committees do not assume functions beyond their quality of care mandate, or at least that such separate activities should be kept separate from the quality of care activities, so that the status of the quality of care information as such is not brought into question.

62   QCIPA, above note 2, s. 1, definition of "quality of care information," clause (c).

extends beyond what is contained in the patient's file, to cover any record that is maintained for the purpose of providing health care to an individual.

b) Record Required by Law

Quality of care information does not include information contained in a record that is required by law[63] to be created or to be maintained. In other words, where a law requires a certain record to be created or maintained for any purpose, any information that is included in that record will not be considered quality of care information.[64]

c) Facts Not in Patient Record

QCIPA also excludes from the scope of quality of care information any "facts contained in a record of an incident involving the provision of health care to an individual" except to the extent that the facts are fully recorded in a health care record, like the patient chart, that will be accessible[65] to the patient, or the patient's family where the patient is deceased or incapacitated.[66] The underlying principle appears to be that facts relating to health care incidents should not be shielded from the patient involved. So where the facts are not included in a record that will be accessible to the patient, they will not be able to be shielded as quality of care information, even if they are recorded in the context of a review by a quality of care committee. Based on the language of the provision, the following appear to be outside the scope of this exclusion, and hence continue to be protected as quality of care information:

---

63 For an explanation of the phrase "required by law," see Chapter 3, Section A(3)(b).

64 *QCIPA*, above note 2, s. 1, definition of "quality of care information," clause (d). This will likely have the effect of allowing certain mandatory disclosure provisions in other legislation or law to continue functioning for the information, despite the non-disclosure provisions of *QCIPA*. If a written report is required by law to be provided to some person, then it would appear likely that the report would be considered "a record that is required by law to be created or maintained" and, if so, the information contained within the record would not fit within the definition of quality of care information, due to this clause (d). As such, the report would not be considered quality of care information, and if another Act required the disclosure of that report, *QCIPA* would not prohibit the disclosure. A record that is required by law to be maintained but not required to be disclosed would also fit within the scope of this exception.

65 Patients and their substitute decision-makers would generally have access to such information about them under the access provisions in Part V of *PHIPA*. See Chapter 13.

66 *QCIPA*, *ibid*, s. 1(e), definition of "quality of care information." This exception is very similar to the exception set out in s. 35.1(4)(a)(ii) of the *Saskatchewan Evidence Act*, above note 20. In the *Quality of Care Information Protection Act Toolkit*, above note 58 at 11, the example is offered that where a quality of care review discovers that a nurse contacted a physician about a certain health care incident involving a patient but no entry was made of this fact in the patient chart, the fact is not quality of care information subject to the restrictions of *QCIPA*.

- unrecorded facts;[67]
- any information that does not relate to "an incident involving the provision of health care to an individual;" and
- information that does not consist of "facts," which apparently refers to opinions and evaluations, for example.

d) Exclusions by Regulation

The definition of quality of care information also contains a provision allowing regulations to create additional exclusions.[68] Any such regulations, however, would take effect only for information received by the committee after the time the regulations were made. This qualification allows people to disclose information to a quality of care committee with the confidence that subsequent regulations will not be able to have the effect of rendering the information no longer protected by *QCIPA*.

As of the time of writing, the regulations exclude the following from the scope of what is considered quality of care information:

- the fact that a quality of care committee met or conducted a review;[69] and
- when the meeting took place.[70]

The exclusion of these types of basic information from the scope of quality of care information suggests that anything that is more descriptive than this of the committee's quality of care functions would tend to be considered quality of care information, and subject to the applicable restrictions. One may perhaps deduce from this that other details about the meeting, that go beyond the fact that the committee met, and when, such as where the committee met, who attended the meeting, and what was on the agenda, may be considered quality of care information.

E. HOW A QUALITY OF CARE COMMITTEE OBTAINS INFORMATION

Under *QCIPA* there is blanket permission for anyone to disclose any information to a quality of care committee for the purposes of the committee.[71] Thus, as long as the information is disclosed to the committee in good faith for the

---

67 Under this clause, only "facts contained *in a record*" are excluded (emphasis added).
68 *QCIPA*, above note 2, s. 1, definition of "quality of care information," clause (f).
69 Reg. 330, above note 32, s. 2(1).
70 *Ibid.*, s. 2(2).
71 *QCIPA*, above note 2, s. 3.

committee to perform its functions in attempting to maintain or improve quality of care within the area of the committee's mandate,[72] the disclosure would be permitted despite any provision to the contrary in *QCIPA* itself,[73] in *PHIPA*,[74] or any other Ontario legislation or regulation.[75] Patient consent is not required to disclose any information to a quality of care committee for the committee's quality of care functions.[76]

Furthermore, a person who discloses information to a quality of care committee is protected against any retaliation. *QCIPA* makes it an offence to "dismiss, suspend, demote, discipline, harass or otherwise disadvantage a person" for disclosing information to the committee under section 4.[77]

72　It may be worth noting that s. 3 permits disclosures of "any information to a quality of care committee for the purposes of the committee" without further limitation. The "purposes of the committee" in this context, however, should almost certainly be interpreted as applying only to the quality of care purposes of the committee, and not to any other purposes the committee may have. It would likely not be considered reasonable to interpret provisions relating to the committee as a quality of care committee as extending to other functions of the committee. This is especially evident from the fact that, as discussed below, s. 3 appears to authorize even disclosures of quality of care information originating in one quality of care committee to another committee for the purposes of the receiving committee. It would hardly be reasonable to think that s. 3 was intended to operate so as to authorize the disclosure of quality of care information to a committee for unspecified non-quality of care functions.

73　As discussed below, from the fact that s. 3 states "despite this Act" it would appear that even quality of care information from another committee may be disclosed to a quality of care committee to assist it with its quality of care functions.

74　*PHIPA* is like other Ontario legislation in this respect.

75　This is due to the fact that *QCIPA* prevails over other Ontario legislation in case of a conflict, unless a regulation under *QCIPA* specifies otherwise: *QCIPA*, above note 2, s. 2. The one exception is the *Independent Health Facilities Act*: Reg. 330, above note 32, s. 1.

76　The disclosure can be made without consent though this is not explicitly stated in s. 3, since s. 3 allows the disclosure without imposing any condition. Additionally, because of s. 3, the disclosure of any personal health information from a health information custodian under *PHIPA* to a quality of care committee is permitted without consent due to *PHIPA*, ss. 29 & 43(1)(h). A person subject to the recipient rules in *PHIPA*, s. 49(1) can also disclose personal health information without consent under the exception set out in that subsection. An agent of a health information custodian can disclose without the authorization of the custodian, under the exception set out in *PHIPA*, s. 17(2).

77　*QCIPA*, above note 2, s. 6. The reference in this provision to s. 4 may be an error, since it is s. 3 and not s. 4 that permits the person to disclose information to a quality of care committee. This is further apparent from the fact that the reference to s. 4 does not identify a subsection, though that section is divided into subsections. The prohibition in s. 6 may nevertheless be effective, however, since the reference in s. 4(1) to no person disclosing quality of care information except as permitted by *QCIPA* can be read as including permission under s. 3 for a person to disclose to a quality of care committee for the purposes of the committee.

A person disclosing information to the committee in good faith, either at the request of the committee or on the person's own initiative for the purpose of assisting the committee in carrying out its quality of care function, is protected against any proceedings[78] for doing so.[79]

It is worth noting that *PHIPA* contains its own provisions allowing a broader range of internal disclosures[80] and uses of personal health information within a health information custodian's organization "for the purpose of risk management, error management or for the purpose of activities to improve or maintain the quality of care or to improve or maintain the quality of any related programs or services of the custodian."[81] These provisions allow information collected by a health information custodian for any purpose to be used and transferred within the custodian's organization[82] for those purposes without patient consent, whether or not a quality of care committee has been designated or is involved. Of course, where a quality of care committee designated under *QCIPA* is not involved, the protections and restrictions in *QCIPA* will not apply. Conversely, where a quality of care committee is involved, and the information is quality of care information, the restrictions in *QCIPA* will prevail over any provisions in *PHIPA*. But there is nothing in either Act that requires that this type of activity be conducted only by a quality of care committee.

F. PROHIBITED AND PERMITTED DISCLOSURES

1) Prohibited Disclosures

No person is permitted to disclose quality of care information except as specifically authorized by *QCIPA*.[83] The term "disclose" with respect to quality of care information is defined as providing or making the information available to someone who is not a member of the relevant quality of care committee.[84]

---

78   As defined in *QCIPA*, *ibid.*, s. 1.

79   *QCIPA*, *ibid.*, s. 8(1).

80   Recall that under *PHIPA* the transfer of information between a health information custodian and its agents, or between the agents of a custodian, is considered a "use" and not a "disclosure," and is subject to the rules under s. 37 of that Act. The term "disclosure" is defined differently in *QCIPA*.

81   *PHIPA*, s. 37(1)(d).

82   The term "organization" is used loosely here to refer to any health information custodian, including any agents of the custodian.

83   *QCIPA*, above note 2, s. 4(1).

84   *Ibid.*, s. 1. Note that the definition of "disclose" in *QCIPA* is different from the definition of the same term in *PHIPA*, where any transfer of information within the organi-

The regulation further specifies that the expression "member of a quality of care committee," as used for example in this definition, includes every person who participates or assists with the committee's quality of care functions.[85] This interpretative provision effectively allows quality of care information to be shared with persons assisting the committee with its quality of care functions (a stenographer, for example) without that being considered a disclosure under QCIPA, and without the need for the committee or the associated health facility to formally make the person a member of the committee. This allows the committee to get the help it needs to do its job in a practical manner. Other possible examples of persons who may be treated as members of the committee are

- experts retained or requested by the committee to assist the committee in addressing quality of care matters; and
- members of another committee in the facility who have been delegated by the quality of care committee with the performance of a task related to the committee's quality of care functions, or who have been asked by the committee to participate in some manner in the committee's quality of care functions.

Sharing information with such persons to further the quality of care functions of the committee is not considered a disclosure by the committee, and hence is not prohibited by QCIPA. Conversely, providing or making available quality of care information to a person who does not participate in or assist with the committee's quality of care functions may be considered a disclosure of the information.

2) Permitted Disclosures

The prohibition on the disclosure of quality of care information is subject to four exceptions, as outlined below.

a) Disclosures to Management

A quality of care committee that is established by a health care organization is authorized under QCIPA to disclose quality of care information to the management of that organization where the committee considers it appropriate to do so for the purpose of improving or maintaining the quality of health care pro-

---

zation of a health information custodian is considered a "use" of the information and not a "disclosure." The QCIPA definition is more expansive and hence makes the prohibition on disclosures more restrictive.

85 Reg. 330, above note 32, s. 3. It appears to be implicit here that the participation or assistance must be with the support or at least the acquiescence of the quality of care committee. Without this interpretation, the committee may lose control over who will be permitted to receive quality of care information.

vided in or by the organization.[86] For example, if the committee discovers a condition within the organization that detracts from the quality of care provided by the organization, it may report that fact to the management of the organization together with any recommendations for remedial steps to be taken. The term "management" is broadly defined in the Act to include both the governing board and the senior management staff of the organization.[87]

A quality of care committee established by a health oversight body[88] is similarly authorized to disclose to management for the purpose of improving or maintaining the quality of care, but in this case the disclosure would be to the management of a health care facility or provider with respect to which the committee was exercising quality of care functions, rather than to the management of the organization that established or designated the committee.[89]

A member of management who receives quality of care information under this provision is in turn authorized to disclose the information to an agent or employee of the organization if the disclosure is necessary for the purposes of improving or maintaining the quality of health care provided in or by the organization.[90]

It is worth noting that this type of disclosure is permitted to be made specifically by the quality of care committee. This suggests that it is the committee, rather than individual members of the committee, that has the power and responsibility of determining what kind of disclosure is appropriate to be authorized pursuant to this provision.[91] Therefore, it appears appropriate to establish a committee protocol or policy for authorizing such disclosures, since individuals who disclose quality of care information without the authorization of the committee risk being found in breach of the non-disclosure provisions of the Act, which is an offence subject to a significant fine.[92]

---

86 *QCIPA*, above note 2, s. 4(3)(a).

87 *Ibid.*, s. 4(2).

88 Under para. (a)(iii) of the definition of "quality of care committee" in *QCIPA*, *ibid.*, s. 1.

89 *Ibid.*, s. 4(3)(b).

90 *Ibid.*, s. 4(6).

91 The language of s. 8(2)(a) may be read to suggest that any member of the committee may exercise this power, independently of the committee. However, the more cautious approach would be to interpret this to mean that the committee member will indeed typically be the one making the disclosure, but the disclosure must still be authorized by the committee to meet the requirements of s. 4(3). Either way, so long as the disclosure by the committee member is in good faith, the immunity provision in s. 8(2)(a) would act as a shield against prosecutions or other proceedings.

92 *QCIPA*, above note 2, s. 7 sets out offences and maximum fines, up to $50,000 for an individual or $250,000 for an organization. But note the immunity provision discussed in the preceding footnote, which may provide comfort to anyone acting in good faith.

b)   Harm Disclosures

The second kind of disclosure of quality of care information that *QCIPA* permits is a disclosure that "is necessary for the purposes of eliminating or reducing a significant risk of serious bodily harm to a person or group of persons."[93] In contrast to the "management" disclosure, the "harm" disclosure is permitted to be made by any person.[94] This disclosure provision mirrors the disclosure provisions for personal health information set out in *PHIPA*.[95] A disclosure of this type may be justified, for example, where the incompetence of a health care professional in the facility is reported by the quality of care committee to the management of the facility, but the management takes no steps to address the problem. In such case, a person may be justified in disclosing the information to an appropriate body outside the facility (e.g., the professional's regulatory college) where the body to whom the disclosure is made has the power to take steps to prevent the professional from practising in a manner that endangers the health or well-being of patients.

Both of the above disclosure powers are subject to good-faith immunity protections for authorized persons who disclose under either of these provisions in good faith, though the disclosure to prevent harm must also be "reasonable in the circumstances" in order to qualify for the immunity.[96] Both of these disclosure powers are also subject to a proviso that a member of a quality of care committee cannot be held legally responsible for "the failure of the committee" to make such a disclosure.[97]

---

93   *QCIPA*, *ibid.*, s. 4(4).

94   In *R. v. McCraw*, [1991] 3 S.C.R. 72, the court defined "serious bodily harm," for the purposes of s. 264.1(1)(a) of the *Criminal Code*, R.S.C. 1985, c. C-46, which makes it an offence to threaten to "cause death or serious bodily harm," as "any hurt or injury, whether physical or psychological, that interferes in a substantial way with the physical or psychological integrity, health or well-being of the complainant." Causing harm to oneself would also appear to fall within the concept, as evident from *Conway v. Fleming*, [1996] O.J. No. 1242, (Gen. Div.), upheld in 173 D.L.R. (4th) 372 (Ont. Div. Ct.), leave to appeal to C.A. denied, 12 July 1999, which deals with the power under the *Mental Health Act* to restrain certain persons to prevent serious bodily harm. A similar power to impose restraints exists at common law, and for hospitals under the *Patient Restraints Minimization Act, 2001*, S.O. 2001, c. 16, s. 6.

95   *PHIPA*, s. 40(1). See the discussion in Chapter 10, Section K(1).

96   *QCIPA*, above note 2, s. 8(2).

97   *Ibid.*, s. 8(3). In the case of a disclosure to avoid harm, however, it could be argued that the immunity only applies to the "committee's" failure to disclose, and not to the individual's failure to disclose, since as noted s. 4(4), unlike s. 4(3), permits anyone to disclose the information, not just the committee, nor even just a committee member.

c) Disclosures to Another Committee

The third type of permitted disclosure is a disclosure to another quality of care committee for the purposes of the receiving committee. The provision allowing such a disclosure[98] is very broadly worded and allows the provision of "any information" by any person "to a quality of care committee for the purposes of the committee."[99] Since the provision states "despite this Act," it seems clear that it stands as an exception to *QCIPA's* general rule[100] that disclosure of quality of care information is prohibited except as permitted by the Act. This exception would appear to be broad enough in appropriate circumstances to allow a disclosure of quality of care information from one organization to a separate quality of care committee in the same organization or in another organization. Also, there is no provision requiring the disclosure to be authorized by the quality of care committee from which the information generated.

d) Disclosures under Prevailing Legislation

The fourth type of permitted disclosure of quality of care information is a disclosure that is permitted or required under any other legislation that prevails over *QCIPA*. Where two laws have conflicting requirements or prohibitions, so that one cannot comply with both, the law that one is obligated to follow in that case is said to "prevail." As a general rule, the provisions of *QCIPA*, including its non-disclosure rules, prevail over other Ontario legislation.[101] *QCIPA* contains a general power under which regulations can be made by the Lieutenant Governor in Council to specify that other Acts, or specified provisions of those Acts, will prevail over *QCIPA*.[102] As of the time of writing, the regulations

---

98 *Ibid.*, s. 3.

99 See Section E, above.

100 Under *QCIPA*, *ibid.*, s. 4(1).

101 *QCIPA*, *ibid.*, s. 2 contains an unusually strong conflicts provision that provides that *QCIPA* and its regulations prevail in the case of a conflict with any other Act or regulations "unless this Act [*QCIPA*] or its regulations specifically provide otherwise." (In *PHIPA*, by contrast, the other Act itself can provide that it prevails over *PHIPA*: s. 7(2) of *PHIPA*.) This appears to mean that *QCIPA* may prevail over any other Act even if that other Act has provisions to indicate that it prevails over other Acts, unless regulations under *QCIPA* specifically provide otherwise. However, where another Act expressly provides that it prevails over *QCIPA*, that may be effective, even without a regulation under *QCIPA*, having regard to the general principle of legislative supremacy.

102 *QCIPA*, *ibid.*, s. 9(1)(c). It may be worth noting that unlike the power to make regulations excluding certain information from the scope of quality of care information, which has the effect of setting such information outside the protections of *QCIPA*, and hence has been specifically provided (in clause (f) of the definition of "quality of care information" in s. 1) not to be retroactive, a regulation providing that other legislation prevails over *QCIPA* could have the effect of rendering previously existing quality of care information liable to be disclosed under the newly prevailing provisions.

under *QCIPA* currently provide that the *Independent Health Facilities Act* will prevail over *QCIPA* for any quality of care information collected by or prepared for a quality of care committee of an independent health facility.[103]

Furthermore, federal legislation is not subject to the rule that *QCIPA* prevails, and hence it would appear that any disclosures permitted or required by or under federal legislation would not be prohibited by *QCIPA*.[104]

Another possibility is that legislation from a jurisdiction outside Ontario may in certain instances prevail over, or apply instead of, *QCIPA*, particularly in circumstances where quality of care information is taken outside of Ontario. *QCIPA* does not prohibit removing quality of care information from Ontario, and when it is removed from Ontario it may become subject to the laws of the jurisdiction to which it is taken.[105]

3) Disclosures to Patients and Their Families

There is no provision in *QCIPA* that allows quality of care information to be disclosed to a patient, or the family of a patient, even where the patient's care was the subject of a review by a quality of care committee. Even if the committee wishes to disclose quality of care information to the patient, it is not permitted to do so unless the disclosure falls within the scope of one of the exceptions set out above, which in most instances would not be the case.[106]

---

103 Reg. 330, above note 32, s. 1. In the draft regulations, the *Laboratory and Specimen Collection Centre Licensing Act*, above note 41 was also specified to prevail over *QCIPA*, but this reference was deleted in the regulation as finalized. The prevailing of the *Independent Health Facilities Act*, R.S.O. 1990, c. I.3 may relate to the disclosures permitted or required under that Act. A detailed discussion and analysis of all the disclosure provisions and implications under the *Independent Health Facilities Act* is beyond the scope of this work, but it may be notable that s. 37.2(1) of that Act provides for broad mandatory disclosures that can be required by the responsible regulatory official from operators of such facilities.

104 Under Canadian constitutional law, even valid provincial legislation cannot override valid federal legislation, and in case it is not possible to comply with both simultaneously, the federal legislation takes precedence (i.e., is "paramount"): P. Hogg, *Constitutional Law of Canada*, looseleaf (Toronto: Carswell, 1997) c. 16.

105 Cross-jurisdictional considerations may eventually call for federal/provincial co-operation in creating seamless, consistent quality of care information protection across the country. In doing so, it may be appropriate to consider putting restrictions on removing quality of care information outside the protected area. Federal legislation would also be necessary to shield quality of care information from disclosure in proceedings that are under federal jurisdiction. The possibility of international transfers of quality of care information raises still further complications and challenges.

106 The patient is also not entitled to access quality of care information by way of an access request under *PHIPA*: see *PHIPA* s. 51(1)(a).

Though quality of care information cannot be disclosed to patients, information that falls outside the scope of quality of care information may be disclosed to the patient or his or her substitute decision-maker. Such information may include the following:

- information in patient health care records;[107]
- recorded facts relating to a health care incident involving the patient.[108] Even if such facts were discovered and documented only in the context of a quality of care review, they are not shielded as quality of care information except to the extent that they are also recorded as part of a patient health care record. If they are recorded in the patient health care record, then they can be disclosed to the patient as part of that record. If they are recorded only in the context of the quality of care review and not as part of the patient's record, then the facts themselves, as distinct from any related opinions, etc., are not considered quality of care information and may hence be disclosed to the patient as appropriate;[109]
- information about follow-up action taken by the organization, as long as it does not include information about the review, or the findings or recommendations of the quality of care committee that led up to the follow-up action being taken; and
- the fact that a quality of care committee met or conducted a review, and when the meeting or review took place, without indicating more than this (e.g., who was involved or what was being reviewed).[110]

To the extent that information described in any of the above exceptions is recorded personal health information, the patient to whom it relates would be able to access a record of the information under *PHIPA*, unless an exception to the access rights there applied.[111]

4) Incident Reports

It is common practice for many health care organizations to make "incident reports" about adverse events involving patients who received health care from

---

107 *QCIPA*, above note 2, clause (c) of definition of "quality of care information" in s. 1.

108 *Ibid.*, clause (d) of definition of "quality of care information" in s. 1.

109 Where the information is not quality of care information it may be disclosed to the patient on an access request under *PHIPA*, assuming that the patient is not otherwise prohibited from having access to the records or information due to the operation of one of the exceptions to access rights set out in ss. 51 or 52 of *PHIPA*. See Chapter 13.

110 Reg. 330, above note 32, s. 2.

111 *PHIPA*, s. 52(1). See Chapter 13.

the organization. It is important to understand the status of such reports under QCIPA.

If the report is not prepared by or for a properly designated quality of care committee, then it would not be considered quality of care information and would hence not be shielded from disclosure under QCIPA.

If such a report is prepared by or for a quality of care committee, then the report would in principle be considered quality of care information, but any facts in the report would not be considered quality of care information unless the facts are also contained in a health care record, which would be potentially accessible to the patient.[112]

The Ontario Hospital Association in its *Quality of Care Information Protection Act Toolkit* (September 2004)[113] advises hospitals that, although incident reports are universally used by hospitals, usually such reports are not protected from disclosure in proceedings by either QCIPA or common law legal privilege.[114] Furthermore, the Toolkit advises that "for serious/critical incidents," staff should not complete an incident report on a routine basis, but should rather notify their manager or the hospital's Quality/Risk Manager, the person co-ordinating quality of care processes within the hospital, who will determine the appropriate way to review and report the incident.[115] Where an incident report is deemed to be appropriate, the Toolkit recommends that it be limited to factual information and avoid speculation about or attribution of the causes of the incident. In the same way, the Toolkit recommends that any such report not contain any recommendations for follow-up, which should rather be made in the context of a properly constituted quality of care review.[116]

5) Restrictions on Recipients of Quality of Care Information

Quality of care information does not cease to be quality of care information simply because it has been disclosed in an authorized manner set out above or even in an unauthorized manner. Where the disclosure was under the management or harm exceptions discussed above, QCIPA specifically provides that the recipient of the disclosure can use the information only for the purposes

---

112 Such access could be in the course of discovery in a proceeding, or pursuant to the *PHIPA* access provisions, unless an exemption to access applies.

113 See online: <www.oha.com/Client/OHA/OHA_LP4W_LND_WebStation.nsf/resources/ QCIPAToolkit/$file/QCIPAToolkit.pdf>.

114 *Ibid.*

115 *Ibid.*

116 *Ibid.*

for which it was disclosed to the person,[117] and the recipient is not permitted to disclose the information except as authorized under either of those exceptions.[118] Information disclosed to another quality of care committee for quality of care purposes[119] is subject to the regular rules in *QCIPA* concerning subsequent uses and disclosures by the quality of care committee. To the extent that another Act prevails over *QCIPA*[120] *and* authorizes or requires a use or disclosure by the recipient, that use or disclosure would also be permitted. Apart from those exceptions, the prohibition against the recipient's using or disclosing quality of care information would apply to prohibit the use or disclosure, even where the disclosure was apparently permitted or required by another law.[121]

6) Disclosure Prohibited in Proceedings

In addition to the qualified prohibition on disclosures generally set out under *QCIPA*,[122] the Act[123] provides an absolute[124] prohibition on the use of quality of care information in proceedings. Not only is quality of care information not

---

117   *QCIPA*, above note 2, s. 4(5). Based on the wording of s. 4(5), this restriction on use does not seem to apply, however, to those who receive the information under s. 4(6), or who received the information in an unauthorized manner. This gap may have been unintentional however, since there does not appear to be a reason for being less restrictive with recipients under s. 4(6) than recipients under s. 4(3), and even less reason for extending leniency to those who received the information in an unauthorized manner. Until this is clarified it would probably be prudent to interpret the restriction on use under s. 4(5) as applying equally to recipients under s. 4(6), in accordance with the apparent underlying intention of the provisions.

118   *QCIPA*, *ibid.*, s. 4(7). Disclosures of quality of care information by any person are also prohibited by s. 4(1), except as otherwise permitted by *QCIPA*.

119   Under *QCIPA*, *ibid.*, s. 3, as discussed above.

120   Ontario provincial legislation other than the *Independent Health Facilities* Act does not prevail over *QCIPA*. See the discussion in Section F(2)(d) above regarding permitted disclosures for more details of which legislation prevails over *QCIPA*.

121   *QCIPA*, *ibid.*, s. 4(1). The restriction on subsequent uses under s. 4(5) only applies where the information was received through a disclosure under ss. 4(3) or (4) (the "management" and "harm" categories of permitted disclosures), so if the information was received under another Act that prevails over *QCIPA*, it would appear that the recipient would be permitted to use the information for the purposes of the disclosure, and possibly other purposes depending on the provisions of that other legislation.

122   *QCIPA*, *ibid.*, s. 4.

123   *Ibid.*, s. 5.

124   The prohibition in s. 5 on disclosing quality of care information in a proceeding does not appear to be subject to the exceptions to the prohibition of disclosure outside proceedings set out in s. 4. This is apparent since the exceptions set out in ss. 4(3) & (4) both open with the phrase "despite subsection (1)," which refers to s. 4(1), which by implication appears to mean that these exceptions are subject to the prohibition in s.

admissible in evidence in a proceeding,[125] no one is even permitted to ask a witness in a proceeding about quality of care information, and a court or tribunal holding a proceeding is prohibited from permitting or requiring a witness to disclose any quality of care information in the proceeding.[126]

To understand the scope of the prohibition on disclosure in proceedings, it is necessary to look carefully at the definition of "proceeding," which is defined in *QCIPA* as follows:

> "proceeding" includes a proceeding that is within the jurisdiction of the Legislature and that is held in, before or under the rules of a court, a tribunal, a commission, a justice of the peace, a coroner, a committee of a College within the meaning of the *Regulated Health Professions Act, 1991*, a committee of the Board of Regents continued under the *Drugless Practitioners Act*, a committee of the Ontario College of Social Workers and Social Service Workers under the *Social Work and Social Service Work Act, 1998*, an arbitrator or a mediator, but does not include any activities carried on by a quality of care committee ....[127]

This is a very broad definition, but it is subject to the significant qualification that it only refers to proceedings within the jurisdiction of the Ontario Legislature.[128] Given the Ontario government's lack of authority to legislate with respect to proceedings that are not within its jurisdiction (e.g., proceedings under federal legislation like the *Criminal Code*) or proceedings being conducted in other jurisdictions, it may be that this qualification would be read into the legislation even if it were not there explicitly.

G. OFFENCES

As already alluded to, it is an offence under *QCIPA* to contravene the non-disclosure provisions of the Act.[129] Such contraventions would include disclosing

---

5. The prohibition in s. 5 would only be subject to any exceptions in legislation that prevail over *QCIPA*, either because the regulations prescribe it to prevail or because it is federal legislation.

125 *QCIPA*, above note 2, s. 5(2).

126 *Ibid.*, s. 5(1). Also relevant here is the definition of "witness" in s. 1 that includes "anyone competent or compellable to be examined," which appears to include virtually everyone.

127 *Ibid.*, s. 1.

128 This restriction is similar to that found in Ontario's *Evidence Act*, R.S.O. 1990, c. E.23, s. 2, which provides: "This Act applies to all actions and other matters whatsoever respecting which the Legislature has jurisdiction."

129 *QCIPA*, above note 2, s. 7(1), referring to the non-disclosure provisions under s. 4.

quality of care information in a manner not permitted under the Act, or for a recipient of a disclosure of quality of care information under the disclosure provisions of *QCIPA* to use the information for a purpose other than the purpose for which the information was disclosed to the person.[130]

Making a disclosure in contravention of *QCIPA* is an offence even in the absence of any knowledge that the disclosure is prohibited by the Act.[131] However, as noted above, a member of a committee who discloses quality of care information in good faith to management for quality of care purposes is immune from prosecution for an offence.[132] Furthermore, a person who makes a reasonable disclosure in good faith to eliminate or reduce a risk of serious bodily harm to any person is also immune from prosecution.[133] Obviously these immunities are intended to apply even if the provision that the person thought authorized the disclosure turned out not to apply in the circumstances, because, if the provision applied as was thought, there would be no need for an immunity provision in the first place. Disclosures based on other grounds, however, would apparently not be covered by the immunity provisions in *QCIPA*. Examples of such disclosures would include a disclosure based on the mistaken belief that the disclosure was authorized by a federal statute, or a disclosure based on a mistaken belief that the recipient of the information was a duly constituted quality of care committee to which disclosures are permitted. In such cases, it would appear that the person who made the mistaken disclosure might be liable to be convicted unless the person could show that he or she had taken all reasonable care in the circumstances to comply with the law.[134]

It is also an offence for anyone to dismiss, discipline, or otherwise disadvantage any person for disclosing information to a quality of care committee as permitted under section 3 of *QCIPA*.[135] This offence is only established where the accused can be shown to have taken the steps against the person "by reason that" the person disclosed information to a quality of care committee as permitted under *QCIPA*.[136]

---

130 *Ibid.*, s. 4(5). See Section F(5) above for a discussion on the restrictions *QCIPA* imposes on recipients of quality of care information.

131 *Provincial Offences Act*, R.S.O. 1990, c. P.33, s. 81.

132 *QCIPA*, above note 2, s. 8(2)(a).

133 *Ibid.*, s. 8(2)(b).

134 *R. v. Sault Ste. Marie*, [1978] 2 S.C.R. 1299 at 1325. See the discussion on strict liability offences in the context of offences for collecting, using, or disclosing the health number contrary to *PHIPA* in Chapter 15, Section D(2)(d).

135 *QCIPA*, above note 2, ss. 6 & 7(1).

136 *Ibid.*, s. 6.

Though a contravention of the Act, it is not an offence for a person to permit or require a witness in a proceeding to disclose quality of care information.[137] The witness who makes the disclosure would be committing an offence, however.[138] Furthermore, the provisions that prohibit courts and tribunals from permitting or requiring a witness to disclose quality of care information in a proceeding, and that render such information inadmissible in a proceeding, are not enforceable by way of offence provisions.[139] Apparently contraventions of these provisions are expected to be dealt with in other ways; for example, by way of appeals or procedural motions within the relevant proceeding.

QCIPA contains provisions for fines of up to $50,000 for an individual or $250,000 for a corporation,[140] and for the liability of officers and agents of a corporation for the offences of the corporation,[141] that are identical with the corresponding provisions in *PHIPA*.[142]

H. REGULATIONS UNDER *QCIPA*

Like *PHIPA*, *QCIPA* contains extensive regulation-making powers that allow regulations to fine-tune or otherwise alter the application of the legislation. Notable regulation-making powers include the powers of the Lieutenant Governor in Council[143] to

- specify certain types of information not to be quality of care information,[144] though without the power to make information quality of care information that would not otherwise fall into the definition of that term set out in *QCIPA*;
- specify provisions of other legislation that will prevail over *QCIPA*;[145] and

---

137   A contravention of s. 5(1) is not specified as an offence under *QCIPA*.

138   This assumes that the disclosure is prohibited under s. 4. See s. 7(1).

139   Contraventions of ss. 5(1) & (2) are not specified as offences under *QCIPA*.

140   *QCIPA*, above note 2, s. 7(2).

141   *Ibid.*, s. 7(3).

142   See Chapter 15, Section D(3) discussing parties to offences under *PHIPA* which is equally applicable to *QCIPA* offences.

143   In practice, a power of the Lieutenant Governor in Council requires a formal decision by the provincial Cabinet.

144   *QCIPA*, above note 2, s. 9(1)(b). As discussed above, however, such a regulation may not have the effect of excluding from protection information that was protected when received by the committee, as set out in clause (f) of the definition of "quality of care information" in s. 1.

145   *Ibid.*, s. 9(1)(c).

- define any otherwise undefined term in *QCIPA*.[146]

In addition to these powers, the Minister of Health and Long-Term Care can make regulations to

- specify additional[147] classes of health care providing organizations or health care oversight bodies that are permitted to designate quality of care committees;[148] and
- set criteria that a committee must meet before it can be considered a quality of care committee under *QCIPA*.[149]

Regulations made under these powers have the potential to significantly affect the nature and scope of the legislation.[150]

In order to address concerns expressed about the breadth of the regulation powers, a provision was set out in *QCIPA*,[151] as in *PHIPA*, requiring the Minister to conduct a public consultation on the regulations. The substance of those provisions is virtually identical with the corresponding provisions of *PHIPA*, which were discussed above in Chapter 16,[152] except for the fact that the *QCIPA* Minister's regulations are not subject to the mandatory public consultation. As a practical matter, though, the Minister in fact consulted publicly on the entire first set of proposed regulations brought forward under *QCIPA*, both the Minister's regulations and the Lieutenant Governor in Council regulations.[153]

---

146 *Ibid.*, s. 9(1)(a).

147 There is no power to remove organizations from the list of organizations under the definition of "health facility" in the Act that can designate a quality of care committee.

148 *QCIPA*, above note 2, s. 9(2) and clause (a) of the definition of "quality of care committee" under s. 1.

149 *Ibid.*, s. 9(2) and clause (b) of the definition of "quality of care committee" under s. 1.

150 All five of the above types of regulation powers were exercised in the initial set of regulations made under *QCIPA*. Apart from the extension of the Act to long-term care facilities and medical laboratories and specimen centres, however, the first regulations could be characterized as fine-tuning rather than greatly altering the nature and scope of *QCIPA*.

151 *QCIPA*, *ibid.*, s. 10.

152 See Chapter 16, Sections C and D.

153 "Notice of Minister of Health and Long-Term Care, Notice of Proposed Regulations, under the *Personal Health Information Protection Act, 2004* and the *Quality of Care Information Protection Act, 2004*," *Ontario Gazette* (3 July 2004).

I. *RHPA* AMENDMENTS

1) Quality Assurance Information Protection

QCIPA also includes amendments to the Regulated Health Professions Code, Schedule 2 to the *Regulated Health Professions Act, 1991*,[154] that provide protection similar to that provided in the main body of *QCIPA*. The protections in the *RHPA* Code apply to "quality assurance information" generated by a quality assurance committee of one of the *RHPA* Colleges.[155] These amendments replace the *RHPA* Code's previously existing "evidence in proceedings" provision.[156] These provisions are outlined here. Much of the discussion set out above on *QCIPA* will be relevant to a greater or lesser extent to these *RHPA* amendments, but a detailed analysis of these provisions of the *RHPA* is beyond the scope of this book.

2) Quality Assurance Committees and Programs

Quality Assurance Committees and quality assurance programs are not new to the *RHPA*. Every *RHPA* College has long been required to establish a quality assurance committee, which has responsibility for its quality assurance pro-

---

154 Above note 19 [*RHPA* Code].

155 *QCIPA*, above note 2, s. 11, adding a new s. 83.1 to the *Regulated Health Professions Act, 1991*, above note 19. These amendments were not part of the first reading version of Bill 31, but were added during clause-by-clause consideration by the Standing Committee on General Government in response to several submissions of regulated health professional Colleges that the quality assurance information should be given comparable protection as set out for quality of care information in *QCIPA*.

156 Prior to 1 November 2004, s. 83.1 of the Code provided that certain types of information connected with a quality assurance committee were "not admissible in evidence in a civil proceeding except in a proceeding under a health profession Act and to the extent permitted by that Act or a regulation made under that Act." (This was set out in s. 83(5), now repealed by s. 11(1) of *QCIPA*.) This restriction applied to information that was supplied to such a committee by a professional who was subject to the jurisdiction of the committee, whether the information was provided voluntarily or under compulsion. The restriction also applied to information that such a professional created or kept for the purpose of complying with the requirements of a prescribed quality assurance program. There was no general prohibition for disclosure of information provided to the College or for information created by the member in compliance with the quality assurance program. These amendments had been added to the Code in 2000 and, as a result, Bill 159 did not include specific reference to this type of privilege, in contrast to the 1997 draft *Personal Health Information Protection Act*, which did. See above note 19.

gram.[157] The Council of each *RHPA* College is required to make regulations governing the College's quality assurance program.[158] A "quality assurance program" of an *RHPA* College is defined to mean a program to assure the quality of the practice of the profession and to promote continuing competence among the members of the profession regulated.[159] Although quality assurance programs differ from one *RHPA* College to another, the components of each program generally include self-assessment, peer assessment, practice review, and remediation. Self-assessment may require a member to keep a portfolio or log for self-reflection where a member records his or her strengths, as well as areas for improvement. By asking for feedback from peers, members of a profession can learn about aspects of their practice that would help them enhance their practice. The members are also often required to have learning plans in place. Colleges may randomly select members to review their self-assessment materials. Other members or patients may be asked to provide feedback to the College about the member's practice. Some such evaluations will lead to more formal assessments by "assessors"[160] who may take such steps as visiting the member's practice, observing the setting, and reviewing and discussing patient records. Some members could then be identified as needing remediation where the level of their competency falls below acceptable standards for the profession.[161]

Under a number of regulated health profession Acts and regulations, professional misconduct includes failing to co-operate with the Quality Assurance Committee or failing to participate in aspects of a regulated health College's quality assurance program.[162]

---

157 *RHPA* Code, above note 154, s. 10(1)[6].

158 *Ibid.*, s. 80. The regulation-making authority, including a number of different elements and remedial powers that a quality assurance committee may be authorized to exercise, are set out in s. 95(1)(r) and (2.1) of the Code.

159 *RHPA* Code, *ibid.*, s. 1(1).

160 A quality assurance committee may appoint assessors for the purpose of assisting the committee to carry out a quality assurance program: *RHPA* Code, *ibid.*, s. 81.

161 These components of quality assurance programs have been summarized from fact sheets published by the Royal College of Dental Surgeons of Ontario, online: <www.rcdso.org>, the College of Nurses of Ontario, online: <www.cno.org>, the College of Physicians and Surgeons of Ontario, online: <www.cpso.on.ca>, and the College of Occupational Therapists of Ontario, online: <www.coto.org>.

162 For example, see *Professional Misconduct*, O. Reg. 680/93, s. 1(37), made under the *Dietetics Act, 1991*, S.O. 1991, c. 26; and *Professional Misconduct*, O. Reg. 199/98, s. 1(12.1), made under the *Medical Radiation Technology Act, 1991*, S.O. 1991, c. 29.

3) The Need for Enhanced Protections

Prior to 1 November 2004, the *RHPA* Code provided some protections for information that a member of a regulated health profession gathered in order to comply with the requirements of a quality assurance program, and for information that a quality assurance committee or an assessor collected. However, the Federation of Health Regulatory Colleges, in its submission to the Standing Committee on General Government, asked for stronger protections for such information comparable to the protections established in *QCIPA* with respect to quality of care information:

> Quality assurance could in fact be considered a misnomer. It's more so an assessment and enhancement process to ensure that, through voluntary disclosure in a co-operative and non-penalizing format, members or registrants can actually identify their own shortcomings, both on an individual basis and on a profession-wide basis so that those shortcomings can actually be addressed to ensure that there is continuous quality improvement in the health care sector. But to do that effectively, it does have to be voluntary and there does have to be buy-in, which means that information has to be protected so members do not feel they are in jeopardy should they disclose information to the Colleges in that regard.[163]

As a result, a number of amendments were made to the Code, similar to the provisions of *QCIPA*, as outlined in the following sections.

4) Protecting the Information Flow to the Quality Assurance Committee

Despite any restrictions on disclosure imposed by *PHIPA* (but subject to any restrictions imposed by *QCIPA*[164]) any person may disclose any information to a quality assurance committee for the purposes of the committee.[165] A person disclosing any information to such a committee in good faith either on the request of the committee or for the purposes of its functions is immune from any legal action for doing so.[166] No one is permitted to retaliate against a person for disclosing information to a quality assurance committee for the pur-

---

163 Ontario, Legislative Assembly, Standing Committee on General Government, *Official Report of Debates (Hansard)*, G-71 (27 January 2004) (Michelle Kennedy, Federation of Regulated Health Colleges).

164 *QCIPA*, above note 2, s. 2.

165 *RHPA* Code, above note 154, s. 83.1(3).

166 *Ibid.*, s. 83.1(8).

pose of its functions, though a discloser may be disciplined for disclosing false information to the committee.[167]

5) Definition of "Quality Assurance Information"

The *QCIPA* amendments to the *RHPA* Code added new provisions for the identification and protection of "quality assurance information." The amendments define "quality assurance information" as information that

- is collected by or prepared for the quality assurance committee for the sole or primary purpose of assisting the committee in carrying out its functions,[168]
- relates solely or primarily to any activity that the quality assurance committee carries on as part of these functions,[169]
- is prepared by a professional who is a regulated member of the College or on behalf of such a member for the purpose of complying with the requirements of the quality assurance program (as prescribed under each health profession Act),[170] or
- is provided to the quality assurance committee.[171]

Quality assurance information does not include the following:

- the name of a professional who is a regulated member of the College and allegations that the member may have committed an act of professional misconduct, or may be incompetent or incapacitated;[172]
- information that was referred to the quality assurance committee from another committee of the College or the Health Professions Appeal and Review Board;[173] or
- information that a regulation made under the Code specifies is not quality assurance information and that the quality assurance committee receives after the day on which that regulation is made.[174]

---

167 *Ibid.*, s. 83.1(7).
168 *Ibid.*, s. 83.1(1)(a), definition of "quality assurance information."
169 *Ibid.*, s. 83.1(1)(b).
170 *Ibid.*, s. 83.1(1)(c).
171 *Ibid.*, s. 83.1(1)(d).
172 *Ibid.*, s. 83.1(1)(e). Such information has long been permitted to be provided by a quality assurance committee to the executive committee of the relevant College: *ibid.*, s. 83(3).
173 *Ibid.*, s. 83.1(1)(f), definition of "quality assurance information."
174 *Ibid.*, s. 83.1(1)(g). No such regulations are currently in place, at the time of writing.

6) Legal Privilege in Proceedings

Under the *RHPA* amendments set out in *QCIPA*, quality assurance information is privileged in legal proceedings in much the same way as is quality of care information under *QCIPA*. Quality assurance information is deemed not admissible in evidence in any proceeding.[175] "Proceeding" is defined essentially as it is in *QCIPA*, and includes a proceeding of a committee of an *RHPA* College; for example, a discipline committee.[176] Furthermore, no person is permitted even to ask a witness to disclose quality assurance information, and no court or other body conducting a proceeding may permit or require any witness in the proceeding to disclose quality assurance information except as permitted or required by the provisions on the quality assurance program.[177] "Witness" is defined as in *QCIPA*.[178]

7) Prohibited Disclosures of Quality Assurance Information

Despite the provisions in *PHIPA* that authorize various type of disclosures of personal health information with or without consent, no person is permitted to disclose quality assurance information except as permitted by the *RHPA*, the *RHPA* Code, a health profession Act referred to in the *RHPA*, or regulations or bylaws made under the *RHPA* or a health profession Act.[179] The term "disclose," as it relates to quality assurance information, is defined to mean, to provide or make the information available to a person who is not

- a member of the quality assurance committee;
- an assessor appointed by the quality assurance committee, a person engaged on its behalf as a mentor, or a person conducting an assessment program on its behalf; or

---

175 *Ibid.*, s. 83.1(6).
176 *Ibid.*, s. 83.1(1), definition of "proceeding." The main difference between the definition of "proceeding" in *QCIPA* and that in s. 83.1 of the *RHPA* Code is that in the *QCIPA* definition "proceeding" is defined to exclude activities carried out by the quality of care committee, while in the *RHPA* Code it excludes activities carried out by the quality assurance committee. In both cases, this reflects that the intention of the provisions is to enhance, and not to restrict, the powers of the applicable committee to acquire and use information relevant to its tasks.
177 *Ibid.*, s. 83.1(5).
178 *Ibid.*, s. 83.1(1), definition of "witness."
179 *Ibid.*, s. 83.1(4). For this reason, the patient does not have a right of access to a record containing personal health information that might be quality assurance information under *PHIPA*, see Part V, s. 51(1)(b). See Chapter 13 for further discussion of the right of access provisions.

- a person providing administrative support to the quality assurance committee or the Registrar of the applicable *RHPA* College or the committee's legal counsel.[180]

As with the provisions of *QCIPA*, these new protections in the *RHPA* should enhance existing processes for improving the quality of health care being provided in Ontario.

J.   CHECKLIST FOR ORGANIZATIONS WISHING TO RELY ON *QCIPA* PROTECTIONS

- Is our organization eligible to designate a quality of care committee? If not, is there an oversight body that may be authorized to establish a quality of care committee that could operate within the organization?
- Establish or designate a quality of care committee with the appropriate members, mandate, and supporting policies. Consider
  - existing committee functions and quality of care processes
  - whether it is feasible to designate only one quality of care committee dedicated primarily to quality of care matters (as appears to be preferable under *QCIPA*)
- Ensure that there are policies in place, and communicated to employees and agents of the organization, about
  - the need to refer quality of care issues through the proper channels to a quality of care committee, to ensure that any quality of care review will be eligible to claim the protections set out in *QCIPA*
  - the prohibition on disclosing any quality of care information to anyone outside the quality of care committee (i.e., who is not participating as authorized by the committee in the quality of care functions of the committee) except as permitted under *QCIPA*
  - restrictions on recipients of quality of care information using or disclosing the information for other purposes

---

180   *RHPA* Code, above note 154, s. 83.1(1), definition of "disclose." These persons, in turn, are subject to the secrecy provision of s. 36 of the *RHPA*, above note 19.

K. ADDITIONAL RESOURCES RELATING TO *QCIPA*

- Ministry of Health and Long-Term Care website, online: <www.health.gov. on.ca>. For the broadest range of materials be sure to access the part of the site identified for "health care providers."
- Ontario Hospital Association *Quality of Care Information Act Toolkit* (September 2004), online: <www.oha.com/Client/OHA/OHA_LP4W_LND_ WebStation.nsf/page/Publications+PSSS>.
- For the latest updates to *QCIPA* and its regulations see the Ontario government legislation and regulations, online: <www.e-laws.gov.on.ca>.

Appendix 1:
Glossary of Terms Defined in or Relating to *PHIPA*

The main definitions section of *PHIPA* defines thirty-three terms. Further interpretive provisions are found in various sections of *PHIPA* and its regulation. Understanding the definitions and keeping them in mind when reading the Act is necessary in order to have an accurate understanding of *PHIPA*.

In addition to the terms defined in *PHIPA*, we use a few other special terms in referring to important concepts or relevant legislation in a concise and convenient manner. These terms are also set out and explained below. For statute citations, which are not provided here, we ask readers to refer to the Table of Statutes, Bills, Regulations, Orders, and Abbreviations found after the Appendices. All section references are to *PHIPA* unless otherwise noted.

Term and Definition	Section References, Cross-references, and Notes
"Agent," in relation to a health information custodian, means a person that, with the authorization of the custodian, acts for or on behalf of the custodian in respect of personal health information for the purposes of the custodian, and not for the agent's own purposes, whether or not the agent has the authority to bind the custodian, whether or not the agent is employed by the custodian, and whether or not the agent is being remunerated.	Section 2. A health information custodian's use of agents is subject to rules primarily set out in s. 17. (See Chapter 2.)

Term and Definition	Section References, Cross-references, and Notes
"Assistant Commissioner" means the Assistant Commissioner for Personal Health Information appointed under the *Freedom of Information and Protection of Privacy Act*.	Section 2. This new officer was created by the amendments to *FIPPA* set out in *PHIPA*, s. 81, and has a role in the enforcement of *PHIPA*. (See Chapter 15.)
"Attorney for personal care" means an attorney under a power of attorney for personal care made in accordance with the *Substitute Decisions Act, 1992*.	Section 2. This term is used only in that part of *PHIPA* that deals with substitute decision-making, particularly ss. 26–27. (See Chapter 6.)
"Attorney for property" means an attorney under a continuing power of attorney for property made in accordance with the *Substitute Decisions Act, 1992*.	Section 2. This term is used only in that part of *PHIPA* that deals with substitute decision-making, particularly ss. 26–27. (See Chapter 6.)
"Board" means the Consent and Capacity Board constituted under the *Health Care Consent Act, 1996*.	Section 2. This Board reviews matters relating to findings of incapacity and the appointment of substitute decision-makers. (See Chapter 6.)
"Capable" means mentally capable, and "capacity" has a corresponding meaning.	Section 2. This relates to the ability to provide a consent. (See Chapter 6.)
"Collect," in relation to personal health information, means to gather, acquire, receive, or obtain the information by any means from any source, and "collection" has a corresponding meaning.	Section 2. This central term in *PHIPA* is explained in detail in Chapter 2. Limits on collection are set out in Chapter 7. Direct and indirect collections are outlined in Chapter 8. (See Chapters 2, 7, and 8.)
"Commissioner" means the Information and Privacy Commissioner appointed under the *Freedom of Information and Protection of Privacy Act*.	Section 2. The Commissioner is primarily referred to in the Administration and Enforcement provisions (see Chapter 15), but has a role in some other contexts also.[1]

1　Such other activities include authorizing indirect collections under s. 37(1)(f); approving privacy-related practices and procedures of a prescribed planning entity under s. 45(3) and of a health data institute under s. 47(9); reviewing Minister's disclosure proposals under s. 47(4); approving disclosures in the public interest by a health data institute to the Minister under s. 48; and receiving the registration of archives under s. 14(1)(d) of the Regulation.

Term and Definition	Section References, Cross-references, and Notes
"CSA Privacy Code" is the term commonly used to refer to the Code incorporated in Schedule 1 of the *Personal Information Protection and Electronic Documents Act*. The Schedule is officially entitled "Principles Set Out in the National Standard of Canada Entitled Model Code for the Protection of Personal Information, CAN/CSA-Q830-96."	Not defined in *PHIPA* or *PHIPA* Regulation. This term is used for ease of reference in this Guide.
"Custodian"	Not defined in *PHIPA* or *PHIPA* Regulation. This term is used in *PHIPA* and in this Guide as shorthand for "health information custodian," which is a defined term under *PHIPA*, s. 3.
"De-identify," in relation to the personal health information of an individual, means to remove any information that identifies the individual or for which it is reasonably foreseeable in the circumstances that it could be utilized, either alone or with other information, to identify the individual. "De-identification" has a corresponding meaning.	Section 47(1). This term corresponds closely to the definition of "identifying information" in s. 4(2). The term "de-identify" is used only in s. 47 in describing what the health data institute must do to personal health information before reporting to the Minister. (See Chapter 11.)
"Disclose," in relation to personal health information in the custody or under the control of a health information custodian or a person, means to make the information available or to release it to another health information custodian or to another person, but does not include using the information. "Disclosure" has a corresponding meaning.	Section 2. This central term in *PHIPA* is explained in Chapter 2. Limits on disclosure are addressed in Chapter 7. Permitted disclosures are generally outlined in Chapter 10. Section 1(3) of the Regulation is also relevant to this definition:[2] see also the definition of "use." (See Chapters 2, 7, and 10.)
"FIPPA" refers to the *Freedom of Information and Protection of Privacy Act*, Ontario's provincial public sector access to information and privacy legislation.	Not defined in *PHIPA* or *PHIPA* Regulation. This term is used for ease of reference in this Guide.

2   Section 1(3) of the *PHIPA* Regulation provides:

> (3) In the definition of "disclose" in section 2 of the Act, the expression "to make the information available or to release it to another health information custodian or to another person" does not include a person's providing personal health information to someone who provided it to or disclosed it to the person, whether or not the personal health information has been manipulated or altered, if it does not contain any additional identifying information.

Term and Definition	Section References, Cross-references, and Notes
"*FIPPA/MFIPPA* custodian" is a shorthand term that refers to a health information custodian that is also either an "institution" or a part of an "institution," as that term is defined in either the *Freedom of Information and Protection of Privacy Act* or the *Municipal Freedom of Information and Protection of Privacy Act*, that is subject to either of those Acts.	Not defined in *PHIPA* or *PHIPA* Regulation. This term is used for ease of reference in this Guide.
"Guardian of property" means a guardian of property or a statutory guardian of property under the *Substitute Decisions Act, 1992*.	Section 2. This term is used only in that part of *PHIPA* that deals with substitute decision-making, particularly ss. 26–27. (See Chapter 6.)
"Guardian of the person" means a guardian of the person appointed under the *Substitute Decisions Act, 1992*.	Section 2. This term is used only in that part of *PHIPA* that deals with substitute decision-making, particularly ss. 26–27. (See Chapter 6.)
"Health care" means any observation, examination, assessment, care, service, or procedure that is done for a health-related purpose and that a) is carried out or provided to diagnose, treat, or maintain an individual's physical or mental condition; b) is carried out or provided to prevent disease or injury or to promote health, or c) is carried out or provided as part of palliative care; and includes, d) the compounding, dispensing, or selling of a drug, a device, equipment, or any other item to an individual, or for the use of an individual, pursuant to a prescription; and e) a community service that is described in s. 2(3) of the *Long-Term Care Act, 1994* and provided by a service provider within the meaning of that Act.	Section 2. The *PHIPA* Regulation further provides: 1(1) In the definition of "health care" in section 2 of the Act, "a procedure that is done for a health-related purpose" includes taking a donation of blood or blood products from an individual. The term "health care" is important in understanding several aspects of *PHIPA*, including the terms "health care practitioner" and "personal health information" (see Chapter 2). The term "health care" also appears in the context of a health information custodian's collection, use, and disclosure of personal health information without consent of the patient. (See Chapters 8–10.)
"Health care practitioner" means a) a person who is a member within the meaning of the *Regulated Health Professions Act, 1991* and who provides health care, b) a person who is registered as a drugless practitioner under the *Drugless Practitioners Act* and who provides health care,	Section 2. A health care practitioner is a type of health information custodian, unless certain exceptions apply. (See Chapter 2.)

Term and Definition	Section References, Cross-references, and Notes
"Health care practitioner" ... c) a person who is a member of the Ontario College of Social Workers and Social Service Workers and who provides health care, or d) any other person whose primary function is to provide health care for payment.	
"Health information custodian" has the meaning set out in section 3.	Section 2. This central term in the Act is explained in detail in Chapter 2.
"Health information network provider" or **"provider"** means a person who provides services to two or more health information custodians where the services are provided primarily to custodians to enable the custodians to use electronic means to disclose personal health information to one another, whether or not the person is an agent of any of the custodians.	Section 6(2) of Regulation. Section 6(3) of the *PHIPA* Regulation sets out requirements that apply to such persons. (See Chapter 2.)
"Health number" means the number, the version code, or both of them assigned to an insured person within the meaning of the *Health Insurance Act* by the General Manager within the meaning of that Act.	Section 2. Section 34 of *PHIPA* regulates the collection, use, and disclosure of the health number by all persons. (See Chapter 2.)
"Identifying information" means information that identifies an individual or for which it is reasonably foreseeable in the circumstances that it could be utilized, either alone or with other information, to identify an individual.	Section 4(2). This definition is a component of the definition of "personal health information." Only identifying information can be personal health information.[3] (See Chapter 2.)
"Incapable" means mentally incapable. **"Incapacity"** has a corresponding meaning.	Section 2. This term relates to a patient's ability to provide a consent. (See Chapter 6.)
"Individual," in relation to personal health information, means the individual, whether living or deceased, with respect to whom the information was or is being collected or created.	Section 2. In the Guide, we often use the more concrete term "patient" in place of "individual." See glossary entry for "patient."

---

3   In other words, if information is not identifying information, then it is therefore also not personal health information. On the other hand, information can be identifying information without being personal health information. Personal health information is a subset of identifying information.

Term and Definition	Section References, Cross-references, and Notes
"Information practices," in relation to a health information custodian, means the policy of the custodian for actions involving personal health information, including a) when, how, and the purposes for which the custodian routinely collects, uses, modifies, discloses, retains, or disposes of personal health information; and b) the administrative, technical, and physical safeguards and practices that the custodian maintains with respect to the information.	Section 2. Health information custodians are obliged to have in place and follow information practices that comply with *PHIPA* and its regulation (s. 10), and they must make a general description of these available to the public (s. 16). (See Chapter 4.)
"*Krever Report*" refers to the three-volume *Report of the Commission of Inquiry into the Confidentiality of Health Information*, commissioned in 1977 and submitted to the Ontario Minister of Health in 1980 by the Honourable Mr. Justice Krever.	Not defined in *PHIPA* or *PHIPA* Regulation. This term is used for ease of reference in this Guide.
"Marketing" does not include a) a communication by a health care practitioner who provides insured services within the meaning of the *Health Insurance Act* to an individual or a member of the individual's family or household by which the practitioner makes available to those persons an arrangement whereby they may receive ancillary uninsured services for a block fee or on the basis of a set fee for service, or b) a communication by the Canadian Blood Services for the purpose of recruiting donors of blood, blood products, or hematopoietic progenitor cells.	*PHIPA* Regulation, s. 1(2). This provision interprets the term "marketing," which is not defined in *PHIPA*, but which is used in s. 33 of the Act. A health information custodian requires the patient's express consent to collect, use, or disclose personal health information about the patient for marketing purposes. (See Chapter 5.)
"MFIPPA" refers to the *Municipal Freedom of Information and Protection of Privacy Act*, Ontario's municipal public sector access to information and privacy legislation.	Not defined in *PHIPA* or *PHIPA* Regulation. This term is used for ease of reference in this Guide.
"Minister" means the Minister of Health and Long-Term Care.	Section 2. The Minister is a custodian under s. 3[4] and has various other roles under *PHIPA*.[5]

4   Under s. 3, the list of health information custodians includes "the Minister, together with the Ministry of the Minister if the context so requires." This may reflect that under *FIPPA* it is the Ministry rather than the Minister that is the "institution" covered by that Act. If so, the flexibility in the reference to the Minister in the listing of custodians in s. 3 may be intended to allow the "Minister" covered by *PHIPA* to include the "Ministry" covered by *FIPPA*, rather than suggesting that the two are separate entities.

5   For example, as well as acting as a health information custodian, the Minister approves applications to be permitted to act as a single custodian under s. 3(8), directs

Term and Definition	Section References, Cross-references, and Notes
"**Partner**" means either of two persons who have lived together for at least one year and have a close personal relationship that is of primary importance in both persons' lives.	Section 2. This term is referred to in the provisions on substitute decision-makers,[6] and in provisions on the disclosure of a deceased individual's personal health information.[7] (See Chapter 6.)
"**Patient**" is used largely throughout this book as the most immediately understandable term to refer to the person who is the subject of personal health information. *PHIPA* uses the term "individual" to refer to the subject of personal health information. "Individual" is defined to mean "the individual, whether living or deceased, with respect to whom the information was or is being collected." Of course, not all persons and entities in the health sector use the word "patient" in all contexts to describe recipients of health care services. Depending on the context, the subject of the personal health information may more appropriately be called a "client" or "resident," etc. or may be a patient, out-patient, former patient, or deceased patient. Nevertheless, for consistency and ease of reference, this Guide commonly uses the term "patient" to refer to all of these. Furthermore, when referring to a "patient" or "individual" providing a consent, making a request (e.g., for access or correction), providing an instruction, or taking some other step, the word "patient" or "individual" also can be read as including the patient's "substitute decision-maker" (see *PHIPA*, s. 25, and Chapter 6). The Guide does not repeat the phrase "patient or his or her substitute decision-maker, as the case may be," but in general, references to "patient" include references to the patient's substitute decision-maker.	Not defined in *PHIPA* or *PHIPA* Regulation. See definition of "individual" in *PHIPA*, as set out above in this glossary.

---

disclosures of personal health information under ss. 46 or 47, subject to the restrictions set out there, and approves a health data institute for the purposes of s. 47.

6   *PHIPA*, s. 26.
7   *Ibid.*, s. 38(4)(c).

Term and Definition	Section References, Cross-references, and Notes
"Person" includes a partnership, association, or other entity.	Section 2. "Person" is further defined in the *Interpretation Act*[8] as "includ[ing] a corporation and the heirs, executors, administrators or other legal representatives of a person to whom the context can apply according to law."
"Personal health information" has the meaning set out in s. 4.	Section 2. This central term in the Act is explained in detail in Chapter 2. Sections 1(4)[9] and 4[10] of the *PHIPA* Regulation are also relevant to this definition. See also entry on "identifying information."
"PHIPA" means the *Personal Health Information Protection Act, 2004*, which is the focus of this book.	Not defined in *PHIPA* or *PHIPA* Regulation. This term is used for ease of reference in this Guide.
"PHIPA Regulation" refers to Ontario Regulation 329/04[11] made under *PHIPA* and filed on 21 October 2004.	Not defined in *PHIPA* or *PHIPA* Regulation. This term is used for ease of reference in this Guide.
"PIPEDA" is the federal *Personal Information Protection and Electronic Documents Act*, which has applied since 1 January 2004, to organizations collecting, using, or disclosing personal health information in the course of commercial activities.	Not defined in *PHIPA* or *PHIPA* Regulation. This term is used for ease of reference in this Guide.
"Prescribed" means prescribed by the regulations made under this Act.	Section 2.
"Prescribed health registry" refers to a person prescribed pursuant to s. 39(1)(c) who compiles or maintains a registry of personal health information for the purposes of facilitating or improving the provision of health care or relating to the storage or donation of body parts or bodily substances.	Not defined in *PHIPA* or *PHIPA* Regulation. This term is used for ease of reference in this Guide. (See Chapter 11.)

8   Section 29(1).

9   There it provides that "(4) For the purposes of clause 4(1)(d) of the Act, the expression 'eligibility for health care' includes eligibility for coverage under the *Health Insurance Act* or for any other insurance or payment arrangement with respect to health care."

10 There it states: "4. Except for the purposes of subsection 8(4) of the Act, 'personal health information' as defined under subsection 4(1) of the Act includes all identifying information that is contained in a record that contains information of the type referred to in any one or more of clauses (a) to (g) of subsection 4(1)."

11 Abbreviated as O. Reg. 329/04.

Term and Definition	Section References, Cross-references, and Notes
"Prescribed planning entity" is an entity that is prescribed in the regulations, pursuant to *PHIPA*, s. 45, to which a health information custodian is permitted to disclose personal health information for the purpose of analysis or compiling statistical information for the management, evaluation, or monitoring of the allocation of resources to, or planning for, all or part of the health system, including the delivery of services.	Not defined in *PHIPA* or *PHIPA* Regulation. This term is used for ease of reference in this Guide. (See Chapter 11.)
"Proceeding" includes a proceeding held in, before, or under the rules of a court, a tribunal, a commission, a justice of the peace, a coroner, a committee of a College within the meaning of the *Regulated Health Professions Act, 1991*, a committee of the Board of Regents continued under the *Drugless Practitioners Act*, a committee of the Ontario College of Social Workers and Social Service Workers under the *Social Work and Social Service Work Act, 1998*, an arbitrator, or a mediator.	Section 2. This term is used in various provisions relating to collection, use, and disclosure (Chapters 8–10) and exceptions to the right of access (Chapter 13).
"Professional governing bodies" refers to the *RHPA* Colleges and also the Board of Regents under the *Drugless Practitioners Act* and the Ontario College of Social Workers and Social Service Workers under the *Social Work and Social Service Work Act, 1998*.	Not defined in *PHIPA* or *PHIPA* Regulation. This term is used for ease of reference in this Guide.
"QCIPA" is the *Quality of Care Information Protection Act, 2004*, which is the subject of Chapter 17 of this Guide and which is referred to occasionally in *PHIPA*.	Not defined in *PHIPA* or *PHIPA* Regulation. This term is used for ease of reference in this Guide. See Chapter 17 for a full explanation of this Act.
"Quality of care information" has the same meaning as in the *Quality of Care Information Protection Act, 2004*.	Section 2. In *PHIPA* this term comes up as information excluded from the access provisions and from IPC[12] investigations. See Chapter 17 for a full discussion of the meaning of this term.
"Recipient" refers to "a person who is not a health information custodian and to whom a health information custodian discloses personal health information."	Sections 49(1) and (2). The term "recipient" is found in the heading to s. 49(1), so it is not a term of the legislation itself. Recipients are subjects to restrictions on their use and disclosure of the personal health information they have received from a custodian.

12   IPC: Ontario Information and Privacy Commissioner.

Term and Definition	Section References, Cross-references, and Notes
	Health information custodians are subject to similar restrictions with respect to their employee or agent information under s. 49(3).
	(See Chapter 12.)
"**Record**" means a record of information in any form or in any medium, whether in written, printed, photographic, or electronic form or otherwise, but does not include a computer program or other mechanism that can produce a record.	Section 2.
	(See Chapter 2.)
"**Relative**" means either of two persons who are related to each other by blood, marriage, or adoption.	Section 2.
	This term is used in substitute decision-maker provisions,[13] and a disclosure provision.[14]
	(See Chapters 6 and 10.)
"**Research**" means a systematic investigation designed to develop or establish principles, facts, or generalizable knowledge, or any combination of them, and includes the development, testing, and evaluation of research.	Section 2.
	If a use of personal health information is considered research then a custodian can use or disclose the information for that purpose under the research rules with research ethics board approval.
	(See Chapter 11.)
"**Researcher**" means a person who conducts research.	Section 2.
	(See Chapter 11.)
"**Research ethics board**" means a board of persons that is established for the purpose of approving research plans under s. 44 and that meets the prescribed requirements.	Section 2.
	The requirements for such a board are set out in s. 15 of the *PHIPA* Regulation.
	(See Chapter 11.)
"**RHPA**" refers to the *Regulated Health Professions Act, 1991*,[15] which provides a framework for the regulation of twenty-three health professions in Ontario, including physicians, nurses, and dentists.	Not defined in *PHIPA* or *PHIPA* Regulation.
	This term is used for ease of reference in this Guide.
"**RHPA College**" refers to a College within the meaning of the *Regulated Health Professions Act, 1991*, which provides a framework for the regulation of twenty-three health professions in Ontario, including physicians, nurses, and dentists. Such a College is the governing body of the profession to which it relates.	Not defined in *PHIPA* or *PHIPA* Regulation.
	This term is used for ease of reference in this Guide.

13   *PHIPA*, s. 26(1)[8].
14   *Ibid.*, s. 38(1)(c).
15   S.O. 1991, c. 18.

Term and Definition	Section References, Cross-references, and Notes

"Spouse" means either of two persons who
a) are married to each other, or
b) live together in a conjugal relationship outside marriage and
  i) have cohabited for at least one year,
  ii) are together the parents of a child, or
  iii) have together entered into a cohabitation agreement under s. 53 of the *Family Law Act*,
unless they are living separate and apart as a result of a breakdown of their relationship.
	Section 2.
	
	This term is referred to in the provisions on substitute decision-makers,[16] and in provisions relating to the disclosure of a deceased individual's personal health information.[17]
	
	(See Chapters 6 and 10.)

"Substitute decision-maker" has the meaning set out in s. 5 [which states in s. 5(1)]: **"Substitute decision-maker"** in relation to an individual, means, unless the context requires otherwise, a person who is authorized under [*PHIPA*] to consent on behalf of the individual to the collection, use, or disclosure of personal health information about the individual.	Section 2. Sections 5, 23, 25, and 26 set out further provisions related to who may act as a substitute and in which circumstances. (See Chapter 6.)
"Use," in relation to personal health information in the custody or under the control of a health information custodian or a person, means to handle or deal with the information, subject to s. 6(1), but does not include to disclose the information; "use," as a noun, has a corresponding meaning.	Section 2. This central term is explained in Chapter 2. Section 6(1) is also important for this definition.[18] (See Chapters 2, 7, and 9.)

Note: Those of the above interpretation provisions that are set out in *PHIPA* or the *PHIPA* Regulation do not apply insofar as any such provision is inconsistent with the intent or object of *PHIPA* or would give to a word, expression, or provision of *PHIPA* an interpretation inconsistent with the context.[19]

---

16   *PHIPA*, s. 26.
17   *Ibid.*, s. 38(4)(c).
18   That provision states: "For the purposes of this Act, the providing of personal health information between a health information custodian and an agent of the custodian is a use by the custodian, and not a disclosure by the person providing the information or a collection by the person to whom the information is provided.
19   *Interpretation Act*, ss. 1–2. Note that the implied provisions set out in s. 28 of that Act may also apply to *PHIPA*, unless a contrary intention appears in *PHIPA*.

Ten Things to Know to Make Compliance with *PHIPA* Easier

© *Irwin Law Inc., 2005, from* Guide to the Ontario Personal Health Information Protection Act, *by Halyna Perun, Michael Orr, and Fannie Dimitriadis, published by Irwin Law Inc.*

Permission is granted for the non-commercial reproduction and further distribution of this list provided that it is copied in its entirety including this notice, without any modification.

This material does not reflect the opinions of the Ontario Government or its Ministries, and is not intended as legal advice.

The following list outlines ten things that health information custodians should keep in mind to help simplify their compliance with *PHIPA*. For full details of these points, see the noted sections of *PHIPA*, and the cross-referenced Chapters of this Guide.

1. Implied consent concerning personal health information for health care purposes is simplified for some health information custodians under *PHIPA*. A health information custodian whose core business is providing health care[1] can *assume* the patient's implied consent to collect, use, or dis-

---

[1] More precisely, *PHIPA*, s. 20(2) refers to the health information custodians described in paras. 1, 2, 3, or 4 of the definition of "health information custodian" in s. 3(1) of the Act. This includes all health care practitioners (i.e., physicians, nurses, etc.), and institutions that provide health care (like hospitals, long-term care facilities, etc.).

close personal health information the custodian received from the patient, the patient's substitute decision-maker, or another health information custodian, for the purposes of providing health care or assisting in providing health care to the patient, unless the custodian is aware that the patient has expressly withheld or withdrawn the consent.[2] The custodian need not take additional steps before assuming implied consent.[3]

2. Unless it is not reasonable in the circumstances, a health information custodian can rely on a person's statement that he or she

   • is a person authorized to request access to a record of personal health information;[4] or

   • is entitled to act as a substitute decision-maker with respect to personal health information.[5]

It is prudent, however, to require identification and a signed statement to this effect from the person.

3. A consent provided before *PHIPA* came into force (on 1 November 2004) for the collection, use, or disclosure of personal health information[6] remains valid, whether written or oral, express or implied, provided that it meets the requirements of *PHIPA* — most importantly that at the time of giving the consent it was reasonable to believe that the patient knew the purposes of the collection, use, or disclosure that was the subject of the consent, and knew that he or she was entitled to give or withhold the consent.[7] The consent does not have to reference *PHIPA* or be in any particular form.

---

2   *PHIPA*, s. 20(2).

3   See Chapter 5, Section C for more details. It is not necessary to give a notice described in s. 18(6), which is an optional way in which to establish that it is reasonable to believe that a patient's consent is knowledgeable, as required by s. 18(1)(b). Whether or not a custodian wishes to rely on implied consent, *PHIPA* requires the custodian to make publicly available a written public statement setting out, among other things, a general description of its information practices, which includes the custodian's policy on when, how, and the purposes for which the custodian routinely collects, uses, modifies, discloses, retains, or disposes of personal health information: s. 16(1)(a) and s. 2, definition of "information practices." This written public statement can fulfil other purposes too, as discussed in item 4 below.

4   *PHIPA*, s. 71(4)(a). See Chapter 13, Section E for more details.

5   *Ibid.*, ss. 71(4)(b), (c), & (d). See Chapter 6, Section C for more details.

6   A consent to the collection, use, or disclosure of *personal* information that meets the requirements of *PHIPA* would be sufficient, since personal health information is a subset of personal information.

7   *Ibid.*, s. 18(7). The consent must also "relate to the information," (s. 18(1)(c)), so it would have to be a consent that contemplated future ongoing collections, uses, and

4. Where a health information custodian uses or discloses personal health information about a patient, without the patient's consent, outside the scope of the custodian's written public statement describing the custodian's routine uses and disclosures etc. (which a custodian must make publicly available under *PHIPA*[8]), the custodian is obliged to inform the patient of that fact.[9] A custodian should make sure that the written public statement is comprehensive and worded so as to minimize the need for any such notifications; for example, by ensuring that it contains a general statement such as that "personal health information is collected, used, and disclosed by [the custodian] as permitted or required by law."[10] To ensure the written public statement is as useful as possible, it should also incorporate the following:

   - a notice describing the purposes of typical collections, uses, and disclosures of personal health information by the custodian, so that the notice may fulfil the functions of a notice under *PHIPA* that provide the custodian with a reasonable basis to believe that the patient knows the purposes of a collection, use, or disclosure of personal health information, as required generally for consents;[11]

   - a notice for implied consent for fundraising where the custodian is a charitable organization that can conduct fundraising;[12] and

   - in the case of health facilities, a notice to patients offering them the opportunity to opt out from disclosures otherwise permitted to anyone of the patient's name, location in the facility, and general health status;[13] or to religious or other organizations with which the patient has indicated an affiliation, of the patient's name, location in the facility, and applicable affiliation.[14]

---

disclosures rather than just one collection, use, or disclosure that took place before *PHIPA* came into force. See Chapter 5 for more information.

8   *PHIPA*, s. 16(1).

9   *Ibid.*, s. 16(2). The patient need not be informed, however, where the patient does not have a right of access to a record containing the information under Part V of *PHIPA*.

10   It is arguable that such a general "catch-all" description of routine collections, uses, and disclosures is too general to meet the requirements of s. 16(1)(a) read together with the definition of "information practices" in s. 2. However, this language will, at least, provide arguable coverage after the fact where a custodian's collections, uses, or disclosures are not otherwise included in the summary of information practices in the written public statement.

11   *PHIPA*, s. 18(6).

12   See Chapter 5, Section F(7)(a) for a sample text of an implied-consent notice for fundraising purposes.

13   *PHIPA*, s. 38(3).

14   *Ibid.*, s. 20(4).

5. A contact person, which *PHIPA* requires every health information custodian to have,[15] can perform the function of contact person for several custodians, as long as the contact person does not disclose personal health information pertaining to one custodian to another custodian without proper authority for the disclosure. Appointing a common contact person may be especially useful for related health information custodians; for example, health care practitioners providing health care and employed by the same non-custodian, like nurses and social workers employed by a children's aid society or speech-language pathologists and psychologists employed by a school board.[16]

6. There are important limitations on a health information custodian's obligations to ensure the accuracy of personal health information. First, a health information custodian need only ensure that personal health information it uses is as accurate, complete, and up-to-date as is necessary for the purposes for which it uses the information.[17] Furthermore, when disclosing personal health information, a health information custodian has an obligation to take reasonable steps to ensure that the information is as accurate, complete, and up-to-date as is necessary for the purposes of the disclosure that are known to the custodian at the time of the disclosure.[18] However, the custodian can minimize the scope of this obligation when making a disclosure by clearly setting out for the recipient of the disclosure any limitations on the accuracy, completeness, or up-to-date character of the information. For example, the custodian may note, when appropriate, when making a disclosure: "We cannot give any assurance that the information we are providing is accurate, complete, or up-to-date for any particular purpose. Please verify this information before relying upon it. We do not assume responsibility for the consequences of any reliance on this information."[19] Such a qualification may be prudent where the custodian is unsure about the quality of the information, or is not fully knowledgeable about the purposes for which the disclosed information is needed.

---

15 *PHIPA*, s. 15. A custodian who is a natural person has the option of not designating a contact person, but then the custodian must perform the functions of a contact person him-or herself.

16 See Chapter 2, Section B(1)(b)(iii), for more information on facilitating *PHIPA* compliance for such practitioners.

17 *PHIPA*, s. 11(1).

18 *Ibid.*, s. 11(2).

19 See Chapter 4, Section H(2)(d).

7. Where another Act or regulation applicable in Ontario permits or requires a collection, use, or disclosure of personal health information without the patient's consent, that collection, use, or disclosure is thereby permitted under *PHIPA*.[20]

8. A custodian that lawfully disclosed personal health information to a researcher between 1 November 2001 and 1 November 2004 for the purposes of research may continue to disclose personal health information to the researcher for that research without complying with the detailed requirements for research set out in *PHIPA*,[21] including the requirement for research ethics board approval, until 1 November 2007.[22] Similarly, a custodian that lawfully used personal health information between 1 November 2001 and 1 November 2004 for the purposes of research may continue doing so[23] without complying with the detailed requirements for research set out in *PHIPA* until 1 November 2007. Therefore, effectively, research projects commenced before 1 November 2004 will be allowed to continue until 1 November 2007, at which time full compliance with the research provisions of *PHIPA* will be required.

9. A health information custodian has no obligation to correct a record of personal health information:
    - to which the custodian has not granted the patient access;[24]
    - that, though incomplete or inaccurate in some respects, is not inaccurate or incomplete for any purpose for which the custodian uses the information;[25]
    - that was not originally created by the custodian, unless the custodian has sufficient knowledge, expertise, and authority to make the correction;[26] or

---

20 *PHIPA*, s.s 36(1)(g), 37(1)(k), and 43(1)(h). See Chapter 3, Section B(3) for a detailed explanation of the implications of these provisions.

21 The standard requirements are set out in *PHIPA*, ss. 44(1)–(6).

22 *Ibid.*, s. 44(12).

23 The personal health information being used after 1 November 2004 is apparently not required to be the same personal health information that was used before then. The research, however, must evidently be the same or part of the same research project or endeavour.

24 *PHIPA*, s. 55(1).

25 *Ibid.*, s. 55(8).

26 *Ibid.*, s. 55(9)(a).

- consisting of a professional opinion or observation that a custodian has made in good faith about the patient.[27]

10. *PHIPA* provides immunity from damage claims for health information custodians and others who do or omit anything in good faith in the exercise, or intended exercise, of their powers or duties under *PHIPA*, where the act or omission was reasonable in the circumstances.[28]

---

27 *Ibid.*, s. 55(9)(b). For full detail on the obligation to correct records of personal health information based on a patient request, see Chapter 14.

28 Section 71(1). The immunity provision does not apply to offences under *PHIPA*, but the offences typically require that significant wrongful intention be shown: *PHIPA*, s. 72(1). The immunity also does not apply to reviews by the Information and Privacy Commissioner, but the Commissioner has discretion to discontinue or refuse to start a review, or to refrain from making an order, for any reason the Commissioner deems appropriate, including that the person complained about acted reasonably and in good faith in the circumstances: *PHIPA*, s. 57(4). See Chapter 15, Section C(4) for more detail.

Appendix 3:
Online *PHIPA* Resources

Material related to *PHIPA* can be found at a number of online sources, the most important of which are, at the time of writing:

- *Ontario Information and Privacy Commissioner website, online: <www.ipc.on.ca>.* This site contains considerable explanatory material on *PHIPA* and is expected to be a source for ongoing material, including copies of orders made under *PHIPA*. The material on this site related to the Ontario public sector privacy legislation is also sometimes useful in interpreting *PHIPA* obligations.
- *Ministry of Health and Long-Term Care website, online: <www.health.gov.on.ca>.* This site includes materials that the Ministry of Health and Long-Term Care has developed to help inform both the public and health sector stakeholders about both *PHIPA* and *QCIPA*. In the past, the Ministry has also used this site to post a notice of proposed regulations. For the broadest range of materials, be sure to access the part of the site identified for "health care providers."

Both of the sites above contain a link to the Ontario Hospital Association's *PHIPA* Privacy Toolkit[1] and *QCIPA* Toolkit,[2] which can be accessed directly, along with various other privacy-related material, online: <www.oha.com>.

---

1   Ontario Hospital Association, *Hospital Privacy Toolkit: Guide to the Ontario Personal Health Information Protection Act* (Toronto: Ontario Hospital Association, 2004).
2   Ontario Hospital Association, *Quality of Care Information Protection Act Toolkit* (Toronto: Ontario Hospital Association, 2004).

Appendix 4:

Personal Health Information Protection Act, 2004

S.O. 2004, Chapter 3
Schedule A

CONTENTS

PART I
INTERPRETATION AND APPLICATION

PURPOSES, DEFINITIONS AND INTERPRETATION

APPLICATION OF ACT

PART II
PRACTICES TO PROTECT PERSONAL HEALTH INFORMATION

GENERAL

10. Information practices
11. Accuracy
12. Security

RECORDS

13. Handling of records
14. Place where records kept

ACCOUNTABILITY AND OPENNESS

15. Contact person
16. Written public statement
17. Agents and information

PART III
CONSENT CONCERNING PERSONAL HEALTH INFORMATION

GENERAL

18. Elements of consent
19. Withdrawal of consent
20. Assumption of validity

CAPACITY AND SUBSTITUTE DECISION-MAKING

21. Capacity to consent
22. Determination of incapacity
23. Persons who may consent
24. Factors to consider for consent
25. Authority of substitute decision-maker
26. Incapable individual: persons who may consent
27. Appointment of representative
28. Transition, representative appointed by Board

PART IV
COLLECTION, USE AND DISCLOSURE OF PERSONAL HEALTH INFORMATION

GENERAL LIMITATIONS AND REQUIREMENTS

29. Requirement for consent
30. Other information
31. Use and disclosure of personal health information

PART VI
ADMINISTRATION AND ENFORCEMENT

PART VII
GENERAL

PART I
INTERPRETATION AND APPLICATION

PURPOSES, DEFINITIONS AND INTERPRETATION

Purposes

1. The purposes of this Act are,

(a) to establish rules for the collection, use and disclosure of personal health information about individuals that protect the confidentiality of that information and the privacy of individuals with respect to that information, while facilitating the effective provision of health care;

(b) to provide individuals with a right of access to personal health information about themselves, subject to limited and specific exceptions set out in this Act;

(c) to provide individuals with a right to require the correction or amendment of personal health information about themselves, subject to limited and specific exceptions set out in this Act;

(d) to provide for independent review and resolution of complaints with respect to personal health information; and

(e) to provide effective remedies for contraventions of this Act. 2004, c. 3, Sched. A, s. 1.

Definitions

2. In this Act,

"agent", in relation to a health information custodian, means a person that, with the authorization of the custodian, acts for or on behalf of the custodian in respect of personal health information for the purposes of the custodian, and not the agent's own purposes, whether or not the agent has the authority to bind the custodian, whether or not the agent is employed by the custodian and whether or not the agent is being remunerated; ("mandataire")

"Assistant Commissioner" means the Assistant Commissioner for Personal Health Information appointed under the *Freedom of Information and Protection of Privacy Act*; ("commissaire adjoint")

"attorney for personal care" means an attorney under a power of attorney for personal care made in accordance with the *Substitute Decisions Act, 1992*; ("procureur au soin de la personne")

"attorney for property" means an attorney under a continuing power of attorney for property made in accordance with the *Substitute Decisions Act, 1992*; ("procureur aux biens")

"Board" means the Consent and Capacity Board constituted under the *Health Care Consent Act, 1996*; ("Commission")

"capable" means mentally capable, and "capacity" has a corresponding meaning; ("capable", "capacité")

"collect", in relation to personal health information, means to gather, acquire, receive or obtain the information by any means from any source, and "collection" has a corresponding meaning; ("recueillir", "collecte")

"Commissioner" means the Information and Privacy Commissioner appointed under the *Freedom of Information and Protection of Privacy Act*; ("commissaire")

"disclose", in relation to personal health information in the custody or under the control of a health information custodian or a person, means to make the information available or to release it to another health information custodian or to another person, but does not include to use the information, and "disclosure" has a corresponding meaning; ("divulguer", "divulgation")

"guardian of property" means a guardian of property or a statutory guardian of property under the *Substitute Decisions Act, 1992*; ("tuteur aux biens")

"guardian of the person" means a guardian of the person appointed under the *Substitute Decisions Act, 1992*; ("tuteur à la personne")

"health care" means any observation, examination, assessment, care, service or procedure that is done for a health-related purpose and that,
   (a) is carried out or provided to diagnose, treat or maintain an individual's physical or mental condition,
   (b) is carried out or provided to prevent disease or injury or to promote health, or
   (c) is carried out or provided as part of palliative care,

   and includes,
   (d) the compounding, dispensing or selling of a drug, a device, equipment or any other item to an individual, or for the use of an individual, pursuant to a prescription, and
   (e) a community service that is described in subsection 2 (3) of the *Long-Term Care Act, 1994* and provided by a service provider within the meaning of that Act; ("soins de santé")

"health care practitioner" means,
   (a) a person who is a member within the meaning of the *Regulated Health Professions Act, 1991* and who provides health care,
   (b) a person who is registered as a drugless practitioner under the *Drugless Practitioners Act* and who provides health care,
   (c) a person who is a member of the Ontario College of Social Workers and Social Service Workers and who provides health care, or
   (d) any other person whose primary function is to provide health care for payment; ("praticien de la santé")

"health information custodian" has the meaning set out in section 3; ("dépositaire de renseignements sur la santé")

"health number" means the number, the version code or both of them assigned to an insured person within the meaning of the *Health Insurance Act* by the General Manager within the meaning of that Act; ("numéro de la carte Santé")

"incapable" means mentally incapable, and "incapacity" has a corresponding meaning; ("incapable", "incapacité")

"individual", in relation to personal health information, means the individual, whether living or deceased, with respect to whom the information was or is being collected or created; ("particulier")

"information practices", in relation to a health information custodian, means the policy of the custodian for actions in relation to personal health information, including,

    (a) when, how and the purposes for which the custodian routinely collects, uses, modifies, discloses, retains or disposes of personal health information, and

    (b) the administrative, technical and physical safeguards and practices that the custodian maintains with respect to the information; ("pratiques relatives aux renseignements")

"Minister" means the Minister of Health and Long-Term Care; ("ministre")

"partner" means either of two persons who have lived together for at least one year and have a close personal relationship that is of primary importance in both persons' lives; ("partenaire")

"person" includes a partnership, association or other entity; ("personne")

"personal health information" has the meaning set out in section 4; ("renseignements personnels sur la santé")

"prescribed" means prescribed by the regulations made under this Act; ("prescrit")

"proceeding" includes a proceeding held in, before or under the rules of a court, a tribunal, a commission, a justice of the peace, a coroner, a committee of a College within the meaning of the *Regulated Health Professions Act, 1991*, a committee of the Board of Regents continued under the *Drugless Practitioners Act*, a committee of the Ontario College of Social Workers and Social Service Workers under the *Social Work and Social Service Work Act, 1998,* an arbitrator or a mediator; ("instance")

"quality of care information" has the same meaning as in the *Quality of Care Information Protection Act, 2004;* ("renseignements sur la qualité des soins")

"record" means a record of information in any form or in any medium, whether in written, printed, photographic or electronic form or otherwise, but does not include a computer program or other mechanism that can produce a record; ("dossier")

"relative" means either of two persons who are related to each other by blood, marriage or adoption; ("parent")

"research" means a systematic investigation designed to develop or establish principles, facts or generalizable knowledge, or any combination of them, and includes the development, testing and evaluation of research; ("recherche")

"researcher" means a person who conducts research; ("chercheur")

"research ethics board" means a board of persons that is established for the purpose of approving research plans under section 44 and that meets the prescribed requirements; ("commission d'éthique de la recherche")

"spouse" means either of two persons who,
    (a)   are married to each other, or
    (b)   live together in a conjugal relationship outside marriage and,
        (i)   have cohabited for at least one year,
        (ii) are together the parents of a child, or
        (iii) have together entered into a cohabitation agreement under section 53 of the *Family Law Act,*
unless they are living separate and apart as a result of a breakdown of their relationship; ("conjoint")

"substitute decision-maker" has the meaning set out in section 5; ("mandataire spécial")

"use", in relation to personal health information in the custody or under the control of a health information custodian or a person, means to handle or deal with the information, subject to subsection 6 (1), but does not include to disclose the information, and "use", as a noun, has a corresponding meaning. ("utiliser", "utilisation") 2004, c. 3, Sched. A, s. 2.

Health information custodian

3. (1) In this Act,

"health information custodian", subject to subsections (3) to (11), means a person or organization described in one of the following paragraphs who has custody or control of personal health information as a result of or in connection with performing the person's or organization's powers or duties or the work described in the paragraph, if any:

1.   A health care practitioner or a person who operates a group practice of health care practitioners.

2.   A service provider within the meaning of the *Long-Term Care Act, 1994* who provides a community service to which that Act applies.

3.   A community care access corporation within the meaning of the *Community Care Access Corporations Act, 2001*.

4.   A person who operates one of the following facilities, programs or services:

   i.   A hospital within the meaning of the *Public Hospitals Act*, a private hospital within the meaning of the *Private Hospitals Act*, a psychiatric facility within the meaning of the *Mental Health Act*, an institution within the meaning of the *Mental Hospitals Act* or an independent health facility within the meaning of the *Independent Health Facilities Act*.

   ii.   An approved charitable home for the aged within the meaning of the *Charitable Institutions Act*, a placement co-ordinator described in subsection 9.6 (2) of that Act, a home or joint home within the meaning of the *Homes for the Aged and Rest Homes Act*, a placement co-ordinator described in subsection 18 (2) of that Act, a nursing home within the meaning of the *Nursing Homes Act*, a placement co-ordinator described in subsection 20.1 (2) of that Act or a care home within the meaning of the *Tenant Protection Act, 1997*.

   iii.   A pharmacy within the meaning of Part VI of the *Drug and Pharmacies Regulation Act*.

   iv.   A laboratory or a specimen collection centre as defined in section 5 of the *Laboratory and Specimen Collection Centre Licensing Act*.

   v.   An ambulance service within the meaning of the *Ambulance Act*.

   vi.   A home for special care within the meaning of the *Homes for Special Care Act*.

   vii.   A centre, program or service for community health or mental health whose primary purpose is the provision of health care.

5. An evaluator within the meaning of the *Health Care Consent Act, 1996* or an assessor within the meaning of the *Substitute Decisions Act, 1992*.

6. A medical officer of health or a board of health within the meaning of the *Health Protection and Promotion Act*.

7. The Minister, together with the Ministry of the Minister if the context so requires.

8. Any other person prescribed as a health information custodian if the person has custody or control of personal health information as a result of or in connection with performing prescribed powers, duties or work or any prescribed class of such persons. 2004, c. 3, Sched. A, s. 3 (1).

Interpretation, officer in charge

(2) For the purposes of subparagraph 4 i of the definition of "health information custodian" in subsection (1), the officer in charge of an institution within the meaning of the *Mental Hospitals Act* shall be deemed to be the person who operates the institution. 2004, c. 3, Sched. A, s. 3 (2).

Exceptions

(3) Except as is prescribed, a person described in any of the following paragraphs is not a health information custodian in respect of personal health information that the person collects, uses or discloses while performing the person's powers or duties or the work described in the paragraph, if any:

1. A person described in paragraph 1, 2 or 5 of the definition of "health information custodian" in subsection (1) who is an agent of a health information custodian.

2. A person who is authorized to act for or on behalf of a person that is not a health information custodian, if the scope of duties of the authorized person does not include the provision of health care.

3. The Minister when acting on behalf of an institution within the meaning of the *Freedom of Information and Protection of Privacy Act* or the *Municipal Freedom of Information and Protection of Privacy Act* that is not a health information custodian. 2004, c. 3, Sched. A, s. 3 (3).

Other exceptions

(4) A health information custodian does not include a person described in one of the following paragraphs who has custody or control of personal health information as a result of or in connection with performing the work described in the paragraph:

1. An aboriginal healer who provides traditional healing services to aboriginal persons or members of an aboriginal community.

2. An aboriginal midwife who provides traditional midwifery services to aboriginal persons or members of an aboriginal community.

3. A person who treats another person solely by prayer or spiritual means in accordance with the tenets of the religion of the person giving the treatment. 2004, c. 3, Sched. A, s. 3 (4).

Multiple facilities

(5) Subject to subsection (6) or an order of the Minister under subsection (8), a health information custodian that operates more than one facility described in one of the subparagraphs of paragraph 4 of the definition of "health information custodian" in subsection (1) shall be deemed to be a separate custodian with respect to personal health information of which it has custody or control as a result of or in connection with operating each of the facilities that it operates. 2004, c. 3, Sched. A, s. 3 (5).

Single custodian

(6) Despite subsection (5), the following persons shall be deemed to be a single health information custodian with respect to all the functions described in the applicable paragraph, if any:

1. A person who operates a hospital within the meaning of the *Public Hospitals Act* and any of the facilities, programs or services described in paragraph 4 of the definition of "health information custodian" in subsection (1).

2. A community care access corporation that provides a community service within the meaning of subsection 2 (3) of the *Long Term Care Act, 1994* and acts as a placement co-ordinator as described in subsection 9.6 (2) of the *Charitable Institutions Act*, subsection 18 (2) of the *Homes for the Aged and Rest Homes Act* or subsection 20.1 (2) of the *Nursing Homes Act*.

3. Health information custodians or facilities that are prescribed. 2004, c. 3, Sched. A, s. 3 (6).

Application to act as one custodian

(7) A health information custodian that operates more than one facility described in one of the subparagraphs of paragraph 4 of the definition of "health information custodian" in subsection (1) or two or more health information custodians may apply to the Minister, in a form approved by the Minister, for an order described in subsection (8). 2004, c. 3, Sched. A, s. 3 (7).

Minister's order

(8) Upon receiving an application described in subsection (7), the Minister may make an order permitting all or some of the applicants to act as a single health information custodian on behalf of those facilities, powers, duties or

work that the Minister specifies, subject to the terms that the Minister considers appropriate and specifies in the order, if the Minister is of the opinion that it is appropriate to make the order in the circumstances, having regard to,

(a) the public interest;

(b) the ability of the applicants to provide individuals with reasonable access to their personal health information;

(c) the ability of the applicants to comply with the requirements of this Act; and

(d) whether permitting the applicants to act as a single health information custodian is necessary to enable them to effectively provide integrated health care. 2004, c. 3, Sched. A, s. 3 (8).

Scope of order

(9) In an order made under subsection (8), the Minister may order that any class of health information custodians that the Minister considers to be situated similarly to the applicants is permitted to act as a single health information custodian, subject to the terms that the Minister considers appropriate and specifies in the order, if the Minister is of the opinion that it is appropriate to so order, having regard to,

(a) the public interest;

(b) the ability of the custodians that are subject to the order made under this subsection to provide individuals with reasonable access to their personal health information;

(c) the ability of the custodians that are subject to the order made under this subsection to comply with the requirements of this Act; and

(d) whether permitting the custodians that are subject to the order made under this subsection to act as a single health information custodian is necessary to enable them to effectively provide integrated health care. 2004, c. 3, Sched. A, s. 3 (9).

No hearing required

(10) The Minister is not required to hold a hearing or to afford to any person an opportunity for a hearing before making an order under subsection (8). 2004, c. 3, Sched. A, s. 3 (10).

Duration

(11) Subject to subsection (12), a health information custodian does not cease to be a health information custodian with respect to a record of personal health information until complete custody and control of the record, where applicable, passes to another person who is legally authorized to hold the record. 2004, c. 3, Sched. A, s. 3 (11).

Death of custodian

(12) If a health information custodian dies, the following person shall be deemed to be the health information custodian with respect to records of personal health information held by the deceased custodian until custody and control of the records, where applicable, passes to another person who is legally authorized to hold the records:

1. The estate trustee of the deceased custodian.

2. The person who has assumed responsibility for the administration of the deceased custodian's estate, if the estate does not have an estate trustee. 2004, c. 3, Sched. A, s. 3 (12).

Personal health information

4. (1) In this Act,

"personal health information", subject to subsections (3) and (4), means identifying information about an individual in oral or recorded form, if the information,

(a) relates to the physical or mental health of the individual, including information that consists of the health history of the individual's family,

(b) relates to the providing of health care to the individual, including the identification of a person as a provider of health care to the individual,

(c) is a plan of service within the meaning of the *Long-Term Care Act, 1994* for the individual,

(d) relates to payments or eligibility for health care in respect of the individual,

(e) relates to the donation by the individual of any body part or bodily substance of the individual or is derived from the testing or examination of any such body part or bodily substance,

(f) is the individual's health number, or

(g) identifies an individual's substitute decision-maker. 2004, c. 3, Sched. A, s. 4 (1).

Identifying information

(2) In this section,

"identifying information" means information that identifies an individual or for which it is reasonably foreseeable in the circumstances that it could be utilized, either alone or with other information, to identify an individual. 2004, c. 3, Sched. A, s. 4 (2).

Mixed records

(3) Personal health information about an individual includes identifying information about the individual that is not personal health information described in subsection (1) but that is contained in a record that contains personal health information described in that subsection about the individual. 2004, c. 3, Sched. A, s. 4 (3).

Exception

(4) Personal health information does not include identifying information contained in a record that is in the custody or under the control of a health information custodian if,

(a) the identifying information contained in the record relates primarily to one or more employees or other agents of the custodian; and

(b) the record is maintained primarily for a purpose other than the provision of health care or assistance in providing health care to the employees or other agents. 2004, c. 3, Sched. A, s. 4 (4).

Substitute decision-maker

5. (1) In this Act,

"substitute decision-maker", in relation to an individual, means, unless the context requires otherwise, a person who is authorized under this Act to consent on behalf of the individual to the collection, use or disclosure of personal health information about the individual. 2004, c. 3, Sched. A, s. 5 (1).

Decision about treatment

(2) A substitute decision-maker of an individual within the meaning of section 9 of the *Health Care Consent Act, 1996* shall be deemed to be a substitute decision-maker of the individual in respect of the collection, use or disclosure of personal health information about the individual if the purpose of the collection, use or disclosure is necessary for, or ancillary to, a decision about a treatment under Part II of that Act. 2004, c. 3, Sched. A, s. 5 (2).

Admission to a care facility

(3) A substitute decision-maker of an individual within the meaning of section 39 of the *Health Care Consent Act, 1996* shall be deemed to be a substitute decision-maker of the individual in respect of the collection, use or disclosure of personal health information about the individual if the purpose of the collection, use or disclosure is necessary for, or ancillary to, a decision about admission to a care facility under Part III of that Act. 2004, c. 3, Sched. A, s. 5 (3).

Personal assistance services

(4) A substitute decision-maker of an individual within the meaning of section 56 of the *Health Care Consent Act, 1996* shall be deemed to be a substitute decision-maker of the individual in respect of the collection, use or disclosure of personal health information about the individual if the purpose of the collection, use or disclosure is necessary for, or ancillary to, a decision about a personal assistance service under Part IV of that Act. 2004, c. 3, Sched. A, s. 5 (4).

Interpretation

6. (1) For the purposes of this Act, the providing of personal health information between a health information custodian and an agent of the custodian is a use by the custodian, and not a disclosure by the person providing the information or a collection by the person to whom the information is provided. 2004, c. 3, Sched. A, s. 6 (1).

Provisions based on consent

(2) A provision of this Act that applies to the collection, use or disclosure of personal health information about an individual by a health information custodian with the consent of the individual, whatever the nature of the consent, does not affect the collection, use or disclosure that this Act permits or requires the health information custodian to make of the information without the consent of the individual. 2004, c. 3, Sched. A, s. 6 (2).

Permissive disclosure

(3) A provision of this Act that permits a health information custodian to disclose personal health information about an individual without the consent of the individual,

(a) does not require the custodian to disclose it unless required to do so by law;

(b) does not relieve the custodian from a legal requirement to disclose the information; and

(c) does not prevent the custodian from obtaining the individual's consent for the disclosure. 2004, c. 3, Sched. A, s. 6 (3).

APPLICATION OF ACT

Application of Act

7. (1) Except if this Act or its regulations specifically provide otherwise, this Act applies to,

(a) the collection of personal health information by a health information custodian on or after the day this section comes into force;

(b) the use or disclosure of personal health information, on or after the day this section comes into force, by,

  (i) a health information custodian, even if the custodian collected the information before that day, or

  (ii) a person who is not a health information custodian and to whom a health information custodian disclosed the information, even if the person received the information before that day; and

(c) the collection, use or disclosure of a health number by any person on or after the day this section comes into force. 2004, c. 3, Sched. A, s. 7 (1).

Conflict

(2) In the event of a conflict between a provision of this Act or its regulations and a provision of any other Act or its regulations, this Act and its regulations prevail unless this Act, its regulations or the other Act specifically provide otherwise. 2004, c. 3, Sched. A, s. 7 (2).

Interpretation

(3) For the purpose of this section, there is no conflict unless it is not possible to comply with both this Act and its regulations and any other Act or its regulations. 2004, c. 3, Sched. A, s. 7 (3).

Exception

(4) This Act and its regulations do not prevail in the event of a conflict between a provision of this Act or its regulations and a provision of the *Quality of Care Information Protection Act, 2004* or its regulations. 2004, c. 3, Sched. A, s. 7 (4).

Freedom of information legislation

8. (1) Subject to subsection (2), the *Freedom of Information and Protection of Privacy Act* and the *Municipal Freedom of Information and Protection of Privacy Act* do not apply to personal health information collected by a health information custodian or in the custody or under the control of a health information custodian unless this Act specifies otherwise. 2004, c. 3, Sched. A, s. 8 (1).

Exceptions

(2) Sections 11, 12, 15, 16, 17 and 33, subsection 35 (2) and sections 36 and 44 of the *Freedom of Information and Protection of Privacy Act* and sections 5, 9, 10, 24, 25, 26 and 34 of the *Municipal Freedom of Information and Protection of Privacy Act* apply in respect of records of personal health information in the custody or under the control of a health information custodian that is an institution within the meaning of either of those Acts, as the case may be, or that is acting as part of such an institution. 2004, c. 3, Sched. A, s. 8 (2).

Same

(3) A record of personal health information prepared by or in the custody or control of an institution within the meaning of the *Freedom of Information and Protection of Privacy Act* or the *Municipal Freedom of Information and Protection of Privacy Act* shall be deemed to be a record to which clause 32 (b) of the *Freedom of Information and Protection of Privacy Act* or clause 25 (1) (b) of the *Municipal Freedom of Information and Protection of Privacy Act* applies, as the case may be. 2004, c. 3, Sched. A, s. 8 (3).

Access

(4) This Act does not limit a person's right of access under section 10 of the *Freedom of Information and Protection of Privacy Act* or section 4 of the *Municipal Freedom of Information and Protection of Privacy Act* to a record of personal health information if all the types of information referred to in subsection 4 (1) are reasonably severed from the record. 2004, c. 3, Sched. A, s. 8 (4).

Transition

(5) This Act does not apply to a collection, use or disclosure of personal health information, a request for access or an appeal made under the *Freedom of Information and Protection of Privacy Act* or the *Municipal Freedom of Information and Protection of Privacy Act* before the day this section comes into force, and the applicable Act continues to apply to the collection, use, disclosure, request or appeal. 2004, c. 3, Sched. A, s. 8 (5).

Non-application of Act

9. (1) This Act does not apply to personal health information about an individual after the earlier of 120 years after a record containing the information was created and 50 years after the death of the individual. 2004, c. 3, Sched. A, s. 9 (1).

Other rights and Acts

(2) Nothing in this Act shall be construed to interfere with,

(a) anything in connection with a subrogated claim or a potential subrogated claim;

(b) any legal privilege, including solicitor-client privilege;

(c) the law of evidence or information otherwise available by law to a party or a witness in a proceeding;

(d) the power of a court or a tribunal to compel a witness to testify or to compel the production of a document;

(e) the regulatory activities of a College under the *Regulated Heath Professions Act, 1991*, the College under the *Social Work and Social Service Work Act, 1998* or the Board under the *Drugless Practitioners Act*; or

(f) any provision of any Act of Ontario or Canada or any court order, if the provision or order, as the case may be, prohibits a person from making information public or from publishing information. 2004, c. 3, Sched. A, s. 9 (2).

PART II
PRACTICES TO PROTECT PERSONAL HEALTH INFORMATION

GENERAL

Information practices

10. (1) A health information custodian that has custody or control of personal health information shall have in place information practices that comply with the requirements of this Act and its regulations. 2004, c. 3, Sched. A, s. 10 (1).

Duty to follow practices

(2) A health information custodian shall comply with its information practices. 2004, c. 3, Sched. A, s. 10 (2).

Use of electronic means

(3) A health information custodian that uses electronic means to collect, use, modify, disclose, retain or dispose of personal health information shall comply with the prescribed requirements, if any. 2004, c. 3, Sched. A, s. 10 (3).

Providers to custodians

(4) A person who provides goods or services for the purpose of enabling a health information custodian to use electronic means to collect, use, modify, disclose, retain or dispose of personal health information shall comply with the prescribed requirements, if any. 2004, c. 3, Sched. A, s. 10 (4).

Accuracy

11. (1) A health information custodian that uses personal health information about an individual shall take reasonable steps to ensure that the information is as accurate, complete and up-to-date as is necessary for the purposes for which it uses the information. 2004, c. 3, Sched. A, s. 11 (1).

Same, disclosure

(2) A health information custodian that discloses personal health information about an individual shall,

(a) take reasonable steps to ensure that the information is as accurate, complete and up-to-date as is necessary for the purposes of the disclosure that are known to the custodian at the time of the disclosure; or

(b) clearly set out for the recipient of the disclosure the limitations, if any, on the accuracy, completeness or up-to-date character of the information. 2004, c. 3, Sched. A, s. 11 (2).

Security

12. (1) A health information custodian shall take steps that are reasonable in the circumstances to ensure that personal health information in the custodian's custody or control is protected against theft, loss and unauthorized use or disclosure and to ensure that the records containing the information are protected against unauthorized copying, modification or disposal. 2004, c. 3, Sched. A, s. 12 (1).

Notice of loss, etc.

(2) Subject to subsection (3) and subject to the exceptions and additional requirements, if any, that are prescribed, a health information custodian that has custody or control of personal health information about an individual shall notify the individual at the first reasonable opportunity if the information is stolen, lost, or accessed by unauthorized persons. 2004, c. 3, Sched. A, s. 12 (2).

Exception

(3) If the health information custodian is a researcher who has received the personal health information from another health information custodian under subsection 44 (1), the researcher shall not notify the individual that the information is stolen, lost or accessed by unauthorized persons unless the health information custodian under that subsection first obtains the individual's consent to having the researcher contact the individual and informs the researcher that the individual has given the consent. 2004, c. 3, Sched. A, s. 12 (3).

RECORDS

Handling of records

13. (1) A health information custodian shall ensure that the records of personal health information that it has in its custody or under its control are retained, transferred and disposed of in a secure manner and in accordance with the prescribed requirements, if any. 2004, c. 3, Sched. A, s. 13 (1).

Retention of records subject to a request

(2) Despite subsection (1), a health information custodian that has custody or control of personal health information that is the subject of a request for

access under section 53 shall retain the information for as long as necessary to allow the individual to exhaust any recourse under this Act that he or she may have with respect to the request. 2004, c. 3, Sched. A, s. 13 (2).

Place where records kept

14. (1) A health information custodian may keep a record of personal health information about an individual in the individual's home in any reasonable manner to which the individual consents, subject to any restrictions set out in a regulation, by-law or published guideline under the *Regulated Health Professions Act, 1991*, an Act referred to in Schedule 1 of that Act, the *Drugless Practitioners Act* or the *Social Work and Social Service Work Act, 1998.* 2004, c. 3, Sched. A, s. 14 (1).

Records kept in other places

(2) A health care practitioner may keep a record of personal health information about an individual in a place other than the individual's home and other than a place in the control of the practitioner if,

(a) the record is kept in a reasonable manner;

(b) the individual consents;

(c) the health care practitioner is permitted to keep the record in the place in accordance with a regulation, by-law or published guideline under the *Regulated Health Professions Act, 1991*, an Act referred to in Schedule 1 to that Act, the *Drugless Practitioners Act* or the *Social Work and Social Service Work Act, 1998*, if the health care practitioner is described in any of clauses (a) to (c) of the definition of "health care practitioner" in section 2; and

(d) the prescribed conditions, if any, are satisfied. 2004, c. 3, Sched. A, s. 14 (2).

ACCOUNTABILITY AND OPENNESS

Contact person

15. (1) A health information custodian that is a natural person may designate a contact person described in subsection (3). 2004, c. 3, Sched. A, s. 15 (1).

Same

(2) A health information custodian that is not a natural person shall designate a contact person described in subsection (3). 2004, c. 3, Sched. A, s. 15 (2).

Functions of contact person

(3) A contact person is an agent of the health information custodian and is authorized on behalf of the custodian to,

(a) facilitate the custodian's compliance with this Act;

(b) ensure that all agents of the custodian are appropriately informed of their duties under this Act;

(c) respond to inquiries from the public about the custodian's information practices;

(d) respond to requests of an individual for access to or correction of a record of personal health information about the individual that is in the custody or under the control of the custodian; and

(e) receive complaints from the public about the custodian's alleged contravention of this Act or its regulations. 2004, c. 3, Sched. A, s. 15 (3).

If no contact person

(4) A health information custodian that is a natural person and that does not designate a contact person under subsection (1) shall perform on his or her own the functions described in clauses (3) (b), (c), (d) and (e). 2004, c. 3, Sched. A, s. 15 (4).

Written public statement

16. (1) A health information custodian shall, in a manner that is practical in the circumstances, make available to the public a written statement that,

(a) provides a general description of the custodian's information practices;

(b) describes how to contact,

   (i) the contact person described in subsection 15 (3), if the custodian has one, or

   (ii) the custodian, if the custodian does not have that contact person;

(c) describes how an individual may obtain access to or request correction of a record of personal health information about the individual that is in the custody or control of the custodian; and

(d) describes how to make a complaint to the custodian and to the Commissioner under this Act. 2004, c. 3, Sched. A, s. 16 (1).

Notification

(2) If a health information custodian uses or discloses personal health information about an individual, without the individual's consent, in a manner that is outside the scope of the custodian's description of its information practices under clause (1) (a), the custodian shall,

(a) inform the individual of the uses and disclosures at the first reasonable opportunity unless, under section 52, the individual does not have a right of access to a record of the information;

(b) make a note of the uses and disclosures; and

(c) keep the note as part of the records of personal health information about the individual that it has in its custody or under its control or in a form that is linked to those records. 2004, c. 3, Sched. A, s. 16 (2).

Agents and information

17. (1) A health information custodian is responsible for personal health information in the custody or control of the health information custodian and may permit the custodian's agents to collect, use, disclose, retain or dispose of personal health information on the custodian's behalf only if,

(a) the custodian is permitted or required to collect, use, disclose, retain or dispose of the information, as the case may be;

(b) the collection, use, disclosure, retention or disposition of the information, as the case may be, is in the course of the agent's duties and not contrary to the limits imposed by the custodian, this Act or another law; and

(c) the prescribed requirements, if any, are met. 2004, c. 3, Sched. A, s. 17 (1).

Restriction on agents

(2) Except as permitted or required by law and subject to the exceptions and additional requirements, if any, that are prescribed, an agent of a health information custodian shall not collect, use, disclose, retain or dispose of personal health information on the custodian's behalf unless the custodian permits the agent to do so in accordance with subsection (1). 2004, c. 3, Sched. A, s. 17 (2).

Responsibility of agent

(3) An agent of a health information custodian shall notify the custodian at the first reasonable opportunity if personal health information handled by the agent on behalf of the custodian is stolen, lost or accessed by unauthorized persons. 2004, c. 3, Sched. A, s. 17 (3).

PART III
CONSENT CONCERNING PERSONAL HEALTH INFORMATION

GENERAL

Elements of consent

18. (1) If this Act or any other Act requires the consent of an individual for the collection, use or disclosure of personal health information by a health information custodian, the consent,

(a) must be a consent of the individual;

(b) must be knowledgeable;

(c) must relate to the information; and

(d) must not be obtained through deception or coercion. 2004, c. 3, Sched. A, s. 18 (1).

Implied consent

(2) Subject to subsection (3), a consent to the collection, use or disclosure of personal health information about an individual may be express or implied. 2004, c. 3, Sched. A, s. 18 (2).

Exception

(3) A consent to the disclosure of personal health information about an individual must be express, and not implied, if,

(a) a health information custodian makes the disclosure to a person that is not a health information custodian; or

(b) a health information custodian makes the disclosure to another health information custodian and the disclosure is not for the purposes of providing health care or assisting in providing health care. 2004, c. 3, Sched. A, s. 18 (3).

Same

(4) Subsection (3) does not apply to,

(a) a disclosure pursuant to an implied consent described in subsection 20 (4);

(b) a disclosure pursuant to clause 32 (1) (b); or

(c) a prescribed type of disclosure that does not include information about an individual's state of health. 2004, c. 3, Sched. A, s. 18 (4).

Knowledgeable consent

(5) A consent to the collection, use or disclosure of personal health information about an individual is knowledgeable if it is reasonable in the circumstances to believe that the individual knows,

(a) the purposes of the collection, use or disclosure, as the case may be; and

(b) that the individual may give or withhold consent. 2004, c. 3, Sched. A, s. 18 (5).

Notice of purposes

(6) Unless it is not reasonable in the circumstances, it is reasonable to believe that an individual knows the purposes of the collection, use or disclosure of personal health information about the individual by a health information custodian if the custodian posts or makes readily available a notice describing the purposes where it is likely to come to the individual's attention or provides the individual with such a notice. 2004, c. 3, Sched. A, s. 18 (6).

Transition

(7) A consent that an individual gives, before the day that subsection (1) comes into force, to a collection, use or disclosure of information that is personal health information is a valid consent if it meets the requirements of this Act for consent. 2004, c. 3, Sched. A, s. 18 (7).

Withdrawal of consent

19. (1) If an individual consents to have a health information custodian collect, use or disclose personal health information about the individual, the individual may withdraw the consent, whether the consent is express or implied, by providing notice to the health information custodian, but the withdrawal of the consent shall not have retroactive effect. 2004, c. 3, Sched. A, s. 19 (1).

Conditional consent

(2) If an individual places a condition on his or her consent to have a health information custodian collect, use or disclose personal health information about the individual, the condition is not effective to the extent that it purports to prohibit or restrict any recording of personal health information by a health information custodian that is required by law or by established standards of professional practice or institutional practice. 2004, c. 3, Sched. A, s. 19 (2).

Assumption of validity

20. (1) A health information custodian who has obtained an individual's consent to a collection, use or disclosure of personal health information about the individual or who has received a copy of a document purporting to record the individual's consent to the collection, use or disclosure is entitled to assume that the consent fulfils the requirements of this Act and the individual has not withdrawn it, unless it is not reasonable to assume so. 2004, c. 3, Sched. A, s. 20 (1).

Implied consent

(2) A health information custodian described in paragraph 1, 2, 3 or 4 of the definition of "health information custodian" in subsection 3 (1), that receives personal health information about an individual from the individual, the individual's substitute decision-maker or another health information custodian for the purpose of providing health care or assisting in the provision of health care to the individual, is entitled to assume that it has the individual's implied consent to collect, use or disclose the information for the purposes of providing health care or assisting in providing health care to the individual, unless the custodian that receives the information is aware that the individual has expressly withheld or withdrawn the consent. 2004, c. 3, Sched. A, s. 20 (2).

Limited consent

(3) If a health information custodian discloses, with the consent of an individual, personal health information about the individual to a health information custodian described in paragraph 1, 2, 3 or 4 of the definition of "health information custodian" in subsection 3 (1) for the purpose of the provision of health care to the individual and if the disclosing custodian does not have the consent of the individual to disclose all the personal health information about the individual that it considers reasonably necessary for that purpose, the disclosing custodian shall notify the custodian to whom it disclosed the information of that fact. 2004, c. 3, Sched. A, s. 20 (3).

Implied consent, affiliation

(4) If an individual who is a resident or patient in a facility that is a health information custodian provides to the custodian information about his or her religious or other organizational affiliation, the facility may assume that it has the individual's implied consent to provide his or her name and location in the facility to a representative of the religious or other organization, where the custodian has offered the individual the opportunity to withhold or withdraw the consent and the individual has not done so. 2004, c. 3, Sched. A, s. 20 (4).

CAPACITY AND SUBSTITUTE DECISION-MAKING

Capacity to consent

21. (1) An individual is capable of consenting to the collection, use or disclosure of personal health information if the individual is able,

(a) to understand the information that is relevant to deciding whether to consent to the collection, use or disclosure, as the case may be; and

(b) to appreciate the reasonably foreseeable consequences of giving, not giving, withholding or withdrawing the consent. 2004, c. 3, Sched. A, s. 21 (1).

Different information

(2) An individual may be capable of consenting to the collection, use or disclosure of some parts of personal health information, but incapable of consenting with respect to other parts. 2004, c. 3, Sched. A, s. 21 (2).

Different times

(3) An individual may be capable of consenting to the collection, use or disclosure of personal health information at one time, but incapable of consenting at another time. 2004, c. 3, Sched. A, s. 21 (3).

Presumption of capacity

(4) An individual is presumed to be capable of consenting to the collection, use or disclosure of personal health information. 2004, c. 3, Sched. A, s. 21 (4).

Non-application

(5) A health information custodian may rely on the presumption described in subsection (4) unless the custodian has reasonable grounds to believe that the individual is incapable of consenting to the collection, use or disclosure of personal health information. 2004, c. 3, Sched. A, s. 21 (5).

Determination of incapacity

22. (1) A health information custodian that determines the incapacity of an individual to consent to the collection, use or disclosure of personal health information under this Act shall do so in accordance with the requirements and restrictions, if any, that are prescribed. 2004, c. 3, Sched. A, s. 22 (1).

Information about determination

(2) If it is reasonable in the circumstances, a health information custodian shall provide, to an individual determined incapable of consenting to the collection, use or disclosure of his or her personal health information by the custodian, information about the consequences of the determination of incapacity, including the information, if any, that is prescribed. 2004, c. 3, Sched. A, s. 22 (2).

Review of determination

(3) An individual whom a health information custodian determines is incapable of consenting to the collection, use or disclosure of his or her personal health information by a health information custodian may apply to the Board for a review of the determination unless there is a person who is entitled to act as the substitute decision-maker of the individual under subsection 5 (2), (3) or (4). 2004, c. 3, Sched. A, s. 22 (3).

Parties

(4) The parties to the application are:

1. The individual applying for the review of the determination.
2. The health information custodian that has custody or control of the personal health information.
3. All other persons whom the Board specifies. 2004, c. 3, Sched. A, s. 22 (4).

Powers of Board

(5) The Board may confirm the determination of incapacity or may determine that the individual is capable of consenting to the collection, use or disclosure of personal health information. 2004, c. 3, Sched. A, s. 22 (5).

Restriction on repeated applications

(6) If a determination that an individual is incapable with respect to consenting to the collection, use or disclosure of personal health information is confirmed on the final disposition of an application under this section, the individual shall not make a new application under this section for a determination with respect to the same or a similar issue within six months after the final disposition of the earlier application, unless the Board gives leave in advance. 2004, c. 3, Sched. A, s. 22 (6).

Grounds for leave

(7) The Board may give leave for the new application to be made if it is satisfied that there has been a material change in circumstances that justifies reconsideration of the individual's capacity. 2004, c. 3, Sched. A, s. 22 (7).

Procedure

(8) Sections 73 to 81 of the *Health Care Consent Act, 1996* apply with necessary modifications to an application under this section. 2004, c. 3, Sched. A, s. 22 (8).

Persons who may consent

23. (1) If this Act or any other Act refers to a consent required of an individual to a collection, use or disclosure of personal health information about the individual, a person described in one of the following paragraphs may give, withhold or withdraw the consent:

1. If the individual is capable of consenting to the collection, use or disclosure of the information,
    i. the individual, or
    ii. if the individual is at least 16 years of age, any person who is capable of consenting, whom the individual has authorized in writing to act on his or her behalf and who, if a natural person, is at least 16 years of age.

2. If the individual is a child who is less than 16 years of age, a parent of the child or a children's aid society or other person who is lawfully entitled to give or refuse consent in the place of the parent unless the information relates to,
    i. treatment within the meaning of the *Health Care Consent Act, 1996*, about which the child has made a decision on his or her own in accordance with that Act, or
    ii. counselling in which the child has participated on his or her own under the *Child and Family Services Act*.

3. If the individual is incapable of consenting to the collection, use or disclosure of the information, a person who is authorized under subsection 5 (2), (3) or (4) or section 26 to consent on behalf of the individual.

4. If the individual is deceased, the deceased's estate trustee or the person who has assumed responsibility for the administration of the deceased's estate, if the estate does not have an estate trustee.

5. A person whom an Act of Ontario or Canada authorizes or requires to act on behalf of the individual. 2004, c. 3, Sched. A, s. 23 (1).

Definition

(2) In subsection (1),

"parent" does not include a parent who has only a right of access to the child. 2004, c. 3, Sched. A, s. 23 (2).

Conflict if child capable

(3) If the individual is a child who is less than 16 years of age and who is capable of consenting to the collection, use or disclosure of the information and if there is a person who is entitled to act as the substitute decision-maker of the child under paragraph 2 of subsection (1), a decision of the child to give, withhold or withdraw the consent or to provide the information prevails over a conflicting decision of that person. 2004, c. 3, Sched. A, s. 23 (3).

Factors to consider for consent

24. (1) A person who consents under this Act or any other Act on behalf of or in the place of an individual to a collection, use or disclosure of personal health information by a health information custodian, who withholds or withdraws such a consent or who provides an express instruction under clause 37 (1) (a), 38 (1) (a) or 50 (1) (e) shall take into consideration,

(a) the wishes, values and beliefs that,
(i)   if the individual is capable, the person knows the individual holds and believes the individual would want reflected in decisions made concerning the individual's personal health information, or
(ii) if the individual is incapable or deceased, the person knows the individual held when capable or alive and believes the individual would have wanted reflected in decisions made concerning the individual's personal health information;

(b) whether the benefits that the person expects from the collection, use or disclosure of the information outweigh the risk of negative consequences occurring as a result of the collection, use or disclosure;

(c) whether the purpose for which the collection, use or disclosure is sought can be accomplished without the collection, use or disclosure; and

(d) whether the collection, use or disclosure is necessary to satisfy any legal obligation. 2004, c. 3, Sched. A, s. 24 (1).

Determination of compliance

(2) If a substitute decision-maker, on behalf of an incapable individual, gives, withholds or withdraws a consent to a collection, use or disclosure of personal health information about the individual by a health information custodian or provides an express instruction under clause 37 (1) (a), 38 (1) (a) or 50 (1) (e) and if the custodian is of the opinion that the substitute decision-maker has not complied with subsection (1), the custodian may apply to the Board for a determination as to whether the substitute decision-maker complied with that subsection. 2004, c. 3, Sched. A, s. 24 (2).

Parties

(3) The parties to the application are:

1. The health information custodian.
2. The incapable individual.
3. The substitute decision-maker.
4. Any other person whom the Board specifies. 2004, c. 3, Sched. A, s. 24 (3).

Power of Board

(4) In determining whether the substitute decision-maker complied with subsection (1), the Board may substitute its opinion for that of the substitute decision-maker. 2004, c. 3, Sched. A, s. 24 (4).

Directions

(5) If the Board determines that the substitute decision-maker did not comply with subsection (1), it may give him or her directions and, in doing so, shall take into consideration the matters set out in clauses (1) (a) to (d). 2004, c. 3, Sched. A, s. 24 (5).

Time for compliance

(6) The Board shall specify the time within which the substitute decision-maker must comply with its directions. 2004, c. 3, Sched. A, s. 24 (6).

Deemed not authorized

(7) If the substitute decision-maker does not comply with the Board's directions within the time specified by the Board, he or she shall be deemed not to meet the requirements of subsection 26 (2). 2004, c. 3, Sched. A, s. 24 (7).

Public Guardian and Trustee

(8) If the substitute decision-maker who is given directions is the Public Guardian and Trustee, he or she is required to comply with the directions and subsection (6) does not apply to him or her. 2004, c. 3, Sched. A, s. 24 (8).

Procedure

(9) Sections 73 to 81 of the *Health Care Consent Act, 1996* apply with necessary modifications to an application under this section. 2004, c. 3, Sched. A, s. 24 (9).

Authority of substitute decision-maker

25. (1) If this Act permits or requires an individual to make a request, give an instruction or take a step and a substitute decision-maker is authorized to consent on behalf of the individual to the collection, use or disclosure of personal health information about the individual, the substitute decision-maker may make the request, give the instruction or take the step on behalf of the individual. 2004, c. 3, Sched. A, s. 25 (1).

Same

(2) If a substitute decision-maker makes a request, gives an instruction or takes a step under subsection (1) on behalf of an individual, references in this Act to the individual with respect to the request made, the instruction given or the step taken by the substitute decision-maker shall be read as references to the substitute decision-maker, and not to the individual. 2004, c. 3, Sched. A, s. 25 (2).

Incapable individual: persons who may consent

26. (1) If an individual is determined to be incapable of consenting to the collection, use or disclosure of personal health information by a health information custodian, a person described in one of the following paragraphs may, on the individual's behalf and in the place of the individual, give, withhold or withdraw the consent:

1. The individual's guardian of the person or guardian of property, if the consent relates to the guardian's authority to make a decision on behalf of the individual.
2. The individual's attorney for personal care or attorney for property, if the consent relates to the attorney's authority to make a decision on behalf of the individual.
3. The individual's representative appointed by the Board under section 27, if the representative has authority to give the consent.
4. The individual's spouse or partner.

5. A child or parent of the individual, or a children's aid society or other person who is lawfully entitled to give or refuse consent in the place of the parent. This paragraph does not include a parent who has only a right of access to the individual. If a children's aid society or other person is lawfully entitled to consent in the place of the parent, this paragraph does not include the parent.

6. A parent of the individual with only a right of access to the individual.

7. A brother or sister of the individual.

8. Any other relative of the individual. 2004, c. 3, Sched. A, s. 26 (1).

Requirements

(2) A person described in subsection (1) may consent only if the person,

(a) is capable of consenting to the collection, use or disclosure of personal health information by a health information custodian;

(b) in the case of an individual, is at least 16 years old or is the parent of the individual to whom the personal health information relates;

(c) is not prohibited by court order or separation agreement from having access to the individual to whom the personal health information relates or from giving or refusing consent on the individual's behalf;

(d) is available; and

(e) is willing to assume the responsibility of making a decision on whether or not to consent. 2004, c. 3, Sched. A, s. 26 (2).

Meaning of "available"

(3) For the purpose of clause (2) (d), a person is available if it is possible, within a time that is reasonable in the circumstances, to communicate with the person and obtain a consent. 2004, c. 3, Sched. A, s. 26 (3).

Ranking

(4) A person described in a paragraph of subsection (1) may consent only if no person described in an earlier paragraph meets the requirements of subsection (2). 2004, c. 3, Sched. A, s. 26 (4).

Same

(5) Despite subsection (4), a person described in a paragraph of subsection (1) who is present or has otherwise been contacted may consent if the person believes that,

(a) no other person described in an earlier paragraph or the same paragraph exists; or

(b) although such other person exists, the other person is not a person described in paragraph 1 or 2 of subsection (1) and would not object to the person who is present or has otherwise been contacted making the decision. 2004, c. 3, Sched. A, s. 26 (5).

Public Guardian and Trustee

(6) If no person described in subsection (1) meets the requirements of subsection (2), the Public Guardian and Trustee may make the decision to consent. 2004, c. 3, Sched. A, s. 26 (6).

Conflict between persons in same paragraph

(7) If two or more persons who are described in the same paragraph of subsection (1) and who meet the requirements of subsection (2) disagree about whether to consent, and if their claims rank ahead of all others, the Public Guardian and Trustee may make the decision in their stead. 2004, c. 3, Sched. A, s. 26 (7).

Transition, representative appointed by individual

(8) Where an individual, to whom personal health information relates, appointed a representative under section 36.1 of the *Mental Health Act* before the day this section comes into force, the representative shall be deemed to have the same authority as a person mentioned in paragraph 2 of subsection (1). 2004, c. 3, Sched. A, s. 26 (8).

Limited authority

(9) The authority conferred on the representative by subsection (8) is limited to the purposes for which the representative was appointed. 2004, c. 3, Sched. A, s. 26 (9).

Revocation

(10) An individual who is capable of consenting with respect to personal health information may revoke the appointment mentioned in subsection (8) in writing. 2004, c. 3, Sched. A, s. 26 (10).

Ranking

(11) A person who is entitled to be the substitute decision-maker of the individual under this section may act as the substitute decision-maker only in circumstances where there is no person who may act as the substitute decision-maker of the individual under subsection 5 (2), (3) or (4). 2004, c. 3, Sched. A, s. 26 (11).

Appointment of representative

27. (1) An individual who is 16 years old or older and who is determined to be incapable of consenting to the collection, use or disclosure of personal

health information may apply to the Board for appointment of a representative to consent on the individual's behalf to a collection, use or disclosure of the information by a health information custodian. 2004, c. 3, Sched. A, s. 27 (1).

Application by proposed representative

(2) If an individual is incapable of consenting to the collection, use or disclosure of personal health information, another individual who is 16 years old or older may apply to the Board to be appointed as a representative to consent on behalf of the incapable individual to a collection, use or disclosure of the information. 2004, c. 3, Sched. A, s. 27 (2).

Exception

(3) Subsections (1) and (2) do not apply if the individual to whom the personal health information relates has a guardian of the person, a guardian of property, an attorney for personal care, or an attorney for property, who has authority to give or refuse consent to the collection, use or disclosure. 2004, c. 3, Sched. A, s. 27 (3).

Parties

(4) The parties to the application are:

1. The individual to whom the personal health information relates.
2. The proposed representative named in the application.
3. Every person who is described in paragraph 4, 5, 6 or 7 of subsection 26 (1).
4. All other persons whom the Board specifies. 2004, c. 3, Sched. A, s. 27 (4).

Appointment

(5) In an appointment under this section, the Board may authorize the representative to consent, on behalf of the individual to whom the personal health information relates, to,

(a) a particular collection, use or disclosure at a particular time;

(b) a collection, use or disclosure of the type specified by the Board in circumstances specified by the Board, if the individual is determined to be incapable of consenting to the collection, use or disclosure of personal health information at the time the consent is sought; or

(c) any collection, use or disclosure at any time, if the individual is determined to be incapable of consenting to the collection, use or disclosure of personal health information at the time the consent is sought. 2004, c. 3, Sched. A, s. 27 (5).

Criteria for appointment

(6) The Board may make an appointment under this section if it is satisfied that the following requirements are met:

1. The individual to whom the personal health information relates does not object to the appointment.

2. The representative consents to the appointment, is at least 16 years old and is capable of consenting to the collection, use or disclosure of personal health information.

3. The appointment is in the best interests of the individual to whom the personal health information relates. 2004, c. 3, Sched. A, s. 27 (6).

Powers of Board

(7) Unless the individual to whom the personal health information relates objects, the Board may,

(a) appoint as representative a different individual than the one named in the application;

(b) limit the duration of the appointment;

(c) impose any other condition on the appointment; or

(d) on any person's application, remove, vary or suspend a condition imposed on the appointment or impose an additional condition on the appointment. 2004, c. 3, Sched. A, s. 27 (7).

Termination

(8) The Board may, on any person's application, terminate an appointment made under this section if,

(a) the individual to whom the personal health information relates or the representative requests the termination;

(b) the representative is no longer capable of consenting to the collection, use or disclosure of personal health information;

(c) the appointment is no longer in the best interests of the individual to whom the personal health information relates; or

(d) the individual to whom the personal health information relates has a guardian of the person, a guardian of property, an attorney for personal care, or an attorney for property, who has authority to give or refuse consent to the types of collections, uses and disclosures for which the appointment was made and in the circumstances to which the appointment applies. 2004, c. 3, Sched. A, s. 27 (8).

Procedure

(9) Sections 73 to 81 of the *Health Care Consent Act, 1996* apply with necessary modifications to an application under this section. 2004, c. 3, Sched. A, s. 27 (9).

Transition, representative appointed by Board

28. (1) This Act applies to a representative whom the Board appointed under section 36.2 of the *Mental Health Act* or who was deemed to be appointed under that section before the day this section comes into force for an individual with respect to the individual's personal health information, as if the representative were the individual's representative appointed by the Board under section 27. 2004, c. 3, Sched. A, s. 28 (1).

Limited authority

(2) The authority conferred on the representative by subsection (1) is limited to the purposes for which the representative was appointed. 2004, c. 3, Sched. A, s. 28 (2).

PART IV
COLLECTION, USE AND DISCLOSURE OF PERSONAL HEALTH INFORMATION

General Limitations and Requirements

Requirement for consent

29. A health information custodian shall not collect, use or disclose personal health information about an individual unless,

(a) it has the individual's consent under this Act and the collection, use or disclosure, as the case may be, to the best of the custodian's knowledge, is necessary for a lawful purpose; or

(b) the collection, use or disclosure, as the case may be, is permitted or required by this Act. 2004, c. 3, Sched. A, s. 29.

Other information

30. (1) A health information custodian shall not collect, use or disclose personal health information if other information will serve the purpose of the collection, use or disclosure. 2004, c. 3, Sched. A, s. 30 (1).

Extent of information

(2) A health information custodian shall not collect, use or disclose more personal health information than is reasonably necessary to meet the purpose of the collection, use or disclosure, as the case may be. 2004, c. 3, Sched. A, s. 30 (2).

Exception

(3) This section does not apply to personal health information that a health information custodian is required by law to collect, use or disclose. 2004, c. 3, Sched. A, s. 30 (3).

Use and disclosure of personal health information

31. (1) A health information custodian that collects personal health information in contravention of this Act shall not use it or disclose it unless required by law to do so. 2004, c. 3, Sched. A, s. 31 (1).

Express instruction to public hospitals, etc.

(2) An express instruction that an individual, before November 1, 2005, gives to a health information custodian that is a public hospital within the meaning of the *Public Hospitals Act* or a person described in paragraph 1 of subsection 3 (6) with respect to the use or disclosure of personal health information about the individual is not an express instruction for the purpose of clause 37 (1) (a), 38 (1) (a) or 50 (1) (e). 2004, c. 3, Sched. A, s. 31 (2).

Same

(3) Nothing in subsection (2) prevents the custodian from refraining, in accordance with an express instruction that an individual gives as described in that subsection, to use or disclose the information under clause 37 (1) (a), 38 (1) (a) or 50 (1) (e). 2004, c. 3, Sched. A, s. 31 (3).

Repeal

(4) Subsections (2) and (3) are repealed on November 1, 2005. 2004, c. 3, Sched. A, s. 31 (4).

Fundraising

32. (1) Subject to subsection (2), a health information custodian may collect, use or disclose personal health information about an individual for the purpose of fundraising activities only where,

(a) the individual expressly consents; or

(b) the individual consents by way of an implied consent and the information consists only of the individual's name and the prescribed types of contact information. 2004, c. 3, Sched. A, s. 32 (1).

Requirements and restrictions

(2) The manner in which consent is obtained under subsection (1) and the resulting collection, use or disclosure of personal health information for the purpose of fundraising activities shall comply with the requirements and restrictions that are prescribed, if any. 2004, c. 3, Sched. A, s. 32 (2).

Marketing

33. A health information custodian shall not collect, use or disclose personal health information about an individual for the purpose of marketing anything or for the purpose of market research unless the individual expressly consents and the custodian collects, uses or discloses the information, as the case may be, subject to the prescribed requirements and restrictions, if any. 2004, c. 3, Sched. A, s. 33.

Health cards and health numbers

34. (1) In this section,

"health card" means a card provided to an insured person within the meaning of the *Health Insurance Act* by the General Manager of the Ontario Health Insurance Plan; ("carte Santé")

"provincially funded health resource" means a service, thing, subsidy or other benefit funded, in whole or in part, directly or indirectly by the Government of Ontario, if it is health related or prescribed. ("ressource en matière de santé subventionnée par la province") 2004, c. 3, Sched. A, s. 34 (1).

Collection or use

(2) Despite subsection 49 (1), a person who is not a health information custodian shall not collect or use another person's health number except,

(a) for purposes related to the provision of provincially funded health resources to that other person;

(b) for the purposes for which a health information custodian has disclosed the number to the person;

(c) if the person is the governing body of health care practitioners who provide provincially funded health resources and is collecting or using health numbers for purposes related to its duties or powers; or

(d) if the person is prescribed and is collecting or using the health number, as the case may be, for purposes related to health administration, health planning, health research or epidemiological studies. 2004, c. 3, Sched. A, s. 34 (2).

Disclosure

(3) Despite subsection 49 (1) and subject to the exceptions and additional requirements, if any, that are prescribed, a person who is not a health information custodian shall not disclose a health number except as required by law. 2004, c. 3, Sched. A, s. 34 (3).

Confidentiality of health cards

(4) No person shall require the production of another person's health card, but a person who provides a provincially funded health resource to a person who has a health card may require the production of the health card. 2004, c. 3, Sched. A, s. 34 (4).

Exceptions

(5) Subsections (2) and (3) do not apply to,

(a) a person who collects, uses or discloses a health number for the purposes of a proceeding;

(b) a prescribed entity mentioned in subsection 45 (1) that collects, uses or discloses the health number in the course of carrying out its functions under section 45; or

(c) a health data institute that the Minister approves under subsection 47 (9) and that collects, uses or discloses the health number in the course of carrying out its functions under sections 47 and 48. 2004, c. 3, Sched. A, s. 34 (5).

Fees for personal health information

35. (1) A health information custodian shall not charge a person a fee for collecting or using personal health information except as authorized by the regulations made under this Act. 2004, c. 3, Sched. A, s. 35 (1).

Same, for disclosure

(2) When disclosing personal health information, a health information custodian shall not charge fees to a person that exceed the prescribed amount or the amount of reasonable cost recovery, if no amount is prescribed. 2004, c. 3, Sched. A, s. 35 (2).

COLLECTION

Indirect collection

36. (1) A health information custodian may collect personal health information about an individual indirectly if,

(a) the individual consents to the collection being made indirectly;

(b) the information to be collected is reasonably necessary for providing health care or assisting in providing health care to the individual and it is not reasonably possible to collect, directly from the individual,

    (i) personal health information that can reasonably be relied on as accurate, or

    (ii) personal health information in a timely manner;

(c) the custodian is an institution within the meaning of the *Freedom of Information and Protection of Privacy Act* or the *Municipal Freedom of Information and Protection of Privacy Act*, or is acting as part of such an institution, and the custodian is collecting the information for a purpose related to,

    (i) investigating a breach of an agreement or a contravention or an alleged contravention of the laws of Ontario or Canada,

    (ii) the conduct of a proceeding or a possible proceeding, or

    (iii) the statutory function of the custodian;

(d) the custodian collects the information from a person who is not a health information custodian for the purpose of carrying out research conducted in accordance with subsection 37 (3) or research that a research ethics board has approved under section 44 or that meets the criteria set out in clauses 44 (10) (a) to (c), except if the person is prohibited by law from disclosing the information to the custodian;

(e) the custodian is a prescribed entity mentioned in subsection 45 (1) and the custodian is collecting personal health information from a person who is not a health information custodian for the purpose of that subsection;

(f) the Commissioner authorizes that the collection be made in a manner other than directly from the individual;

(g) the custodian collects the information from a person who is permitted or required by law or by a treaty, agreement or arrangement made under an Act or an Act of Canada to disclose it to the custodian; or

(h) subject to the requirements and restrictions, if any, that are prescribed, the health information custodian is permitted or required by law or by a treaty, agreement or arrangement made under an Act or an Act of Canada to collect the information indirectly. 2004, c. 3, Sched. A, s. 36 (1).

Direct collection without consent

(2) A health information custodian may collect personal health information about an individual directly from the individual, even if the individual is incapable of consenting, if the collection is reasonably necessary for the provision of health care and it is not reasonably possible to obtain consent in a timely manner. 2004, c. 3, Sched. A, s. 36 (2).

USE

Permitted use

37. (1) A health information custodian may use personal health information about an individual,

(a) for the purpose for which the information was collected or created and for all the functions reasonably necessary for carrying out that purpose, but not if the information was collected with the consent of the individual or under clause 36 (1) (b) and the individual expressly instructs otherwise;

(b) for a purpose for which this Act, another Act or an Act of Canada permits or requires a person to disclose it to the custodian;

(c) for planning or delivering programs or services that the custodian provides or that the custodian funds in whole or in part, allocating resources to any of them, evaluating or monitoring any of them or detecting, monitoring or preventing fraud or any unauthorized receipt of services or benefits related to any of them;

(d) for the purpose of risk management, error management or for the purpose of activities to improve or maintain the quality of care or to improve or maintain the quality of any related programs or services of the custodian;

(e) for educating agents to provide health care;

(f) in a manner consistent with Part II, for the purpose of disposing of the information or modifying the information in order to conceal the identity of the individual;

(g) for the purpose of seeking the individual's consent, when the personal health information used by the custodian for this purpose is limited to the individual's name and contact information;

(h) for the purpose of a proceeding or contemplated proceeding in which the custodian or the agent or former agent of the custodian is, or is expected to be, a party or witness, if the information relates to or is a matter in issue in the proceeding or contemplated proceeding;

(i) for the purpose of obtaining payment or processing, monitoring, verifying or reimbursing claims for payment for the provision of health care or related goods and services;

(j) for research conducted by the custodian, subject to subsection (3), unless another clause of this subsection applies; or

(k) subject to the requirements and restrictions, if any, that are prescribed, if permitted or required by law or by a treaty, agreement or arrangement made under an Act or an Act of Canada. 2004, c. 3, Sched. A, s. 37 (1).

Agents

(2) If subsection (1) authorizes a health information custodian to use personal health information for a purpose, the custodian may provide the infor-

mation to an agent of the custodian who may use it for that purpose on behalf of the custodian. 2004, c. 3, Sched. A, s. 37 (2).

Research

(3) Under clause (1) (j), a health information custodian may use personal health information about an individual only if the custodian prepares a research plan and has a research ethics board approve it and for that purpose subsections 44 (2) to (4) and clauses 44 (6) (a) to (f) apply to the use as if it were a disclosure. 2004, c. 3, Sched. A, s. 37 (3).

Mixed uses

(4) If a research plan mentioned in subsection (3) proposes that a health information custodian that is an institution within the meaning of the *Freedom of Information and Protection of Privacy Act* or the *Municipal Freedom of Information and Protection of Privacy Act* or that is acting as part of such an institution use personal health information, together with personal information within the meaning of those two Acts that is not personal health information, those two Acts do not apply to the use and this section applies to the use. 2004, c. 3, Sched. A, s. 37 (4).

Disclosure

Disclosures related to providing health care

38. (1) A health information custodian may disclose personal health information about an individual,

(a) to a person described in paragraph 1, 2, 3 or 4 of the definition of "health information custodian" in subsection 3 (1), if the disclosure is reasonably necessary for the provision of health care and it is not reasonably possible to obtain the individual's consent in a timely manner, but not if the individual has expressly instructed the custodian not to make the disclosure;

(b) in order for the Minister or another health information custodian to determine or provide funding or payment to the custodian for the provision of health care; or

(c) for the purpose of contacting a relative, friend or potential substitute decision-maker of the individual, if the individual is injured, incapacitated or ill and unable to give consent personally. 2004, c. 3, Sched. A, s. 38 (1).

Notice of instruction

(2) If a health information custodian discloses personal health information about an individual under clause (1) (a) and if an instruction of the individual made under that clause prevents the custodian from disclosing all the

personal health information that the custodian considers reasonably necessary to disclose for the provision of health care or assisting in the provision of health care to the individual, the custodian shall notify the person to whom it makes the disclosure of that fact. 2004, c. 3, Sched. A, s. 38 (2).

Facility that provides health care

(3) A health information custodian that is a facility that provides health care may disclose to a person the following personal health information relating to an individual who is a patient or a resident in the facility if the custodian offers the individual the option, at the first reasonable opportunity after admission to the facility, to object to such disclosures and if the individual does not do so:

1. The fact that the individual is a patient or resident in the facility.
2. The individual's general health status described as critical, poor, fair, stable or satisfactory, or in similar terms.
3. The location of the individual in the facility. 2004, c. 3, Sched. A, s. 38 (3).

Deceased individual

(4) A health information custodian may disclose personal health information about an individual who is deceased, or is reasonably suspected to be deceased,

(a) for the purpose of identifying the individual;

(b) for the purpose of informing any person whom it is reasonable to inform in the circumstances of,

   (i) the fact that the individual is deceased or reasonably suspected to be deceased, and

   (ii) the circumstances of death, where appropriate; or

(c) to the spouse, partner, sibling or child of the individual if the recipients of the information reasonably require the information to make decisions about their own health care or their children's health care. 2004, c. 3, Sched. A, s. 38 (4).

Disclosures for health or other programs

39. (1) Subject to the requirements and restrictions, if any, that are prescribed, a health information custodian may disclose personal health information about an individual,

(a) for the purpose of determining or verifying the eligibility of the individual to receive health care or related goods, services or benefits provided under an Act of Ontario or Canada and funded in whole or in part by the Government of Ontario or Canada or by a municipality;

(b) to a person conducting an audit or reviewing an application for accreditation or reviewing an accreditation, if the audit or review relates to services provided by the custodian and the person does not remove any records of personal health information from the custodian's premises; or

(c) to a prescribed person who compiles or maintains a registry of personal health information for purposes of facilitating or improving the provision of health care or that relates to the storage or donation of body parts or bodily substances. 2004, c. 3, Sched. A, s. 39 (1).

Same

(2) A health information custodian may disclose personal health information about an individual,

(a) to the Chief Medical Officer of Health or a medical officer of health within the meaning of the *Health Protection and Promotion Act* if the disclosure is made for a purpose of that Act; or

(b) to a public health authority that is similar to the persons described in clause (a) and that is established under the laws of Canada, another province or a territory of Canada or other jurisdiction, if the disclosure is made for a purpose that is substantially similar to a purpose of the *Health Protection and Promotion Act*. 2004, c. 3, Sched. A, s. 39 (2).

Removal allowed

(3) Despite clause (1) (b), the person described in that clause may remove records of personal health information from the custodian's premises if,

(a) the removal is authorized by or under an Act of Ontario or Canada; or

(b) an agreement between the custodian and the person authorizes the removal and provides that the records will be held in a secure and confidential manner and will be returned when the audit or review is completed. 2004, c. 3, Sched. A, s. 39 (3).

Authorization to collect

(4) A person who is not a health information custodian is authorized to collect the personal health information that a health information custodian may disclose to the person under clause (1) (c). 2004, c. 3, Sched. A, s. 39 (4).

Disclosures related to risks

40. (1) A health information custodian may disclose personal health information about an individual if the custodian believes on reasonable grounds that the disclosure is necessary for the purpose of eliminating or reducing a significant risk of serious bodily harm to a person or group of persons. 2004, c. 3, Sched. A, s. 40 (1).

Disclosures related to care or custody

(2) A health information custodian may disclose personal health information about an individual to the head of a penal or other custodial institution in which the individual is being lawfully detained or to the officer in charge of a psychiatric facility within the meaning of the *Mental Health Act* in which the individual is being lawfully detained for the purposes described in subsection (3). 2004, c. 3, Sched. A, s. 40 (2).

Same

(3) A health information custodian may disclose personal health information about an individual under subsection (2) to assist an institution or a facility in making a decision concerning,

(a)   arrangements for the provision of health care to the individual; or

(b)   the placement of the individual into custody, detention, release, conditional release, discharge or conditional discharge under Part IV of the *Child and Family Services Act*, the *Mental Health Act*, the *Ministry of Correctional Services Act*, the *Corrections and Conditional Release Act* (Canada), Part XX.1 of the *Criminal Code* (Canada), the *Prisons and Reformatories Act* (Canada) or the *Youth Criminal Justice Act* (Canada). 2004, c. 3, Sched. A, s. 40 (3).

Disclosures for proceedings

41. (1) A health information custodian may disclose personal health information about an individual,

(a)   subject to the requirements and restrictions, if any, that are prescribed, for the purpose of a proceeding or contemplated proceeding in which the custodian or the agent or former agent of the custodian is, or is expected to be, a party or witness, if the information relates to or is a matter in issue in the proceeding or contemplated proceeding;

(b)   to a proposed litigation guardian or legal representative of the individual for the purpose of having the person appointed as such;

(c)   to a litigation guardian or legal representative who is authorized under the Rules of Civil Procedure, or by a court order, to commence, defend or continue a proceeding on behalf of the individual or to represent the individual in a proceeding; or

(d)   for the purpose of complying with,

(i)   a summons, order or similar requirement issued in a proceeding by a person having jurisdiction to compel the production of information, or

(ii)   a procedural rule that relates to the production of information in a proceeding. 2004, c. 3, Sched. A, s. 41 (1).

Disclosure by agent or former agent

(2) An agent or former agent who receives personal health information under subsection (1) or under subsection 37 (2) for purposes of a proceeding or contemplated proceeding may disclose the information to the agent's or former agent's professional advisor for the purpose of providing advice or representation to the agent or former agent, if the advisor is under a professional duty of confidentiality. 2004, c. 3, Sched. A, s. 41 (2).

Disclosure to successor

42. (1) A health information custodian may disclose personal health information about an individual to a potential successor of the custodian, for the purpose of allowing the potential successor to assess and evaluate the operations of the custodian, if the potential successor first enters into an agreement with the custodian to keep the information confidential and secure and not to retain any of the information longer than is necessary for the purpose of the assessment or evaluation. 2004, c. 3, Sched. A, s. 42 (1).

Transfer to successor

(2) A health information custodian may transfer records of personal health information about an individual to the custodian's successor if the custodian makes reasonable efforts to give notice to the individual before transferring the records or, if that is not reasonably possible, as soon as possible after transferring the records. 2004, c. 3, Sched. A, s. 42 (2).

Transfer to archives

(3) Subject to the agreement of the person who is to receive the transfer, a health information custodian may transfer records of personal health information about an individual to,

(a) the Archives of Ontario; or

(b) in the prescribed circumstances, a prescribed person whose functions include the collection and preservation of records of historical or archival importance, if the disclosure is made for the purpose of that function. 2004, c. 3, Sched. A, s. 42 (3).

Disclosures related to this or other Acts

43. (1) A health information custodian may disclose personal health information about an individual,

(a) for the purpose of determining, assessing or confirming capacity under the *Health Care Consent Act, 1996,* the *Substitute Decisions Act, 1992* or this Act;

(b) to a College within the meaning of the *Regulated Health Professions Act, 1991* for the purpose of the administration or enforcement of the *Drug and*

Pharmacies Regulation Act, the *Regulated Health Professions Act, 1991* or an Act named in Schedule 1 to that Act;

(c) to the Board of Regents continued under the *Drugless Practitioners Act* for the purpose of the administration or enforcement of that Act;

(d) to the Ontario College of Social Workers and Social Service Workers for the purpose of the administration or enforcement of the *Social Work and Social Service Work Act, 1998;*

(e) to the Public Guardian and Trustee, the Children's Lawyer, a children's aid society, a Residential Placement Advisory Committee established under subsection 34 (2) of the *Child and Family Services Act* or the Registrar of Adoption Information appointed under subsection 163 (1) of that Act so that they can carry out their statutory functions;

(f) in the circumstances described in clause 42 (c), (g) or (n) of the *Freedom of Information and Protection of Privacy Act* or clause 32 (c), (g) or (l) of the *Municipal Freedom of Information and Protection of Privacy Act*, if the custodian is subject to either of those Acts;

(g) subject to the requirements and restrictions, if any, that are prescribed, to a person carrying out an inspection, investigation or similar procedure that is authorized by a warrant or by or under this Act or any other Act of Ontario or an Act of Canada for the purpose of complying with the warrant or for the purpose of facilitating the inspection, investigation or similar procedure;

(h) subject to the requirements and restrictions, if any, that are prescribed, if permitted or required by law or by a treaty, agreement or arrangement made under an Act or an Act of Canada. 2004, c. 3, Sched. A, s. 43 (1).

Interpretation

(2) For the purposes of clause (1) (h) and subject to the regulations made under this Act, if an Act, an Act of Canada or a regulation made under any of those Acts specifically provides that information is exempt, under stated circumstances, from a confidentiality or secrecy requirement, that provision shall be deemed to permit the disclosure of the information in the stated circumstances. 2004, c. 3, Sched. A, s. 43 (2).

Disclosure for research

44. (1) A health information custodian may disclose personal health information about an individual to a researcher if the researcher,

(a) submits to the custodian,

(i) an application in writing,

(ii) a research plan that meets the requirements of subsection (2), and

      (iii) a copy of the decision of a research ethics board that approves the research plan; and

(b) enters into the agreement required by subsection (5). 2004, c. 3, Sched. A, s. 44 (1).

Research plan

      (2) A research plan must be in writing and must set out,

(a) the affiliation of each person involved in the research;

(b) the nature and objectives of the research and the public or scientific benefit of the research that the researcher anticipates; and

(c) all other prescribed matters related to the research. 2004, c. 3, Sched. A, s. 44 (2).

Consideration by board

      (3) When deciding whether to approve a research plan that a researcher submits to it, a research ethics board shall consider the matters that it considers relevant, including,

(a) whether the objectives of the research can reasonably be accomplished without using the personal health information that is to be disclosed;

(b) whether, at the time the research is conducted, adequate safeguards will be in place to protect the privacy of the individuals whose personal health information is being disclosed and to preserve the confidentiality of the information;

(c) the public interest in conducting the research and the public interest in protecting the privacy of the individuals whose personal health information is being disclosed; and

(d) whether obtaining the consent of the individuals whose personal health information is being disclosed would be impractical. 2004, c. 3, Sched. A, s. 44 (3).

Decision of board

      (4) After reviewing a research plan that a researcher has submitted to it, the research ethics board shall provide to the researcher a decision in writing, with reasons, setting out whether the board approves the plan, and whether the approval is subject to any conditions, which must be specified in the decision. 2004, c. 3, Sched. A, s. 44 (4).

Agreement respecting disclosure

      (5) Before a health information custodian discloses personal health information to a researcher under subsection (1), the researcher shall enter into an agreement with the custodian in which the researcher agrees to comply with the conditions and restrictions, if any, that the custodian imposes relating to

the use, security, disclosure, return or disposal of the information. 2004, c. 3, Sched. A, s. 44 (5).

Compliance by researcher

(6) A researcher who receives personal health information about an individual from a health information custodian under subsection (1) shall,

(a) comply with the conditions, if any, specified by the research ethics board in respect of the research plan;

(b) use the information only for the purposes set out in the research plan as approved by the research ethics board;

(c) not publish the information in a form that could reasonably enable a person to ascertain the identity of the individual;

(d) despite subsection 49 (1), not disclose the information except as required by law and subject to the exceptions and additional requirements, if any, that are prescribed;

(e) not make contact or attempt to make contact with the individual, directly or indirectly, unless the custodian first obtains the individual's consent to being contacted;

(f) notify the custodian immediately in writing if the researcher becomes aware of any breach of this subsection or the agreement described in subsection (5); and

(g) comply with the agreement described in subsection (5). 2004, c. 3, Sched. A, s. 44 (6).

Mixed disclosures

(7) If a researcher submits a research plan under subsection (1) that proposes that a health information custodian that is an institution within the meaning of the *Freedom of Information and Protection of Privacy Act* or the *Municipal Freedom of Information and Protection of Privacy Act* or that is acting as part of such an institution disclose to the researcher personal health information, together with personal information within the meaning of those two Acts that is not personal health information, those two Acts do not apply to the disclosure and this section applies to the disclosure. 2004, c. 3, Sched. A, s. 44 (7).

Transition

(8) Despite subsection (7), nothing in this section prevents a health information custodian that is an institution within the meaning of the *Freedom of Information and Protection of Privacy Act* or the *Municipal Freedom of Information and Protection of Privacy Act* or that is acting as part of such an institution from disclosing to a researcher personal health information, that is personal

information within the meaning of those two Acts, if, before the day this section comes into force, the researcher has entered into an agreement that requires the custodian to comply with clause 21 (1) (e) of the *Freedom of Information and Protection of Privacy Act* or clause 14 (1) (e) of the *Municipal Freedom of Information and Protection of Privacy Act* as a condition of disclosing the information. 2004, c. 3, Sched. A, s. 44 (8).

Disclosure under other Acts

(9) Despite any other Act that permits a health information custodian to disclose personal health information to a researcher for the purpose of conducting research, this section applies to the disclosure as if it were a disclosure for research under this section unless the regulations made under this Act provide otherwise. 2004, c. 3, Sched. A, s. 44 (9).

Research approved outside Ontario

(10) Subject to subsection (11), a health information custodian may disclose personal health information to a researcher or may use the information to conduct research if,

(a) the research involves the use of personal health information originating wholly or in part outside Ontario;

(b) the research has received the prescribed approval from a body outside Ontario that has the function of approving research; and

(c) the prescribed requirements are met. 2004, c. 3, Sched. A, s. 44 (10).

Same

(11) Subsections (1) to (4) and clauses (6) (a) and (b) do not apply to a disclosure or use made under subsection (10) and references in the rest of this section to subsection (1) shall be read as references to this subsection with respect to that disclosure or use. 2004, c. 3, Sched. A, s. 44 (11).

Transition

(12) Despite anything in this section, a health information custodian that lawfully disclosed personal health information to a researcher for the purpose of conducting research in the three-year period before the day this section comes into force may continue to disclose personal health information to the researcher for the purposes of that research for a period of three years after the day this section comes into force. 2004, c. 3, Sched. A, s. 44 (12).

Same, use

(13) Despite anything in this section, a health information custodian that lawfully used personal health information for the purpose of conducting

research in the three-year period before the day this section comes into force may continue to use personal health information for the purposes of that research for a period of three years after the day this section comes into force. 2004, c. 3, Sched. A, s. 44 (13).

Repeal

(14) Subsections (12) and (13) are repealed on the third anniversary of the day they came into force. 2004, c. 3, Sched. A, s. 44 (14).

Note: Subsections (12) and (13) came into force on November 1, 2004. See: 2004, c. 3, Sched. A, s. 99 (2).

Disclosure for planning and management of health system

45. (1) A health information custodian may disclose to a prescribed entity personal health information for the purpose of analysis or compiling statistical information with respect to the management of, evaluation or monitoring of, the allocation of resources to or planning for all or part of the health system, including the delivery of services, if the entity meets the requirements under subsection (3). 2004, c. 3, Sched. A, s. 45 (1).

Exception

(2) Subsection (1) does not apply to,

(a) notes of personal health information about an individual that are recorded by a health information custodian and that document the contents of conversations during a private counselling session or a group, joint or family counselling session; or

(b) prescribed information in circumstances that are prescribed. 2004, c. 3, Sched. A, s. 45 (2).

Approval

(3) A health information custodian may disclose personal health information to a prescribed entity under subsection (1) if,

(a) the entity has in place practices and procedures to protect the privacy of the individuals whose personal health information it receives and to maintain the confidentiality of the information; and

(b) the Commissioner has approved the practices and procedures, if the custodian makes the disclosure on or after the first anniversary of the day this section comes into force. 2004, c. 3, Sched. A, s. 45 (3).

Review by Commissioner

(4) The Commissioner shall review the practices and procedures of each prescribed entity every three years from the date of its approval and advise the

health information custodian whether the entity continues to meet the requirements of subsection (3). 2004, c. 3, Sched. A, s. 45 (4).

Authorization to collect

(5) An entity that is not a health information custodian is authorized to collect the personal health information that a health information custodian may disclose to the entity under subsection (1). 2004, c. 3, Sched. A, s. 45 (5).

Use and disclosure

(6) Subject to the exceptions and additional requirements, if any, that are prescribed and despite subsection 49 (1), an entity that receives personal health information under subsection (1) shall not use the information except for the purposes for which it received the information and shall not disclose the information except as required by law. 2004, c. 3, Sched. A, s. 45 (6).

Monitoring health care payments

46. (1) A health information custodian shall, upon the request of the Minister, disclose to the Minister personal health information about an individual for the purpose of monitoring or verifying claims for payment for health care funded wholly or in part by the Ministry of Health and Long-Term Care or for goods used for health care funded wholly or in part by the Ministry of Health and Long-Term Care. 2004, c. 3, Sched. A, s. 46 (1).

Disclosure by Minister

(2) The Minister may disclose information collected under subsection (1) to any person for a purpose set out in that subsection if the disclosure is reasonably necessary for that purpose. 2004, c. 3, Sched. A, s. 46 (2).

Disclosure for analysis of health system

47. (1) In this section,

"de-identify", in relation to the personal health information of an individual, means to remove any information that identifies the individual or for which it is reasonably foreseeable in the circumstances that it could be utilized, either alone or with other information, to identify the individual, and "de-identification" has a corresponding meaning. 2004, c. 3, Sched. A, s. 47 (1).

Same

(2) Subject to the restrictions, if any, that are prescribed, a health information custodian shall, upon the request of the Minister, disclose personal health information to a health data institute that the Minister approves under subsection (9) for analysis with respect to the management of, evaluation or monitor-

ing of, the allocation of resources to or planning for all or part of the health system, including the delivery of services, if the requirements of this section are met. 2004, c. 3, Sched. A, s. 47 (2).

Form, manner and time of disclosure

(3) The Minister may specify the form and manner in which and the time at which the health information custodian is required to disclose the personal health information under subsection (2). 2004, c. 3, Sched. A, s. 47 (3).

Requirements for Minister

(4) Before requesting the disclosure of personal health information under subsection (2), the Minister shall submit a proposal to the Commissioner and, in accordance with this section, allow the Commissioner to review and comment on the proposal. 2004, c. 3, Sched. A, s. 47 (4).

Contents of proposal

(5) The proposal must identify a health data institute to which the personal health information would be disclosed under this section and must set out the prescribed matters. 2004, c. 3, Sched. A, s. 47 (5).

Review by Commissioner

(6) Within 30 days after the Commissioner receives the proposal, the Commissioner shall review the proposal and may comment in writing on the proposal. 2004, c. 3, Sched. A, s. 47 (6).

Consideration by Commissioner

(7) In reviewing the proposal, the Commissioner shall consider the public interest in conducting the analysis and the privacy interest of the individuals to whom the personal health information relates in the circumstances. 2004, c. 3, Sched. A, s. 47 (7).

Consideration by Minister

(8) The Minister shall consider the comments, if any, made by the Commissioner within the time specified in subsection (6), and may amend the proposal if the Minister considers it appropriate. 2004, c. 3, Sched. A, s. 47 (8).

Approval of health data institute

(9) The Minister may approve a health data institute for the purposes of a disclosure made under this section if,

(a) the corporate objects of the institute include performing data analysis of personal health information, linking the information with other information and de-identifying the information for the Minister; and

(b) the institute has in place practices and procedures to protect the privacy of the individuals whose personal health information it receives and to maintain the confidentiality of the information and the Commissioner has approved those practices and procedures. 2004, c. 3, Sched. A, s. 47 (9).

Review by Commissioner

(10) The Commissioner shall review the practices and procedures of each health data institute every three years from the date of its approval and advise the Minister whether the institute continues to meet the requirements of clauses (9) (a) and (b). 2004, c. 3, Sched. A, s. 47 (10).

Withdrawal of approval

(11) The Minister shall withdraw the approval of a health data institute that ceases to meet the requirements of clauses (9) (a) and (b) or to carry out its objects mentioned in clause (9) (a), unless the Minister requires the institute to take immediate steps to satisfy the Minister that it will meet the requirements or that it will carry out the objects. 2004, c. 3, Sched. A, s. 47 (11).

Effect of withdrawal of approval

(12) If the Minister withdraws the approval of a health data institute, the institute shall,

(a) make no further use or disclosure of any personal health information that a health information custodian has disclosed to it under subsection (2) or any information derived from that personal health information; and

(b) comply with the written directions of the Minister that the Commissioner has approved in writing with respect to information described in clause (a). 2004, c. 3, Sched. A, s. 47 (12).

If institute ceases to exist

(13) If a health data institute ceases to exist, the persons holding the personal health information that the institute received under subsection (2) and held when it ceased to exist shall comply with the written directions of the Minister that the Commissioner has approved in writing with respect to the information. 2004, c. 3, Sched. A, s. 47 (13).

Disclosure by Minister

(14) The Minister may disclose to the health data institute that receives personal health information under subsection (2) other personal health information for the purposes of the analysis and linking that the Minister requires if the disclosure is included in the Minister's proposal, as amended under subsection (8), if applicable. 2004, c. 3, Sched. A, s. 47 (14).

Duties of health data institute

(15) A health data institute that receives personal health information under subsection (2) or (14) shall,

(a) follow the practices and procedures described in clause (9) (b) that the Commissioner has approved;

(b) perform the analysis and linking with other data that the Minister requires;

(c) de-identify the information;

(d) provide the results of the analysis and linking, using only de-identified information, to the Minister or to the persons that the Minister approves;

(e) not disclose the information to the Minister or to the persons that the Minister approves except in a de-identified form; and

(f) subject to clauses (d) and (e), not disclose to any persons the information, even in a de-identified form, or any information derived from the information. 2004, c. 3, Sched. A, s. 47 (15).

Transition

(16) If the Minister has lawfully required the disclosure of personal health information for a purpose described in subsection (2) in the 18 months before this section comes into force, this section does not apply with respect to a disclosure the Minister requires for a substantially similar purpose after this section comes into force until the first anniversary of the coming into force of this section. 2004, c. 3, Sched. A, s. 47 (16).

Notification

(17) If the Minister requires a disclosure for a substantially similar purpose under subsection (16) after this section comes into force, the Minister shall notify the Commissioner within the later of the time of requiring the disclosure and 90 days after this section comes into force. 2004, c. 3, Sched. A, s. 47 (17).

No hearing required

(18) The Minister is not required to hold a hearing or to afford to any person an opportunity for a hearing before making a decision under this section. 2004, c. 3, Sched. A, s. 47 (18).

Disclosure with Commissioner's approval

48. (1) A health data institute to which a health information custodian has disclosed personal health information under section 47, shall, upon the request of the Minister and in accordance with the Commissioner's approval given under this section, disclose the information to the Minister or another person approved by the Minister if the Minister is of the opinion that it is in the public interest to request the disclosure and the requirements of this section have been met. 2004, c. 3, Sched. A, s. 48 (1).

Non-application of section

(2) The personal health information mentioned in subsection (1) is not,

(a) notes of personal health information about an individual that are recorded by a health information custodian and that document the contents of conversations during a private counselling session or a group, joint or family counselling session; or

(b) information that is prescribed. 2004, c. 3, Sched. A, s. 48 (2).

Commissioner's approval required

(3) The Minister shall not request the disclosure of personal health information under subsection (1) unless the Minister has submitted to the Commissioner a proposal for the disclosure and the Commissioner has approved the proposal. 2004, c. 3, Sched. A, s. 48 (3).

Contents of proposal

(4) The proposal must include,

(a) a statement as to why the disclosure is reasonably required in the public interest and why the disclosure under section 47 was insufficient to meet the public interest;

(b) the extent of the identifiers that the Minister proposes be part of the information disclosed and a statement as to why the use of those identifiers is reasonably required for the purpose of the disclosure;

(c) a copy of all proposals and comments previously made or received under section 47 in respect of the information, if any; and

(d) all other information that the Commissioner requires. 2004, c. 3, Sched. A, s. 48 (4).

Terms of approval

(5) If the Commissioner approves the proposal, the Commissioner may specify terms, conditions or limitations for the disclosure. 2004, c. 3, Sched. A, s. 48 (5).

Restrictions on recipients

49. (1) Except as permitted or required by law and subject to the exceptions and additional requirements, if any, that are prescribed, a person who is not a health information custodian and to whom a health information custodian discloses personal health information, shall not use or disclose the information for any purpose other than,

(a) the purpose for which the custodian was authorized to disclose the information under this Act; or

(b) the purpose of carrying out a statutory or legal duty. 2004, c. 3, Sched. A, s. 49 (1).

Extent of use or disclosure

(2) Subject to the exceptions and additional requirements, if any, that are prescribed, a person who is not a health information custodian, and to whom a health information custodian discloses personal health information, shall not use or disclose more of the information than is reasonably necessary to meet the purpose of the use or disclosure, as the case may be, unless the use or disclosure is required by law. 2004, c. 3, Sched. A, s. 49 (2).

Employee or agent information

(3) Except as permitted or required by law and subject to the exceptions and additional requirements, if any, that are prescribed, if a health information custodian discloses information to another health information custodian and the information is identifying information of the type described in subsection 4 (4) in the custody or under the control of the receiving custodian, the receiving custodian shall not,

(a) use or disclose the information for any purpose other than,

    (i) the purpose for which the disclosing custodian was authorized to disclose the information under this Act, or

    (ii) the purpose of carrying out a statutory or legal duty; or

(b) use or disclose more of the information than is reasonably necessary to meet the purpose of the use or disclosure, as the case may be. 2004, c. 3, Sched. A, s. 49 (3).

Same

(4) The restrictions set out in clauses (3) (a) and (b) apply to a health information custodian that receives the identifying information described in subsection (3) even if the custodian receives the information before the day that subsection comes into force. 2004, c. 3, Sched. A, s. 49 (4).

Freedom of information legislation

(5) Except as prescribed, this section does not apply to an institution within the meaning of the *Freedom of Information and Protection of Privacy Act* or the *Municipal Freedom of Information and Protection of Privacy Act* that is not a health information custodian. 2004, c. 3, Sched. A, s. 49 (5).

Disclosure outside Ontario

50. (1) A health information custodian may disclose personal health information about an individual collected in Ontario to a person outside Ontario only if,

(a) the individual consents to the disclosure;

(b) this Act permits the disclosure;

(c) the person receiving the information performs functions comparable to the functions performed by a person to whom this Act would permit the custodian to disclose the information in Ontario under subsection 40 (2) or clause 43 (1) (b), (c), (d) or (e);

(d) the following conditions are met:

(i) the custodian is a prescribed entity mentioned in subsection 45 (1) and is prescribed for the purpose of this clause,

(ii) the disclosure is for the purpose of health planning or health administration,

(iii) the information relates to health care provided in Ontario to a person who is resident of another province or territory of Canada, and

(iv) the disclosure is made to the government of that province or territory;

(e) the disclosure is reasonably necessary for the provision of health care to the individual, but not if the individual has expressly instructed the custodian not to make the disclosure; or

(f) the disclosure is reasonably necessary for the administration of payments in connection with the provision of health care to the individual or for contractual or legal requirements in that connection. 2004, c. 3, Sched. A, s. 50 (1).

Notice of instruction

(2) If a health information custodian discloses personal health information about an individual under clause (1) (e) and if an instruction of the individual made under that clause prevents the custodian from disclosing all the personal health information that the custodian considers reasonably necessary to disclose for the provision of health care to the individual, the custodian shall notify the person to whom it makes the disclosure of that fact. 2004, c. 3, Sched. A, s. 50 (2).

PART V
ACCESS TO RECORDS OF PERSONAL HEALTH INFORMATION AND CORRECTION

ACCESS

Application of Part

51. (1) This Part does not apply to a record that contains,

(a) quality of care information;

(b) personal health information collected or created for the purpose of complying with the requirements of a quality assurance program within the meaning of the Health Professions Procedural Code that is Schedule 2 to the *Regulated Health Professions Act, 1991;*

(c) raw data from standardized psychological tests or assessments; or

(d) personal health information of the prescribed type in the custody or under the control of a prescribed class or classes of health information custodians. 2004, c. 3, Sched. A, s. 51 (1).

Severable record

(2) Despite subsection (1), this Part applies to that part of a record of personal health information that can reasonably be severed from the part of the record that contains the information described in clauses (1) (a) to (d). 2004, c. 3, Sched. A, s. 51 (2).

Agent of a non-custodian

(3) This Part does not apply to a record in the custody or under the control of a health information custodian acting as an agent of an institution within the meaning of the *Freedom of Information and Protection of Privacy Act* or the *Municipal Freedom of Information and Protection of Privacy Act* that is not a health information custodian if the individual has the right to request access to the record under one of those Acts. 2004, c. 3, Sched. A, s. 51 (3).

Individual's right of access

52. (1) Subject to this Part, an individual has a right of access to a record of personal health information about the individual that is in the custody or under the control of a health information custodian unless,

(a) the record or the information in the record is subject to a legal privilege that restricts disclosure of the record or the information, as the case may be, to the individual;

(b) another Act, an Act of Canada or a court order prohibits disclosure to the individual of the record or the information in the record in the circumstances;

(c) the information in the record was collected or created primarily in antici-pation of or use in a proceeding, and the proceeding, together with all appeals or processes resulting from it, have not been concluded;

(d) the following conditions are met:

    (i) the information was collected or created in the course of an inspec-tion, investigation or similar procedure authorized by law, or under-taken for the purpose of the detection, monitoring or prevention of a person's receiving or attempting to receive a service or benefit, to which the person is not entitled under an Act or a program operated by the Minister, or a payment for such a service or benefit, and

    (ii) the inspection, investigation, or similar procedure, together with all proceedings, appeals or processes resulting from them, have not been concluded;

(e) granting the access could reasonably be expected to,

    (i) result in a risk of serious harm to the treatment or recovery of the indi-vidual or a risk of serious bodily harm to the individual or another per-son,

    (ii) lead to the identification of a person who was required by law to pro-vide information in the record to the custodian, or

    (iii) lead to the identification of a person who provided information in the record to the custodian explicitly or implicitly in confidence if the cus-todian considers it appropriate in the circumstances that the name of the person be kept confidential; or

(f) the following conditions are met:

    (i) the custodian is an institution within the meaning of the *Freedom of Information and Protection of Privacy Act* or the *Municipal Freedom of Information and Protection of Privacy Act* or is acting as part of such an institution, and

    (ii) the custodian would refuse to grant access to the part of the record,

        (A) under clause 49 (a), (c) or (e) of the *Freedom of Information and Protection of Privacy Act*, if the request were made under that Act and that Act applied to the record, or

        (B) under clause 38 (a) or (c) of the *Municipal Freedom of Information and Protection of Privacy Act*, if the request were made under that Act and that Act applied to the record. 2004, c. 3, Sched. A, s. 52 (1).

Severable record

(2) Despite subsection (1), an individual has a right of access to that part of a record of personal health information about the individual that can reasonably be

severed from the part of the record to which the individual does not have a right of access as a result of clauses (1) (a) to (f). 2004, c. 3, Sched. A, s. 52 (2).

Same

(3) Despite subsection (1), if a record is not a record dedicated primarily to personal health information about the individual requesting access, the individual has a right of access only to the portion of personal health information about the individual in the record that can reasonably be severed from the record for the purpose of providing access. 2004, c. 3, Sched. A, s. 52 (3).

Individual's plan of service

(4) Despite subsection (1), a health information custodian shall not refuse to grant the individual access to his or her plan of service within the meaning of the *Long-Term Care Act, 1994*. 2004, c. 3, Sched. A, s. 52 (4).

Consultation regarding harm

(5) Before deciding to refuse to grant an individual access to a record of personal health information under subclause (1) (e) (i), a health information custodian may consult with a member of the College of Physicians and Surgeons of Ontario or a member of the College of Psychologists of Ontario. 2004, c. 3, Sched. A, s. 52 (5).

Informal access

(6) Nothing in this Act prevents a health information custodian from,

(a) granting an individual access to a record of personal health information, to which the individual has a right of access, if the individual makes an oral request for access or does not make any request for access under section 53; or

(b) with respect to a record of personal health information to which an individual has a right of access, communicating with the individual or his or her substitute decision-maker who is authorized to consent on behalf of the individual to the collection, use or disclosure of personal health information about the individual. 2004, c. 3, Sched. A, s. 52 (6).

Duty of health information custodian

(7) Nothing in this Part relieves a health information custodian from a legal duty to provide, in a manner that is not inconsistent with this Act, personal health information as expeditiously as is necessary for the provision of health care to the individual. 2004, c. 3, Sched. A, s. 52 (7).

Request for access

53. (1) An individual may exercise a right of access to a record of personal health information by making a written request for access to the health information custodian that has custody or control of the information. 2004, c. 3, Sched. A, s. 53 (1).

Detail in request

(2) The request must contain sufficient detail to enable the health information custodian to identify and locate the record with reasonable efforts. 2004, c. 3, Sched. A, s. 53 (2).

Assistance

(3) If the request does not contain sufficient detail to enable the health information custodian to identify and locate the record with reasonable efforts, the custodian shall offer assistance to the person requesting access in reformulating the request to comply with subsection (2). 2004, c. 3, Sched. A, s. 53 (3).

Response of health information custodian

54. (1) A health information custodian that receives a request from an individual for access to a record of personal health information shall,

(a) make the record available to the individual for examination and, at the request of the individual, provide a copy of the record to the individual and if reasonably practical, an explanation of any term, code or abbreviation used in the record;

(b) give a written notice to the individual stating that, after a reasonable search, the custodian has concluded that the record does not exist or cannot be found, if that is the case;

(c) if the custodian is entitled to refuse the request, in whole or in part, under any provision of this Part other than clause 52 (1) (c), (d) or (e), give a written notice to the individual stating that the custodian is refusing the request, in whole or in part, providing a reason for the refusal and stating that the individual is entitled to make a complaint about the refusal to the Commissioner under Part VI; or

(d) if the custodian is entitled to refuse the request, in whole or in part, under clause 52 (1) (c), (d) or (e), give a written notice to the individual stating that the custodian is refusing to confirm or deny the existence of any record subject to any of those provisions and that the individual is entitled to make a complaint about the refusal to the Commissioner under Part VI. 2004, c. 3, Sched. A, s. 54 (1).

Time for response

(2) Subject to subsection (3), the health information custodian shall give the response required by clause (1) (a), (b), (c) or (d) as soon as possible in the circumstances but no later than 30 days after receiving the request. 2004, c. 3, Sched. A, s. 54 (2).

Extension of time for response

(3) Within 30 days after receiving the request for access, the health information custodian may extend the time limit set out in subsection (2) for a further period of time of not more than 30 days if,

(a) meeting the time limit would unreasonably interfere with the operations of the custodian because the information consists of numerous pieces of information or locating the information would necessitate a lengthy search; or

(b) the time required to undertake the consultations necessary to reply to the request within 30 days after receiving it would make it not reasonably practical to reply within that time. 2004, c. 3, Sched. A, s. 54 (3).

Notice of extension

(4) Upon extending the time limit under subsection (3), the health information custodian shall give the individual written notice of the extension setting out the length of the extension and the reason for the extension. 2004, c. 3, Sched. A, s. 54 (4).

Expedited access

(5) Despite subsection (2), the health information custodian shall give the response required by clause (1) (a), (b), (c) or (d) within the time period that the individual specifies if,

(a) the individual provides the custodian with evidence satisfactory to the custodian, acting on a reasonable basis, that the individual requires access to the requested record of personal health information on an urgent basis within that time period; and

(b) the custodian is reasonably able to give the required response within that time period. 2004, c. 3, Sched. A, s. 54 (5).

Frivolous or vexatious requests

(6) A health information custodian that believes on reasonable grounds that a request for access to a record of personal health information is frivolous or vexatious or is made in bad faith may refuse to grant the individual access to the requested record. 2004, c. 3, Sched. A, s. 54 (6).

Effect of non-compliance

(7) If the health information custodian does not respond to the request within the time limit or before the extension, if any, expires, the custodian shall be deemed to have refused the individual's request for access. 2004, c. 3, Sched. A, s. 54 (7).

Right to complain

(8) If the health information custodian refuses or is deemed to have refused the request, in whole or in part,

(a) the individual is entitled to make a complaint about the refusal to the Commissioner under Part VI; and

(b) in the complaint, the burden of proof in respect of the refusal lies on the health information custodian. 2004, c. 3, Sched. A, s. 54 (8).

Identity of individual

(9) A health information custodian shall not make a record of personal health information or a part of it available to an individual under this Part or provide a copy of it to an individual under clause (1) (a) without first taking reasonable steps to be satisfied as to the individual's identity. 2004, c. 3, Sched. A, s. 54 (9).

Fee for access

(10) A health information custodian that makes a record of personal health information or a part of it available to an individual under this Part or provides a copy of it to an individual under clause (1) (a) may charge the individual a fee for that purpose if the custodian first gives the individual an estimate of the fee. 2004, c. 3, Sched. A, s. 54 (10).

Amount of fee

(11) The amount of the fee shall not exceed the prescribed amount or the amount of reasonable cost recovery, if no amount is prescribed. 2004, c. 3, Sched. A, s. 54 (11).

Waiver of fee

(12) A health information custodian mentioned in subsection (10) may waive the payment of all or any part of the fee that an individual is required to pay under that subsection if, in the custodian's opinion, it is fair and equitable to do so. 2004, c. 3, Sched. A, s. 54 (12).

CORRECTION

Correction

55. (1) If a health information custodian has granted an individual access to a record of his or her personal health information and if the individual believes that the record is inaccurate or incomplete for the purposes for which the custodian has collected or used the information, the individual may request in writing that the custodian correct the record. 2004, c. 3, Sched. A, s. 55 (1).

Informal request

(2) If the individual makes an oral request that the health information custodian correct the record, nothing in this Part prevents the custodian from making the requested correction. 2004, c. 3, Sched. A, s. 55 (2).

Reply

(3) As soon as possible in the circumstances but no later than 30 days after receiving a request for a correction under subsection (1), the health information custodian shall, by written notice to the individual, grant or refuse the individual's request or extend the deadline for replying for a period of not more than 30 days if,

(a) replying to the request within 30 days would unreasonably interfere with the activities of the custodian; or

(b) the time required to undertake the consultations necessary to reply to the request within 30 days would make it not reasonably practical to reply within that time. 2004, c. 3, Sched. A, s. 55 (3).

Extension of time for reply

(4) A health information custodian that extends the time limit under subsection (3) shall,

(a) give the individual written notice of the extension setting out the length of the extension and the reason for the extension; and

(b) grant or refuse the individual's request as soon as possible in the circumstances but no later than the expiry of the time limit as extended. 2004, c. 3, Sched. A, s. 55 (4).

Deemed refusal

(5) A health information custodian that does not grant a request for a correction under subsection (1) within the time required shall be deemed to have refused the request. 2004, c. 3, Sched. A, s. 55 (5).

Frivolous or vexatious requests

(6) A health information custodian that believes on reasonable grounds that a request for a correction under subsection (1) is frivolous or vexatious or is made in bad faith may refuse to grant the request and, in that case, shall provide the individual with a notice that sets out the reasons for the refusal and that states that the individual is entitled to make a complaint about the refusal to the Commissioner under Part VI. 2004, c. 3, Sched. A, s. 55 (6).

Right to complain

(7) The individual is entitled to make a complaint to the Commissioner under Part VI about a refusal made under subsection (6). 2004, c. 3, Sched. A, s. 55 (7).

Duty to correct

(8) The health information custodian shall grant a request for a correction under subsection (1) if the individual demonstrates, to the satisfaction of the custodian, that the record is incomplete or inaccurate for the purposes for which the custodian uses the information and gives the custodian the information necessary to enable the custodian to correct the record. 2004, c. 3, Sched. A, s. 55 (8).

Exceptions

(9) Despite subsection (8), a health information custodian is not required to correct a record of personal health information if,

(a) it consists of a record that was not originally created by the custodian and the custodian does not have sufficient knowledge, expertise and authority to correct the record; or

(b) it consists of a professional opinion or observation that a custodian has made in good faith about the individual. 2004, c. 3, Sched. A, s. 55 (9).

Duties upon correction

(10) Upon granting a request for a correction under subsection (1), the health information custodian shall,

(a) make the requested correction by,

   (i) recording the correct information in the record and,

     (A) striking out the incorrect information in a manner that does not obliterate the record, or

     (B) if that is not possible, labelling the information as incorrect, severing the incorrect information from the record, storing it separately from the record and maintaining a link in the record that enables a person to trace the incorrect information, or

    (ii) if it is not possible to record the correct information in the record, ensuring that there is a practical system in place to inform a person who accesses the record that the information in the record is incorrect and to direct the person to the correct information;

(b) give notice to the individual of what it has done under clause (a);

(c) at the request of the individual, give written notice of the requested correction, to the extent reasonably possible, to the persons to whom the custodian has disclosed the information with respect to which the individual requested the correction of the record, except if the correction cannot reasonably be expected to have an effect on the ongoing provision of health care or other benefits to the individual. 2004, c. 3, Sched. A, s. 55 (10).

Notice of refusal

    (11) A notice of refusal under subsection (3) or (4) must give the reasons for the refusal and inform the individual that the individual is entitled to,

(a) prepare a concise statement of disagreement that sets out the correction that the health information custodian has refused to make;

(b) require that the health information custodian attach the statement of disagreement as part of the records that it holds of the individual's personal health information and disclose the statement of disagreement whenever the custodian discloses information to which the statement relates;

(c) require that the health information custodian make all reasonable efforts to disclose the statement of disagreement to any person who would have been notified under clause (10) (c) if the custodian had granted the requested correction; and

(d) make a complaint about the refusal to the Commissioner under Part VI. 2004, c. 3, Sched. A, s. 55 (11).

Rights of individual

    (12) If a health information custodian, under subsection (3) or (4), refuses a request for a correction under subsection (1), in whole or in part, or is deemed to have refused the request, the individual is entitled to take the actions described in any of clauses (11) (a), (b), (c) and (d). 2004, c. 3, Sched. A, s. 55 (12).

Custodian's duty

    (13) If the individual takes an action described in clause (11) (b) or (c), the health information custodian shall comply with the requirements described in the applicable clause. 2004, c. 3, Sched. A, s. 55 (13).

PART VI

ADMINISTRATION AND ENFORCEMENT

COMPLAINTS, REVIEWS AND INSPECTIONS

Complaint to Commissioner

56. (1) A person who has reasonable grounds to believe that another person has contravened or is about to contravene a provision of this Act or its regulations may make a complaint to the Commissioner. 2004, c. 3, Sched. A, s. 56 (1).

Time for complaint

(2) A complaint that a person makes under subsection (1) must be in writing and must be filed within,

(a) one year after the subject-matter of the complaint first came to the attention of the complainant or should reasonably have come to the attention of the complainant, whichever is the shorter; or

(b) whatever longer period of time that the Commissioner permits if the Commissioner is satisfied that it does not result in any prejudice to any person. 2004, c. 3, Sched. A, s. 56 (2).

Same, refusal of request

(3) A complaint that an individual makes under subsection 54 (8) or 55 (7) or (12) shall be in writing and shall be filed within six months from the time at which the health information custodian refuses or is deemed to have refused the individual's request mentioned in the applicable subsection. 2004, c. 3, Sched. A, s. 56 (3).

Non-application

(4) The *Ombudsman Act* does not apply to any matter in respect of which a complaint may be made to the Commissioner under this Act or to the Commissioner or his or her employees or delegates acting under this Act. 2004, c. 3, Sched. A, s. 56 (4).

Response of Commissioner

57. (1) Upon receiving a complaint made under this Act, the Commissioner may inform the person about whom the complaint is made of the nature of the complaint and,

(a) inquire as to what means, other than the complaint, that the complainant is using or has used to resolve the subject-matter of the complaint;

(b) require the complainant to try to effect a settlement, within the time period that the Commissioner specifies, with the person about which the complaint is made; or

(c) authorize a mediator to review the complaint and to try to effect a settlement, within the time period that the Commissioner specifies, between the complainant and the person about which the complaint is made. 2004, c. 3, Sched. A, s. 57 (1).

Dealings without prejudice

(2) If the Commissioner takes an action described in clause (1) (b) or (c) but no settlement is effected within the time period specified,

(a) none of the dealings between the parties to the attempted settlement shall prejudice the rights and duties of the parties under this Act;

(b) none of the information disclosed in the course of trying to effect a settlement shall prejudice the rights and duties of the parties under this Act; and

(c) none of the information disclosed in the course of trying to effect a settlement and that is subject to mediation privilege shall be used or disclosed outside the attempted settlement, including in a review of a complaint under this section or in an inspection under section 60, unless all parties expressly consent. 2004, c. 3, Sched. A, s. 57 (2).

Commissioner's review

(3) If the Commissioner does not take an action described in clause (1) (b) or (c) or if the Commissioner takes an action described in one of those clauses but no settlement is effected within the time period specified, the Commissioner may review the subject-matter of a complaint made under this Act if satisfied that there are reasonable grounds to do so. 2004, c. 3, Sched. A, s. 57 (3).

No review

(4) The Commissioner may decide not to review the subject-matter of the complaint for whatever reason the Commissioner considers proper, including if satisfied that,

(a) the person about which the complaint is made has responded adequately to the complaint;

(b) the complaint has been or could be more appropriately dealt with, initially or completely, by means of a procedure, other than a complaint under this Act;

(c) the length of time that has elapsed between the date when the subject-matter of the complaint arose and the date the complaint was made is such that a review under this section would likely result in undue prejudice to any person;

(d) the complainant does not have a sufficient personal interest in the subject-matter of the complaint; or

(e) the complaint is frivolous or vexatious or is made in bad faith. 2004, c. 3, Sched. A, s. 57 (4).

Notice

(5) Upon deciding not to review the subject-matter of a complaint, the Commissioner shall give notice of the decision to the complainant and shall specify in the notice the reason for the decision. 2004, c. 3, Sched. A, s. 57 (5).

Same

(6) Upon deciding to review the subject-matter of a complaint, the Commissioner shall give notice of the decision to the person about whom the complaint is made. 2004, c. 3, Sched. A, s. 57 (6).

Commissioner's self-initiated review

58. (1) The Commissioner may, on his or her own initiative, conduct a review of any matter if the Commissioner has reasonable grounds to believe that a person has contravened or is about to contravene a provision of this Act or its regulations and that the subject-matter of the review relates to the contravention. 2004, c. 3, Sched. A, s. 58 (1).

Notice

(2) Upon deciding to conduct a review under this section, the Commissioner shall give notice of the decision to every person whose activities are being reviewed. 2004, c. 3, Sched. A, s. 58 (2).

Conduct of Commissioner's review

59. (1) In conducting a review under section 57 or 58, the Commissioner may make the rules of procedure that the Commissioner considers necessary and the *Statutory Powers Procedure Act* does not apply to the review. 2004, c. 3, Sched. A, s. 59 (1).

Evidence

(2) In conducting a review under section 57 or 58, the Commissioner may receive and accept any evidence and other information that the Commissioner sees fit, whether on oath or by affidavit or otherwise and whether or not it is or would be admissible in a court of law. 2004, c. 3, Sched. A, s. 59 (2).

Inspection powers

60. (1) In conducting a review under section 57 or 58, the Commissioner may, without a warrant or court order, enter and inspect any premises in accordance with this section if,

(a) the Commissioner has reasonable grounds to believe that,

(i) the person about whom the complaint was made or the person whose activities are being reviewed is using the premises for a purpose related to the subject-matter of the complaint or the review, as the case may be, and

(ii) the premises contains books, records or other documents relevant to the subject-matter of the complaint or the review, as the case may be;

(b) the Commissioner is conducting the inspection for the purpose of determining whether the person has contravened or is about to contravene a provision of this Act or its regulations; and

(c) the Commissioner does not have reasonable grounds to believe that a person has committed an offence. 2004, c. 3, Sched. A, s. 60 (1).

Review powers

(2) In conducting a review under section 57 or 58, the Commissioner may,

(a) demand the production of any books, records or other documents relevant to the subject-matter of the review or copies of extracts from the books, records or other documents;

(b) inquire into all information, records, information practices of a health information custodian and other matters that are relevant to the subject-matter of the review;

(c) demand the production for inspection of anything described in clause (b);

(d) use any data storage, processing or retrieval device or system belonging to the person being investigated in order to produce a record in readable form of any books, records or other documents relevant to the subject-matter of the review; or

(e) on the premises that the Commissioner has entered, review or copy any books, records or documents that a person produces to the Commissioner, if the Commissioner pays the reasonable cost recovery fee that the health information custodian or person being reviewed may charge. 2004, c. 3, Sched. A, s. 60 (2).

Entry to dwellings

(3) The Commissioner shall not, without the consent of the occupier, exercise a power to enter a place that is being used as a dwelling, except under the authority of a search warrant issued under subsection (4). 2004, c. 3, Sched. A, s. 60 (3).

Search warrants

(4) Where a justice of the peace is satisfied by evidence upon oath or affirmation that there is reasonable ground to believe it is necessary to enter a place that is being used as a dwelling to investigate a complaint that is the subject of a review under section 57, he or she may issue a warrant authorizing the entry by a person named in the warrant. 2004, c. 3, Sched. A, s. 60 (4).

Time and manner for entry

(5) The Commissioner shall exercise the power to enter premises under this section only during reasonable hours for the premises and only in such a manner so as not to interfere with health care that is being provided to any person on the premises at the time of entry. 2004, c. 3, Sched. A, s. 60 (5).

No obstruction

(6) No person shall obstruct the Commissioner who is exercising powers under this section or provide the Commissioner with false or misleading information. 2004, c. 3, Sched. A, s. 60 (6).

Written demand

(7) A demand for books, records or documents or copies of extracts from them under subsection (2) must be in writing and must include a statement of the nature of the things that are required to be produced. 2004, c. 3, Sched. A, s. 60 (7).

Obligation to assist

(8) If the Commissioner makes a demand for any thing under subsection (2), the person having custody of the thing shall produce it to the Commissioner and, at the request of the Commissioner, shall provide whatever assistance is reasonably necessary, including using any data storage, processing or retrieval device or system to produce a record in readable form, if the demand is for a document. 2004, c. 3, Sched. A, s. 60 (8).

Removal of documents

(9) If a person produces books, records and other documents to the Commissioner, other than those needed for the current health care of any person, the Commissioner may, on issuing a written receipt, remove them and may review or copy any of them if the Commissioner is not able to review and copy them on the premises that the Commissioner has entered. 2004, c. 3, Sched. A, s. 60 (9).

Return of documents

(10) The Commissioner shall carry out any reviewing or copying of documents with reasonable dispatch, and shall forthwith after the reviewing or copying return the documents to the person who produced them. 2004, c. 3, Sched. A, s. 60 (10).

Admissibility of copies

(11) A copy certified by the Commissioner as a copy is admissible in evidence to the same extent, and has the same evidentiary value, as the thing copied. 2004, c. 3, Sched. A, s. 60 (11).

Answers under oath

(12) In conducting a review under section 57 or 58, the Commissioner may, by summons, in the same manner and to the same extent as a superior court of record, require the appearance of any person before the Commissioner and compel them to give oral or written evidence on oath or affirmation. 2004, c. 3, Sched. A, s. 60 (12).

Inspection of record without consent

(13) Despite subsections (2) and (12), the Commissioner shall not inspect a record of, require evidence of, or inquire into, personal health information without the consent of the individual to whom it relates, unless,

(a) the Commissioner first determines that it is reasonably necessary to do so, subject to any conditions or restrictions that the Commissioner specifies, which shall include a time limitation, in order to carry out the review and that the public interest in carrying out the review justifies dispensing with obtaining the individual's consent in the circumstances; and

(b) the Commissioner provides a statement to the person who has custody or control of the record to be inspected, or the evidence or information to be inquired into, setting out the Commissioner's determination under clause (a) together with brief written reasons and any restrictions and conditions that the Commissioner has specified. 2004, c. 3, Sched. A, s. 60 (13).

Limitation on delegation

(14) Despite subsection 67 (1), the power to make a determination under clause (13) (a) and to approve the brief written reasons under clause (13) (b) may not be delegated except to the Assistant Commissioner. 2004, c. 3, Sched. A, s. 60 (14).

Document privileged

(15) A document or thing produced by a person in the course of an inquiry is privileged in the same manner as if the inquiry were a proceeding in a court. 2004, c. 3, Sched. A, s. 60 (15).

Protection

(16) Except on the trial of a person for perjury in respect of his or her sworn testimony, no statement made or answer given by that or any other person in the course of a review by the Commissioner is admissible in evidence in any court or at any inquiry or in any other proceedings, and no evidence in respect of proceedings before the Commissioner shall be given against any person. 2004, c. 3, Sched. A, s. 60 (16).

Protection under federal Act

(17) The Commissioner shall inform a person giving a statement or answer in the course of a review by the Commissioner of the person's right to object to answer any question under section 5 of the *Canada Evidence Act*. 2004, c. 3, Sched. A, s. 60 (17).

Representations

(18) The Commissioner shall give the person who made the complaint, the person about whom the complaint is made and any other affected person an opportunity to make representations to the Commissioner. 2004, c. 3, Sched. A, s. 60 (18).

Representative

(19) A person who is given an opportunity to make representations to the Commissioner may be represented by counsel or another person. 2004, c. 3, Sched. A, s. 60 (19).

Access to representations

(20) The Commissioner may permit a person to be present during the representations that another person makes to the Commissioner or to have access to them unless doing so would reveal,

(a) the substance of a record of personal health information, for which a health information custodian claims to be entitled to refuse a request for access made under section 53; or

(b) personal health information to which an individual is not entitled to request access under section 53. 2004, c. 3, Sched. A, s. 60 (20).

Proof of appointment

(21) If the Commissioner or Assistant Commissioner has delegated his or her powers under this section to an officer or employee of the Commissioner, the officer or employee who exercises the powers shall, upon request, produce the certificate of delegation signed by the Commissioner or Assistant Commissioner, as the case may be. 2004, c. 3, Sched. A, s. 60 (21).

Powers of Commissioner

61. (1) After conducting a review under section 57 or 58, the Commissioner may,

(a) if the review relates to a complaint into a request by an individual under subsection 53 (1) for access to a record of personal health information, make an order directing the health information custodian about whom the complaint was made to grant the individual access to the requested record;

(b) if the review relates to a complaint into a request by an individual under subsection 55 (1) for correction of a record of personal health information, make an order directing the health information custodian about whom a complaint was made to make the requested correction;

(c) make an order directing any person whose activities the Commissioner reviewed to perform a duty imposed by this Act or its regulations;

(d) make an order directing any person whose activities the Commissioner reviewed to cease collecting, using or disclosing personal health information if the Commissioner determines that the person is collecting, using or disclosing the information, as the case may be, or is about to do so in contravention of this Act, its regulations or an agreement entered into under this Act;

(e) make an order directing any person whose activities the Commissioner reviewed to dispose of records of personal health information that the Commissioner determines the person collected, used or disclosed in contravention of this Act, its regulations or an agreement entered into under this Act but only if the disposal of the records is not reasonably expected to adversely affect the provision of health care to an individual;

(f) make an order directing any health information custodian whose activities the Commissioner reviewed to change, cease or not commence an information practice specified by the Commissioner, if the Commissioner determines that the information practice contravenes this Act or its regulations;

(g) make an order directing any health information custodian whose activities the Commissioner reviewed to implement an information practice specified by the Commissioner, if the Commissioner determines that the information practice is reasonably necessary in order to achieve compliance with this Act and its regulations;

(h) make an order directing any person who is an agent of a health information custodian, whose activities the Commissioner reviewed and that an order made under any of clauses (a) to (g) directs to take any action or to refrain from taking any action, to take the action or to refrain from taking the action if the Commissioner considers that it is necessary to make the order against the agent to ensure that the custodian will comply with the order made against the custodian; or

(i) make comments and recommendations on the privacy implications of any matter that is the subject of the review. 2004, c. 3, Sched. A, s. 61 (1).

Terms of order

(2) An order that the Commissioner makes under subsection (1) may contain the terms that the Commissioner considers appropriate. 2004, c. 3, Sched. A, s. 61 (2).

Copy of order, etc.

(3) Upon making comments, recommendations or an order under subsection (1), the Commissioner shall provide a copy of them, including reasons for any order made, to,

(a) the complainant and the person about whom the complaint was made, if the Commissioner made the comments, recommendations or order after conducting a review under section 57 of a complaint;

(b) the person whose activities the Commissioner reviewed, if the Commissioner made the comments, recommendations or order after conducting a review under section 58;

(c) all other persons to whom the order is directed;

(d) the body or bodies that are legally entitled to regulate or review the activities of a health information custodian directed in the order or to whom the comments or recommendations relate; and

(e) any other person whom the Commissioner considers appropriate. 2004, c. 3, Sched. A, s. 61 (3).

No order

(4) If, after conducting a review under section 57 or 58, the Commissioner does not make an order under subsection (1), the Commissioner shall give the complainant, if any, and the person whose activities the Commissioner reviewed a notice that sets out the Commissioner's reasons for not making an order. 2004, c. 3, Sched. A, s. 61 (4).

Appeal of order

62. (1) A person affected by an order of the Commissioner made under any of clauses 61 (1) (c) to (h) may appeal the order to the Divisional Court on a question of law in accordance with the rules of court by filing a notice of appeal within 30 days after receiving the copy of the order. 2004, c. 3, Sched. A, s. 62 (1).

Certificate of Commissioner

(2) In an appeal under this section, the Commissioner shall certify to the Divisional Court,

(a) the order and a statement of the Commissioner's reasons for making the order;

(b) the record of all hearings that the Commissioner has held in conducting the review on which the order is based;

(c) all written representations that the Commissioner received before making the order; and

(d) all other material that the Commissioner considers is relevant to the appeal. 2004, c. 3, Sched. A, s. 62 (2).

Confidentiality of information

(3) In an appeal under this section, the court may take precautions to avoid the disclosure by the court or any person of any personal health information about an individual, including, where appropriate, receiving representations without notice, conducting hearings in private or sealing the court files. 2004, c. 3, Sched. A, s. 62 (3).

Court order

(4) On hearing an appeal under this section, the court may, by order,

(a) direct the Commissioner to make the decisions and to do the acts that the Commissioner is authorized to do under this Act and that the court considers proper; and

(b) if necessary, vary or set aside the Commissioner's order. 2004, c. 3, Sched. A, s. 62 (4).

Compliance by Commissioner

(5) The Commissioner shall comply with the court's order. 2004, c. 3, Sched. A, s. 62 (5).

Enforcement of order

63. An order made by the Commissioner under this Act that has become final as a result of there being no further right of appeal may be filed with the Superior Court of Justice and on filing becomes and is enforceable as a judgment or order of the Superior Court of Justice to the same effect. 2004, c. 3, Sched. A, s. 63.

Further order of Commissioner

64. (1) After conducting a review under section 57 or 58 and making an order under subsection 61 (1), the Commissioner may rescind or vary the order or may make a further order under that subsection if new facts relating to the subject-matter of the review come to the Commissioner's attention or if there is a material change in the circumstances relating to the subject-matter of the review. 2004, c. 3, Sched. A, s. 64 (1).

Circumstances

(2) The Commissioner may exercise the powers described in subsection (1) even if the order that the Commissioner rescinds or varies has been filed with the Superior Court of Justice under section 63. 2004, c. 3, Sched. A, s. 64 (2).

Copy of order, etc.

(3) Upon making a further order under subsection (1), the Commissioner shall provide a copy of it to the persons described in clauses 61 (3) (a) to (e) and shall include with the copy a notice setting out,

(a) the Commissioner's reasons for making the order; and

(b) if the order was made under any of clauses 61 (1) (c) to (h), a statement that the persons affected by the order have the right to appeal described in subsection (4). 2004, c. 3, Sched. A, s. 64 (3).

Appeal

(4) A person affected by an order that the Commissioner rescinds, varies or makes under any of clauses 61 (1) (c) to (h) may appeal the order to the Divisional Court on a question of law in accordance with the rules of court by filing a notice of appeal within 30 days after receiving the copy of the order and subsections 62 (2) to (5) apply to the appeal. 2004, c. 3, Sched. A, s. 64 (4).

Damages for breach of privacy

65. (1) If the Commissioner has made an order under this Act that has become final as the result of there being no further right of appeal, a person affected by the order may commence a proceeding in the Superior Court of Justice for damages for actual harm that the person has suffered as a result of a contravention of this Act or its regulations. 2004, c. 3, Sched. A, s. 65 (1).

Same

(2) If a person has been convicted of an offence under this Act and the conviction has become final as a result of there being no further right of appeal, a person affected by the conduct that gave rise to the offence may commence a proceeding in the Superior Court of Justice for damages for actual harm that the person has suffered as a result of the conduct. 2004, c. 3, Sched. A, s. 65 (2).

Damages for mental anguish

(3) If, in a proceeding described in subsection (1) or (2), the Superior Court of Justice determines that the harm suffered by the plaintiff was caused by a contravention or offence, as the case may be, that the defendants engaged in wilfully or recklessly, the court may include in its award of damages an award, not exceeding $10,000, for mental anguish. 2004, c. 3, Sched. A, s. 65 (3).

COMMISSIONER

General powers

66. The Commissioner may,

(a) engage in or commission research into matters affecting the carrying out of the purposes of this Act;

(b) conduct public education programs and provide information concerning this Act and the Commissioner's role and activities;

(c) receive representations from the public concerning the operation of this Act;

(d) on the request of a health information custodian, offer comments on the custodian's actual or proposed information practices;

(e) assist in investigations and similar procedures conducted by a person who performs similar functions to the Commissioner under the laws of Canada, except that in providing assistance, the Commissioner shall not use or disclose information collected by or for the Commissioner under this Act;

(f) in appropriate circumstances, authorize the collection of personal health information about an individual in a manner other than directly from the individual. 2004, c. 3, Sched. A, s. 66.

Delegation

67. (1) The Commissioner may in writing delegate any of the Commissioner's powers, duties or functions under this Act, including the power to make orders, to the Assistant Commissioner or to an officer or employee of the Commissioner. 2004, c. 3, Sched. A, s. 67 (1).

Subdelegation by Assistant Commissioner

(2) The Assistant Commissioner may in writing delegate any of the powers, duties or functions delegated to him or her under subsection (1) to any other officers or employees of the Commissioner, subject to the conditions and restrictions that the Assistant Commissioner specifies in the delegation. 2004, c. 3, Sched. A, s. 67 (2).

Limitations re personal health information

68. (1) The Commissioner and any person acting under his or her authority may collect, use or retain personal health information in the course of carrying out any functions under this Part solely if no other information will serve the purpose of the collection, use or retention of the personal health information and in no other circumstances. 2004, c. 3, Sched. A, s. 68 (1).

Extent of information

(2) The Commissioner and any person acting under his or her authority shall not in the course of carrying out any functions under this Part collect, use or retain more personal health information than is reasonably necessary to enable the Commissioner to perform his or her functions relating to the administration of this Act or for a proceeding under it. 2004, c. 3, Sched. A, s. 68 (2).

Confidentiality

(3) The Commissioner, the Assistant Commissioner and persons acting on behalf of or under the direction of either of them shall not disclose any information that comes to their knowledge in the course of exercising their functions under this Act unless,

(a) the disclosure is required for the purpose of exercising those functions;

(b) the information relates to a health information custodian, the disclosure is made to a body that is legally entitled to regulate or review the activities of the custodian and the Commissioner or the Assistant Commissioner is of the opinion that the disclosure is justified;

(c) the Commissioner obtained the information under subsection 60 (12) and the disclosure is required in a prosecution for an offence under section 131 of the *Criminal Code* (Canada) in respect of sworn testimony; or

(d) the disclosure is made to the Attorney General, the information relates to the commission of an offence against an Act or an Act of Canada and the Commissioner is of the view that there is evidence of such an offence. 2004, c. 3, Sched. A, s. 68 (3).

Same

(4) Despite anything in subsection (3), the Commissioner, the Assistant Commissioner and persons acting on behalf of or under the direction of either of them shall not disclose,

(a) any quality of care information that comes to their knowledge in the course of exercising their functions under this Act; or

(b) the identity of a person, other than a complainant under subsection 56 (1), who has provided information to the Commissioner and who has requested the Commissioner to keep the person's identity confidential. 2004, c. 3, Sched. A, s. 68 (4).

Information in review or proceeding

(5) The Commissioner in a review under section 57 or 58 and a court, tribunal or other person, including the Commissioner, in a proceeding mentioned in section 65 or this section shall take every reasonable precaution,

including, when appropriate, receiving representations without notice and conducting hearings that are closed to the public, to avoid the disclosure of any information for which a health information custodian is entitled to refuse a request for access made under section 53. 2004, c. 3, Sched. A, s. 68 (5).

Not compellable witness

(6) The Commissioner, the Assistant Commissioner and persons acting on behalf of or under the direction of either of them shall not be required to give evidence in a court or in a proceeding of a judicial nature concerning anything coming to their knowledge in the exercise of their functions under this Act that they are prohibited from disclosing under subsection (3) or (4). 2004, c. 3, Sched. A, s. 68 (6).

Immunity

69. No action or other proceeding for damages may be instituted against the Commissioner, the Assistant Commissioner or any person acting on behalf of or under the direction of either of them for,

(a) anything done, reported or said in good faith and in the exercise or intended exercise of any of their powers or duties under this Act; or

(b) any alleged neglect or default in the exercise in good faith of any of their powers or duties under this Act. 2004, c. 3, Sched. A, s. 69.

PART VII

GENERAL

Non-retaliation

70. No one shall dismiss, suspend, demote, discipline, harass or otherwise disadvantage a person by reason that,

(a) the person, acting in good faith and on the basis of reasonable belief, has disclosed to the Commissioner that any other person has contravened or is about to contravene a provision of this Act or its regulations;

(b) the person, acting in good faith and on the basis of reasonable belief, has done or stated an intention of doing anything that is required to be done in order to avoid having any person contravene a provision of this Act or its regulations;

(c) the person, acting in good faith and on the basis of reasonable belief, has refused to do or stated an intention of refusing to do anything that is in contravention of a provision of this Act or its regulations; or

(d) any person believes that the person will do anything described in clause (a), (b) or (c). 2004, c. 3, Sched. A, s. 70.

Immunity

71. (1) No action or other proceeding for damages may be instituted against a health information custodian or any other person for,

(a) anything done, reported or said, both in good faith and reasonably in the circumstances, in the exercise or intended exercise of any of their powers or duties under this Act; or

(b) any alleged neglect or default that was reasonable in the circumstances in the exercise in good faith of any of their powers or duties under this Act. 2004, c. 3, Sched. A, s. 71 (1).

Crown liability

(2) Despite subsections 5 (2) and (4) of the *Proceedings Against the Crown Act*, subsection (1) does not relieve the Crown of liability in respect of a tort committed by a person mentioned in subsection (1) to which it would otherwise be subject. 2004, c. 3, Sched. A, s. 71 (2).

Substitute decision-maker

(3) A person who, on behalf of or in the place of an individual, gives or refuses consent to a collection, use or disclosure of personal health information about the individual, makes a request, gives an instruction or takes a step is not liable for damages for doing so if the person acts reasonably in the circumstances, in good faith and in accordance with this Act and its regulations. 2004, c. 3, Sched. A, s. 71 (3).

Reliance on assertion

(4) Unless it is not reasonable to do so in the circumstances, a person is entitled to rely on the accuracy of an assertion made by another person, in connection with a collection, use or disclosure of, or access to, the information under this Act, to the effect that the other person,

(a) is a person who is authorized to request access to a record of personal health information under section 53;

(b) is a person who is entitled under section 5 or 23 or subsection 26 (1) to consent to the collection, use or disclosure of personal health information about another individual;

(c) meets the requirement of clauses 26 (2) (b) and (c); or

(d) holds the beliefs described in subsection 26 (5). 2004, c. 3, Sched. A, s. 71 (4).

Offences

72. (1) A person is guilty of an offence if the person,

(a) wilfully collects, uses or discloses personal health information in contravention of this Act or its regulations;

(b) makes a request under this Act, under false pretences, for access to or correction of a record of personal health information;

(c) in connection with the collection, use or disclosure of personal health information or access to a record of personal health information, makes an assertion, knowing that it is untrue, to the effect that the person,

    (i) is a person who is entitled to consent to the collection, use or disclosure of personal health information about another individual,

    (ii) meets the requirement of clauses 26 (2) (b) and (c),

    (iii) holds the beliefs described in subsection 26 (5), or

    (iv) is a person entitled to access to a record of personal health information under section 52;

(d) disposes of a record of personal health information in the custody or under the control of the custodian with an intent to evade a request for access to the record that the custodian has received under subsection 53 (1);

(e) wilfully disposes of a record of personal health information in contravention of section 13;

(f) contravenes subsection 34 (2), (3) or (4) or clause 47 (15) (a), (e) or (f);

(g) wilfully obstructs the Commissioner or a person known to be acting under the authority of the Commissioner in the performance of his or her functions under this Act;

(h) wilfully makes a false statement to mislead or attempt to mislead the Commissioner or a person known to be acting under the authority of the Commissioner in the performance of his or her functions under this Act;

(i) wilfully fails to comply with an order made by the Commissioner or a person known to be acting under the authority of the Commissioner under this Act; or

(j) contravenes section 70. 2004, c. 3, Sched. A, s. 72 (1).

Penalty

(2) A person who is guilty of an offence under subsection (1) is liable, on conviction,

(a) if the person is a natural person, to a fine of not more than $50,000; and

(b) if the person is not a natural person, to a fine of not more than $250,000. 2004, c. 3, Sched. A, s. 72 (2).

Officers, etc.

(3) If a corporation commits an offence under this Act, every officer, member, employee or other agent of the corporation who authorized the offence, or who had the authority to prevent the offence from being committed but knowingly refrained from doing so, is a party to and guilty of the offence and is

liable, on conviction, to the penalty for the offence, whether or not the corporation has been prosecuted or convicted. 2004, c. 3, Sched. A, s. 72 (3).

No prosecution

(4) No person is liable to prosecution for an offence against this or any other Act by reason of complying with a requirement of the Commissioner under this Act. 2004, c. 3, Sched. A, s. 72 (4).

Commencing a prosecution

(5) No person other than the Attorney General or a counsel or agent acting on behalf of the Attorney General may commence a prosecution for an offence under subsection (1). 2004, c. 3, Sched. A, s. 72 (5).

Regulations

73. (1) Subject to section 74, the Lieutenant Governor in Council may make regulations,

(a) prescribing or specifying anything that this Act describes as being prescribed, specified, described, provided for, authorized or required in the regulations made under this Act;

(b) exempting persons or classes of persons from the persons described in clause (d) of the definition of "health care practitioner" in section 2;

(c) specifying persons or classes of persons who shall not be included in the definition of "health information custodian" in subsection 3 (1);

(d) specifying that certain types of information shall or shall not be included in the definition of "personal health information" in subsection 4 (1);

(e) defining, for the purposes of this Act and its regulations, any word or expression used in this Act that has not already been expressly defined in this Act;

(f) making any provision of this Act or its regulations, that applies to some but not all health information custodians, applicable to a prescribed person mentioned in paragraph 8 of the definition of "health information custodian" in subsection 3 (1) or a member of a prescribed class of persons mentioned in that paragraph;

(g) specifying requirements with respect to information practices for the purposes of subsection 10 (1), including conditions that a health information custodian is required to comply with when collecting, using or disclosing personal health information or classes of personal health information, or specifying procedural processes or requirements for setting requirements with respect to information practices for the purposes of that subsection;

(h) specifying requirements, or a process for setting requirements, for the purposes of subsection 10 (3) with which a health information custodian is required to comply when using electronic means to collect, use, modify, disclose, retain or dispose of personal health information, including standards for transactions, data elements for transactions, code sets for data elements and procedures for the transmission and authentication of electronic signatures;

(i) specifying requirements for the purposes of subsection 17 (1), including requiring that a health information custodian and its agent enter into an agreement that complies with the regulations made under clause (k) before the custodian provides personal health information to the agent;

(j) specifying requirements that an agreement entered into under this Act or its regulations must contain;

(k) specifying requirements, restrictions or prohibitions with respect to the collection, use or disclosure of any class of personal health information by any person in addition to the requirements, restrictions or prohibitions set out in this Act;

(l) specifying requirements that an express instruction mentioned in clause 37 (1) (a), 38 (1) (a) or 50 (1) (e) must meet;

(m) permitting notices, statements or any other things, that under this Act are required to be provided in writing, to be provided in electronic or other form instead, subject to the conditions or restrictions that are specified by the regulations made under this Act;

(n) prescribing under what circumstances the Canadian Blood Services may collect, use and disclose personal health information, the conditions that apply to the collection, use and disclosure of personal health information by the Canadian Blood Services and disclosures that may be made by a health information custodian to the Canadian Blood Services;

(o) specifying information relating to the administration or enforcement of this Act that is required to be contained in a report made under subsection 58 (1) of the *Freedom of Information and Protection of Privacy Act;*

(p) respecting any matter necessary or advisable to carry out effectively the purposes of this Act. 2004, c. 3, Sched. A, s. 73 (1).

General or specific application

(2) A regulation made under this Act may be of general application or specific to any person or persons or class or classes in its application. 2004, c. 3, Sched. A, s. 73 (2).

Classes

(3) A class described in the regulations made under this Act may be described according to any characteristic or combination of characteristics and may be described to include or exclude any specified member, whether or not with the same characteristics. 2004, c. 3, Sched. A, s. 73 (3).

Public consultation before making regulations

74. (1) Subject to subsection (7), the Lieutenant Governor in Council shall not make any regulation under section 73 unless,

(a) the Minister has published a notice of the proposed regulation in *The Ontario Gazette* and given notice of the proposed regulation by all other means that the Minister considers appropriate for the purpose of providing notice to the persons who may be affected by the proposed regulation;

(b) the notice complies with the requirements of this section;

(c) the time periods specified in the notice, during which members of the public may exercise a right described in clause (2) (b) or (c), have expired; and

(d) the Minister has considered whatever comments and submissions that members of the public have made on the proposed regulation in accordance with clause (2) (b) or (c) and has reported to the Lieutenant Governor in Council on what, if any, changes to the proposed regulation the Minister considers appropriate. 2004, c. 3, Sched. A, s. 74 (1).

Contents of notice

(2) The notice mentioned in clause (1) (a) shall contain,

(a) a description of the proposed regulation and the text of it;

(b) a statement of the time period during which members of the public may submit written comments on the proposed regulation to the Minister and the manner in which and the address to which the comments must be submitted;

(c) a description of whatever other rights, in addition to the right described in clause (b), that members of the public have to make submissions on the proposed regulation and the manner in which and the time period during which those rights must be exercised;

(d) a statement of where and when members of the public may review written information about the proposed regulation;

(e) all prescribed information; and

(f) all other information that the Minister considers appropriate. 2004, c. 3, Sched. A, s. 74 (2).

Time period for comments

(3) The time period mentioned in clauses (2) (b) and (c) shall be at least 60 days after the Minister gives the notice mentioned in clause (1) (a) unless the Minister shortens the time period in accordance with subsection (4). 2004, c. 3, Sched. A, s. 74 (3).

Shorter time period for comments

(4) The Minister may shorten the time period if, in the Minister's opinion,

(a) the urgency of the situation requires it;

(b) the proposed regulation clarifies the intent or operation of this Act or the regulations; or

(c) the proposed regulation is of a minor or technical nature. 2004, c. 3, Sched. A, s. 74 (4).

Discretion to make regulations

(5) Upon receiving the Minister's report mentioned in clause (1) (d), the Lieutenant Governor in Council, without further notice under subsection (1), may make the proposed regulation with the changes that the Lieutenant Governor in Council considers appropriate, whether or not those changes are mentioned in the Minister's report. 2004, c. 3, Sched. A, s. 74 (5).

No public consultation

(6) The Minister may decide that subsections (1) to (5) should not apply to the power of the Lieutenant Governor in Council to make a regulation under section 73 if, in the Minister's opinion,

(a) the urgency of the situation requires it;

(b) the proposed regulation clarifies the intent or operation of this Act or the regulations; or

(c) the proposed regulation is of a minor or technical nature. 2004, c. 3, Sched. A, s. 74 (6).

Same

(7) If the Minister decides that subsections (1) to (5) should not apply to the power of the Lieutenant Governor in Council to make a regulation under section 73,

(a) those subsections do not apply to the power of the Lieutenant Governor in Council to make the regulation; and

(b) the Minister shall give notice of the decision to the public and to the Commissioner as soon as is reasonably possible after making the decision. 2004, c. 3, Sched. A, s. 74 (7).

Contents of notice

(8) The notice mentioned in clause (7) (b) shall include a statement of the Minister's reasons for making the decision and all other information that the Minister considers appropriate. 2004, c. 3, Sched. A, s. 74 (8).

Publication of notice

(9) The Minister shall publish the notice mentioned in clause (7) (b) in *The Ontario Gazette* and give the notice by all other means that the Minister considers appropriate. 2004, c. 3, Sched. A, s. 74 (9).

Temporary regulation

(10) If the Minister decides that subsections (1) to (5) should not apply to the power of the Lieutenant Governor in Council to make a regulation under section 73 because the Minister is of the opinion that the urgency of the situation requires it, the regulation shall,

(a) be identified as a temporary regulation in the text of the regulation; and

(b) unless it is revoked before its expiry, expire at a time specified in the regulation, which shall not be after the second anniversary of the day on which the regulation comes into force. 2004, c. 3, Sched. A, s. 74 (10).

No review

(11) Subject to subsection (12), neither a court, nor the Commissioner shall review any action, decision, failure to take action or failure to make a decision by the Lieutenant Governor in Council or the Minister under this section. 2004, c. 3, Sched. A, s. 74 (11).

Exception

(12) Any person resident in Ontario may make an application for judicial review under the *Judicial Review Procedure Act* on the grounds that the Minister has not taken a step required by this section. 2004, c. 3, Sched. A, s. 74 (12).

Time for application

(13) No person shall make an application under subsection (12) with respect to a regulation later than 21 days after the day on which,

(a) the Minister publishes a notice with respect to the regulation under clause (1) (a) or subsection (9), where applicable; or

(b) the regulation is filed, if it is a regulation described in subsection (10). 2004, c. 3, Sched. A, s. 74 (13).

Review of Act

75. A committee of the Legislative Assembly shall,

(a) begin a comprehensive review of this Act not later than the third anniversary of the day on which this section comes into force; and

(b) within one year after beginning that review, make recommendations to the Assembly concerning amendments to this Act. 2004, c. 3, Sched. A, s. 75.

76.–98. OMITTED (AMENDS OR REPEALS OTHER ACTS). 2004, c. 3, Sched. A, ss. 76–98.

99. OMITTED (PROVIDES FOR COMING INTO FORCE OF PROVISIONS OF THIS ACT). 2004, c. 3, Sched. A, s. 99.

100. OMITTED (ENACTS SHORT TITLE OF THIS ACT). 2004, c. 3, Sched. A, s. 100.

© Queen's Printer for Ontario, 2004.

This is an unofficial version of Government of Ontario legal materials.

Appendix 5:
Ontario Regulation
329/04 under *PHIPA*

No Amendments

GENERAL

This is the English version of a bilingual regulation.

Definitions for the purposes of the Act

1. (1) In the definition of "health care" in section 2 of the Act,

"a procedure that is done for a health-related purpose" includes taking a donation of blood or blood products from an individual. O. Reg. 329/04, s. 1 (1).

(2) For the purposes of the Act,

"marketing" does not include,

(a) a communication by a health care practitioner who provides insured services within the meaning of the *Health Insurance Act* to an individual or a member of the individual's family or household by which the practitioner makes available to those persons an arrangement whereby they may receive ancillary uninsured services for a block fee or on the basis of a set fee for service, or

(b) a communication by the Canadian Blood Services for the purpose of recruiting donors of blood, blood products or hematopoietic progenitor cells. O. Reg. 329/04, s. 1 (2).

(3) In the definition of "disclose" in section 2 of the Act, the expression "to make the information available or to release it to another health information custodian or to another person" does not include a person's providing personal health information to someone who provided it to or disclosed it to the person, whether or not the personal health information has been manipulated or altered, if it does not contain any additional identifying information. O. Reg. 329/04, s. 1 (3).

(4) For the purposes of clause 4 (1) (d) of the Act, the expression "eligibility for health care" includes eligibility for coverage under the *Health Insurance Act* or for any other insurance or payment arrangement with respect to health care. O. Reg. 329/04, s. 1 (4).

(5) For the purposes of subsection 7 (3) of the Act, if the Act or its regulations provides that an action, including a collection, use or disclosure, may be taken, and another Act or regulation provides that it may not be taken, then "it is not possible to comply with both". O. Reg. 329/04, s. 1 (5).

(6) For the purposes of clause 18 (4) (c) of the Act,

"information about an individual's state of health" does not include information about medication or related goods or services provided by a member of the Ontario College of Pharmacists to the individual that the member discloses to a third party who is being requested to provide payment for the medication or related goods or services. O. Reg. 329/04, s. 1 (6).

(7) For the purposes of paragraph 5 of subsection 23 (1) of the Act,

"a person whom an Act of Ontario or Canada authorizes or requires to act on behalf of the individual" includes a person who is an agent for the purposes of section 157 of the *Drug and Pharmacies Regulation Act* where the consent under section 23 of the *Personal Health Information Protection Act, 2004* relates to a prescription being presented to a pharmacist to be dispensed. O. Reg. 329/04, s. 1 (7).

(8) For the purposes of subsections 34 (2) and (3) of the Act,

"a person who is not a health information custodian" does not include,

(a) a custodian's agent who is using or disclosing the information on behalf of the custodian in accordance with the Act, or

(b) the individual or the individual's substitute decision-maker in respect of the individual's health number. O. Reg. 329/04, s. 1 (8).

(9) For the purposes of clause 39 (1) (a) of the Act, the expression "eligibility of the individual to receive health care or related goods, services or benefits provided under an Act of Ontario or Canada and funded in whole or in part by the Government of Ontario or Canada or by a municipality" includes eligibility of the individual for coverage under the *Health Insurance Act* or for any other insurance or payment arrangement with respect to health care or related goods, services or benefits that are provided under the authority of an Act of Ontario or Canada and are funded in whole or in part by the Government of Ontario or Canada or by a municipality. O. Reg. 329/04, s. 1 (9).

(10) For the purposes of subsections 42 (1) and (2) of the Act, "potential successor" and "successor" mean a potential successor or a successor that is a health information custodian or that will be a health information custodian if it becomes the successor. O. Reg. 329/04, s. 1 (10).

Exemptions, "health care practitioner"

2. The following persons are not health care practitioners under clause (d) of the definition of "health care practitioner" in section 2 of the Act:

1.   Persons providing fitness or weight-management services. O. Reg. 329/04, s. 2.

Health information custodians

3. (1) The Canadian Blood Services is prescribed as a health information custodian, and is prescribed as a single health information custodian with respect to all its functions. O. Reg. 329/04, s. 3 (1).

(2) Despite paragraph 6 of subsection 3 (1) of the Act, the medical officer of health of a board of health within the meaning of the *Health Protection and Promotion Act* is prescribed as a single health information custodian with respect to the performance of his or her duties under that or any other Act. O. Reg. 329/04, s. 3 (2).

(3) Each public health laboratory established by the Minister under section 79 of the *Health Protection and Promotion Act*,
   (a)   is a single health information custodian in respect of all its functions; and
   (b)   shall be deemed to be included in the list of types of custodians referred to in subsections 20 (2) and (3) and clause 38 (1) (a) of the Act. O. Reg. 329/04, s. 3 (3).

Mixed records

4. Except for the purposes of subsection 8 (4) of the Act, "personal health information" as defined under subsection 4 (1) of the Act includes all identifying information that is contained in a record that contains information of the

type referred to in any one or more of clauses (a) to (g) of subsection 4 (1). O. Reg. 329/04, s. 4.

Prevail over Act

5. The confidentiality requirements in the following provisions prevail over the Act:

1. Section 165 and subsection 168 (3) of the *Child and Family Services Act*.
2. Subsection 85.3 (4) of the Health Professions Procedural Code set out in Schedule 2 to the *Regulated Health Professions Act, 1991*.
3. Subsection 19 (8) of the *Remedies for Organized Crime and Other Unlawful Activities Act, 2001*.
4. Subsection 181 (3) of the *Workplace Safety and Insurance Act, 1997*. O. Reg. 329/04, s. 5.

Persons who provide to custodians

6. (1) Except as otherwise required by law, the following are prescribed as requirements for the purposes of subsection 10 (4) of the Act with respect to a person who supplies services for the purpose of enabling a health information custodian to use electronic means to collect, use, modify, disclose, retain or dispose of personal health information, and who is not an agent of the custodian:

1. The person shall not use any personal health information to which it has access in the course of providing the services for the health information custodian except as necessary in the course of providing the services.
2. The person shall not disclose any personal health information to which it has access in the course of providing the services for the health information custodian.
3. The person shall not permit its employees or any person acting on its behalf to be able to have access to the information unless the employee or person acting on its behalf agrees to comply with the restrictions that apply to the person who is subject to this subsection. O. Reg. 329/04, s. 6 (1).

(2) In subsection (3),

"health information network provider" or "provider" means a person who provides services to two or more health information custodians where the services are provided primarily to custodians to enable the custodians to use electronic means to disclose personal health information to one another, whether or not the person is an agent of any of the custodians. O. Reg. 329/04, s. 6 (2).

(3) The following are prescribed as requirements with respect to a health information network provider in the course of providing services to enable a

health information custodian to use electronic means to collect, use, disclose, retain or dispose of personal health information:

1. The provider shall notify every applicable health information custodian at the first reasonable opportunity if,

    i.   the provider accessed, used, disclosed or disposed of personal health information other than in accordance with paragraphs 1 and 2 of subsection (1), or

    ii. an unauthorized person accessed the personal health information.

2. The provider shall provide to each applicable health information custodian a plain language description of the services that the provider provides to the custodians, that is appropriate for sharing with the individuals to whom the personal health information relates, including a general description of the safeguards in place to protect against unauthorized use and disclosure, and to protect the integrity of the information.

3. The provider shall make available to the public,

    i.   the description referred to in paragraph 2,

    ii. any directives, guidelines and policies of the provider that apply to the services that the provider provides to the health information custodians to the extent that these do not reveal a trade secret or confidential scientific, technical, commercial or labour relations information, and

    iii. a general description of the safeguards implemented by the person in relation to the security and confidentiality of the information.

4. The provider shall to the extent reasonably practical, and in a manner that is reasonably practical, keep and make available to each applicable health information custodian, on the request of the custodian, an electronic record of,

    i.   all accesses to all or part of the personal health information associated with the custodian being held in equipment controlled by the provider, which record shall identify the person who accessed the information and the date and time of the access, and

    ii. all transfers of all or part of the information associated with the custodian by means of equipment controlled by the provider, which record shall identify the person who transferred the information and the person or address to whom it was sent, and the date and time it was sent.

5. The provider shall perform, and provide to each applicable health information custodian a written copy of the results of, an assessment of the services provided to the health information custodians, with respect to,

    i.   threats, vulnerabilities and risks to the security and integrity of the personal health information, and

ii.   how the services may affect the privacy of the individuals who are the subject of the information.

6.   The provider shall ensure that any third party it retains to assist in providing services to a health information custodian agrees to comply with the restrictions and conditions that are necessary to enable the provider to comply with this section.

7.   The provider shall enter into a written agreement with each health information custodian concerning the services provided to the custodian that,

i.   describes the services that the provider is required to provide for the custodian,

ii.   describes the administrative, technical and physical safeguards relating to the confidentiality and security of the information, and

iii.   requires the provider to comply with the Act and the regulations. O. Reg. 329/04, s. 6 (3).

(4) A health information custodian who uses goods or services supplied by a person referred to in subsection 10 (4) of the Act, other than a person who is an agent of the custodian, for the purpose of using electronic means to collect, use, modify, disclose, retain or dispose of personal health information shall not be considered in so doing to make the information available or to release it to that person for the purposes of the definition of "disclose" in section 2 of the Act if,

(a)   the person complies with subsections (1) and (3), to the extent that either is applicable, in supplying services; and

(b)   in the case of a person supplying goods to the health information custodian, the custodian does not, in returning the goods to the person, enable the person to access the personal health information except where subsection (1) applies and is complied with. O. Reg. 329/04, s. 6 (4).

Exception to s. 17 (2) of the Act

7. The following are prescribed as exceptions to subsection 17 (2) of the Act:

1.   An agent of a health information custodian to whom the custodian provides information to use for the purposes of clause 37 (1) (d) of the Act may use that information, together with other such information that the agent has received from other custodians to use for the purposes of that clause, for the purposes of systemic risk management analysis if,

i.   the agent is the Canadian Medical Protective Association or the Healthcare Insurance Reciprocal of Canada, and

ii.   the agent does not disclose personal health information provided to it by one health information custodian to another custodian.

2.   An agent of a health information custodian may disclose personal health information acquired in the course of the agent's activities for or on behalf of the custodian, as if the agent were a health information custodian for the purposes of,

    i.   subsection 40 (1) of the Act,

    ii.   clauses 43 (1) (b), (c) and (d) of the Act, or

    iii. disclosures to the Public Guardian and Trustee or a children's aid society under clause 43 (1) (e) of the Act. O. Reg. 329/04, s. 7.

s. 18 (4) (c) of the Act

8. The disclosure of information by a member of the Ontario College of Pharmacists to a third party who is being requested to provide payment for medication or related goods or services provided to an individual is a prescribed type of disclosure for the purposes of clause 18 (4) (c) of the Act. O. Reg. 329/04, s. 8.

Substitute decision maker

9. An application to the Board under subsection 24 (2), 27 (1) or (2) of the Act shall be deemed to include an application to the Board under subsection 22 (3) of the Act with respect to the individual's capacity to consent to the collection, use or disclosure of his or her personal health information unless the individual's capacity has been determined by the Board within the previous six months. O. Reg. 329/04, s. 9.

Fundraising

10. (1) The type of contact information that is prescribed for the purposes of clause 32 (1) (b) of the Act is the individual's mailing address. O. Reg. 329/04, s. 10 (1).

(2) For the purposes of subsection 32 (2) of the Act, the following are prescribed as requirements and restrictions on the manner in which consent is obtained and the resulting collection, use or disclosure of personal health information:

1.   Personal health information held by a health information custodian may only be collected, used or disclosed for the purpose of fundraising activities undertaken for a charitable or philanthropic purpose related to the custodian's operations.

2.   Consent under clause 32 (1) (b) of the Act may only be inferred where,

    i.   the custodian has at the time of providing service to the individual, posted or made available to the individual, in a manner likely to come to the attention of the individual, a brief statement that unless he or she requests otherwise, his or her name and contact information may

be disclosed and used for fundraising purposes on behalf of the custodian, together with information on how the individual can easily
opt-out of receiving any future fundraising solicitations on behalf of
the custodian, and

ii.   the individual has not opted out within 60 days of when the statement
provided under subparagraph i was made available to him or her.

3.   All solicitations for fundraising must provide the individual with an easy
way to opt-out of receiving future solicitations.

4.   A communication from the custodian or a person conducting fundraising
on its behalf to an individual for the purpose of fundraising must not
include any information about the individual's health care or state of
health. O. Reg. 329/04, s. 10 (2).

(3) The name and mailing address of the individual's substitute decision
maker are prescribed contact information for the purposes of clause 32 (1) (b)
of the Act. O. Reg. 329/04, s. 10 (3).

Health number collection

11. The following are prescribed persons for the purposes of clause 34 (2)
(d) of the Act:

1.   The Workplace Safety and Insurance Board.

2.   Every person that is prescribed under section 13.

3.   Every entity that is prescribed under section 18.

4.   A researcher mentioned in paragraph 2 of section 12, for the purposes of
the research. O. Reg. 329/04, s. 11.

Disclosure of health number

12. The following are prescribed as exceptions for the purposes of subsection 34 (3) of the Act:

1.   A person who is not a health information custodian may disclose a health
number for a purpose related to the provision of provincially funded
health resources.

2.   A researcher who has custody or control of personal health information,
including a health number, by reason of a disclosure authorized under section 44 of the Act, or that the researcher uses pursuant to clause 37 (1) (j)
of the Act, may disclose the health number to a person that is a prescribed
person for the purposes of clause 39 (1) (c) of the Act, an entity prescribed
for the purposes of subsection 45 (1) of the Act or another researcher if,

i.   the disclosure is part of a research plan approved under section 44 of
the Act, or

ii.   the disclosure is necessary for the purpose of verifying or validating the information or the research.

3.   A person that is prescribed for the purposes of clause 39 (1) (c) of the Act may disclose the health number for the purposes of its functions under clause 39 (1) (c).

4.   The Workplace Safety and Insurance Board may disclose the health number in the course of exercising its powers under section 159 of the *Workplace Safety and Insurance Act, 1997.* O. Reg. 329/04, s. 12.

Registries of personal health information

13. (1) The following are prescribed persons for the purposes of clause 39 (1) (c) of the Act:

1.   Cardiac Care Network of Ontario in respect of its registry of cardiac services.

2.   INSCYTE (Information System for Cytology etc.) Corporation in respect of CytoBase.

3.   London Health Sciences Centre in respect of the Ontario Joint Replacement Registry.

4.   Canadian Stroke Network in respect of the Canadian Stroke Registry. O. Reg. 329/04, s. 13 (1).

(2) A person that is a prescribed person for the purposes of clause 39 (1) (c) of the Act shall put in place practices and procedures approved by the Commissioner to protect the privacy of the individuals whose personal health information it receives and to maintain the confidentiality of the information, except that the practices and procedures are not required to be approved by the Commissioner until the first anniversary of the day that section 45 of the Act comes into force. O. Reg. 329/04, s. 13 (2).

(3) A person that is a prescribed person for the purposes of clause 39 (1) (c) of the Act shall make publicly available a plain language description of the functions of the registry compiled or maintained by the person, including a summary of the practices and procedures described in subsection (2). O. Reg. 329/04, s. 13 (3).

(4) A person that is a prescribed person for the purposes of clause 39 (1) (c) of the Act may use personal health information as if it were a health information custodian for the purposes of clause 37 (1) (j) or subsection 37 (3) of the Act. O. Reg. 329/04, s. 13 (4).

(5) A person that is a prescribed person for the purposes of clause 39 (1) (c) of the Act may disclose personal health information as if it were a health

information custodian for the purposes of sections 44, 45 and 47 of the Act. O. Reg. 329/04, s. 13 (5).

Archives

14. (1) Subject to clause 42 (3) (b) of the Act, a health information custodian may transfer records of personal health information under that clause to a person who,

(a) has put in place reasonable measures to ensure that personal health information in the person's custody or control is protected against theft, loss and unauthorized use or disclosure and to ensure that the records containing the information are protected against unauthorized copying, modification or disposal;

(b) has put in place measures to allow an individual to have reasonable access to the individual's own record of personal health information held by the person;

(c) has made available to the public a written statement that,

   (i)   provides a general description of the person's information practices,

   (ii) describes how an individual may obtain access to a record of personal health information about the individual that is in the custody or control of the person,

   (iii) describes the mandate, and organizational links and affiliations, of the person in maintaining the archive, and

   (iv) describes how to make a complaint to the person and to the Commissioner under the Act; and

(d) has registered with the Commissioner the intention to act as a recipient of information under this section, and provided to the Commissioner the statement set out in (c), and any further information reasonably requested by the Commissioner. O. Reg. 329/04, s. 14 (1).

(2) If a person that received records under clause 42 (3) (b) of the Act ceases to exercise the functions of collecting and preserving records of historical or archival importance or ceases to comply with the conditions set out in subsection (1), the person shall immediately transfer the records, including any health number contained in the records, to another person who is authorized to receive transfers of records under clause 42 (3) (a) or (b) of the Act, subject to the agreement of the person who is to receive the transfer. O. Reg. 329/04, s. 14 (2).

(3) Despite subsection 49 (1) of the Act, and subject to the agreement of the person who is to receive the transfer, a person who is not a health information custodian to whom a health information custodian disclosed personal health information may transfer any records containing the personal health information, including any health number contained in the records to,

(a) the Archives of Ontario; or

(b) a person prescribed under subsection (1), if the disclosure is made for the purpose of that function. O. Reg. 329/04, s. 14 (3).

(4) A person who receives a transfer of records of personal health information under subsection (2) or (3) or under clause 42 (3) (b) of the Act may,

(a) collect any health number contained in the records incidentally to receiving the transfer of the records;

(b) use personal health information contained in the records, including any health number contained in the records, as if it were a health information custodian for the purposes of clause 37 (1) (j) and subsection 37 (3) of the Act; and

(c) disclose personal health information contained in the records, including any health number contained in the records, as if it were a health information custodian for the purposes of sections 44, 45 and 47 of the Act. O. Reg. 329/04, s. 14 (4).

(5) A person who, before November 1, 2004, received a transfer of a record of personal health information to which subsection (4) would have applied on or after November 1, 2004, may disclose and use it, including any health number contained in the record, for research as if it were a health information custodian under the Act. O. Reg. 329/04, s. 14 (5).

Research ethics boards

15. The following are prescribed as requirements that must be met by a research ethics board:

1. The board must have at least five members, including,

   i. at least one member with no affiliation with the person or persons that established the research ethics board,

   ii. at least one member knowledgeable in research ethics, either as a result of formal training in research ethics, or practical or academic experience in research ethics,

   iii. at least two members with expertise in the methods or in the areas of the research being considered, and

   iv. at least one member knowledgeable in considering privacy issues.

2. The board may only act with respect to a proposal to approve a research plan where there is no conflict of interest existing or likely to be perceived between its duty under subsection 44 (3) of the Act and any participating board member's personal interest in the disclosure of the personal health information or the performance of the research. O. Reg. 329/04, s. 15.

Requirements for research plans

16. The following are prescribed as additional requirements that must be set out in research plans for the purposes of clause 44 (2) (c) of the Act:

1. A description of the research proposed to be conducted and the duration of the research.

2. A description of the personal health information required and the potential sources.

3. A description of how the personal health information will be used in the research, and if it will be linked to other information, a description of the other information as well as how the linkage will be done.

4. An explanation as to why the research cannot reasonably be accomplished without the personal health information and, if it is to be linked to other information, an explanation as to why this linkage is required.

5. An explanation as to why consent to the disclosure of the personal health information is not being sought from the individuals to whom the information relates.

6. A description of the reasonably foreseeable harms and benefits that may arise from the use of the personal health information and how the researchers intend to address those harms.

7. A description of all persons who will have access to the information, why their access is necessary, their roles in relation to the research, and their related qualifications.

8. The safeguards that the researcher will impose to protect the confidentiality and security of the personal health information, including an estimate of how long information will be retained in an identifiable form and why.

9. Information as to how and when the personal health information will be disposed of or returned to the health information custodian.

10. The funding source of the research.

11. Whether the researcher has applied for the approval of another research ethics board and, if so the response to or status of the application.

12. Whether the researcher's interest in the disclosure of the personal health information or the performance of the research would likely result in an actual or perceived conflict of interest with other duties of the researcher. O. Reg. 329/04, s. 16.

Disclosure by researcher

17. Despite clause 44 (6) (d) of the Act, a researcher may disclose the information to an entity prescribed under subsection 45 (1) of the Act, to a person prescribed for the purposes of clause 39 (1) (c) of the Act for use in a registry compiled or maintained by that person, or to another researcher if,

(a) the disclosure is part of a research plan approved under section 44 of the Act; or

(b) the disclosure is necessary for the purpose of verifying or validating the information or the research. O. Reg. 329/04, s. 17.

Prescribed entities for the purposes of s. 45 (1) of the Act

18. (1) Each of the following entities, including any registries maintained within the entity, is a prescribed entity for the purposes of subsection 45 (1) of the Act:

1.   Cancer Care Ontario.
2.   Canadian Institute for Health Information.
3.   Institute for Clinical Evaluative Sciences.
4.   Pediatric Oncology Group of Ontario. O. Reg. 329/04, s. 18 (1).

(2) An entity that is a prescribed entity for the purposes of subsection 45 (1) of the Act shall make publicly available a plain language description of the functions of the entity including a summary of the practices and procedures described in subsection 45 (3) of the Act. O. Reg. 329/04, s. 18 (2).

(3) Despite subsection 45 (6) of the Act, every entity that is a prescribed entity for the purposes of subsection 45 (1) of the Act may use personal health information as if it were a health information custodian for the purposes of clause 37 (1) (j) and subsection 37 (3) of the Act. O. Reg. 329/04, s. 18 (3).

(4) Despite subsection 45 (6) of the Act, every entity that is a prescribed entity for the purposes of subsection 45 (1) of the Act may disclose personal health information as if it were a health information custodian for the purposes of clause 39 (1) (c) and sections 44, 45 and 47 of the Act. O. Reg. 329/04, s. 18 (4).

(5) An entity that is a prescribed entity for the purposes of subsection 45 (1) of the Act may disclose the information that it receives under subsection 45 (1) of the Act to a health information custodian who provided it to or disclosed it directly or indirectly to the person from whom the entity collected the information, whether or not the information has been manipulated or altered, if it does not contain any additional identifying information. O. Reg. 329/04, s. 18 (5).

(6) An entity that is a prescribed entity for the purposes of subsection 45 (1) of the Act may disclose the information that it receives under subsection 45 (1) of the Act to a governmental institution of Ontario or Canada as if the enti-

ty were a health information custodian for the purposes of clause 43 (1) (h) of the Act. O. Reg. 329/04, s. 18 (6).

(7) Despite subsection 45 (6) of the Act, the Canadian Institute for Health Information may disclose personal health information about an individual to a person outside Ontario where,

(a) the disclosure is for the purpose of health planning or health administration;
(b) the information relates to health care provided in Ontario to a person who is a resident of another province or territory of Canada; and
(c) the disclosure is made to the government of that province or territory. O. Reg. 329/04, s. 18 (7).

Collection by institution

19. An institution within the meaning of the *Freedom of Information and Protection of Privacy Act* or the *Municipal Freedom of Information and Protection of Privacy Act* that is not a health information custodian may collect personal health information from a health information custodian if and only if the custodian has authority to disclose the information to the institution under the Act. O. Reg. 329/04, s. 19.

Information received before commencement

20. For the purposes of subsection 49 (1) of the Act, a person who is not a health information custodian and to whom a health information custodian disclosed personal health information prior to November 1, 2004 may use or disclose the information for the purpose for which it was disclosed to the person, except where otherwise prohibited by law. O. Reg. 329/04, s. 20.

Exceptions to restrictions on recipients

21. (1) Section 49 of the Act does not apply,

(a) to an individual or a substitute decision maker of an individual in respect of personal health information about the individual; or
(b) to prevent a person who received personal health information from a health information custodian from using or disclosing the information pursuant to a valid consent. O. Reg. 329/04, s. 21 (1).

(2) Despite subsection 49 (1) of the Act, a person who is not a health information custodian and who provides coverage for payment to or on behalf of individuals in respect of medications or related goods or services may, where a claim is made to the person through a member of the Ontario College of Pharmacists for such a payment to or on behalf of an individual, disclose personal health infor-

mation about the individual to the member to assist the member in advising the individual or providing health care to the individual. O. Reg. 329/04, s. 21 (2).

(3) Despite subsection 49 (1) of the Act, a person who is not a health information custodian and to whom a health information custodian discloses personal health information shall not disclose the personal health information where the disclosure is otherwise prohibited by law. O. Reg. 329/04, s. 21 (3).

Extent of use or disclosure by recipient

22. Subsection 49 (2) of the Act does not apply to,

(a) a College under the *Regulated Health Professions Act, 1991,* the College under the *Social Work and Social Service Work Act, 1998* or the Board under the *Drugless Practitioners Act*;

(b) a children's aid society or any person providing services on behalf of or on the request of a children's aid society; or

(c) a foster parent. O. Reg. 329/04, s. 22.

Freedom of information legislation

23. (1) Subsections 49 (1) and (2) of the Act do not apply to a person employed by or acting for an institution within the meaning of the *Freedom of Information and Protection of Privacy Act* or the *Municipal Freedom of Information and Protection of Privacy Act,* to the extent that the person is acting within the scope of one of those Acts. O. Reg. 329/04, s. 23 (1).

(2) Subsection 49 (3) of the Act does not apply to an institution within the meaning of the *Freedom of Information and Protection of Privacy Act* or the *Municipal Freedom of Information and Protection of Privacy Act* that is a health information custodian. O. Reg. 329/04, s. 23 (2).

Exclusions from access provisions

24. (1) The following types of personal health information in the custody or control of the following types of health information custodians are not subject to Part V of the Act:

1.   Personal health information that a researcher uses solely for the purposes of research, where the research is conducted in accordance with a research plan approved under subsection 44 (4) of the Act, or has been approved under clause 44 (10) (b) of the Act.

2.   Personal health information that is in the custody or control of a laboratory in respect of a test requested by a health care practitioner for the purpose of providing health care to the individual where the following conditions apply:

    i.   the individual has a right of access to the information through the health care practitioner, or will have such a right when the information is provided by the laboratory to the health care practitioner within a reasonable time, and

   ii.   the health care practitioner has not directed the laboratory to provide the information directly to the individual. O. Reg. 329/04, s. 24 (1).

(2) For the purposes of paragraph 2 of subsection (1),

"laboratory" means,

   (a) a laboratory or a specimen collection centre as defined in section 5 of the *Laboratory and Specimen Collection Centre Licensing Act*, or

   (b) a laboratory operated by a ministry of the Crown in right of Ontario. O. Reg. 329/04, s. 24 (2).

(3) Part V of the Act does not apply to entitle a person to a right of access to information about the person that is contained in a record that is dedicated primarily to the personal health information of another person. O. Reg. 329/04, s. 24 (3).

Canadian Blood Services

25. (1) The Canadian Blood Services may indirectly collect personal health information about an individual who donates or attempts to donate blood or blood products, if the information is reasonably necessary to ensure the safety of the blood system and it is not reasonably possible to collect, directly from the individual,

(a) personal health information that can reasonably be relied on as accurate; or

(b) personal health information in a timely way. O. Reg. 329/04, s. 25 (1).

(2) The Canadian Blood Services may use the personal health information of an individual who donates or attempts to donate blood or blood products for the purpose of ensuring the safety of the blood system. O. Reg. 329/04, s. 25 (2).

(3) The Canadian Blood Services may collect personal health information from, and disclose personal health information to, Héma-Québec as necessary for the purpose of ensuring the safety of the supply of blood and blood products, where the personal health information relates to an individual who donates or attempts to donate blood or blood products. O. Reg. 329/04, s. 25 (3).

(4) The Canadian Blood Services shall not disclose personal health information for the purpose of recruiting donors of blood, blood products or

hematopoietic progenitor cells without the express consent of the individual, despite subsection 18 (2) of the Act. O. Reg. 329/04, s. 25 (4).

(5) The Canadian Blood Services may disclose personal health information about a deceased individual who has received blood or blood products to a relative of the individual or the executor or administrator of the individual's estate for the purpose of determining eligibility for compensation. O. Reg. 329/04, s. 25 (5).

26. OMITTED (PROVIDES FOR COMING INTO FORCE OF PROVISIONS OF THIS REGULATION). O. Reg. 329/04, s. 26.

Appendix 6:
Quality of Care Information Protection Act, 2004

S.O. 2004, Chapter 3
Schedule B

CONTENTS

Definitions

1. In this Act,

"disclose" means, with respect to quality of care information, to provide or make the information available to a person who is not a member of the quality of care committee with which the information is associated, and "disclosure" has a corresponding meaning; ("divulguer", "divulgation")

"health care" means any observation, examination, assessment, care, service or procedure that is done for a health-related purpose and that,

(a) is carried out or provided to diagnose, treat or maintain an individual's physical or mental condition,

(b) is carried out or provided to prevent disease or injury or to promote health, or

(c) is carried out or provided as part of palliative care,

and includes,

(d) the compounding, dispensing or selling of a drug, a device, equipment or any other item to an individual, or for the use of an individual, pursuant to a prescription, and

(e) a prescribed type of service; ("soins de santé")

"health facility" means a hospital within the meaning of the *Public Hospitals Act*, a private hospital within the meaning of the *Private Hospitals Act*, a psychiatric facility within the meaning of the *Mental Health Act*, an institution within the meaning of the *Mental Hospitals Act* or an independent health facility within the meaning of the *Independent Health Facilities Act*; ("établissement de santé")

"information" includes personal health information as defined in the *Personal Health Information Protection Act, 2004*; ("renseignements")

"Minister" means the Minister of Health and Long-Term Care; ("ministre")

"proceeding" includes a proceeding that is within the jurisdiction of the Legislature and that is held in, before or under the rules of a court, a tribunal, a commission, a justice of the peace, a coroner, a committee of a College within the meaning of the *Regulated Health Professions Act, 1991*, a committee of the Board of Regents continued under the *Drugless Practitioners Act*, a committee of the Ontario College of Social Workers and Social Service Workers under the *Social Work and Social Service Work Act, 1998*, an arbitrator or a mediator, but does not include any activities carried on by a quality of care committee; ("instance") "quality of care committee" means a body of one or more individuals,

    (a) that is established, appointed or approved,

        (i) by a health facility,

        (ii) by an entity that is prescribed by the regulations and that provides health care, or

        (iii) by an entity that is prescribed by the regulations and that carries on activities for the purpose of improving or maintaining the quality of care provided by a health facility, a health care provider or a class of health facility or health care provider,

    (b) that meets the prescribed criteria, if any, and

    (c) whose functions are to carry on activities for the purpose of studying, assessing or evaluating the provision of health care with a view to improving or maintaining the quality of the health care or the level of skill, knowledge and competence of the persons who provide the health care; ("comité de la qualité des soins")

"quality of care information" means information that,

    (a) is collected by or prepared for a quality of care committee for the sole or primary purpose of assisting the committee in carrying out its functions, or

    (b) relates solely or primarily to any activity that a quality of care committee carries on as part of its functions,

but does not include,

    (c) information contained in a record that is maintained for the purpose of providing health care to an individual,

    (d) information contained in a record that is required by law to be created or to be maintained,

    (e) facts contained in a record of an incident involving the provision of health care to an individual, except if the facts involving the incident are also fully recorded in a record mentioned in clause (c) relating to the individual, or

    (f) information that a regulation specifies is not quality of care information and that a quality of care committee receives after the day on which that regulation is made; ("renseignements sur la qualité des soins")

"regulations" mean the regulations made under this Act; ("règlements")

"use", with respect to quality of care information, does not include to disclose the information and "use", as a noun, does not include disclosure of the information; ("utiliser", "utilisation") "witness" means a person, whether or not a party to a proceeding, who, in the course of the proceeding,

(a) is examined or cross-examined for discovery, either orally or in writing,

(b) makes an affidavit, or

(c) is competent or compellable to be examined or cross-examined or to produce a document, whether under oath or not. ("témoin") 2004, c. 3, Sched. B, s. 1.

Conflict

2. In the event of a conflict between a provision of this Act or its regulations and a provision of any other Act or its regulations, this Act and its regulations prevail unless this Act or its regulations specifically provide otherwise. 2004, c. 3, Sched. B, s. 2.

Disclosure to quality of care committee

3. Despite this Act and the *Personal Health Information Protection Act, 2004*, a person may disclose any information to a quality of care committee for the purposes of the committee. 2004, c. 3, Sched. B, s. 3.

Quality of care information

4. (1) Despite the *Personal Health Information Protection Act, 2004*, no person shall disclose quality of care information except as permitted by this Act. 2004, c. 3, Sched. B, s. 4 (1).

Definition

(2) In subsections (3) and (4),

"management", with respect to a health facility or entity, includes members of the senior management staff, the board of directors, governors or trustees and members of the commission or other governing body or authority of the facility or entity. 2004, c. 3, Sched. B, s. 4 (2).

Exception, quality of care committee

(3) Despite subsection (1) and the *Personal Health Information Protection Act, 2004*, a quality of care committee may disclose quality of care information to,

(a) the management of the health facility or entity mentioned in subclause (a) (ii) of the definition of "quality of care committee" in section 1 that established, appointed or approved the committee if the committee considers it appropriate to do so for the purpose of improving or maintaining the quality of health care provided in or by the facility or entity; or

(b) the management of a health facility or health care provider, where an entity mentioned in subclause (a) (iii) of the definition of "quality of care committee" in section 1 carries on activities for the purpose of improving or maintaining the quality of health care provided by the facility, the provider or a class including the facility or the provider, if the committee considers it appropriate to do so for the purpose of improving or maintaining the quality of health care provided in or by the facility, provider or class. 2004, c. 3, Sched. B, s. 4 (3).

Exception, any person

(4) Despite subsection (1) and the *Personal Health Information Protection Act, 2004,* a person may disclose quality of care information if the disclosure is necessary for the purposes of eliminating or reducing a significant risk of serious bodily harm to a person or group of persons. 2004, c. 3, Sched. B, s. 4 (4).

Use of information

(5) A person to whom information is disclosed under subsection (3) or (4) shall not use the information except for the purposes for which the information was disclosed to the person. 2004, c. 3, Sched. B, s. 4 (5).

Further disclosure of information

(6) A member of the management of a health facility or entity described in subsection (3) to whom quality of care information is disclosed under that subsection may disclose the information to an agent or employee of the facility or entity if the disclosure is necessary for the purposes of improving or maintaining the quality of health care provided in or by the facility or entity. 2004, c. 3, Sched. B, s. 4 (6).

Same

(7) A person to whom information is disclosed under subsection (3), (4) or (6) shall not disclose the information except if subsection (4) or (6) permits the disclosure. 2004, c. 3, Sched. B, s. 4 (7).

Non-disclosure in proceeding

5. (1) No person shall ask a witness and no court or other body holding a proceeding shall permit or require a witness in the proceeding to disclose quality of care information. 2004, c. 3, Sched. B, s. 5 (1).

Non-admissibility of evidence

(2) Quality of care information is not admissible in evidence in a proceeding. 2004, c. 3, Sched. B, s. 5 (2).

Non-retaliation

6. No one shall dismiss, suspend, demote, discipline, harass or otherwise disadvantage a person by reason that the person has disclosed information to a quality of care committee under section 4. 2004, c. 3, Sched. B, s. 6.

Offence

7. (1) Every person who contravenes section 4 or 6 is guilty of an offence. 2004, c. 3, Sched. B, s. 7 (1).

Penalty

(2) A person who is guilty of an offence under subsection (1) is liable, on conviction,

(a) to a fine of not more than $50,000, if the person is an individual; or

(b) to a fine of not more than $250,000, if the person is not an individual. 2004, c. 3, Sched. B, s. 7 (2).

Officers, etc.

(3) If a corporation commits an offence under this Act, every officer, member, employee or other agent of the corporation who authorized the offence, or who had the authority to prevent the offence from being committed but knowingly refrained from doing so, is a party to and guilty of the offence and is liable, on conviction, to the penalty for the offence, whether or not the corporation has been prosecuted or convicted. 2004, c. 3, Sched. B, s. 7 (3).

Immunity

8. (1) No action or other proceeding may be instituted against a person who in good faith discloses information to a quality of care committee at the request of the committee or for the purposes of assisting the committee in carrying out its functions. 2004, c. 3, Sched. B, s. 8 (1).

Same, committee member

(2) No action or other proceeding, including a prosecution for an offence under section 7, may be instituted in respect of,

(a) a member of a committee who, in good faith, discloses quality of care information for a purpose described in subsection 4 (3); or

(b) a person who, in good faith, discloses information for a purpose described in subsection 4 (4), if the disclosure is reasonable in the circumstances. 2004, c. 3, Sched. B, s. 8 (2).

Same, failure to disclose

(3) No action or other proceeding may be instituted against a member of a committee in respect of the failure of the committee to make a disclosure described in subsection 4 (3) or (4). 2004, c. 3, Sched. B, s. 8 (3).

Regulations

9. (1) Subject to section 10, the Lieutenant Governor in Council may make regulations,

(a) defining any term used in this Act that is not defined in this Act;

(b) specifying information for the purpose of clause (f) of the definition of "quality of care information" in section 1;

(c) specifying a provision of another Act or its regulations that prevails over this Act or its regulations for the purpose of section 2;

(d) prescribing information for the purpose of clause 10 (2) (e). 2004, c. 3, Sched. B, s. 9 (1).

Minister's regulations

(2) The Minister may make regulations prescribing anything that the definition of "health care" or "quality of care committee" in section 1 mentions as being prescribed. 2004, c. 3, Sched. B, s. 9 (2).

Public consultation before making regulations

10. (1) Subject to subsection (7), the Lieutenant Governor in Council shall not make any regulation under section 9 unless,

(a) the Minister has published a notice of the proposed regulation in *The Ontario Gazette* and given notice of the proposed regulation by all other means that the Minister considers appropriate for the purpose of providing notice to the persons who may be affected by the proposed regulation;

(b) the notice complies with the requirements of this section;

(c) the time periods specified in the notice, during which members of the public may exercise a right described in clause (2) (b) or (c), have expired; and

(d) the Minister has considered whatever comments and submissions that members of the public have made on the proposed regulation in accordance with clause (2) (b) or (c) and has reported to the Lieutenant Governor in Council on what, if any, changes to the proposed regulation the Minister considers appropriate. 2004, c. 3, Sched. B, s. 10 (1).

Contents of notice

(2) The notice mentioned in clause (1) (a) shall contain,

(a) a description of the proposed regulation and the text of it;

(b) a statement of the time period during which members of the public may submit written comments on the proposed regulation to the Minister and the manner in which and the address to which the comments must be submitted;

(c) a description of whatever other rights, in addition to the right described in clause (b), that members of the public have to make submissions on the proposed regulation and the manner in which and the time period during which those rights must be exercised;

(d) a statement of where and when members of the public may review written information about the proposed regulation;

(e) all prescribed information; and

(f) all other information that the Minister considers appropriate. 2004, c. 3, Sched. B, s. 10 (2).

Time period for comments

(3) The time period mentioned in clauses (2) (b) and (c) shall be at least 60 days after the Minister gives the notice mentioned in clause (1) (a) unless the Minister shortens the time period in accordance with subsection (4). 2004, c. 3, Sched. B, s. 10 (3).

Shorter time period for comments

(4) The Minister may shorten the time period if, in the Minister's opinion,

(a) the urgency of the situation requires it;

(b) the proposed regulation clarifies the intent or operation of this Act or the regulations; or

(c) the proposed regulation is of a minor or technical nature. 2004, c. 3, Sched. B, s. 10 (4).

Discretion to make regulations

(5) Upon receiving the Minister's report mentioned in clause (1) (d), the Lieutenant Governor in Council, without further notice under subsection (1), may make the proposed regulation with the changes that the Lieutenant Governor in Council considers appropriate, whether or not those changes are mentioned in the Minister's report. 2004, c. 3, Sched. B, s. 10 (5).

No public consultation

(6) The Minister may decide that subsections (1) to (5) should not apply to the power of the Lieutenant Governor in Council to make a regulation under section 9 if, in the Minister's opinion,

(a) the urgency of the situation requires it;

(b) the proposed regulation clarifies the intent or operation of this Act or the regulations; or

(c) the proposed regulation is of a minor or technical nature. 2004, c. 3, Sched. B, s. 10 (6).

Same

(7) If the Minister decides that subsections (1) to (5) should not apply to the power of the Lieutenant Governor in Council to make a regulation under section 9,

(a) those subsections do not apply to the power of the Lieutenant Governor in Council to make the regulation; and

(b) the Minister shall give notice of the decision to the public as soon as is reasonably possible after making the decision. 2004, c. 3, Sched. B, s. 10 (7).

Contents of notice

(8) The notice mentioned in clause (7) (b) shall include a statement of the Minister's reasons for making the decision and all other information that the Minister considers appropriate. 2004, c. 3, Sched. B, s. 10 (8).

Publication of notice

(9) The Minister shall publish the notice mentioned in clause (7) (b) in *The Ontario Gazette* and give the notice by all other means that the Minister considers appropriate. 2004, c. 3, Sched. B, s. 10 (9).

Temporary regulation

(10) If the Minister decides that subsections (1) to (5) should not apply to the power of the Lieutenant Governor in Council to make a regulation under section 9 because the Minister is of the opinion that the urgency of the situation requires it, the regulation shall,

(a) be identified as a temporary regulation in the text of the regulation; and

(b) unless it is revoked before its expiry, expire at a time specified in the regulation, which shall not be after the second anniversary of the day on which the regulation comes into force. 2004, c. 3, Sched. B, s. 10 (10).

No review

(11) Subject to subsection (12), a court shall not review any action, decision, failure to take action or failure to make a decision by the Lieutenant Governor in Council or the Minister under this section. 2004, c. 3, Sched. B, s. 10 (11).

Exception

(12) Any person resident in Ontario may make an application for judicial review under the *Judicial Review Procedure Act* on the grounds that the Minister has not taken a step required by this section. 2004, c. 3, Sched. B, s. 10 (12).

Time for application

(13) No person shall make an application under subsection (12) with respect to a regulation later than 21 days after the day on which,

(a) the Minister publishes a notice with respect to the regulation under clause (1) (a) or subsection (9), where applicable; or

(b) the regulation is filed, if it is a regulation described in subsection (10). 2004, c. 3, Sched. B, s. 10 (13).

11. OMITTED (AMENDS OR REPEALS OTHER ACTS). 2004, c. 3, Sched. B, s. 11.

12. OMITTED (PROVIDES FOR COMING INTO FORCE OF PROVISIONS OF THIS ACT). 2004, c. 3, Sched. B, s. 12.

13. OMITTED (ENACTS SHORT TITLE OF THIS ACT). 2004, c. 3, Sched. B, s. 13.

Appendix 7:
Ontario Regulation 297/04 under *QCIPA*

No Amendments

DEFINITION OF "QUALITY OF CARE COMMITTEE"

This is the English version of a bilingual regulation.

Prescribed entity, health care provider

1. The following are prescribed as entities for the purposes of subclause (a) (ii) of the definition of "quality of care committee" in section 1 of the Act:

1. An approved charitable home for the aged within the meaning of the *Charitable Institutions Act*.
2. A home or joint home within the meaning of the *Homes for the Aged and Rest Homes Act*.
3. A nursing home within the meaning of the *Nursing Homes Act*.
4. A laboratory or a specimen collection centre as defined in section 5 of the *Laboratory and Specimen Collection Centre Licensing Act*. O. Reg. 297/04, s. 1.

Prescribed entity, quality of care improver

2. The following are prescribed as entities for the purposes of subclause (a) (iii) of the definition of "quality of care committee" in section 1 of the Act:

1. The Ontario Medical Association, in respect of its activities under the *Laboratory and Specimen Collection Centre Licensing Act*.

2. The Canadian Blood Services in respect of its laboratory and specimen collection centres and its other health care services. O. Reg. 297/04, s. 2.

Prescribed criteria

3. The following are prescribed as criteria for the purposes of clause (b) of the definition of "quality of care committee" in section 1 of the Act:

1. Before acting as a quality of care committee, it must be designated in writing, by the health facility or entity that established, appointed or approved it, as a quality of care committee for the purposes of the Act.

2. The terms of reference of the committee and its designation must be available on request to members of public. O. Reg. 297/04, s. 3.

4. Omitted (provides for coming into force of this Regulation). O. Reg. 297/04, s. 4.

Appendix 8:
Ontario Regulation 330/04 under *QCIPA*

No Amendments

GENERAL

This is the English version of a bilingual regulation.

Prevail over Act

1. The *Independent Health Facilities Act* prevails over the Act with respect to any quality of care information collected by or prepared for a quality of care committee established, appointed or approved by an independent health facility. O. Reg. 330/04, s. 1.

Not quality of care information

2. The following information is not "quality of care information" for the purposes of the Act:

1. The fact that a quality of care committee met or conducted a review.

2. When the meeting or review took place. O. Reg. 330/04, s. 2.

Member

3. For the purposes of the Act,

"member of the quality of care committee" includes every person who participates or assists with the committee's functions as set out in clause (c) of the definition of "quality of care committee" in section 1 of the Act. O. Reg. 330/04, s. 3.

Meaning of "functions"

4. For the purposes of clauses (a) and (b) of the definition of "quality of care information" in section 1 of the Act,

"functions" means the functions described in clause (c) of the definition of "quality of care committee" in section 1 of the Act. O. Reg. 330/04, s. 4.

5. OMITTED (PROVIDES FOR COMING INTO FORCE OF THIS REGULATION). O. Reg. 330/04, s. 5.

© Queen's Printer for Ontario, 2004.

This is an unofficial version of Government of Ontario legal materials.

Table of Statutes, Bills, Regulations, and Abbreviations

Statutes

Aeronautics Act, R.S.C. 1985, c. A-2

Age of Majority and Accountability Act, R.S.O. 1990, c. A.7

Alberta Evidence Act, R.S.A. 2000, c. A-18

Ambulance Act, R.S.O. 1990, c. A.19

An Act respecting Health Services and Social Services, R.S.Q., c. S-4.2

Arbitrations Act, 1991, S.O. 1991, c. 17

Archives Act, R.S.O 1990, c. A.27

Audit Statute Law Amendment Act, S.O. 2004, c. 17

Auditor General Act, R.S.O. 1990, c. A.35

Business Corporations Act, R.S.O. 1990, c. B.1

Canadian Charter of Rights and Freedoms, Part I of the *Constitution Act, 1982*, being Schedule B to the *Canada Act, 1982* (U.K.), 1982, c. 11 [*Charter*]

Cancer Act, R.S.O. 1990, c. C.1

Charitable Institutions Act, R.S.O. 1990, c. C.9 [*CIA*]

Child and Family Services Act, R.S.O 1990, c. 11 [*CFSA*]

Children's Law Reform Act, R.S.O. 1990, c. 12 [*CLRA*]

Commitment to the Future of Medicare Act, 2004, S.O. 2004, c. 5

Community Care Access Corporations Act, 2001, S.O. 2001, c. 33 [*CCACA*]

Constitution Act, 1867 (U.K.), 30 & 31 Vict., c. 3

Coroner's Act, R.S.O. 1990, c. 37
Corporations Act, R.S.O. 1990, c. C.38
Corrections and Conditional Release Act (Canada), S.C. 2002, c. 20
Courts of Justice Act, R.S.O. 1990, c. C.43
Criminal Code (Canada), R.S.C. 1985, c. C-46
Crown Estates Administration Act, R.S.O. 1990, c. 47

Dental Hygiene Act, 1991, S.O. 1991, c. 22
Dentistry Act, 1991, S.O. 1991, c. 24
Development Corporations Act, R.S.O. 1990, c. D.10
Dietetics Act, 1991, S.O. 1991, c. 26
Drug and Pharmacies Regulation Act, R.S.O. 1990, c. H.4 [*DPRA*]
Drugless Practitioners Act, R.S.O. 1990, c. D.18 [*DPA*]

Electronic Commerce Act, 2000, S.O. 2000, c. 17
Environmental Bill of Rights, 1993, S.O 1993, c. 28
Evidence Act, C.C.S.M., c. E150
Evidence Act, R.S.B.C. 1996, c. 124
Evidence Act, R.S.N.B. 1973, c. E-11
Evidence Act, R.S.N.L. 1990, c. E-16
Evidence Act, R.S.N.S. 1989, c. 154
Evidence Act, R.S.O. 1990, c. E.23

Family Law Act, R.S.O. 1990, c. F.3
Freedom of Information and Protection of Privacy Act, R.S.O. 1990, c. F.31
   [*FIPPA*]

Highway Traffic Act, R.S.O. 1990, c. H.8
Health Cards and Numbers Control Act, 1991, S.O. 1991, c. 1 [*HCNCA*]
Health Care Consent Act, 1996, S.O. 1996, c. 2, Sch. A [*HCCA*]
Health Information Act, R.S.A. 2000, c. H-5 [*HIA*]
Health Information Act, S.A. 1999, c. H-4.8
Health Information Protection Act, 1999, S.S. 1999, c. H-0.021
Health Insurance Act, R.S.O. 1990, c. H.6
Health Protection and Promotion Act, R.S.O. 1990, c. H.7 [*HPPA*]
Homes for Special Care Act, R.S.O. 1990, c. H.12 [*HSCA*]
Homes for the Aged and Rest Homes Act, R.S.O. 1990, c. H.13 [*HARHA*]

Independent Health Facilities Act, R.S.O. 1990, c. I.3 [*IHFA*]
Interest Act, R.S.C. 1985, c. I-15
Interpretation Act, R.S.O. 1990, c. I.11

Judicial Review Procedure Act, R.S.O. 1990, c. J.1

Laboratory and Specimen Collection Centre Licensing Act, R.S.O. 1990, c. L.1
Limitations Act, 2002, S.O. 2002, c. 24, Sch. B
Long-Term Care Act, 1994, S.O. 1994, c. 26 [*LTCA*]

Massage Therapy Act, 1991, S.O. 1991, c. 27
Medical Act, R.S.P.E.I. 1988, c. M-5
Medical Laboratory Technology Act, 1991, S.O. 1991, c. 28
Medical Radiation Technology Act, 1991, S.O. 1991, c. 29
Medicine Act, 1991, S.O. 1991, c. 30
Mental Health Act, R.S.O. 1990, c. M.7 [*MHA*]
Mental Hospitals Act, R.S.O. 1990, c. M.8
Midwifery Act, 1991, S.O. 1991, c. 31
Ministry of Correctional Services Act, R.S.O. 1990, c. M.22
Ministry of Health and Long-Term Care Act, R.S.O. 1990, c. M.26
Municipal Freedom of Information and Protection of Privacy Act, R.S.O. 1990,
  c. M.56 [*MFIPPA*]
Municipal Freedom of Information Statute Law Amendment Act, 1989, S.O.
  1989, c. 64

Nursing Act, 1991, S.O. 1991, c. 32
Nursing Homes Act, R.S.O. 1990, c. N.7 [*NHA*]

Occupational Health and Safety Act, R.S.O. 1990, c. O.1
Occupational Therapy Act, 1991, S.O. 1991, c. 33
Ombudsman Act, R.S.O. 1990, c. O.6
Ontario Disability Support Program Act, 1997, S.O. 1997, c. 25, Sch. B
Ontario Drug Benefit Act, R.S.O. 1990, c. O.10 [*ODBA*]
Optometry Act, 1991, S.O. 1991, c. 35

Patient Restraints Minimization Act, 2001, S.O. 2001, c. 16
Personal Health Information Act, C.C.S.M., c. P33.5
Personal Health Information Protection Act, 2004, Schedule A to the *Health
  Information Protection Act*, S.O. 2004, c. 3 [*PHIPA*]
Personal Information Protection and Electronic Documents Act, S.C. 2000, c. 5
  [*PIPEDA*]
Pharmacy Act, 1991, S.O. 1991, c. 36
Police Services Act, R.S.O. 1990, c. P.15

*Principles Set Out in the National Standard of Canada Entitled Model Code for
   the Protection of Personal Information*, CAN/CSA-Q830-96 set out in
   Schedule 1 of *PIPEDA* [CSA Privacy Code]
Prisons and Reformatories Act (Canada), R.S.C. 1985, c. P-20
Private Hospitals Act, R.S.O. 1990, c. P.24
Provincial Offences Act, R.S.O. 1990, c. P.33
Public Guardian and Trustee Act, R.S.O. 1990, c. P.51
Public Hospitals Act, R.S.O. 1990, c. P.40 [*PHA*]
Public Inquiries Act, R.S.O. 1990, c. P.41

Quality of Care Information Protection Act, 2004, Schedule B to the *Health
   Information Protection Act, 2004*, S.O. 2004, c. 3 [*QCIPA*]

Regulated Health Professions Act, 1991, S.O. 1991, c. 18 [*RHPA*]
Regulations Act, R.S.O. 1990, c. R.21
Remedies for Organized Crime and Other Unlawful Activities Act, 2001, S.O.
   2001, c. 28
Respiratory Therapy Act, 1991, S.O. 1991, c. 39

Saskatchewan Evidence Act, R.S.S. 1978, c. S-16, as amended by S.S. 1989–90,
   c. 57, s.3
Social Housing Reform Act, 2000, S.O. 2000, c. 27
Social Work and Social Service Workers Act, 1998, S.O. 1998, c. 3 [*SWSSWA*]
Statutory Powers Procedures Act, R.S.O. 1990, c. S.22
Substitute Decisions Act, 1992, S.O. 1992, c. 30 [*SDA*]

Tenant Protection Act, 1997, S.O. 1997, c. 24 [*TPA*]
Trillium Gift of Life Network Act, R.S.O. 1990, c. H.10

Workplace Safety and Insurance Act, 1997, S.O. 1997, c. 16

Youth Criminal Justice Act (Canada), S.C. 2002, c. 1

Bills

Bill C-54   *An Act to support and promote electronic commerce by protecting per-
            sonal information that is collected, used or disclosed in certain circum-
            stances, by providing for the use of electronic means to communicate or
            record information or transactions and by amending the Canada Evi-
            dence Act, the Statutory Instruments Act and the Statute Revision Act*,
            1st Sess., 36th Parl., 1997–98

Bill C-6   *An Act to support and promote electronic commerce by protecting personal information that is collected, used or disclosed in certain circumstances, by providing for the use of electronic means to communicate or record information or transactions and by amending the Canada Evidence Act, the Statutory Instruments Act and the Statute Revision Act,* 2d Sess., 36th Parl., 1999

Bill 31   *An Act to enact and amend various Acts with respect to the protection of health information,* 1st Sess., 38th Leg., Ontario, 2003

Bill 159   *An Act respecting personal health information and related matters,* 1st Sess., 37th Leg., Ontario, 2000

Bill 124   *An Act to amend the Health Protection and Promotion Act,* 1st Sess., 38th Leg., Ontario, 2004

Bill 110   *An Act to require the disclosure of information to police respecting persons being treated for gunshot wounds,* 1st Sess., 38th Leg., Ontario, 2004

Bill 190   *An Act to promote good government by amending or repealing certain Acts and by enacting one new Act,* 1st Sess., 38th Leg, Ontario, 2005

Regulations

Capacity Assessment, O. Reg. 238/00, made under the *SDA*
Classification of Hospitals, O. Reg. 321/01, made under the *PHA*

Evaluators, O. Reg. 104/96, made under the *HCCA*

Food and Drug Regulations, C.R.C., c. 870, Part C, Division 5 (Drugs for Clinical Trials Involving Human Subjects)

General, O. Reg. 57/92, made under the *IHFA*
General, R.R.O. 1990, Reg. 69, made under the *CIA*
General, O. Reg. 114/94, made under the *Medicine Act, 1991*
General, O. Reg. 119/94, made under the *Optometry Act, 1991*
General, O. Reg. 194/98, made under the *TPA*
General, O. Reg. 218/94, made under the *Dental Hygiene Act, 1991*
General, O. Reg. 257/00, made under the *Ambulance Act*
General, O. Reg. 329/04, made under the *PHIPA* [*PHIPA* Regulation]
General, O. Reg. 330/04, made under the *QCIPA*
General, R.R.O. 1990, Reg. 460, made under *FIPPA*
General, O. Reg. 544/94, made under the *Massage Therapy Act, 1991*
General, R.R.O. 1990, Reg. 551, made under the *DPRA*
General, R.R.O. 1990, Reg. 552, made under the *HIA*

General, R.R.O. 1990, Reg. 636, made under the *HSCA*

General, R.R.O. 1990, Reg. 637, made under the *HARHA*

General, R.R.O. 1990, Reg. 741, made under the *MHA*

General, R.R.O. 1990, Reg. 823, made under the *MFIPPA*

General, R.R.O. 1990, Reg. 832, made under the *NHA*

Hospital Management, R.R.O. 1990, Reg. 965, made under the *PHA*

Institutions, O. Reg. 372/91, made under the *MFIPPA*

Laboratories, R.R.O. 1990, Reg. 682, made under the *Laboratory and Specimen Collection Centre Licensing Act*

Professional Misconduct, O. Reg. 199/98, made under the *Medical Radiation Technology Act*

Professional Misconduct, O. Reg. 203/00, made under the *Dietetics Act, 1991*

Professional Misconduct, O. Reg. 384/00, made under the *SWSSWA*

Professional Misconduct, O. Reg. 680/93, made under the *Dietetics Act, 1991*

Professional Misconduct, O. Reg. 681/93, made under the *DPRA*

Professional Misconduct, O. Reg. 752/93, made under the *Medical Laboratory Technology Act, 1991*

Professional Misconduct, O. Reg. 753/93, made under the *Respiratory Therapy Act, 1991*

Professional Misconduct, O. Reg. 853/93, made under the *Dentistry Act, 1991*

Professional Misconduct, O. Reg. 856/93, made under the *Medicine Act, 1991*

Professional Misconduct, O. Reg. 858/93, made under the *Midwifery Act, 1991*

Quality of Care Committee, O. Reg. 297/04, made under the *QCIPA*

Rules of Civil Procedure, R.R.O. 1990, Reg. 194, made under the *Courts of Justice Act*

Smart Systems for Health Agency, O. Reg. 43/02, made under the *Development Corporations Act*

Specification of Communicable Diseases, O. Reg. 558/91, made under the *HPPA*

Specification of Reportable Diseases, O. Reg. 559/91, made under the *HPPA*

Specification of Virulent Diseases, O. Reg. 95/03, made under the *HPPA*

Table of Cases

Index

About the Authors

Linia

Halyna Perun is counsel with the Legal Services Branch of the Ministry of Health and Long-Term Care. In her seventeen years of practice with the Ministry's Legal Services Branch, Halyna has had responsibility for a variety of portfolios including regulated health professions, public hospitals, mental health, freedom of information, and protection of privacy. She has been involved in health privacy issues at the Ministry since 1996. She was instrumental in developing the Ministry's 1997 draft health information legislation, which became the model for health information legislation in Manitoba, Alberta, Saskatchewan, and ultimately, Ontario. In the mid-1990s, Halyna was instrumental in the creation of the *Health Care Consent Act*.

Michael Orr has been counsel with the Legal Services Branch of the Ministry of Health and Long-Term Care since 2001, advising the Ministry on health sector information, privacy matters, and matters relating to long-term care and hospitals. He was also the principal lawyer advising the Ministry on the drafting of the *Quality of Care Information Protection Act, 2004*. In 2000–2001 Michael was with the Legal Services Branch of the Ministry of Municipal Affairs and Housing. He served at Ombudsman Ontario as Counsel and Policy Advisor from 1991–2000.

Fannie Dimitriadis began her legal career with the Legal Services Branch of the Ministry of Health and Long-Term Care in 2000. She has been counsel to the Ministry since her call to the Ontario Bar in 2001. Fannie has been involved in the development of Ontario's health information privacy legislation since 2000 and provides the Ministry with legal advice on a wide range of privacy-related matters, including the impact of new information technology initiatives.

MEMBRE DU GROUPE SCABRINI

Québec, Canada
2005